Macroeconomics

Macroeconomics

PRINCIPLES FOR A CHANGING WORLD

FIFTH EDITION

Eric P. Chiang

worth publishers
Macmillan Learning
New York

Senior Vice President, Content Strategy: Charles Linsmeier
Program Director: Shani Fisher
Program Manager: Sarah Seymour
Senior Development Editors: Valerie Raymond and Bruce Kaplan
Assessment Manager: Kristyn Brown
Marketing Manager: Clay Bolton
Marketing Assistant: Steven Huang
Director of Media Editorial and Assessment: Noel Hohnstine
Senior Media Editor: Lindsay Neff
Assistant Editor: Amanda Gaglione
Director, Content Management Enhancement: Tracey Kuehn
Senior Managing Editor: Lisa Kinne
Content Project Manager: Edgar Doolan
Director of Design, Content Management: Diana Blume
Design Services Manager: Natasha Wolfe
Interior Design: Dirk Kaufman
Cover Design: John Callahan
Media Permissions Manager: Christine Buese
Photo Researcher: Donna Ranieri, Lumina Datamatics, Inc.
Senior Workflow Project Manager: Paul W. Rohloff
Production Supervisor: Robert Cherry
Media Project Manager: Jason Perkins
Composition: Lumina Datamatics, Inc.
Printing and Binding: LSC Communications
Cover Image: Mopic/Shutterstock

ISBN-13: 978-1-319-21927-7
ISBN-10: 1-319-21927-6

Library of Congress Control Number: 2019946844

Printed in the United States of America

1 2 3 4 5 6   23 22 21 20 19

Worth Publishers
One New York Plaza
Suite 4600
New York, NY 10004-1562
www.macmillanlearning.com

To John and Tina Chiang:
my parents, who instilled in me a work ethic that allows me to pursue endless opportunities

Tribute to Jerry Stone

Jerry Stone long believed that the best principles of economics textbooks are authored by people invested in their students' classroom experience. The decisions made in the shaping of the first two editions of this textbook were influenced by Jerry's 30-plus years in the classroom. The foundation of this edition is a testament to Jerry's accomplishment: a book envisioned, designed, and executed to be the principles of economics book that teaches better than any other textbook on the market.

Jerry had a remarkable career as a longtime teacher at Metropolitan State University of Denver and as an author of two successful principles of economics textbooks. Those who knew Jerry miss his steadfast commitment to the teaching of economics, a legacy that lives on in each new edition of *Economics: Principles for a Changing World*. Jerry Stone passed away after a difficult battle with cancer in August 2010.

About the Author

Eric P. Chiang received his bachelor's degree in economics from the University of Nevada Las Vegas and his master's and doctorate in economics from the University of Florida. His first academic position was at New Mexico State University. Currently, Eric is an associate professor and graduate director of the Department of Economics at Florida Atlantic University. Eric also serves as the director of instructional technology for the College of Business.

In 2009 Eric was the recipient of Florida Atlantic University's highest teaching honor, the Distinguished Teacher of the Year Award. Among numerous other teaching awards, he also was named the Stewart Distinguished Professor at the College of Business. He has written over 35 articles in peer-reviewed journals on a range of subjects, including technology spillovers, intellectual property rights, telecommunications, and health care. His research has appeared in leading journals, including the *Review of Economics and Statistics, Journal of Technology Transfer*, and *Southern Economic Journal*. He is a frequent presenter at major economics conferences and at universities across the country and around the world.

As an instructor who teaches both face-to-face and online courses, Eric uses a variety of technological tools, including clickers, Web-based polling, lecture capture, and homework management systems to complement his active-learning-style lectures. As an administrator in the College of Business, Eric's role as director of instructional technology involves assisting instructors with effectively implementing classroom technologies. In this position, Eric also ensures that the quality of online courses meets accreditation standards, including those set by the Association to Advance Collegiate Schools of Business (AACSB).

In addition to his dedication to teaching economic principles and his administrative duties, Eric devotes time to new research in economic education. His current research focuses on student learning outcomes in economics education based on the different methods of instruction in use today. The fifth edition of *Economics: Principles for a Changing World* embodies Eric's devotion to economics education and the benefits of adapting to the new, often creative ways in which students learn and instructors teach.

In his spare time, Eric enjoys studying cultures and languages. He has visited all fifty U.S. states and over eighty countries, often taking long jogs in the cities he visits to experience local life to the fullest. A more quirky fact: Eric is a professional mini-golf player, having competed in both the Pro Mini Golf U.S. Open and Masters tournaments. In 2019, he was a contestant on ABC's extreme mini-golf game show *Holey Moley*.

The Vision for *Economics*, Fifth Edition

Every time I teach an introductory economics class, I keep in mind that many of my students are learning about economics for the first time. How they perceive my course may influence their perceptions and understanding of economics for a long time. This was the guiding principle behind the first edition of this text, and it continues through the fifth edition.

Today's students represent many ethnicities and backgrounds, each bringing their unique life experiences into the classroom. Similarly, over half of all new economics instructors in the United States were born in another country, bringing with them a wealth of unique stories. People from all over the world face similar economic problems yet seek to solve these problems in different ways. Economics is not a tool for one political system or point of view; its theories are based in facts and offer possible solutions to problems of our complex world. In turbulent days, economics provides a steadying hand. This book celebrates the diversity of our global society with topics and examples woven through every chapter.

Instructors and students face two types of problems in each class. Instructors ask, "How many students can I reach today? Can I reach each one?" Students ask, "How does this affect *my* life?" I have taught over 20,000 students since 2001 in a variety of settings—small classrooms, large auditoriums, online, hybrid, daytime, evening, and in other countries. The diversity of my students provides abundant opportunities to learn from experience. Each setting is a laboratory for innovative teaching techniques to motivate students.

The challenge of reaching each and every student is made especially difficult by the sheer amount of information available to students and the increasing number of ways in which students learn. Each edition of this book has been written with active learning methodologies in mind. Instructors often encourage or even require students to read their textbook prior to class. If students do, class time can be used more effectively to refine the knowledge. The problem is that students often don't read the book prior to class.

When I started doing research on learning outcomes, I came to the conclusion that using a textbook in such a way may not be very effective. Instead, I was inspired to create short tutorials that students watch before class as a friendlier approach to introducing to economic concepts. By piquing students' interest in the topic early, they are more likely to participate in class and to use the textbook to explore concepts more deeply. As a result, the textbook and its technology play a critical role in the learning process.

Still, each chapter still must stand on its own in its delivery of content. My experience has led me to believe there are three key aspects to this. First, students retain more information when presented with multiple channels, for example, words, images, and application. Every chapter in this book contains a wealth of vivid examples, intuitive explanations, and visuals to build stronger comprehension and long-term retention of concepts. Each major section concludes with a Checkpoint summary and application question. Each chapter concludes with a two-page visual summary, connecting concepts with images. Moreover, each chapter presents topical issues that challenge students to think about and debate economic issues confronting our world today.

The second aspect involves the explanation of WHY we are studying each concept. Each major topic, such as demand or consumer and producer surplus, begins with an introduction that breaks down the concept to a very fundamental idea. For demand, we show how it is derived from many individuals valuing a good or service differently (their willingness and ability to pay). For consumer and producer surplus, we begin with one consumer and one producer before proceeding to the entire market. These additional examples (which seldom appear in other textbooks) help to answer the "why?" question that students have as they approach each topic.

The final key aspects involves the ability to read and manipulate data. To this end, each chapter presents a wealth of data to enhance literacy and clarify how it is woven into economic issues. A By the Numbers feature in each chapter presents key data in graphical form along with the source of the data, a discussion of the data's relevance to the chapter topic, a related news headline, and questions to assess data literacy.

In today's classrooms, whether in-person or virtual, it is no longer enough to write a good or even a great textbook. The book is just one medium for delivering information when students are accustomed to consuming information from many different sources. To reach students, it's now essential to deliver information in a variety of formats beyond the textbook or lecture. Therefore, I have worked with Worth Publishers to develop each of the technological elements for *Economics: Principles for a Changing World*, allowing it to be a much more effective teaching tool for instructors.

—*Eric P. Chiang*

Macroeconomics

Connecting Text and Technology

When it comes to the classroom, we know there isn't one single path to reaching the summit of teaching and learning success. That's why Eric Chiang and Macmillan Learning are committed to helping teachers teach the way they want and students learn in the most effective way possible, all with flexible and affordable options. It begins with a text filled with compelling examples and supported by pedagogy to make the concepts memorable. And, built on learning science, and co-designed with thousands of students and instructors, the text's features are supported by author-driven and text-specific technology. Here are the key features of what this text has to offer.

DATA LITERACY

Reconceptualized for the Fifth Edition, the **By the Numbers** feature is now a practical tool. It encourages greater appreciation for and familiarity with data and graphs by tying them to a key topic discussed in the chapter. Moreover, it is supported by an autogradeable *digital activity* to apply the data.

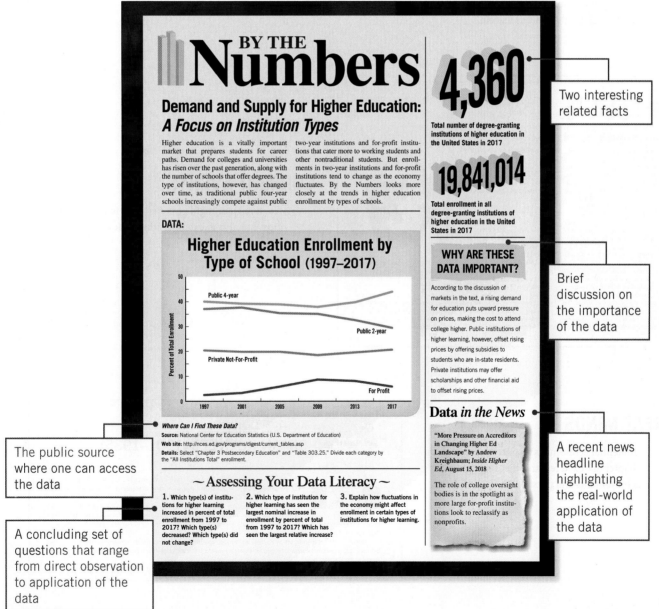

Two interesting related facts

Brief discussion on the importance of the data

A recent news headline highlighting the real-world application of the data

The public source where one can access the data

A concluding set of questions that range from direct observation to application of the data

GLOBAL FOCUS

One of the unique things about Eric Chiang is his philosophy on travel. Years ago, he started his "Around the World in 80 Hours" trips, where he would circumnavigate the globe, briefly stopping off in international spots, and film himself talking about the local economy. Why? World economies are intertwined. In many cases the health of one economy depends on the health of another. While people around the world are faced with many of the same economic problems, they solve them in surprisingly different ways.

Eric started these journeys on his own accord to help illustrate this concept to his students. His experiences have been developed into the Around the World feature in every chapter. Students read a synopsis of an international issue, view media to further their understanding (some videos featuring Eric himself), and are asked to answer a question on how that issue is resolved in different places throughout the world. New to the 5th edition are autogradeable *digital activities* designed to help students understand and apply the information gleaned from this feature.

 **AROUND THE WORLD**

Singapore: Resolving Traffic Jams and Reducing Pollution Using Price Controls

How did Singapore use economic tools to intervene in the market to improve traffic flow and to correct a potential market failure?

How much time is spent waiting in gridlock traffic in major cities? According to a study by the transportation analytics firm INRIX, in 2018, American drivers spent over 8 billion hours stuck in traffic. Traffic creates an opportunity cost that leads to reduced productivity. Moreover, traffic jams reduce fuel efficiency and generate more air pollution. Is there an economic solution to these problems? Singapore may have the answer.

Singapore uses an electronic road-pricing system that charges drivers a toll on dozens of its major roads and highways. Unlike traditional toll roads, Singapore's road charges vary throughout the day. During times when roads are less subject to congestion, the fee is very minimal or

even zero, while during times of the day when roads are likely to be congested, the fee is higher. As it becomes more expensive to drive during certain periods of the day, drivers are incentivized to drive less, to drive during off-peak times, or to find alternative means of transportation. The outcome is a road system that is less prone to congestion, reducing an inefficiency.

Singapore is not the only city that uses congestion charges. It costs approximately $15 to drive in Central London between the hours of 7 A.M. and 6 P.M. Even in the

United States, the introduction of express lanes in Los Angeles, Atlanta, Miami, and other cities has allowed motorists to pay a toll to bypass traffic. Similar to Singapore, these tolls vary throughout the day, with prices rising as roads become more congested.

Not only do congestion charges incentivize people to drive less, they also encourage companies to change the way they operate. Companies that do not need to operate during traditional business hours might encourage their employees to arrive at work later and return home later, avoiding times when congestion charges are at their peak. By reducing traffic congestion, less time is wasted, productivity rises, and pollution is reduced. Furthermore, the fees collected are a valuable source of government revenue.

Many economists believe that market-based pricing mechanisms such as congestion charges can lead to increased efficiency and equity.

GO ONLINE TO PRACTICE THE ECONOMIC CONCEPTS IN THIS STORY

 **ISSUE**

A 0% Credit Card Offer: Is It Too Good to Be True?

Credit card debt is one of the most common forms of consumer debt in the United States. The average U.S. household carries over $8,000 in credit card debt, often at interest rates higher than what is paid on home mortgages, car loans, or student loans. However, many credit card companies offer new credit card subscribers 0% financing for a limited period of time. These offers are attractive for individuals with debt, many of whom might transfer debt from another credit card. Do credit card companies profit by giving customers such a great deal? Yes, more than you might think.

Nearly all 0% financing offers are teaser strategies, and not all are created equal. They vary in terms of the length of the offer, the initial transfer fees, and whether finance charges are accrued. Zero percent interest offers generally vary from 6 to 18 months from the opening of a new credit card, and most are *balance transfer*

offers that pay off another credit card balance but require an initial transfer fee of 3% to 5%. Therefore, if one pays a 5% fee to enjoy a 0% interest rate for 6 months, that is the equivalent of a 10% annual interest rate. Finally, some credit card companies *accrue* finance charges over the promotional period if the balance is not paid off. For example, if one has a $1,000 balance at 0% for 12 months, which then increases to 15% after 12 months, an accrued finance charge means that if the $1,000 balance is not paid off in 12 months, the 15% rate is charged from day 1, eliminating any benefit from the 0% offer. One should always read the terms of a 0% offer to avoid unexpected fees.

Finally, there is an income effect. When a consumer can buy goods at a 0% interest rate, a consumer *feels* wealthier, which may lead to greater spending. Since credit card companies charge

Zero percent interest lending rate deals abound to attract new customers, but beware, they do not last for long!

businesses around 2% to 3% on every purchase for processing the transaction, they will still earn money on every purchase, even if you never pay a penny in finance charges.

CURRENT EVENTS

- Each chapter highlights a current issue in a separate box, but also in examples throughout and in end-of-chapter questions.

GREAT MINDS

- Influential economists are introduced in each chapter in boxed features that highlight their achievements and personalize their stories.

NOBEL PRIZE
SIMON KUZNETS (1901–1985)

Simon Kuznets was awarded the Nobel Prize in Economics in 1971 for devising systematic approaches to the compilation and analysis of national economic data. Kuznets is credited with developing gross national product as a measurement of economic output.

Kuznets developed methods for calculating the size and changes in national income known as the national income and product accounts (NIPA). Caring little for abstract models, he sought to define concepts that could be observed empirically and measured statistically. Thanks to Kuznets, economists have had a large amount of data with which to test their economic theories.

Another important contribution by Kuznets is the hypothesis that as countries develop, income inequality initially rises but then falls as incomes continue to grow. The simple inverted U-shaped graph that represents this relationship became known as the Kuznets curve.

SECTION AND END-OF-CHAPTER SUMMARIES

- End-of-section Checkpoint summaries include an application question, an example of how the text speaks to, not at, the student.

- End-of-chapter Visual Summaries reinforce key concepts with words and images to help cement the ideas.

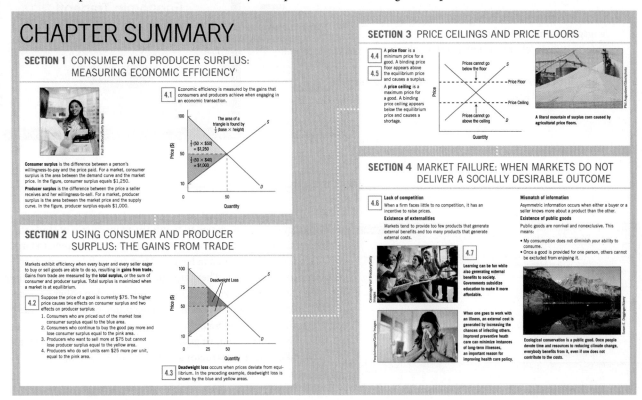

CONCEPT REVIEW AND APPLICATION

- End-of-chapter Questions and Problems in the text ask students to manipulate the concepts and are also available in *digital format*:

  - Check Your Understanding—concept review
  - Apply the Concepts—scenario application
  - In the News—real-world events application
  - Solving Problems/Work It Out—interactive activity

Completing the Learning Program

Eric Chiang has conducted a great deal of research on pedagogy in economic education. Much of this research has focused on increasing student retention and engagement. He writes the text, develops the visual program, and assembles the resources for the homework system at the same time. These threads come together for a complete learning program.

Animated prelecture tutorials provide a base-level understanding of core economic topics before students ever "set foot" in a class.

- Straightforward animations provide information in an engaging format without distraction.
- Information is "chunked" into short, easily remembered segments.
- Embedded questions and a pacing system put learning in the students' hands.

Bridge questions are designed to inform an instructor of students' level of understanding before they come into class, helping to target what needs to be covered in lecture. They are useful as lead-ins to discussion and review. They "bridge" prelecture time to lecture time.

- Students first answer a question designed to either be open-ended, address a typical misconception, or otherwise lead to further discussion in the lecture.
- Students then must explain the rationale behind their answer, allowing the instructor a deep level of insight into their understanding.

An e-book fully integrates text with activities and quizzes.

LearningCurve Adaptive Quizzing helps students target what they've learned and what they need more work to learn. Embraced by students and instructors alike, this incredibly popular and effective adaptive quizzing engine offers individualized question sets and feedback tailored to each student based on correct and incorrect responses. LearningCurve questions are hyperlinked to relevant e-book sections, encouraging students to read and use the resources at hand to enrich their understanding.

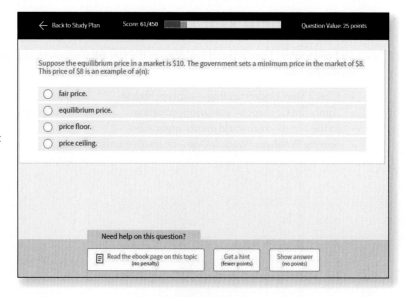

Author Lecture Videos offer a chance for the students to hear from the author directly. This hugely popular feature now provides concise and engaging explanations for every chapter along with assessment.

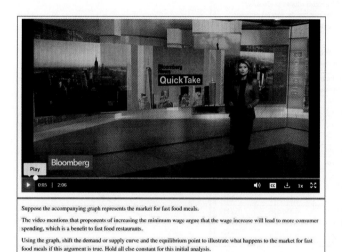

Video Activities expand the real-world examples in the text with video activities powered by Bloomberg videos. These unique activities pair Bloomberg content related to key topics and examples covered in the text with an assignment built around Bloom's taxonomy. By completing these exercises, students will gain practice applying economic analysis to today's news.

For Assessment

End-of-Chapter Problems have been converted to a digital format which provides students with feedback targeted to their specific mistakes, guiding them through the problem-solving process. Questions are often multi-part and utilize a variety of question types including numeric entry, multiple-choice, multiple-select, sorting, labeling, and ranking. In graphing exercises, students are asked to demonstrate their understanding of economic models by simply clicking, dragging, and dropping a line to a predetermined location. The graphs have been designed so that the student's entire focus is on moving the correct curve in the correct direction, virtually eliminating grading issues for instructors. Online homework sets utilize the same technology to provide additional problem-solving practice.

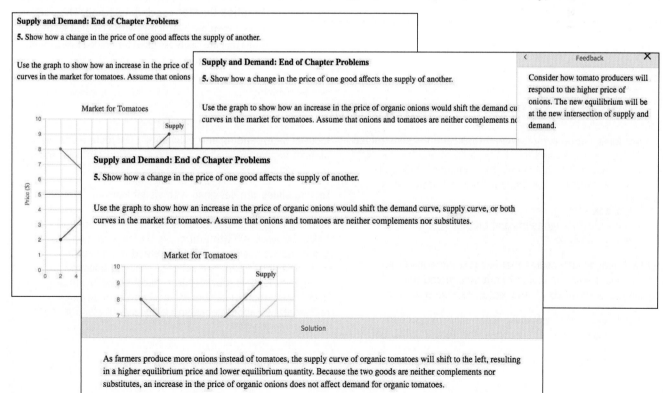

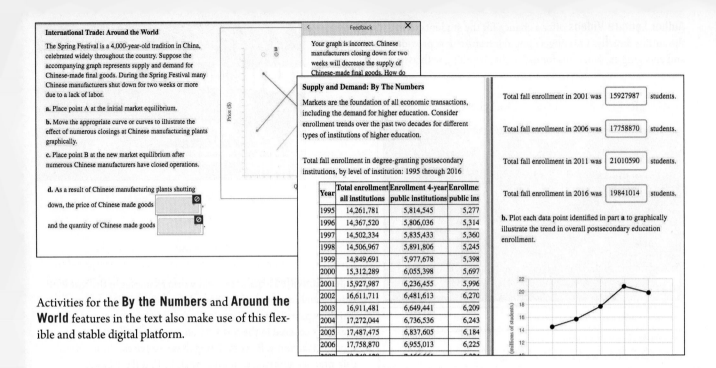

Activities for the **By the Numbers** and **Around the World** features in the text also make use of this flexible and stable digital platform.

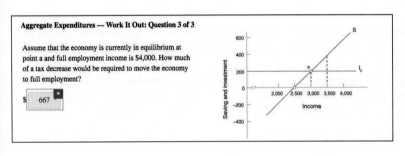

Work It Out skill-building activities pair sample end-of-chapter problems with targeted feedback and video explanations to help students solve problems step-by-step. This approach allows students to work independently, tests their comprehension of concepts, and prepares them for class and exams.

Practice Quizzes conclude each unit. These are pre-built, providing instructors with a curated set of questions that are easily assigned for graded assessment.

POWERFUL SUPPORT FOR INSTRUCTORS

Test Bank contains more than 8,000 carefully constructed, thoroughly edited and revised, and comprehensively accuracy-checked questions. Each chapter's test bank contains "anchor" questions written by the author himself.

Gradebook offers clear feedback to students and instructors on individual assignments and on performance in the course as a whole.

LMS Integration ensures that is easily integrated into a school's learning management system and that an instructor's gradebook and roster are always in sync.

Instructor's Teaching Manual is the ideal resource for many classroom teaching styles. The Teaching Manual focuses on expanding and enlivening classroom lectures by highlighting varied ways to bring real-world examples into the classroom.

Lecture Slides are designed with visual learning in mind. This set of slides contains fully animated graphs, visual learning images, and additional examples and created links. *Economics,* Fifth Edition, is the only principles of economics textbook with slides created by the author.

In addition, a separate set of slides with questions to engage students is provided to support active learning in your classroom. Ask your Macmillan Learning sales representative about packaging iClicker with *Principles for a Changing World.*

Major Updates to the Fifth Edition

COVERAGE OF CURRENT TRENDS REVEAL ECONOMICS BASICS

- Statistics and examples throughout reflect the latest economic landscape.
- New "Apply the Concepts" and "In the News" questions in each chapter touch on topics in the news.
- New photos throughout give visual support to key concepts.

CHAPTER 1

New examples include Sheryl Sandberg and the effects of choosing one's academic major. New *In the News* topic: consequences of banning plastic straws.

CHAPTER 2

Wholly rewritten sections: *Absolute and Comparative Advantage, Gains From Trade,* and *Practical Constraints on Trade.* New *In the News* topics: impact on production and allocative efficiency of new forms of biodegradable plastics; impact of China's growing demand for U.S. automobiles along with food and agricultural goods, such as lobsters.

CHAPTER 3

New example of online markets. Addition of a brief description of substitution and income effects. Rewritten section on the demand curve. New *In the News* topics: StubHub and Super Bowl ticket prices through the playoffs; effects of recalls on self-balancing scooters.

CHAPTER 4

Wholly rewritten section *Price Floors* and a major section, *Market Failure: When Markets Do Not Deliver a Socially Desirable Outcome,* including new coverage of addressing market failure in three key societal issues: climate change, health care, and education. New *In the News* topics: economic impact of legalizing recreational marijuana; impact of 2018 Massachusetts minimum wage rate increase to $15.

CHAPTER 5

New *Issue: Will the Next Recession Feel Like a Recession?* Heavy revision focuses on the importance of and the current state of the global marketplace.

CHAPTER 6

New material on the personal consumption expenditures. Wholly revised section: *Marginally Attached Workers and Underemployment.* New *Around the World* box: *A New Cuban Renaissance: The Rise of American "Tourism" in Cuba.* New example of Venezuela and the dangers of printing money to offset deficits. New key term: labor force participation rate. New *In the News* topic: impact on unemployment of hotel chains automating the check-in process.

CHAPTER 7

New *In the News* topic: The United Kingdom's slowing growth rate and Brexit.

CHAPTER 8

Wholly rewritten section on recessionary and inflationary gaps, including new key term and heading: GDP gap. New *In the News* topics: effects of tax cuts; effects of infrastructure spending when the economy is experiencing expansion vs. recession.

CHAPTER 9

Wholly revised section: *Short Run.* New *In the News* topics: what happens to the multiplier effect when government increases spending and reduces taxes at a time when unemployment is below the natural rate, as in 2019; how a trade dispute, such as between the United States and China, can lead to a slowing of aggregate output in both countries.

CHAPTER 10

Wholly revised sections: *Investment in Infrastructure, Capital, and Research and Development* and *Reducing Tax Rates and Regulations.* New *In the News* topics: the long-term implications of the 2.1% rise in interest rates on 30-year Treasury bonds; implications of counting the estimated output of informal activities as part of GDP.

CHAPTER 11

New section: *Cryptocurrency.* New *In the News* topics: potential change in incentives to work and save of raising the minimum age for when one can begin collecting Social Security benefits from 62 to 65; investing in SpaceX vs. other investments.

CHAPTER 12

Expanded explanation of the structure of the Federal Reserve. New *In the News* topic: what would be the risks to the economy if the Federal Reserve were abolished?

CHAPTER 13

Wholly rewritten section: *Monetary Policy Challenges* and its subsections *Joining Versus Leaving a Common Currency* and *Politicization of Monetary Policy*. New *In the News* topics: potential impact of bringing in board members with strong political views; austerity measures in Greece to deal with the debt crisis.

CHAPTER 14

Wholly rewritten section: *From Recession to Recovery: The Government in Action* and its subsections *From the Housing Bubble to the Financial Crisis, The Government's Policy Response*, and *The U.S. Economy: A Decade Later*. Wholly rewritten section, *Macroeconomic Issues That Confront Our Future*, including the new section *Automation and Its Effect on the Macroeconomy*. New key term: automation. New *In*

the News topic: implications of greater transparency from the Fed.

CHAPTER 15

Wholly rewritten section *Absolute and Comparative Advantage* and its subsections *Gains From Trade, The Terms of Trade,* and *Effects of Tariffs and Quotas*. New *In the News* topic: the possible connection between restricting migrant workers and restricting international trade.

CHAPTER 16

New *In the News* topics: how the increasing tourist trade affects foreign exchange of the Icelandic krona; American tourism in Cuba and the 10% tax of foreign exchange transactions.

NEW ONLINE CHAPTER A: *Economics of Health Care*: analysis of the supply and demand for health care; divergent incentives between stakeholders; current health care policy and debate.

NEW ONLINE CHAPTER B: *Economics of Food and Agriculture*: Characteristics of the U.S. agricultural industry; price fluctuations; government intervention; international trade disputes.

Acknowledgments

No project of this scope is accomplished alone. *Economics: Principles for a Changing World* and its suite of learning resources came together as a result of the dedication of many individuals who devoted incredible amounts of time to the project. These include reviewers of manuscript chapters, workshop participants, accuracy checkers, digital resource contributors, project specialists, and the production and editorial staff at Worth Publishers.

I want to thank the following individuals who provided valuable feedback and suggestions through formal reviews as well as from casual emails, conversations over coffee, and meetings during campus visits and conferences:

Kenneth Baker, *University of Tennessee, Knoxville*

Mongoljin Batsaikhan, *Georgetown University in Qatar*

William Bosshardt, *Florida Atlantic University*

Emilio Bruna, *Santa Fe College*

Jeff Buser, *Ohio State University*

Joe Craig, *University of Colorado at Colorado Springs*

John Cullis, *Iowa State University*

Peter S. Cunningham, *Mt. Hood Community College*

Monica Escaleras, *Florida Atlantic University*

Debbie Evercloud, *University of Colorado Denver*

Maurita Fawls, *Portland Community College, Sylvania*

Louis Foglia, *Suffolk University*

Jonathan Haughton, *Suffolk University*

John Homer, *Olivet College*

Karen Kressenberg, *Martin Methodist College*

Daniel D. Kuester, *Kansas State University*

Susan Laury, *Georgia State University*

Eric Levy, *Florida Atlantic University*

Ting Levy, *Florida Atlantic University*

Ishuan Li, *Minnesota State University, Mankato*

Bryan Lynch, *Lake Land College*

Christos Makriyannis, *Suffolk University*

Charles Meyrick, *Housatonic Community College*

Erick M. Perez, *Broward College*

Dennis Petruska, *Youngstown State University*

Susan Russell, *Saddleback College*

Jeff Salavitabar, *Delaware County Community College*

Olga Shemyakina, *Georgia Institute of Technology*

Robert D. Simonson, *Minnesota State University, Mankato*

Leticia Starkov, *Elgin Community College*

John S. Thompson, *University of Texas at Austin*

Caleb Watkins, *University of Tennessee at Chattanooga*

My current and former students (over 20,000 and counting) have influenced my career tremendously. They made this book possible. Their comments, body language, and facial expressions provide cues to whether my concept explanations and applications are clear and provide guidance on how to approach these topics in the book. Many have provided feedback and shared ideas for examples that resonate with students today. I especially thank Jonathan Lu, Felicia Lu, Yoko Uyehara, Andrew Hetzel, Michael Schwob, and Anne Isman for their passion for economics and desire to explore concepts at a deeper level.

I am thankful to have a friend and colleague in Vicky Chiu-Irion of Honolulu Community College, who has contributed to this edition in more ways than I can adequately describe. Vicky meticulously examined every chapter, line by line, catching errors as well as suggesting alternative explanations to improve the clarity of each concept. In addition to her eagle eye for detail, she provided many new examples used in this edition and is always willing to class-test new features developed for this book.

I also thank Thomas Dunn for his remarkable skills as a data and fact-checker. From revisions in terms used by government organizations to recent changes in the name of a country's capital city, Thomas was able to catch these hard-to-notice errors that allow the book to be as accurate and up-to-date as possible.

Macmillan's team of technology specialists who manage the online resources and customer experience are truly instrumental to the success of this product. I thank Travis Long, learning solutions specialist, for his tireless efforts in working with instructors setting up their courses, resolving issues, and connecting with prospective and current users. I also thank Andrew Robinson, Client Success Specialist, and Thomas Acox, Customer Experience, for always responding quickly and thoughtfully whenever I have a suggestion or a gripe related to improving the student and/or instructor's digital experience.

A tremendous amount of gratitude goes to Lindsay Neff and the supplements authors. Lindsay always finds the very best people to author each component of the suite of resources for this book. I thank Jaclyn Lindo and Janet Wolcutt, who managed the revision of the Test Bank; Andrea Valenzuela for authoring questions for the Around the World and Author Video features; AJ Sumell and Debbie Evercloud who prepared the classroom questions slides; Jesse Liebman and Joe Nowakowski who worked on lecture video activities and Bloomberg video activities respectively; Smit Vasquez Caballero, Matt Carlson and

Joe Nowakowski who worked on the online version of end-of-chapter material; and Amanda Dunaway who made sure everything was completed on time. Thanks also to Kristyn Brown for managing the development of the excellent assessment program.

I am truly indebted to Jeremy Brown, who over the years taught me the tools and tricks of digital technology that are indispensable in a media driven world. These tools include video editing, animation, and other visual effects, creating a professional Web site, and maximizing the effectiveness of social media. Whenever I have a technology-related question, I can count on Jeremy for an answer. His influence has given me the confidence to use cutting-edge technology to its maximum potential to the benefit of the fifth edition's suite of resources.

The production team at Worth is truly the best in the industry. My heartfelt thanks go to the entire team, including Natasha Wolfe, senior designer manager, and John Callahan for the fantastic set of interior and cover designs; Edgar Doolan, senior content project manager, for skillfully managing the copyediting and proofing of the book; Bruce Owens for his superb copyediting; photo editors Christine Buese and Donna Ranieri for researching and obtaining rights to hundreds of beautiful photos used in the book; Paul W. Rohloff, Senior Workflow Project Manager and Ronald D'Souza, senior project manager at Lumina Datamatics, Inc.; Katie Pachnos; and Tracey Kuehn, director, content management and enhancement. Each of these individuals made sure each part of the production process went smoothly. Thank you very much for a job well done.

It is a true pleasure working with Valerie Raymond, senior development editor. Valerie has remarkable insight for how books are portrayed in a culturally diverse society with many unique perspectives on economic issues. She made sure this book provides a foundation for discussing and debating issues from any viewpoint a student may have. I also thank Sarah Seymour, program manager, for her tireless efforts in ensuring that this book meets the needs of today's instructors and students. She is always gathering feedback from the book's users to enhance its ability to improve the learning experience. I thank Shani Fisher, publisher, for her determination to broaden the appeal of this book to a wider market, and Chuck Linsmeier, vice president, social sciences, who signed me as an author and provides continuous support with each edition.

You could not ask for a better marketing team than that at Worth. Over 150 sales representatives, technology specialists, and regional managers all work seamlessly to match each instructor with the best resources to meet the needs of students. I thank Andrew Zierman, marketing manager, for his talent and enthusiasm in providing current and prospective users innovative experiences such as the annual EconED conference, regional events, campus visits, webinars, community groups, and social media campaigns.

Finally, I thank Bruce Kaplan and Jerry Stone, two friends who had profound influence in my career as an author. Bruce was my former development editor who guided me through earlier editions of this book. His decades of experience was instrumental to this book's success. Many of the features in the fifth edition are the result of Bruce's insights that were implemented with each new edition. Jerry is a friend and colleague who put his full trust in me when he asked me to assume authorship of this book and carry it forward to a new generation of students and instructors. I will never cease my efforts to make *Economics: Principles for a Changing World* a long-lasting legacy of Jerry's brilliance and dedication to students and instructors.

Brief Contents

Contents

6 Measuring Inflation and Unemployment • 135

7 Economic Growth • 163

Macroeconomics

Exploring Economics

Understanding how economics explains everyday decisions made by individuals, businesses, and governments

magine jumping over open pits of fire, being chased by crazed people with sticks, diving through muddy pools of water under barbed wire, and climbing over a series of rocky walls. This does not describe a war zone or a military boot camp. Instead, these are typical challenges found in the increasingly popular sport of obstacle course racing. Also known as Warrior Dash, Tough Mudder, and Spartan Race, obstacle course racing incorporates demanding physical and mental obstacles to challenge individuals over the standard 3- to 5-mile (or longer) length of the course.

Does this sound thrilling? Or perhaps crazy? These are common thoughts that come to mind when people talk about the increasing popularity of new adventure sports. Would you imagine that whether or not to participate in such an activity is an economic question? Most people probably would not. But this example resembles an economic problem in many ways. Obstacle course racing involves a challenge, one with a *benefit* (a sense of accomplishment) and a *cost* (including monetary costs, physical demands on the body, and a risk of injury). It involves *tradeoffs* such as the countless hours spent practicing and training in order to be successful. And it involves societal beliefs about whether such activities should be regulated or restricted to persons of a minimum age and well-being. Benefits, costs, tradeoffs, and regulation: These are the foundations for making an economic decision. Nearly all decisions made by individuals, firms, and governments in pursuit of an objective or goal can be understood using these economic concepts.

By the end of this course, you will come to understand that economics involves all types of decisions, from small everyday decisions on how to manage one's time to life-changing decisions made by world leaders. Consumers make decisions about what clothes to buy and what foods to eat. Businesses must decide what products to make and how much of each product to stock on store shelves. Indeed, one cannot escape making decisions, and the outcomes of these decisions affect not only our own lives but also those of entire societies and countries.

You still might be asking yourself: Why should I study economics? First, you will spend roughly the next 40 years working in an economic environment: paying taxes, experiencing ups and downs in the overall economy, investing money, and voting on various economic issues. It will benefit you to know how the economy works. More important, economic analysis gives you a structure from which you can make decisions in a more rational manner. Economics teaches you how to make better and wiser decisions given your limited resources. This course may well change the way you look at the world. It can open your eyes to how you make everyday decisions, from what to buy to where you choose to live.

Like our opening example, economic analysis involves decisions that are not just "economic" in the general sense of the term. Certainly, economic thinking may change your views on spending and saving, on how you feel about government debt, and on your opinions of environmental policies and globalization. But you also may develop a different perspective on how much time to study for each of your courses this term or where you might go for spring break this year. Such is the wide scope of economic analysis.

Economics as a Career and a Valuable Tool for Life

Economics is one of the most popular college majors in the country. This is because so much of what we do, the decisions we face, and the issues we confront involve economics. But what do economists do as a career? The answer is wide ranging, another reason for its popularity as a major of study. Some economics majors go on to law school, others to a graduate business program, and others to public policy programs. Some pursue teaching careers, work in government organizations, consult or invest in the financial sector, or work in one of thousands of corporations that use economists to forecast revenues and costs, analyze demand and pricing data, and make strategic decisions to stay ahead of the competition. Truly, economics is a well-rounded subject that leads to many career choices. This By the Numbers looks more closely at careers that economists pursue.

DATA:

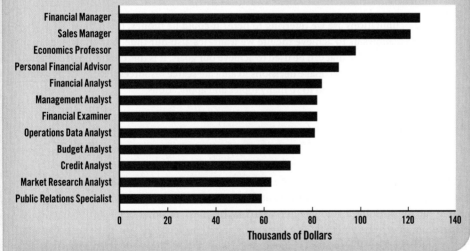

Popular Jobs Held by Economists and Their Median Annual Salaries in 2017 (in thousands of dollars)

Where Can I Find These Data?

Source: Bureau of Labor Statistics; U.S. Department of Labor **Web site:** https://www.bls.gov/bls/blswage.htm

Details: In the National Wage Data section, links are provided for wage data by occupation. One can then download a spreadsheet containing detailed data, including median wages by occupation.

~ Assessing Your Data Literacy ~

1. Based on the list of popular jobs held by economists, what is the median salary of a financial manager? What is the median salary of a public relations specialist?

2. What factors might explain the large difference in median salary between a financial manager and a public relations specialist?

3. Based on the introduction at the top of this page, what types of jobs (other than those listed in the graph) might economists hold?

47,092

Total number of economics bachelor's degrees awarded in the United States in 2018

$112,800

The median salary of workers with economics degrees after 15 years of work experience in 2018

WHY ARE THESE DATA IMPORTANT?

According to the discussion in the text, economics is about making choices and tradeoffs. Choosing one's major is one of the most important decisions in college and requires a tradeoff of other subjects in which one can major. The good news is that the data show many well-paying careers that economics majors can pursue after graduating.

Data *in the News*

"Picking Your College Major Could Mean Big Money" by Adam Tamburin; *Tennessean*, June 5, 2015

Picking a major could have a bigger influence on future earnings than deciding to go to college in the first place, according to a new study. Workers with college degrees earn an average of $1 million more than high school graduates over the course of their lifetimes. But the gap between the highest- and lowest-paying college majors is wider.

This introductory chapter takes a broad look at economics. First, we study a key method of economic analysis: model building. Economists use stylized facts and the technique of holding some variables constant to develop testable theories about how consumers, businesses, and governments make decisions. Then we turn to a short discussion of some key principles of economics to give you a sense of the guiding concepts you will encounter in this book.

This chapter will give you a sense of what economics is, what concepts it uses, and what it finds to be important. Do not go into this chapter thinking you have to memorize these concepts. Rather, use this chapter to get a sense of the expansive scope of economics. You will be given many opportunities to understand and use these concepts throughout this course. Return to this chapter at the end of the course and see if everything has now become crystal clear.

WHAT IS ECONOMICS ABOUT?

Economics is a very dynamic and comprehensive subject. It often seems that economics has something important to say about almost everything.

economics The study of how individuals, firms, and society make decisions to allocate limited resources to many competing wants.

To boil it down to a simple definition, **economics** is about making choices. Economics studies how individuals, firms, and societies make decisions to maximize their well-being given limitations. In other words, economics attempts to address the problem of having too many wants but too few resources to achieve them all, an important concept called **scarcity**. Note that scarcity is not the same thing as something being *scarce*. Although all resources are scarce, certain goods are less scarce than others. For example, cars are not very scarce—there are car dealerships around the country filled with cars ready to be sold, but that doesn't mean you can go out tonight and buy three. Scarcity refers to the fact that people must make choices given the resource limitations they face.

scarcity Our unlimited wants clash with limited resources, leading to scarcity. Everyone (rich or poor) faces scarcity because, at a minimum, our time on earth is limited. Economics focuses on the allocation of scarce resources to satisfy unlimited wants as fully as possible.

What kind of limitations are we referring to here? It could be money, but money is not the only resource that allows us to achieve the life we want. It's also our time, our knowledge, our work ethic, and anything else that can be used to achieve our goals. It is this definition of economics being the study of how people make decisions to allocate scarce resources to competing wants that allows the subject to be applied to so many topics and applications.

Why Study Economics?

The first answer that might come to mind as to why you are taking this course is "because I have to." Although economics is a required course for many college students, economics should be thought of as something much, much more. For example, studying economics can prepare you for many types of careers in major industries and government. Studying economics also is a great launching pad for pursuing a graduate degree in law, business, or other fields. More practically speaking, economics helps you to think more clearly about the decisions you make every day and to understand better how the economy functions and why certain things happen the way they do.

For example, economics has some important things to say about the environment. Most people care about the environment to some degree and do their part by recycling, not littering, and turning off the lights when leaving a room. But not all people make decisions in the same way: Some might do much more to conserve resources, such as driving less, avoiding disposable plastic, or writing to policymakers to support sustainability legislation. The extent to which people participate in environmental activities depends on the benefit they perceive when pursuing such actions compared to the costs, which can include monetary costs, time and effort, and forgone opportunities such as driving a larger, more comfortable car. A challenge, however, is that these costs are more immediate, while the benefits of a cleaner environment may not fully materialize until later. But the consequences of doing nothing now may result in significant future costs. Economics looks at all of these factors to determine how people make decisions that affect the environment, which affects us all. Economics is a way of thinking about an issue, not just a discipline that has money as its chief focus.

The way in which economists think often focuses on how individuals respond to **incentives**. Incentives are the factors, both good and bad, that influence how people make decisions. For example, tough admissions requirements for graduate school provide an incentive for students to study harder in college, while lucrative commissions push car salespeople to sell even the ugliest or most unreliable car. Economists begin most questions by considering how rational people would respond to the incentives that specific situations provide. Sometimes this analysis leads us down an unexpected path.

incentives The factors that motivate individuals and firms to make decisions in their best interest.

Microeconomics Versus Macroeconomics

Economics is split into two broad categories: microeconomics and macroeconomics. **Microeconomics** deals with decision making by individuals, businesses, and industries. It is concerned with issues such as which orange juice to buy, which job to take, and where to go on vacation as well as which items a business should produce and what price it should charge and whether a market should be left on its own or be regulated.

microeconomics The study of the decision-making by individuals, businesses, and industries.

Microeconomics looks at how markets are structured. Some markets are very competitive, where many firms offer similar products. Other markets have only one or two large firms, offering little choice. What decisions do businesses make under different market structures? Microeconomics also extends to such topics as labor laws, environmental policy, and health care policy. How can we use the tools of microeconomics to analyze the costs and benefits of differing policies?

Macroeconomics, on the other hand, focuses on the broader issues we face as a nation. Most of us don't care whether an individual buys Brooks or Sperry shoes. We *do* care whether prices of *all* goods and services rise. Inflation—a general increase in prices economy-wide—affects all of us. So does unemployment (virtually every person will at some point in their life be unemployed, even if it's just for a short time when switching from one job to another) and economic growth. What decisions do governments make to deal with macroeconomic problems such as inflation and recessions?

macroeconomics The study of the broader issues in the economy such as inflation, unemployment, and national output of goods and services.

Macroeconomics uses microeconomic tools to answer some questions, but its main focus is on the aggregate variables of the economy. Macroeconomics has its own terms and topics, such as business cycles, recession, and unemployment. Macroeconomics looks at policies that increase economic growth, the impact of government spending and taxation, the effect of monetary policy on the economy, and inflation. It also looks closely at theories of international trade and international finance. All of these topics impact our economy and our standard of living.

Still not clear? Here's an easy way to remember the difference between microeconomics and macroeconomics. Only one letter separates the two terms, so just remember that the "i" in microeconomics refers to "individual" entities (such as a person or a firm), while the "a" in macroeconomics refers to "aggregate" entities (such as cities or a nation as a whole).

Although we break economics into microeconomics and macroeconomics, there is considerable overlap in the analysis. Both involve the analysis of how individuals, firms, and governments make decisions that affect the lives of people. We use simple supply and demand analysis to understand *both* individual markets and the general economy as a whole. You will find yourself using concepts from microeconomics to understand fluctuations in the macroeconomy.

Economics is a social science that uses many facts and figures to develop and express ideas. This inevitably involves numbers. For macroeconomics, this means getting used to talking and thinking in huge numbers: billions (nine zeros) and trillions (twelve zeros). Today, we are talking about a federal government budget of over $4 trillion. To conceptualize such a huge number, consider how long it would take to spend a trillion dollars if you spent a dollar every second, or $86,400 per day. To spend $1 trillion would require almost 32,000 years. And the federal government now spends over 4 times this much in one year.

Economic Theories and Reality

If you flip through any economics text, you'll likely see a multitude of graphs, charts, and equations. This book is no exception. The good news is that all of the graphs and charts become relatively easy to understand since they all basically read the same way. The few equations in this book stem from elementary algebra. Once you get through one equation, the rest are similar.

Graphs, charts, and equations are often the simplest and most efficient ways to express data and ideas. Equations are used to express relationships between two variables. Complex and wordy discussions can often be reduced to a simple graph or figure. These are efficient techniques for expressing economic ideas.

Model Building As you study economics this term, you will encounter stylized approaches to a number of issues. By *stylized,* we mean that economists boil down facts to their basic relevant elements and use assumptions to develop a stylized (simple) model to analyze the issue. There are always situations that lie outside these models, but they are exceptions.

We begin with relatively simple models, then gradually build to more difficult ones. For example, the most important model in this book is supply and demand, which begins as a simple illustration with two lines but has profound implications on the role of free markets and prices. We can then add more dimensions to make the model more applicable to complex situations, but often the insights are still based on the simplest notion of the model.

ceteris paribus Assumption used in economics (and other disciplines as well) that other relevant factors or variables are held constant.

Ceteris Paribus: **All Else Held Constant** To aid in our model building, economists use the *ceteris paribus* assumption: "Holding all other things equal." That means we will hold some important variables constant. For example, to determine how many songs you might be willing to download from iTunes in any given month, we would hold your monthly income constant. We then would change song prices to see the impact on the number purchased (again holding your monthly income constant).

Though model building can lead to surprising insights into how economic actors and economies behave, it is not the end of the story. Economic insights lead to economic theories, but these theories must then be tested. In some cases, such as the extent to which a housing bubble could lead to a financial crisis, economic predictions turned out to be false. Thus, model building is a *process*—models are created and then tested. If models fail to explain reality, new models are constructed.

Efficiency Versus Equity

efficiency How well resources are used and allocated. Do people obtain the goods and services they want at the lowest possible resource cost? This is the chief focus of efficiency.

Efficiency deals with how well resources are used and allocated. No one likes waste. Much of economic analysis is directed toward ensuring that the most efficient outcomes result from public policy. There are different ways in which efficiency is measured. *Production efficiency* occurs when goods are produced at the lowest cost. *Allocative efficiency* occurs when individuals who desire a product the most obtain those goods and services. And *Pareto efficiency* occurs when society improves the well-being of as many individuals as possible without making anyone worse off. Each of these measures of efficiency is important when debating policies that affect the lives of many people.

equity The fairness of various issues and policies.

The other way we evaluate how resources are used and allocated is **equity,** or fairness. Is it fair that the CEOs of large companies make hundreds of times more money than their service workers? Is it fair that some have so much and others have so little? Should society take care of the homeless and disabled? There are many divergent views about fairness until we get to extreme cases. When just a few people earn nearly all of the income and control nearly all of a society's wealth, most people agree that this is unfair.

Throughout this course, you will see instances where efficiency and equity collide. You may agree that a specific policy is efficient but think it is unfair to some group of people. This will be especially evident when you consider tax policy and its impact on income distribution. Fairness, or equity, is a subjective concept, and each of us has different ideas about what is just and fair. When it comes to public policy issues, economics will help you see the tradeoffs between equity and efficiency, but you will ultimately have to make up your own mind about the wisdom of the policy given these tradeoffs.

ISSUE

Do Economists Ever Agree on Anything?

Give me a one-handed economist! All my economists say, "on one hand . . . on the other."

—Harry S. Truman

President Truman once exclaimed that the country needed more *one-handed economists*. What did he mean by that? He was saying that anytime an economist talks about a solution to an economic problem, the economist will often follow that statement by saying, "on the other hand. . . ."

Economics is about making choices with scarce resources and the tradeoffs that result. Because individuals place different values on the benefits and costs within these tradeoffs, nearly every economic issue can be viewed from different perspectives, so much so that economists seemingly disagree with one another on everything.

For example, suppose we debate whether gasoline taxes are too high.

On the one hand, higher gasoline taxes will reduce oil consumption, reduce pollution, reduce traffic congestion, and generate money to promote public transportation such as buses, subways, and high-speed trains. *On the other hand*, higher gasoline taxes raise the cost of commuting to work and school, make travel more expensive, and result in higher prices for many consumer goods due to higher shipping costs.

Different opinions about the relative weights of benefits and costs make economic policymaking challenging. Economic conditions are always changing. This is why economists rely so much on models and assumptions in order to prescribe a solution based on the conditions facing the economy.

But despite differences and frequent disagreements in economic policy, economists do agree on many things, such as the value of specialization, the efficiency

John Lund/Getty Images

of markets, and the role of incentives. These areas of consensus are grounded in the key economic principles described in the next section of this chapter.

Positive Versus Normative Questions

Returning to the example in the chapter opener, we ask ourselves many questions whenever a decision needs to be made or an issue is debated. Some questions involve the understanding of basic facts, such as how risky a particular sport is or how much enjoyment one receives from participating in the sport. Economists call these types of questions **positive questions**. Positive questions (which need not be positive or upbeat in the literal sense) are questions that can be answered one way or another as long as the information is available. This does not mean that people will always agree on an answer because presentation of facts and information can differ.

Another type of question that arises is how something ought to be, such as whether extreme sports should be banned or whether additional safety measures should be required. Economists call these types of questions **normative questions**. Normative questions involve societal beliefs on what should or should not be done; differing opinions on an issue can sometimes make normative questions difficult to resolve.

Throughout this book, positive and normative questions will arise, which will play an important role in how individuals and firms make decisions and how governments form policy proposals that may or may not become law. Indeed, economics encompasses many ideas and questions that affect everyone.

positive question A question that can be answered using available information or facts.

normative question A question whose answer is based on societal beliefs on what should or should not take place.

✅ CHECKPOINT

WHAT IS ECONOMICS ABOUT?

- Economics is about making decisions under scarcity, in which wants are unlimited but resources are limited.

- Economics is separated into two broad categories: microeconomics and macroeconomics.

- *Microeconomics* deals with individuals, firms, and industries and how they make decisions.

- *Macroeconomics* focuses on broader economic issues such as inflation, employment and unemployment, and economic growth.

- Economics uses a stylized approach, creating simple models that hold all other relevant factors constant (*ceteris paribus*).

- Economists and policymakers often face a tradeoff between efficiency and equity.

- Positive questions can be answered with facts and information, while normative questions ask how something should or ought to be.

QUESTION: In each of the following situations, determine whether it is a microeconomic or macroeconomic issue.

1. Hewlett-Packard announces that it is lowering the price of its printers by 15%.
2. The president proposes a tax cut.
3. You decide to look for a new job.
4. The economy is in a recession, and the job market is worsening.
5. The Federal Reserve announces that it is raising interest rates because it fears inflation.
6. You receive a nice raise.
7. Average wages grew by 2% last year.

Answers to the Checkpoint questions can be found at the end of this chapter.

KEY PRINCIPLES OF ECONOMICS

Economics has a set of key principles that show up continually in economic analysis. Some are more restricted to specific issues, but most apply universally. In the following, we summarize eight key principles that will be applied throughout the entire book. By the end of this course, these principles should be crystal clear, and you will likely find yourself using these principles throughout your life, even if you never take another economics course.

Principle 1: Economics Is Concerned With Making Choices With Limited Resources

Economics deals with nearly every type of decision we face each day. But when a typical person is asked what economics is about, the most common answer is "money." Why is economics commonly misconceived as dealing only with money? This may be due in part to how economics is portrayed in the news—dealing with financial issues, jobs and wages, and the cost of living, among other money matters. While money matters are indeed an important issue studied in economics, you now know that economics involves much, much more.

Economics is about making decisions on allocating limited resources to maximize an individual or society's well-being. Money is just one source of well-being, assuming that more money makes a person happier, all else equal. But other factors also improve a person's well-being, such as receiving a day off from work with pay. Even if one does not have a lot of money or free time, satisfaction can come from other activities or events, such as participating in a fun activity with friends or family or watching one's favorite team win.

In sum, many aspects of life contribute to the well-being of individuals and of society. Unfortunately, often these are limited by various resource constraints. Therefore, one must think of economics in a broad sense of determining how best to manage all of society's resources (not just money) in order to maximize well-being. This involves tradeoffs and opportunity costs, which we consider next.

Principle 2: When Making Decisions, One Must Take Into Account Tradeoffs and Opportunity Costs

Wouldn't it be great if we all had the resources of Sheryl Sandberg, the chief operating officer at Facebook and a billionaire who is one of the most powerful women in business? That amount of wealth can buy just about any material possession one could possibly want. Still, everyone has limited resources, including Ms. Sandberg, because resources comprise more than just money. For example, we all face time limitations: There are only 24 hours in a day, and some of that must be spent sleeping. The fact that we have many wants but limited resources (scarcity) means that we must make tradeoffs in nearly everything we do. In other words, we have to decide between alternatives, which always exist whenever we make a decision.

How is this accomplished? What factors determine whether you buy a nicer car or use extra money to pay down debt? Or whether you should spend the weekend at a local music festival or use the time to study for an exam? Economists use an important term to help weigh the benefits and costs of every decision we make, and that term is **opportunity cost**. In fact, economics is often categorized as the discipline that always weighs benefits against costs.

At its very core, opportunity cost is determined by asking yourself, in any situation, "What could I be doing right now if I weren't _____ (fill in the activity)?" or "What could I have bought if I hadn't bought this _____ (fill in the last good or service you bought)?" Opportunity cost measures the value of the next best alternative use of your time or money, or what you *give up* when you make an economic decision. And since there are always alternatives, one cannot avoid opportunity costs.

A common mistake that people make is that they sometimes do not fully take their opportunity cost into account. Have you ever waited in a very long line to buy the latest smartphone or concert ticket? Have you ever spent a copious amount of time to dispute a parking ticket? When making decisions that involve your time and effort, opportunity cost includes the value of everything you give up in order to make that purchase, including the money spent and the time, because these are all resources that could be used for other purposes. The sum of all opportunity costs can sometimes outweigh the benefits, especially if the product is sold out or if you are not successful at disputing that parking ticket.

Every activity involves opportunity costs. Sleeping, eating, studying, partying, running, hiking, and so on all require that we spend resources that could be used on another activity. Opportunity cost varies from person to person. A company president rushing from meeting to meeting has a higher opportunity cost than a retired senior citizen and therefore is more likely to choose the quickest option to accomplish day-to-day activities.

Opportunity costs apply to us as individuals and to societies as a whole. For example, if a country chooses to spend more on environmental conservation, it must use resources that otherwise could be used to promote other objectives, such as education and health care.

Principle 3: Specialization Leads to Gains for All Involved

Whenever we pursue an activity or a task, we use time that could be used for other activities or tasks. However, sometimes these other tasks are best left to others to perform. Life would be much more difficult if we all had to grow our own food. This highlights the idea that tradeoffs (especially with one's time) can lead to better outcomes if one is able to specialize in activities in which she or he is more proficient.

Suppose you and your roommate can each cook your own dinner and clean your own rooms. Alternatively, you might have your roommate clean both rooms (he's better at it than you) in exchange for you preparing dinner for two (you're a better cook). Using this arrangement, both tasks are completed in less time since each of you is specializing in the activity you're better at, plus both of you will benefit from a cleaner apartment and a tastier dinner.

Another example of specialization begins when you select an academic major. Taking a large number of courses in one subject helps you to become an expert and subsequently more attractive to potential employers. A cautionary note: When choosing a major, be sure it is a subject that you are actually good at! Specializing in something that you are not passionate about may lead to disappointment down the road.

opportunity cost The value of the next best alternative; what you give up to do something or purchase something.

Charles Krupa/AP Images

Even Sheryl Sandberg, one of wealthiest women in the world, faces tradeoffs.

Specialization in tasks in which one is more proficient can lead to gains for all parties as long as exchange is possible and those involved trade in a mutually beneficial manner. Each person is acting on the opportunity to improve his or her well-being, an example of how incentives affect people's lives. The following Around the World feature describes how specialization is vital in the Canadian province of Nunavut, where resources are very limited and its residents depend on other regions for their daily necessities.

Principle 4: People Respond to Incentives, Both Good and Bad

Each time an individual or a firm makes a decision, that person or firm is acting on an incentive that drives the individual or firm to choose an action. These incentives often occur naturally. For example, we choose to eat every day because we face an incentive to survive, and we study and work hard because we face an incentive to be successful in our careers. However, incentives also can be formed by policies set by government to encourage individuals and firms to act in certain ways and by businesses to encourage consumers to change their consumption habits.

For example, tax policy rests on the idea that people respond to incentives. Do we want to encourage people to save for their retirement? Then let them deduct a certain amount that they can put into a tax-deferred retirement account. Do we want businesses to spend more to stimulate the economy? Then give them tax credits for new investment. Do we want people to go to college? Then give them tax advantages for setting up education savings accounts.

AROUND THE WORLD

Nunavut: Land of Abundance and Scarcity

How does the condition of scarcity determine the economic tradeoffs observed in Canada's newest and largest province?

What products is Canada known for? Canada is a northern country known for its lakes and forests. And what are forests made of? Trees, of course. How important are trees? Just ask the 38,000 residents in the newest Canadian province of Nunavut. They know because they have no trees!

With a landmass roughly equal to Alaska and California combined, Nunavut has many natural resources but lacks the

one resource most often associated with Canada: trees. With much of Nunavut's landmass situated above the tree line, it must rely on goods supplied by other provinces and imported from other countries for its building materials and agricultural products. A visit to Nunavut highlights the

prevalence of scarcity and the necessity of specialization and trade.

For example, nearly all of Nunavut's food, household goods, and building materials must be flown in to its sparsely populated communities accessible only by air or snowmobile, resulting in extremely high prices for most goods. However, Nunavut has many gold mines and fisheries that allow it to specialize and export precious metals and its famous Arctic char fish, a close relative to the salmon.

Residents of even the most remote places of the world can solve the challenge of scarcity and gain access to many goods and services by engaging in specialization and trade.

GO ONLINE TO PRACTICE THE ECONOMIC CONCEPTS IN THIS STORY

ISSUE

Would a City Change Its Name for a Game Show?

Driving along Interstate 25 in central New Mexico, one encounters a city with a very peculiar name, one that required the state's Department of Transportation to order extra-long road signs: Truth or Consequences. Originally named Hot Springs, the small city is popular for its natural hot springs and small quaint lodges that dot the landscape in this remote part of the desert. How did the city of Hot Springs end up changing its name?

In 1950 a popular radio game show called *Truth or Consequences*, hosted by Ralph Edwards, offered a challenge. If any city was willing to rename itself Truth or Consequences, Mr. Edwards would host his show from that location. Hot Springs

saw this as an opportunity to raise its city profile and therefore acted on the incentive to be the first and only city to accept the challenge. It subsequently changed its official name to Truth or Consequences, New Mexico, a name that remains in use.

Truth or Consequences has benefited from its name change long after it. The city continues to host an annual fiesta that welcomed Mr. Edwards in person every year for the 50 years that followed the name change. Today, Truth or Consequences remains a small city of 6,500 residents and is still popular for its natural springs. But on the horizon is another famous person, Sir Richard Branson, the founder of Virgin Galactic, who plans to

develop a commercial space flight industry in New Mexico. The location, Spaceport America, is just 25 miles from Truth or Consequences, another attraction that will add to the city's unique character.

Tax policy is an obvious example in which people follow incentives. But this principle can be seen in action wherever you look. Want to encourage people to fly during the slow travel season? Offer price discounts or bonus frequent flyer miles for flying during that period. Want to increase business at restaurants? Give early-bird discounts to those willing to eat at 5:00 P.M., before peak dining time.

Note that in saying that people follow incentives, economists do not claim that everyone follows each incentive every time. Though you may not want to eat dinner at 5:00 P.M., there might be other people who are willing to eat earlier in return for a price discount.

If not properly constructed, incentives might lead to harmful outcomes. During the 2008 financial crisis, it became clear that the incentives for traders and executives offered by Wall Street investment banks were misguided. Traders and executives were paid bonuses based on short-term profits. This encouraged them to take extreme risks to generate quick profits and high bonuses with little regard for the long-term viability of the bank. The bank might have shut down the next day, but these people still had those huge bonuses.

Responding to badly designed incentives is often described as greed, but they are not always the same. If you found a $20 bill on the sidewalk, would you pick it up? You may, but would that make you a greedy person? The stranger who accidentally dropped the bill an hour ago might think so, but you are just responding to an incentive to pick up the money before the next lucky person does. Could incentives ever be designed to prevent people from picking up money they find? It may surprise you that one industry has: In many casinos, it is prohibited to keep chips or money you find on the floor.

The natural tendency for society to respond to incentives leads individuals and firms to work hard and generate ideas that increase productivity, a measure of a society's capacity to produce that determines our standard of living. A worker who can do twice as much as another is likely to earn a higher salary because productivity and pay tend to go together. The same is true for nations. Countries with the highest standards of living are also the most productive.

Principle 5: Rational Behavior Requires Thinking on the Margin

Have you ever noticed that when you eat at an all-you-can-eat buffet, you always go away fuller than when you order and eat at a nonbuffet restaurant? Is this phenomenon unique to you, or is there something more fundamental? Remember, economists look at facts to find incentives to economic behavior.

In this case, people are just rationally responding to the price of *additional* food. They are thinking on the margin. In a nonbuffet restaurant, dessert costs extra, and you make a decision as to whether the enjoyment you receive from the dessert (the marginal benefit) is worth the extra cost (the marginal cost). At the buffet, dessert is included, which means the marginal cost is zero. Even so, you still must ask yourself if dessert will give you satisfaction. If the dessert tastes terrible or adds unwanted calories to your diet, then you might pass on dessert even if it is free. But the fact that one is more likely to have dessert at a buffet than at a menu-based restaurant highlights the notion that people tend to think on the margin.

The idea of thinking on the margin applies to a society as well. Like asking ourselves whether we want another serving of dessert, a society must ask itself whether it wants a little bit more or a little bit less of something, and policymakers and/or citizens vote on such policy proposals. An example of society thinking on the margin is whether an increase in taxes should be used to pay for a new domestic project such as high-speed trains or space exploration or maybe not be raised at all.

Throughout this book, we will see examples of thinking on the margin. A business uses marginal analysis to determine how much of its products it is willing to supply to the market. Individuals use marginal analysis to determine how many hours to exercise or study. And governments use marginal analysis to determine how much pollution should be permitted.

Principle 6: Markets Are Generally Efficient; When They Aren't, Government Can Sometimes Correct the Failure

Individuals and firms make decisions that maximize their well-being, and markets bring buyers and sellers together. Private markets and the incentives they provide are the best mechanisms

Markets can be crowded and chaotic, but they generally promote an efficient outcome by bringing buyers and sellers together.

known today for providing products and services. There is no government food board that makes sure that bread, cereal, coffee, and all the other food products you demand are on your plate during the day. The vast majority of products we consume are privately provided.

Competition for the consumer dollar forces firms to provide products at the lowest possible price, or some other firm will undercut their high price. New products enter the market and old products die out. Such is the dynamic characteristic of markets.

What drives and disciplines markets? Prices and profits are the keys. Profits drive entrepreneurs to provide new products (think of Apple) or existing products at lower prices (think of Walmart). When prices and profits become too high in any market, new firms jump in with lower prices to grab away customers. This competition, or sometimes even the threat of competition, keeps markets from exploiting consumers.

Individuals and firms respond to prices in markets by altering the choices and quantities of goods they purchase and sell, respectively. These actions highlight the ability of markets to provide an efficient outcome for all. Markets can achieve this efficiency without a central planner mandating what people should buy or what firms should sell. This phenomenon that markets promote efficiency through the incentives faced by individuals and firms (as if they were guided by an omnipotent force) is referred to as the *invisible hand*, a term coined by Adam Smith, considered the father of modern economics.

As efficient as markets usually are, society does not desire a market for everything, such as hard drugs or child pornography. In other cases, a market may not provide enough of a good or service, such as public parks or public education. For these products and services, markets can fail to provide an optimal outcome.

But when markets do fail, they tend to do so in predictable ways. Where consumers have no choice but to buy from one firm (such as a local water company), the market will fail to provide the best solution, and government regulation is often used to protect consumers. Another example is pollution: Left unregulated, companies often will pollute the air and water. Governments then intervene to deal with this market failure. Finally, people rely on information to make rational decisions. When information is not readily available or is known only to one side of the market, markets again can fail to produce the socially desirable outcome.

We also can extend the idea of market efficiency to the greater economy. The market forces of supply and demand generally keep the economy in equilibrium. But occasionally, fluctuations in the macroeconomy will occur, and markets take time to readjust on their own. In some cases, the economy becomes stuck in a severe downturn. In these instances, government can smooth the fluctuations in the overall economy by using policies such as government spending or tax cuts. But remember, just because the government *can* successfully intervene does not mean it *always* successfully intervenes. The macroeconomy is not a simple machine. Successful policymaking is a tough task.

Principle 7: Economic Growth, Low Unemployment, and Low Inflation Are Economic Goals That Do Not Always Coincide

The reliance on private markets and reasonable government intervention aims to maximize societal gains in terms of higher incomes and standards of living. The key to higher standards of living is economic growth, which can be measured a number of ways, most commonly by estimating the change in a country's real gross domestic product per capita. Yet, other measures of economic growth include average household income, quality of education, infrastructure development, improvement in technology and innovation, environmental sustainability, and poverty reduction.

The goal of economic growth is fostered by policies set by government, including fiscal policy and monetary policy. But things are not always so simple, given the two persistent economic obstacles that naturally occur in the economy: unemployment and inflation. Unemployment and inflation often run opposite to one another; for example, when unemployment is high, inflation is generally low, and vice versa. When either unemployment or inflation is too high, economic growth can be inhibited. Government policy is therefore used to correct one problem at the potential expense of exacerbating the other.

In 2018, U.S. unemployment reached a low point of 3.7%, but the growing economy was pushing inflation higher. As a result, the U.S. Federal Reserve faced an important decision on how quickly to raise interest rates to prevent inflation from rising too quickly. But by making policy to keep inflation in check, the risk is that economic growth can slow down, causing unemployment to rise. Determining economic policy is like walking a tightrope: One must stay balanced to prevent toppling over to one side.

Principle 8: Institutions and Human Creativity Help Explain the Wealth of Nations

We have seen how individuals and firms make decisions to maximize their well-being and how tradeoffs, specialization, incentives, and marginal analysis play an important role. We then saw how markets bring buyers and sellers together to promote better outcomes and that governments sometimes step in when markets fail to produce the best outcome. But how does all of this affect the overall wealth of a nation? Two important factors influencing the wealth of nations are good institutions and human creativity.

Institutions include a legal system to enforce contracts and laws and to protect the rights of citizens and the ideas they create. It also includes a legislative process to develop laws and policies that provide incentives to individuals and firms to work hard, a government free of corruption, and a strong monetary system.

Equally as important as institutions is the ability of societies to create ideas. Ideas change civilizations. Ideas are the basis for creating new products and finding new ways to improve existing goods and services. Human creativity starts with a strong educational system, and builds with proper incentives that allow innovation and creativity to flourish into marketable outcomes to improve the lives of all.

ADAM SMITH (1723–1790)

When Adam Smith was 4 years old, he was kidnapped and held for ransom. Had his captors not taken fright and returned the boy unharmed, the history of economics might well have turned out differently.

Born in Kirkcaldy, Scotland, in 1723, Smith graduated from the University of Glasgow at age 17 and was awarded a scholarship to Oxford. Smith considered his time at Oxford to be largely wasted. Returning to Scotland in 1751, Smith was named Professor of Moral Philosophy at the University of Glasgow.

After 12 years at Glasgow, Smith began tutoring the son of a wealthy Scottish nobleman. This job provided him with the opportunity to spend several years touring the European continent with his young charge. In Paris, Smith met some of the leading French economists of the day, which helped stoke his own interest in political economy. While there, he wrote a friend, "I have begun to write a book in order to pass the time."

Returning to Kirkcaldy in 1766, Smith spent the next decade finishing An Inquiry Into the Nature and Causes of the Wealth of Nations. Before publication in 1776, he read sections of the text to Benjamin Franklin. Smith's genius was in taking the existing forms of economic analysis available at the time and putting them together in a systematic fashion to make sense of the national economy as a whole. Smith demonstrated how individuals left free to pursue their own economic interests end up acting in ways that enhance the welfare of all. This is Smith's famous "invisible hand." In Smith's words, "By directing that industry in such a manner as its produce may be of the greatest value, he intends only his own gain, and he is in this, as in many other cases, led by an invisible hand to promote an end which was no part of his intention."

How important was Adam Smith? He has been called the "father of political economy." Many of the foundations of economic analysis we still use today are based on Adam Smith's writings of several centuries ago.

Information from Howard Marshall, *The Great Economists: A History of Economic Thought* (New York: Pitman Publishing), 1967; Paul Strathern, *A Brief History of Economic Genius* (New York: Texere), 2002; Ian Ross, *The Life of Adam Smith* (Oxford: Clarendon Press), 1995.

Summing It All Up: Economics Is All Around Us

The examples presented in these key principles should have convinced you that economic decisions are a part of our everyday lives. Anytime we make a decision involving a purchase or decide what we plan to eat, study, or do with our day, we are making economic decisions. Just keep in mind that economics is broader than an exclusive concern with money despite the great emphasis placed on money in our everyday economic discussions.

Instead, economics is about making decisions when we can't have everything we want and how we interact with others to maximize our well-being given limitations. The existence of well-functioning markets allows individuals and firms to come together to achieve good outcomes, and government institutions and policies provide incentives that can lead to a better standard of living for all residents.

The key principles discussed in this chapter will be repeated throughout this book, and you will learn more about these important principles as the term progresses. For now, realize that economics rests on the foundation of a limited number of important principles. Once you fully grasp these basic ideas, the study of economics will be both rewarding and exciting because after this course you will discover and appreciate how much more you understand the world around you.

 CHECKPOINT

KEY PRINCIPLES OF ECONOMICS

- Economics is concerned with making choices with limited resources.
- When making decisions, one must take into account tradeoffs and opportunity costs.
- Specialization leads to gains for all involved.
- People respond to incentives, both good and bad.
- Rational behavior requires thinking on the margin.
- Markets are generally efficient; when they aren't, government can sometimes correct the failure.
- Economic growth, low unemployment, and low inflation are economic goals that do not always coincide.
- Institutions and human creativity help explain the wealth of nations.

QUESTION: McDonald's introduced a premium blend of coffee that sells for more than its standard coffee. How does this represent thinking at the margin?

Answers to the Checkpoint questions can be found at the end of this chapter.

CHAPTER SUMMARY

SECTION 1 WHAT IS ECONOMICS ABOUT?

1.1 **Economics** is the study of how individuals, firms, and societies make decisions to improve their well-being given limitations.

AP Images/YVES LOGGHE

Scarcity is the idea that people have unlimited wants but limited resources. Resources can be money, time, ability, work ethic, or anything that can be used to generate productive outcomes.

Scarce versus scarcity: Large uncut diamonds are scarce—only a few are found in the world each year—and are sold for millions of dollars each. A car, on the other hand, is less scarce, as car dealerships around the country have lots full of them. But both large diamonds and cars are subject to scarcity—many people want them but can only buy what they can afford.

REUTERS/Mike Blake

1.2 **What Is the Difference Between Microeconomics and Macroeconomics?**

- M"i"croeconomics deals with individual entities, such as individuals, firms, and industries. (Remember "i" = "individual.")
- M"a"croeconomics deals with aggregate entities, such as cities or the nation. (Remember "a" = "aggregate" or "all.")

1.3 Economic analysis uses a stylized approach: models boil issues and facts down to their basic relevant elements.

How governments deal with pollution is an important problem that can be addressed using economic analysis.

1.4 To build models means that we make use of the *ceteris paribus* assumption and hold some important variables constant. This useful device often provides surprising insights about economic behavior.

1.5 Economists and policymakers often confront the trade-off between efficiency and equity. Efficiency reflects how well resources are used and allocated. Equity (or fairness) of an outcome is a subjective matter, where differences of opinion exist.

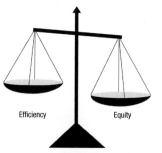

Efficiency   Equity

Fernando Jose Vascocelos Soares/Dreamstime.com

SECTION 2 KEY PRINCIPLES OF ECONOMICS

1.6

1.7

1. Economics Is Concerned With Making Choices With Limited Resources

Economics involves making decisions to maximize one's well-being, which can come from many sources, including money, time, happiness, or a fortuitous event.

"We should have done something different this weekend. . . ."

4. People Respond to Incentives, Both Good and Bad

Incentives encourage people to work hard and be more productive.

Rewarding the top salesperson in the company creates a valuable incentive to work hard.

6. Markets Are Generally Efficient; When They Aren't, Government Can Sometimes Correct the Failure

Markets bring buyers and sellers together. Competition forces firms to provide products at the lowest possible price. New products are introduced to the market and old products disappear. This dynamism makes markets efficient. In some instances, though, markets might fail, such as in dealing with pollution, leading governments to intervene to correct the failure.

Market equilibrium often is achieved by letting market participants make decisions freely.

2. When Making Decisions, One Must Take Into Account Tradeoffs and Opportunity Costs

Choice and scarcity force tradeoffs because we face unlimited wants but limited resources. We must make tradeoffs in nearly everything we do. Opportunity costs are resources (e.g., time and money) that could be used in another activity. Everything we do involves opportunity costs, the value of the next best alternative use of our resources.

3. Specialization Leads to Gains for All Involved

Specializing in tasks in which one is comparatively better at doing than another allows individuals to achieve productivity gains as long as the work is shared in a mutually beneficial manner.

5. Rational Behavior Requires Thinking on the Margin

When making a decision involving benefits and costs, one should continue to consume or produce as long as the marginal (additional) benefit exceeds the marginal (additional) cost.

Maximizing your food intake at a buffet is not thinking at the margin if you end up bloated from overeating.

7. Economic Growth, Low Unemployment, and Low Inflation Are Economic Goals That Do Not Always Coincide

Economic growth is an important factor in improving the standard of living in a country. A government uses various policies to promote economic growth by keeping unemployment and inflation low. However, addressing one goal (unemployment) often comes at the expense of the other (inflation).

8. Institutions and Human Creativity Help Explain the Wealth of Nations

Institutions include the legal system, laws and policies, a government free of corruption, and a strong monetary system. Ideas and innovation lead to new products and improve on existing ones, raising the standard of living of all residents.

Key Concepts

economics, p. 4

scarcity, p. 4

incentives, p. 5

microeconomics, p. 5

macroeconomics, p. 5

ceteris paribus, p. 6

efficiency, p. 6

equity, p. 6

positive question, p. 7

normative question, p. 7

opportunity cost, p. 9

Questions and Problems

Check Your Understanding

1. What is wrong with the statement "Economics is everything to do with money"?

2. Does your going to college have anything to do with expanding choices or reducing scarcity? Explain.

3. What is the difference between a positive question and a normative question?

4. You normally stay at home on Wednesday nights and study. Next Wednesday night, your best friend is having his big 21st birthday party. What is the opportunity cost of going to the party?

5. What is the incentive to spend four years of one's life and tens of thousands of dollars to earn a college degree?

6. Why do markets typically lead to an efficient outcome for buyers and sellers?

Apply the Concepts

7. Many companies offer employees health savings accounts (HSAs) instead of traditional health care plans. HSAs provide each employee with money (usually between $500 and $1,000 per year) that can be used for any health care expense but then requires employees to cover a much higher portion of expenses beyond that. Describe an issue of efficiency and an issue of equity that arises from this policy.

8. Stores depend on feedback from their customers as a way to improve their business practices and to market their products. To encourage customers to offer feedback, stores will sometimes offer an incentive, such as a discount on a future purchase or additional reward points in a frequent shopper program. Why do some customers, but not all, take advantage of the incentive to leave feedback? Does the actual shopping experience of the customer affect his or her willingness to do so?

9. The black rhinoceros is extremely endangered. Its horn is considered a powerful aphrodisiac in many Asian countries, and a single horn fetches many thousands of dollars on the black market, creating a great incentive for poachers. Unlike other stories of endangered species, this one might have a simple solution. Conservationists could capture as many rhinos as possible and remove their horns, reducing the incentive to poach. Do you think this will help reduce poaching? Why or why not?

10. Most amusement parks in the United States charge a fixed price for admission, which includes unlimited roller coaster rides for the day. Some people attempt to ride the roller coasters as often as possible in order to maximize the value of their admission. Why is riding a roller coaster at an amusement park over and over to "get your money's worth" not considered *thinking on the margin*?

11. Because the U.S. government wants to reduce the nation's reliance on fossil fuels, greater use of solar panels has been encouraged among households and businesses. However, the cost of installing solar panels can be prohibitively expensive for most people. Because people follow incentives, what can the government do to encourage more households and businesses to install solar panels?

12. Some colleges and universities charge tuition by the credit hour, while others charge tuition by the term, allowing students to take as many classes as they desire. How do these tuition structures affect the incentives students face when deciding how many classes to take? Provide an example of a beneficial effect and an example of a potentially harmful effect resulting from the incentives created with each system. How does marginal analysis affect the incentives with each system?

In the News

13. The *New York Times* reported in an article titled "What the Top 1% of Earners Majored In" that 8.2% of Americans who majored in economics for their undergraduate degree are in the top 1% of salary earners. Only those who majored in pre-med had a higher percentage in the top 1%. What might be some reasons why economics majors have done well in the job market?

14. In 2018, Seattle and San Francisco passed laws banning the use of plastic disposable straws because they are harmful to the environment (because plastic does not easily biodegrade) and to marine life (which ingest straws that end up in the ocean). But opponents point out that such bans may result in unintended monetary costs as well as external costs. Describe two potential costs that may arise as a result of these new laws.

Solving Problems

15. Suppose your favorite band is on tour and coming to your area. Tickets are $100, and you take a day off from work for which you could have earned $60. What is your opportunity cost of going to the concert?

Work It Out

 interactive activity

16. At your local family fun center, miniature golf is $12 per person for unlimited rounds in a day, while each go-kart session is $8. If you played three rounds of miniature golf and rode the go-karts three times, what was the marginal cost of the third round of miniature golf? What was the marginal cost of the third go-kart session?

Answers to Questions in Checkpoints

Checkpoint: What Is Economics About? 8

(1) microeconomics (2) macroeconomics (3) microeconomics (4) macroeconomics (5) macroeconomics (6) microeconomics (7) macroeconomics

Checkpoint: Key Principles of Economics 15

McDonald's is adding one more product (premium coffee) to its line. Thinking at the margin entails thinking about how you can improve an operation (or increase profits) by adding to your existing product line or reducing costs.

Appendix
Working With Graphs and Formulas

You can't watch the news on television or read a newspaper without seeing a graph of some sort. If you have flipped through this book, you have seen a large number of graphs, charts, and tables and a few simple equations. This is the language of economics. Economists deal with data for all types of issues. Just looking at data in tables often doesn't help you discern the trends or relationships in the data.

Economists develop theories and models to explain economic behavior and levels of economic activity. These theories or models are simplified representations of real-world activity. Models are designed to distill the most important relationships between variables, and then these relationships are used to predict future behavior of individuals, firms, and industries or to predict the future course of the overall economy.

In this short section, we will explore the different types of graphs you are likely to see in this course (and in the media) and then turn to an examination of how graphs are used to develop and illustrate models. This second topic leads us into a discussion of modeling relationships between data and how to represent these relationships with simple graphs and equations.

GRAPHS AND DATA

The main forms of data graphs are time series, scatter plots, pie charts, and bar charts. Time series, as the name suggests, plot data over time. Most of the figures you will encounter in publications are time series graphs.

Time Series

Time series graphs involve plotting time (minutes, hours, days, months, quarters, or years) on the horizontal axis and the value of some variable on the vertical axis. Figure APX-1 illustrates a time series plot for civilian employment of those 16 years and older. Notice that since the early 1990s, employment has grown by over 35 million for this group. The vertical strips in the figure designate the last three recessions. Notice that in each case when the recession hit, employment fell, then rebounded after the recession ended.

Scatter Plots

Scatter plots are graphs in which two variables (neither variable being time) are plotted against each other. Scatter plots often give us a hint if the two variables are related to each other in some consistent way. Figure APX-2 plots one variable, median household income, against another variable, percentage of Americans holding a college degree.

Two things can be seen in this figure. First, these two variables appear to be related to each other in a positive way. A rising percentage of college graduates leads to a higher median household income. It is not surprising that college degrees and earnings are related because increased education leads to a more productive workforce, which translates into more income. Second, given that the years for the data are listed next to the dots, we can see that the percentage of the population with college degrees has risen significantly over the last half-century. From this simple scatter plot, we can see a lot of information and ideas about how the two variables are related.

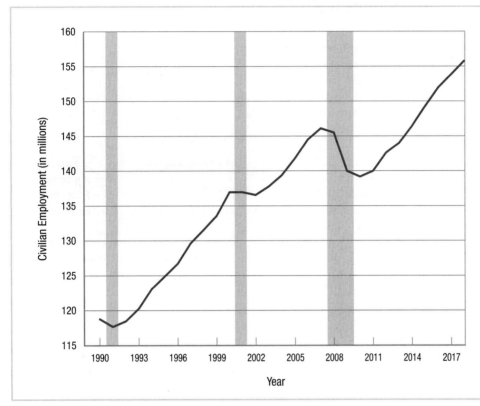

This time series graph shows the number of civilians 16 years and older employed in the United States since 1990. Employment has grown steadily over this period, except in times of recession, indicated by the vertical strips. Note that employment fell during the recession and then bounced back after each recession ended.

Figure APX-2 • The Relationship Between the Median Household Income and the Percentage of Americans Holding a College Degree ··········

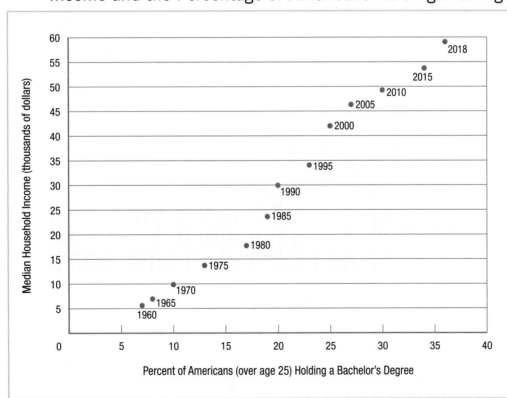

This scatter plot shows the relationship between median household income and the percentage of Americans holding a college degree. Median household income increased as a greater proportion of Americans earn college degrees. Note that the percentage of Americans earning college degrees has increased significantly in the last half-century.

Figure APX-3 • Relative Importance of Consumer Price Index (CPI) Components (2018)

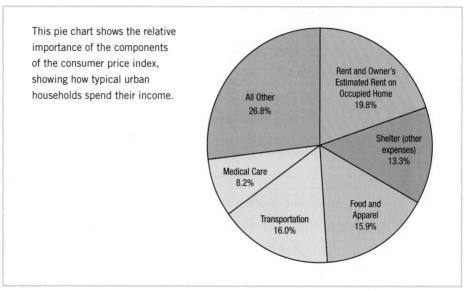

This pie chart shows the relative importance of the components of the consumer price index, showing how typical urban households spend their income.

Rent and Owner's Estimated Rent on Occupied Home
19.8%

All Other
26.8%

Shelter (other expenses)
13.3%

Medical Care
8.2%

Food and Apparel
15.9%

Transportation
16.0%

Pie Charts

Pie charts are simple graphs showing a circular pie cut into wedges, where each wedge represents a percentage of the whole. A simple pie chart for the relative importance of components in the consumer price index (CPI) is shown in Figure APX-3. It reveals how the typical urban household budget is allocated. By looking at each slice of the pie, we see a picture of how typical families spend their income.

Bar Charts

Bar charts use bars to show the value of specific data points. Figure APX-4 is a bar chart showing the annual percentage changes in real (adjusted for inflation) gross domestic product

Figure APX-4 • Percent Change in Real (Inflation Adjusted) GDP

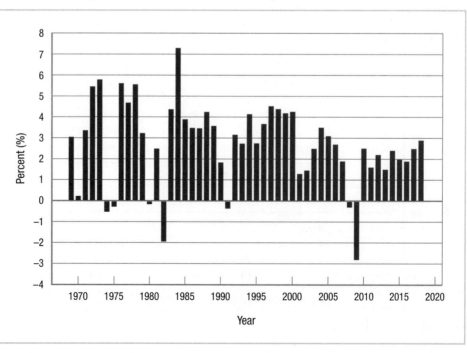

This bar chart shows the annual percent change in real (adjusted for inflation) gross domestic product (GDP) over the last 50 years. Over this period, GDP declined only seven times.

Percent (%)

Year

····· Figure APX-5 • Social Media Usage Across Age Groups ····················

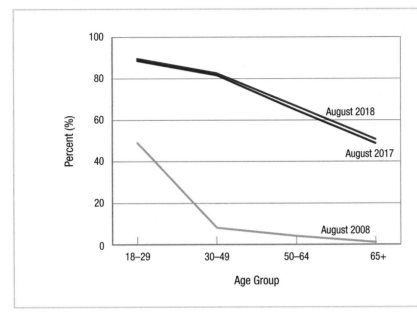

These curves show the percentage of Americans using a social media site by age. The curves slope downward because older Americans are less likely to use social media than younger Americans. However, over time, more Americans in all age groups are using social media, as evidenced by each point on the August 2017 curve being higher than the corresponding point on the August 2008 curve and each point on the August 2018 curve being higher than the corresponding point on the August 2017 curve.

(GDP). Notice that over the last 50 years, the United States has had only seven years when GDP declined.

Simple Graphs Can Pack in a Lot of Information It is not unusual for graphs and figures to have several things going on at once. Look at Figure APX-5, illustrating the number of social media users as a percent of each age group. On the horizontal axis are the age groups in years. On the vertical axis is the percent of each age group that regularly used social media. Figure APX-5 shows the relationship between age and social media penetration for different periods. They include the most recent period shown (August 2018), a year previous (August 2017), and ten years prior (August 2008).

You should notice two things in this figure. First, the relationship between the variables slopes downward. This means that older Americans are less likely to use social media than younger Americans. Second, use of social media has increased across all ages over the three periods studied (from August 2008 to August 2017 to August 2018) as shown by the position of the curves. Each point on the August 2018 curve is above the corresponding point on the August 2017 curve, which is subsequently above each point on the August 2008 curve.

A Few Simple Rules for Reading Graphs Looking at graphs of data is relatively easy if you follow a few simple rules. First, read the title of the figure to get a sense of what is being presented. Second, look at the label for the horizontal axis (x axis) to see how the data are being presented. Make sure you know how the data are being measured. Is it months or years or hours worked or hundreds of hours worked? Third, examine the label for the vertical axis (y axis). This is the value of the variable being plotted on that axis; make sure you know what it is. Fourth, look at the graph itself to see if it makes logical sense. Are the curves (bars, dots) going in the right direction?

Look the graph over and see if you notice something interesting going on. This is really the fun part of looking closely at figures both in this text and in other books, magazines, and newspapers. Often, simple data graphs can reveal surprising relationships between variables. Keep this in mind as you examine graphs throughout this course.

One more thing. Graphs in this book are always accompanied by explanatory captions. Examine the graph first, making your preliminary assessment of what is going on. Then carefully read the caption, making sure it accurately reflects what is shown in the graph. If the caption refers to movement between points, follow this movement in the graph. If you think there is a discrepancy between the caption and the graph, reexamine the graph to make sure you have not missed anything.

····· Figure APX-6 • Studying and Your GPA ···

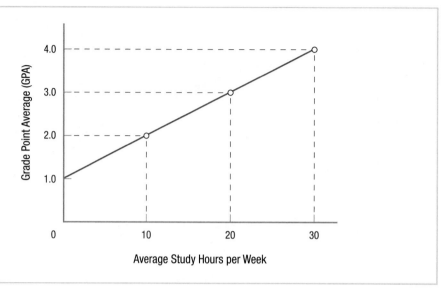

This figure shows a hypothetical linear relationship between average study hours and GPA. Without studying, a D average results, and with 10 hours of studying, a C average is obtained, and so on.

GRAPHS AND MODELS

Let's now take a brief look at how economists use graphs and models, and how graphs are constructed. Economists use what are called "stylized graphs" to represent relationships between variables. These graphs are a form of modeling to help us simplify our analysis and focus on those relationships that matter. Figure APX-6 is one such model.

Linear Relationships

Figure APX-6 shows a linear relationship between average study hours and grade point average (GPA), indicating a higher GPA the more you study. By a linear relationship, we mean that the "curve" is a straight line. In this case, if you don't study at all, we assume you are capable of making D's and your GPA will equal 1.0, not enough to keep you in school for long. If you hit the books for an average of 10 hours a week, your GPA rises to 2.0, a C average. Studying for additional hours raises your GPA up to its maximum of 4.0.

The important point here is that the curve is linear; any hour of studying yields the same increase in GPA. All hours of studying provide equal yields from beginning to end. This is what makes linear relationships unique.

Computing the Slope of a Linear Line Looking at the line in Figure APX-6, we can see two things: The line is straight, so the slope is constant, and the slope is positive. As average hours of studying increase, GPA increases. Computing the slope of the line tells us how much GPA increases for every hour of additional studying. Computing the slope of a linear line is relatively easy and is shown in Figure APX-7.

The simple rule for computing slope is: Slope is equal to rise over run (or rise ÷ run). Since the slope is constant along a linear line, we can select any two points and determine the slope for the entire curve. In Figure APX-7, we have selected points *a* and *b*, where GPA moves from 2.0 to 3.0 when studying increases from 10 to 20 hours per week.

Your GPA increases by 1.0 for an additional 10 hours of study. This means that the slope is equal to 0.1 (1.0 ÷ 10 = 0.1). So for every additional hour of studying you add each week, your GPA will rise by 0.1. Thus, if you would like to improve your GPA from 3.0 to 3.5, you would have to study five more hours per week.

····· Figure APX-7 • Computing Slope for a Linear Line ·····

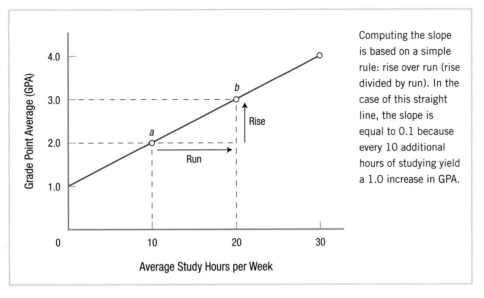

Computing the slope is based on a simple rule: rise over run (rise divided by run). In the case of this straight line, the slope is equal to 0.1 because every 10 additional hours of studying yield a 1.0 increase in GPA.

Computing slope for negative relations that are linear is done exactly the same way, except that when computing the changes from one point to another, one of the values will be negative, making the relationship negative.

Nonlinear Relationships

It would be nice for model builders if all relationships were linear, but that is not the case. It is probably not really the case with the amount of studying and GPA either. Figure APX-8 depicts a more realistic nonlinear and positive relationship between studying and GPA. Again, we assume that one can get a D average (1.0) without studying and reach a maximum of straight A's (4.0) with 30 hours of studying per week.

Figure APX-8 suggests that the first few hours of study per week are more important to raising GPA than are the others. The first 10 hours of studying yield more than the last 10 hours.

····· Figure APX-8 • Studying and Your GPA (Nonlinear) ·····

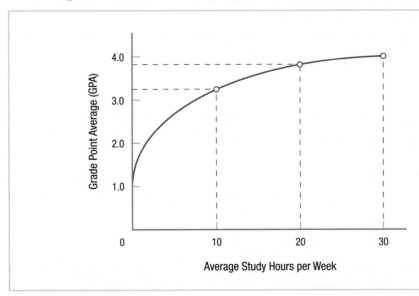

This nonlinear graph of study hours and GPA is probably more typical than the one shown in Figures APX-6 and APX-7. Like many other things, studying exhibits diminishing returns. The first few hours of studying result in greater improvements to GPAs than further hours of studying.

····· Figure APX-9 • Computing Slope for a Nonlinear Curve ······················

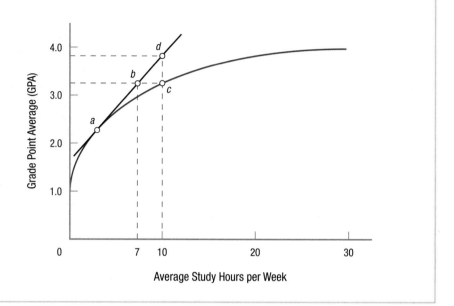

Computing the slope of a nonlinear curve requires that you compute the slope of the tangent line at each point on the curve.

The first 10 hours of study raise one's GPA from 1.0 to 3.3 (a gain of 2.3), while the 20th to the 30th hours raise GPA from 3.8 to 4.0 (a gain of only 0.2). This curve exhibits what economists call diminishing returns. Just as the first bite of pizza tastes better than the 100th, so the first five hours of studying bring a bigger jump in GPA than the 25th to 30th hours.

Computing the Slope of a Nonlinear Curve As you might suspect, computing the slope of a nonlinear curve is more complex than computing the slope of a straight line. But it is not that much more difficult. In fact, we use essentially the same rise over run approach that is used for linear lines.

Looking at the curve in Figure APX-8, it should be clear that the slope changes at each point on the curve. It starts out very steep, then begins to level out above 20 hours of studying. Figure APX-9 shows how to compute the slope at any point on the curve.

Computing the slope at point *a* requires drawing a line tangent to that point, then computing the slope of that line. For point *a*, the slope of the line tangent to it is found by computing rise over run again. In this case, it is length $dc \div bc$ or $[(3.8 - 3.3) \div (10 - 7)] = 0.5 \div 3 = 0.167$. Notice that this slope is significantly larger than the original linear relationship of 0.1. The slope near 30 hours of studying approaches zero (the slope of a horizontal line is zero).

CETERIS PARIBUS, SIMPLE EQUATIONS, AND SHIFTING CURVES

Hold on while we beat this GPA and studying example into the ground. Inevitably, when we simplify analysis to develop a graph or model, important factors or influences must be controlled. We do not ignore them, we hold them constant. These are known as *ceteris paribus* assumptions.

Ceteris Paribus: All Else Equal

By *ceteris paribus*, we mean "holding all other things equal." This means that all other relevant factors, elements, or influences are held constant. When economists define your demand for a

Figure APX-10 • Studying and Your GPA: A Simple Equation

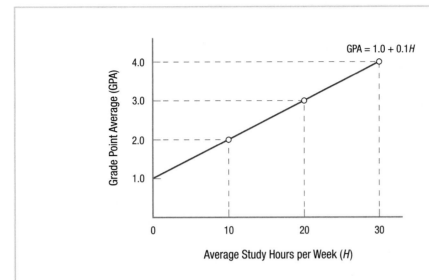

The formula for a linear relationship is $Y = a + bX$, where Y is the y axis variable, X is the x axis variable, and a and b are constants. For the original relationship between study hours and GPA, this equation is $GPA = 1.0 + 0.1H$.

product, they want to know how much or how many units you will buy at different prices. For example, to determine how many swimsuits you will buy at various prices (your demand for swimsuits), we hold your income and the price of shoes and shirts constant. If your income suddenly jumped, you would be willing to buy more swimsuits at all prices, but this is a whole new demand curve. *Ceteris paribus* assumptions are a way to simplify analysis; then the analysis can be extended to include those factors held constant, as we will see next.

Simple Linear Equations

Simple linear equations can be expressed as $Y = a + bX$. This is read as Y equals a plus b times X, where Y is the variable plotted on the y axis and a is a constant (unchanging) and b is a different constant that is multiplied by X, the value on the x axis. The formula for our studying and GPA example introduced in Figure APX-6 is shown in Figure APX-10.

The constant a is known as the vertical intercept because it is the value of GPA when study hours (X) is zero, and therefore it lies on (intercepts) the vertical axis at the value of 1.0 (D average). Now each time you study another hour on average, your GPA rises by 0.1, so the constant b (the slope of the line) is equal to 0.1. Letting H represent hours of studying, the final equation is $GPA = 1.0 + 0.1H$. You start with a D average without studying, and as your hours of studying increase, your GPA goes up by 0.1 times the hours of studying. If we plug 20 hours of studying into the equation, the answer is a GPA of 3.0 $[1.0 + (0.1 \times 20) = 1.0 + 2.0 = 3.0]$.

Shifting Curves

Now let's introduce a couple of factors that we have been holding constant (the *ceteris paribus* assumption). These two elements are tutoring and partying. So, our new equation now becomes $GPA = 1.0 + 0.1H + Z$, where Z is our variable indicating whether you have a tutor or whether you are excessively partying. When you have a tutor, $Z = 1$, and when you party too much, $Z = -1$. Tutoring adds to the productivity of your studying (hence $Z = 1$), while excessive late-night partying reduces the effectiveness of studying because you are always tired (hence $Z = -1$). Figure APX-11 shows the impact of adding these factors to the original relationship.

With tutoring, your GPA-studying curve has moved upward and to the left. Now, because $Z = 1$, you begin with a C average (2.0), and with just 20 hours of studying (because of tutoring),

····· Figure APX-11 • The Impact of Tutoring and Partying on Your GPA ···········

The effects of tutoring and partying on our simple model of studying and GPA are shown. Partying harms your academic efforts and shifts the relationship down and to the right, making it harder to maintain your previous average (you now have to study more hours). Tutoring, on the other hand, improves the relationship (shifts the curve up and to the left).

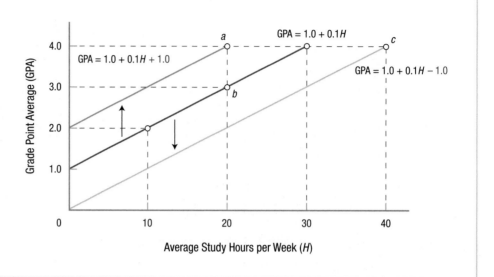

you can reach a 4.0 GPA (point *a*). Alternatively, when you don't have tutoring and you party every night, your GPA–studying relationship has worsened (shifted downward and to the right). Now you must study 40 hours (point *c*) to accomplish a 4.0 GPA. Note that you begin with failing grades.

The important point here is that we can simplify relationships between different variables and use a simple graph or equation to represent a model of behavior. In doing so, we often have to hold some things constant. When we allow those factors to change, the original relationship is now changed and often results in a shift in the curves. You will see this technique applied over and over as you study economics this term.

CORRELATION IS NOT CAUSATION

Just because two variables seem related or appear related on a scatter plot does not mean that one causes another. Economists 100 years ago correlated business cycles (the ups and downs of the entire economy) with sunspots. Because they appeared related, some suggested that sunspots caused business cycles. The only rational argument was that agriculture was the dominant industry and sunspots affected the weather; therefore, sunspots caused the economy to fluctuate.

Other examples of erroneously assuming that correlation implies causality abound, some of which can be preposterous or humorous. For example, did Spotify cause a spike in college tuition? Both the number of Spotify subscribers and average college tuition increased significantly between 2010 and 2018, but that doesn't mean one has anything to do with the other. Just because two variables appear to be related does not mean that one causes the other to change.

Understanding graphs and using simple equations are a key part of learning economics. Practice helps.

2

Production, Economic Growth, and Trade

Understanding how economies grow based on the goods and services they choose to produce

Can a speck of sand be the most significant driver of economic growth of the last generation? Just about every piece of electronic and computing equipment contains a microchip, a tiny piece of circuitry that allows devices to function and to store immense amounts of data and multimedia. Most chips are made of silicon, which is nothing more than a basic element found in sand, and aside from oxygen is the most abundant element in the Earth's crust.

Extracting silicon from sand, melting it, and creating silicon wafers on which transistors are produced to create a functioning microchip is a complex process. More impressive is how efficient the process has become. A single chip smaller than the size of a dime can hold billions of transistors, enough to store and display all of the music, videos, and photos you could ever want on a single device.

Arguably, no invention has transformed the economy more in the past 30 years than the development and advancement of the silicon chip. Technological change has made production methods more efficient, allowing countries to produce more goods and services using fewer physical and natural resources. And as we emphasized in the previous chapter on the importance of scarcity, determining how to achieve more using less—fewer resources—is one of the important goals of economics.

An industry that has experienced significant technological change is telecommunications. In 1950 long-distance phone calls were placed with the assistance of live operators, every minute on the line costing the average consumer the equivalent of several hours' pay. Today, with Internet communications technology allowing one to call virtually anyone in the world for pennies or less, it seems the world is getting smaller as communications brings us closer together and contributes to greater productivity.

Another driver of economic growth is trade. Several centuries ago, individuals produced most of what they consumed. Today, most of us produce little of what we consume. Instead, we work at specialized jobs, then use our wages to purchase the goods we desire.

Nearly every country engages in commercial trade with other countries to expand the opportunities for consumption and production by its people. As products are consumed, new products must be produced, allowing increased consumption in one country to spur economic growth in another. Given the ability of global trade to open economic doors and raise incomes, trade is vital for economic growth in all nations.

This chapter gives you a framework for understanding economic growth. It provides a simple model for thinking about production, then applies this model to economies at large so you will know how to think about economic growth and its determinants. It then goes on to analyze international trade as a special case of economic growth. By the time you finish this chapter, you should understand the importance of economic growth and what drives it.

12.1%

Percentage of the U.S. total production that is exported

5,385,365

Number of American brand cars sold in China in 2018, contributing significantly to U.S. exports and job creation in the automobile industry

Specialization and Trade:
The Importance of a Globalized Economy

Specialization and trade are important contributors to productivity and growth in an economy. Countries trade for many reasons. First, they must import goods that they are unable to produce themselves (for example, with the exception of a few locations, the United States does not have the ability to produce coffee or cocoa). Second, countries trade because their citizens desire a variety of foreign and domestic brands to choose from. And third, countries trade in order to take advantage of specialization, allowing countries to consume at points beyond their production possibilities frontier. This By the Numbers looks at the growth of trade over the past 20 years and the vital role it plays in the growth of the economy.

WHY ARE THESE DATA IMPORTANT?

According to the discussion of specialization and trade in the text, all countries gain when each country specializes in goods and services in which they have a comparative advantage. When countries export these goods and import goods in which they have a comparative disadvantage, total production increases and consumers enjoy a greater variety of goods at lower prices.

DATA:

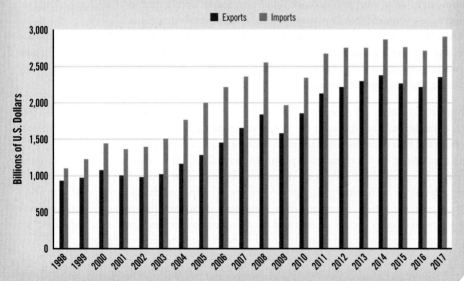

Total Exports and Imports in Goods and Services (1998–2017)

Where Can I Find These Data?

Source: U.S. Census Bureau (U.S. Department of Commerce)

Web site: http://www.census.gov/foreigntrade/data/index.html

Details: Select "Historical Series," then "U.S. International Trade in Goods and Services," and finally "Annual" data.

Data *in the News*

~ Assessing Your Data Literacy ~

1. From 1998 to 2017, how many years did exports rise from the previous year? How many years did imports rise from the previous year?

2. Between which two years did exports increase the most? Imports?

3. Recessions occurred in 2001 and 2007–2009. What was the general trend in trade during these recessions? Why do you think this trend occurs?

BASIC ECONOMIC QUESTIONS AND PRODUCTION

Regardless of the country, its circumstances, or its precise economic structure, every economy must answer three basic questions.

Basic Economic Questions

The three basic economic questions that each society must answer are:

- What goods and services are to be produced?
- How are these goods and services to be produced?
- Who will receive these goods and services?

The response an economy makes to the first question—What goods and services should it produce?—depends on the goods and services a society wants. In a communist state, the government decides what a society wants, but in a capitalist economy, consumers signal what products they want by way of their demands for specific commodities. In the next chapter, we investigate how consumer demand for individual products is determined and how markets meet these demands. For now, we assume that consumers, individually and as a society, are able to decide on the mix of goods and services they most want and that producers supply these items at acceptable prices.

Once we know what goods a society wants, the next question its economic system must answer is, How are these goods and services to be produced? In the end, this problem comes down to the simple question of how land, labor, and capital should be combined to produce the desired products. If a society demands a huge amount of corn, for example, we can expect the use of its resources will be different from a society that demands digital equipment. But even an economy devoted to corn production could be organized in different ways, perhaps relying on extensive use of human labor or perhaps relying on automated equipment.

Once an economy has determined what goods and services to produce and how to produce them, it is faced with the distribution question: Who will get the resulting products? *Distribution* refers to the way an economy allocates the goods and services it produces to consumers. How this is done depends on how the economy is organized.

Economic Systems All economies have to answer the three basic economic questions. How that is done depends on who owns the factors of production (land, labor, capital, and entrepreneurship) and how decisions are made to coordinate production and distribution.

In *capitalist* or *market* economies, private individuals and firms own most of the resources. The what, how, and who decisions are determined by individual desires for products and profit-making decisions by firms. Product prices are the principal mechanism for communicating information in the system. Based on prices, consumers decide whether to buy or not, and firms decide how to employ their resources and what production technology to use. This competition between many buyers and sellers leads to highly efficient production of goods and services. Producers are free to survive or perish based on their efficiency and the quality of their products. The government's primary roles are protecting property rights, enforcing contracts between private parties, providing public goods such as national defense, and establishing and ensuring the appropriate operating environment for competitive markets. Today, the U.S. economy is not a pure *laissez-faire* ("leave it alone," or minimal government role) market economy but more of a mixed economy with many regulations and an extended role for government.

In contrast, *planned* or *command* economies are systems in which most of the productive resources are owned by the government and most economic decisions are made by central governments. Much like how market economies vary in terms of the role of government, planned economies also vary in the extent to which governments control businesses and allocate resources. The former Soviet Union was a highly centralized economy before it broke up into many countries in 1991, of which most (such as Latvia and Kazakhstan) are no longer planned economies. China is another country that was highly centralized until recently. Although the Chinese government still controls many resources and regulates businesses, a market economy has thrived and, along with it, strong economic growth as entrepreneurs build businesses to cater to the rapid rise of middle-class Chinese consumers. Today, very few planned economies remain (North Korea and Cuba being the most prominent examples).

Although there is a distinct difference between market and planned economies, this distinction does not always coincide with political freedom. On the one hand, China is still a communist country with a one-party government despite its growing market-based economy. On the other hand, people in socialist countries such as Sweden and Denmark enjoy a high degree of political freedom, but pay high taxes so that government can play a large role in providing services.

Resources and Production

Having examined the three basic economic questions, let's take a look at the production process. **Production** involves turning **resources** into products and services that people are willing and able to buy. Let's begin our discussion of this process by examining the scarce resources used to produce goods and services.

Land For economists, the term **land** includes both land in the usual sense as well as all other natural resources that are used in production. Natural resources such as mineral deposits, oil and natural gas, and water are all included by economists in the definition of land. Economists refer to the payment for use of land as a resource as *rent*.

Labor **Labor** as a factor of production includes both the mental and physical talents of people. Few goods and services can be produced without labor resources. Improvement to labor capabilities from training, education, and apprenticeship programs—typically called "human capital"—all add to labor's productivity and ultimately to a higher standard of living. Labor is paid *wages*.

Capital **Capital** includes all manufactured products that are used to produce other goods and services. This includes equipment such as drill presses, blast furnaces for making steel, and other tools used in the production process. It also includes trucks and automobiles used by businesses, as well as office equipment such as copiers, computers, and telephones. Any manufactured product that is used to produce other products is included in the category of capital. The payment to owners of capital is *interest*.

Note that the term "capital" as used by economists refers to real (or physical) capital—actual manufactured products used in the production process—not money or financial capital. Money and financial capital are important in that they are used to purchase the real capital that is used to produce products.

Entrepreneurial Ability **Entrepreneurs** *combine* land, labor, and capital to produce goods and services, and they assume the *risks* associated with running a business. Entrepreneurs combine and manage the inputs of production and manage the day-to-day marketing, finance, and production decisions. The risks of running a business are often significant, including the possibility of bankruptcies and lawsuits. Globalization has opened many opportunities as well as risks. For undertaking these activities and assuming the risks associated with business, entrepreneurs earn *profit*.

Production and Efficiency

Production turns *resources*—land, labor, capital, and entrepreneurial ability—into products and services. The necessary production factors vary for different products. To produce corn, for instance, one needs arable land, seed, fertilizer, water, and farm equipment, and the workers to operate that equipment. Farmers looking to produce corn would need to devote hundreds of acres of open land to this crop, plow the land, plant and nurture the corn, and finally harvest the crop. Producing digital equipment, in contrast, requires less land but more capital and more highly skilled labor.

As we have seen, every country has to decide what to produce, how to produce it, and who receives the output. Countries desire to do the first two as efficiently as possible by choosing the production method that results in the greatest output using the least amount of resources.

production The process of converting resources (factors of production)—land, labor, capital, and entrepreneurial ability—into goods and services.

resources Productive resources include land (land and natural resources), labor (mental and physical talents of people), capital (manufactured products used to produce other products), and entrepreneurial ability (the combining of the other factors to produce products and assume the risk of the business).

land Includes natural resources such as mineral deposits, oil, natural gas, water, and land in the usual sense of the word. The payment for use of land as a resource is rent.

labor Includes the mental and physical talents of individuals who produce products and services. The payment to labor is wages.

capital Includes manufactured products such as tractors, welding equipment, and computers that are used to produce other goods and services. The payment to owners of capital is interest.

entrepreneurs Entrepreneurs combine land, labor, and capital to produce goods and services. They absorb the risk of being in business, including the risk of bankruptcy and other liabilities associated with doing business. Entrepreneurs earn profit for their effort.

····· Figure 1 • From Factors of Production to Output ····································

Each of the four factors of production is employed in a production method in order to generate goods and services. The ability to use factors of production efficiently within a production method increases the amount of output given a fixed amount of inputs.

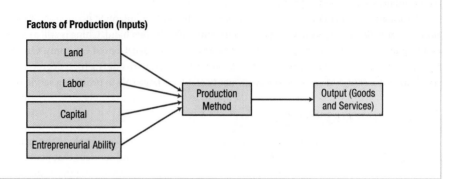

Figure 1 shows how factors of production enter into a production method to generate goods and services. Determining the production method is the role of a manager, who must decide how factors of production are best used. Economists refer to this actual choice as the production function, a concept that will be discussed in greater detail in a later chapter. In addition to the amount of resources available for production, the type of resources also plays an important role. Physical capital and entrepreneurship can enhance the productivity of other resources, as we will see in the following Around the World feature describing the beginnings of the Industrial Revolution.

AROUND THE WORLD

Ironbridge: The Beginnings of the Industrial Revolution

How did the town of Ironbridge solve a logistical problem using factors of production, and how did it lead to enhanced production and economic growth?

What is arguably the most important building material in modern societies? It's steel, which is made primarily from iron ore. Prior to the Industrial Revolution, the use of iron was mostly limited to producing coins and other small trinkets. The Industrial Revolution began with the mass production of iron, and the town of Ironbridge, England, claims to be one of the birthplaces of the Industrial Revolution. Why Ironbridge?

Abraham Darby was an 18th-century British entrepreneur. He developed

innovative ways to power machinery using water. In the mid-18th century, Darby built a large aqueduct to harness the natural flow of the river to power his iron furnace. In 1779, when iron began to be produced on a large scale, Darby began building an iron bridge, which was completed in 1781.

How was this bridge revolutionary in design? Made of cast iron, the Iron Bridge was sturdier than any other bridge built

before it. A single span allowed large boats to easily pass underneath its high arch. In fact, the original bridge remains open today, setting the standard for constructing bridges and buildings for centuries to come. The Iron Bridge represents a feat of engineering that led to the development of physical capital as a key factor of production.

Today, it's difficult to imagine production without the use of machines and other modern tools and the creative ideas that employ these resources to produce goods efficiently. Physical capital and entrepreneurship are two key factors of production that greatly enhance the other factors of production: land and labor. Combining all of the factors of production has allowed economic growth to flourish over the past two centuries, and this can be traced back to a small Victorian town that bears the name of its most famous landmark.

GO ONLINE TO PRACTICE THE ECONOMIC CONCEPTS IN THIS STORY

Productivity is a measure of efficiency determined by the amount of output produced given the amount of inputs used. But economists also use specific concepts to describe two different aspects of efficiency: production efficiency and allocative efficiency.

Production efficiency occurs when the mix of goods is produced at the lowest possible resource or opportunity cost. Alternatively, production efficiency occurs when as much output as possible is produced with a given amount of resources. Firms use the best technology available and combine the other resources to create products at the lowest cost to society.

production efficiency Goods and services are produced at their lowest resource (opportunity) cost.

Allocative efficiency occurs when the mix of goods and services produced is the most desired by society. In capitalist countries, this is determined by consumers and businesses and their interaction through markets. The next chapter explores this interaction in some detail. Needless to say, it would be inefficient (a waste of resources) to be producing cassette tapes in the age of digital music players. Allocative efficiency requires that the right mix of goods be produced at the lowest cost.

allocative efficiency The mix of goods and services produced is just what society desires.

Every economy faces constraints or limitations. Land, labor, capital, and entrepreneurship are all limited. No country has an infinite supply of available workers or the space and machinery that would be needed to put them all to work efficiently. No country can break free of these natural restraints. Such limits are known as production possibilities frontiers, and they are the focus of the next section.

CHECKPOINT

BASIC ECONOMIC QUESTIONS AND PRODUCTION

- Every economy must decide what to produce, how to produce it, and who will receive what is produced.

- Production is the process of converting factors of production (resources)— land, labor, capital, and entrepreneurial ability—into goods and services.

- To the economist, land includes both land and natural resources. Labor includes the mental and physical resources of humans. Capital includes all manufactured products used to produce other goods and services. Entrepreneurs combine resources to manufacture products, and they assume the risk of doing business.

- Production efficiency requires that products be produced at the lowest cost. Allocative efficiency occurs when the mix of goods and services produced is just what society desires.

QUESTION: The one element that really seems to differentiate entrepreneurship from the other resources is the fact that entrepreneurs shoulder the *risk* of the failure of the enterprise. Is this important? Explain.

Answers to the Checkpoint questions can be found at the end of this chapter.

PRODUCTION POSSIBILITIES AND ECONOMIC GROWTH

As we discovered in the previous section, all countries and all economies face constraints on their production capabilities. Production can be limited by the quantity of the various factors of production in the country and its current technology. Technology includes such considerations as the country's infrastructure, its transportation and education systems, and the economic freedom it allows. Although perhaps going beyond the everyday meaning of the word "technology," for simplicity, we will assume that all of these factors help determine the state of a country's technology.

To further simplify matters, production possibilities analysis assumes that the quantity of resources available and the technology of the economy remain constant and that the economy produces only two products. Although a two-product world sounds far-fetched, this simplification allows us to analyze many important concepts regarding production and tradeoffs. Further, the conclusions drawn from this simple model will not differ fundamentally from a more complex model of the real world.

Production Possibilities

production possibilities frontier (PPF) Shows the combinations of two goods that are possible for a society to produce at full employment. Points on or inside the PPF are attainable, and those outside of the frontier are unattainable.

Assume that our simple economy produces backpacks and tablet computers. Figure 2 with its accompanying table shows the production possibilities frontier for this economy. The table shows seven possible production levels (*a–g*). These seven combinations, which range from 12,000 backpacks and zero tablets to zero backpacks and 6,000 tablets, are graphed in Figure 2.

When we connect the seven production possibilities, we delineate the **production possibilities frontier (PPF)** for this economy (some economists refer to this curve as the production possibilities curve). All points on the PPF are considered *attainable* by our economy. Everything to the left of the PPF is also attainable but is an inefficient use of resources—the economy can make more of one good or both goods. Everything to the right of the curve is considered *unattainable*. Therefore, the PPF maps out the economy's limits; it is impossible for the economy to produce at levels beyond the PPF without an increase in resources or technology, or both.

What the PPF in Figure 2 shows is that, given an efficient use of limited resources and taking technology into account, this economy can produce any of the seven combinations of tablets and backpacks listed, each of which represents a combination where the economy cannot produce another unit without giving up something. If society wants to produce 1,000 tablets, it will only be able to produce 10,000 backpacks, as shown by point *b* on the PPF. Should the society decide that mobile Internet access is important, it might decide to produce 4,000 tablets, which would force backpack production to be cut to 4,000, shown by point *e*. At each of these points, resources are fully employed in the economy, and therefore increasing production of one good requires giving up some production of the other. Also, the economy can produce any combination of the two products on or within the PPF, but not any combination beyond it.

Contrast points *c* and *e* with production at point *i*. At point *i*, the economy is only producing 2,000 tablets and 4,000 backpacks. Clearly, some resources are not being used. When fully employed, the economy's resources could produce more of both goods (point *d*).

Because the PPF represents combinations of goods using resources fully, the economy could not produce 4,000 tablets and still produce 10,000 backpacks. This situation, shown by point *h*,

Figure 2 • Production Possibilities Frontier

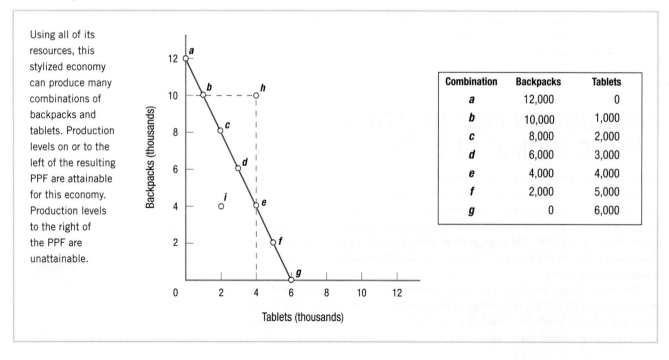

Using all of its resources, this stylized economy can produce many combinations of backpacks and tablets. Production levels on or to the left of the resulting PPF are attainable for this economy. Production levels to the right of the PPF are unattainable.

Combination	Backpacks	Tablets
a	12,000	0
b	10,000	1,000
c	8,000	2,000
d	6,000	3,000
e	4,000	4,000
f	2,000	5,000
g	0	6,000

lies to the right of the PPF and hence outside the realm of possibility. Anything to the right of the PPF is impossible for the economy to attain.

Opportunity Cost Whenever a country reallocates resources to change production patterns, it does so at the **opportunity cost.** Recall from Chapter 1 that opportunity cost is what you *give up* when making an economic decision. Here, society is deciding how many backpacks and tablets to produce. If society decides to produce more tablets, it gives up the ability to produce more backpacks. Shown through the PPF, the opportunity cost of producing more of one good is determined by the amount of the other good that is given up. In moving from point *b* to point *e* in Figure 2, tablet production increases by 3,000 units, from 1,000 units to 4,000 units. However, the country must forgo producing 6,000 backpacks because production falls from 10,000 backpacks to 4,000 backpacks. Giving up 6,000 backpacks for 3,000 more tablets represents an opportunity cost of 6,000 backpacks for these 3,000 tablets, or two backpacks for each tablet.

> **opportunity cost** The cost paid for one product in terms of the output (or consumption) of another product that must be forgone.

Opportunity cost thus represents the tradeoff required when an economy wants to increase its production of any single product. Governments must choose between infrastructure and national parks or between military spending and social spending. Since there are limits to what taxpayers are willing to pay, spending choices are necessary. Think of opportunity costs as what you or the economy must give up to have more of a product or service.

Increasing Opportunity Cost In most cases, land, labor, and capital cannot easily be shifted from producing one good or service to another. You cannot take a semitrailer and use it to plow a field, even though the semi and a top-of-the-line tractor cost about the same. The fact is that some resources are suited to specific sorts of production, just as some people seem to be better suited to performing one activity over another. Some people have a talent for music or art, and they would be miserable—and inefficient—working as accountants or computer programmers. Some people find they are more comfortable working outside, while others require the amenities of an environmentally controlled, ergonomically designed office.

Thus, a more realistic production possibilities frontier is shown in Figure 3. This PPF is concave to (or bowed away from) the origin because opportunity costs rise as more factors are used to produce increasing quantities of one product. Another way of saying this is that resources are

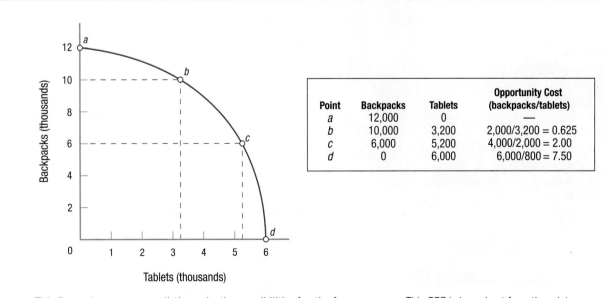

······ Figure 3 • Production Possibilities Frontier (Increasing Opportunity Cost) ······

Point	Backpacks	Tablets	Opportunity Cost (backpacks/tablets)
a	12,000	0	—
b	10,000	3,200	2,000/3,200 = 0.625
c	6,000	5,200	4,000/2,000 = 2.00
d	0	6,000	6,000/800 = 7.50

This figure shows a more realistic production possibilities frontier for an economy. This PPF is bowed out from the origin since opportunity cost rises as more factors are used to produce increasing quantities of one product or the other.

subject to diminishing returns as more resources are devoted to the production of one product. Let's consider why this is so.

Let's begin at a point at which the economy's resources are strictly devoted to backpack production (point *a*). Now assume that society decides to produce 3,200 tablets. This will require a move from point *a* to point *b*. As we can see, 2,000 backpacks must be given up to obtain the added 3,200 tablets. This means the opportunity cost of 1 tablet is 0.625 backpacks (2,000 ÷ 3,200 = 0.625). This is a low opportunity cost because those resources that are better suited to producing tablets will be the first ones shifted into this industry.

But what happens when this society decides to produce an additional 2,000 tablets, or moves from point *b* to point *c* on the graph? As Figure 3 illustrates, each additional tablet costs 2 backpacks because producing 2,000 more tablets requires the society to sacrifice 4,000 backpacks. Thus, the opportunity cost of tablets has more than tripled due to diminishing returns on the tablet side, which arise because added resources are not as well suited to the production of tablets.

To describe what has happened in plain terms, when the economy was producing 12,000 backpacks, all its resources went into backpack production. Those members of the labor force who are engineers and electronic assemblers were probably not well suited to producing backpacks. As the economy reduced backpack production and began producing tablets, the opportunity cost of producing tablets was low because resources (including workers) that were more suited to tablet production than backpack production were used first. Eventually, however, as tablets became the dominant product, manufacturing more tablets required shifting workers skilled in backpack production to the tablet industry. Employing these less suitable resources drives up the opportunity costs of tablets.

You may be wondering which point along the PPF is the best for society. Economists have no grounds for stating unequivocally which mixture of goods and services would be ideal. The perfect mixture of goods depends on the tastes and preferences of the members of society. In a capitalist economy, resource allocation is determined largely by individual choices and the workings of private markets. We consider these markets and their operations in the next chapter.

Economic Growth

We have seen that PPFs map out the maximum that an economy can produce: Points to the right of the PPF are unattainable. But what if the PPF can be shifted to the right? This shift would give economies new maximum frontiers. In fact, we will see that economic growth can be viewed as an outward shift of the PPF. In this section, we use the production possibilities model to determine some of the major reasons for economic growth. Understanding these reasons for growth will enable us to suggest some broad economic policies that could lead to expanded growth.

The production possibilities model holds resources and technology constant to derive the PPF. These assumptions suggest that economic growth has two basic determinants: expanding resources and improving technologies. The expansion of resources allows producers to increase production of all goods and services in an economy. Specific technological improvements, however, often affect only one industry directly. The development of a new color printing process, for instance, will directly affect only the printing industry.

Nevertheless, ripples from technological improvements can spread out through an entire economy, just like ripples in a pond. Specifically, improvements in technology can lead to new products, improved goods and services, and increased productivity.

Sometimes technological improvements in one industry allow other industries to increase their production with existing resources. This means producers can increase output without using added labor or other resources. Alternatively, they can get the same

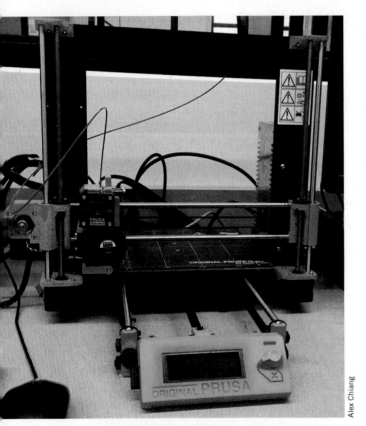

"Beaming" objects might not be restricted to *Star Trek* fantasy with the development of 3D printers capable of reproducing objects. Could this be the next big technological advancement in printing?

Alex Chiang

production levels as before by using fewer resources than before. This frees up resources in the economy for use in other industries.

When the electric lightbulb was invented, it not only created a new industry (someone had to produce lightbulbs) but also revolutionized other industries. Factories could stay open longer since they no longer had to rely on the sun for light. Workers could see better, thus improving the quality of their work. The result was that resources operated more efficiently throughout the entire economy.

The modern-day equivalent of the lightbulb might be the smartphone. Widespread use of these mobile devices enables people all across the world to produce goods and services more efficiently. Insurance agents can file claims instantly from disaster sites, deals can be closed while one is stuck in traffic, and communications have been revolutionized. Thus, this new technology has ultimately expanded time, the most finite of our resources. A similar argument could be made for the Internet. It has profoundly changed how many products are bought, sold, and delivered and has expanded communications and the flow of information.

Expanding Resources The PPF represents the possible output of an economy at a specific time. But economies are constantly changing, and so are PPFs. Capital and labor are the principal resources that can be changed through government action. Land and entrepreneurial talent are important factors of production, but neither is easy to change by government policies. The government can make owning a business easier or more profitable by reducing regulations or by offering low-interest loans or favorable tax treatment to small businesses. However, it is difficult to turn people into risk takers through government policy.

Increasing Labor and Human Capital A clear increase in population, the number of households, or the size of the labor force shifts the PPF outward, as shown in Figure 4. With added labor, the production possibilities available to the economy expand from PPF_0 to PPF_1. Such a labor increase can be caused by higher birthrates, increased immigration, or an increased willingness of people to enter the labor force. This last type of increase has occurred over the past several decades as more women have entered the labor force on a permanent basis. America's high level of immigration (both legal and illegal) fuels a strong rate of economic growth.

Rather than simply increasing the number of people working, however, the labor factor can also be increased by improving workers' skills. Economists refer to this as *investment in human capital*. Education, on-the-job training, and other professional training fit into this category.

Figure 4 • Economic Growth by Expanding Resources

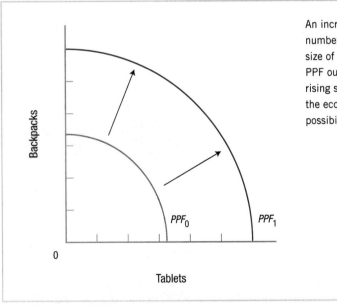

An increase in population, the number of households, or the size of the labor force shifts the PPF outward. In this figure, a rising supply of labor expands the economy's production possibilities from PPF_0 to PPF_1.

Improving human capital means people are more productive, resulting in higher wages, a higher standard of living, and an expanded PPF for society.

Capital Accumulation Increasing the capital used throughout the economy, usually brought about by investment, similarly shifts the PPF outward, as shown in Figure 4. Additional capital makes each unit of labor more productive and thus results in higher possible production throughout the economy. Adding robotics and computer-controlled machines to production lines, for example, means each unit of labor produces many more units of output.

The production possibilities model and the economic growth associated with capital accumulation suggest a tradeoff. Figure 5 illustrates the tradeoff all nations face between current consumption and capital accumulation.

Let's first assume that a nation selects a product mix in which the bulk of goods produced are consumption goods—that is, goods that are immediately consumable and have short life spans, such as food and entertainment. This product mix is represented by point b in Figure 5. Consuming most of what it produces, a decade later the economy is at PPF_b. Little growth has occurred because the economy has done little to improve its productive capacity—the present generation has essentially decided to consume rather than to invest in the economy's future.

Contrast this decision with one in which the country at first decides to produce at point a. In this case, more capital goods such as machinery and tools are produced, while fewer consumption goods are available for current consumption. Selecting this product mix results in a much further expanded PPF a decade later (PPF_a) because the economy steadily built up its productive capacity during those 10 years.

Technological Change Figure 6 illustrates what happens when an economy experiences a technological change in one of its industries, in this case, the tablet industry. As the figure shows, the economy's potential output of tablets expands greatly, although its maximum production of backpacks remains unchanged. The area between the two curves represents an improvement in the society's standard of living. People can produce and consume more of both goods than before: more tablets because of the technological advancement and more backpacks because some of the resources once devoted to tablet production can be shifted to backpack production, even as the economy is turning out more tablets than before.

This example reflects the United States today, where the computer industry is exploding with new technologies. Companies such as Apple and Intel lead the way by relentlessly developing newer, faster, and more powerful products. Consequently, consumers have seen home computers

Figure 5 • Consumption Goods, Capital Goods, and the Expansion of the Production Possibilities Frontier

If a nation selects a product mix in which most of the goods produced are consumption goods, it will initially produce at point b. The small investment made in capital goods has the effect of expanding the nation's productive capacity only to PPF_b over the following decade. If the country decides to produce at point a, however, devoting more resources to producing capital goods, its productive capacity will expand much more rapidly, pushing the PPF out to PPF_a over the following decade.

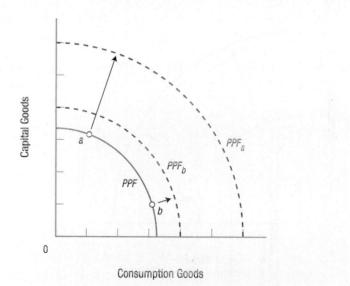

..... Figure 6 • Technological Change and Expansion ......
of the Production Possibilities Frontier

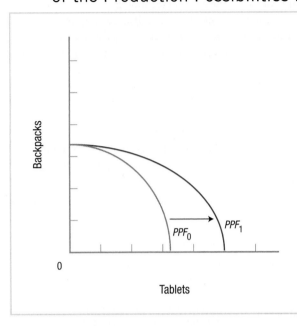

In this figure, an economy's potential output of tablets expanded greatly, while its maximum production of backpacks remained unchanged. The area between the two curves represents an improvement in the society's standard of living since more of both goods can be produced and consumed than before. Some of the resources once used for tablet production can be diverted to backpack production, even as the number of tablets produced increases.

go from clunky conversation pieces to powerful, fast, indispensable machines. Today's computers are more powerful than the mainframe supercomputers of just a few decades ago. And the latest developments in smartphones allow them to do much more than what powerful computers did a decade ago.

● ISSUE

Is the Ocean the Next Frontier? Land Reclamation and Underwater Cities

Can a city exist underneath the ocean surface? A team of engineers in Japan say that such cities can become a reality by 2030. They created a proposal for an underwater city that is powered by a process called *ocean thermal energy conversion*, in which power is generated from the differences in seawater temperatures at different depths. Can a self-sustained underwater city be a reality? If so, it could generate a vast amount of new territory around the world since the majority of the Earth is covered by oceans that could become the next frontier.

In fact, using the vast expanse of the ocean has already become a reality in some countries. Japan, Singapore, and the United Arab Emirates have built islands

off of their coastlines using a process called *land reclamation,* in which sand is moved from other parts of the ocean to create new land above the ocean's surface. More recently, China made headlines by building islands *far* from its coastline, which brings into question the role of property rights.

One of the concerns with underwater cities or land reclamation is who actually owns the right to live in the ocean. Because international waters begin 12 nautical miles beyond a country's coastline, some have questioned whether creating underwater cities or new islands in the ocean is merely a way for a country to acquire new territory and subsequently the resources

Underwater hotels are already a reality in Singapore.

deriving from that territory, such as fish, natural resources, or a strategic geographic location for military purposes.

Besides new products, technology has dramatically reduced the cost of producing tablets and other high-tech items, allowing countries to produce and consume more of other products, expanding the entire PPF outward. However, the effect of technology on an economy also depends on how well its important trade centers are linked together. If a country has mostly dirt paths rather than paved highways, you can imagine how this deficiency would affect its economy: Distribution will be slow, and industries will be slow to react to changes in demand. In such a case, improving the roads might be the best way to stimulate economic growth.

As you can see, there are many ways to stimulate economic growth. A society can expand its output by using more resources, perhaps by encouraging more people to enter the workforce or raising educational levels of workers. The government can encourage people to invest more, as opposed to devoting their earnings to immediate consumption. The public sector can spur technological advances by providing incentives to private firms to do research and development or underwrite research investments of its own. Another important contributor to economic growth is specialization and trade, which we turn to next.

 CHECKPOINT

PRODUCTION POSSIBILITIES AND ECONOMIC GROWTH

- A production possibilities frontier (PPF) depicts the different combinations of goods that a fully employed economy can produce, given its available resources and current technology (both assumed fixed in the short run).

- Production levels inside and on the frontier are possible, but those outside the curve are unattainable.

- Because production on the frontier represents the maximum output attainable when all resources are fully employed, reallocating production from one product to another involves *opportunity costs*: The output of one product must be reduced to get the added output of the other. The more of one product that is desired, the higher its opportunity cost because of diminishing returns and the unsuitability of some resources for producing some products.

- The PPF model suggests that economic growth can arise from an expansion in resources or improvements in technology. Economic growth is an outward shift of the PPF.

QUESTION: Taiwan is a small mountainous island with 23 million inhabitants, little arable land, and few natural resources, while Nigeria is a much larger country with 8 times the population, 40 times more arable land, and tremendous deposits of oil. Given Nigeria's sizable resource advantage, why is Nigeria's total annual production less than that of Taiwan's?

Answers to the Checkpoint questions can be found at the end of this chapter.

SPECIALIZATION, COMPARATIVE ADVANTAGE, AND TRADE

As we have seen, economics has a lot to do with voluntary production and exchange. People and nations do business with one another because all expect to gain from the transactions. Centuries ago, European merchants ventured to the Far East to ply the lucrative spice trade. These days, American consumers buy wines from Italy, cars from Japan, electronics from South Korea, and millions of other products from countries around the world. The goods we buy from other countries are **imports**, while the goods we sell to other countries are **exports**.

Many people mistakenly assume that trade between nations is a zero-sum game—a game in which, for one party to gain, another party must lose. This is how poker works. If one player walks away from the table a winner, someone else must have lost. But this is not how voluntary trade works. Voluntary trade is a positive-sum game: Both parties to a transaction score positive gains. After all, who would voluntarily enter into an exchange if he or she did not believe there was some gain from it? To understand how all parties to an exchange (whether individuals or nations) can

imports Goods and services that are purchased from abroad.

exports Goods and services that are sold abroad.

DAVID RICARDO (1772–1823)

David Ricardo's rigorous, dispassionate evaluation of economic principles influenced generations of theorists, including such vastly different thinkers as John Stuart Mill and Karl Marx. Ricardo was born in London as the third of 17 children. At age 14, he joined his father's trading business on the London Stock Exchange. At 21, he started his own brokerage and within five years had amassed a small fortune.

While vacationing in Bath, England, he chanced upon a copy of Adam Smith's *The Wealth of Nations* and decided to devote his energies to studying economics and writing. He once wrote to his lifelong friend Thomas Malthus (another prominent economist of the time) that he was "thankful for the miserable English climate because it kept him at his desk writing." Ricardo and Malthus corresponded on a regular basis, and their exchanges led to the development of many economic concepts still used today.

Later, as a member of the British Parliament, Ricardo was an outspoken critic of the 1815 Corn Laws, which placed high tariffs on imported grain to protect British landowners. Ricardo was a strong advocate of free trade, and his writings reflected this view. His theory of "comparative advantage" suggested that countries would mutually benefit from trade by specializing in export goods they could produce at a lower opportunity cost than another country. His classic example was trade in cloth and wine between England and Portugal.

Ricardo died in 1823 of an ear infection, leaving an enduring legacy of classical (pre-1930s) economic analysis.

Information from E. Ray Canterbery, *A Brief History of Economics* (Hackensack, NJ: World Scientific), 2001; Howard Marshall, *The Great Economists: A History of Economic Thought* (New York: Pitman Publishing), 1967; Steven Pressman, *Fifty Major Economists,* 2nd ed. (New York: Routledge), 2006.

gain from it, we need to consider the concept of comparative advantage developed by David Ricardo roughly 200 years ago and how this concept differs from the concept of absolute advantage.

Absolute and Comparative Advantage

Table 1 presents a hypothetical production rate for Haiti and the Dominican Republic, two countries with similar populations. Both countries produce cocoa (used to make chocolate) and coffee. As shown in the table, Haiti is able to produce 16 tons of cocoa or 20 tons of coffee using its resources

TABLE 1	COMPARING PRODUCTION AND OPPORTUNITY COSTS FOR COCOA AND COFFEE (IN TONS)			
	Absolute Advantage		**Comparative Advantage**	
	Cocoa	**Coffee**	**Opp. Cost of 1 Cocoa**	**Opp. Cost of 1 Coffee**
Haiti	16	20	20 ÷ 16 = 1.25 coffee	16 ÷ 20 = 0.8 cocoa
Dominican Republic	20	40	40 ÷ 20 = 2 coffee	20 ÷ 40 = 0.5 cocoa
Advantage	Dominican Republic	Dominican Republic	Haiti	Dominican Republic

A country has an absolute advantage if it can produce more of a good than another country using the same amount of resources. The Dominican Republic has an absolute advantage in producing both cocoa and coffee. Even so, Haiti has a comparative advantage over the Dominican Republic in producing cocoa because its opportunity cost of producing 1 ton of cocoa is 1.25 tons of coffee, which is lower than the Dominican Republic's opportunity cost (2 tons of coffee). The Dominican Republic, however, has a lower opportunity cost of producing 1 ton of coffee (0.5 vs. 0.8 for Haiti), thus giving it a comparative advantage in coffee production.

absolute advantage A country can produce more of a good than another country using the same amount of resources.

comparative advantage A country has a lower opportunity cost of producing a good than another country.

over a fixed time period, while the Dominican Republic is able to produce 20 tons of cocoa or 40 tons of coffee in the same time period. Based on this comparison, the Dominican Republic has an **absolute advantage** over Haiti in producing both products. An absolute advantage exists when one country can produce more of a good than another country using the same amount of resources.

At first glance, one might wonder why the Dominican Republic would trade with Haiti if it is able to produce more of both goods. Wouldn't the Dominican Republic just produce all of its own cocoa and coffee? The answer lies in comparative advantage. One country has a **comparative advantage** in producing a good if its opportunity cost is lower than another country's opportunity cost for that good.

In Table 1, we calculate the opportunity cost of each good for each country. First, we compare the opportunity costs of producing 1 ton of cocoa. In Haiti, the opportunity cost of producing 1 ton of cocoa is 1.25 tons of coffee. This is calculated by dividing 20 (tons of coffee) by 16. We then do the same for the Dominican Republic, except we divide 40 (tons of coffee) by 20, such that producing 1 ton of cocoa means giving up producing 2 tons of coffee. We can now compare the opportunity cost of producing 1 ton of cocoa in both countries to find that Haiti has a lower opportunity cost of 1.25 tons of coffee versus 2 tons of coffee in the Dominican Republic. Because Haiti's opportunity cost is lower, it has a comparative advantage in producing cocoa.

To determine who has the comparative advantage in producing coffee, we compute the opportunity cost of producing 1 ton of coffee in each country. As Table 1 shows, 1 ton of coffee in Haiti means giving up producing 0.8 ton of cocoa, while 1 ton of coffee in the Dominican Republic means giving up producing 0.5 ton of cocoa. In this case, the Dominican Republic has a lower opportunity cost of coffee production and therefore a comparative advantage.

Note that while we are comparing production between countries, the concepts of absolute advantage and comparative advantage apply to individuals as well. Suppose that in one minute, I can run 300 meters or swim 50 meters, while you can run 320 meters or swim 80 meters. Because you can run and swim faster than me, you have an absolute advantage in both sports. However, my comparative advantage would be running because for every meter that we run, I give up only 0.17 meter of swimming while you give up 0.25. Meanwhile, for every meter that we swim, I give up 6 meters of running while you give up only 4.

Now that our understanding of comparative advantage is clearer, how does this translate into gains from trade to both countries? We will need to use the PPF model to illustrate how countries can gain by specializing in producing the good in which it has a comparative advantage.

Gains from Trade

Figure 7 shows production possibilities frontiers for Haiti and the Dominican Republic based on the production rates shown in Table 1. For simplicity, we assume that the opportunity costs

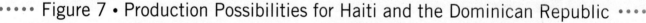

····· Figure 7 • Production Possibilities for Haiti and the Dominican Republic ····

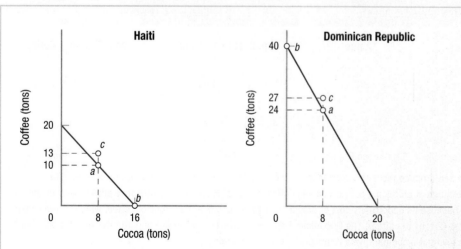

Haiti and the Dominican Republic initially produce and consume at point *a* (in autarky) on their respective PPFs. When each country specializes according to their comparative advantage, each country moves to point *b* on their PPF. Finally, by trading with each other, each country ends up at point *c*, which is beyond their original PPFs. Comparative advantage leads to gains for both countries from specialization and trade.

TABLE 2	INITIAL PRODUCTION AND CONSUMPTION WITHOUT TRADE	
	Cocoa	Coffee
Haiti	8	10
Dominican Republic	8	24
Total	16	34

in both countries are constant. This means that the PPFs will be straight lines. The intercepts of the PPF correspond to the amount of cocoa and coffee that each country can produce. Note that the intercepts indicate the maximum amount of output that can be produced if all resources are devoted to producing that one product. For example, Haiti can produce 16 tons of cocoa *or* 20 tons of coffee or any combination along its PPF. Similarly, the Dominican Republic can produce 20 tons of cocoa *or* 40 tons of coffee or any combination along its PPF. The slopes of the PPFs for each country correspond to the opportunity cost.

Let's assume that both countries are in **autarky,** which means they do not trade at all. Haiti and the Dominican Republic both produce and consume at point *a* on their respective PPFs. This means that Haiti will produce and consume 8 tons of cocoa and 10 tons of coffee, while the Dominican Republic will produce and consume 8 tons of cocoa and 24 tons of coffee. Table 2 summarizes these initial conditions.

Now assume that Haiti focuses on producing cocoa (its comparative advantage), producing the maximum that it can: 16 tons. The Dominican Republic focuses on producing coffee (its comparative advantage), producing the most that it can: 40 tons. These amounts are shown as point *b* in Figure 7. Table 3 shows each country's production when both countries completely specialize according to their comparative advantage. Although the combined production of cocoa remained constant at 16 tons, the total production of coffee increased by 6 (from 34 to 40) tons.

Now suppose that the two countries agree to trade and to share the additional 6 tons of coffee produced. Haiti will export 8 tons of cocoa to the Dominican Republic in exchange for 13 tons of coffee. The resulting mix of products consumed in each country is shown in Table 4 and at points *c* in Figure 7. Compared to the autarky situation from Table 2, both countries

autarky A country that does not engage in international trade, also known as a closed economy.

TABLE 3	PRODUCTION AFTER SPECIALIZATION BUT BEFORE TRADE	
	Cocoa	Coffee
Haiti	16	0
Dominican Republic	0	40
Total	16	40

TABLE 4	FINAL CONSUMPTION AFTER TRADE	
	Cocoa	Coffee
Haiti	8	13
Dominican Republic	8	27
Total	16	40

Would you pay extra for shoes that are "Made in USA"? New Balance's 990 collection is made in the USA, but prices are about double compared to imported models, reflecting the higher labor cost that goes into making them.

are now better off, having engaged in specialized production and trade. In fact, both countries are now consuming at points beyond their PPFs, which means trade allows these countries to achieve an outcome that could not be achieved on their own given the amount of resources they have. The important point to remember here is that even when one country has an absolute advantage over another in the production of both goods, both countries can still benefit from trading with one another.

Practical Constraints on Trade

Before leaving the subject of international trade and how it contributes to growth, we should take a moment to note some practical constraints on trade. First, every transaction involves costs, including transportation, communications, and the general cost of doing business. Because these costs have fallen in recent decades, global trade continues to increase. Second, PPFs for nations are not linear but rather are governed by increasing costs and diminishing returns. Therefore, countries do not completely specialize in one product. Not only is it risky, but rising resource costs make it impractical to do so.

Finally, although countries that trade benefit overall, there are still winners and losers from trade within each country. For example, industries that compete against imported goods face lower prices, making it difficult to stay in business. Workers in these industries may lose their jobs. However, trade increases demand for goods that are exported, which creates more high-paying jobs.

For example, China is now the biggest consumer of American cars, benefiting the U.S. auto industry and its workers tremendously. Also, consumers benefit from the lower prices and greater variety of goods that trade provides. In some cases, trade is the only option—for example, the United States produces practically no coffee or cocoa, making your morning coffee or hot chocolate nearly impossible without trade. Finally, many American industries depend on imported raw materials in order to produce items in the United States.

Although trade does not benefit everyone equally, there are clearly more winners than losers. Trade agreements between countries (such as the recent USMCA agreement with Canada, Mexico, and the United States) help to promote greater trade by reducing tariffs and other barriers. For the United States, opening up more markets to American products in countries like China and India (with 2.8 billion potential customers) will lead to significant benefits from trade over time.

●ISSUE

Do We Really Specialize in That? Comparative Advantage in the United States and China

What do tofu, edamame, ink, soy sauce, livestock feed, and soy milk have in common? They are all products commonly made from soybeans. Although direct human consumption of soybeans in the United States is often confined to health food products and food in Asian restaurants, soybeans are much more important to the U.S. economy than most people think. The United States has a comparative advantage in soybean production.

How can a rich, technologically advanced country like the United States end up with a comparative advantage in an agricultural product like soybeans? Several factors play a role. First, the United States has an abundance of farmland ideal in climate and soil for soybean production. Second, modern fertilizers and seed technologies have made soybean production a much more innovative industry than in the past, allowing farms to increase soybean yields per acre of land. And third, a strong appetite for soy-based products, particularly in Asia has made soybeans a very lucrative industry.

China is the largest trading partner to the United States, trading $680 billion worth of goods in 2018. Yet the top five U.S. export goods (items sold) and import goods (items bought) with China, listed below, may be surprising.

Dušan Kostić/iStockphoto

Top Five Exports to China (2018)
1. Aircraft ($16.3 billion)
2. Soybeans ($15.4 billion)
3. Automobiles ($13.7 billion)
4. Industrial machinery ($13.2 billion)
5. Electrical goods ($12.7 billion)

Top Five Imports from China (2018)
1. Electrical goods ($147.8 billion)
2. Machinery ($110.0 billion)
3. Furniture ($32.5 billion)
4. Toys/sporting goods ($26.2 billion)
5. Plastics ($16.1 billion)

Although the United States sells a lot of machines and electrical goods to China (mostly specialized machinery and electronics used in factories and research labs), it buys significantly greater amounts of these products *from* China. In other words, the United States is a net buyer of machinery and electrical goods, industries that include many consumer technology goods we use, such as smartphones, computers, and digital equipment. Besides soybeans, wood pulp, copper, and wood are three other resource industries (not listed here but in the top 10) that constitute a large portion of U.S. sales *to* China.

In sum, specialization and trade are not as simple as they used to be. Products such as computers and electronics that once were the purview of "rich" countries like the United States are now being manufactured in China and other countries, while improved technology in the agricultural and natural resource industries has given the United States a comparative advantage that would have been unheard of 50 years ago.

✔ CHECKPOINT

SPECIALIZATION, COMPARATIVE ADVANTAGE, AND TRADE

- An absolute advantage exists when a country can produce more of some good than another country using the same amount of resources.

- A comparative advantage exists when one country has a lower opportunity cost of producing a good than another country. Both countries gain from trade if each focuses on producing those goods with which it has a comparative advantage.

- Voluntary trade is a positive-sum game because both countries benefit.

QUESTION: Why do Hollywood stars (and many other rich individuals)—unlike most people—have full-time personal assistants who manage their personal affairs?

Answers to the Checkpoint questions can be found at the end of this chapter.

CHAPTER SUMMARY

SECTION 1 BASIC ECONOMIC QUESTIONS AND PRODUCTION

2.1

Every economy must decide:
1. What to produce.
2. How to produce it.
3. Who will receive the goods and services produced.

Bloomberg/Getty Images

Using scarce resources productively leads to:

Production efficiency: Goods and services are produced at their lowest possible resource cost.

Allocative efficiency: Goods are produced according to what society desires.

2.2

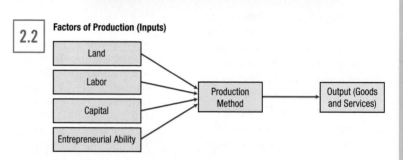

Factors of Production (Inputs)

Land
Labor
Capital
Entrepreneurial Ability
→ Production Method → Output (Goods and Services)

SECTION 2 PRODUCTION POSSIBILITIES AND ECONOMIC GROWTH

2.3 The **production possibilities frontier (PPF)** shows the different combinations of goods that a fully employed economy can produce, given its available resources and current technology.

2.4 Production possibilities frontiers (PPFs) illustrate tradeoffs—if an economy operates at full employment (on the PPF), producing more of one good requires producing less of the other. A concave PPF shows how opportunity costs rise due to diminishing returns.

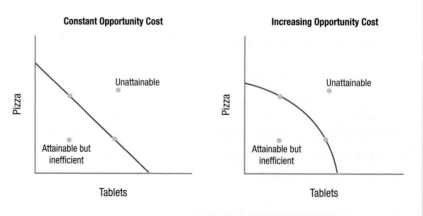

Some pizza makers were never meant to produce computers and some computer workers were never meant to produce pizza, which increases the opportunity cost of production as more of one good is produced.

The production possibilities model shows how economic growth can arise from an expansion in resources or from improvements in technology, or both.

2.5 | **Changes in the *PPF***: From *PPF$_A$* to *PPF$_B$*: An increase in productivity in the production of one good (e.g., an increase in the number of students studying computer engineering).

From *PPF$_A$* to *PPF$_C$*: An increase in productive capacity of both goods (e.g., an increase in overall technology, or an increase in labor or capital resources).

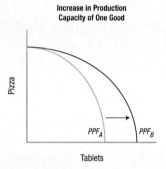

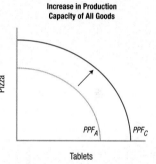

SECTION 3 SPECIALIZATION, COMPARATIVE ADVANTAGE, AND TRADE

2.6 | An **absolute advantage** exists when one country can produce more of a good than another country using the same amount of resources. A **comparative advantage** exists when one country can produce a good at a lower opportunity cost than another country.

Gains from trade result when a country specializes in the production of goods in which it has a comparative advantage, and trades these goods with another country. Trade is a positive-sum game. Both countries can benefit even if one country has an absolute advantage in both goods.

Calculating Opportunity Costs Using Production Numbers (units produced per day per worker)

	Boomerangs	Kiwi
Australia	20	12
New Zealand	8	16

- Opportunity cost of 1 boomerang:
  Australia: 12 kiwi/20 boomerangs = 0.6 kiwi per boomerang.
  New Zealand: 16 kiwi/8 boomerangs = 2 kiwi per boomerang.
  Australia has a lower opportunity cost of producing boomerangs.

- Opportunity cost of 1 kiwi:
  Australia: 20 boomerangs/12 kiwi = 1.7 boomerangs per kiwi.
  New Zealand: 8 boomerangs/16 kiwi = 0.5 boomerangs per kiwi.
  New Zealand has a lower opportunity cost of producing kiwi.

2.7 | Countries export goods for which they have a comparative advantage and import goods for which they have a comparative disadvantage, leading to gains from trade to both countries.

Key Concepts

Questions and Problems

Check Your Understanding

1. When can an economy increase the production of one good without reducing the output of another?

2. In which of the three basic questions facing any society does technology play the greatest role?

3. Explain the important difference between a straight-line PPF and a PPF that is concave to (bowed away from) the origin.

4. How would unemployment be shown on the PPF?

5. List three factors that can contribute to an economy's growth.

6. How can a country that does not have an absolute advantage in producing goods still benefit from trade?

Apply the Concepts

7. Innovation and technology has allowed for new forms of biodegradable plastics to be created that are less harmful to the environment. How might such inventions impact production efficiency and allocative efficiency (if at all) of industries that use a lot of plastics, such as the construction and automobile industries?

8. Describe how a country producing more capital goods than consumption goods ends up in the future with a PPF that is farther out than that of a country that produces more consumption goods and fewer capital goods.

9. The United States has an absolute advantage in making many goods, such as short-sleeved golf shirts. Why do Indonesia and Bangladesh make these shirts and export them to the United States?

10. Why is it that the United States uses heavy street-cleaning machines driven by one person to clean the streets, while China and India use many people with brooms to do the same job?

11. If specialization and trade as discussed in this chapter lead to a win-win situation in which both countries gain, why is there often opposition to trade agreements and globalization?

12. China's rising middle class has resulted in a surge of luxury food imports such as lobsters from the United States. China's demand for U.S. lobsters is so great that fishermen in Maine (where most U.S. lobsters are caught) have a tough time filling orders. Explain how China's increased demand for lobsters affects consumers and producers of lobsters in the United States.

In the News

13. In 2017, Hurricane Harvey caused more than $100 billion in damage to homes, businesses, and farms in Texas and Louisiana. The production capacity of this region was subsequently affected for several months. Explain how such a natural disaster can affect a region's PPF. How might it affect economic growth?

14. In 2017, a $500 million private-public initiative was announced for the purpose of boosting STEM (science, technology, engineering, and math) education, as the United States contin-ues to fall behind other industrialized nations in student achievement in these fields. How would spending on STEM initiatives today, which leads to higher costs in the near term, pay off in future benefits to the economy?

Solving Problems

Work It Out

 interactive activity

15. Iceland and Denmark both produce skis and sleds. Iceland can produce 3 skis or 6 sleds using one day of labor, while Denmark can produce 4 skis or 12 sleds using one day of labor. Which country has an absolute advantage in producing skis? Sleds? Which country has a comparative advantage in produc-ing skis? Sleds? Are gains from trade possible between Iceland and Denmark? If yes, which good should each country special-ize in producing?

16. The following table shows the potential output combinations of oranges and jars of prickly pear jelly (from the flower of the prickly pear cactus) for Florida and Arizona.

   a. Compute the opportunity cost of oranges in Florida in terms of jars of prickly pear jelly. Do the same for prickly pear jelly in terms of oranges.
   b. Compute the opportunity cost of oranges in Arizona in terms of jars of prickly pear jelly. Do the same for prickly pear jelly in terms of oranges.
   c. Would it make sense for Florida to specialize in producing oranges and for Arizona to special-ize in producing prickly pear jelly and then trade? Why or why not?

Florida		Arizona	
Oranges	Prickly Pear Jelly	Oranges	Prickly Pear Jelly
0	10	0	500
50	8	20	400
100	6	40	300
150	4	60	200
200	2	80	100
250	0	100	0

✅ Answers to Questions in Checkpoints

Checkpoint: Basic Economic Questions and Production 35

Typically, entrepreneurs put not only their time and effort into a business but also their money, often pledging private assets as collateral for loans. Should the business fail, they stand to lose more than their jobs, rent from the land, or interest on capital loaned to the firm. Workers can get other jobs, landowners can rent to others, and capital can be used in other enterprises. The entre-preneur must suffer the loss of personal assets and move on.

Checkpoint: Production Possibilities and Economic Growth 42

Although Nigeria has significantly more natural resources and labor (two important factors of production) than Taiwan, these resources alone do not guarantee a higher ability to produce goods and services. Factors of production also include physical capital (machinery), human capital (education), and technology (research and development), all of which Taiwan has in great abundance. Thus, despite the lack of land, labor, and natural resources, Taiwan is able to use its resources efficiently and expand its production possibilities beyond those of Nigeria.

Checkpoint: Specialization, Comparative Advantage, and Trade 47

For Hollywood stars and other rich people, the opportunity cost of their time is high. As a result, they hire people at lower cost to do the mundane chores that each of us is accustomed to doing because our time is relatively less valuable. Specializing in one's comparative advantage is a way to maximize utility when time is limited.

Supply and Demand

Using the basic tools of supply and demand to determine how prices and quantities are set in a market economy

What $100+ billion global industry sells a product that many people typically can obtain easily from another source free of charge? The bottled water industry! This industry began its meteoric rise in the early 1990s, and today, the ubiquitous bottle of water has changed the way we live. It also has created new concerns regarding the environmental impact of the billions of plastic bottles used and discarded.

The bottled water industry took off as consumers changed their hydration habits, spurred by greater awareness of the health benefits of drinking water, including weight loss, illness prevention, and overall health maintenance. As water consumption increased, people started wanting something more than just ordinary water from the tap. They desired water that was purer, more consistent in taste, or infused with flavor or minerals. Plus, consumers wanted water that was easy to carry. Bottled water was the product consumers wanted, and the market was willing to provide it.

Bottled water comes from many sources, both domestic and foreign, and consists of either spring water (from natural springs underneath the Earth's surface) or purified water (ordinary tap water that undergoes a complex purification process). As the industry grew, new varieties of water were made available. Water from exotic faraway springs, vitamin-infused water, flavored water, and carbonated water were some of the choices consumers were given. The total amount of water produced for the bottled water industry continued to increase as long as there were customers willing to pay for it in the market.

In the late 2000s, rising concerns about the harmful effects of discarded plastic bottles on the environment, increased use of home water purification devices, and even some laws against the use of bottled water eventually slowed the market's growth. The bottled water industry has since responded to the environmental concerns by using bottles made from recycled plastic or by using new technologies to reduce the plastic content in water bottles, again responding to the desires of consumers.

Consumers have many choices of what water to buy and where to buy it. Even so, the bottled water market is one in which prices vary considerably depending on the location of purchase. A single bottle of water of the same brand might cost $0.69 at a grocery store, $0.99 at a convenience store, $1.25 from a vending machine, $1.49 at a local coffee shop, and $3.00 or more at a theme park, sports stadium, or movie theater. How can the same product be sold in different places at so many different prices?

This chapter analyzes the various factors influencing how consumers value goods in different settings and circumstances. We also study how producers take costs and incentives into account in determining what products to produce, how much to produce, and what prices to charge. The interaction between consumers and producers within a market determines the prices we pay.

In any given market, prices are determined by "what the market will bear." Which factors determine what the market will bear, and what happens when events that occur in the marketplace cause prices to change? For answers to these questions, economists turn to supply and demand analysis. The basic model of supply and demand presented in this chapter will let you determine why product sales rise and fall, in what direction prices move, and how many goods will be offered for sale when certain events happen in the marketplace. Later chapters use this same model to explain complex phenomena such as how wages are set and how personal income is distributed.

BY THE Numbers

Demand and Supply for Higher Education:
A Focus on Institution Types

Higher education is a vitally important market that prepares students for career paths. Demand for colleges and universities has risen over the past generation, along with the number of schools that offer degrees. The type of institutions, however, has changed over time, as traditional public four-year schools increasingly compete against public two-year institutions and for-profit institutions that cater more to working students and other nontraditional students. But enrollments in two-year institutions and for-profit institutions tend to change as the economy fluctuates. By the Numbers looks more closely at the trends in higher education enrollment by types of schools.

4,360

Total number of degree-granting institutions of higher education in the United States in 2017

19,841,014

Total enrollment in all degree-granting institutions of higher education in the United States in 2017

DATA:

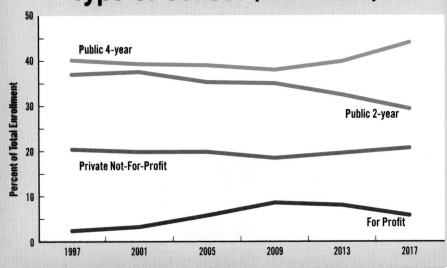

Higher Education Enrollment by Type of School (1997–2017)

Where Can I Find These Data?

Source: National Center for Education Statistics (U.S. Department of Education)

Web site: http://nces.ed.gov/programs/digest/current_tables.asp

Details: Select "Chapter 3 Postsecondary Education" and "Table 303.25." Divide each category by the "All Institutions Total" enrollment.

WHY ARE THESE DATA IMPORTANT?

According to the discussion of markets in the text, a rising demand for education puts upward pressure on prices, making the cost to attend college higher. Public institutions of higher learning, however, offset rising prices by offering subsidies to students who are in-state residents. Private institutions may offer scholarships and other financial aid to offset rising prices.

Data *in the News*

"More Pressure on Accreditors in Changing Higher Ed Landscape" by Andrew Kreighbaum; *Inside Higher Ed*, August 15, 2018

The role of college oversight bodies is in the spotlight as more large for-profit institutions look to reclassify as nonprofits.

~ Assessing Your Data Literacy ~

1. Which type(s) of institutions for higher learning increased in percent of total enrollment from 1997 to 2017? Which type(s) decreased? Which type(s) did not change?

2. Which type of institution for higher learning has seen the largest nominal increase in enrollment by percent of total from 1997 to 2017? Which has seen the largest relative increase?

3. Explain how fluctuations in the economy might affect enrollment in certain types of institutions for higher learning.

MARKETS

markets Institutions that bring buyers and sellers together so that they can interact and transact with each other.

A **market** is an institution that enables buyers and sellers to interact and transact with one another. A lemonade stand is a market because it allows people to exchange money for a product, in this case, lemonade. Ticket scalping, which remains illegal or highly restricted in some states, similarly represents market activity since it leads to the exchange of money for tickets, whether it takes place in person outside the stadium or online.

The Internet, without a physical location, has dramatically expanded the notion of markets. Online market sites, such as eBay, OfferUp, and Amazon, permit firms and individuals to sell a variety of products, both new and used. There are also online markets for virtual goods, such as virtual tools, cash, and animals, in popular games. And the recent rise of cryptocurrencies, such as Bitcoin and Ethereum, has increased the use of speculation in markets.

Even though all markets have the same basic component—the transaction—they can differ in a number of ways. Some markets are quite limited because of their geographical location or because they offer only a few different products for sale. The New York Stock Exchange serves as a market for just a single type of financial instrument, stocks, but it facilitates exchanges worth billions of dollars daily. Compare this to the neighborhood flea market, which is much smaller and may operate only on weekends but offers everything from food and crafts to T-shirts and electronics. Cement manufacturers are typically restricted to local markets due to high transportation costs, whereas Internet firms can easily do business with customers around the world.

The Price System

When buyers and sellers exchange money for goods and services, accepting some offers and rejecting others, they are also doing something else: They are communicating their individual desires. Much of this communication is accomplished through the prices of items. If buyers

Do Markets Exist for Everyone, Including Dogs and Cats?

Over 89 million dogs and 95 million cats call the United States home, with many times more finding homes around the world. Over four in ten U.S. households include at least one pet, which is often treated as a beloved member of the family. The expenses associated with pet ownership often extend beyond the basic necessities of food and veterinarian checkups.

Total spending on pet-related products in the United States has increased every year since 2001, surpassing $70 billion in 2018. Even the severe recession of 2007–2009 did not dampen the growth in spending on pets. The seeming immunity of the pet goods market to economic hardships raises an interesting question of to whom the market is geared: the pets or their sometimes fanatical owners?

Manufacturers of pet goods have increased the types of "consumer" goods and services for pets. These include a greater selection of pet foods and toys, but increasingly sellers are being more creative in their offerings. For example, the number of pet spas, pet hotels, and even pet airlines, allowing pets to bathe in luxury as they or their owners travel, has boomed over the past decade.

Pet consumerism has even gone high-tech. Since the introduction of tablets, programmers have introduced new tablet apps designed for cats, including games that are played feline versus human. Such apps highlight the ability of businesses to turn pets into consumers, whose desires (even if imagined by their owners) turn into actual purchases.

Jefferson Graham

The power of consumer decisions extending beyond the wants of humans demonstrates the broad reach of markets. Because humans share a deep connection with their furry loved ones, they will often incorporate their pets' desires into real consumption choices. And based on the growth of this market, it's likely that dogs and cats will continue to be avid consumers.

value a particular item sufficiently, they will quickly pay its asking price. If they do not buy it, they are indicating they do not believe the item to be worth its asking price.

Prices also give buyers an easy means of comparing goods that can substitute for each other. If the price of margarine falls to half the price of butter, this will suggest to many consumers that margarine is a better deal. Similarly, sellers can determine what goods to sell by comparing their prices. When prices rise for tennis rackets, this tells sporting goods store operators that the public wants more tennis rackets, leading the store operators to order more. Prices, therefore, contain a considerable amount of useful information for both consumers and sellers. For this reason, economists often call our market economy the **price system.**

price system A name given to the market economy because prices provide considerable information to both buyers and sellers.

✅ CHECKPOINT

MARKETS

- Markets are institutions that enable buyers and sellers to interact and transact business.

- Markets differ in geographical location, products offered, and size.

- Prices contain a wealth of information for both buyers and sellers.

- Through their purchases, consumers signal their willingness to exchange money for particular products at particular prices. These signals help businesses decide what to produce and how much to produce.

- The market economy is also called the price system.

QUESTION: What are the important differences between the markets for financial securities such as the New York Stock Exchange and your local farmer's market?

Answers to the Checkpoint questions can be found at the end of this chapter.

DEMAND

Whenever you purchase a product, you are voting with your money. You are typically selecting one product out of many and supporting one firm out of many, both of which signal to the business community what sorts of products satisfy your wants as a consumer.

Economists typically focus on wants rather than needs because it is so difficult to determine what we truly need. Theoretically, you could survive on tofu and vitamin pills, living in a lean-to made of cardboard and buying all your clothes from thrift stores. Most people in our society, however, choose not to live in such austere fashion. Rather, they want something more, and in most cases they are willing and able to pay for more.

Willingness-to-Pay: The Building Block of Market Demand

Imagine sitting in your economics class around mealtime. In your rush to class, you didn't eat, and now you're hungry. You think about foods that sound appealing to you (just about anything at this point) and plan to go to the cafeteria immediately after class and buy a sandwich. Given your growling stomach, you think more about what you want on your sandwich and less about how much the sandwich will cost. In your mind, your **willingness-to-pay (WTP)** for that sandwich can be quite high, say, $10 or even more.

Economists refer to WTP as the maximum amount one is willing and able to pay for a good or service, which represents the highest value that a consumer believes the good or service is worth. Of course, one always hopes that the actual price would be much lower. In your case, WTP is the cutoff between buying a sandwich and not buying a sandwich.

WTP varies from person to person due to the circumstances each person is in and the number of items one chooses to buy. Suppose your classmate ate a full meal before she came to class. Her WTP for a sandwich would be much lower than yours because she isn't hungry at that moment. Similarly, after you buy and consume your first sandwich, your WTP for a second sandwich

willingness-to-pay An individual's valuation of a good or service, equal to the most an individual is willing and able to pay.

····· Figure 1 • From Individual Willingness-to-Pay to Market Demand ············

In panel A, you are willing and able to pay up to $10 for your first sandwich and $4 for the second. Jane, however, is only willing to pay up to $6 for her first sandwich and $2 for a second (panel B). Placing the WTP for sandwiches by you and Jane in order from the highest to lowest value, we generate a market with two consumers shown in panel C. As more and more individuals are added to the market, the demand for sandwiches becomes a smooth downward-sloping line, shown in panel D.

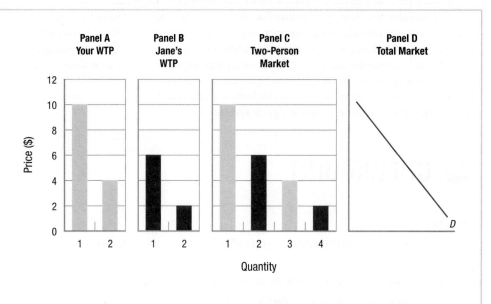

would decrease because you would be less hungry. The desires consumers have for goods and services are expressed through their purchases in the market.

Figure 1 illustrates how individuals' WTP is used to derive market demand curves. Suppose you are willing to pay up to $10 for the first sandwich and $4 for the second sandwich (shown in panel A), while Jane, your less hungry classmate, would pay up to $6 for her first sandwich and only $2 for her second sandwich (shown in panel B). If we take the WTP for your two sandwiches and the WTP of Jane's two sandwiches and place all four values in order from highest to lowest, a two-person market for sandwiches is created as shown in panel C. Notice how the distance between steps becomes smaller in the two-person market. Now suppose we combine the WTPs for everybody in the class (or for an entire city or country) into a single market. What would that diagram look like? In large markets, the difference in WTP between each unit of a good becomes so small that it becomes a straight line, as shown in panel D.

These illustrations show how ordinary demand curves, which we will discuss in detail in the remainder of this section, are developed from the perceptions of what individual consumers believe a good or service is worth to them (their WTP). Let's now discuss an important characteristic of market demand.

The Law of Demand: The Relationship Between Quantity Demanded and Price

demand The maximum amount of a product that buyers are willing and able to purchase over some time period at various prices, holding all other relevant factors constant (the *ceteris paribus* condition).

law of demand Holding all other relevant factors constant, as price increases, quantity demanded falls, and as price decreases, quantity demanded rises.

Demand refers to the goods and services people are willing and able to buy during a certain period of time at various prices, holding all other relevant factors constant (the *ceteris paribus* condition). Typically, when the price of a good or service increases (say your favorite café raises its prices), the quantity demanded will decrease because fewer and fewer people will be willing and able to spend their money on such things. However, when prices of goods or services decrease (think of sales offered the day after Thanksgiving), the quantity demanded increases.

In a market economy, there is a negative relationship between price and quantity demanded. This relationship, in its most basic form, states that as price increases, the quantity demanded falls, and conversely, as price falls, the quantity demanded increases.

This principle, when all other factors are held constant, is known as the **law of demand.** The law of demand explains why prices are inversely related to the quantity demanded. More specifically, the relationship is explained by the *substitution effect* and *income effect*. The substitution effect states that as the price of a good falls, consumers will buy more of this good in place of alternative goods that are now relatively more expensive. The income effect states that as the price of a good falls, less money is spent on that good, freeing up income that can be used to buy more of all goods, including the good that has fallen in price. Both the substitution and income effects lead to a consumer buying more of a good when the price falls, and vice versa. But technical descriptions aside, the law of demand is very intuitive—when prices of goods fall (such as in a sale), people buy more. When prices of goods rise, people buy less.

Time is an important component in the demand for many products. Consuming many products—watching a movie, eating a pizza, playing tennis—takes some time. Thus, the price of these goods includes not only their monetary cost but also the opportunity cost of the time needed to consume them.

Bloomberg/Getty Images

The day after Thanksgiving, dubbed "Black Friday," is when stores offer steep discounts to jumpstart the holiday shopping season. This leads to massive quantities of goods sold, in an example of the law of demand.

The Demand Curve

The law of demand states that as price decreases, quantity demanded increases. When we translate demand information into a graph, we create a **demand curve.** This demand curve, which slopes down and to the right, graphically illustrates the law of demand. A demand curve shows both the willingness-to-pay for any given quantity and what the quantity demanded will be at any given price. In Figure 1, we saw how individual demands (measured by willingness-to-pay) can be combined to represent market demand, which can consist of many consumers. For simplicity, from now on we will assume that all demand curves, including those for individuals, are linear (straight lines).

Consider the market for gaming apps. The mobile gaming industry is a $70 billion industry. Although each gaming app costs no more than a few dollars to download, sales of gaming apps have surpassed all other forms of gaming, including PC and console games. Let's examine the relationship between the price of gaming apps and the quantity demanded by individual consumers and the market. For simplicity, assume that all gaming apps are the same price.

Suppose Ahmad and Binah are the only two consumers in the market for gaming apps. Figure 2 shows each of their annual demands using a demand schedule and a demand curve. A **demand schedule** is a table indicating the quantities consumers are willing and able to purchase at each price. We can see that both Ahmad and Binah are willing to buy more gaming apps as the price decreases. When the price is $10, Ahmad is willing to buy 10 apps, while Binah buys none. When the price falls to $8, Ahmad is willing to buy 15 apps, and Binah would buy 5.

We can take the values from the demand schedule in the table and graph them with price on the vertical axis and quantity demanded of gaming apps on the horizontal axis, following the convention in economics of always placing price on the vertical axis and quantity on the horizontal axis. By doing so, we can create a demand curve for each consumer as well as a market demand curve. Both the table and the graph convey the same information as well as exhibit the law of demand.

Although individual demand curves are interesting, market demand curves are far more important to economists, as they can be used to predict changes in product price and quantity. Further, one can observe what happens to a product's price and quantity and infer what changes have occurred in the market. Market demand is the sum of individual demands—the number of units of a product all consumers will purchase at each price. This process is known as **horizontal summation.**

In Figure 2, the individual demand curves for Ahmad and Binah are shown as D_a and D_b, respectively. Because Binah will not buy any apps at a price of $10, the market demand at $10 or higher is equal to Ahmad's demand. At prices below $10, we add Ahmad's and Binah's demands at each price to obtain the market demand. For example, at $8, individual demand is 15 for Ahmad and 5 for Binah, and market demand is therefore 20 (point c). At $4, market demand sums to 40 (point e). The heavier curve, D_{Mkt}, represents the market demand curve, or the horizontal summation of the two individual demand curves.

demand curve A graphical illustration of the law of demand, which shows the relationship between the price of a good and the quantity demanded.

demand schedule A table that shows the quantity of a good a consumer purchases at each price.

horizontal summation The process of adding the number of units of the product purchased or supplied at each price to determine market demand or supply.

Figure 2 • Market Demand: Horizontal Summation of Individual Demand Curves

Ahmad's and Binah's demand schedules (the table) and their individual demand curves (the graph) for gaming apps are shown. Ahmad will purchase 15 gaming apps when the price is $8, 25 apps when the price falls to $4, and buy more as prices continue to fall. Binah will purchase 5 gaming apps when the price is $8 and buy 15 when the price falls to $4. The individual demand curves for Ahmad and Binah are shown as D_a and D_b, respectively, and are horizontally summed to get market demand, D_{Mkt}. Horizontal summation involves adding the quantities demanded by each individual at each possible price.

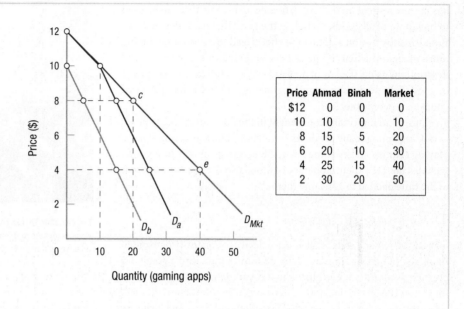

Price	Ahmad	Binah	Market
$12	0	0	0
10	10	0	10
8	15	5	20
6	20	10	30
4	25	15	40
2	30	20	50

This is a simple example with just two consumers, but the process works the same for any number of consumers in a market. In the real world, markets are made up of millions of consumers, and economic analysts and marketing professionals use sophisticated statistical techniques to estimate market demand for goods and services in the industries they represent.

The market demand curve shows the maximum amount of a product consumers are willing and able to purchase during a given time period at various prices, all other relevant factors being held constant (*ceteris paribus*). Economists use the term *determinants of demand* to refer to these other, nonprice factors that are held constant.

Determinants of Demand

Up to this point, we have discussed only how price affects the quantity demanded. When prices fall, consumers purchase more of a product; thus, quantity demanded rises. When prices rise, consumers purchase less of a product; thus, quantity demanded falls. These two situations are shown as a movement from one point on a demand curve to another point on the same demand curve. But several other factors besides the price of that item also affect demand, including what people like, what their income is, and how much related products cost. More specifically, there are five key **determinants of demand:** (1) tastes and preferences, (2) income, (3) prices of related goods, (4) the number of buyers, and (5) expectations regarding future prices, income, and product availability. When one of these determinants changes, the *entire* demand curve changes by either shifting to the right (an increase in demand) or shifting to the left (a decrease in demand). Let's see why.

determinants of demand

Nonprice factors that affect demand, including tastes and preferences, income, prices of related goods, number of buyers, and expectations.

Tastes and Preferences We all have preferences for certain products over others, easily perceiving subtle differences in styling and quality. Automobiles, clothing, phones, and music are just a few of the products that are subject to the whims of the consumer.

Whenever a new fad begins, a spike in demand ensues. But this increase in demand is not because the *price* was lowered; instead, consumers buy more at *all* prices because the good is in style. This effect is shown in Figure 3, where the initial demand curve of D_0 shifts to the right to D_1. At D_1, the quantity purchased at every price is higher than at D_0. However, fads come and go, and

····· Figure 3 · Shifts of the Demand Curve ················

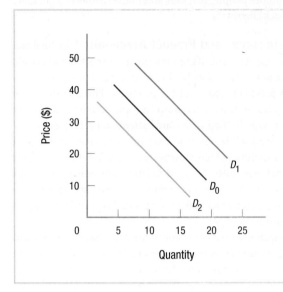

A new fad shifts the demand curve from D_0 to D_1 as consumers are willing and able to purchase more at *all* prices. Once the fad cools off, the demand curve shifts leftward to D_2 as consumers want less at each price. When a determinant such as tastes and preferences changes, the *entire* demand curve shifts.

once the popularity of the good falls, the demand curve will shift to the left, perhaps to D_2. It is important to keep in mind that when one of the determinants changes, such as tastes and preferences, the *entire* demand curve shifts.

Income Income is another important factor influencing consumer demand. Generally speaking, as income rises, demand for most goods will likewise increase. Get a raise, and you are more likely to buy more clothes and acquire the latest technology gadgets. Your demand curve for these goods will shift to the right (such as from D_0 to D_1 in Figure 3). Products for which demand is positively linked to income—when income rises, demand for the product also rises—are called **normal goods.**

There are also some products for which demand declines as income rises, and the demand curve shifts to the left. Economists call these products **inferior goods.** As income grows, for instance, the consumption of discount clothing and cheap motel stays will likely fall as individuals upgrade their wardrobes and stay in more comfortable hotels when traveling. Similarly, when you graduate from college and your income rises, your consumption of ramen noodles will fall as you begin to cook tastier dinners and eat out more frequently.

Prices of Related Goods The prices of related commodities also affect consumer decisions. You may be an avid concertgoer, but with concert ticket prices often topping $100, further rises in the price of concert tickets may entice you to see more movies and fewer concerts. Movies, concerts, plays, and sporting events are good examples of **substitute goods** because consumers can substitute one for another depending on their respective prices. When the *price* of concerts rises, your *demand* for movies increases, and vice versa. These are substitute goods.

Movies and popcorn, on the other hand, are examples of **complementary goods.** These are goods that are generally consumed together, such that an increase or decrease in the consumption of one will similarly result in an increase or decrease in the consumption of the other—see fewer movies, and your consumption of popcorn will decline. Other complementary goods include cars and gasoline, hot dogs and hot dog buns, and ski lift tickets and ski rentals. Thus, when the *price* of lift tickets increases, the quantity of lift tickets demanded falls, which causes your *demand* for ski rentals to fall as well (shifts to the left), and vice versa.

The Number of Buyers Another factor influencing market demand for a product is the number of potential buyers in the market. Clearly, the more consumers there are who would be likely to buy a particular product, the higher its market demand will be (the demand curve will shift

normal good A good for which an increase in income results in rising demand.

inferior good A good for which an increase in income results in declining demand.

substitute goods Goods consumers will substitute for one another. When the *price* of one good rises, the *demand* for the other good increases, and vice versa.

complementary goods Goods that are typically consumed together. When the *price* of a complementary good rises, the *demand* for the other good declines, and vice versa.

rightward). As our average life span steadily rises, the demand for medical services and retirement communities likewise increases. As more people than ever enter universities and graduate schools, demand for textbooks and backpacks increases.

Expectations About Future Prices, Incomes, and Product Availability The final factor influencing demand involves consumer expectations. If consumers expect shortages of certain products or increases in their prices in the near future, they tend to rush out and buy these products immediately, thereby increasing the present demand for the products. The demand curve shifts to the right. During the hurricane season, when a large storm forms and begins moving toward the coast, the demand for plywood, nails, bottled water, and batteries quickly rises.

The expectation of a rise in income, meanwhile, can lead consumers to take advantage of credit in order to increase their present consumption. Department stores and furniture stores, for example, often run "no payments until next year" sales designed to attract consumers who want to "buy now, pay later." These consumers expect to have more money later, when they can pay, so they go ahead and buy what they want now, thereby increasing their present demand for the promoted items. Again, the demand curve shifts to the right.

The key point to remember from this section is that when one of the determinants of demand changes, the *entire* demand curve shifts rightward (an increase in demand) or leftward (a decrease in demand). A quick look back at Figure 3 shows that when demand increases, consumers are willing to buy more at all prices, and when demand decreases, they will buy less at each and every price.

Changes in Demand Versus Changes in Quantity Demanded

When the price of a product rises, consumers buy fewer units of that product. This is a movement along an existing demand curve. However, when one or more of the determinants changes, the entire demand curve is altered. Now at any given price, consumers are willing to purchase more or less depending on the nature of the change. This section focuses on this important distinction between *changes in demand* versus *changes in quantity demanded*.

change in demand Occurs when one or more of the determinants of demand changes, shown as a shift of the entire demand curve.

A **change in demand** occurs whenever one or more of the determinants of demand changes and the entire demand curve shifts. When demand changes, the demand curve shifts either to the right or to the left. Let's look at each shift in turn.

Demand increases when the entire demand curve shifts to the right. At all prices, consumers will purchase more of the product in question. Figure 4 shows an increase in demand for gaming apps; the demand curve shifts from D_0 to D_1. Notice that more gaming apps are purchased at all prices along D_1 as compared to D_0.

Now look at a decrease in demand, when the entire demand curve shifts to the left. At all prices, consumers will purchase less of the product in question. A drop in consumer income is normally associated with a decrease in demand (the demand curve shifts to the left from D_0 to D_2 in Figure 4).

change in quantity demanded Occurs when the price of the product changes, shown as a movement along an existing demand curve.

Whereas a change in demand can be brought about by many different factors, a **change in quantity demanded** can be caused by only one thing: *a change in product price*. This is shown in Figure 4 as a reduction in price from $8 to $4, resulting in sales (quantity demanded) increasing from 20 (point *a*) to 40 (point *c*) apps. This distinction between a change in demand and a change in quantity demanded is important. Reducing price to increase sales is different from spending a few million dollars on Super Bowl advertising to increase sales at all prices.

These concepts are so important that a quick summary is in order. As Figure 4 illustrates, given the initial demand D_0, increasing sales from 20 to 40 apps can occur in either of two ways. First, changing a determinant (say, increasing advertising) could shift the demand curve to D_1 so that 40 apps would be sold at $8 (point *b*). Alternatively, 40 apps could be sold by reducing the price to $4 (point *c*). Selling more by increasing advertising causes an increase in demand, or a shift of the entire demand curve. Simply reducing the price, on the other hand, causes an increase in quantity demanded, or a movement along the existing demand curve, D_0, from point *a* to point *c*.

..... Figure 4 • Changes in Demand Versus Changes .... in Quantity Demanded

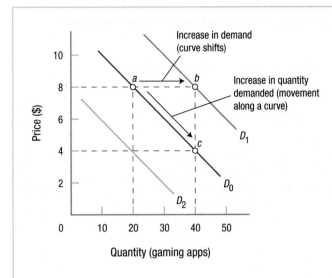

A shift in the demand curve from D_0 to D_1 represents an *increase in demand*, and consumers will buy more of the product at each price. A shift from D_0 to D_2 reflects a *decrease in demand*. A movement along D_0 from point *a* to point *c* indicates an *increase in quantity demanded*; this type of movement can only be caused by a change in the price of the product.

 CHECKPOINT

DEMAND

- A person's willingness-to-pay is the maximum amount she or he values a good to be worth at a particular moment in time and is the building block for demand.

- Demand refers to the quantity of products people are willing and able to purchase at various prices during some specific time period, all other relevant factors being held constant.

- The law of demand states that price and quantity demanded have an inverse (negative) relation. As price rises, consumers buy fewer units; as price falls, consumers buy more units. It is depicted as a downward-sloping demand curve.

- Demand curves shift when one or more of the determinants of demand changes.

- The determinants of demand are consumer tastes and preferences, income, prices of substitutes and complements, the number of buyers in a market, and expectations about future prices, incomes, and product availability.

- A shift of a demand curve is a *change in demand* and occurs when a determinant of demand changes.

- A *change in quantity demanded* occurs only when the price of a product changes, leading consumers to adjust their purchases along the existing demand curve.

QUESTIONS: Sales of electric plug-in cars, such as the Tesla, have risen in recent years. Despite their relatively high price compared to gasoline-powered cars and the limited distance the cars can travel before requiring a recharge, other manufacturers are adding new models of plug-ins to their lines. What has led to the rising popularity of plug-in cars? Is this an increase in demand or an increase in quantity demanded?

Answers to the Checkpoint questions can be found at the end of this chapter.

SUPPLY

The analysis of a market economy rests on two foundations: supply and demand. So far, we've covered the demand side of the market. Let's focus now on the decisions businesses make regarding production numbers and sales. These decisions cause variations in product supply.

The Law of Supply: The Relationship Between Quantity Supplied and Price

supply The maximum amount of a product that sellers are willing and able to provide for sale over some time period at various prices, holding all other relevant factors constant (the *ceteris paribus* condition).

Supply is the maximum amount of a product that producers are willing and able to offer for sale at various prices, all other relevant factors being held constant. The quantity supplied will vary according to the price of the product.

What explains this relationship? As we saw in the previous chapter, businesses inevitably encounter rising opportunity costs as they attempt to produce more and more of a product. This is due in part to diminishing returns from available resources and in part to the fact that when producers increase production, they must either have existing workers put in overtime (at a higher hourly pay rate) or hire additional workers away from other industries (again at premium pay).

Producing more units, therefore, makes it more expensive to produce each individual unit. These increasing costs give rise to the positive relationship between product price and quantity supplied to the market.

law of supply Holding all other relevant factors constant, as price increases, quantity supplied rises, and as price declines, quantity supplied falls.

Unfortunately for producers, they can rarely charge whatever they would like for their products; they must charge whatever the market will permit. But producers can decide how much of their product to produce and offer for sale. The **law of supply** states that higher prices will lead producers to offer more of their products for sale during a given period. Conversely, if prices fall, producers will offer fewer products to the market. The explanation is simple: The higher the price, the greater the potential for higher profits and thus the greater the incentive for businesses to produce and sell more products. Also, given the rising opportunity costs associated with increasing production, producers need to charge these higher prices to increase the quantity supplied profitably.

Let's return to our market for gaming apps. Why do programmers spend countless hours developing new gaming apps? Because they have an incentive to do so. Much like how consumers download more gaming apps when the price goes down, the opposite is true for suppliers. As the price rises, programmers are more willing to create new games, enhance existing games, and provide more server capacity (to ensure games operate smoothly) and technical support, all to increase the quantity of gaming apps supplied. Although gaming apps are not a physical good, the law of supply still applies. This is no different than an oil producer drilling for more oil when the price rises. In each case, producers respond to changes in price.

The Supply Curve

supply curve A graphical illustration of the law of supply, which shows the relationship between the price of a good and the quantity supplied.

Just as demand curves graphically display the law of demand, **supply curves** provide a graphical representation of the law of supply. The supply curve shows the maximum amounts of a product a producer will furnish at various prices during a given period of time. While the demand curve slopes *down* to the right, the supply curve slopes *up* to the right.[1] This illustrates the positive relationship between price and quantity supplied: The higher the price, the greater the quantity supplied.

Market Supply Curves

As with demand, economists are more interested in market supply than in the supplies offered by individual firms. To compute market supply, use the same method that was used to calculate market demand: horizontally summing the supplies of individual producers. A hypothetical market

---

[1] There are some exceptions to positively sloping supply curves. But for our purposes, we will ignore them for now.

Figure 5 • Supply of Gaming Apps

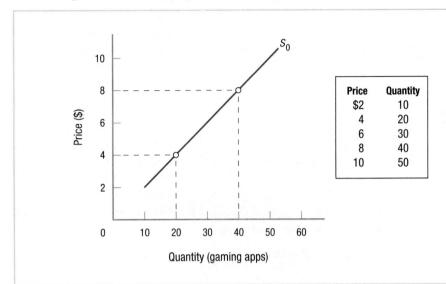

Price	Quantity
$2	10
4	20
6	30
8	40
10	50

This supply curve graphs the supply schedule and shows the maximum quantity of gaming apps that producers will offer for sale over some defined period of time. The supply curve is positively sloped, reflecting the law of supply. In other words, as prices rise, quantity supplied increases; as prices fall, quantity supplied decreases.

supply curve for gaming apps is depicted in Figure 5. The quantity of gaming apps that producers will offer for sale increases as the price of gaming apps rises. The opposite would happen if the price of gaming apps falls. These two situations are shown as a movement from one point on a supply curve to another point on the same supply curve.

Determinants of Supply

Like demand, several nonprice factors help to determine the supply of a product. Specifically, there are six **determinants of supply:** (1) production technology, (2) costs of resources, (3) prices of related commodities, (4) expectations, (5) the number of sellers (producers) in the market, and (6) taxes and subsidies. When one of these determinants of supply changes, the *entire* supply curve changes by shifting to either the right (an increase in supply) or the left (a decrease in supply).

determinants of supply
Nonprice factors that affect supply, including production technology, costs of resources, prices of related commodities, expectations, number of sellers, and taxes and subsidies.

Production Technology Technology determines how much output can be produced from given quantities of resources. If a factory's equipment is old and can produce only 50 units of output per hour, then no matter how many other resources are employed, those 50 units are the most the factory can produce in an hour. If the factory is outfitted with newer, more advanced equipment capable of turning out 100 units per hour, the firm can supply more of its product at the same price as before or even at a lower price. In Figure 6, this would be represented by a shift in the supply curve from S_0 to S_1. At every single price, more would be supplied.

Technology further determines the nature of products that can be supplied to the market. A hundred years ago, the supply of computers on the market was zero because computers did not yet exist. More recent advances in microprocessing and miniaturization brought a wide array of products to the market that were not available just a few years ago, including tablets, automobile engines that go 100,000 miles between tune-ups, and constant-monitoring insulin pumps that automatically keep a diabetic patient's glucose levels under control.

Costs of Resources Resource costs clearly affect production costs and supply. If resources such as raw materials or labor become more expensive, production costs will rise and supply will be reduced (the supply curve shifts to the left, from S_0 to S_2 in Figure 6). The reverse is true if resource costs drop (the supply curve shifts to the right, from S_0 to S_1). The growing power of microchips along with their falling cost has resulted in cheap and plentiful electronics and computers. Nanotechnology—manufacturing processes that fashion new products

····· Figure 6 • Shifts of the Supply Curve ················

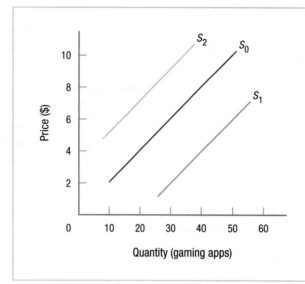

The supply of gaming apps originally is S_0. If supply increases, the supply curve shifts rightward to S_1. Producers are willing to sell more at *all* prices. If supply falls, supply shifts leftward to S_2. Now firms are willing to sell less at each price. When a determinant of supply changes, the *entire* supply curve shifts.

through the combination of individual atoms—may soon usher in a new generation of inexpensive products.

However, when the cost of resources (such as oil and farm products) rise, the cost of products using those resources in their manufacture will go up, leading to the supply being reduced (the supply curve shifts leftward). If labor costs rise because immigration is restricted, this drives up production costs of California vegetables (fewer farmworkers) and software in Silicon Valley (fewer software engineers from abroad) and leads to a shift in the supply curve to the left in Figure 6.

Prices of Related Commodities Most firms have some flexibility in the portfolio of goods they produce. A vegetable farmer, for example, might be able to grow celery or radishes, or some combination of the two. Given this flexibility, a change in the price of one item may influence the quantity of other items brought to market. If the price of celery should rise, for instance, most farmers will start growing more celery. And since they all have a limited amount of land on which to grow vegetables, this reduces the quantity of radishes they can produce. Hence, in this case, the rise in the price of celery may well cause a reduction in the supply of radishes (the supply curve for radishes shifts leftward).

Expectations The effects of future expectations on market supplies can be confusing, but it need not be. When sellers expect prices of a good to rise in the future, they are likely to restrict their supply in the current period in anticipation of receiving higher prices in some future period. Examples include homes and stocks—if you believe prices are going up, you'd be less likely to sell today, which decreases the supply of such goods (supply shifts to the left). Similarly, expectations of price reductions can increase supply as sellers try to sell off their inventories before prices drop (supply shifts to the right).

Eventually, if prices do rise in the next period, producers would increase the quantity supplied of the good; however, this would be due to the law of supply, not due to a shift of the supply curve. In other words, rising prices result in a movement along the supply curve. Only when producers anticipate a change in a future price, causing a reaction now, does supply shift.

Number of Sellers Everything else being held constant, if the number of sellers in a particular market increases, the market supply of their product increases. It is no great mystery why: Ten dim sum chefs can produce more dumplings in a given period than five dim sum chefs.

Taxes and Subsidies For businesses, taxes and subsidies affect costs. An increase in taxes (property, excise, or other fees) will shift supply to the left and reduce it. Subsidies are the opposite of taxes. If the government subsidizes the production of a product, supply will increase and the supply curve will shift to the right. A proposed new tax on expensive health care insurance plans will reduce supply (the tax is equivalent to an increase in production costs), while today's subsidies to ethanol producers expand ethanol production.

Changes in Supply Versus Changes in Quantity Supplied

A **change in supply** results from a change in one or more of the determinants of supply; it causes the entire supply curve to shift. An increase in the supply of a product, perhaps because advancing technology has made it cheaper to produce, means that more of the commodity will be offered for sale at every price. This causes the supply curve to shift to the right, as illustrated in Figure 7 by the shift from S_0 to S_1. A decrease in supply, conversely, shifts the supply curve to the left since fewer units of the product are offered at every price. Such a decrease in supply is represented by the shift from S_0 to S_2.

A change in supply involves a shift of the entire supply curve. In contrast, the supply curve does not move when there is a **change in quantity supplied.** Only a change in the price of a product can cause a change in the quantity supplied; hence, it involves a movement along an existing supply curve rather than a shift to an entirely different curve. In Figure 7, for example, an increase in price from $4 to $8 results in an increase in quantity supplied from 20 to 40 apps, represented by the movement from point a to point c along S_0.

In summary, a change in supply is represented in Figure 7 by the shift from S_0 to S_1 or S_2, which involves a shift of the entire supply curve. For example, an increase in supply from S_0 to S_1 results in an increase in supply from 20 gaming apps (point a) to 40 (point b) provided at a price of $4. More apps are provided at the same price. In contrast, a change in quantity supplied is shown in Figure 7 as a movement along an existing supply curve, S_0, from point a to point c caused by an increase in the price of the product from $4 to $8.

change in supply Occurs when one or more of the determinants of supply change, shown as a shift in the entire supply curve.

change in quantity supplied Occurs when the price of the product changes, shown as a movement along an existing supply curve.

Figure 7 • Changes in Supply Versus Changes in Quantity Supplied

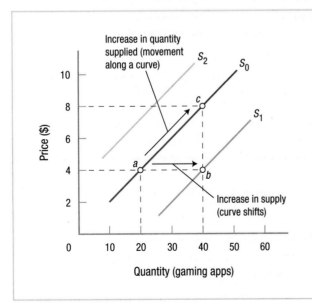

A shift in the supply curve from S_0 to S_1 represents an *increase in supply* because businesses are willing to offer more of the product to consumers at *all* prices. A shift from S_0 to S_2 reflects a decrease in supply. A movement along S_0 from point a to point c represents an *increase in quantity supplied*; this type of movement can only be caused by a change in the price of the product.

As on the demand side, this distinction between changes in supply and changes in quantity supplied is crucial. It means that when a product's price changes, only quantity supplied changes—the supply curve does not move. A summary of the determinants for both supply and demand is shown in Figure 8.

Figure 8 • Summary of Changes in Demand and Supply and their Determinants

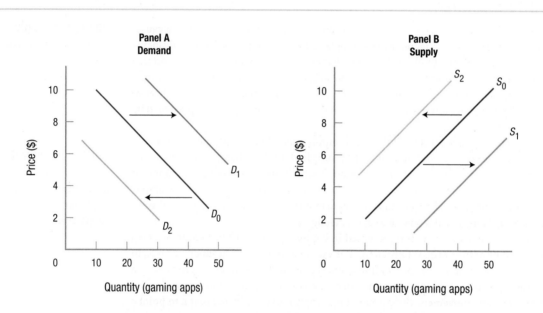

Determinants of Demand		Determinants of Supply	
Decrease in Demand	**Increase in Demand**	**Decrease in Supply**	**Increase in Supply**
Tastes and preferences fall.	Tastes and preferences rise.	Technology deteriorates.	Technology improves.
Income falls (for normal goods). Income rises (for inferior goods).	Income rises (for normal goods). Income falls (for inferior goods).	Resource costs rise.	Resource costs fall.
Price of substitutes falls.	Price of substitutes rises.	Price of production substitute rises.	Price of production substitute falls.
Price of complements rises.	Price of complements falls.	Price expectations for future rise.	Price expectations for future fall.
Number of buyers falls.	Number of buyers rises.	Number of sellers falls.	Number of sellers rises.
Price expectations for future fall.	Price expectations for future rise.	Taxes rise or subsidies fall.	Taxes fall or subsidies rise.

Various factors cause a market demand curve to shift to the left (decrease in demand) or shift to the right (increase in demand) in panel A. Similarly, various factors cause a market supply curve to shift to the left (decrease in supply) or shift to the right (increase in supply) in panel B. The table summarizes the factors influencing demand and supply shifts.

CHECKPOINT

SUPPLY

- Supply is the quantity of a product producers are willing and able to put on the market at various prices, all other relevant factors being held constant.

- The law of supply reflects the positive relationship between price and quantity supplied: The higher the market price, the more goods supplied, and the lower the market price, the fewer goods supplied.

- As with demand, market supply is derived by horizontally summing the individual supplies of all of the firms in the market.

- A change in supply occurs when one or more of the determinants of supply changes.

- The determinants of supply are production technology, the cost of resources, prices of related commodities, expectations about future prices, the number of sellers or producers in the market, and taxes and subsidies.

- A *change in supply* is a shift of the supply curve. A shift to the right reflects an increase in supply, while a shift to the left represents a decrease in supply.

- A *change in quantity supplied* is caused only by a change in the price of the product; it results in a movement along the existing supply curve.

QUESTIONS: Ride-sharing services such as Uber and Lyft charge a higher price (called "surge pricing" and "Prime Time," respectively) when demand for rides is higher than normal. When drivers react to higher prices by working more hours, is this a change in supply or quantity supplied? Suppose that bad weather causes many drivers to take the day off. How does this affect the supply curve for rides?

Answers to the Checkpoint questions can be found at the end of this chapter.

MARKET EQUILIBRIUM

Supply and demand together determine the prices and quantities of goods bought and sold. Neither factor alone is sufficient to determine the market price and quantity. It is through their interaction that supply and demand do their work, just as two blades of a scissors are required to cut paper.

A market will determine the price at which the quantity of a product demanded is equal to the quantity supplied. At this price, the market is said to be cleared or to be in **equilibrium,** meaning that the amount of the product that consumers are willing and able to purchase is matched exactly by the amount that producers are willing and able to sell. This is the **equilibrium price** and the **equilibrium quantity.** The equilibrium price is also called the market-clearing price.

Figure 9 puts together Figures 2 and 5, showing the market supply and demand for gaming apps. It illustrates how supply and demand interact to determine equilibrium price and quantity. Clearly, the quantities demanded and supplied equal one another only where the supply and demand curves cross, at point *e*. From the table in Figure 9, you can see that quantity demanded and quantity supplied are the same at only one price. At $6 per app, sellers are willing to provide exactly the same quantity as consumers would like to purchase, 30 units. Hence, at this price, the market clears since buyers and sellers both want to transact the same number of units. But how is an equilibrium actually achieved? Or will it in every circumstance?

Markets work by encouraging buyers and sellers to react to prices until the equilibrium is reached. This occurs automatically as long as buyers and sellers are free to act in their own self-interests. For example, suppose gaming developers choose to price gaming apps at $8. As we can see by comparing points *a* and *b*, sellers are willing to supply more apps at this price than consumers are willing to buy. Economists characterize such a situation as one of excess supply, or **surplus.** In this case, at $8, sellers supply 40 apps to the market (point *b*), yet buyers want to purchase only 20 (point *a*). This leaves an excess of 20 apps overhanging the market; these unsold apps ultimately become surplus inventories.

Here is where the market kicks in to restore equilibrium. As inventories rise, most firms cut production. Some firms, moreover, start reducing their prices to increase sales. Other firms must then cut their own prices to remain competitive. This process continues, with firms cutting their

equilibrium Market forces are in balance when the quantities demanded by consumers just equal the quantities supplied by producers.

equilibrium price The price at which the quantity demanded is just equal to the quantity supplied.

equilibrium quantity The output that results when the quantity demanded is just equal to the quantity supplied.

surplus Occurs when the price is above market equilibrium and quantity supplied exceeds quantity demanded.

..... Figure 9 • Equilibrium Price and Quantity of Gaming Apps ....

Market equilibrium is achieved when quantity demanded and quantity supplied are equal at the market price. In this graph, that equilibrium occurs at point *e*, at an equilibrium price of $6 and an equilibrium output of 30. If the market price is above equilibrium, say $8, a surplus of 20 gaming apps will result (*b* − *a*), and market forces would drive the price back down to $6. When the market price is too low ($4), a shortage of 20 gaming apps will result (*d* − *c*), and businesses will raise the offering prices until equilibrium is again restored.

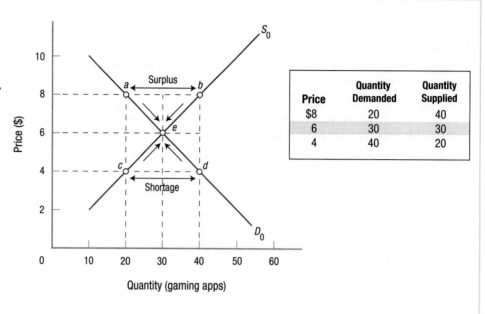

Price	Quantity Demanded	Quantity Supplied
$8	20	40
6	30	30
4	40	20

shortage Occurs when the price is below market equilibrium and quantity demanded exceeds quantity supplied.

prices and production, until most firms have managed to exhaust their surplus inventories. This happens when prices reach $6 and quantity supplied equals 30 because consumers are once again willing to buy up the entire quantity supplied at this price, and the market is restored to equilibrium.

In general, therefore, when prices are set too high, surpluses result, which drive prices back down to their equilibrium levels. If, conversely, a price is initially set too low, say, at $4, a **shortage** results. In this case, buyers want to purchase 40 apps (point *d*), but sellers are only providing 20 (point *c*), creating a shortage of 20 apps. Because consumers are willing to pay more than $4 to obtain the few apps available on the market, they will start bidding up the price of gaming apps. Sensing an opportunity to make some money, firms will start raising their prices and increasing production once again until equilibrium is restored. Hence, in general, a shortage causes firms to raise prices and increase production.

When there is a shortage in a market, economists speak of a tight market or a seller's market. Under these conditions, producers have no difficulty selling off all their output. On the other hand, when a surplus of goods exists, this gives rise to a buyer's market because buyers can buy all the goods they want at attractive prices.

We have now seen how changing prices naturally works to clear up shortages and surpluses, thereby returning markets to equilibrium. Some markets, once disturbed, will return to equilibrium quickly. Examples include the stock, bond, and money markets, where trading is nearly instantaneous and extensive information abounds. Other markets react very slowly. Consider the labor market, for instance. When workers lose their jobs due to a plant closing, most will search for new jobs that pay at least as much as the salary at their previous jobs. Some will be successful, while others might struggle, having to settle for a lower-paying position after a long job search. Similarly, real estate markets can be slow to adjust because sellers will often refuse to accept a price below what they are asking, until the lack of sales over time convinces sellers to adjust the price downward.

These automatic market adjustments can make some buyers and sellers feel uncomfortable: It seems as if prices and quantities are being set by forces beyond anyone's control. In fact, this phenomenon is precisely what makes market economies function so efficiently. Without anyone needing to be in control, prices and quantities naturally gravitate toward equilibrium levels.

Given the self-correcting nature of the market, long-term shortages or surpluses are often the result of government intervention or actions by firms with market power, such as the example of

ALFRED MARSHALL (1842–1924)

British economist Alfred Marshall is considered the father of the modern theory of supply and demand—that price and output are determined by both supply *and* demand. He noted that the two go together like the blades of a scissors that cross at equilibrium. He assumed that changes in quantity demanded were only affected by changes in price and that all other factors remained constant. Marshall also is credited with developing the ideas of the laws of demand and supply and the concepts of consumer surplus and producer surplus—concepts we will study in the next chapter.

With financial help from his uncle, Marshall attended St. John's College, Cambridge, to study mathematics and physics. However, after long walks through the poorest sections of several European cities and seeing their horrible conditions, he decided to focus his attention on political economy.

In 1890 he published *Principles of Economics*. In it he introduced many new ideas, though he would never boast about them as being novel. In hopes of appealing to the general public, Marshall buried his diagrams in footnotes. And, although he is credited with many economic theories, he would always clarify them with various exceptions and qualifications. He expected future economists to flesh out his ideas.

Above all, Marshall loved teaching and his students. His lectures were known to never be orderly or systematic because he tried to get students to think *with* him and ultimately think for themselves. At one point near the turn of the 20th century, essentially all of the leading economists in England had been his students. More than anyone else, Marshall is given credit for establishing economics as a discipline of study. He died in 1924.

Information from E. Ray Canterbery, *A Brief History of Economics: Artful Approaches to the Dismal Science* (Hackensack, NJ: World Scientific), 2001; Robert Skidelsky, *John Maynard Keynes: Volume 2, The Economist as Saviour 1920–1937* (New York: Penguin Press), 1992; and John Maynard Keynes, *Essays in Biography* (New York: Norton), 1951.

Tokyo Disneyland discussed in the Around the World feature. But these situations aside, markets are efficient at moving to a new equilibrium when external factors cause the demand or supply curves (or both) to change.

Moving to a New Equilibrium: Changes in Supply and Demand

Once a market is in equilibrium and the forces of supply and demand balance one another out, the market will remain there unless an external factor changes. But when the supply curve or demand curve shifts (some determinant changes), equilibrium also shifts, resulting in a new equilibrium price and/or output. The ability to predict new equilibrium points is one of the most useful aspects of supply and demand analysis.

Predicting the New Equilibrium When One Curve Shifts When only supply or only demand changes, the change in equilibrium price and equilibrium output can be predicted. We begin with changes in supply.

Changes in Supply Figure 10 shows what happens when supply changes. Equilibrium initially is at point *e*, with equilibrium price and quantity at $9 and 30, respectively. But let us assume that a rise in wages or the bankruptcy of a key business in the market (the number of sellers falls) causes a decrease in supply. When supply declines (the supply curve shifts from S_0 to S_2), equilibrium price rises to $12, while equilibrium output falls to 20 (point *a*).

If, on the other hand, supply increases (the supply curve shifts from S_0 to S_1), equilibrium price falls to $6, while equilibrium output rises to 40 (point *b*). This is what has happened in the electronics industry: Falling production costs have resulted in more electronic products being sold at lower prices.

AROUND THE WORLD

Tokyo Disneyland: Is THAT the Line for Space Mountain?!

What are some factors that cause Tokyo Disneyland to be so crowded even during the middle of winter?

How long are you willing to wait to experience your favorite ride at a theme park? 20 minutes? 60 minutes? How about 3 hours? On an ordinary day at Tokyo Disneyland, one of the most popular theme parks in the world, the line for its famous attractions such as Space Mountain, Splash Mountain, and Tower of Terror can reach 200 minutes. . . . That's over a 3-hour wait to enjoy a 3-minute ride! What causes lines to form at theme parks?

Theme park rides have lines because the quantity of rides demanded exceeds the quantity supplied. Why is that? Because most theme parks charge a fixed admission fee for unlimited rides, visitors

typically demand more rides than the theme park is able to supply, even if a ride is operating at full capacity. The extent of the shortage and consequently the length of wait time are influenced largely by market factors.

First, consider the role of preferences. Disneyland has a worldwide following, and for those living in Japan, visiting Tokyo Disneyland is certainly easier than visiting Disney parks in California or Florida. Second, consider the number

of potential buyers. Tokyo Disneyland is located in a metropolitan area with over 30 million people. The sheer number of potential visitors will lead to higher demand. And third, consider the role of pricing. Given its popularity, Tokyo Disneyland could charge higher prices to reduce the quantity demanded. Yet, in 2019 a one-day adult admission to Tokyo Disneyland cost only $65, while its counterparts in California and Florida charged around $130.

The combination of preferences, proximity to potential buyers, and relatively low prices cause demand for Tokyo Disneyland rides to far exceed the park's reasonable capacity (at least by U.S. standards), creating very long lines. But rather than raise prices sharply, Tokyo Disneyland offers many attractions besides rides, such as an abundance of photo-taking opportunities with Disney characters. Despite the crowds, it's still the "Happiest Place on Earth!"

GO ONLINE TO PRACTICE THE ECONOMIC CONCEPTS IN THIS STORY

····· Figure 10 • Equilibrium Price, Output, and Shifts in Supply ················

When supply alone shifts, the effects on both equilibrium price and output can be predicted. When supply increases (S_0 to S_1), equilibrium price will fall and output will rise. When supply declines (S_0 to S_2), the opposite happens: Equilibrium price will rise and output will fall.

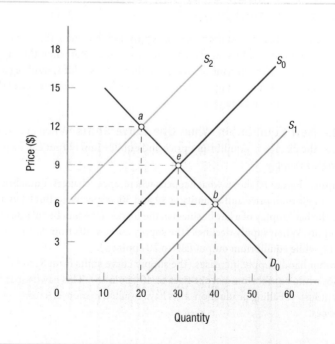

We have seen how equilibrium price and quantity will change when supply changes. When supply increases, equilibrium price will fall and output will rise; when supply decreases, equilibrium price will rise and output will fall.

Changes in Demand The effects of demand changes are shown in Figure 11. Again, equilibrium is initially at point *e*, with equilibrium price and quantity at $9 and 30, respectively. But let us assume that the economy then enters a recession and incomes sink, or perhaps the price of some complementary good soars; in either case, demand falls. As demand decreases (the demand curve shifts from D_0 to D_2), equilibrium price falls to $6, while equilibrium output falls to 20 (point *a*).

Meanwhile, a recession would cause the demand for inferior goods (beans and bologna) to rise, as falling incomes force people to switch to less expensive substitutes. For these products, as demand increases (shifting the demand curve from D_0 to D_1), equilibrium price rises to $12, and equilibrium output grows to 40 (point *b*).

Like changes in supply, we can predict how equilibrium price and quantity will change when demand changes. When demand increases, both equilibrium price and output will rise; when demand decreases, both equilibrium price and output will fall.

Predicting the New Equilibrium When Both Curves Shift

When both supply and demand change, things get tricky. We can predict what will happen with price in some cases and output in other cases but not what will happen to both.

Figure 12 portrays an increase in both demand and supply. Consider the market for corn. Suppose that an increase in corn-based ethanol production causes demand for corn to increase. Meanwhile, suppose that bioengineering results in a new corn hybrid that uses less fertilizer and generates 50% higher yields, causing supply to also increase. When demand increases from D_0 to D_1 and supply increases from S_0 to S_1, output grows to Q_1.

When Universal Studios in Florida expanded its popular Wizarding World of Harry Potter attraction with the opening of Diagon Alley and Hogwarts Express, demand for Universal Studios tickets increased. A one-day ticket (allowing entry to both parks) now exceeds $160. And that doesn't include the wand (another $30 to $40) needed to operate many of the Harry Potter experiences!

..... Figure 11 • Equilibrium Price, Output, ...
and Shifts in Demand

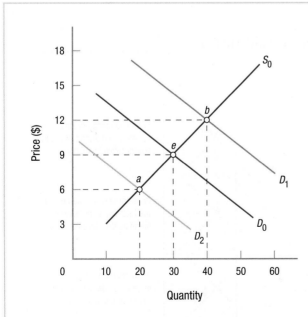

When demand alone changes, the effects on both equilibrium price and output can again be determined. When demand grows (D_0 to D_1), both price and output rise. Conversely, when demand falls (D_0 to D_2), both price and output fall.

ISSUE

Two-Buck Chuck: Will People Drink $2-a-Bottle Wine?

The great California wines of the 1990s put California vineyards on the map. Demand, prices, and exports grew rapidly. Overplanting of new grapevines was a result. When driving along Interstate 5 or Highway 101 north of Los Angeles, one can see vineyards extending for miles, and most were planted in the mid- to late 1990s. The 2001 recession reduced the demand for California wine, and a rising dollar made imported wine relatively cheaper. The result was a sharp drop in demand for California wine and a huge surplus of grapes.

Bronco Wine Company CEO Fred Franzia made an exclusive deal with Trader Joe's, an unusual supermarket that features innovative food and wine products. He bought the excess grapes at distressed prices and in his company's modern plant produced inexpensive wines—chardonnay, merlot, cabernet sauvignon, shiraz, and sauvignon blanc—under the Charles Shaw label. Consumers flocked to Trader Joe's for wine costing $1.99 a bottle and literally hauled cases of wine out by the carload. In less than a

Joel zatz Alamy

decade, 400 million bottles of Two-Buck Chuck, as it is known, have been sold. This is not rotgut: The 2002 shiraz beat out 2,300 other wines to win a double gold medal at the 28th Annual International Eastern Wine Competition in 2004. Still, to many Napa Valley vintners, it is known as Two-Buck Upchuck.

Two-Buck Chuck was such a hit that other supermarkets were forced to offer their own discount wines. This good,

low-priced wine has had the effect of opening up markets. People who previously avoided wine because of the cost have begun consuming more. However, the influence of Two-Buck Chuck may be waning. Because of the rising costs of producing the wine in recent years, Two-Buck Chuck is now sold between $2.99 and $3.79 per bottle. Although the price is still a bargain, the product that changed the wine industry may need a new nickname.

Figure 12 • Increase in Supply, Increase in Demand, and Equilibrium

When both demand and supply increase, output will clearly rise, but what happens to the new equilibrium price is uncertain. If demand grows relatively more than supply, price will rise, but if supply grows relatively more than demand, price will fall.

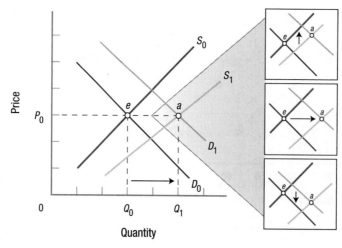

Price increases because the increase in demand exceeds the increase in supply.

Price remains the same because the increase in demand is the same as the increase in supply.

Price decreases because the increase in demand is less than the increase in supply.

But what happens to the price of corn is not so clear. If demand and supply grow the same, output increases, but price remains at P_0 (also captured in the middle panel to the right). If demand grows relatively more than supply, the new equilibrium price will be higher (top panel on the right). Conversely, if demand grows relatively less than supply, the new equilibrium price will be lower (bottom panel on the right). Figure 12 is just one of the four possibilities when both supply and demand change. The other three possibilities are shown in Table 1 along with the four possibilities when just one curve shifts. When only one curve shifts, the direction of change in equilibrium price and quantity is certain. But when both curves shift, the direction of change in either the equilibrium price or quantity will be indeterminate.

TABLE 1	THE EFFECT OF CHANGES IN DEMAND OR SUPPLY ON EQUILIBRIUM PRICES AND QUANTITIES			
	Change in Demand	Change in Supply	Change in Equilibrium Price	Change in Equilibrium Quantity
One Curve Shifting	No change	Increase	Decrease	Increase
	No change	Decrease	Increase	Decrease
	Increase	No change	Increase	Increase
	Decrease	No change	Decrease	Decrease
Both Curves Shifting	Increase	Increase	Indeterminate	Increase
	Decrease	Decrease	Indeterminate	Decrease
	Increase	Decrease	Increase	Indeterminate
	Decrease	Increase	Decrease	Indeterminate

 CHECKPOINT

MARKET EQUILIBRIUM

- Together, supply and demand determine market equilibrium, which occurs when the quantity supplied exactly equals quantity demanded.

- The equilibrium price is also called the market-clearing price.

- When quantity demanded exceeds quantity supplied, a shortage occurs and prices are bid up toward equilibrium. When quantity supplied exceeds quantity demanded, a surplus occurs and prices are pushed down toward equilibrium.

- When supply and demand change, equilibrium price and output change.

- When only one curve shifts, the resulting changes in equilibrium price and quantity can be predicted.

- When both curves shift, we can predict the change in equilibrium price in some cases or the change in equilibrium quantity in others but never both. We have to determine the relative magnitudes of the shifts before we can predict both equilibrium price and quantity.

QUESTIONS: In China, where lines are a routine part of everyday life, a growing industry of professional line waiters has developed. Exactly as it sounds, these people are paid an average of $3 an hour to wait in line for others, a wage that is higher than what a typical factory worker in China earns. Today, the professional line waiter has popped up in cities around the world, including New York, though at significantly higher prices than in China. Given that one can pay someone to wait, what might happen in the market for goods and services most prone to long waiting lines, such as prime concert tickets or the latest technology gadget?

Answers to the Checkpoint questions can be found at the end of this chapter.

CHAPTER SUMMARY

SECTION 1 MARKETS

3.1 A **market** is an institution that enables buyers and sellers to interact and transact with one another.

Corbis/SuperStock

Stars and Stripes/Alamy

Markets can be as simple as a lemonade stand, as large as an automobile lot, as valuable as the stock market, as virtual as an Internet shopping site, or as illegal as a ticket scalping operation.

Buyers and sellers communicate their desires in a market through the prices at which goods and services are bought and sold. Hence, a market economy is called a **price system.**

SECTION 2 DEMAND

3.2 **Demand** refers to the goods and services people are willing and able to buy during a period of time. It is a horizontal summation of individual demand curves in a defined market.

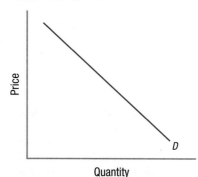

The **law of demand** states that as prices increase, quantity demanded falls, and vice versa, resulting in a downward-sloping demand curve.

Roller coasters are a lot of fun, but riding the same one over and over gives less satisfaction with each ride; therefore, willingness-to-pay falls with each ride.

3.3 **Determinants of Demand: How Demand Curves Shift**

- ↑ Tastes and preferences: Demand shifts right.
- ↑ Income: Demand for normal goods shifts right, while demand for inferior goods shifts left.
- ↑ Price of substitutes: Demand shifts right.
- ↑ Price of complements: Demand shifts left.
- ↑ Number of buyers: Demand shifts right.
- ↑ Price expectations: Demand shifts right.

When investors expect stock prices to increase, demand for stock increases.

Bryan Smith/ZUMA Press

3.4 **A Common Confusion in Terminology**

A "change in demand" is a shift of the entire demand curve and is caused by a change in one of the determinants of demand.

A "change in quantity demanded" is a movement from one point to another on the same demand curve and is caused only by a change in price of that good.

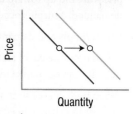

SECTION 3 SUPPLY

3.5 Supply analysis works the same way as demand but looking at the market from the firm's point of view.

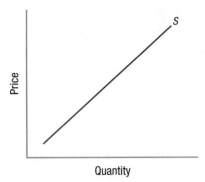

Philip Gostelow/Aurora Photos

The **law of supply** states that as price increases, firms want to supply more, and vice versa. It leads to an upward-sloping supply curve.

3.6 Determinants of Supply: How Supply Curves Shift

- ↑ Production technology: Supply shifts right.
- ↑ Cost of resources: Supply shifts left.
- ↑ Price of related commodities: Supply shifts left.
- ↑ Price expectations: Supply shifts left.
- ↑ Number of sellers: Supply shifts right.
- ↑ Taxes: Supply shifts left.
- ↑ Subsidies: Supply shifts right.

SECTION 4 MARKET EQUILIBRIUM

3.7 **Market equilibrium** occurs at the price at which the quantity supplied is equal to quantity demanded and is where the demand and supply curves intersect.

How does equilibrium change?

Which curve slopes up and which slopes down? Two tricks to aid in memory:

- S"up"ply contains the word "up" for upward-sloping.
- Only the fingers on your right hand can make a "d" for demand. Hold that hand up in front of you!

3.8 A shift in demand or supply will change equilibrium price and quantity.

Neil Emmerson/robertharding/Getty Images

Higher oil prices raise the cost of resins used to produce surfboards.

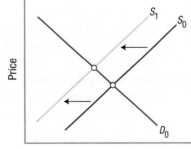

Summary of Demand and Supply Shifts on Equilibrium Price and Quantity:

D shifts right:	$P\uparrow$	$Q\uparrow$
D shifts left:	$P\downarrow$	$Q\downarrow$
S shifts right:	$P\downarrow$	$Q\uparrow$
S shifts left:	$P\uparrow$	$Q\downarrow$

Supply of surfboards shifts left, raising equilibrium price and lowering equilibrium quantity.

Key Concepts

Questions and Problems

Check Your Understanding

1. Product prices give consumers and businesses a lot of information besides just the price. What kinds of information?

2. Provide an example of a factor that might increase the demand for frozen slushies. What might decrease the demand for frozen slushies?

3. Assume there is a positive relationship between aging and cholesterol levels. As the world population ages, will the demand for cholesterol drugs increase, decrease, or remain the same? Would this cause a change in demand or a change in quantity demanded?

4. If incomes are rising in an economy, why would we see a decrease in demand for certain goods?

5. Explain how an increase in the price of organic onions can affect the supply of organic tomatoes that use the same land to grow. How will this affect the equilibrium price and quantity of organic tomatoes?

6. Suppose the market for tomatoes is in equilibrium and events occur that simultaneously shift both the demand and supply curves to the right. Is it possible to determine how the equilibrium price and/or quantity would change? Explain.

Apply the Concepts

7. Suppose that high temperatures and a lack of rain in Wisconsin causes a shortage of cranberries, leading to a rise in cranberry prices. Explain how this would affect the equilibrium price and quantity for other products that use cranberries, such as cranberry sauce and cranberry juice?

8. Suppose the price of monthly data plans required to access the Internet anywhere using a tablet computer falls. How would this affect the market for tablet computers?

9. Using the accompanying figures, answer the following questions:
    a. On the Demand panel:
        - Show an increase in demand and label it D_1.
        - Show a decrease in demand and label it D_2.
        - Show an increase in quantity demanded.
        - Show a decrease in quantity demanded.
        - What causes demand to change?
        - What causes quantity demanded to change?

b. On the Supply panel:
- Show an increase in supply and label it S_1.
- Show a decrease in supply and label it S_2.
- Show an increase in quantity supplied.
- Show a decrease in quantity supplied.
- What causes supply to change?
- What causes quantity supplied to change?

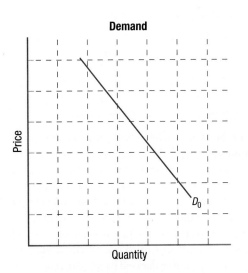

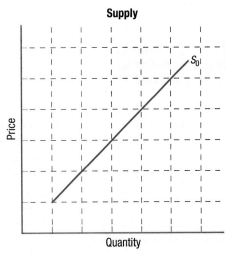

10. Several medical studies have shown that drinking red wine in moderation is good for the heart. How would such a study affect the public's demand for wine? Would it have an impact on the type of grapes planted in new vineyards?

11. Disneyland has an exclusive members-only club called Club 33 where celebrities and wealthy Disney fans dine on fine food. Although annual membership fees are reported to be upwards of $30,000, there is still a 14-year waiting list to join. How would this market for memberships be represented in a supply and demand diagram? In what ways can the shortage be eliminated, especially if Disney controls the price and the supply of memberships?

12. Over the past decade, cruise ship companies have dramatically increased the number of mega-ships (those that carry 3,000 passengers or more), increasing the supply of cruises. At the same time, the popularity of cruising has increased among consumers, increasing demand. Explain how these two effects can coincide with a decrease in the average price of cruise travel.

In the News

13. In January 2018, the online ticket market StubHub reported record high average prices for Super Bowl tickets as the Minnesota Vikings advanced through the playoffs and was one game away from playing in the Super Bowl in their home stadium in Minneapolis. However, when the Vikings lost to the Eagles in the last game before the Super Bowl, ticket prices plummeted. Explain why prices for Super Bowl tickets on StubHub reacted in this way after the Vikings lost using demand and supply analysis.

14. In 2014, self-balancing scooters (known as hoverboards) saw a huge spike in sales as their popularity rose and more companies started producing them. In 2015, a safety risk was exposed when it was reported that over 100 incidences of hoverboards catching fire or exploding occurred, causing injuries. This led to a massive recall of hoverboards as manufacturers had to retool their products and fix existing products. Also, it led to a ban on hoverboards on airlines and in many schools. Explain how these two events affected the equilibrium price and quantity of hoverboards.

Solving Problems

Work It Out

≋ interactive activity

15. A popular tradition when traveling to Hawaii is to receive a *lei*, a wreath of flowers to welcome guests. Although a lei can be made of flowers, leaves, nuts, or even candy and money, orchids remain the most popular flower used to create them. Suppose that supply and demand in the orchid lei market in Hawaii are as represented in the table below:

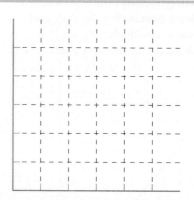

Price ($/unit)	Quantity Demanded (thousands)	Quantity Supplied (thousands)
5	24	8
10	20	12
15	16	16
20	12	20
25	8	24

a. Graph both the supply (S_0) and demand (D_0) curves. What is the current equilibrium price? Label the equilibrium point *a*.

b. Assume that the Hawaiian lei industry increases its use of orchids from Thailand (where they are grown at a lower price), allowing orchid lei supply to increase by 8,000 units at every price. Illustrate the increase in the supply in your graph. Label the new supply curve (S_1). What will the new equilibrium price in the market be? Label that point *b*.

c. Now assume that luxury hotels in Hawaii begin cost-cutting measures by no longer presenting guests with a lei upon check-in, reducing orchid lei demand by 8,000 units at every price. Label the new demand curve (D_1). What will the new equilibrium price be? Label this new equilibrium point *c*.

d. Subsequently assume that severe monsoons and civil unrest in Thailand lead to a reduction in orchid production, reducing supply back to the original curve (S_0). What will the new equilibrium price be? Label this new equilibrium point *d*.

16. The following figure shows the supply and demand for strawberries. Answer the questions that follow.

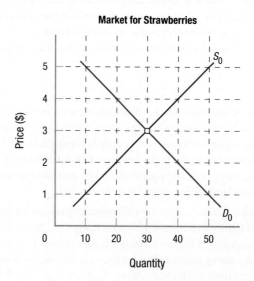

Market for Strawberries

a. Indicate the equilibrium price and equilibrium quantity.
b. Suppose sellers try to sell strawberries at $4. How much of a shortage or a surplus of strawberries would result?
c. Now suppose that the demand for strawberries falls by 10 units at every price. Draw the new demand curve in the figure and estimate what the new equilibrium price and equilibrium quantity would be.
d. If sellers still try to sell strawberries at $4, would the shortage or the surplus increase or decrease?

Answers to Questions in Checkpoints

Checkpoint: Markets 57

The market for financial securities is a huge, well-organized, and regulated market compared to local farmer's markets. Trillions of dollars change hands each week in the financial markets, and products are standardized.

Checkpoint: Demand 63

The ability to avoid high gasoline prices, a general rise in environmental consciousness, incentives such as preferred parking and reduced tolls offered by some states, an increase in the availability of charging stations (reducing opportunity cost), and improvements in quality have all led to an increase in demand for plug-in electric cars. These factors led to a change in demand because factors other than the price of the car itself have led to an increase in demand for these cars. However, as the costs of production eventually fall, prices will decrease, which will result in an increase in quantity demanded.

Checkpoint: Supply 69

A higher price for rides encourages drivers to work more hours, which results in an increase in the quantity supplied. In other words, drivers are reacting to a change in price. However, if drivers react to bad weather by working less, this will cause the supply curve to shift left. In this case, the change is due to a factor other than price.

Checkpoint: Market Equilibrium 75

Waiting in line for a new product or a good deal adds to the cost of acquiring a good. For those with higher opportunity costs of time, hiring a professional line waiter reduces this cost, making the product more affordable. Therefore, professional line waiters would cause an increase in demand for goods and services more prone to lines, causing even greater lines and shortages if prices do not adjust upward.

4

Markets and Government

Analyzing the conditions that determine when markets are efficient and when markets might fail

Learning Objectives

4.1 Define the concepts of consumer surplus and producer surplus and explain how they are used to measure the benefits and costs of market transactions.

4.2 Use consumer surplus and producer surplus to describe the gains from trade.

4.3 Explain the causes of deadweight loss and how markets can mitigate them.

4.4 Describe what an effective price ceiling or price floor does to a market and how it creates shortages or surpluses.

4.5 Identify the winners and losers when price ceilings and price floors are implemented.

4.6 Understand why markets sometimes fail to provide an optimal outcome.

4.7 Apply the concept of market failure to the important issues of climate change, health care, and education.

Once an exotic food from the Orient eaten by few outside Asia, sushi has become part of the U.S. diet in all parts of the country, available in sushi bars, cafés, buffets, and even grocery stores. The popularity of sushi stems largely from the known health benefits of eating fish, providing omega-3-rich, low-fat, and low-calorie meals. But to have sushi, one must have access to fresh fish, not easy for those not living near a coastline. Or is it?

To provide fresh sushi to inland consumers, fish must be caught, processed, and then transported to destinations in a short period of time in order to maintain its freshness. In most cases, fish is flown around the world to meet the demand. The largest fish market in the world is the Toyosu Market in Tokyo. Over 5 million pounds of fish are auctioned each morning and flown to wholesalers and restaurants around the globe.

Why would fishermen, fish market operators, wholesalers, and restaurant owners go through so much trouble just to provide fresh sushi to customers in faraway places whom they will never meet? Because the market provides incentives for each person to do so. Every person in the sushi supply chain acts in his or her own best interest by supplying what the market wants (as determined by the prices received for their goods), and that leads to an efficiently functioning market. Adam Smith's notion of the *invisible hand* works to ensure that consumers get what they want in a market society.

Hamachi, Unagi, Maguro, Toro. . . . Fish from an ocean halfway around the world to a dinner plate in a rural inland town highlights the ability of efficient markets to provide what consumers want.

BY THE Numbers

Price Controls in the Economy: *A Focus on the Minimum Wage*

Efficient markets are an essential part of modern societies. However, freely operating markets sometimes result in market failure, when markets do not generate an outcome that society deems desirable. One example occurs in the labor market, with wages representing the price of labor. In lesser-skilled industries, the equilibrium wage under a free market may be viewed as too low to support a basic living standard. Therefore, the federal government imposes a minimum wage, a price floor, in the labor market. In 2019, the federal minimum wage was $7.25 per hour. However, many states and municipalities set their minimum wage higher than the federal level. This By The Numbers looks more closely at the minimum wage and its effects on the economy.

2.3%

Percentage of all hourly paid workers in the United States who work at the federal minimum wage rate in 2019 (U.S. Bureau of Labor Statistics)

$16.00

The minimum wage in Seattle, Washington, the highest minimum wage among major U.S. cities. Some exceptions apply

WHY ARE THESE DATA IMPORTANT?

According to the discussion of price controls in the text, price floors create surpluses when they are effective (that is, higher than the market equilibrium). A surplus in the labor market creates unemployment, which is undesirable if too extensive. But if the minimum wage is effective in only a small number of lesser-skilled industries, the effect on overall unemployment is much smaller.

DATA:

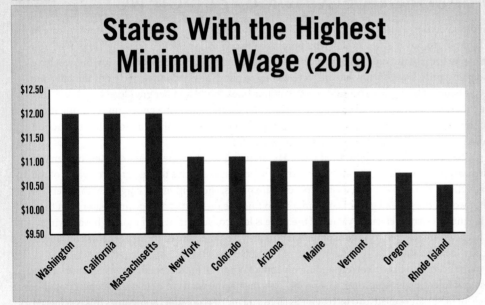

States With the Highest Minimum Wage (2019)

Where Can I Find These Data?

Source: U.S. Department of Labor   **Web site:** http://www.dol.gov/whd/minwage/america.htm

Details: The map on this Web page shows each state's minimum wage. Historical minimum wage data are also provided in tables.

~ Assessing Your Data Literacy ~

1. How much would you earn in one year if you worked 2,000 hours (50 weeks × 40 hours) at the federal minimum wage? How much more would you earn per year if you worked at the minimum wage in Washington?

2. How much must a person earn per hour in order to support a household of three people at the federal poverty guidelines of $21,330 in 2019? In which states would the minimum wage be enough?

3. What factors might explain why states pass minimum wages higher than the federal level? There are many correct answers, including economic and noneconomic reasons.

Data *in the News*

"A Smarter Minimum Wage" by Jonathan Cowan and Jim Kessler; *New York Times*, November 17, 2017

EGGS over easy, home fries, bacon, and toast. It's $9.99 at Tops Diner in Newark but $5.79 at Pop's Diner near Oklahoma City. If the same meal in two parts of the country has such a different price, should America have a single national minimum wage?

Everywhere we look in the world there are markets, and not just the big markets for fish or other major industries. Countless smaller markets dot our local landscapes, and many new virtual markets are springing up on the Internet. All play a similar role in terms of providing what consumers want, using prices as a way to signal the values placed on goods and services.

The previous chapter considered how supply and demand work together to determine the quantities of various products sold and the equilibrium prices consumers must pay for them in a market economy. The markets we have studied thus far have been stylized versions of competitive markets: They have featured many buyers and sellers, a uniform product, consumers and sellers who have complete information about the market, and few barriers to market entry or exit.

In this chapter, we start with this stylized competitive market and introduce tools for measuring the efficiency of competitive markets. We then use these tools to analyze the effects in markets when prices are not in equilibrium and why governments choose to use price controls to intervene in markets. There are sometimes complexities inherent in markets that may lead to a market failure, in which a free market does not produce a socially desirable price or quantity. We apply this concept to the discussion of climate change, health care, and education, three important issues that are often debated in government policy.

CONSUMER AND PRODUCER SURPLUS: MEASURING ECONOMIC EFFICIENCY

Suppose you find a rare comic book on eBay that you believe is worth $100 and start putting in bids hoping to buy it. After a week, you purchase the comic book with a winning bid of $80. You are happy because not only will you receive the comic book you've been looking for, but you have also paid a price lower than what you were willing to pay. However, you're likely not the only one who is happy. The person who sold you that comic book found it in her granddad's old trunk that she inherited and had hoped to receive at least $60 for it. In fact, she ended up receiving more money than the minimum amount she had hoped to receive. In this situation, the transaction took place, and both the buyer and seller are better off.

consumer surplus The difference between what consumers (as individuals or collectively as the market) would be willing to pay and the market price. It is equal to the area above market price and below the demand curve.

When consumers go about their everyday shopping or when they seek out their next major purchase, their objective typically is to find the lowest price relative to the perceived value of the product. It is the reason why consumers compare prices, shop online, or bargain with sellers. In other words, the general goal of consumers is to find the product at a price no greater than their willingness-to-pay (perceived value); if the price is less, consumers benefit more. These "savings," so to speak, are referred to as **consumer surplus** and are a measure of the net benefits consumers receive in the market.

Producers also have a corresponding objective. When an entrepreneur opens up a new business, her intention is to maximize its profit. This means she wants to obtain the highest possible price for her product relative to its cost for as large a quantity as possible. Sometimes this is achieved by selling fewer units at a higher markup (such as rare art), while other times it is achieved through the sale of mass quantities of products at relatively small markups (such as goods sold at Walmart). Regardless of the strategy used, the general goal of producers is to obtain a price at least equal to their willingness-to-sell; if the price is higher, producers benefit more. These gains are called **producer surplus** and are a measure of the net benefits producers receive in the market.

producer surplus The difference between the market price and the price at which firms are willing to supply the product. It is equal to the area below market price and above the supply curve.

Now that you have an intuitive sense of what consumer surplus and producer surplus are, let's look more carefully into how they are measured. We begin with a single case of a buyer and a seller at a car dealership. Suppose you are the buyer, and you find a car that interests you. Let's assume that the most you would be willing to pay for that car is $20,000. In other words, you find the car to be worth $20,000, but paying that price would be the worst-case scenario other than not buying the car at all. You would rather get a better deal by negotiating with the sales manager. But now let's look at the other side: Assume that the sales manager has a minimum price of $15,000 at which he is willing to sell the car. Selling the car at this price would be his worst-case scenario other than not selling the car.

····· Figure 1 • Willingness-to-Pay and Willingness-to-Sell ·····················

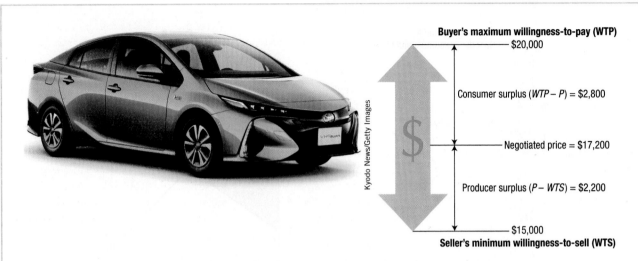

In a transaction with a single buyer and a single seller, consumer surplus ($2,800) is the difference between the maximum amount the buyer was willing to pay ($20,000) and the actual price paid ($17,200). Producer surplus ($2,200) is the difference between the actual price received ($17,200) and the minimum amount the seller was willing to accept ($15,000).

We have now determined a potential "gain" of $5,000 that can be shared by the buyer and seller depending on the final negotiated price for this car. Figure 1 shows this gain as the difference between the buyer's willingness-to-pay (WTP) and the seller's willingness-to-sell (WTS). Assume that the final negotiated price of the car is $17,200. We can now use this information to calculate consumer surplus ($WTP - P = \$20,000 - \$17,200 = \$2,800$) and producer surplus ($P - WTS = \$17,200 - \$15,000 = \$2,200$).

This example is unique in that the price of the car is negotiated between the buyer and seller. In most of our daily transactions, however, the prices of goods and services are not negotiated. When you go to the grocery store, the prices that appear are what you pay unless you have a coupon or a rewards card. You don't negotiate over the price of milk, bread, or chicken. Nonetheless, the measurements of consumer surplus and producer surplus remain the same.

Suppose that instead of just one buyer and one seller, the market contains dozens or even thousands of buyers and sellers. What would change? Let's look at the market for hockey pucks. First, each of the many buyers would have a different WTP, which would be represented as a downward-sloping demand curve (by definition, demand is a collection of WTPs of all consumers in a market). Second, each of the many sellers would have a different WTS, which would be represented as an upward-sloping supply curve. But the definition of consumer surplus ($WTP - P$) and producer surplus ($P - WTS$) remains the same, except that now we apply it to the entire market. Figure 2 illustrates how consumer and producer surplus is determined in a small market for hockey pucks with specific consumers and firms and for the overall market.

Panel A in Figure 2 represents a small market with 6 individual buyers and 6 individual sellers, with an equilibrium price of $6 (from equilibrium point e) at which 6 units of output are sold. In this market, Amy has the highest willingness-to-pay because she values a hockey puck to be worth $11. Because the market determines that $6 is the price everyone pays, Amy clearly gets a bargain by purchasing the unit and receiving a consumer surplus equal to $5 ($11 − $6). Denis, however, values a hockey puck a little less at $10 but still receives a consumer surplus of $4 ($10 − $6). And so on for Quin, Lily, and Gabby, who receive a consumer surplus of $3, $2, and $1, respectively. Only Greg, who values a hockey puck to be worth exactly the same amount as the market price, earns no consumer surplus. Total consumer surplus for the 6 consumers in panel A is found by adding all of the individual consumer surpluses for each unit purchased. Thus, total consumer surplus in panel A is equal to $5 + $4 + $3 + $2 + $1 + $0 = $15.

Figure 2 • Consumer and Producer Surplus

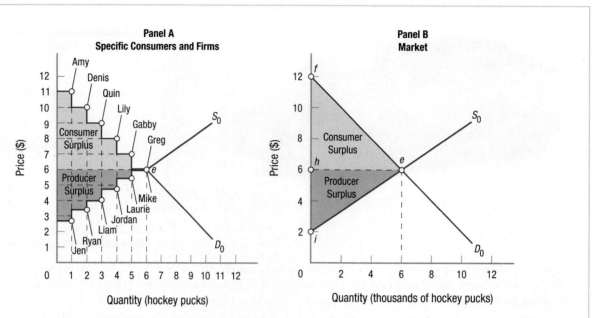

Panel B shows a market consisting of many more of the specific consumers and firms shown in panel A. This market determines equilibrium price to be $6 (point *e*), and total sales for the market are 6,000 hockey pucks. Consumer surplus is equal to the area under the demand curve but above the equilibrium price of $6. Producer surplus is the area under the equilibrium price but above the supply curve.

In a similar way, assume that each point on the supply curve represents a specific seller, each with a hockey puck to sell but each with a different willingness-to-sell. Equilibrium price is still $6; therefore, Jen, who is willing to sell her hockey puck for just $2.67, receives a producer surplus of $3.33 ($6 − $2.67). Ryan, Liam, Jordan, and Laurie, who each have a higher willingness-to-sell, receive a correspondingly smaller producer surplus equal to $2.67, $2.00, $1.33, and $0.67, respectively. And Mike, who has a willingness-to-sell of $6, receives no producer surplus for his sale. Total producer surplus in panel A is equal to $3.33 + $2.67 + $2.00 + $1.33 + $0.67 + $0 = $10.

Panel B illustrates consumer and producer surplus for an entire market. For convenience, we have assumed that the market is 1,000 times larger than that shown in panel A. Whereas in panel A we had discrete buyers and sellers, we now have one big market. Therefore, consumer surplus is equal to the area under the demand curve and above equilibrium price, or the area of the shaded triangle labeled "consumer surplus."

To put a number to the consumer surplus triangle (*feh*) in panel B, we can compute the area of the triangle using the formula $\frac{1}{2}$(base × height). Thus, total market consumer surplus in panel B is [$\frac{1}{2}$ × (6,000) × ($12 − $6)] = $18,000. The shaded triangle labeled "producer surplus" (area *hei*) is found in the same way by computing the value of the triangle. Producer surplus is equal to [$\frac{1}{2}$ × (6,000) × ($6 − $2)] = $12,000.

Although we simplify the calculation of consumer and producer surplus using the area of the triangle, remember that it is still the sum of many individual consumer and producer surpluses. It is because of the fact that markets have thousands of buyers and sellers that the steps in panel A of Figure 2 become very small, thus resulting in the smooth demand and supply curves in panel B.

We have now defined consumer surplus and producer surplus for individuals and for markets. But how do we know whether the market leads to an ideal outcome for consumers and producers? The next section goes on to reveal the efficiency of markets.

✓ CHECKPOINT

CONSUMER AND PRODUCER SURPLUS: MEASURING ECONOMIC EFFICIENCY

- Consumers and producers attempt to maximize their well-being by achieving the greatest gains in their market transactions.

- Consumer surplus occurs when consumers would have been willing to pay more for a good or service than the actual price paid. It represents a form of savings to consumers.

- Producer surplus occurs when businesses would have been willing to provide a good or service at a price lower than the market price. It represents a form of earnings to producers.

QUESTION: At the end of the semester, four college students list their economics textbooks for sale on the bulletin board in the student union. The minimum price Alex is willing to accept is $20, Caroline wants at least $25, Kira wants at least $30, and Will wants at least $35. Now assume that four college students taking an economics class next semester are searching for a deal on the textbook. Cole wishes to pay no more than $50, Jacqueline no more than $55, Sienna no more than $60, and Tessa no more than $65. Suppose that the actual sales price for each of the four textbooks is $40. What is the total consumer surplus received by the four buyers and the total producer surplus received by the four sellers?

Answers to the Checkpoint questions can be found at the end of the chapter.

USING CONSUMER AND PRODUCER SURPLUS: THE GAINS FROM TRADE

Markets are efficient when they generate the largest possible amount of net benefits to all parties involved. When transactions between a buyer and a seller take place, each party is better off than before the transaction, leading to gains from trade. We had previously looked at gains from trade in an earlier chapter from the perspectives of individuals, firms, and countries specializing in activities and engaging in mutually beneficial transactions. This is no different from our present market examples, in which buyers and sellers mutually gain when transacting with one another.

At the equilibrium price, shortages and surpluses are nonexistent, and all consumers wanting to buy a good at that price are able to find a seller willing to sell at that price. The market efficiency that results maximizes the sum of consumer surplus and producer surplus, referred to as **total surplus.** Total surplus is a measure of the total net benefits a society achieves when both consumers and producers are valued components of an economy.

To see why markets are efficient at equilibrium, we need to analyze what happens to total surplus when markets deviate from equilibrium.

total surplus The sum of consumer surplus and producer surplus; it is a measure of the overall net benefit gained from a market transaction.

The Consequences of Deviating From Market Equilibrium

The market mechanism ensures that goods and services get to where they are most needed because consumers desiring them bid up the price, while suppliers eager to earn profit supply them. Adam Smith termed this process the *invisible hand* to describe how resources are allocated efficiently through individual decisions made in markets.

But not all markets end up in equilibrium, especially if buyers or sellers hold inadequate information about products or if buyers or sellers hold unrealistic or inaccurate expectations about market prices and behavior. Let's examine two scenarios in the market for treadmills in which prices deviate from the equilibrium price.

When Price Exceeds Equilibrium Figure 3 illustrates a market for treadmills with an equilibrium price of $300. Suppose that due to unrealistic expectations of demand, prices for treadmills are set at $400, above the equilibrium price. We know from the previous chapter that a price above equilibrium leads to surplus because consumers only demand 10,000 units, while producers desire to sell 30,000. Our tools of consumer surplus and producer surplus allow us to evaluate the effects on buyers and sellers in this market.

Figure 3 • Consumer and Producer Surplus When Price Exceeds Equilibrium

Compared to the equilibrium price, a price of $400 would prevent some consumers from purchasing the product. A loss of consumer surplus equal to the blue area occurs. Further, consumers who still purchase the product pay $100 more than the equilibrium price, causing an additional loss of consumer surplus equal to the pink area. Producers, meanwhile, lose producer surplus equal to the yellow area resulting from the units that consumers no longer buy but earn additional producer surplus equal to the pink area as a result of the higher price. The total amount of surplus lost is represented by the blue and yellow areas, and is called deadweight loss. The pink area is surplus transferred from consumers to producers because of the higher price.

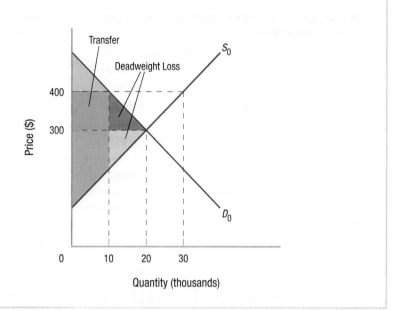

When prices are above equilibrium, consumer surplus shrinks due to two effects. First, a price of $400 causes some consumers to not make a purchase because these consumers were only willing to pay between $300 and $400. The area shown in blue represents the lost consumer surplus from these forgone purchases. Second, the consumers who still are willing and able to purchase a unit pay $100 more, which represents a loss in consumer surplus equal to the pink area. In sum, the pink and blue regions represent the total reduction in consumer surplus from the higher price.

Producers, on the other hand, will likely benefit from the higher price but face two opposing effects. First, the fact that the higher price causes some consumers to not purchase a unit causes a loss in producer surplus equal to the yellow area. However, this is offset by the additional money earned from the consumers who buy the unit at the higher price, which is represented by the pink area.

Therefore, the pink area represents a transfer of surplus from consumers to producers. The blue and yellow areas represent **deadweight loss,** the loss of consumer surplus and producer surplus caused by the inefficiency of a market not operating at equilibrium. Nobody receives the blue or yellow areas. Deadweight loss represents a loss in total surplus because both buyers and sellers would have benefited from these transactions.

deadweight loss The reduction in total surplus that results from the inefficiency of a market not in equilibrium.

When Price Falls Below Equilibrium When prices are below equilibrium, the opposite effects happen as a result of a shortage. Figure 4 shows the market for treadmills in which the price of $200 is below the equilibrium price. At that price, sellers provide 10,000 units for sale, while buyers demand 30,000 units, causing a shortage.

At a price of $200, producers are clearly worse off. Some producers are unwilling to sell at that low price, causing a loss of producer surplus equal to the yellow area, while those who still sell the product earn $100 less per unit, resulting in a loss of producer surplus equal to the pink area.

At first, you might believe consumers are better off with the lower price, and some in fact are. But these gains, shown by the pink area, are limited to consumers lucky enough to purchase the good. The rest of the consumers who are affected by the shortage are worse off because consumer surplus equal to the blue area is lost because of trades never made. In sum, deadweight loss equals the sum of the blue and yellow areas.

The two scenarios shown in Figures 3 and 4 demonstrate that whenever prices deviate from equilibrium, total surplus as measured by the sum of consumer surplus and producer surplus falls,

Figure 4 • Consumer and Producer Surplus When Price Is Below Equilibrium

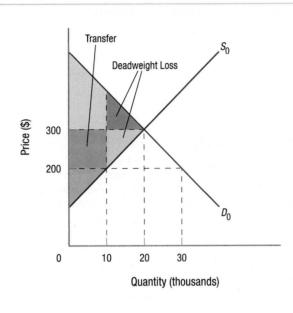

Compared to the equilibrium price, a price of $200 causes some producers to not sell the product. A loss of producer surplus equal to the yellow area occurs. Further, producers who still sell the product earn $100 less than before, causing an additional loss of producer surplus equal to the pink area. Consumers, meanwhile, lose consumer surplus equal to the blue area resulting from the shortage but receive additional consumer surplus equal to the pink area as a result of the lower price for those lucky enough to find units for sale. Once again, deadweight loss is the blue and yellow areas, and the pink area is surplus that is transferred.

NOBEL PRIZE
PAUL A. SAMUELSON (1915–2009)

In 1970 Paul Samuelson became the first American to win the Nobel Prize in Economics. One could say that Paul Samuelson literally wrote the book on economics. In 1948, when he was a young professor at the Massachusetts Institute of Technology (MIT), the university asked him to write a text for the junior-year course in economics. Seventy years later, more than 4 million copies of his textbook *Economics* have been sold.

Samuelson's interests were wide ranging, and his contributions include everything from the highly technical and mathematical to a popular column for *Newsweek* magazine. He made breakthrough contributions to virtually all areas of economics.

Born in Gary, Indiana, in 1915, Samuelson attended the University of Chicago. He received the university's Social Science Medal and was awarded a graduate fellowship, which he used at Harvard, where he published eleven papers while in the graduate program.

He wanted to remain at Harvard but was only offered an instructor's position. However, MIT soon made a better offer and, as he describes it, "On a fine October day in 1940 an *enfant terrible emeritus* packed up his pencil and moved three miles down the Charles River, where he lived happily ever after." He often remarked that a pencil was all he needed to theorize. Seven years later, he published his Ph.D. dissertation *Foundations of Economic Analysis,* a major contribution to the area of mathematical economics.

Harvard made several attempts to lure him back, but he spent his entire career at MIT and is often credited with developing a department as good as or better than Harvard's. Samuelson was an informal adviser to President John F. Kennedy. A prolific writer, his *Collected Scientific Papers* takes up seven volumes and includes nearly 400 articles. He was an active economist until his death in 2009 at the age of 94. As you read through this book, keep in mind that in virtually every chapter, Paul Samuelson created or added to the analysis in substantial ways.

Information from David Warsh, *Knowledge and the Wealth of Nations: A Story of Economic Discovery* (New York: Norton), 2006; Paul Samuelson, "Economics in My Time," in William Breit and Roger Spencer, *Lives of the Laureates: Seven Nobel Economists* (Cambridge, MA: MIT Press), 1986.

resulting in a deadweight loss from mutually beneficial transactions between buyers and sellers not taking place. But why would markets not achieve equilibrium? One reason is because governments may choose to intervene in markets to achieve an outcome that may be more socially desirable or equitable, even at the cost of deadweight loss that results. The next section discusses the effects of price controls in a market.

 CHECKPOINT

USING CONSUMER AND PRODUCER SURPLUS: THE GAINS FROM TRADE

- The sum of consumer surplus and producer surplus is total surplus, a measure of the overall net benefit for an economy.
- Markets are efficient when all buyers and all sellers willing to buy and sell at the market price are able to do so.
- When buyers and sellers engage in a market transaction, gains from trade are created from consumer surplus and producer surplus.
- Total surplus is maximized when the market is in equilibrium.
- Deadweight loss is created when markets deviate from equilibrium.

QUESTION: Waiting for an organ transplant is an ordeal for patients. Some wait years for a compatible donor organ to become available. Some economists have suggested that offering monetary compensation to organ donors would increase the quantity supplied of available organs. Would such a system lead to gains from trade? Why are such incentives difficult to implement?

Answers to the Checkpoint questions can be found at the end of this chapter.

PRICE CEILINGS AND PRICE FLOORS

laissez-faire A market that is allowed to function without any government intervention.

To this point, we have assumed that competitive markets are allowed to operate freely, without any government intervention. Economists refer to freely functioning markets as **laissez-faire,** a French term meaning "let it be." The justification for this type of economic policy is that when competitive markets are left to determine equilibrium price and output, they "clear." This means that businesses provide consumers with the quantity of goods they want to purchase at the equilibrium price; there are no shortages or surpluses. Consumer and producer surplus together, or total surplus, is maximized.

As we saw in the previous section, when the price of a good deviates from the market equilibrium, inefficiencies in the form of deadweight loss can result. In these cases, a competitive market would push the price toward equilibrium. But what happens when government policy prevents that from occurring? Governments sometimes intervene in markets in order to achieve an objective that people may consider to be more equitable, such as preventing energy prices from rising too high or ensuring that farm products are priced high enough to support a comfortable living for farmers. Therefore, governments use price ceilings and price floors on certain goods and services to keep prices below or above market equilibrium. But what really happens when governments control prices? This section will study the effects more closely.

Price Ceilings

price ceiling A maximum price established by government for a product or service. When the price ceiling is set below equilibrium, a shortage results.

When the government sets a **price ceiling,** it is legally mandating the maximum price that can be charged for a product or service. This is a legal maximum; regardless of market forces, price cannot exceed this level. An historical example of a price ceiling is the establishment of rent-controlled apartments in New York City during World War II, some of which still exist today. However, more common examples of price ceilings include limits on what insurance companies can charge customers, price caps on telecommunications and electric services to customers in rural or remote locations, and limits on tuition hikes at public universities.

Panel A in Figure 5 shows a binding (or effective) price ceiling, or one in which the ceiling price is set below the equilibrium price. In this case, equilibrium price is P_e, but the government

Figure 5 • A Price Ceiling Set Below Equilibrium Creates a Shortage

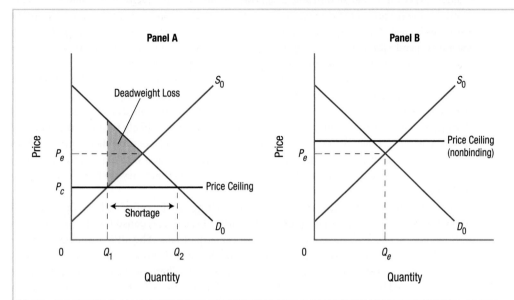

When the government enacts a price ceiling below equilibrium (panel A), consumers will demand Q_2 and businesses will supply only Q_1, creating a shortage equal to $Q_2 - Q_1$ and causing deadweight loss equal to the shaded area. If the price ceiling is set above equilibrium (panel B), the price ceiling has no effect, and the market price and quantity prevail with no deadweight loss created.

has set a price ceiling at P_c. Quantity supplied at the ceiling price is Q_1, whereas consumers want Q_2; therefore, the result is a shortage of $Q_2 - Q_1$ units of the product. As we saw in the previous section, setting a price below equilibrium alters consumer and producer surplus, and results in a deadweight loss indicated by the shaded area. If the price ceiling is raised toward equilibrium, the shortage is reduced along with the deadweight loss. If the price ceiling is set above P_e (as shown in panel B), the market simply settles at P_e, and the price ceiling has no impact; it is nonbinding, and no deadweight loss occurs. A price ceiling can also *become* nonbinding if market factors cause supply to increase or demand to fall, pushing the equilibrium price below the ceiling.

A common mistake when analyzing the effect of price ceilings is assuming that effective price ceilings appear above the market equilibrium because the word "ceiling" refers to something *above you*. Instead, think of ceilings as something that keep you from moving higher. Suppose you build a makeshift skateboarding ramp in your apartment hallway and tempt your friends to test it out. If the ceiling is too low, some of your friends might end up with a severe headache. In other words, a binding (effective) ceiling is one that is kept lower than normal. If the ceiling can be raised by 5 feet, then all of your friends would achieve their jumps without bumping their heads. In sum, price ceilings have their strongest effects when kept very low, preventing the price from reaching equilibrium; as the ceiling is raised, the effect of the policy diminishes, and the ceiling becomes nonbinding once the equilibrium price is reached.

Given the price ceiling, one might argue that although shortages might exist, at least prices will be kept lower and therefore more "fair." The question is, fairer to whom? Suppose your university places a new price ceiling on the rents of all existing apartments located on campus, one that is below the rents of similar apartments off campus. This might sound like a great idea, but often what sounds like a great idea comes with costs.

A price ceiling increases the quantity demanded for on-campus apartments, and without an increase in supply, a shortage results. Those lucky enough to obtain an on-campus apartment benefit from the lower rents. But what about those who couldn't? Because

The ability to jump on one's bed depends on the height of the ceiling. The lower the ceiling, the more it restricts this fun activity. Similarly, price ceilings below equilibrium (rather than above equilibrium) restrict the market and lead to shortages.

Dr. Peter Chiang

misallocation of resources
Occurs when a good or service is not consumed by the person who values it the most and typically results when a price ceiling creates an artificial shortage in the market.

some students who really could have benefited from lower rents (those with lower incomes or without cars) cannot find an on-campus apartment while other students who could have easily afforded a higher-priced off-campus apartment managed to snatch one up, a **misallocation of resources** is created. Further, when on-campus apartments do open up, students eager to obtain one might spend a lot of time and resources trying. These resources (an opportunity cost) end up offsetting some or all of the savings from finding an on-campus apartment.

Besides the misallocation of resources and potential opportunity costs of long waits and search costs, price ceilings also lead to some unintended long-term consequences. For example, if a landlord owns some apartments on campus (where rents are controlled) and some apartments off campus (where rents are higher), on which apartments is she likely to spend more money for upgrades and/or maintenance? The quality of goods and services subjected to price ceilings tends to deteriorate over time, as the incentives shift toward products with higher prices. Further, when it comes time to invest in new apartments, where do you think they are likely to be built—on campus or off?

The key point to remember here is that price ceilings are intended to keep the price of a product below its market or equilibrium level. When this happens, consumer surplus increases for those able to purchase the good, while producer surplus falls. The ultimate effect of a price ceiling, however, is that the quantity of the product demanded exceeds the quantity supplied, thereby producing a shortage of the product in the market. When shortages occur, deadweight losses are created because some mutually beneficial transactions do not take place, causing a reduction in total surplus.

Price Floors

price floor A minimum price established by government for a product or service. When the price floor is set above equilibrium, a surplus results.

A **price floor** is a government-mandated minimum price that sellers must charge for a product or service. Regardless of market forces, product price cannot legally fall below this level. One of the most familiar examples of a price floor actually occurs not in the market for goods but rather in the market for labor with the implementation of minimum wage laws. Price floors are also used in agricultural markets to ensure that prices are sufficient to support an adequate standard of living for farmers. But similar to our analysis of price ceilings, the effects of price floors lead to some unintended consequences.

Figure 6 shows the economic impact of a price floor. In panel A, the price floor, P_f, is set above equilibrium, P_e. At the higher price, suppliers are incentivized by the law of supply to

Figure 6 • A Price Floor Set Above Equilibrium Creates a Surplus

When the government sets a price floor above equilibrium (panel A), businesses try to sell Q_2 at a price of P_f, but consumers are willing to purchase only Q_1 at that price. This results in a surplus equal to $Q_2 - Q_1$. When a price floor is set below equilibrium (panel B), it becomes nonbinding.

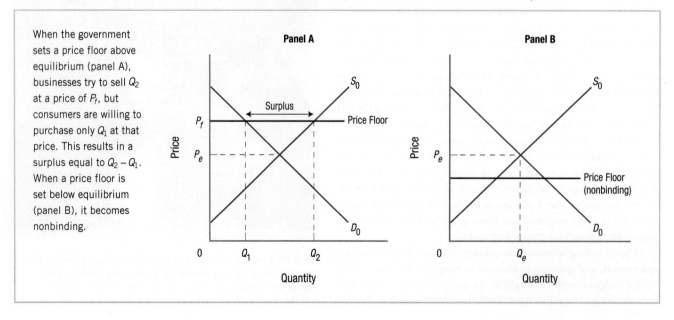

produce more units (Q_2) than at the equilibrium price. However, consumers act according to the law of demand and are willing to buy fewer units (Q_1) at the mandated price floor. The result is a surplus of $Q_2 - Q_1$ units. Whenever the price floor is above the equilibrium price, it is binding, which results in a surplus of goods. If the price floor is below the equilibrium price (shown in panel B), it has no effect on the market because goods can continue to be sold at the equilibrium price; in this case, the price floor is nonbinding, and no deadweight loss occurs.

The surplus of units caused by a binding price floor creates inefficiency in the market. Because consumers buy fewer units at the higher price, fewer transactions take place in the market, creating deadweight loss. Although suppliers are willing to sell many more units at the higher price, they are unable to find consumers willing to buy all of the units. Unlike in a market without the price floor, suppliers cannot simply lower their price to sell their excess units without violating the law. Therefore, the resulting surplus of goods either goes unsold (which results in a loss of resources) or are sold in a black market at prices below the price floor.

ISSUE

Are Price-Gouging Laws Good for Consumers?

During the summer hurricane season, residents along the Atlantic and Gulf coasts brace for hurricanes that can wreak havoc on the unprepared. The routine is well known: Buy plywood and shutters to protect windows, fill up gas tanks in cars and buy extra gas for generators, and stock up on batteries, bottled water, and nonperishable foods. Because of the huge spike in demand, numerous states have introduced price-gouging laws, which prevent stores from raising prices above the average price of the past 30 days. Penalties for violating such laws are severe.

Price-gouging laws generally pass with huge majority votes from both major political parties. The logic seems clear—to prevent businesses from exploiting a bad situation to their benefit by raising prices. Passing such laws always appears to be a victory for the consumer. But is it really?

Price-gouging laws are price ceilings placed at the price last existing when times were normal. But during a natural disaster, the market is far from normal—demand is higher, and supplies are often restricted due to plant closures. The figure shows what happens when these two

A cargo plane can carry a tremendous amount of supplies to address supply shortages, as long as an incentive exists to use that plane for this purpose.

effects come together—the market price spikes upward. But price-gouging laws require that prices remain at the *original* level, resulting in a shortage when demand increases to D_1 and supply falls to S_1.

What happens during a shortage? Huge lines form at home improvement stores, gas stations, and grocery stores. Time spent waiting in line is time that could be

spent completing other tasks in preparation for the storm. What might be a better solution?

Instead of capping prices and causing a shortage, efforts can be made to provide incentives to businesses to generate more supply. If supply shifts enough to the right to compensate for the increase in demand, then prices need not increase, regardless of the price ceiling. But the question is, How do we incentivize supply? Subsidies to offset increased transportation costs might be an example. Imagine how many supplies could be flown in on a single cargo plane from a non–hurricane-prone area. Quite a bit, but firms aren't willing to spend that money. If the incentive is provided, supply will increase, reducing shortages and costs to everyone.

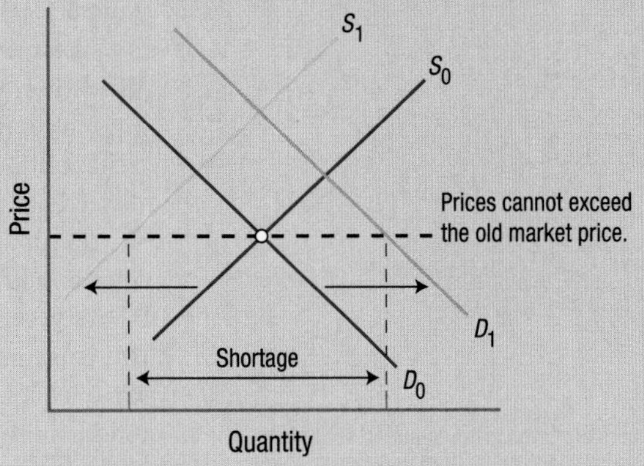

Figure: Axes labeled Price (vertical) and Quantity (horizontal). Curves labeled S_1, S_0, D_1, D_0. A dashed line labeled "Prices cannot exceed the old market price." A bracket labeled "Shortage."

Minimum Wage Policy With respect to the labor market, a minimum wage that is set higher than the equilibrium wage causes a surplus of labor, similar to panel A in Figure 6. But remember that workers (not firms) supply labor, and a surplus of labor leads to unemployment. Fortunately, the labor market is made up of many careers, and usually only jobs that require the least amount of skills end up in markets in which the minimum wage is binding. For nearly all other skilled jobs (especially the ones you are aiming for with a college degree), the equilibrium is far higher than the minimum wage, and therefore the minimum wage will be nonbinding.

Still, several million workers earn the minimum wage, and this policy has the benefit of reducing income inequality by raising the incomes of low-wage workers. Many people believe that the minimum wage should be even higher so that an individual working full-time at the minimum wage is able to keep a family out of poverty. Subsequently, many states and cities have raised their minimum wage above the federal level. However, the potential consequence of a higher minimum wage is a greater surplus of workers in lesser-skilled labor markets. One remedy is to provide education and job-training incentives to encourage workers to seek higher-paying careers. But there are a variety of reasons why many workers remain in low-paying jobs. Therefore, minimum wage policy remains an issue subject to much debate among policymakers.

Agricultural Price Support Policy The agricultural industry is another market in which price floors (also called price supports) are common. Governments use price floors to smooth out the incomes of farmers, which often fluctuate due to annual variations in crop prices. The United States, the European Union, and Japan have long protected their agricultural industries by ensuring a minimum price level for many types of crops.

Although not all crops are subject to binding price floors, those that do face the effects described earlier in which suppliers produce more crops than consumers are willing to buy, creating a surplus. Because unsold crops will eventually spoil, the unintended effect of unsold crops resulting from the price floor can lead to *lower* incomes, the exact opposite of the policy's objective. To prevent this, the government will buy up surplus crops affected by price floors.

But what does the government do with the crops it buys? It cannot sell them because that would push prices below the price floor. It can store certain crops for use in the event of future shortages, but storage costs money, and many crops spoil quickly. Another common use of surplus crops is for the government to give them to public schools. This has the benefit of keeping lunch prices affordable (or even free for certain students), but nutritionists voice concern that the types of foods being provided under these programs (wheat, grains, and corn) are not the most nutritious foods for children to eat.

Surplus foods resulting from government price floors are often given to public schools to be used in school lunches.

Another criticism of agricultural price supports comes from developing countries that depend on the export of crops for their economic output. These countries claim that price supports hamper their economic development by preventing them from selling goods in which they have a comparative advantage. In other words, agricultural price supports restrict gains from trade.

Despite their questionable economic justification, political pressures have ensured that agricultural price supports and related programs still command a sizable amount of the domestic federal budget.

In sum, price ceilings and price floors are policies aimed at promoting equity or fairness in a society, such as preventing rapid price increases for consumers or ensuring fair wages for workers. Price controls are one tool that governments use to address situations when a competitive market does not generate an outcome that some people believe to be desirable. The next section presents several situations in which nearly all governments choose to intervene in markets to some extent. Because these policies involve a tradeoff between efficiency and equity, consensus among people is often difficult to achieve, leading to vigorous economic and political debates.

✓ CHECKPOINT

PRICE CEILINGS AND PRICE FLOORS

- Governments use price floors and price ceilings to intervene in markets.

- A price ceiling is a maximum legal price that can be charged for a product. Price ceilings set below the equilibrium price result in shortages.

- A price floor is a minimum legal price that must be charged for a product. Price floors set above market the equilibrium price result in surpluses.

QUESTION: The day after Thanksgiving, also known as *Black Friday,* is a day on which retailers advertise very steep discounts on selected items such as televisions or laptops. Assuming the number of units available at the discounted price is limited, in what ways are the effects of this pricing strategy similar to a price ceiling set by the government? In what ways do they differ?

Answers to the Checkpoint questions can be found at the end of the chapter.

MARKET FAILURE: WHEN MARKETS DO NOT DELIVER A SOCIALLY DESIRABLE OUTCOME

Markets are inherently efficient mechanisms for allocating resources due to the incentives that drive consumers and firms to act in their own best interests. However, there are times when many people consider the equilibrium price and quantity to be undesirable. When freely functioning markets fail to provide an optimal amount of goods and services, a **market failure** occurs. What exactly does this mean?

In the supply and demand diagram in Figure 7, an equilibrium occurs in a free market at the price of $3,000 and quantity of 1 million. However, suppose that this market represents shark fins, a delicacy used to make a popular soup in certain countries, but has the consequence of killing sharks, often inhumanely, for the sake of harvesting their fins. Thus, despite the fact that this

market failure Occurs when a free market does not lead to a socially desirable outcome.

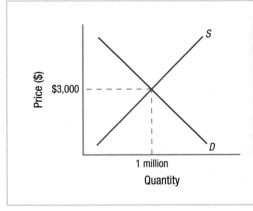

······ Figure 7 • A Free Market Quantity That Is Not Socially Optimal ··············

A free market for shark fins will generate an equilibrium price of $3,000 and an equilibrium quantity of 1 million. However, many people believe this quantity is too high. Because the socially desirable quantity is less than the market equilibrium quantity, a market failure occurs.

market offers a price and quantity that maximizes total surplus, there are many people, organizations, and governments around the world that desire a much smaller quantity of shark fins to be sold or even an outright ban. In other words, the socially desirable quantity is less than the market equilibrium quantity. A market failure occurs because of the discrepancy between what a free market says ought to happen and what society believes should happen. This, however, leads to a normative question: Should the sale of shark fins be restricted?

Causes of Market Failure

The market for shark fins is one of many real-life examples that societies must address that involve a potential market failure. There are four major reasons why markets fail: a lack of competition, a mismatch of information, the existence of externalities, and the existence of public goods.

Lack of Competition When a market has many buyers and sellers, no one seller has the ability to raise its price above that of its competitors. But when a market lacks competition, such as a town with only one water provider that faces no competition, inefficient production is more likely to occur, along with a desire to increase profits. Both of these factors would lead to higher prices to consumers.

asymmetric information
Occurs when one party to a transaction has significantly better information than another party.

Mismatch of Information An important condition for efficient markets is that buyers and sellers possess adequate information about products. When one party knows more about a product than the other, **asymmetric information** results. For example, a seller of a used car knows more about the true condition of the car than a potential buyer. Conversely, an antiques buyer may know more about the value of items than the seller at an estate sale. In these cases, a mismatch of information can lead to prices being set too high or too low.

Existence of Externalities Externalities are the external benefits or external costs generated by the actions of others. For example, driving your car creates external costs in terms of traffic congestion and pollution, while obtaining a flu shot creates external benefits by reducing the probability of inflicting others since you are less likely to become sick. The existence of externalities leads to outcomes in which a free market leads to the production and consumption of what people believe to be too much or too little of a good or service.

Existence of Public Goods Most goods we buy are private goods, such as meals and clothing; once you buy them, they are yours to do as you please. Public goods, however, are goods that one person can consume without diminishing what is left for others. Public television, for example, is a public good that exhibits nonrivalry (my watching of PBS does not mean there is less PBS for you to watch) and nonexclusivity (once a good is provided, others cannot be excluded from enjoying it). Because of these characteristics, public goods are difficult to provide in the private market.

The factors that lead to a market failure are common in societies that must choose how to allocate resources across individuals facing different circumstances. Because the government plays an important role in allocating certain goods and services, significant debates will arise with respect to what society deems to be a socially desirable outcome. We turn next to three key debates.

Addressing Market Failure in Three Key Societal Issues

Much of the economic debate surrounding key issues discussed in government and politics relates to a market failure issue and the extent to which governments should intervene. In a democratic society, it's often difficult to achieve consensus on normative questions, and heated debate can arise between those with opposing viewpoints. Among the most contentious issues include climate change, health care policy, and the provision of education.

Climate Change Every person on the planet is affected by changes in our climate, which have become more apparent in recent years. Efforts to combat climate change can be viewed as a large public good—everybody benefits without rivalry or exclusion. Therefore, climate change policy illustrates a market failure because the actions that protect against climate change are costly, but the benefits of such actions are enjoyed by all Earthlings, including those who do not pay (known as free riders). This is a common problem inherent with public goods.

Moreover, actions that affect climate change exhibit externalities. The amount of carbon emissions emitted by countries vary significantly. If one country pollutes more due to greater industrialization, an external cost is generated on the rest of the world. On the other hand, countries that promote sustainable production generate external benefits. Clearly, some countries do more to combat climate change than others, which illustrates the challenges of mitigating the issue. While nearly everyone desires a cleaner planet, not everyone wishes to pay to achieve that goal.

Governments have come together to address climate change by forming agreements to combat the problem in an equitable manner. One recent example is the Paris Agreement, which was

🌍AROUND THE WORLD

Singapore: Resolving Traffic Jams and Reducing Pollution Using Price Controls

> How did Singapore use economic tools to intervene in the market to improve traffic flow and to correct a potential market failure?

How much time is spent waiting in gridlock traffic in major cities? According to a study by the transportation analytics firm INRIX, in 2018, American drivers spent over 8 billion hours stuck in traffic. Traffic creates an opportunity cost that leads to reduced productivity. Moreover, traffic jams reduce fuel efficiency and generate more air pollution. Is there an economic solution to these problems? Singapore may have the answer.

Singapore uses an electronic road-pricing system that charges drivers a toll on dozens of its major roads and highways. Unlike traditional toll roads, Singapore's road charges vary throughout the day. During times when roads are less subject to congestion, the fee is very minimal or

even zero, while during times of the day when roads are likely to be congested, the fee is higher. As it becomes more expensive to drive during certain periods of the day, drivers are incentivized to drive less, to drive during off-peak times, or to find alternative means of transportation. The outcome is a road system that is less prone to congestion, reducing an inefficiency.

Singapore is not the only city that uses congestion charges. It costs approximately $15 to drive in Central London between the hours of 7 A.M. and 6 P.M. Even in the

United States, the introduction of express lanes in Los Angeles, Atlanta, Miami, and other cities has allowed motorists to pay a toll to bypass traffic. Similar to Singapore, these tolls vary throughout the day, with prices rising as roads become more congested.

Not only do congestion charges incentivize people to drive less, they also encourage companies to change the way they operate. Companies that do not need to operate during traditional business hours might encourage their employees to arrive at work later and return home later, avoiding times when congestion charges are at their peak. By reducing traffic congestion, less time is wasted, productivity rises, and pollution is reduced. Furthermore, the fees collected are a valuable source of government revenue.

Many economists believe that market-based pricing mechanisms such as congestion charges can lead to increased efficiency and equity.

〽 GO ONLINE TO PRACTICE THE ECONOMIC CONCEPTS IN THIS STORY

signed by nearly every country in the world, including the United States, in 2016. But because opinions change, in 2017 the United States announced its intent to pull out of the Paris Agreement. Although official U.S. government policy may take one position, many American individuals and firms remain strong proponents of reducing climate change, with many corporations taking the lead in reducing their carbon footprint.

Another strategy used to confront climate change is to implement incentives to promote resource conservation. The Around the World feature describes a strategy implemented by some cities to reduce traffic gridlock, a major contributor to carbon emissions.

Health Care What is the socially desirable allocation of health care? Should everybody have health care coverage provided by the government? Or should health care be provided in a private market where consumers and providers make decisions based on their own situations? Or should it be somewhere in between? Health care is among the most expensive outlays among individuals, firms, and the government. This is especially the case in technologically-advanced countries where treatments are available for even the rarest illnesses, albeit at a very high cost.

One of the resulting normative questions is whether every person should have access to health care regardless of their ability to pay for it. In the United States, this issue is mitigated for those age 65 and over, when Medicare (a government-run health care program) becomes available. In many other countries, a similar program is provided to all citizens regardless of age. Much like climate change policy, health care policy generates many external benefits and external costs. For example, providing better health care reduces illnesses and subsequent sick days, which can boost worker productivity and overall happiness (who likes lying in bed with the flu?), a clear external benefit.

The counterargument to providing health care to everyone relates to rising costs as people live longer, experience more illnesses due to modern lifestyle factors (stress, poor nutrition, and environmental toxins), or have access to expensive treatments that can cure more diseases. These high costs can potentially impede growth as a larger portion of the budget is spent on health care. This would create an external cost. Therefore, resolving the market failure in health care is a challenge that may require other strategies, such as focusing on preventive care (to prevent major illnesses from developing) or providing incentives to individuals (such as through health savings accounts) to make more market-driven health care choices.

Education The provision of education is another issue that generates externalities. A more educated society leads to greater productivity, which benefits all people. Because of the high cost of providing education, a market-determined equilibrium quantity of education is often viewed as too little, which means that governments must intervene to make education more affordable. Because education is not free, societies must determine how much education to provide, and how to finance it.

In the United States, public school education is funded by the government from preschool or kindergarten to the 12th grade. The price of public education is determined not in a free market but instead by individual state legislatures that determine the amount of public funds to allocate to education. Some states provide more funds for education than others. Some provide subsidized tuition to in-state residents at public colleges and universities or free tuition at community colleges. In other states, public college tuition are set at rates that exceed $16,000 per year. In many European nations, the price of attending college is negligible due to generous government subsidies. Again, the external benefits and external costs that education policy creates is one that generates significant debate among voters as each policy creates benefits and costs that vary among individuals.

In sum, the importance of markets and the efficiency they provide in the allocation of goods and services is of utmost importance in all economies. We saw how markets can generate an equilibrium price that individuals in society believe to be too high or too low or an equilibrium quantity that is too much or too little. As a result, governments intervene in certain markets in order to achieve outcomes that people believe to be more equitable. However, governments must be careful when intervening in markets to prevent the costs of such policies to exceed the potential benefits.

CHECKPOINT

MARKET FAILURE: WHEN MARKETS DO NOT DELIVER A SOCIALLY DESIRABLE OUTCOME

- Markets are typically efficient, although sometimes they fail by not providing the socially optimal amount of goods and services.

- Market failure is caused by a lack of competition, mismatch of information, existence of externalities, and existence of public goods.

- Climate change, health care, and education are important issues facing societies that involve debate of how to resolve market failures.

QUESTION: One proposal to reduce auto pollution would be to implement a gas tax on drivers that would subsequently make all public transportation available at little to no cost to riders. Opponents of these proposals argue that they simply provide subsidies (a form of welfare) to those without cars, without providing any benefit to those who must pay the tax. Thinking about externalities, are there any external benefits that might result to those paying the gas tax?

Answers to the Checkpoint questions can be found at the end of this chapter.

CHAPTER SUMMARY

SECTION 1 CONSUMER AND PRODUCER SURPLUS: MEASURING ECONOMIC EFFICIENCY

Paul Bradbury/Getty Images

Consumer surplus is the difference between a person's willingness-to-pay and the price paid. For a market, consumer surplus is the area between the demand curve and the market price. In the figure, consumer surplus equals $1,250.

Producer surplus is the difference between the price a seller receives and her willingness-to-sell. For a market, producer surplus is the area between the market price and the supply curve. In the figure, producer surplus equals $1,000.

4.1 Economic efficiency is measured by the gains that consumers and producers achieve when engaging in an economic transaction.

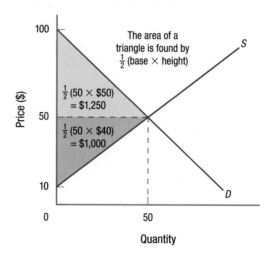

SECTION 2 USING CONSUMER AND PRODUCER SURPLUS: THE GAINS FROM TRADE

Markets exhibit efficiency when every buyer and every seller eager to buy or sell goods are able to do so, resulting in **gains from trade.** Gains from trade are measured by the **total surplus,** or the sum of consumer and producer surplus. Total surplus is maximized when a market is at equilibrium.

4.2 Suppose the price of a good is currently $75. The higher price causes two effects on consumer surplus and two effects on producer surplus:

1. Consumers who are priced out of the market lose consumer surplus equal to the blue area.
2. Consumers who continue to buy the good pay more and lose consumer surplus equal to the pink area.
3. Producers who want to sell more at $75 but cannot lose producer surplus equal to the yellow area.
4. Producers who do sell units earn $25 more per unit, equal to the pink area.

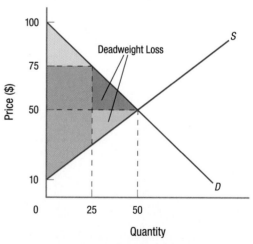

4.3 **Deadweight loss** occurs when prices deviate from equilibrium. In the preceding example, deadweight loss is shown by the blue and yellow areas.

SECTION 3 PRICE CEILINGS AND PRICE FLOORS

4.4 A **price floor** is a minimum price for a good. A binding price floor appears above the equilibrium price and causes a surplus.

4.5 A **price ceiling** is a maximum price for a good. A binding price ceiling appears below the equilibrium price and causes a shortage.

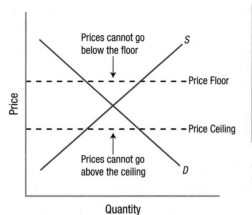

Prices cannot go below the floor

Price Floor

Price Ceiling

Prices cannot go above the ceiling

Price

Quantity

S

D

A literal mountain of surplus corn caused by agricultural price floors.

Phil Augustavo/iStockphoto

SECTION 4 MARKET FAILURE: WHEN MARKETS DO NOT DELIVER A SOCIALLY DESIRABLE OUTCOME

4.6

Lack of competition

When a firm faces little to no competition, it has an incentive to raise prices.

Existence of externalities

Markets tend to provide too few products that generate external benefits and too many products that generate external costs.

Caiaimage/Paul Bradbury/Getty Images

4.7

Learning can be fun while also generating external benefits to society. Governments subsidize education to make it more affordable.

PeopleImages/Getty Images

When one goes to work with an illness, an external cost is generated by increasing the chances of infecting others. Improved preventive heath care can minimize instances of long-term illnesses, an important reason for improving health care policy.

Mismatch of information

Asymmetric information occurs when either a buyer or a seller knows more about a product than the other.

Existence of public goods

Public goods are nonrival and nonexclusive. This means:

- My consumption does not diminish your ability to consume.
- Once a good is provided for one person, others cannot be excluded from enjoying it.

Susan E. Degginger/Alamy

Ecological conservation is a public good. Once people devote time and resources to reducing climate change, everybody benefits from it, even if one does not contribute to the costs.

Key Concepts

consumer surplus, p. 86

producer surplus, p. 86

total surplus, p. 89

deadweight loss, p. 90

laissez-faire, p. 92

price ceiling, p. 92

misallocation of resources, p. 94

price floor, p. 94

market failure, p. 97

asymmetric information, p. 98

Questions and Problems

Check Your Understanding

1. Describe how consumer surplus and producer surplus are measured.

2. Using the following graph, show what happens to consumer surplus when a new technology reduces the cost of production.

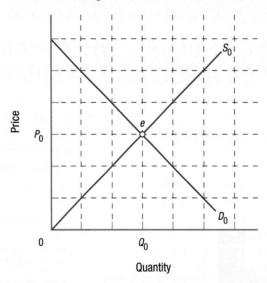

3. Explain why deadweight loss can occur with a price below equilibrium even when some consumers benefit from it.

4. Why does an effective price ceiling appear below the equilibrium rather than above it?

5. If a price floor is reduced toward equilibrium but not below it, explain what happens to the total surplus and deadweight loss.

6. Why does the quantity of public college education determined in a free market (without government intervention) represent a market failure?

Apply the Concepts

7. An increasing number of charities have turned to online auctions as a way to raise money by selling unique experiences donated by celebrities (such as a *meet-and-greet* with a celebrity before a concert or a walk-on role on a television show). Why would the use of auctions lead to a better outcome for the charity as opposed to just setting a fixed price? Explain using the concepts of consumer surplus and producer surplus.

8. Luigi's is the only pizzeria in a small town in northern Alaska. It is constantly busy, but there is never a wait for a table. One of Luigi's friends suggests that he would earn much more money if he raised his menu prices by 25% because no one is likely to open a new pizzeria in the near future. If Luigi follows his friend's advice, what would happen to consumer and producer surplus and efficiency?

9. Over the past decade, many American candy companies, including The Hershey Company, Brach's Confections, and Ferrara Candy Company, opened factories in Mexico and Canada to produce candy that is then shipped back to the United States for sale. Although lower wages in Mexico might explain part of this move, wages in Canada are comparable to U.S. wages. Explain how U.S. government agricultural policy in the sugar industry may have encouraged these moves.

10. Government and employer subsidies to reduce the price of health insurance have important benefits to the individual in terms of improved health. In addition, society overall can benefit from higher levels of health care coverage. Provide three examples of external benefits that may result from increased health care coverage.

11. In cities around the country, the government provides assistance to families with low incomes to rent apartments at prices capped by the U.S. Department of Housing and Urban Development (HUD), essentially setting a price ceiling on apartments. These designated apartments tend to rent quickly, and tenants are less likely to move once they find an apartment. Explain how rent controls affect market prices for non–rent-controlled apartments. How are incentives by landlords affected in terms of maintaining rent-controlled and non–rent-controlled apartments? How would your answer change if the government provided a subsidy payment to landlords to offset the difference between the price ceiling and the market price?

12. The U.S. Department of Labor reports that of the roughly 150 million people employed, just over half are paid by the hour, but fewer than 5% earn the minimum wage or less; 95% of wage earners earn more. And of those earning the minimum wage or less, 25% are teenagers living at home. If so few people are affected by the minimum wage, why does it often seem to be such a contentious political issue?

In the News

13. Over the past few years, several U.S. states have either legalized recreational marijuana or at least decriminalized its use ("Would Legalizing Marijuana Help the Economy?," Debate.org). Proponents argue that legalizing the use of marijuana would help the economy by boosting economic activity and reducing costs. Do you agree? Why or why not? Use the concepts of supply and demand and consumer and producer surplus to support your answer.

14. In 2018, Governor Baker of Massachusetts signed a bill to raise the state's minimum wage to $15 per hour by 2023 ("Massachusetts Governor Signs Bill Raising Minimum Wage to $15," *The Hill*, June 29, 2018). Proponents argue that this policy helps the working poor who hold full-time jobs yet are not able to pull their families out of poverty. Meanwhile, opponents argue that the policy would cause harm in the labor market. Provide an example of a situation that would support each side's argument.

Solving Problems

15. Consider the market shown in the following graph.

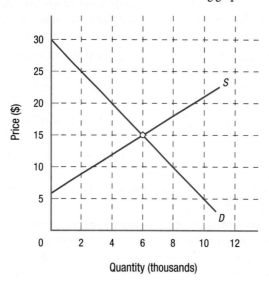

Quantity (thousands)

a. Compute the consumer surplus.
b. Compute the producer surplus.

Now assume that government puts a price floor on this product at $20 a unit.

c. Compute the new consumer surplus.
d. Compute the new producer surplus.
e. Would consumers or producers be more likely to have their advocates or lobbyists support price floors? Explain.

Work It Out

 interactive activity

16. Suppose the U.S. government places a price ceiling on the sale of gasoline at $2 per gallon, as shown in the accompanying figure.

   a. Would a shortage or surplus result? How large is it?
   b. Calculate the effects of this policy in terms of the changes in consumer surplus and producer surplus.
   c. How much deadweight loss is created?
   d. What would happen if the price ceiling were raised to $5 per gallon?

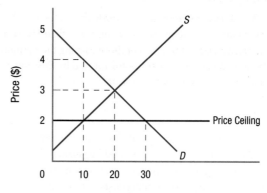

Quantity (in millions of gallons)

✔ Answers to Questions in Checkpoints

Checkpoint: Consumer and Producer Surplus:
Measuring Economic Efficiency 89

Cole's consumer surplus is ($50−$40)=$10, Jacqueline's is ($55−$40)=$15, Sienna's is ($60−$40)=$20, and Tessa's is ($65−$40)=$25. Total consumer surplus is $10+$15+$20+$25=$70. Alex's producer surplus is ($40−$20)=$20, Caroline's is ($40−$25)=$15, Kira's is ($40−$30)=$10, and Will's is ($40−$35)=$5. Total producer surplus is $20+$15+$10+$5=$50.

Checkpoint: Using Consumer and Producer Surplus:
The Gains From Trade 92

Although many people voluntarily become organ donors because of the goodwill they feel knowing that their actions can potentially save a life, still many others choose not to become organ donors because they do not see any monetary benefit from doing so. Compensating individuals for becoming organ donors, thereby raising the "price" of organs, would be a way to increase the quantity supplied of organs, allowing the shortage to dissipate until equilibrium is reached. In doing so, organ donors and recipients both benefit, resulting in gains from trade. However, moral objections to selling body parts have led to many laws preventing organ donors from being compensated. As a result, shortages continue to be a problem.

Checkpoint: Price Ceilings and Price Floors 97

Black Friday specials are typically deeply discounted in order to attract customers into the store, which is why such specials are prominently shown on the first page of sales circulars. Like a price ceiling that is set below the equilibrium price, the quantity demanded for the discounted good increases, while stores limit the number of units available for sale, creating a shortage. Some buyers will be fortunate to find units available to purchase, while subsequent shoppers will find that the product has sold out. Deadweight loss is generated because some customers who would have been willing to pay a little more are unable to purchase the good. However, unlike a price ceiling, stores strategically choose to advertise goods with many alternatives, such as different brands of televisions and laptops, so that when the discounted product sells out, customers may consider buying a nondiscounted product. Therefore, the pricing strategy leads to a strategic shortage that is designed to attract customers into the store to buy goods in addition to those that are advertised.

Checkpoint: Market Failure: When Markets Do Not Deliver a Socially Desirable Outcome 101

If the gas tax and subsidized public transportation encourage people to drive less and use more public transportation, those who continue to drive will likely experience less traffic congestion, which saves both time and gas. Moreover, there would be fewer cars competing for limited parking spaces. And because gas-powered cars generate significant carbon emissions, reducing the number of cars on the road can improve air quality. These are all external benefits that help to offset the higher monetary cost paid by drivers.

Introduction to Macroeconomics

*Understanding how the economy is measured and why
recessions periodically occur over time*

The decade from 2010 to 2020 was remarkable in many respects for the U.S. economy. Over 20 million jobs were created, the unemployment rate fell from around 10% to 4%, major stock market indexes tripled in value, and wages increased in nearly every industry. Yet in terms of the sentiment of the typical household, these benefits have not been shared equally. The decade of robust growth followed the Great Recession, which ended officially in 2009. But this economic downturn had ravished the economy so much that a large portion of the growth over this decade was simply recovering from the Great Recession.

Moreover, the economic growth over the past decade did not occur on its own. Government actions, including historically low interest rates, record government spending, and tax cuts, were used to stimulate the economy. And while the economy has prospered as a result, there are potential long-term costs with rising national debt; higher costs of essentials, such as health care, food, and energy; and growing income inequality.

The ability for a country to maintain economic growth depends on the ability of companies to sell products not only domestically but also to foreign consumers as part of international trade. Countries in today's global economy are highly interconnected. Therefore, recent economic slowdowns in China and Brazil, along with continued financial struggles facing many European nations in managing their unified currency (the euro) make it difficult for the U.S. economy to expand.

A significant challenge facing countries today is determining the best path to long-run prosperity. Over the course of the past century, two dominant schools of thought have frequently been debated: the classical view and the Keynesian view. Classical economists believe that rising debt is unsustainable and that it creates an undue burden on future generations that can prevent them from achieving their economic goals. These economists believe in paring the size of government and relying more on markets to dictate economic actions. In contrast, Keynesian economists believe that an active government role is needed to ensure that economic activity is promoted in areas where markets cannot do it alone. Keynesians believe that using government tools to manage economic downturns will promote growth and that debt incurred in the short run will eventually be reduced by an expanding economy.

Classical economics was the dominant form of thinking a century ago when macroeconomic policy was largely based on microeconomic analysis. That all changed during the Great Depression of the 1930s, when John Maynard Keynes explained the causes of the Great Depression and set forth a framework on which to develop policies to avoid future severe macroeconomic downturns. This led to the development of macroeconomics as a discipline. Today, the use of Keynesian policy is common, as evidenced by government actions taken to minimize the effects of past recessions.

BY THE Numbers

From the Great Recession to the Record Recovery and Expansion

The 2007–2009 recession was the most severe economic downturn to face the United States in over 70 years. Although this recession officially lasted only 18 months, it took about 60 months for the economy to return to the level of employment and growth seen prior to the recession. And since then, the economy has continued to grow, setting the record for the longest period of recovery and expansion since business cycles began to be recorded. This By the Numbers analyzes U.S. real GDP growth and the unemployment rate since 2005 to show how these critical measures change during a recession and in the subsequent recovery and expansion.

DATA:

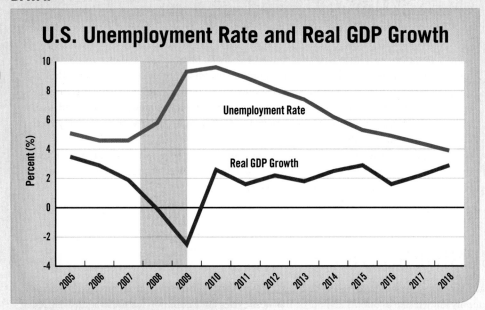

U.S. Unemployment Rate and Real GDP Growth

Unemployment Rate

Real GDP Growth

y-axis: Percent (%) — 10, 8, 6, 4, 2, 0, -2, -4

x-axis: 2005, 2006, 2007, 2008, 2009, 2010, 2011, 2012, 2013, 2014, 2015, 2016, 2017, 2018

Where Can I Find These Data?

Source: Bureau of Economic Analysis (U.S. Department of Commerce) and Bureau of Labor Statistics (U.S. Department of Labor)

Web sites: GDP Growth: https://www.bea.gov/tools/
Unemployment Rate: https://www.bls.gov/data

Details: Use the BEA's Interactive Data Tool to view national data for "GDP and personal income". Use the BLS's data tools to view historical data series for unemployment.

~ Assessing Your Data Literacy ~

1. In which years did the size of the economy contract (exhibit negative real GDP growth)?

2. Describe what happened to real GDP growth and the unemployment rate during the economic recession of 2007–2009.

3. Describe how real GDP growth and the unemployment rate changed during the period of recovery and expansion from 2010 to 2018.

$20,865,100,000,000

U.S. gross domestic product (GDP) in 2018

$84,835,460,000,000

Gross world product (sum of GDP from every country in the world) in 2018

WHY ARE THESE DATA IMPORTANT?

According to the discussion of business cycles in the text, recessions and recoveries are a normal part of any economy. But each stage of the business cycle has important effects on the lives of many people. GDP growth generally leads to rising wages but recessions lead to periods of temporary joblessness for millions of people.

Data *in the News*

"Bond Investors Prepare for Next U.S. Recession" by Robin Wigglesworth; *Financial Times*, July 25, 2018

Next summer the current US economic expansion will become the longest in history, but it will still pale next to the runs of some other major countries. What nurtures long bouts of growth, and could the US enjoy a similar spell?

Figure 1 • Markets and Institutions in the Macroeconomy

Labor, capital, and product markets, along with financial and government institutions, come together to influence macroeconomic outcomes, such as the unemployment rate.

Managing the economy is not an easy task. Changes in the macroeconomy occur every day, and many changes are beyond the control of government. Because the world has become more connected, recessions in one country have an effect on other countries. Competition for jobs intensifies with greater labor mobility through immigration and with more companies seeking to pay lower wages by moving production facilities overseas. Population growth means more jobs are needed for a country just to remain at its same employment level. And pressure to earn profits in a competitive global economy force businesses to find more efficient means of production, including the use of automation, leading to some job loss as workers are replaced by machines.

These factors help to explain why economies fluctuate up and down over time and how economists have developed tools to manage the severity of these fluctuations. Macroeconomics describes how individuals, businesses, financial institutions, and government institutions interact to achieve the goals of job growth, low inflation, and economic growth. It is not just the conditions of one industry or group of workers that influence macroeconomic outcomes but rather the conditions of all. Figure 1 illustrates how different markets and institutions come together to influence macroeconomic outcomes, such as the unemployment rate and economic growth.

This chapter deals with how the macroeconomy is analyzed and measured, and how these measures relate to our standard of living. The foundation established in this chapter will apply to topics covered throughout the course.

BUSINESS CYCLES

business cycles Alternating increases and decreases in economic activity that include four phases: peak, recession, trough, and recovery (or expansion).

Macroeconomics is concerned with **business cycles,** those short-run fluctuations in the macroeconomy known also as booms and busts. Business cycles are a common feature of industrialized economies and are important to study because they emphasize the idea that markets are intertwined with one another. What happens in one market is not usually independent from other markets.

Defining Business Cycles

Economies fluctuate up and down as part of the normal pattern of market activity. During periods of strong economic growth, rising demand pushes prices higher as consumers buy more goods and services and businesses demand more inputs. Eventually, rising prices slow an economy, which can lead to lower business expectations, reduced consumer confidence, and ultimately higher unemployment until prices adjust again. This is all part of the regularly occurring business cycle of the macroeconomy.

Figure 2 shows the four phases of the business cycle. These phases include the peak, followed by a recession (often referred to as a downturn or contraction), leading to the trough, finally followed by a recovery and expansion to another peak.

····· Figure 2 • Typical Business Cycle ····················

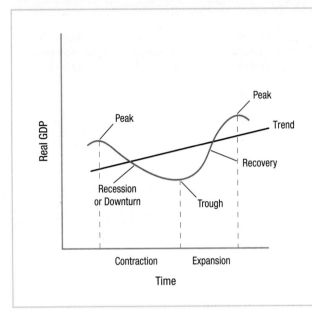

The four phases of the business cycle are the peak, followed by a recession (often called a downturn or contraction), leading to the trough, followed by a recovery and expansion leading to another peak. The various phases of the business cycle vary widely in duration and intensity, but they fluctuate around a long-term trend of economic growth.

A peak in the business cycle usually means that the economy is operating at its capacity. Peaks are followed by downturns or recessions. This change can happen simply because the economy runs out of steam and business investment begins to decline, causing economic growth to slow or turn negative.

Once a recession is under way, businesses react by curtailing hiring and perhaps even laying off workers, thus adding to the recession's depth. Eventually a trough is reached, and economic activity begins to pick up as businesses and consumers become more optimistic about the economy. Often, the federal government or the Federal Reserve Bank institutes fiscal or monetary policies to help reverse the recession. We will look at government actions in future chapters.

Figure 2 suggests that business cycles are fairly regular, but in fact the various phases of the cycle can vary dramatically in duration and intensity. As Table 1 shows, the recessions of the last 65 years have lasted anywhere from 6 months to 18 months. Expansions or recoveries have varied even more, lasting from 1 year to as many as 10 years. Some countries have experienced even longer expansions (Australia had a 28-year expansion). Moreover, some recessions have been truly intense, bringing about major declines in income, while others have been little more than potholes in the road, causing no declines in real income.

A good metaphor for the wide variation in business cycles is a roller coaster. Some roller coasters rise higher than others, fall faster than others, or climb slower than others. Some roller coasters have one large dip followed by a series of smaller ups and downs, while others may have a large dip followed by another large dip. This is true with business cycles—some business cycles are higher, faster, or longer than others, but all have the same four phases described earlier. An important difference between a business cycle and a roller coaster, however, is that a roller coaster typically ends at the same level as it starts, while business cycles tend to have an upward long-run trend in most countries, indicating a growing economy over time.

Unemployment has shown a similar variability: The more severe the recession, the higher the unemployment rate goes. In the recessions of 1990–1991 and 2001, the economy as a whole showed remarkable resiliency, but the recoveries were termed *jobless recoveries* because the economic growth following the recessions did not coincide with strong levels of job growth. In fact, sometimes an economy's recovery falls short and enters another recession before it fully recovers;

TABLE 1	SELECTED DATA FOR U.S. BUSINESS CYCLES SINCE 1953					
Years	Peak	Trough	Recession Length (months)	Expansion Length (months)	Percentage Change in Real GDP	Maximum Unemployment Rate (%)
1953–1954	July 1953	May 1954	10	39	−2.2	5.9
1957–1958	Aug. 1957	April 1958	8	24	−3.6	7.4
1960–1961	April 1960	Feb. 1961	10	106	−0.6	7.1
1969–1970	Dec. 1969	Nov. 1970	11	36	+0.2	6.1
1973–1975	Nov. 1973	March 1975	16	58	−1.8	9.0
1980	Jan. 1980	July 1980	6	12	−2.3	7.8
1981–1982	July 1981	Nov. 1982	16	92	−2.2	10.8
1990–1991	July 1990	March 1991	8	120	−1.0	6.9
2001	March 2001	Nov. 2001	8	73	+0.5	5.8
2007–2009	Dec. 2007	June 2009	18	—	−4.1	10.0

Business cycles resemble roller coasters—some are higher, faster, or longer than others, but all are similar in terms of the up-and-down nature of the ride.

double-dip recession A recession that begins after only a short period of economic recovery from the previous recession.

this is referred to as a **double-dip recession.** The last double-dip recession occurred in the early 1980s. However, the slow recovery following the 2007–2009 recession caused many economists to worry that another double-dip recession would occur. Fortunately, it did not.

Dating Business Cycles

Business cycles are officially dated by the National Bureau of Economic Research (NBER), a non-profit research organization founded in 1920. The NBER assigns a committee of economists the task of dating "turning points"—times at which the economy switches from peak to downturn or from trough to recovery. The committee looks for clusters of aggregate data pointing either up or down. Committee members date turning points when they reach a consensus that the economy has switched directions.

The committee's work has been met with some criticism because the decisions rest on the consensus of six eminent economists, who often bring different methodologies to the table. The committee's deliberations, moreover, are not public; the committee announces only its final decision. Finally, the NBER dates peaks and troughs only after the fact: Their decisions appear several months after the turning points have been reached. By waiting, the panel can use updated or revised data to avoid premature judgments. But some argue that the long lag renders the NBER's decisions less useful to policymakers.

Nonetheless, the work of the NBER in dating the turning points is important for investors and businesses alike, as they help form expectations of how the economy might perform based on the phase of the business cycle it has reached. Businesses are more likely to invest during a time of expansion, and they don't want to be investing in greater production capacity at a time of recession when sales might fall.

Alternative Measures of the Business Cycle

Because the NBER focuses on historical data to date phases of the business cycle *after* they occur, economists have developed tools to analyze trends in an effort to predict phases of the business cycle *before* they occur. The following are three examples of methods used to predict business cycle movements.

Figure 3 • The Chicago Fed National Activity Index

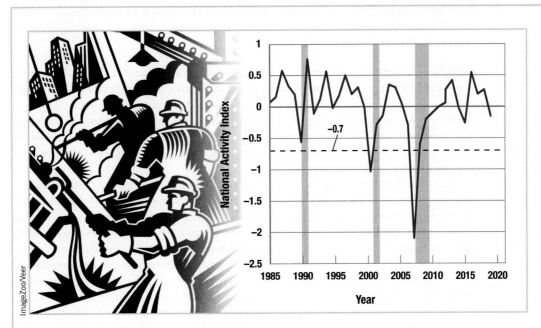

The Chicago Fed National Activity Index is a weighted average of 85 indicators of economic activity in the economy. When the index moves below −0.70 (dashed line), the economy is probably moving into a recession (indicated by the shaded bars). This index appears to track the official NBER business cycle turning points.

Chicago Fed National Activity Index The Chicago Fed National Activity Index is a weighted average of 85 indicators of national economic activity. These indicators are drawn from a huge swath of economic activity including production, income, employment, unemployment, hours worked, personal consumption, housing, sales, orders, and inventories.

Figure 3 shows the index since 1985. When the index has a zero value, the economy is growing at its historical trend rate of growth. Negative values mean that the economy is growing slower and positive rates imply it's growing faster than its long-term trend. When the index moves below −0.70 following a period of expansion, this suggests a high likelihood that the economy has moved into a recession (indicated by the shaded bars). The index has done a remarkable job in pinpointing the signs of recessions in a reasonably current time frame.

Conference Board Leading Economic Index The Leading Economic Index (or LEI) established by The Conference Board, an independent business and research association, is another index that economists look to when predicting movements in the business cycle. The LEI uses ten important leading indicators to produce a weighted index. Because each indicator is a predictor of how the economy should perform in the near future, any change in the LEI today is supposed to reflect how the economy will change tomorrow.

Indicators in the LEI
Average weekly hours, manufacturing
Average weekly initial claims for unemployment insurance
Manufacturers' new orders, consumer goods and materials
Index of new orders from consumers
Manufacturers' new orders, nondefense capital goods excluding aircraft orders
Building permits, new private housing units
Stock prices, 500 common stocks
Index of credit conditions in the economy
Interest rate spread, 10-year Treasury bonds less federal funds
Average consumer expectations for business conditions

The LEI predicts a recession whenever the index falls for three months in a row (compared to the same month the previous year). In fact, it has successfully predicted the last seven recessions since 1969, although critics point to the fact that it has also provided some false warnings of recessions (a funny adage shared among economists is that forecasters have predicted ten of the last seven recessions).

Yield Curve Perhaps the simplest, and surprisingly accurate, predictor of changes in the business cycle is the yield curve. A **yield curve** shows the interest rates for bonds (shown on the vertical axis) with different maturity rates (shown on the horizontal axis). A yield curve has a positive slope in most cases because investors typically demand a higher interest rate the longer their money is tied up. Related to the yield curve is the Treasury spread, which represents the difference in interest rates between a long-term bond and a short-term bond, with a positive value indicating a normal yield curve.

One approach economists have used to predict recessions is to calculate the Treasury spread, shown in Figure 4 as the interest of a long-term 10-year bond less the interest rate on a short-term three-month bill. Whenever this value turns negative, which means interest rates on short-term bills exceed those on long-term bonds, an *inverted yield curve* results, and a recession is likely to occur. Why? When investors believe an economic slowdown may occur, they buy long-term bonds to lock in interest rates, pushing interest rates on long-term bonds lower. This has been true for seven of the last eight recessions. However, some economists remain skeptical, pointing to several false warnings of the yield curve that did not result in actual recessions.

Each of the three indices is one of many methods economists use to predict the movements of the business cycle. Although a perfect predictor of booms and busts is not possible, many people follow these indices because of the importance of the business cycle in the macroeconomy.

The duration and intensity of business cycles are measured using data collected by the Bureau of Economic Analysis and the U.S. Department of Labor. These data for aggregate income and output come from the national income and product accounts. We turn in a moment to see how these data are collected and analyzed and consider how well they measure our standard of living. Keep in mind that these data are the key ingredients economists use to determine the state of the macroeconomy.

yield curve Shows the relationship between the interest rate earned on a bond (measured on the vertical axis) and the length of time until the bond's maturity date (shown on the horizontal axis).

····· Figure 4 • Treasury Spread ··

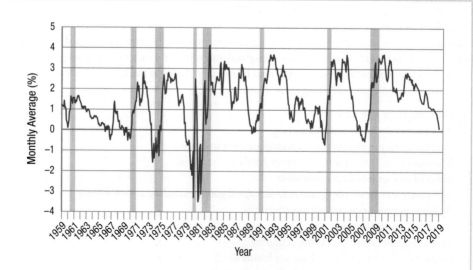

The Treasury spread shown is calculated as the 10-year bond rate minus 3-month bill rate (monthly average). Shaded bars indicate recessions. In all but one recession since 1960, the difference in rates turned negative prior to the recession.

Data from New York Federal Reserve: https://www.newyorkfed.org/research /capital_markets/ycfaq.html.

ISSUE

Will the Next Recession *Feel* Like a Recession?

According to the National Bureau of Economic Research (NBER), the last U.S. recession officially ended in June 2009. Since then, the U.S. economy has embarked on a record-long period of recovery and expansion that has produced significant growth in GDP and a sharp reduction in the unemployment rate. The economy is in such robust shape that when the next recession begins, it may not actually feel like a recession. How could this be?

Part of the explanation is how economists date the business cycle. The NBER looks at "turning points" when the economy goes from a peak to a downturn or from a trough to a recovery. A recession officially begins when the economy is at its peak, which occurs when the economy is in its best (or near best) condition.

This means that for a portion of the recession, the economy will appear healthy in terms of employment and wages. But it's the trend that matters. At the start of a recession, life is still good for most people, but the trend is turning negative as companies begin to cut production and lay off workers as consumer confidence erodes.

Even when the economy is booming, the next recession may be around the corner.

Toward the end of the recession and into the start of the recovery is when most people feel the effects of the recession at its worst. The start of the recovery occurs right after the trough, when unemployment is usually high and wages are depressed. A comparison of key statistics at the start and end of the Great Recession tells the story: In December 2007, the unemployment rate was 5.0%, and GDP was $13.4 trillion. At the start of the recovery in June 2009, the unemployment rate was 9.5%, and GDP was $12.8 trillion.

What does this suggest about the prospects of the next recession? When the next recession begins, it may not actually feel like a recession because of how recessions and recoveries are dated based on turning points in the business cycle.

✅ CHECKPOINT

BUSINESS CYCLES

- Business cycles are alternating increases and decreases in economic activity.

- The four phases of the business cycle include the peak, recession (or contraction), trough, and recovery (or expansion).

- Business cycles vary in intensity, duration, and speed.

- Business cycles are dated by the National Bureau of Economic Research (NBER). Business cycles are usually dated some time after the trough and peak have been reached.

- Economists have developed different methods to predict movements in the business cycle, including the use of the Chicago Fed National Activity Index, the Conference Board Leading Economic Index, and the yield curve.

QUESTION: Do you think that the business cycle has a bigger impact on automobile and capital goods manufacturers or on grocery stores? Explain.

Answers to the Checkpoint questions can be found at the end of this chapter.

NATIONAL INCOME ACCOUNTING

The national income and product accounts (NIPA) let economists judge our nation's economic performance, compare U.S. income and output to that of other nations, and track the economy's condition over the course of the business cycle.

Before World War I, estimating the output of various sectors of the economy—and to some extent the output of the economy as a whole—was a task left to individual scholars. Government agencies tried to measure various sorts of economic activity, but little came of these efforts. When the Great Depression struck, the lack of reliable economic data made it difficult for the administration and Congress to design timely and appropriate policy responses. Much of the information that was available at the time was anecdotal: newspaper reports of plant shutdowns, stories of home and farm foreclosures, and observations of the rapid meltdown of the stock market.

In 1933 Congress directed the Department of Commerce (DOC) to develop estimates of "total national income for the United States for each of the calendar years 1929, 1930, and 1931, including estimates of the portions of national income originating from [different sectors] and estimates of the distribution of the national income in the form of wages, rents, royalties, dividends, profits and other types of payments." This directive was the beginning of the NIPA.

In 1934 a small group of economists working under the leadership of Simon Kuznets and in collaboration with the NBER produced a report for the Senate. The report defined many standard economic aggregates still in use today, including gross national product, gross domestic product, consumer spending, and investment spending. Kuznets was later awarded a Nobel Prize for his lifetime of work in this area.

Work continued on the NIPA through World War II, and by 1947 the basic components of the present-day income and product accounts were in place. Over the years, the DOC has modified, improved, and updated the data it collects. These data are released on a quarterly basis, with preliminary data being put out in the middle of the month following a given quarter. By the end of a given quarter, the DOC will have collected about two-thirds of the survey data it needs, allowing it to estimate the remaining data to generate preliminary figures.

The Core of the NIPA

The major components of the NIPA can be found in either of two ways: by adding up the income in the economy or by adding up spending. A simple circular flow diagram of the economy shows why either approach can be used to determine the level of economic activity.

NOBEL PRIZE
SIMON KUZNETS (1901–1985)

Simon Kuznets was awarded the Nobel Prize in Economics in 1971 for devising systematic approaches to the compilation and analysis of national economic data. Kuznets is credited with developing gross national product as a measurement of economic output.

Kuznets developed methods for calculating the size and changes in national income known as the national income and product accounts (NIPA). Caring little for abstract models, he sought to define concepts that could be observed empirically and measured statistically. Thanks to Kuznets, economists have had a large amount of data with which to test their economic theories.

Another important contribution by Kuznets is the hypothesis that as countries develop, income inequality initially rises but then falls as incomes continue to grow. The simple inverted U-shaped graph that represents this relationship became known as the Kuznets curve.

Figure 5 • A Simple Circular Flow Diagram

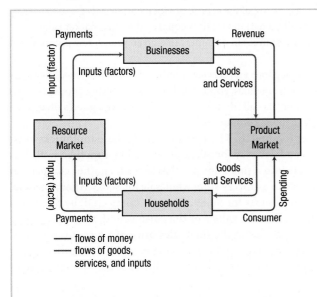

This circular flow diagram illustrates how one entity's spending becomes another entity's income. The blue arrows show the flow of real items. Businesses sell goods and services to households, and households sell inputs (such as one's labor) to businesses. The red arrows show the corresponding flow of money. Household spending becomes revenue to businesses, and factor payments by businesses become wages and earnings to households.

The Circular Flow Diagram Figure 5 illustrates a simple **circular flow diagram** that shows how businesses and households interact in the resource and product markets.

Let us first follow the blue arrows that point in a clockwise direction. Begin at the bottom of the diagram with households. Households supply labor (and other inputs or factors of production) to the resource market; that is, they become employees of businesses. Businesses use this labor (and other inputs) to produce goods and services that are supplied to the product market. Such products find their way back into households through consumer purchases. The blue arrows show the flow of real items: inputs, including labor, and goods and services.

The red arrows pointing counterclockwise represent the corresponding flows of money. Businesses pay for inputs (factors of production): land, labor, capital, and entrepreneurship. Factors are paid rents, wages, interest, and profits. These payments become income for the economy's households, which use these funds to purchase goods and services in the product market. This spending for goods and services becomes sales revenues for the business sector.

Spending and Income: Looking at GDP in Two Ways The circular flow diagram illustrates why economic aggregates in our economy can be determined in either of two ways. All spending by households that occurs in the product market becomes income to businesses, and all spending by businesses that occurs in the resource market becomes income to households.

As in most economic models, this circular flow diagram is a simplification of the real economy. But the main idea is that every dollar spent in an economy becomes a dollar of income to someone else. For example, suppose you spend $5 on a smoothie, and suppose this $5 goes to the following:

$1 to rent and equipment = income to landlord and equipment makers
$1 to fruits and juices = income to farmers
$1 to wages for store workers and managers = income to labor
$1 to taxes = income to government
$1 to profit = income to investors

Therefore, regardless of whether economic activity is measured by the $5 in spending by the consumer or the $5 in income generated to various parties, the resulting measurement is the same.

circular flow diagram
Illustrates how households and firms interact through product and resource markets and shows that economic aggregates can be determined by examining either spending flows or income flows to households.

Gross Domestic Product

gross domestic product (GDP) A measure of the economy's total output; it is the most widely reported value in the national income and product accounts (NIPA) and is equal to the total market value of all final goods and services produced by resources in a country in a given year.

Gross domestic product (GDP) is a measure of the economy's total output; it is the most widely reported value in the NIPA. Technically, a nation's GDP is equal to the total market value of all final goods and services produced by resources in a country in a given year. A few points about this definition need to be noted.

First, GDP reflects the *final* value of goods and services produced. Therefore, measurements of GDP do not include the value of intermediate goods used to produce other products. This distinction helps prevent what economists call "double counting" because a good's final value includes the intermediate values going into its production.

To illustrate, consider a box of toothpicks. The firm producing these toothpicks must first purchase a supply of cottonwood, let's say for $0.22 per unit. The firm then mills this wood into toothpicks, which it puts into a small box purchased from another company at $0.08 each. The completed box is sold to a grocery store wholesale for $0.65. After a markup, the grocery store sells the box of toothpicks for $0.89. The sale raises GDP by $0.89, *not* by $1.84 (0.22 + 0.08 + 0.65 + 0.89), because the values of the cottonwood, the box, and the grocery store's services are already included in the final sales price of a box of toothpicks. Thus, by including only final prices in GDP, double counting is avoided. Another way to think about this is that the final price comprises all of the value added from each stage of production.

A second point to note is that, as the term gross *domestic* product implies, GDP is a measure of the output produced by resources in a given country. For example, to determine U.S. GDP, it does not matter whether the producers are American citizens or foreign nationals as long as the production takes place within the country's borders. GDP does not include goods or services produced abroad, even if the producers are American citizens or companies.

In contrast to GDP is *gross national product* (GNP). GNP reflects the market value of all final goods and services produced domestically and abroad using resources supplied by U.S. citizens while excluding the value of goods and services produced in the United States by foreign-owned businesses. GNP was the DOC's standard measure of output until the early 1990s, when the GDP became the standard because it is a better measure of activity occurring within a country's borders. In an increasingly globalized world where foreign-owned businesses contribute significantly to our economy in terms of jobs and investment, GDP takes these contributions into account while excluding the value of goods produced by U.S. companies in other countries.

The difference between GDP and GNP is small in the United States. But there are countries where the difference is substantial. For example, Japan's GNP is greater than its GDP because many Japanese corporations (e.g., Sony, Toyota, and Panasonic) produce goods in other countries, while Ireland's GDP is greater than its GNP because many foreign corporations operate in Ireland due to its favorable tax laws.

Third, whenever possible, the NIPA uses market values, or the prices paid for products, to compute GDP. Therefore, even if a firm must sell its product at a loss, the product's final sales price is what figures into GDP, not the firm's production cost or the original retail price.

Fourth, the NIPA accounts focus on market-produced goods and services. The major exceptions to this approach include substituting payroll costs for the value of government services and estimating (imputing) the rental value of owner-occupied housing. This focus on market values has been criticized on the grounds that child care services, for instance, when provided by a nanny, are figured into GDP, while the values for these same services when performed by parents are not.

The Expenditures (Spending) Approach to Calculating GDP

Although GDP represents the value of all final goods produced in a country, there are alternative methods of calculating GDP by measuring either all spending or all income in an economy. With the expenditures approach, all spending on final goods and services is added together. The four major categories of spending are personal consumption expenditures, gross private domestic investment (GPDI), government spending, and net exports (exports minus imports).

Personal Consumption Expenditures **Personal consumption expenditures** are the purchases of goods and services by residents and businesses of the United States. These goods and services are divided into three main categories: durable goods, nondurable goods, and services. Durable goods are products that have an average useful life of at least three years. Automobiles, major appliances, books, and musical instruments are all examples of durable goods. Nondurable goods include all other tangible goods, such as canned soft drinks, frozen pizza, toothbrushes, and underwear (all of which should be thrown out before they are three years old). Services are commodities that cannot be stored and are consumed at the time and place of purchase, for example, legal, barber, and repair services. Table 2 gives a detailed account of U.S. personal consumption spending in 2018. Notice that personal consumption is 68% of GDP, by far the most important part of GDP, and services constitute the largest portion of personal consumption.

personal consumption expenditures Goods and services purchased by residents of the United States, whether individuals or businesses; they include durable goods, nondurable goods, and services.

Gross Private Domestic Investment The second major aggregate listed in Table 2 is **gross private domestic investment (GPDI),** which, at 18% of GDP, refers to *fixed investments,* or investments in such things as structures (residential and nonresidential), equipment, and software. It also includes changes in private inventories.

Residential housing represents about one-fifth of GPDI, and nonresidential structures make up most of the rest because inventory changes are small. Nonresidential structures include such diverse structures as hotels and motels, manufacturing plants, mine shafts, oil wells, and fast-food restaurants. Improvements to existing business structures and new construction are counted as fixed investments.

A "change in inventories" refers to a change in the physical volume of the inventory a private business owns, valued at the average prices over the period. If a business increases its inventories (whether intentionally or unintentionally due to weak sales volumes), this change is treated as an investment because the business is adding to the stock of products it has ready

gross private domestic investment (GPDI) Investments in such things as structures (residential and nonresidential), equipment, and software, along with changes in private inventories.

TABLE 2	THE EXPENDITURES APPROACH TO GDP (2018)	
Category	**Billions of $**	**% of GDP**
Personal Consumption Expenditures	**14,188.3**	**68.0**
Durable goods	1,476.0	7.1
Nondurable goods	2,910.5	13.9
Services	9,801.8	47.0
Gross Private Domestic Investment	**3,766.3**	**18.0**
Fixed nonresidential	2,864.8	13.7
Fixed residential	793.9	3.8
Change in inventories	107.5	0.5
Government Purchases of Goods and Services	**3,569.4**	**17.1**
Federal	1,341.9	6.4
State and local	2,227.5	10.7
Net Exports	**−658.9**	**−3.2**
Exports	2,540.6	12.2
Imports	3,199.5	15.4
Gross Domestic Product	**20,865.1**	**100.0**

Data from U.S. Department of Commerce, Bureau of Economic Analysis, www.bea.gov.

for sale. This type of investment is generally the least desirable because excess inventory does not increase productivity and could fall in value if the goods become outdated or if the market price falls.

Gross private domestic investment is a key factor driving economic growth and an important determinant of swings in the business cycle. Figure 6 tracks GPDI as a percentage of GDP since 1980. Recessions are represented by the vertical shaded columns. Notice that during each recession, GPDI turns down, and when the recession ends, GPDI turns up. Therefore, investment is an important factor shaping the turning points of the business cycle, especially at the troughs, and an important determinant of how severe a recession will be.

Government Purchases The government component of GDP measures the impact that **government spending** has on final demand in the economy. As Figure 7 illustrates, government spending is a relatively large component of GDP. It includes the wages and salaries of government employees (federal, state, and local) and the purchase of products and services from private businesses and the rest of the world. Government spending also includes the purchase of new structures and equipment.

Net Exports of Goods and Services **Net exports** of goods and services are equal to exports minus imports for the current period. Exports include all the items we sell overseas, such as agricultural products, movies, pharmaceutical drugs, and military equipment. Our imports are all those items we bring into the country, including vegetables from Mexico, clothing from India, and cars from South Korea. Most years our imports exceed our exports, and therefore net exports are a negative percentage of GDP.

It is important to note that imports do not actually lead to a smaller GDP. The reason that the value of imports is subtracted is because these same values are included in consumer purchases, investment, and government purchases. For example, when you buy a $100 pair of imported shoes, the $100 is included in consumption. But because the shoes are imported and do not count toward GDP, the $100 is subtracted so that the net effect on GDP is zero. Meanwhile, exports must be added because these are goods that are produced in the country (and count toward GDP) but do not appear in the other three categories because these goods are sold to consumers, businesses, and governments in *other* countries.

government spending
Includes the wages and salaries of government employees (federal, state, and local), the purchase of products and services from private businesses and the rest of the world, and government purchases of new structures and equipment.

net exports Exports minus imports for the current period. Exports include all goods and services we sell abroad, while imports include all goods and services we buy from other countries.

····· Figure 6 • Gross Private Domestic Investment (GPDI) as a Percent of GDP ·····

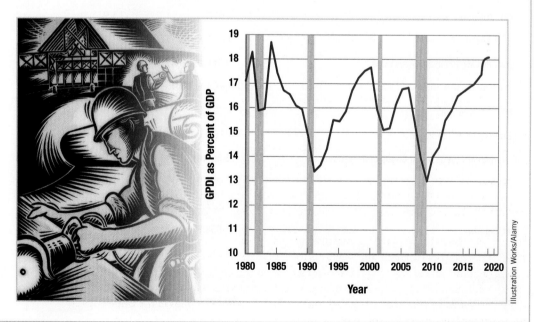

Gross private domestic investment is a key factor driving economic growth and an important determinant of swings in the business cycle. This graph tracks GPDI as a percentage of GDP since 1980. GPDI fell before the start of each recession (indicated by the shaded bars).

····· Figure 7 • Government Spending as a Percent of GDP ·····················

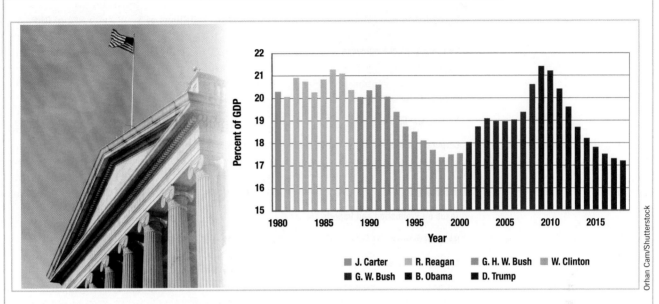

Government spending as a percent of GDP fell in the 1990s, rose in the 2000s until peaking in 2009, and has since fallen every year.

Summing Aggregate Expenditures The four categories just described are commonly abbreviated as C (consumption), I (investment), G (government spending), and $X - M$ (net exports; exports minus imports). Together, these four categories constitute GDP. We summarize this by the following equation:

$$GDP = C + I + G + (X - M)$$

Using the information from Table 2, we can calculate GDP for 2018 (in billions of dollars) as

$$20,865.1 = 14,188.3 + 3,766.3 + 3,569.4 + (-658.9)$$

The Income Approach to Calculating GDP

As we have already seen, spending that contributes to GDP provides an income for one of the economy's various inputs (factors) of production. And in theory, this is how this process works. In practice, however, the national income accounts need to be adjusted to fully account for GDP when we switch from the expenditures to the income approach. Let's work our way through the income side of the NIPA, which Table 3 summarizes.

Compensation of Employees Compensation to employees refers to payments for work done, including wages, salaries, and benefits. Benefits include the social insurance payments made by employers to various government programs, such as Social Security, Medicare, and workers' compensation and unemployment insurance. Some other benefits that count as labor income are employer-provided retirement contributions, profit-sharing plans, group health insurance, and in-kind benefits such as day care services. Employee compensation is 52.8% of GDP.

Proprietors' Income Proprietors' income represents the current income of all sole proprietorships, partnerships, and tax-exempt cooperatives in the country. It includes the imputed (estimated) rental income of owner-occupied farmhouses. Proprietors' income is adjusted by a capital consumption allowance to account for depreciating equipment (equipment that is used up while producing goods and services). Although there are many proprietorships in the United States, their combined income is 7.7% of GDP.

TABLE 3	THE INCOME APPROACH TO GDP (2018)	
Category	**Billions of $**	**% of GDP**
Compensation of Employees	**11,023.0**	**52.8**
Wages and salaries	8,979.2	43.0
Supplements to wages and salaries	2,043.8	9.8
Proprietors' Income	**1,616.7**	**7.7**
Corporate Profits	**2,310.8**	**11.1**
Rental Income	**768.6**	**3.7**
Net Interest	**569.5**	**2.7**
Taxes on Production and Imports	**1,523.6**	**7.3**
National Income	**17,812.2**	**85.4**
Adjustments to National Income	**3,052.9**	**14.6**
Consumption of fixed capital	3,340.6	16.0
Net income payments to rest of world	−254.9	−1.2
Statistical discrepancy	−32.8	−0.2
Gross Domestic Product	**$20,865.1**	**100.0**

Data from U.S. Department of Commerce, Bureau of Economic Analysis, www.bea.gov.

Corporate Profits Corporate profits are defined as the income that flows to corporations, adjusted for inventory valuation and capital consumption allowances. Most corporations are private enterprises, although this category also includes mutual financial institutions, Federal Reserve banks, and nonprofit institutions that mainly serve businesses. Despite the huge profit figures often reported in the news media, corporate profits are about 11% of GDP.

Rental Income Rental income, at 3.7% of GDP, is the income that flows to individuals engaged in renting real property (calculated as rent collected less depreciation, property taxes, maintenance and repairs, and mortgage interest). It does not include the income of real estate agents or brokers, but it does include the imputed rental value of homes occupied by their owners (again, less depreciation, taxes, repairs, and mortgage interest), along with royalties from patents, copyrights, and rights to natural resources.

Net Interest Net interest is the interest paid by businesses less the interest they receive, from the United States and abroad, and is 2.7% of GDP. Interest expense is the payment for the use of capital. Interest income includes payments from home mortgages, home improvement loans, and home equity loans.

Taxes on Production and Imports Indirect business taxes, such as sales and excise taxes along with tariffs on imported goods that are added to the prices of goods when sold, are backed out of payments to factors of production. This is because these taxes are not kept by businesses but instead are collected by the government and therefore are placed into a separate category representing revenues flowing to the government.

Summing Up Income Measures To this point, we have described different measures of income including wages, salaries, and benefits; profits (for sole proprietors, partnerships, and corporations); rental income; and interest. Summing each of these measures along with taxes on production and imports equals the **national income.** But be careful—national income is not the same as GDP. National income is income generated from the use of a country's resources, whether at home or abroad.

In order to complete the calculation of GDP using the income approach, three additional measures need to be included. First, an allowance for the depreciation (or consumption) of fixed capital is added. This is the amount of capital or infrastructure that a country needs to undertake in order to maintain its productivity. Second, income payments made to the rest of the world (when a foreign company produces goods in the United States) less income receipts from the rest of the world (when an American company produces goods in other countries) are added. Recall that GDP includes output produced within the country's borders, regardless of whether the resources are domestic or foreign owned. Finally, a small statistical discrepancy is included because like all macroeconomic measurements, it is difficult to be exactly precise, especially in a country as large as the United States. Once these factors are included, GDP is the same whether it is derived from spending or income.

We have now seen how the national income and product accounts determine the major macroeconomic aggregates. But what does the NIPA tell us about the economy? When GDP rises, are we better off as a nation? Do increases in GDP correlate with a rising standard of living? What impact does rising GDP have on the environment and the quality of life? We conclude this chapter with a brief look at some of these questions.

national income All income, including compensation of employees, profits (from sole proprietorships, partnerships, and corporations), rental income, net interest, and taxes on production and imports collected by the government.

✔ CHECKPOINT

NATIONAL INCOME ACCOUNTING

- The circular flow diagram shows how households and firms interact through product and resource markets.
- GDP can be computed as spending or as income.
- GDP is equal to the total market value of all final goods and services produced by labor and property within a country's borders in a given year.
- Personal consumption expenditures are the purchases of goods and services by individual and business residents of the United States.
- Gross private domestic investment (GPDI) refers to fixed investments such as structures, equipment, and software.
- GDP is equal to consumer expenditures, investment expenditures, government purchases, and net exports (exports minus imports). In equation form, $GDP = C + I + G + (X - M)$.
- GDP can also be computed by adding all of the payments to factors of production. This includes compensation to employees, proprietors' income, rental income, corporate profits, and net interest, along with some statistical adjustments.

QUESTIONS: Each summer, many of the campsites at America's most popular national parks sell out months in advance due to their limited supply, low prices, and prime locations. This had led entrepreneurial individuals to reserve these campsites well in advance and then resell the reservations at a higher price. Does the money earned by these campsite scalpers appear in GDP? Why or why not? Suppose the government attempts to minimize campsite scalping by doubling the price of campsites. Would this affect GDP? Explain.

Answers to the Checkpoint questions can be found at the end of this chapter.

GDP AND OUR STANDARD OF LIVING

GDP data provide us with one way of comparing the productivity of different nations. But it doesn't necessarily give us an accurate picture of the standard of living in each country. For example, China, India, and Brazil each have a GDP that places them among the top ten largest economies in the world. But clearly one would not describe the average citizen in these countries as wealthy. This section describes some of the factors that make it challenging to use GDP measures to compare the standard of living of average citizens across countries.

Different Ways of Comparing GDP Across Countries

The previous section described the two ways of measuring GDP using total expenditures and total income in an economy. But once the value of GDP is determined, does that mean it can be used to compare the size of the overall economy between two countries? To some extent, yes, in that countries with larger GDPs do produce more output based on the final value of goods and services *in that country* and *in a particular year.* Herein lies an important caveat regarding GDP measures: Nominal GDP statistics do not do a good job of factoring changes in the prices of goods and services over time or of taking into account differences in the cost of living between countries.

real GDP The total value of final goods and services produced in a country in a year measured using prices in a base year.

To address the first issue of changing prices, the U.S. Bureau of Economic Analysis reports GDP statistics in both nominal terms as well as in *real* terms. **Real GDP** statistics adjust each year's data to prices in a single base year (such as 2012). Therefore, real GDP does a better job of measuring actual growth in output rather than counting the rise in prices of goods and services over time. The next chapter on inflation discusses nominal and real values in greater detail.

To address the second issue of differences in the cost of living between countries, organizations that report GDP statistics across countries, such as the World Bank's World Development Indicators, also report GDP statistics based on *purchasing-power-parity*–adjusted measures, or GDP-PPP. For example, a haircut in India may cost $3, while that same haircut in Switzerland may cost $30. Since the service is the same, is it accurate to count a haircut ten times more in Switzerland than in India in terms of GDP? By using a GDP-PPP measure, countries in which prices of goods and services (especially nontraded items such as haircuts and restaurant meals) are lower than a representative base country will have their GDP statistics increased, while countries in which prices are higher than the base country will have their GDP statistics lowered.

The effect of using GDP-PPP can be substantial. Although the United States remains the world's largest economy in terms of nominal GDP, it falls to second place behind China when GDP-PPP is used. The reason is because the cost of living in China (on average) is still lower than the cost of living in the United States. But despite this remarkable achievement by China in terms of GDP-PPP, the average Chinese citizen is much less well off than the average American. This is because aggregate GDP measures do not take into account population.

Population and GDP per Capita

GDP per capita A country's GDP divided by its population. GDP per capita provides a useful measure of a country's relative standard of living.

How can GDP measures better reflect a country's population? The most common approach is to divide GDP by a country's population, resulting in a statistic known as **GDP per capita.** GDP per capita is a useful measure of the relative standard of living of citizens in different countries. However, by simply dividing GDP by population, GDP per capita does not take into account the differences in wealth between the rich and poor within a country and therefore might not fully reflect the standard of living of the typical citizen. For example, U.S. GDP per capita is about $63,000, but certainly the typical American family of four does not earn $252,000 a year. Due to the significant variation in income distribution, with the richest 20% earning over 50% of income, this statistic is not representative. Yet, GDP per capita data are fairly easy to measure and thus are a useful measure of relative wealth between countries.

An alternative measure of the standard of living is median household income. Being the median household means that half of all households make less and the other half make more. Using this statistic reduces the effect of outliers (i.e., the very destitute or the superrich) skewing the averages. The U.S. median household income in 2018 was about $60,000, an amount that is closer to what middle-income households make.

Environmental Quality and Other Quality-of-Life Measures

Although GDP measures provide a valuable indicator of a country's overall well-being, they do not account for many nonmonetary factors that affect the standard of living of its citizens. These include environmental quality and other quality-of-life measures.

People around the globe have become increasingly concerned with the impact economic activity has on the natural world. These days, it is difficult to watch a nightly newscast without seeing a report about some ecological disaster or looming environmental problem. U.S. consumers, businesses, and the government spend hundreds of billions of dollars annually to protect the environment at home and abroad. Surprisingly, however, our national income and production statistics do little to account for the environmental benefits or harmful impacts of economic activity.

But from a consumer's perspective, a cleaner environment also provides value. The ability to hike in parks, to suntan on clean beaches, and to swim in lakes and rivers all depend on a level of environmental quality that does not show up in our national accounts.

Besides environmental quality, other quality-of-life measures include average life expectancy, overall health, personal safety, relationships with other people, community activities, and many other nonmonetary factors. These factors improve the overall well-being and happiness of a country's citizens despite not being counted in its GDP. The following Around the World feature focuses on Costa Rica, which, despite having a relatively low GDP, is a very livable country with many happy people.

Roberto Candia/AP Image

Santiago, Chile, is one of the richest cities in Latin America but also one of the most polluted. Should the negative effects of pollution be reflected in Chile's GDP?

AROUND THE WORLD

Costa Rica: *Pura Vida* and Happiness Without a High GDP

What does GDP fail to measure in terms of how well Costa Ricans live?

When one thinks of countries in which citizens live well, rich countries often come to mind, such as Luxembourg, Denmark, and Switzerland. These countries have a high GDP per capita, allowing many of their people to live comfortable and consequently *happy* lives. This contrasts with countries with low GDP per capita, such as Sudan, Bangladesh, or Chad, where many people lack basic necessities and where much suffering takes place.

But does a country need to be materially rich in order to be happy? One country in Central America whose name literally translates to "rich coast" doesn't think so.

Costa Rica's GDP per capita is about $12,000 a year, or one-fifth that of the United States. However, according to the

World Happiness Report by the Sustainable Development Solutions Network, in 2018 Costa Rica ranked 12th in terms of happiness, higher than the United States. What factors allow Costa Ricans to live happy lives despite having modest incomes? First, life expectancy in Costa Rica is slightly higher than in the United States. Good, affordable health care and guaranteed government pension payments make retiring in Costa Rica pleasant. Second, Costa Rica's emphasis on ecotourism has helped preserve its environment and biodiversity. And third, without an army

per its constitution, Costa Rica is able to devote funds otherwise spent on military uses to provide better education to its citizens.

It's no wonder why many companies, including those in the United States, choose to operate production facilities in Costa Rica. With a literacy rate near 100% and a healthy, long-living populace, Costa Rica offers a productive and inexpensive labor force, with manufacturing and service wages averaging $2 to $3 per hour.

Still, low wages means that many families in Costa Rica struggle with daily finances and lack the ability to afford luxuries that richer countries take for granted. But Costa Ricans, in addition to their uplifting country name, also have an uplifting national slogan, "Pura Vida," a phrase used in ordinary everyday conversations to express optimism about life. As long as people are happy, they live productive lives, which bodes well for the future of the country.

GO ONLINE TO PRACTICE THE ECONOMIC CONCEPTS IN THIS STORY

Nonmarket Activities and the Informal Economy

In addition to addressing such concerns as environmental impacts and the value of nonmarket natural resources, the DOC panel's recommendations highlight some of the broader shortcomings of the NIPA. For example, the national accounts ignore nonmarket transactions, investments in human capital, and the use of people's time.

Nonmarket transactions are an important part of our everyday lives. If a maid cleans your apartment, GDP rises, but if you did the same job yourself, GDP is unaffected. The same is true for babysitting, lawn care, and car maintenance. There is one exception—NIPA already imputes (estimates) the rental value, less expenses, of owner-occupied homes and adds this to GDP.

Many people believe that the NIPA should be an index of well-being found within our economy. In that case, it would ideally need to take into account the implications of economic activity the DOC panel noted and more, perhaps including data on life expectancy; business spending on research and development; the stock of human capital, including education and health; greenhouse gas emissions; income distribution; poverty rates; and unemployment rates.

informal economy Includes all transactions that are conducted but are not licensed. This income is not reported to the government so no taxes are collected.

The **informal economy** (the underground or black market) is a large unmeasured component of our economy. The informal economy can be as simple as the money earned from a garage sale or from items sold on eBay that are not reported to the IRS. It also includes transactions dealing with illegal goods and services, such as drugs, prostitution, or unlicensed gambling. Finally, the informal economy includes the income earned by undocumented residents—those working on farms, factories, or restaurants for cash or workers hired for housekeeping or babysitting services who are easily paid "under the table." The size of the informal economy in the United States is estimated at around 10% of GDP. This is relatively small compared to many developing countries that can have an informal economy valued at as much as 50% of their GDP.

The effects of the informal economy can be positive and negative. On the upside, people working in the informal economy are generating and spending income, contributing to national economic activity. Countries with large informal markets have total output that is significantly larger than what is officially reported in their GDP statistics. On the downside, those working in the informal economy do not pay much if any taxes, placing a greater tax burden on the rest of society. Also, the informal economy is less regulated, which increases the probability of corruption and crime.

Although the NIPA has served us well, making adjustments to account for various environmental and other nonmarket considerations might provide us with an even better picture of the health of our economy. But we must keep in mind that an aggregate measure of the economy cannot be all things to all people. As we add complexity to an already complex undertaking, the NIPA may lose some effectiveness as a measure of economic activity, as pointed out earlier in the discussion of environmental quality. This is a difficult balancing act facing policymakers.

The NIPA allows us to track business cycles, compare the domestic economy with that of other nations, and take a crude measure of our standard of living. In the next chapter, we will see how two other important policy variables, unemployment and inflation, are measured.

The next several chapters will focus on developing explanations of short-term movements in the business cycle and long-term economic growth (the trend line in Figure 2). If we can understand why upturns and downturns occur, we may be able to devise policies that reduce the severity of business cycle swings while promoting economic growth. These investigations and policy objectives form the essence of modern macroeconomic analysis.

The informal market ranges from tutoring that students do in their spare time for cash to the multibillion dollar online gambling industry.

✔ CHECKPOINT

GDP AND OUR STANDARD OF LIVING

- Nominal GDP uses current year prices, while real GDP measures output using prices from a base year. GDP-PPP takes into account the cost of living in a country.

- GDP per capita divides GDP by population, providing a useful measure of a country's relative standard of living.

- GDP does not measure certain aspects of qualify of life, including environmental quality, community safety, and life expectancy.

- GDP does not include nonmarket activities or the informal economy.

- Despite the shortcomings of the GDP measure, GDP provides a simple and consistent way of measuring the overall economic activity in an economy.

QUESTION: The small Himalayan country of Bhutan has a GDP per capita of around $3,000 per year, about 1/20th that of the United States. But the constitution of Bhutan focuses less on GDP and instead has developed an alternative measure of well-being called the Gross National Happiness (GNH) index. Search online for details about the GNH index. What are some components in Bhutan's GNH index that do not appear in official measures of GDP?

Answers to the Checkpoint questions can be found at the end of this chapter.

CHAPTER SUMMARY

SECTION 1 BUSINESS CYCLES

5.1 **Business cycles** are the alternating increases and decreases in economic activity typical of market economies.

Business cycles can vary in duration and intensity, just like a roller coaster. These fluctuations take place around a long-run growth trend.

Business cycles are officially dated by the National Bureau of Economic Research, which assigns a committee of economists to determine "turning points" when the economy switches from peak to recession or from trough to recovery. They do this using past data, which means announcements take place after the turning points occur.

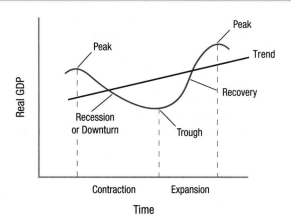

Four Phases of the Business Cycle

- **Peak:** The economy is operating at its capacity.
- **Recession:** Occurs when the economy runs out of steam and business investment falls.
- **Trough:** The lowest point in a business cycle.
- **Recovery:** Economic activity picks up and the economy grows.

5.2 **Alternative Measures of Business Cycles**

- Chicago Fed National Activity Index
- Conference Board Leading Economic Index
- Yield curve

SECTION 2 NATIONAL INCOME ACCOUNTING

5.3 The **national income and product accounts (NIPA)** allow economists to judge our nation's economic performance, compare income and output to that of other nations, and track the economy's condition over the course of the business cycle.

Gross domestic product (GDP) is the total market value of all final goods and services produced in a year within a country's borders, regardless of a firm's nationality. *Gross national product* (GNP) measures goods produced by a country's citizens and firms, regardless of where they are produced.

Caterpillar Tractor
U.S. firm; made in USA
Part of U.S. GDP and GNP

Toyota Camry
Japanese firm; made in USA
Part of U.S. GDP, not GNP

Brooks Running Shoes
U.S. firm; made in China
Part of U.S. GNP, not GDP

5.4 **The circular flow diagram** shows how businesses and households interact through the resource and product markets. It shows spending as well as income.

The major components of the NIPA can be constructed in either of two ways: by summing the spending of the economy or by summing income. Likewise, GDP can be measured by adding together either spending or income.

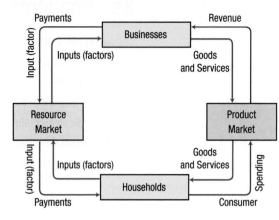

5.5 **Calculating GDP Using Expenditures (% of 2018 U.S. GDP)**

Personal Consumption Expenditures (*C*)	68%	Government Purchases (*G*)	17%
Gross Private Domestic Investment (*I*)	18%	Net Exports (*X – M*)	–3%

5.6 **Calculating GDP Using Income (% of 2018 U.S. GDP)**

Compensation of Employees	53%	Rental Income	4%
Proprietors' Income	8%	Net Interest	3%
Corporate Profits	11%	Other/Adjustments	21%

SECTION 3 GDP AND OUR STANDARD OF LIVING

5.7 **GDP per capita** is measured as GDP divided by the population. It provides a rough measure of a country's standard of living relative to other countries. However, it does not reflect differences in income within a country.

Measures of GDP

- **Nominal GDP:** GDP measured in current year prices
- **Real GDP:** GDP measured using prices from a base year
- **GDP-PPP:** GDP adjusted for cost of living relative to a base country

Countries are placing greater emphasis on protecting the environment. The economic benefits from a clean environment, however, are mostly unmeasured in GDP statistics. This is changing as new measures are introduced to take environmental quality and degradation into account.

Liechtenstein: small GDP but many rich citizens.

India: large GDP but many poor citizens.

5.8 The **informal economy** includes all market transactions that are not officially reported and hence are not included in GDP measures; it creates both positive and negative effects:

- **Positive:** Transactions in an informal economy create jobs and contribute to overall economic activity.
- **Negative:** Taxes are rarely paid on income in the informal economy, putting a greater tax burden on others. Also, the informal economy is less regulated, which can lead to unsafe products or risky job conditions.

Key Concepts

business cycles, p. 112

double-dip recession, p. 114

yield curve, p. 116

circular flow diagram, p. 119

gross domestic product (GDP), p. 120

personal consumption expenditures, p. 121

gross private domestic investment (GPDI), p. 121

government spending, p. 122

net exports, p. 122

national income, p. 125

real GDP, p. 126

GDP per capita, p. 126

informal economy, p. 128

Questions and Problems

Check Your Understanding

1. How are business cycles defined? Describe the four phases of business cycles.

2. Explain the key problem with the way the NBER dates recessions and recoveries?

3. Describe the circular flow diagram. Why must all income equal spending in the economy?

4. Why does GDP accounting include only the final value of goods and services produced? What would be the problem if intermediate products were included?

5. Explain why GDP can be computed using either the expenditures or income approach.

6. What does GDP per capita measure? Why is it not a precise measure of a typical person's standard of living in a country?

Apply the Concepts

7. Explain how it is possible for an economy in the recovery phase of the business cycle to have a lower GDP and a higher unemployment rate than when it was in the recession phase of the business cycle.

8. As a percentage of GDP, government spending tends to increase during recessions and decrease during times of economic expansion. Explain why government spending tends to change depending on the phase of the business cycle and how that affects spending as a percentage of GDP.

9. Critics of the way GDP is measured argue that it fails to fully account for "intangibles" in knowledge-based goods. For example, the value of books are counted in the year they were produced, but when those books are lent out in a library or resold in the used book market, it does not add to GDP despite the benefits and knowledge that the books provide to readers. What might be some problems associated with trying to include intangibles in GDP?

10. GDP and GNP are two different measures of the overall value of production in an economy. Suppose that a country's GDP is much greater than its GNP. What does that mean in terms of investment in and out of the country?

11. Among the major spending categories that make up GDP, why is gross private domestic investment (GPDI) much more volatile than personal consumption expenditures over the business cycle? In your response, provide two examples of an investment purchase that may be put on hold during a recession that may explain this volatility.

12. Suppose that a new method of calculating GDP allows for reductions in GDP as a result of the severity of environmental degradation in a country. If this method is used, which of the following countries might experience the greatest adjustment to their GDP calculation: India, Germany, or Iceland?

In the News

13. For much of the last 20 years, China's GDP has grown around 10% per year but in recent years has fallen to around 6% per year, which is still much higher than the average U.S. growth rate in recent years of about 2% per year. Why would a slowdown in China's GDP growth be a significant concern to the U.S. macroeconomy? If prices of goods and services fall in China due to slower growth, does this help or hurt U.S. GDP? Explain.

14. According to the CIA's *World Factbook*, in 2018 the tiny country of Equatorial Guinea had the highest GDP per capita in Africa (over $30,000 per year), even higher than more developed countries, such as Morocco, Egypt, or South Africa. But despite the significant overall income from the sale of its natural resources, Equatorial Guinea has extreme poverty, with half of the population lacking clean drinking water and one of the highest infant mortality rates in the world. How can a country that looks so good on paper (in terms of GDP per capita) be one of the least desirable places to live on the planet for the average citizen?

Solving Problems

15. The following table lists gross domestic product (*GDP*), consumption (*C*), gross private domestic investment (*I*), government spending (*G*), and net exports (*X − M*). Compute each as a percent of GDP for the six years presented.

Year	GDP	C	I	G	X − M	C (%)	I (%)	G (%)	X − M(%)
1965	719.1	443.8	118.2	151.5	5.6				
1975	1,638.3	1,034.4	230.2	357.7	16.0				
1985	4,220.3	2,720.3	736.2	879.0	115.2				
1995	7,397.7	4,975.8	1,144.0	1,369.2	−91.4				
2005	12,455.8	8,742.4	2,057.4	2,372.8	−716.7				
2015	18,128.2	12,429.0	3,019.2	3,206.5	−526.5				

a. Which category (or categories) has increased as a percent of GDP from 1965 to 2015? Which category (or categories) has decreased? And which category (or categories) has not changed much from 1965 to 2015?
b. Which category has been the most volatile in terms of changes in the percent of GDP?
c. Ignoring net exports, which component has grown the fastest as a percent of GDP since 1965?

Work It Out

 interactive activity

16. Use the following list of GDP components and data (given in millions of $U.S.) to answer the following questions.

Corporate profits	1,300 _____	Consumption of services	4,300 _____
Gross private domestic investment	2,800 _____	Net interest	500 _____
Consumption of nondurable goods	3,100 _____	Compensation of employees	8,000 _____
Exports	1,400 _____	Imports	1,900 _____
Proprietors' income	1,000 _____	Rental income	400 _____
Taxes on production and imports	700 _____	Government spending	2,100 _____
Net income payments to rest of world	200 _____	Consumption of durable goods	1,300 _____
		Consumption of fixed capital	1,200 _____

a. Indicate whether each component is part of the expenditures approach to calculating GDP (put an "E" next to the component) or the income approach to calculating GDP (put an "I" next to the component).
b. Compute the GDP using both expenditures and income approaches. What factor explains the difference between these measures?
c. Calculate the value of national income. Which category (categories) is (are) not included in national income, but are included in the calculation of GDP using the income approach?

 # Answers to Questions in Checkpoints

Checkpoint: Business Cycles 117

Big-ticket (high-priced, high-margin) items such as automobiles are affected by a recession more than grocery stores, where the margins are smaller and prices are lower. Also, people need to eat and can put off purchasing a new car. When the economy turns downward, investment falls; therefore, the capital goods industry is one of the first to feel the pinch.

Checkpoint: National Income Accounting 125

The money earned by the scalpers is not counted in GDP because goods that are resold (such as used goods) are not counted twice. Moreover, the premium that scalpers earn are not likely to be reported on their tax returns and thus are considered part of the informal economy.

If the government doubles the price of campsites and they continue to sell out, then GDP would increase because money paid to the national parks is part of consumption spending in GDP.

Checkpoint: GDP and Our Standard of Living 129

Bhutan's Gross National Happiness (GNH) index includes a number of components that affect one's well-being and standard of living but do not count toward official GDP measures. These include living standards, education, health, environment, community vitality, time-use, psychological well-being, good governance, and cultural resilience and promotion. Some of these components, such as health and education, may contribute to GDP based on the amount of actual spending that goes into these objectives (but in the GNH index, these components are measured not by spending but rather by perceived health and educational outcomes).

GAS 13 $\frac{8}{10}$

TAX 4 ¢

TOTAL 17 $\frac{8}{10}$

17 8/10
Including Tax
GALLONS		COST
1	-	.18
2	-	.36
3	-	.53
4	-	.71
5	-	.89
6	-	1.07
7	-	1.25
8	-	1.42
9	-	1.60
10	-	1.78
11	-	1.96
12	-	2.14
13	-	2.31
14	-	2.49
15	-	2.67

6

Measuring Inflation and Unemployment

Understanding the effects of rising prices and unemployment on the ability of people to save and prepare for the future

Learning Objectives

Sixty years ago, a single dollar bought a lot. A gallon of gasoline cost less than 30 cents, a movie theater ticket cost about 75 cents, and a meal at a relatively new restaurant chain called McDonald's cost about 50 cents.

Today, none of these items can be purchased for a dollar. The general rise in prices in the economy is referred to as inflation. Inflation has fluctuated each year, ranging from less than 5% in the 1960s, to nearly 15% in 1980, to less than 2% in recent years. Inflation reduces the ability of consumers to purchase goods and services. Your dollar just does not go as far. Inflation is a macroeconomic issue because it reduces the purchasing power of both income and savings over time.

Another macroeconomic concern facing the economy is unemployment, which measures the number of workers without a job but who are actively seeking one. Like the inflation rate, the unemployment rate fluctuates over time, falling below 4% in recent years but reaching 10% at the end of the last recession in 2009. Unemployment is a concern because not only does it force unemployed people to cut back on consumption and to use their savings, it influences the employed to cut back on their consumption as well. Unemployment also puts considerable strain on the government as income tax revenues fall but spending on assistance programs for the unemployed increases.

Because inflation and unemployment can negatively affect the economy, they have been called the "twin evils" of the modern macroeconomy. Each alone is bad. Together, they amplify each other, making things worse.

In the 1960s, macroeconomists thought they had these twin evils beaten. Historical data led them to believe that inflation and unemployment were linked in an inverse fashion; when unemployment went up, inflation would go down, and vice versa. Macroeconomists thought policymakers faced a menu of choices. Pick an unemployment rate from column A and get a corresponding inflation rate from column B. Better yet, the rates at issue were thought to be relatively low: An inflation rate of 3% to 4% was thought to be needed to keep unemployment under 4%. For those unemployed in the 2007–2009 recession when unemployment reached 10%, an unemployment rate less than 4% would seem like a dream. Is a 3% to 4% inflation rate so bad?

Unfortunately, the data amassed in the 1960s gave a false reading, as the high unemployment *and* high inflation rates of the 1970s proved. According to the 1960s macroeconomic model, the macroeconomy was just not supposed to witness the twin evils together.

Jump ahead to 2019. After a long recovery since 2009 that saw persistent unemployment for several years, the silver lining was that inflation was low throughout the recovery. This confirmed the trend that unemployment and inflation tend to run opposite of each other. But as the official unemployment rate fell below 4% in 2018, inflation remained below 2%, largely due to low energy prices. Because both unemployment and inflation were low, the twin evils appeared seemingly defeated . . . but were they? Economists have pointed out that the extraordinary measures taken during and after the last recession caused the debt to grow due to the large expenditures on programs and policies; this spending could eventually result in higher inflation. And if the slowdown in the global economy increases unemployment in the near future, we might have to confront the twin evils together again.

BY THE Numbers

The Twin Evils of Inflation and Unemployment

Inflation and unemployment are two statistics that governments monitor carefully. Nearly every country has experienced periods of very high unemployment or inflation at some point in its past, and government policies used to correct these problems vary significantly. This By the Numbers calculates the Misery Index, which is the sum of average inflation and average unemployment by year. The Misery Index is color-coded based on the president in office during that year.

DATA:

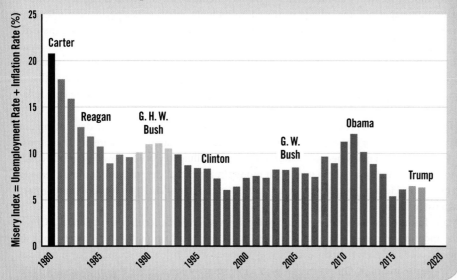

The Misery Index From 1980 to 2018

y-axis: Misery Index = Unemployment Rate + Inflation Rate (%)

Labels on chart: Carter, Reagan, G. H. W. Bush, Clinton, G. W. Bush, Obama, Trump

x-axis years: 1980, 1985, 1990, 1995, 2000, 2005, 2010, 2015, 2020

Where Can I Find These Data?

Source: The Misery Index

Web site: http://www.miseryindex.us

Details: Select "Index by Year." The data for the two components of the index, average inflation and average unemployment, can be obtained from the Bureau of Labor Statistics.

~ Assessing Your Data Literacy ~

1. Excluding Presidents Carter and Trump, under which presidencies did the Misery Index fall (from the first year to the last year of the presidency), and under which presidencies did it rise? Under which presidencies was the average Misery Index highest? Lowest?

2. Based on the graph, did the Misery Index increase in the years during the last three recessions in 1990–1991, 2001, and 2007–2009?

3. Explain why the fluctuations in the Misery Index are less volatile than if we were to look at just the unemployment rate or the inflation rate by itself.

WHY ARE THESE DATA IMPORTANT?

The occurrence of unemployment and inflation impacts the lives of every individual in different ways. While unemployment leads to a loss of income, most individuals experience only short periods of unemployment. However, inflation is a permanent reduction in the purchasing power of one's savings and therefore has greater negative consequences in the long run.

Data *in the News*

The original McDonald's menu in 1955 shows how inflation has increased the prices of goods we buy.

inflation A general rise in prices throughout the economy.

By now, you might be wondering: What is the big deal about inflation? You have a visceral sense that unemployment is bad. Inflation is less tangible. Thus, this chapter will start with inflation, what it is, how it is measured, and why it is bad. Then we will turn to unemployment. How does the government define the unemployment rate? An Uber driver with a Ph.D. is employed, but is he or she really underemployed? Is someone who has given up looking for a job considered unemployed? This chapter concludes by categorizing the types of unemployment, revealing which type can be moderated by government policies and which cannot.

INFLATION

Prices are constantly changing for the goods and services we buy. Prices for items such as concert tickets, fast-food meals, and college tuition have risen steadily over time, making every dollar earned worth a little less in terms of how much it can buy. However, prices for some goods, such as smartphones, laptops, and other technology goods, have fallen. Overall, the prices of a typical "basket" of goods and services we buy rise each year—by 36% over the last 15 years and 608% over the last 50 years. This gradual rise in prices is known as **inflation.** Over time, the effects of inflation can be substantial if one does not take action to protect against rising prices. For example, paying $3.50 for a gallon of milk today is much harder than paying $2.50 a gallon was back in 2002. But it would be even harder if your wages or savings have not increased over that period.

Why should we worry about inflation? Unlike unemployment, which is usually a temporary situation, especially for college-educated individuals, inflation is a permanent phenomenon. When prices increase by 3% over a year, it does not fall back the next year. Instead, inflation builds upon past inflation, causing the purchasing power of money to decrease. And it's not just the money you earn this year: Inflation reduces the purchasing power of your entire life savings. Therefore, inflation acts like a tax on overall savings, which is much harsher than a tax on annual income. For this reason, policymakers are especially careful in making sure inflation remains low.

How do individuals protect themselves against rising prices? First, workers demand higher wages to compensate for higher prices. But in a weak economy, wage increases are not always possible, especially when many people are out of work and willing to work for lower wages. Second, individuals with money saved can invest that money in assets that earn interest or can increase in value over time. Holding cash, for example, does not earn interest and therefore does not protect one against inflation.

Many forms of assets pay interest, including savings accounts, certificates of deposit (CDs), bonds, and money market accounts. But they do not pay equal amounts—safer assets, such as savings accounts, pay less than the average rise in prices, while riskier assets might pay more than the average rise in prices. One asset that pays a rate roughly equal to the rise in prices are TIPS (Treasury Inflation-Protected Securities) bonds, which pay a small fixed interest rate in addition to an adjustment based on how prices change in an economy. Therefore, when prices do not rise much, a TIPS bond would pay little, but when prices rise a lot, a TIPS bond will pay a lot.

What Causes Inflation?

Inflation is a measure of increases in the cost of living. In an economy like ours, prices are constantly changing. Some go up as others go down, and some prices rise and fall seasonally. Inflation is caused by many different factors, but the primary reasons can be attributed to demand factors, supply shocks, and government policy.

First, prices for goods and services are influenced by demand factors such as consumer confidence, income, and wealth. Think of a busy mall or restaurant. When there are plenty of customers, businesses are not pressured to offer discounts to attract buyers. This keeps prices higher than when consumer demand is depressed. For this reason, economic growth tends to coincide with inflation as a result of the demand for goods and services that higher incomes produce.

Second, prices are affected by supply shocks, caused by fluctuations in the price of inputs such as oil, natural resources, and farm crops. Two decades ago, the average price of a gallon of gas was barely over $1 but then a decade later increased demand for oil worldwide (especially in China and India) pushed average gas prices to nearly $4 per gallon. In recent years, a glut of oil production and decreased global demand have allowed average gas prices to fall back below $3 per gallon. Farm products have seen similar fluctuations in prices as droughts and other natural disasters disrupt the supply of crops. When input prices rise, this not only raises the cost of living for individuals but also raises the cost for businesses to produce and transport goods. These higher costs of doing business typically are passed on to consumers in the form of higher prices. When input prices fall, we generally expect the opposite effect on prices to occur.

Lastly, inflation can result from specific government actions. Government has a great power that no one individual has—the power to print money. No doubt you have heard that the federal government runs a budget deficit as it spends more than it receives in tax revenues. How does the government obtain the money to overspend? It borrows by issuing Treasury bonds. When the bonds come due and the government does not have the money to buy them back, it can increase the money supply to buy those bonds. As more money is introduced in the economy, a surplus of dollars is generated in relation to the supply of goods and services. When too much money chases a fixed quantity of goods and services, prices are bid up, which leads to inflation. Governments, like everyone else, have to obey the laws of supply and demand by limiting the growth of the money supply to prevent rampant inflation from occurring.

AP Photo/Daily Chronicle, Eric Sumberg

Now that we have described the main causes of inflation, let's discuss how inflation is measured.

Measuring Inflation: Consumer Price Index, Producer Price Index, and GDP Deflator

The town of Sycamore, Illinois, installed parking meters with prices reminiscent of the 1950s, when the price of parking was 1 cent per 12 minutes or 5 cents per hour. Parking citations were $1.00. The parking meters, stuck in a time long before inflation set in, became a tourist draw for the town.

Each month, the U.S. Department of Labor, through its Bureau of Labor Statistics (BLS), reports several important statistics that provide us with our principal measure of inflation. It does so by reporting changes in the average level of prices over the previous month in terms of the price level. The **price level** is the absolute level of a price index, whether this is the consumer price index (CPI; retail prices), the producer price index (PPI; wholesale prices), or the GDP deflator (average price of all items in GDP). The percentage increase in prices over a 12-month period is referred to as the *rate of inflation*.

Because inflation rates fluctuate up and down, the term **disinflation** is used to describe a reduction in the rate of inflation. Note that an economy going through disinflation still experiences rising prices, just at a slower pace. This was the case from the mid-1980s throughout the 1990s. However, if overall prices in an economy actually fall, this is referred to as **deflation.** Cases of deflation are rare but did occur in the early 1930s and briefly in 2015 as a result of a steep drop in energy prices.

Measuring consumer spending and inflation is one of the oldest data-collection functions of the BLS. The first nationwide survey was conducted in 1888–1891, which at the time emphasized the worker's role as a producer rather than as a consumer. During World War I, surveys of consumer spending were conducted to compute one of the first cost-of-living indices. During the Great Depression, extensive consumer surveys were used to study the welfare of selected groups, notably farmers, rural families, and urban families. The BLS began regular reports of the modern consumer price index in the late 1930s. Today, the consumer price index is the measure of

price level The absolute level of a price index, whether the consumer price index (CPI; retail prices), the producer price index (PPI; wholesale prices), or the GDP deflator (average price of all items in GDP).

disinflation A reduction in the rate of inflation. An economy experiencing disinflation still faces inflation, but at a declining rate.

deflation A decline in overall prices throughout the economy. This is the opposite of inflation.

inflation most Americans are familiar with, although the producer price index and the GDP deflator are also widely followed.

consumer price index (CPI)
An index of the average prices paid by urban consumers for a typical market basket of consumer goods and services.

The Consumer Price Index The **consumer price index (CPI)** is an index of the average prices paid by urban consumers (CPI-U) and urban wage earners and clerical workers (CPI-W) for a market basket of consumer goods and services. The CPI-U covers roughly 93% of the population while the CPI-W covers about 29% of the population.

The CPI is calculated by dividing the market basket's cost in the current period by its cost in the base period. The current CPI is a cost-of-goods index because it measures changes in the price of a fixed basket of goods. The reference or base period used today for the CPI is 1982–1984, but any base year would work just as well.

The CPI is often referred to as a "cost-of-living" index, but the current CPI differs from a true cost-of-living measure. A cost-of-living index compares the cost of maintaining the same standard of living in the current and base periods. A cost-of-goods index, in contrast, merely measures the cost of a fixed bundle of goods and services for an average consumer from one period to the next. This avoids having to measure how consumers react to price changes; for example, if the price of beef rises, people might buy more chicken.

How the BLS Measures Changes in Consumer Prices Measuring consumer prices requires the work of many people. Data collectors record about 80,000 prices in 75 urban areas each month from selected department stores, supermarkets, service stations, doctors' offices, rental offices, and more. Yet, the BLS does not have enough resources to price all goods and services in all retail outlets; therefore, it uses three sample groups to approximate the spending behavior of all urban consumers. These include a *Consumer Expenditure Survey* tracking the spending habits of over 30,000 individuals and households nationwide used to construct the market basket of goods and services, a *Telephone Point of Purchase Survey* that identifies where households purchase goods and services, and census data to select the urban areas where prices are collected.

Goods and services are divided into more than 200 categories, with each category specifying over 200 items for monthly price collection. Data from the three surveys are combined, weighted, and used to compute the cost in the current period required to purchase the fixed market basket of goods. This cost is then compared to the base period to calculate the CPI using the following formula:

$$CPI = (\text{Cost in Current Period} \div \text{Cost in Base Period}) \times 100$$

For example, assume that the market basket of goods cost $5,000 in 2015 and that the same basket of goods now costs $5,750. The CPI for today, using 2015 for the base year, is

$$115.0 = (\$5,750 \div \$5,000) \times 100$$

Therefore, the cost of goods has risen by 15% over this time period because the index in the base year (2015 in this case) is always 100. Again, the choice of base year does not matter as long as the CPI for each year is calculated relative to the cost in the selected base year. In fact, one can use CPI data as reported by the BLS to calculate price changes between any two years, neither of which is the base year, using the following formula:

$$\% \text{ Change in Price} = [(CPI \text{ in Current Year} \div CPI \text{ in Original Year}) \times 100] - 100$$

For example, if the CPI in 2020 was 257.6 and the CPI in 2015 was 234.7, the average change in prices over this five-year period was

$$9.8\% = [(257.6 \div 234.7) \times 100] - 100$$

We now take a quick look at some of the problems inherent in the current approach to measuring the CPI.

Problems in Measuring Consumer Prices The CPI is a *conditional* cost-of-goods index in that it measures only private goods and services; public goods (such as national defense spending) are excluded. Other background environmental factors, meanwhile, are held constant. The current CPI, for instance, does not take into account such issues as the state of the environment, homeland security, life expectancy, crime rates, climate change, or other conditions affecting the quality of life. For these reasons alone, the CPI will probably never be a true cost-of-living index.

But even if we ignore the environmental factors and public services, the CPI still tends to overstate inflation for three key reasons: product substitution, quality improvements, and new products.

- Product substitution: The CPI uses a fixed market basket and assumes that consumers continue to purchase the same goods from one year to the next. We know, however, that as prices change, consumers will often shop for better deals. The CPI does not take these product substitutions into account.

- Quality improvements: In any given year, about 30% of the products in the market basket will disappear from store shelves, and close replacements are available for about two-thirds of these dropped products. This means that about 10% of the original market basket will be replaced by better products (such as a higher-resolution television or a more advanced smartphone). These quality improvements increase our standard of living but are not fully accounted for in the CPI.

- New products: Not too long ago, voice assistant devices did not exist, nor did home virtual reality gaming systems. Because technology is constantly changing, the BLS often waits until a product matures before including it in the market basket. By not measuring the benefits of new products that consumers enjoy, the actual rate of inflation will be overstated.

Due to these criticisms, another measure of inflation has gained traction over the past decade called the Personal Consumption Expenditures (PCE) Price Index, reported by the U.S. Bureau of Economic Analysis. Unlike the CPI, which is based solely on surveys, the PCE uses a system that adjusts the weights for different categories of goods. It also uses actual sales data in its calculation.

The PCE arguably does a better job accounting for product substitution and quality differences that tend to cause the CPI to overstate the true level of inflation. As shown in Figure 1, over the past two decades, the CPI has risen faster than the PCE by about 0.5% per year. The Federal Reserve uses the PCE as its primary measure for setting inflation targets. However, other federal programs, such as Social Security and TIPS bonds, still use the CPI, a policy many people would cheer. Using the CPI allows Social Security payments and returns on TIPS bonds (both of which are tied to the inflation rate) to be higher.

····· Figure 1 • Comparing the CPI and PCE From 2000 to 2018 ················

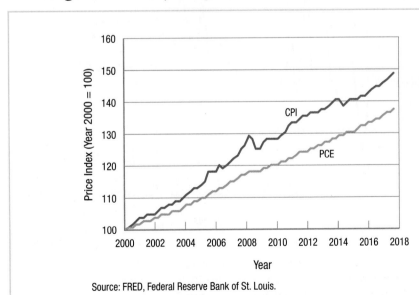

Since 2000, the CPI has exceeded the PCE by about 0.5% per year, which means the difference between the two aggregate price levels continues to widen each year.

Source: FRED, Federal Reserve Bank of St. Louis.

producer price index (PPI)
An index of the average prices received by domestic producers for their output.

GDP deflator An index of the average prices for all goods and services in the economy, including consumer goods, investment goods, government goods and services, and exports. It is the broadest measure of inflation in the national income and product accounts (NIPA).

The Producer Price Index The **producer price index (PPI)** is an index of the average prices received by domestic producers for their output. Before 1978 this index was known as the wholesale price index (WPI). The PPI is compiled by doing extensive sampling of nearly every industry in the mining and manufacturing sectors of the economy.

The PPI contains the following:

- Price indexes for roughly 500 mining and manufacturing industries, including over 10,000 indexes for specific products and product categories
- Over 3,700 commodity price indexes organized by type of product and end use
- About 800 indexes for specific outputs of industries in the service sector and other sectors that do not produce physical products
- Several major aggregate measures of price changes for goods purchased by consumers and businesses as final goods and by businesses as intermediate goods

The PPI measures the net revenue accruing to a representative firm for specific products. Because the PPI measures net revenues received by the firm, excise taxes are excluded, but changes in sales promotion programs, such as rebate offers or zero-interest loans, are included. Moreover, the products measured are the same from month to month, which means the PPI is plagued by the same problems discussed previously for the CPI. These problems include quality changes, deleted products, and some manufacturers exiting the industry.

The GDP Deflator The **GDP deflator** shown in Figure 2 is our broadest measure of inflation. It is an index of the average prices for all goods and services in the economy, including consumer goods, investment goods, government goods and services, and exports. The prices of imports are excluded. Note that *deflation* occurred in the Great Depression. The spike in inflation occurred

Figure 2 • Inflation From 1930 to 2019—GDP Deflator

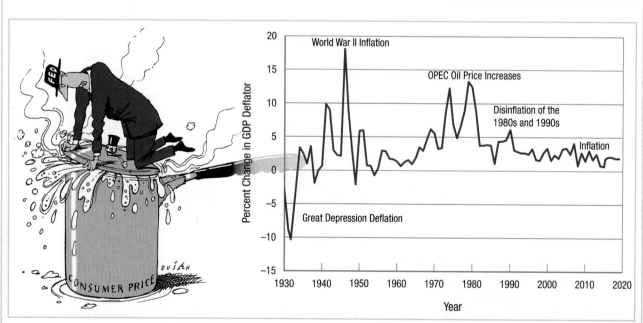

Dusan Petricic/Artizans

The broadest measure of inflation, the GDP deflator, is used to graph inflation from 1930 to the present. Deflation occurred during the Great Depression. The spike in inflation occurred after World War II ended and again in the 1970s. The 1980s saw a period of disinflation as the inflation rate fell from over 10% to below 5%, where it has remained for the past 30 years.

just after the end of World War II, when price controls were lifted. Since the mid-1980s, the economy has witnessed disinflation—inflation was present but generally at a decreasing rate.

Adjusting for Inflation: Escalating and Deflating Series (Nominal Versus Real Values)

Price indexes are used for two primary purposes: escalation and deflation. An escalator agreement modifies future payments, usually increasing them, to take the effects of inflation into account. Deflating a series of data with an index involves adjusting some current value (often called the nominal value) for the impact of inflation, thereby creating what economists call a *real value*. For instance, using the GDP deflator to deflate annual GDP involves adjusting nominal GDP to account for inflation, thereby yielding real GDP.

Escalator Clauses Many contracts, including commercial rental agreements, labor union contracts, and Social Security payments, are subject to escalator clauses. An escalator clause is designed to adjust payments or wages for changes in the price level. Social Security payments, for example, are adjusted upward (and referred to as a cost-of-living adjustment, or COLA) almost every year to account for the rate of inflation.

Escalator clauses become important in times of rising or significant inflation. These clauses protect the real value of wages as well as payments such as Social Security. In fact, voting blocs and organizations such as AARP (an organization whose mission is to enhance the quality of life as people age) have been formed to protect those who depend on escalator clauses to maintain their standards of living.

However, over the past decade, low inflation rates have consequently resulted in tiny increases in benefits. In fact, in 2009, 2010, 2015, and 2016, inflation was so low (around 0%) that no increase in Social Security benefits occurred. This caused some concern among many seniors because the lack of inflation in 2015 and 2016 was due to a large drop in energy prices despite higher prices for food and health care, items on which seniors are more likely to spend their money. In general, though, escalator clauses are important because they do protect people from spikes in the overall price level.

Deflating Series: Nominal Versus Real Values GDP grew by 39% from 2008 to 2018, but should we be celebrating? Not really, because inflation has eroded the purchasing power of that increase. The question is, By how much did GDP really increase?

First, remember that every index is grounded on a base year and that the value for this base year is always 100. For instance, suppose the base year used for the GDP deflator is 2008. The formula for converting a nominal value (or *current dollar value*) to real value (or *constant dollar value*) is

$$\text{Real} = \text{Nominal} \times (\text{Base Year Index} \div \text{Current Year Index})$$

To illustrate, nominal GDP in 2018 was $20,865.1 billion. The GDP deflator, having been 100 in 2008, was 116.9 in 2018. Real GDP for 2018 (in 2008 dollars) was therefore

$$\$17,848.7 \text{ billion} = \$20,865.1 \text{ billion} \times (100.0 \div 116.9)$$

Note that because the economy has faced some inflation— 16.9% from 2008 to 2018—the nominal value of GDP has been reduced by this amount to arrive at the real value. In other words, of the 39% growth in nominal GDP, 16.9% was due to rising prices. If we subtract 16.9% from 39%, real growth of GDP from 2008 to 2018 was about 22%, or about 1.9% per year (taking into account the effect of compounding).

The Effect of Overstating Inflation Many federal benefits, including Social Security payments, food stamps, and veterans' benefits, are indexed to the CPI, which means that if inflation (as measured by the CPI) goes up by 3%, these benefits are increased by 3%. If the CPI overstates inflation, federal expenditures on benefits are higher. Although individuals initially benefit from the higher payments, overstating inflation in the long run makes real earnings appear smaller than what they actually are. For this reason, the use of alternative measures, such as the PCE described earlier, has increased in institutions such as the Federal Reserve.

The Consequences of Inflation

Why do so many policymakers, businesspeople, and consumers dread inflation? Your attitude toward inflation will depend in large part on whether you live on a fixed income, whether you are a creditor or debtor, and whether you have properly anticipated inflation.

Many elderly people live on fixed incomes; often, only their Social Security payments are indexed to inflation. People on fixed incomes are harmed by inflation because the purchasing power of their income declines. If people live long enough on fixed incomes, inflation can reduce them from living comfortably to living in poverty.

Creditors, meanwhile, are harmed by inflation because both the principal on loans and interest payments are usually fixed. Inflation reduces the real value of the payments they receive, while the value of the principal declines in real terms. This means that debtors benefit from inflation; the real value of their payments declines as their wages rise with inflation. Many homeowners in the 1970s and 1980s saw the value of their real estate rise from inflation. At the same time, their wages rose, again partly due to inflation, but their mortgage payments remained fixed. The result was that a smaller part of the typical household's income was needed to pay the mortgage. Inflation thus redistributes income from creditors to debtors.

This result takes place only if the inflation is unanticipated. If lenders foresee inflation, they will adjust the interest rates they offer to offset the inflation expected over the period of the loan. Suppose, for instance, that the interest rate during zero inflation periods is roughly 3%. Now suppose that a lender expects inflation to run 5% a year over the next three years, the life of a proposed loan. The lender will demand an 8% interest rate to adjust for the expected losses caused by inflation. Only when lenders fail to anticipate inflation does it harm them, to the benefit of debtors.

But the effects of unexpected inflation do not stop there. When inflation is unexpected, the incentives individuals and firms face change. For example, if inflation causes prices and wages to increase by 5%, there should be no change in consumption as long as the inflation was expected. But if the price rise was unexpected, consumers might reduce their consumption, leading to lower spending in the economy. Unanticipated inflation leads to faulty signals that can reduce consumer and producer welfare.

Lastly, when inflation becomes rampant, individuals and firms expend resources to protect themselves from the harmful effects of rapidly rising prices, an effect that is especially prevalent in cases of hyperinflation.

Hyperinflation

hyperinflation An extremely high rate of inflation; above 100% per year.

Hyperinflation is an extremely high rate of inflation. Today, most economists refer to an inflation rate above 100% a year as hyperinflation. But in most episodes of hyperinflation, the inflation rates are many times that level. In 2008 in Zimbabwe, prices were more than doubling *every day*, for an annual inflation rate of 231,000,000%.

During Zimbabwe's hyperinflation in 2008, a $100 trillion note was introduced, but even that became nearly worthless after a few months.

ISSUE

The Consequences of Counterfeit Money on Inflation

Each day, hundreds of billions of U.S. dollars exchange hands in everyday transactions. A small fraction of these dollars are counterfeit, circulating throughout the economy as if they were genuine. When counterfeit money is created, who ends up paying for it?

Suppose you receive some money and later realize one of the bills is fake (the ink runs, the paper is too thin, or the watermark is missing). What can you do? Most banks will not replace a fake bill because then the bank would lose the money. Some people pass the fake to the next unsuspecting person, but this is a punishable offense. U.S. law states that a counterfeit bill must be reported to the nearest U.S. Secret Service field office. By doing so, you still lose the money, as there is no compensation for turning in counterfeit money.

Thus, the responsibility lies with individuals and businesses to check the authenticity of the money received and to refuse money that appears to be counterfeit. That is not always as easy as it sounds. A low-quality counterfeit might be detected by the naked eye, by touch, or by the use of devices such as a counterfeit detector pen.

But sophisticated counterfeiters produce high-quality counterfeits that are hard to detect. For example, one counterfeiting method is to remove the ink from a lower-denomination bill and then reprint a higher denomination on the paper. The paper is real, making counterfeit detector pens ineffective, and the bill contains a watermark (however, the wrong one) and a security strip. These counterfeits are nearly indistinguishable from authentic bills and can circulate for years without being noticed.

Restaurants and other businesses often receive counterfeits because cashiers are rushed. Consumers sometimes pass them to businesses thinking it won't hurt them. But businesses that end up with counterfeits incur a loss, raising the cost of doing business, which often leads to higher prices. Therefore, even if individuals do not end up with the counterfeit in their possession, they pay for them in the form of higher prices.

What happens when a high-quality counterfeit circulates for years in the economy? In terms of its economic impact, counterfeit money acts as real money if people accept it as real money. Ultimately,

the government loses. Why? The government (the U.S. Treasury to be specific) is the only institution with the authority to print money. When another entity prints counterfeits, the amount of money in circulation rises, but the government never had the opportunity to use it first.

When more money chases a limited amount of goods and services in an economy, inflation results. Because counterfeits produce the same effect as an increase in the money supply, inflation will occur. In sum, counterfeits hurt everyone, which is why governments invest in new technology to produce money with many security features.

Counterfeit detector pens are commonly used to monitor currency that comes into businesses.

Hyperinflation is not new. It has been around since paper money and debt were invented. During the American Revolutionary War, the Continental Congress issued money until the phrase "not worth a continental" became part of the language. Germany experienced the first modern hyperinflation after World War I. Hungary experienced the highest rate of inflation on record during World War II. By the end of the war, it took over 800 octillion (8 followed by 29 zeros) Hungarian pengos to equal 1 prewar pengo.

Hyperinflation is usually caused by an excess of government spending over tax revenues (extremely high deficits) coupled with the printing of money to finance these deficits. In recent years, Venezuela experienced large government deficits due to falling oil prices (its largest source of revenue) and price controls that required the government to increase its imports to minimize shortages. But as deficits rose and the economy faltered, the government turned to printing more money, causing the value of the bolívar to plummet. In a short amount of time, financial assets in banks and pension accounts became worthless, as they dwindled in value due to hyperinflation.

Stopping hyperinflation requires restoring confidence in the government's ability to bring its budget under control. This usually requires a change in government and a new currency and, most important, a commitment to reduce the growth of the money supply.

Hyperinflation is an extreme case, yet it shows how inflation can have detrimental effects on an economy. This is why it is important to keep track of inflation, as it is an important measure of the health of an economy.

CHECKPOINT

INFLATION

- Inflation is a general rise in prices throughout the economy that affects the cost of living.

- Disinflation is a reduction in the rate of inflation, and deflation is a decline in the overall price level in the economy.

- The CPI is a price index used to measure inflation for urban consumers and is based on a survey of a fixed market basket of goods and services each month.

- The PPI is a price index used to measure price changes for the output of domestic producers.

- The GDP deflator is the broadest measure of inflation and covers all goods and services in GDP.

- Escalator clauses adjust payments (wages, rents, and other payments, such as Social Security) to account for inflation.

- Real (adjusted for inflation) values are found by multiplying the nominal (current dollar) values by the ratio of the base year index to the current year index.

- Hyperinflation is an extremely high rate of inflation, over 100% per year.

QUESTIONS: Suppose you took out $20,000 in student loans at a fixed interest rate of 5%. Assume that after you graduate, inflation rises significantly as you are paying back your loans. Does this rise in inflation benefit you in paying back your student loans? Who is hurt more from unexpected higher inflation—a borrower or a lender?

Answers to the Checkpoint questions can be found at the end of this chapter.

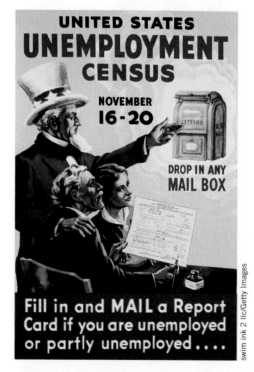

A 1937 Census Bureau poster encouraging compliance with the initial unemployment survey.

UNEMPLOYMENT

Unemployment is a phenomenon that affects nearly all workers at some point in their lives. When people become unemployed, the loss of wages often creates hardships on workers and their families. Moreover, the loss of income reduces consumer spending, which can lead to a ripple effect as businesses cut back production, leading to more workers losing their jobs.

The Historical Record

The Census Bureau began collecting data on wages and earnings in the early 19th century, but it took the Great Depression to focus national attention on the need for consistent data on unemployment rather than specific instances of events such as factory closings. By the 1940s, the Department of Labor began collecting employment data using monthly surveys to obtain a more detailed picture of the labor force. As the BLS has noted,

> *Addressing the issue of unemployment requires information about the extent and nature of the problem. How many people are unemployed? How did they become unemployed? How long have they been unemployed? Are their numbers growing or declining? Are they men or women? Are they young or old? Are they White, or Black, or Asian, or of Hispanic ethnicity? How much education do they have? Are they concentrated in one area of the country more than another?*[1]

[1] From the BLS Web site.

Once the BLS has collected and processed the current employment statistics, policymakers use this information to craft economic policies. Before we discuss how these statistics are defined, collected, used, and made accurate, let's briefly look at the historical record of unemployment and its composition.

Figure 3 shows unemployment rates for the last century. Unemployment has varied from a high of 25% of the labor force in the middle of the Great Depression to a low of just over 1% during World War II. Unemployment during the past 50 years has tended to hover around the 5% to 6% range, although it reached 10% during the 1981–1982 and 2007–2009 recessions.

Table 1 shows a breakdown of unemployment among various groups by gender, race, and education for 1998, 2008, and 2018. For blacks, unemployment has tended to be more than double the rate of white unemployment, and the unemployment rate for Hispanics has usually exceeded that for whites by roughly 50%. Unemployment for college graduates is consistently low. Roughly half of all unemployment is normally from job losses, but this rose to two-thirds during the 2007–2009 downturn. The next largest group involves people who have not worked in some time and are looking to reenter the labor force. Finally, those people who quit their jobs or are new entrants into the labor force constitute a small percentage of the unemployed.

Figure 3 • A Century of Unemployment (1919–2019)

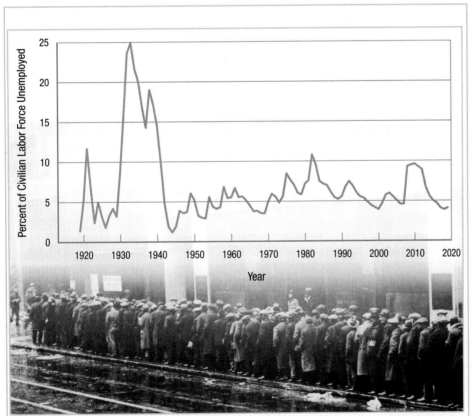

Bettmann/Getty Images

Over the last century, unemployment has varied from a high of 25% of the labor force in the middle of the Great Depression to a low of just over 1% during World War II. During the past 50 years, unemployment hovered around the 5%–6% range.

TABLE 1	UNEMPLOYMENT RATES BY GENDER, RACE, EDUCATION, OCCUPATION, AND REASON FOR UNEMPLOYMENT, 1998, 2008, 2018		
	1998	**2008**	**2018**
Total unemployment	4.4%	7.3%	3.9%
Gender			
Men	4.3	8.0	3.9
Women	4.4	6.5	3.8
Race			
White	3.8	6.7	3.4
Black	7.7	12.1	6.6
Asian	3.5	5.1	3.3
Hispanic	7.7	9.4	4.4
Education			
Less than high school diploma	6.9	11.1	5.8
High school graduate	3.8	7.8	3.8
Some college	2.9	5.7	3.3
College graduate and higher	1.8	3.6	2.1
Occupation			
Managerial and professional	1.9	3.3	2.1
Office and administrative support	3.9	6.1	3.5
Production occupations	5.2	10.5	3.3
Reason Why Unemployed*			
Job loser	2.0	4.3	1.8
Job leaver	0.5	0.6	0.5
Reentrant	1.4	1.8	1.2
New entrant	0.4	0.5	0.4

Data from U.S. Department of Labor, Bureau of Labor Statistics (Historical Data Series, CPS Database).
*The data for this category represent the percentage of the labor force that is unemployed for each reason listed. The sum of the 4 reasons equals the total unemployment rate.

Now that we have some idea of who are unemployed and why they are unemployed, let us consider how these numbers are compiled. First, we need to examine how people get categorized as employed or unemployed.

Defining and Measuring Unemployment

The three major monthly numbers the BLS reports are the size of the labor force, number of people employed, and number unemployed. The unemployment rate is the number of people unemployed divided by the labor force.

Employed People are counted as *employed* if they have performed any work at all for pay or profit during the survey week. Regular full-time work, part-time work, and temporary work are all included. People who have a job but are on vacation, ill, having child care problems, on family leave, on strike, prevented from working because of bad weather, or engaged in some family or personal obligation are treated as employed. These people are considered to be employed because they have jobs to return to once their temporary situations have been resolved.

One other group of people, called *unpaid family workers,* is considered to be employed. These are people who work 15 or more hours a week in a family enterprise, and they usually work in agricultural and retail industries. Unpaid family workers who work fewer than 15 hours a week are not counted as employed.

Unemployed People are counted as *unemployed* if they do not have a job but are available for work and have been *actively* seeking work for the previous four weeks. Actively looking for work includes efforts such as responding to online job ads, sending off résumés, scheduling job interviews, visiting school placement centers, and contacting private or public employment agencies.

Note the emphasis on being active in the job search. A *passive* job search that merely involves browsing online employment openings or talking to friends about jobs is not enough to characterize someone as unemployed. One exception involves workers who have been laid off but are expecting to be recalled; they do not need to seek other work to count as being unemployed. Aside from the only other exception—namely, people suffering a temporary illness—individuals must be engaged in a job search to be counted as unemployed.

Labor Force The **labor force** is the total number of those employed and unemployed. The unemployment rate is the number of unemployed divided by the labor force, expressed as a percent.

The measurement of the labor force has important implications for the unemployment rate. To be counted in the labor force, one must either be employed or not employed but actively seeking work. As a result, a number of groups are not included in the labor force and therefore are not counted in unemployment statistics, including full-time students who do not hold jobs, retirees, children under the age of 16, and persons who are institutionalized. The **labor force participation rate** is the percentage of the adult noninstitutionalized population that is in the labor force. The labor force participation rate in the United States has risen in recent years due to a strengthening economy and is currently around 63%. But as more people enter the labor force, the unemployment rate will increase if not enough jobs are available for these job seekers.

labor force The total number of those employed and unemployed. The unemployment rate is the number of unemployed divided by the labor force, expressed as a percent.

labor force participation rate The percentage of the adult noninstitutionalized population that is in the labor force.

Monthly Employment Surveys

The Census Bureau and the Department of Labor conduct different surveys to measure employment. The Census Bureau surveys households, and the U.S. Department of Labor focuses on the payrolls of businesses and government agencies to produce their monthly reports.

- **The Household Survey** Every month, the Census Bureau, as part of the Current Population Survey (CPS), contacts around 60,000 households in 700 geographical areas to determine the economic activity of people. This survey includes self-employed workers, unpaid family workers, agricultural workers, private household workers, and workers absent without pay. It does not ask interviewees if they are employed but instead uses a set of questions to elicit information that allows the Census Bureau to determine by its standards whether people are employed, unemployed, or not in the labor force.

- **The Payroll Survey** Officially called the Current Employment Statistics (CES) Survey, the payroll or establishment survey focuses on approximately 142,000 companies and government agencies that are asked how many employees they currently have. If jobs are cut, this survey will immediately show a decrease in the number of employees.

Both the household and payroll surveys are used to gain a complete picture of the labor market. The household survey provides a detailed demographic picture of the labor

UNEMPLOYMENT INSURANCE WEEKLY CLAIMS REPORT

<u>Seasonally Adjusted Data</u>

In the week ending April 20, the advance figure for seasonally adjusted **initial claims** was 230,000, an increase of 37,000 from the previous week's level. The 4-week moving average was 206,000, an increase of 4,500 from the previous week...

The Weekly Jobs Report released on April 25, 2019, shows initial unemployment claims of 230,000. Of importance to economists is that the number increased from the previous week (along with the four-week moving average), suggesting that the employment situation for the United States is slightly worsening.

Wall Street Journal

U.S. Hiring Strong in June; Unemployment Rate Rises as More Enter Labor Force

Americans are flocking to the job market . . . employers added 213,000 to their payrolls last month, the Labor Department said Friday. Many of those (new) job seekers . . . were counted as unemployed while they sought out work, which helped push the jobless rate up to 4.0%.

This headline from the *Wall Street Journal* (July 6, 2018) appears odd because the unemployment rate in June 2018 rose despite many jobs being created. This occurred because the labor force increased as more people started looking for work.

market and captures entrepreneurial activity (such as self-employment) missed by the payroll survey. In contrast, the payroll survey provides detailed information by industry and region of the country. Because the payroll survey has a larger sample, it is generally viewed as the most accurate gauge of employment and unemployment changes, but both surveys closely track each other.

Employment Trends

The surveys described in the previous section are important measures of employment and unemployment for the country as a whole as well as for individual states and cities included in the surveys. However, investors and economists are also interested in trends in employment and how they affect the overall health of the economy. Although major companies are highlighted in the news for their decisions on hiring and laying off workers, the majority of jobs in the country are generated by small and mid-sized companies. These employment decisions fluctuate often, and therefore investors are interested in statistics that might capture these short-term trends.

Weekly Jobs Report One report that has gained attention is the Unemployment Insurance Weekly Claims Report, more commonly referred to as the Weekly Jobs Report, released by the U.S. Department of Labor each Thursday. The Weekly Jobs Report contains an estimate of the number of persons filing for unemployment benefits for the first time and is used as a way to estimate trends in layoffs and in hiring. Economists are interested in seeing how the weekly data change from week to week. These data provide a more immediate estimate of unemployment than waiting for the monthly survey report.

Relationship Between Employment and the Unemployment Rate People often generalize the negative relationship between employment and the unemployment rate. Although these terms are negatively related, the relationship is not perfect. For example, it is possible for employment to grow and the unemployment rate to increase at the same time. Recall that the unemployment rate measures the percentage of people in the labor force who are unemployed. The important point to highlight here is that the labor force is constantly changing.

The labor force changes for many reasons. For example, the labor force in the United States grows by around 1.5 million persons each year just from population growth (from natural births as well as from immigration). Therefore, even without considering any other factor influencing the labor force, the United States needs to generate numerous new jobs just to keep the unemployment rate steady. Further, people enter and leave the labor force for many reasons—college, retirement, family reasons, or just frustration with the job market. As a result of these factors, the unemployment rate is not perfectly correlated with employment numbers, as we will analyze in greater detail next.

Problems With Unemployment Statistics

Analyzing issues as complex and personal as employment, unemployment, and job seeking can be expected to generate its share of criticism. When the Department of Labor announces its results each month, commentators often note that these numbers understate unemployment because they do not include chronically unemployed workers who have grown so frustrated and discouraged that they have dropped out of the labor force. Media pundits agonize over the plight of discouraged workers or the underemployed while discussing the impact of the latest numbers on the stock market.

How unemployment is measured depends on the intended use of the resulting measurements. Various uses for unemployment statistics include (1) gauging the state of the economy, (2) determining the divergence of supply and demand in labor markets, and (3) assessing the distribution of unemployment and the extent to which people are suffering from being out of work. In the United States, most unemployment statistics have been developed to gauge the state of the economy. The BLS does, however, publish data about underemployment, discouraged workers, and other marginally attached workers.

Marginally Attached Workers and Underemployment It is not uncommon for people to take jobs that do not fully use their skills. In the early 2000s, the collapse of many Internet start-ups and telecommunications firms eliminated the jobs of many highly skilled workers. The 2007–2009 recession caused by the collapse of the housing market and the subsequent financial crisis put large numbers of construction, real estate, and Wall Street workers out of work. And the steep drop in oil prices from 2014 to 2016 caused domestic oil companies that use a costlier method of extracting oil called *fracking* to lay off many workers.

As a result of these shake-ups, many people were unable to immediately find jobs that paid similar wages. Some of these workers gave up looking for work altogether. The Department of Labor categorizes those who were available for work and actively looked for work during the past 12 months but *not* in the past four weeks as **marginally attached workers.** Marginally attached workers are not counted in the official unemployment statistics because they are not considered part of the labor force.

The reasons that people stop looking for work vary, but the most common reason is a person's belief that there aren't any good jobs available and therefore the search isn't worthwhile until the economy improves. This portion of marginally attached workers is classified as **discouraged workers.** A severe recession will increase the number of discouraged workers. Other reasons for being marginally attached include giving up the search due to family responsibilities, transportation problems, or choosing to go to school.

Another common situation that occurs when people lose their jobs is they accept jobs that do not fully use their education and skills. These workers who take temporary or part-time jobs to earn some money while looking for better work are called **underemployed workers.** For example, many people choose to become Uber or Lyft drivers or Airbnb hosts, allowing them much flexibility as they earn income and continue to search for a better job.

The Census Bureau asks questions of respondents to determine whether they fit into the categories of a discouraged worker, other marginally attached worker, or underemployed worker. Table 2 summarizes these three categories and how they fit into alternative measures of unemployment reported by the BLS. Figure 4 shows how the official unemployment rate, U-3, compare to the alternative measurements, U-4, U-5, and U-6, over the past 18 years. Adding together all of the categories (U-6) nearly doubles the official unemployment rate.

Other countries have different definitions for actively seeking work, classifying individuals engaged in passive searches (such as searching online for jobs without formally applying) as unemployed. In many European countries, 15-year-olds are included in the labor force if they are actively seeking work, and so are those attending college but actively seeking work. These differences make the unemployment rate appear higher. Lastly, countries with large numbers of people working in the informal market (such as street performers or other businesses that do not pay taxes) may have higher official unemployment numbers. The following Around the World feature focuses on the thriving informal labor market in Cuba as a result of the recent influx of American visitors.

marginally attached workers
Workers who were available for work and actively looked for work during the last 12 months but not in the last four weeks.

discouraged workers
Discouraged workers are the portion of marginally attached workers who have given up actively looking for work and, as a result, are not counted as unemployed.

underemployed workers
Workers who are forced to take jobs that do not fully utilize their education, background, or skills. Underemployed workers often hold part-time jobs.

TABLE 2	ALTERNATIVE MEASURES OF UNEMPLOYMENT	
Type of Worker	**Definition**	**Effect on Unemployment**
Marginally attached worker (discouraged workers)	Actively looked for work in the past 12 months but not in the past four weeks due to frustration and/or the belief that there are no good jobs available.	This group of workers is added to the official unemployment rate U-3 to determine U-4.
Other marginally attached workers	Actively looked for work in the past 12 months but not in the past four weeks due to family responsibilities, transportation problems, or choosing to go to school.	This group of workers is added to the U-4 measure to determine U-5.
Underemployed workers	Workers who accept temporary or part-time work that does not fully use their education or skills while seeking more permanent employment.	This group of workers is added to the U-5 measure to determine U-6.

····· Figure 4 • Unemployment Categories (2000–2018) ·························

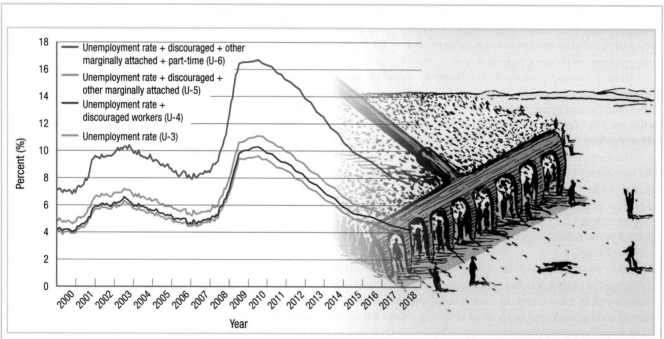

Janusz Kapusta/Illustration Source

The Department of Labor categorizes unemployment into those unemployed and still actively seeking work, those who are discouraged (not looked for work in the last four weeks), those who are marginally attached for other reasons (have looked for work in the past 12 months, but not in the last four weeks due to, for example, family issues or transportation problems), and those working part-time but who would prefer full-time work. The categories U-3 (the official unemployment rate), U-4, U-5, and U-6 correspond to the sum of these respective categories.

AROUND THE WORLD

A New Cuban Renaissance: The Rise of American "Tourism" in Cuba

How has the increase in the number of Americans visiting Cuba impacted its labor market?

For over a half century, Cuba seemed stuck in the past with classic cars from the 1950s roaming the streets and a dearth of modern technologies (such as mobile phones and Internet) that much of the world takes for granted. Much of this is due to a trade embargo with the United States that prevents U.S. companies from conducting business in Cuba and prevents Americans from traveling to Cuba as tourists.

However, with its natural beauty and pristine beaches, being stuck in the past has created a charm that attracts European and Canadian tourists to its shores, along with a few American tourists willing to skirt travel restrictions by entering Cuba from other nations or by applying for an exemption for cultural or academic reasons.

In 2015, the United States and Cuba began to reconcile their differences as most Cubans and Cuban Americans today were not yet born during the Cuban Missile Crisis of 1962 that cemented the embargo. Since 2015, more Americans have visited Cuba as travel restrictions have relaxed. Although tourism to Cuba by Americans is still technically banned, there are more ways around it (such as taking an organized tour or a cruise).

The growth of American tourists to Cuba has dramatically affected private sector employment as Cuban entrepreneurs start up tour guide services, guest houses, cafés, classic car rides, street entertainment, and other attractions. And because Americans are known to be generous tippers, the newly expanded service industry has thrived. This is particularly important given the traditional labor market in Cuba where most citizens work in government-run enterprises at very meager pay. For example, a professor at the University of Havana may earn less than $40 *per month* but can earn more than that in *one day* by giving a private city tour to a visitor.

The growth of private sector jobs, many in the informal market by entrepreneurs, has made many Cubans better off even if these gains are not reflected in official government statistics. But as employment has flourished, prices have also increased as more tourists compete for the limited services available in Cuba. As long as travel rules continue to relax, Cuba will continue to attract tourists where one can take a blast to the past.

 GO ONLINE TO PRACTICE THE ECONOMIC CONCEPTS IN THIS STORY

✔ CHECKPOINT

UNEMPLOYMENT

- People are classified as employed if they are at least 16 years old, not institutionalized, and have worked for pay or profit during the survey week.

- People classified as being unemployed if they do not have a job but are available for work and have been actively seeking work for the previous four weeks.

- The labor force is the sum of the employed and unemployed. The unemployment rate is the percentage of the labor force that is unemployed.

- The official unemployment rate statistics do not account for underemployed, discouraged, and other marginally attached workers.

QUESTIONS: Does it seem reasonable to require that to be counted as unemployed, a person must be actively seeking work? Why not just count those who do not have a job but indicate they would like to work?

Answers to the Checkpoint questions can be found at the end of this chapter.

UNEMPLOYMENT AND THE ECONOMY

Inevitably, our economy will contain some unemployment. People who are reentering the workforce or entering it for the first time will often find that landing a new job can take some time. Then they may find, moreover, that taking the first available job is not always in their best interest—that it might be better to take the time to search for another position better matching their skills and personality. Obtaining information and searching more extensively can extend the period people remain unemployed.

Unemployment can occur because wages are artificially set above the market clearing or equilibrium wage. Both minimum wage laws and union bargaining can have this effect, helping those workers who are employed to earn more but shutting some potential workers out of jobs.

Employers often keep wages above market equilibrium to reduce turnover (and training costs), boost morale, and increase employee productivity. These *efficiency wages* give employees an incentive to work hard and remain with their present employers because at other jobs they could earn only market wages. These higher wages, however, can also prevent employers from hiring additional workers, thus contributing to unemployment.

Changes in the business cycle will also generate unemployment. When the economy falls into a recession, sales decline, and employers are forced to lay off workers; therefore, unemployment grows.

Separating different types of unemployment into distinct categories will help us apply unemployment figures to our analysis of the economy.

Types of Unemployment

There are three types of unemployment: frictional, structural, and cyclical. Each type has different policy ramifications.

Frictional Unemployment Do you recall how many different part-time jobs you held during high school? How about summer jobs while in college? If you have worked several types of jobs, you're not alone, as many reasons exist why one may leave a job. You may get bored, the business may close or reduce the staff it needs, you might move to a new city, or you could have been fired. If you're enrolled in school while working part-time jobs, generally you are not considered unemployed while between jobs because being in school means you're not counted in the labor force. But the reasons for changing jobs are still relevant once you graduate and work full-time.

As you pursue your career, chances are that you'll work for more than one company during your lifetime. **Frictional unemployment** describes the short-term duration of unemployment caused by workers switching jobs, often voluntarily, for a variety of reasons. Some workers quit their jobs to search for better positions. In some cases, these people may already have other jobs, but it may still take several days or weeks before they can report to their new employers. In these cases, people moving from one job to the next are said to be frictionally unemployed.

Frictional unemployment is natural for any economy and, indeed, necessary and beneficial. People need time to search for new jobs, and employers need time to interview and evaluate potential new employees. The Internet has helped to facilitate job searches by expanding access to information; still, frictional unemployment will always exist.

Structural Unemployment Another naturally occurring phenomenon in an economy is **structural unemployment.** Whereas frictional unemployment is assumed to be of rather short duration, structural unemployment is usually associated with extended periods of unemployment.

Structural unemployment is caused by changes in the structure of consumer demands or technology. Many industries and products inevitably decline and become obsolete, and when they do, the skills honed by workers in these industries often become obsolete as well.

Declining demand for cigarettes, for instance, has changed the labor market for tobacco workers. Farm work, textile finishing, and many aspects of manufacturing have all changed drastically in the last several decades. Farms have become more productive, and many sewing and manufacturing jobs have moved overseas due to lower wages there. People who are structurally unemployed are often unemployed for long periods, and then some become discouraged workers.

frictional unemployment
Unemployment resulting from workers who voluntarily quit their jobs to search for better positions or are moving to new jobs but may still take several days or weeks before they can report to their new employers.

structural unemployment
Unemployment caused by changes in the structure of consumer demands or technology. It means that demand for some products declines and the skills of this industry's workers often become obsolete as well. This results in an extended bout of unemployment while new skills are developed.

To find new work, those who are structurally unemployed must often go through extended periods of retraining. But ultimately, the new skills learned make workers more productive in a changing labor market, which make production more efficient. Displaced workers with more education are more likely to retrain easily and adjust to a new occupation. For that reason, governments often provide assistance to workers seeking new skills or more education. One benefit of a growing economy is that retraining is more easily obtained when labor markets are tight.

Cyclical Unemployment **Cyclical unemployment** is the result of changes in the business cycle. If, for example, business investment or consumer spending declines, we would expect the rate of economic growth to slow, in which case the economy would probably enter a recession. Cyclical unemployment is the difference between the current unemployment rate and the full employment rate, defined below.

Music stores selling CDs are a dying breed as consumers stream music, causing structural unemployment in CD manufacturing and in the music retail industry.

Frictional and structural unemployment are difficult problems, and macroeconomic policies provide only limited relief. Most economists agree that combating cyclical unemployment is where public policymakers can have their greatest impact. By keeping the economy on a steady, low-inflationary, solid growth path, policymakers can minimize the costs of cyclical unemployment. Admittedly, this is easier said than done given the various shocks (such as a sharp decline in consumer spending) that can affect the economy.

Defining Full Employment

Economists often describe the health of the economy by comparing its performance to *full employment*. We know full employment cannot be zero unemployment because frictional and structural unemployment will always be present. Full employment today is generally taken to be equivalent to the natural rate of unemployment.

The Natural Rate of Unemployment The **natural rate of unemployment** has come to represent several ideas to economists. First, it is often defined as that level of unemployment at which price and wage decisions are consistent—a level at which the actual inflation rate is equal to people's inflationary expectations. The natural rate of unemployment is also considered to be the unemployment level at which unemployment is only frictional and structural or, alternatively, when cyclical unemployment is zero.

Economists often refer to the natural rate of unemployment as the *nonaccelerating inflation rate of unemployment* (NAIRU), defined as the unemployment rate most consistent with a low rate of inflation. It is the unemployment level at which inflationary pressures in the economy are at their minimum.

Full employment, or the natural rate of unemployment, is determined by such institutional factors as the presence or absence of employment agencies and their effectiveness. Many job seekers today, for example, search online postings on sites such as Indeed or LinkedIn, reducing the time it takes to match available employees with prospective employers. Other factors might include the demographic makeup of the labor force and the incentives associated with various unemployment benefit programs and income tax rates.

Changes in the Unemployment Rate Around the Natural Rate In the previous chapter, we studied how the business cycle leads to both periods of high economic growth and periods of recessions, fluctuating around a long-term trend. The unemployment rate follows a similar pattern, rising during recessions and falling during economic expansions but fluctuating around the natural rate of unemployment. In the United States, the natural rate of unemployment is steady and has fallen slowly over the past 40 years from over 6% to between 4.5% and 5.5% largely due to improvements in labor market efficiencies (such as the use of the Internet in job searches and the increase in part-time and temporary work) that have reduced the unemployment rate associated with low inflation.

cyclical unemployment
Unemployment that results from changes in the business cycle and where public policymakers can have their greatest impact by keeping the economy on a steady, low-inflationary, solid growth path.

natural rate of unemployment The level of unemployment at which price and wage decisions are consistent; a level at which the actual inflation rate is equal to people's inflationary expectations and where cyclical unemployment is zero.

· · · · · Figure 5 • Unemployment Rate and the Natural Rate of Unemployment · · · · · · ·

The average unemployment rate and the natural rate of unemployment are shown from 1968 to 2018. The vertical shaded bars indicate recessions. The rising unemployment line and flatter downward slopes following the last three recessions indicate a longer recovery period for jobs caused by a jobless recovery.

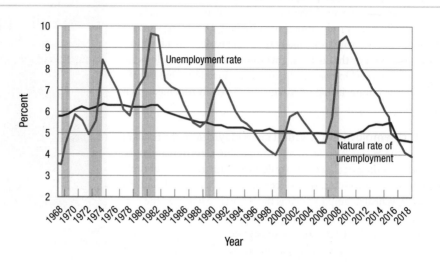

Of particular importance is the length of time it takes the unemployment rate to return to the natural rate when recessions push unemployment higher. To analyze this point, Figure 5 shows the unemployment rate over the past 50 years, along with the natural rate of unemployment. Periods of recession are shaded, most indicating cyclical unemployment as the unemployment rate line rises above the natural rate. It is interesting to note that the time it takes the unemployment rate to return to the natural rate varies. In most economic recoveries prior to 1990, the unemployment rate returned to the natural rate fairly quickly. The 1990–1991 and 2001 recessions did not produce much cyclical unemployment; however, the unemployment rate initially rose during the recovery, leading to a "jobless recovery." One reason for jobless recoveries is automation as companies substitute capital and technology in place of labor following an economic downturn. The longest jobless recovery occurred after the 2007–2009 recession, in which the unemployment rate stayed well above the natural rate for several years.

Jobless Recoveries Prolong Unemployment Above the Natural Rate The previous chapter discussed some of the reasons why unemployment can stay high for so long after a recession is deemed over. It highlighted the four key markets—labor, financial, capital, and output—that influence one another and affect job growth. But the fact that economic growth does not always coincide with job growth deserves an explanation.

In the labor market, recessions tend to send people looking for other options—going back to college, seeking early retirement, or just taking time off until the economy improves. Some who are out of work during these periods take temporary or part-time jobs to support their loved ones until better work can be found. Although all of these people's jobs were affected, the government does not consider them as unemployed because they had either found temporary work or had left the labor force to pursue other options. Thus, the official unemployment rate reported during recessions tends to underestimate the actual number of people seeking work, a problem discussed in the previous section.

During an economic recovery, as jobs are being created, not only do the unemployed seek these jobs, but also many of those who had left the labor force return to compete for these same jobs. When many would-be workers choose to leave the workforce during a prolonged economic downturn, competition for jobs can be more severe during an economic recovery when these workers return to the labor force.

The last few recessions saw many people temporarily leave the workforce to pursue nonwork options, such as schooling, stay-at-home parenting, or volunteer work. These choices may explain why unemployment is slow to fall during economic recoveries and one of the major reasons why jobless recoveries might remain a feature in future recessions.

Inflation, employment, unemployment, and gross domestic product (GDP) are the key macroeconomic indicators of our economic health. Our rising standard of living is closely tied to GDP growth. In the next chapter, we will investigate what causes our economy and living standards to grow over the long term.

ISSUE

Why Do Unemployment Rates Differ So Much Within the United States?

In December 2018, the U.S. unemployment rate was 3.9%. However, in Alaska, it was 6.5%. Meanwhile, in Iowa, it was only 2.4%. Looking at metropolitan area unemployment rates reveals even starker differences. The unemployment rate in El Centro, California, was 17.7%, while in Ames, Iowa, it was 1.5%. Why do such large differences in unemployment exist between states and between cities?

In Europe, where citizens of the European Union are free to live and work in any other country within the union, differences in unemployment rates between member countries remain largely due to cultural reasons. People are hesitant to move to a country where people speak a different language or have a different culture. But in the United States, language and cultural differences between states are considerably less than between European countries—English is the primary language, and Americans all basically watch the same types of movies and television shows.

Aside from the common language and culture, differences do arise in other areas, which helps to explain the differences in the unemployment rate.

First, differences in taxes and regulations exist between states. Some states

The college town of Ames, Iowa, home of Iowa State University, had virtually no unemployment in 2018.

The farming community of El Centro, California, near the southern border with Mexico, had the highest unemployment rate in the nation in 2018.

have lower taxes than others, and some states have environmental and work rules that are more business friendly than others.

Second, many industries tend to form a cluster in order to take advantage of economies of scale and scope. For example, industrial agglomeration in the computer industry centers in greater San Jose ("Silicon Valley"). Detroit has long been the automobile capital of the country, while Gary, Indiana, was once a major steel-producing town (in addition to being the birthplace of Michael Jackson). Economic trends tend to favor some industries over others. Biotechnology, eCommerce, and health care industries have experienced much growth over the past decade, leading

to employment growth in cities home to these industries. However, declines in manufacturing and the oil industry have increased unemployment in cities heavily dependent on those industries for employment.

Finally, and perhaps most obvious, people prefer certain geographic areas to others. Significant population growth has occurred in the South and Mountain West, where warm weather and scenic beauty await, respectively. Many immigrants from Mexico prefer living in states bordering Mexico for cultural reasons. And throughout much of the past century, people have moved from rural areas to urban areas. How much would you sacrifice to live in a preferred area? People often ask themselves this question.

 CHECKPOINT

UNEMPLOYMENT AND THE ECONOMY

- Frictional unemployment is inevitable and natural for any economy as people change jobs and new businesses start up while others close.

- Structural unemployment is typically caused by changes in consumer demands or technology. It is typically of long duration and often requires the unemployed to be retrained for new jobs.

- Cyclical unemployment results from changes in the business cycle. When a recession hits, unemployment rises, then falls when an expansion ensues.

- Macroeconomic policies have the most effect on cyclical unemployment.

- Full employment is typically defined as that level at which cyclical unemployment is zero, or the level associated with a low nonaccelerating inflation rate.

QUESTION: The financial industry experienced a rapid expansion in the mid-2000s as a result of the housing bubble, which created jobs for millions of workers in banks, mortgage companies, financial advising companies, and insurance companies. When the bubble burst, many of these workers became unemployed as the financial industry retrenched. For many, their skills were so specialized that they were unable to find new jobs at their old salaries. Were these people frictionally, structurally, or cyclically unemployed? Explain.

Answers to the Checkpoint questions can be found at the end of this chapter.

CHAPTER SUMMARY

SECTION 1 INFLATION

Inflation is a general rise in prices throughout the economy. Prices for individual goods can fluctuate up or down, but the price level captures the overall trend in the movement of prices.

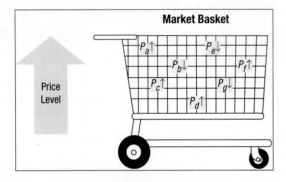

Market Basket

Price Level

$P_a\uparrow$ $P_e\downarrow$ $P_b\downarrow$ $P_f\uparrow$ $P_c\uparrow$ $P_g\downarrow$ $P_d\uparrow$

6.2 **Calculating Inflation Using the CPI**

$$CPI = (\text{Cost in current period}) \div (\text{Cost in base period}) \times 100$$

Example: Suppose a market basket consists of pizza and soda

Base year prices: Pizza = \$6 and Soda = \$2
Current year prices: Pizza = \$8 and Soda = \$3

$$CPI = (\$8 + \$3) \div (\$6 + \$2) \times 100 = 137.5$$
(average prices rose 37.5% since the base year)

6.4 **Disinflation Versus Deflation**

Disinflation occurs when the rate of inflation falls but is still positive.

Deflation occurs when the rate of inflation turns negative.

Hyperinflation is an extremely high rate of inflation, over 100% per year. It typically is caused by excess government spending over tax revenues (high deficits) and the printing of money to finance deficits.

6.1 **How Inflation Is Measured**

- **Consumer price index (CPI):** An index of the average change in prices of a market basket of consumer goods and services.
- **Producer price index (PPI):** An index of the average change in prices received by producers for their output.
- **GDP deflator:** The broadest index used to measure inflation; it includes the prices of all goods and services in the economy.

6.3 **The Main Causes of Inflation**

- **Strong consumer demand:** Consumers spend more money, demand increases, and prices rise.
- **Supply shocks on key inputs:** When prices for goods with inelastic demand (such as food or oil) rise, the higher prices are passed on to other industries and to consumers.
- **Government printing money:** When a government prints money to finance its borrowing, more money is chasing a relatively fixed amount of goods and services, and therefore prices rise.

Melanie Blanding/Alamy

A severe drought can result in a poor harvest for corn, pushing prices higher for corn and any good that uses corn, contributing to inflation.

PHOTOCOPYING SERVICES PRICE LIST

A4 SINGLE SIDE	2 000 000 - 00
A4 BOTH SIDE	3 000 000 - 00
Ids/PASSPORTS	3 000 000 - 00
A3 SINGLE SIDE	6 000 000 - 00
A3 BOTH SIDE	10 000 000 - 00
Lamination	25 000 000 - 00
Spiral Binding (minimum)	45 000 000 - 00

A price list of photocopying services in Zimbabwe in 2008 during hyperinflation.

SECTION 2 UNEMPLOYMENT

The **labor force** is the total number of people employed or unemployed. **Employed** persons are individuals age 16 and over who work for pay, whether full-time, part-time, or even temporary. **Unemployed** persons are those without jobs but actively seeking work.

If you work part-time at the local coffee shop after graduation while looking for a good job, you are not unemployed. Instead, you are underemployed, which still is considered employed.

6.5

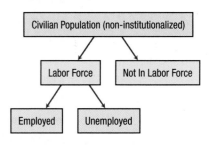

6.6 **Who Are NOT Considered in the Labor Force?**

- **Discouraged workers** are the portion of marginally attached workers who have given up looking for work because they believe there are not enough good jobs.
- Marginally attached workers are those who have looked for work in the past 12 months but not in the last four weeks.
- Students who do not work are not counted in the labor force.
- Retired persons and children under 16 are not counted in the labor force.
- Institutionalized persons including persons in prison also are not counted in the labor force.

SECTION 3 UNEMPLOYMENT AND THE ECONOMY

6.7 **Types of Unemployment**

- **Frictional unemployment:** Includes workers who voluntarily quit their jobs in search of better positions or recent graduates seeking their first full-time job.
- **Structural unemployment:** Longer-term unemployment that is caused by changes in consumer demands or technology and requires workers to use their skills in another industry or to retrain for a new career.

35mm film is rarely used nowadays and has led to structural unemployment as workers in the 35mm film industry find new employment.

- **Cyclical unemployment:** Unemployment that results from the business cycle—when a recession hits, firms lay off workers until the economy recovers.

6.8 The **natural rate of unemployment** or *nonaccelerating inflation rate of unemployment (NAIRU)* is the rate of unemployment that exists when prices and wages are equal to people's expectations. At the natural rate of unemployment, the economy is at "full employment."

Natural rate of unemployment = frictional + structural unemployment

The natural rate of unemployment in the United States has trended downward over the past few decades and is stable between 4.5% and 5.5%.

Key Concepts

inflation, p. 138

price level, p. 139

disinflation, p. 139

deflation, p. 139

consumer price index (CPI), p. 140

producer price index (PPI), p. 142

GDP deflator, p. 142

hyperinflation, p. 144

labor force, p. 149

labor force participation rate, p. 149

marginally attached workers, p. 151

discouraged workers, p. 151

underemployed workers, p. 151

frictional unemployment, p. 154

structural unemployment, p. 154

cyclical unemployment, p. 155

natural rate of unemployment, p. 155

Questions and Problems

Check Your Understanding

1. Describe the three common indices used to measure inflation and the focus of each.

2. Who loses from unanticipated inflation? Who benefits?

3. Why is the inflation rate a positive number when prices of certain goods, such as computers and televisions, fall dramatically due to technological advancement?

4. What is required for a person to be considered unemployed? How is the unemployment rate computed?

5. Why do teenagers and young people have high unemployment rates?

6. Describe the three types of unemployment. What types of government programs would be most effective in combating each type?

Apply the Concepts

7. If you believe that inflation is going to increase significantly over the next few years and you are planning to purchase a new car, would it be advantageous to purchase the car now with a low fixed-interest-rate loan or wait a few years and purchase the car with your savings? Explain.

8. Suppose you work hard at a job after graduation and after your first year, your effort is rewarded with a 3% raise when the average wage increase in your company is 2%. Then, the government releases its inflation report, which states that inflation is running at 5%. Given this information, did your standard of living improve? Why or why not?

9. Suppose Mexico's population grew by 10% over the past two decades due to increased immigration from Central America while Costa Rica's population grew by 10% over the same period primarily due to rising life expectancy. Would the population growth have the same effect on the labor force and unemployment rate in each country? Explain.

10. Assume you just lost your job and have decided to take a monthlong break to travel to Europe before looking for a new position. Just as you return home from your trip, you are interviewed by the Census Bureau about your employment status. How would you be classified (employed, unemployed, or not in the labor force)? Explain why.

11. The Bureau of Labor Statistics categorizes unemployed people into several groups, including job leavers, job losers, and discouraged workers. During a mild recession, which group would tend to increase the most? During a deep recession? During an economic expansion?

12. In the beginning of a recovery after a recession, employment begins to rise, and the news media report these data on job growth. What effect would such a report have on the labor market? How would the report affect the unemployment rate?

In the News

13. A debate that regularly occurs in Congress concerns raising the debt ceiling, allowing the U.S. government to continue paying its obligations. A few years ago, one politician proposed that instead of raising the debt ceiling, the U.S. Treasury should just mint a trillion-dollar coin and use it to "pay off" the federal deficit. If such a coin were to be minted, what would be its potential effects on inflation? Is this a risk-free way of paying off a fiscal deficit? Why or why not?

14. Many hotel chains are automating the check-in process by allowing guests to use their phones to download a scannable code that can be used to unlock their rooms, allowing one to bypass the front desk altogether upon arrival. How will this technological change affect employment in the hotel industry? What type of unemployment might this create? If the hotel industry continues to expand rapidly, what type of jobs could these workers transition to?

Solving Problems

Work It Out

 interactive activity

15. Suppose the country of Snowland uses the following market basket of goods to determine its consumer price index, with Year 1 being the base year with a CPI of 100. Nominal GDP is also provided.

Market Basket Items	Year 1	Year 2	Year 3	Year 4
Loaf of bread	$2.50	$2.80	$3.00	$3.10
Movie ticket	$8.00	$8.80	$9.20	$9.50
Gallon of gasoline	$3.50	$4.20	$4.00	$3.60
Scented candle	$12.00	$13.20	$14.00	$14.30
Nominal GDP	$5 billion	$5.6 billion	$6.1 billion	$6.5 billion

a. Calculate the CPI in Snowland for each year, using Year 1 as the base year with CPI = 100.

b. Calculate the rate of inflation (based on CPI) in Year 2, Year 3, and Year 4.

c. Using the CPI, calculate the real GDP in each of the four years.

d. Between Year 1 and Year 4, what proportion of the total increase in nominal GDP was due to inflation?

16. The town of Villageton has 500 residents, of which 300 are employed, 30 are not working but actively seeking work, 80 are children in school, 40 are retirees, 30 are full-time college students, and 20 are institutionalized.

a. Calculate the unemployment rate in Villageton.

b. Suppose that 10 of the 30 college students graduate and enter the labor force actively seeking work, but only 5 find a job. How does this change the unemployment rate in Villageton?

Answers to Questions in Checkpoints

Checkpoint: Inflation 146

Inflation reduces the purchasing power of a dollar. Therefore, if you borrow money when inflation is low and pay back the loan when inflation is higher, the money you are paying back is worth less than what you received. You benefit by being able to pay back your loans with money that is valued at less than before. Thus, unexpected inflation hurts lenders because the money they are being paid back has less purchasing power than they planned. Alternatively, had the inflation rate unexpectedly fallen, lenders would gain, as the money being paid back would have more purchasing power than was expected.

Checkpoint: Unemployment 153

The reason for the requirement that a person actively seek work is to differentiate empirically those who profess to want a job (at possibly a higher wage than they can earn in the market) from those who are actively trying to obtain work.

Checkpoint: Unemployment and the Economy 157

Many workers became structurally unemployed because the skills they acquired for the financial industry (and, in many cases, specific to the housing industry) were not as useful in other industries. Therefore, as the financial industry became smaller after the housing bubble burst, many workers needed to find work in other industries, which often meant acquiring a new skills set.

7

Economic Growth

Understanding the importance of economic growth and the factors that drive it

Learning Objectives

7.1 Describe how economic growth is measured using real GDP and real GDP per capita.

7.2 Use the Rule of 70 to approximate the number of years it takes for an economy's output to double in size.

7.3 Explain the power of compounding in making small differences much larger over time.

7.4 Explain the difference between short-run and long-run growth.

7.5 List the four factors of production and how each plays a role in the production function.

7.6 Discuss the factors that increase productivity and economic growth.

7.7 Explain total factor productivity and what it measures.

7.8 Explain how the government promotes economic growth through the provision of physical capital and the enhancement of human capital and technology.

7.9 Discuss how strong institutions and economic freedom promotes economic growth.

O n a typical downtown street in Beijing in the 1980s, one would see thousands of bicycles and pedestrians among a trickling of cars owned by the privileged few. The skyline consisted of just a few large buildings.

How times have changed! Today, the bicycles in Beijing have largely been replaced with cars driven by millions of Chinese (now the world's largest consumer of cars) whose incomes have increased enough to afford one, the skyline is dominated by modern sky-scrapers, and the pedestrians have largely moved underground, traveling on one of the world's most extensive and modern subway systems.

China's transformation from a poor, agricultural nation to an emerging world power with a growing middle and upper class has been remarkable. According to data from the World Bank, China's annual growth rate has averaged 9.1% over the past 20 years, compared to the average U.S. annual growth rate of 2.2% over the same period. Although a 7% difference might not seem significant, over 20 years the cumulative growth effect is staggering: China's real GDP grew 565% from 1998 to 2018, while in the United States, real GDP grew 53%.

Economic growth plays a very powerful role in how people live and how standards of living change over time. Even small differences in growth rates compound into large differences in the long run.

One generation ago, the United States, Europe, and the Asian economies of Japan, Singapore, South Korea, Taiwan, and Hong Kong were the leaders of economic growth. These economies had consistent, strong growth, while the rest of the world lagged behind.

Today, a much different picture emerges. Some developing countries are experiencing the highest rates of growth, while many developed countries have seen slower growth rates, especially in the aftermath of the devastating financial crisis and recession of 2007–2009.

Since 2000, a large portion of world economic growth has occurred in the BRIC countries: *Brazil, Russia, India, and China*. These countries transformed their developing economies into more advanced economies and by doing so achieved a remarkable feat: Today, all four countries are among the 12 largest economies in the world, as measured by GDP.

But rapid growth in any country cannot be maintained forever. Although India continued to maintain a high growth rate of over 7% in 2018, China's economy has slowed in recent years, from an average annual growth rate of nearly 10% a decade ago to around 7% in 2018. Even worse, Russia's and Brazil's economies both experienced recessions in 2014–2016 as a result of falling export prices. For example, Russia faced a steep drop in oil

Chang'an Avenue, Beijing (1981)

Chang'an Avenue, Beijing (2018)

BY THE Numbers

Economic Growth and the Standard of Living

Economic growth improves the standard of living of people through higher incomes and greater access to societal resources, such as health care, clean water and sanitation, and education, which generally lead to a longer and more prosperous life. This By the Numbers compares the level of GDP per capita with average life expectancy in 2018.

DATA:

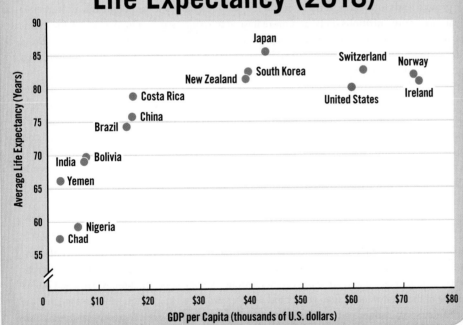

GDP per Capita and Average Life Expectancy (2018)

(Scatter plot. X-axis: GDP per Capita (thousands of U.S. dollars), from $0 to $80. Y-axis: Average Life Expectancy (Years), from 55 to 90.)

Countries plotted: Japan, Switzerland, Norway, South Korea, New Zealand, United States, Ireland, Costa Rica, China, Brazil, India, Bolivia, Yemen, Nigeria, Chad.

Where Can I Find These Data?

Source: CIA World Factbook

Web site: https://www.cia.gov/library/publications/the-world-factbook

Details: Click on the profile of each country. GDP per capita appears in the "Economy" category, and life expectancy appears in the "People and Society" category.

~ Assessing Your Data Literacy ~

1. Which country in the scatter plot has the highest average life expectancy? Which country has the lowest average life expectancy? What is the difference in GDP per capita between these two countries?

2. What trend does the graph show? Why is this not surprising?

3. Does any country appear as an outlier (either low GDP per capita with high average life expectancy, or vice versa)? If not, go to the data source named above to find a country that would be an outlier.

89.4

The average life expectancy in Monaco, the highest in the world and one of the wealthiest nations

72.0

The average life expectancy for the world, which has increased nearly every year over the past century, along with economic growth and development

WHY ARE THESE DATA IMPORTANT?

Economic growth has a cumulative effect on the standard of living. As countries grow and develop economically, more money can be devoted to infrastructure and services that provide opportunities for a better life. Average life expectancy is an important indicator of average well-being, though its relationship with income is not exact. Still, economic growth is a key driver to increasing income and achieving a more comfortable life.

Data *in the News*

"U.S. Life Expectancy Falls Further" by Betsy McKay; *Wall Street Journal*, November 29, 2018

Life expectancy for Americans fell again last year, despite growing recognition of the problems driving the decline and federal and local funds invested in stemming them.

prices that affected its entire economy while Brazil experienced a decline in commodity prices, such as coffee, sugar, and metals.

Although annual growth in the United States has picked up to around 3% in recent years, many of today's fastest-growing countries are concentrated in developing countries in Africa and Central/South Asia, including Ethiopia, Ghana, and Nepal, all of which are growing faster than China and India. This bodes well for bringing many more people out of poverty, just as the BRIC countries have done over the past decade.

This chapter focuses on long-run economic growth and describes the conditions needed to sustain economic growth and improve standards of living. In the long run, all variables in the economy can adjust to changing conditions. The models in this chapter provide a framework for evaluating policies meant to encourage economic growth in the long run.

WHY IS ECONOMIC GROWTH IMPORTANT?

economic growth A change in a country's output or income that leads to an improvement in the standard of living.

Economic growth is tied closely to how well people live. We already saw how a high growth rate in China changed the lives of much of its population—more people now can buy cars, computers, and other goods that previously were either unavailable or unaffordable. Economic growth improves the lives of people of all income levels, from the richest to the poorest citizens.

The benefits of economic growth extend beyond the goods people can buy. For example, economic growth leads to lower poverty rates and longer life expectancies as people can afford better medical care, more nutritious diets, and more leisure to reduce stress. The data speak for themselves. In 1985, the average life expectancies (females and males combined) in China and India were 68 and 56 years, respectively. In 2018, they were 78 and 68 years, respectively. Children born in China and India today can expect to live about a decade longer than their parents.

compounding The ability of growth to build on previous growth. It allows variables such as income and GDP (as well as debt) to increase significantly over time.

Still, according to estimates by the World Bank, nearly 2 billion people in the world live on less than $3.20 per day (about $100 per month). However, the number of people living in poverty has fallen as many countries, such as the BRIC nations, which make up over 40% of the world's population, saw economic growth rates improve over the past two decades. This section analyzes how economic growth is measured and how the power of **compounding**, in which growth builds upon prior growth, can turn small rates of growth into substantial increases in output and income over time, leading to better lives for all.

How Is Economic Growth Measured?

real GDP The total value of final goods and services produced in a country in a year measured using prices in a base year.

Small differences in growth can lead to dramatic differences in income due to the effect of compounding. To show this, we first have to measure economic growth, using the concepts of gross domestic product (GDP) and GDP per capita introduced in an earlier chapter. As we saw, GDP is a measure of the total value of final goods and services produced in a country in one year, or simply a country's total annual output. GDP per capita is a country's GDP divided by its population and provides a rough measure of a typical person's standard of living. Also, recall that **real GDP** and **real GDP per capita** use constant dollars to remove the effects of inflation, allowing for more accurate comparisons in output from year to year.

real GDP per capita Real GDP divided by population. Provides a rough estimate of a country's standard of living.

When a country's real GDP per capita increases, the average output per person is increasing (not just prices), and this generally translates into a higher standard of living for most of its residents. Therefore, this is a good indicator of how an economy grows over time.

In the United States, real GDP is calculated by the Bureau of Economic Analysis (BEA). The BEA produces quarterly reports on the changes in U.S. GDP from the previous quarter and is reported as an annualized rate (quarterly change multiplied by 4). For example, the BEA reported that the U.S. economy grew 2.2% in the fourth quarter of 2018. This means that real GDP in the United States increased 0.55% from the third quarter of 2018 to the fourth quarter of 2018, which equals a rise of 2.2% when annualized.

In addition, the BEA provides GDP growth data *year-over-year*. For example, the BEA reported that the U.S. economy grew 2.9% from the fourth quarter of 2017 to the fourth quarter of 2018. Why

TABLE 1	COMPARING REAL GDP GROWTH DATA IN 2018	
	Annualized GDP Growth Rate	Year-Over-Year Growth Rate
1st quarter	+2.2%	+2.6%
2nd quarter	+4.2%	+2.9%
3rd quarter	+3.4%	+3.0%
4th quarter	+2.2%	+2.9%

Data from BEA Interactive Tables: GDP and the National Income and Product Accounts.

does the BEA report year-over-year growth? Year-over-year growth allows investors and policymakers to compare how the economy has grown over an entire 12-month period, without the seasonal ups and downs most economies experience. Table 1 shows the quarterly real GDP growth rates in 2018 using the annualized and year-over-year methods. The Annualized column shows the seasonal fluctuations that influenced economic growth each quarter, while the Year-Over-Year column shows the growth rate for the preceding 12 months. Both measures are useful depending on whether one is analyzing trends in economic performance for a particular season or for the entire year.

Small Differences in Growth Lead to Large Differences in Income Over Time

When we think of a stark contrast in living standards, we need look no further than the U.S.–Mexican border. For example, driving along Interstate 10 in El Paso, Texas (which is less than 200 yards from the border at its closest point), one can see tremendous differences in the quality of housing in Mexico versus that in the United States. Yet, how did such a difference in standard of living occur? Did the U.S. economy grow that much faster? The surprising answer is that the U.S. growth rate over the past 100 years averaged just 1% higher than Mexico's growth rate. Perhaps more surprising is that Mexico's real GDP per capita is *above average* in the world. Even Mexico appears "rich" to countries such as Nicaragua and Honduras, whose real GDP per capita is only about one-fourth that of Mexico. If growth rates did not differ much between the United States and Mexico or between Mexico and Nicaragua over the past century, why are the economies of these countries so different? The answer is the power of compounding growth.

Power of Compounding Growth Rates Suppose you deposit $1,000 in a high-interest money market account that averages 10% in interest per year. If you simply let the interest accrue without adding any additional money to the account, that $1,000 would turn into $28,102 in 35 years. How is that possible? Money earns interest, in this case 10%. But interest also earns interest. In fact, jump ahead 34 years, when your $1,000 is worth $25,548. In year 35, earning 10% on $25,548 equals over $2,500 in interest, bringing your total to $28,102. In that year, you earned over 2.5 times more in interest than the $1,000 you originally put in. That is the power of compounding growth.

Suppose instead that your money grew at 5% per year. What do you think the return will be? One-half of the 10% amount of $28,102? No . . . saving $1,000 at 5% would result in a total value of $5,516 in 35 years, significantly less than half of the $28,102 had the interest rate been 10%. This example shows that small differences in interest result in big changes

The border between the United States and Mexico offers a glimpse at the sharp contrast between two nations with different growth paths.

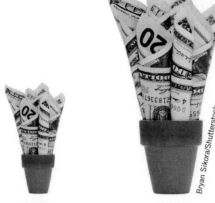

At 5% = $5,516   **At 10% = $28,102**

Doubling the interest rate on a $1,000 deposit generates over 5 times more earnings over 35 years.

Rule of 70 Provides an estimate of the number of years for a value to double and is calculated by dividing 70 by the annual growth rate.

over time. Suppose that your money grew at 9%, just 1% less than 10%. Your $1,000 would be worth $20,414 in 35 years, a drop of almost $8,000 over this period.

These numerical examples highlight the importance of small differences in growth rates over time. Over the past 100 years, the United States grew 2% a year on average, Mexico grew 1.2% a year on average, and Nicaragua grew 0.3% a year on average. These differences are about 1%, but with compounding, U.S. real GDP per capita is about 4 times that of Mexico, and Mexico's real GDP per capita is about 4 times that of Nicaragua.

Rule of 70 Calculating compounding growth over a long period requires the use of a formula and calculator. Fortunately, there is an easy way to *approximate* the number of years it takes for an amount to double in value by using the **Rule of 70.** This rule states that the number of years required for a value (such as a nation's GDP) to double in size is equal to 70 divided by the growth rate:

Number of Years to Double in Value = 70/Growth Rate

For example, if the growth rate is 10%, it would take about 70/10 = 7 years for an initial value of $1,000 to double to $2,000, another 7 years (or 14 years total) to double again to $4,000, another 7 years (or 21 years total) to double again to $8,000, and so on.

The Rule of 70 is fairly accurate for small growth rates. For larger growth rates, especially above 10%, the Rule of 70 becomes slightly less accurate over time. Table 2 provides a comparison between actual values and estimated values using the Rule of 70 for 5% and 10% growth rates. As you see, using the Rule of 70 for the smaller growth rate results in a more accurate estimate.

Although the Rule of 70 does not provide an exact estimate of compounded values over time, its ease of use makes it a valuable tool in understanding the power of compounding growth rates over time.

In all examples so far, we have shown how compounding growth can lead to much improved lives over time. However, it is also important to note that the reverse can be true. The compounding effect also makes debts significantly larger over time.

Do you keep a balance on a credit card? If so, you're not alone. The average American household carries about $10,000 in credit card balances each month. Most credit cards charge interest rates on unpaid balances between 12% and 18%, some even more. Suppose an individual has $10,000 in debt at a 17.5% interest rate. If no payments are made on this debt (let's assume a minimum monthly payment is not required), the Rule of 70 says that the debt will double about every 4 years (70/17.5). If no payment is made on this debt, that $10,000 will turn into $20,000 in 4 years, $40,000 in 8 years, $80,000 in 12 years, and $160,000 in 16 years. Thus, paying off credit card balances can lead to significant savings over time.

In sum, the power of compounding means that policies aimed at increasing the annual rate of economic growth can have powerful long-run effects, resulting in some countries becoming rich while others that do not achieve such growth remain poor. The benefits of economic growth are highlighted through the remarkable rise in income over time that leads to a higher standard of living for all citizens. But what exactly spurs economic growth? That is a question we answer in the next section.

TABLE 2	ACCURACY OF THE RULE OF 70			
	5% Growth Rate		**10% Growth Rate**	
	Actual	**Using Rule of 70**	**Actual**	**Using Rule of 70**
Initial:	$1,000	$1,000	$1,000	$1,000
14 years:	$1,979	$2,000	$3,797	$4,000
28 years:	$3,920	$4,000	$14,421	$16,000

# ISSUE

Can Economic Growth Bring a Billion People Out of Poverty?

Poverty is a global concern. Although definitions of poverty vary from country to country, the World Bank defines *extreme poverty* as a person living on less than $1.90 per day (in real, inflation-adjusted dollars). According to World Bank estimates, in 1994 nearly 2 billion people in the world lived in extreme poverty. Twenty-five years later, that number dropped by 60% even as the world's population grew from 5.5 billion to 7.5 billion over this period.

How did over a billion people find themselves no longer in extreme poverty? Much of the drop can be attributed to economic growth in developing countries such as China and India and, more recently, countries in Africa. In China alone, 25 years of solid growth pulled more than 600 million people above the extreme poverty threshold. Although average wages remain low compared to those in the United States or Europe, a typical factory worker making $500 per month can live a modest life in China, where the cost of living is significantly lower, and clearly a better life than in 1994, when average monthly wages were only $30 per month.

India is another country that has seen significant reductions in extreme poverty. Although poverty rates remain much higher in India than in China, India's growth rate of over 7% led to tens of millions exiting poverty each year. And since 2005, many countries in Africa have begun seeing their poverty rates fall, as greater investment in natural resource industries has led to strong economic growth on the mineral- and oil-rich continent.

Clearly, economic growth is a powerful factor, even during times of economic downturn. During the 2007–2009 global economic downturn, when poverty based on higher thresholds in the United States and in Europe increased, extreme poverty around the world continued to fall. The World Bank's stated goal is to end extreme poverty by 2030.

Economic growth is arguably the most important contributor to reducing extreme poverty worldwide. Yet, not all problems with poverty have been resolved. First, while extreme poverty has fallen precipitously, poverty as defined by higher income thresholds has dropped less than 20% since 1990. In other words, while

Strong economic growth in India over the past 25 years has brought hundreds of millions of people out of poverty, allowing a much more comfortable life for the next generation.

much progress has been made to eliminate extreme poverty, over a quarter of the world's population remains very poor.

Hence, economic growth remains one of the most important, if not the most important, macroeconomic objective pursued by policymakers in order to continue the progress of reducing poverty worldwide.

 # CHECKPOINT

WHY IS ECONOMIC GROWTH IMPORTANT?

- Economic growth is measured by the increase in real GDP and real GDP per capita. In the United States, it is calculated by the BEA on a quarterly basis as an annualized percentage change as well as a year-over-year change.

- Small differences in growth rates translate into large differences in output and income over time. Just a 1% difference in growth over time can make one country appear rich and another country appear poor.

- The Rule of 70 provides an easy way to approximate the number of years required for a value to double.

QUESTIONS: In 2019 the average Chinese manufacturing worker earned about $6,000 a year, while the average U.S. manufacturing worker earned $48,000 a year. Suppose that the U.S. growth rate is 3% per year (income doubles about every 23 years using the Rule of 70), while China's growth rate is 7% per year (income doubles about every 10 years using the Rule of 70). If these growth rates do not change, in what year would the typical Chinese worker earn $48,000 a year? In what year would the typical Chinese worker catch up to the American worker if U.S. wages continue to increase by 3% per year?

Answers to the Checkpoint questions can be found at the end of this chapter.

THINKING ABOUT SHORT-RUN AND LONG-RUN ECONOMIC GROWTH

Up to this point, we have discussed why economic growth is good and how it is measured. Next, we need to discuss the differences between short-run and long-run growth and the factors that determine economic growth.

Short-Run Versus Long-Run Growth

The first step to understanding how growth occurs is to understand the difference between short-run and long-run growth.

Short-Run Growth Involves a Fixed Capacity Short-run growth occurs when an economy makes use of existing but underutilized resources. For example, abandoned shopping centers or malls could easily be reopened with new stores. Idle construction equipment and unemployed workers could quickly be put into use on a new project. In these cases, the resources to produce goods and services are available but are not being used.

Short-run growth is common when countries are recovering from an economic downturn or when obstacles preventing resources from being fully used (such as restrictions on land use or high mandatory benefits for workers) are loosened. But to sustain growth beyond the small fluctuations common in the business cycle, efforts to expand an economy's ability to produce are necessary. This leads to long-run growth.

Long-Run Growth Involves Expanding Capacity Long-run growth occurs when an economy finds new resources or improved ways to use existing resources. In other words, the capacity to produce goods and services increases, leading to long-run growth. For example, suppose natural gas deposits that are estimated to be abundant in the United States are explored, leading to an expansion in production of natural gas vehicles (NGVs). This may lead to an expansion of production capacity in the United States through the development of environmentally-friendly cars that run on domestically-produced natural gas.

In a previous chapter, we introduced the production possibilities frontier (PPF) to illustrate the maximum productive capacity of an economy if all resources are fully utilized. We now use PPF diagrams to show the difference between short-run and long-run economic growth.

In Figure 1, the left panel shows an economy initially producing at point *a* inside of its PPF, indicating underutilized resources, such as idle equipment or excess labor. By putting

····· Figure 1 • Short-Run Versus Long-Run Growth Illustrated on PPF Diagrams ·····

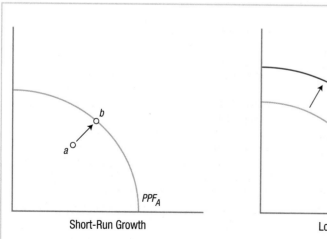
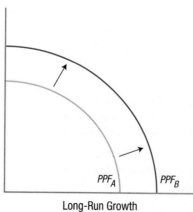

Short-run economic growth occurs when underutilized resources are placed into production. In a PPF diagram, this is shown as a movement from a point inside the PPF to a point closer to or on the PPF (such as from *a* to *b*). Long-run economic growth occurs when new resources are found or existing resources are used more efficiently, thus expanding an economy's capacity to produce. In this case, PPF_A expands outward to PPF_B, allowing for more production possibilities.

Short-Run Growth

Long-Run Growth

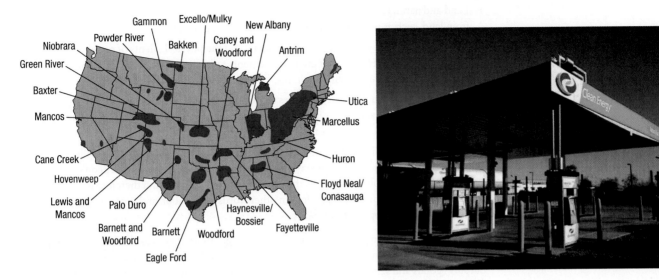

The United States has been called the "Saudi Arabia of Natural Gas" due to its abundance of natural gas deposits.

these resources to work, an economy can work toward production capacity on the PPF line at point *b*, representing short-run growth. Long-run growth, illustrated in the right panel, requires an economy to find new resources, such as new natural resources or improved human capital in its workforce, and/or new ideas and technology to make better use of existing resources. Such improvements in production capacity will shift PPF_A outward to PPF_B, allowing for more production possibilities.

Factors of Production

Achieving long-run growth requires an economy to acquire new resources or to find better ways to use the resources it has to generate goods and services people desire either domestically or abroad through trade. These resources are categorized into the four factors of production, which are the building blocks for production and economic growth. Let's review these factors of production.

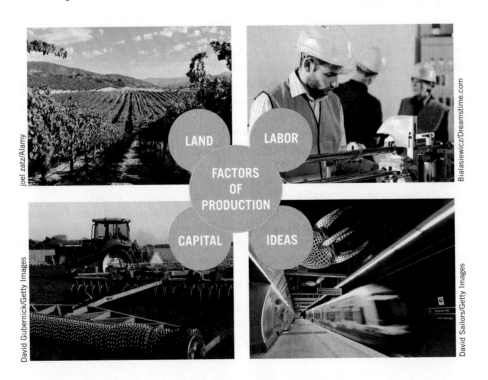

1. Land and natural resources (denoted as N) include land and any raw resources that come from land, such as mineral deposits, oil, natural gas, and water.

2. Labor (denoted as L) includes both the mental and the physical talents of people. Human capital (denoted as H) includes the improvements to labor capabilities from training, education, and apprenticeship programs.

3. Physical capital (denoted as K) includes all manufactured products that are used to produce other goods and services. This includes machinery used in factories, cash registers in stores and restaurants, and communications networks used to track shipments.

4. Entrepreneurial ability and ideas, or technology (denoted as A), describe the ability to take resources and use them in creative ways to produce goods and services that people will buy. For example, technology improves the productivity of all factors and therefore is considered a highly valuable input in production. In other words, land, labor, and physical capital are not useful without entrepreneurial ability.

When factors of production are used to produce goods and services useful for consumption, a measurement tool is needed to calculate the extent to which inputs (resources) are turned into outputs (goods and services). The relationship between the amount of inputs used in production and the amount of output produced is called a production function.

Production Function

production function Measures the output produced using various combinations of inputs and a fixed level of technology.

A **production function** shows the output that is produced using different combinations of inputs combined with existing technology. Although many types of production functions exist, most are variations of the classical form: Output $= f(L, K)$, which means that output is determined by some function of available labor and capital.

Every country, industry, and even firm can have a different production function that measures how much output it can produce given the physical inputs and technology available. No two countries will produce exactly the same type or amount of products given the resources they have. Thus, a production function is a very important tool used to determine whether a country is using its limited resources efficiently and to what extent it can experience long-run growth.

Suppose $f(L, K) = L + K$ for simplicity. This means that if an economy has 10 units of labor and 10 units of capital, total output would equal $10 + 10 = 20$. Although most production functions are not this simple, the idea is that more inputs can produce more output according to some function.

Because inputs are not limited to just labor and capital, a more realistic production function would look like the following:

$$\text{Output} = A \times f(L, K, H, N)$$

where total output equals technology (A) times a function of available labor (L), physical capital (K), human capital (H), and land and natural resources (N).

This equation helps to explain how an entire economy grows. For example, having a more educated labor force or having more capital will contribute to higher productive capacity of the economy (shifting the PPF outward).

But what we are truly interested in is how growth affects the lives of people living in those countries. For example, India's GDP has grown at a very fast pace, but so has its population. The important question is how economic growth affects the standard of living of the average person, or output per person. One way to achieve a close (but not exact) measure of output per person is to revise the previous production function to one that measures output per worker.

To do so, assume that the production function exhibits constant returns to scale (a reasonable assumption). This means that any proportional change in the number of inputs results in the same proportional change in output. For example, if we divide all inputs by L, we would be able to calculate the output per worker as follows:

$$\text{Output per worker} = A \times f(L/L, K/L, H/L, N/L)$$

This equation shows that output per worker equals technology times a function of physical capital per worker, human capital per worker, and land and natural resources per worker. Because we are concerned with output per worker, having more people will not automatically lead to a better standard of living (hence, $L/L=1$). However, having more physical capital per person or more human capital (education) will increase the productivity of labor as each worker produces more output. Therefore, increases in capital will lead to improved standards of living.

To this point, we have discussed the importance of economic growth and defined the building blocks for economic growth using the factors of production that enter into the production function. The next section will use the production function to discuss ways in which an economy grows by increasing productivity.

✅ CHECKPOINT

THINKING ABOUT SHORT-RUN AND LONG-RUN ECONOMIC GROWTH

- Short-run growth occurs from using resources that have been sitting idle or underutilized and is represented in a PPF diagram as a movement from a point within the PPF toward the PPF.

- Long-run growth occurs when the productive capacity of an economy is expanded through more resources or better uses of existing resources (i.e., technological advancements) and is shown in a PPF diagram as an outward shift of the PPF.

- The primary factors of production are land and natural resources, labor (and human capital), physical capital, and technology (entrepreneurial ability and ideas).

- A production function measures the amount of output that can be produced using different combinations of inputs. Production functions vary by firms, industries, and countries.

- Output per person adjusts the production function for changes in population growth in a country.

QUESTION: The Ivory Coast (Côte d'Ivoire) in West Africa is a country with abundant natural resources, a long coastline, and a stable currency that is tied to the euro and managed by the French Treasury. Despite these benefits, it remains an extremely poor country with an unstable government. What does this finding suggest about the Ivory Coast's overall factors of production and its production function compared to a country, say, Iceland, with fewer physical resources but a significantly higher standard of living?

Answers to the Checkpoint questions can be found at the end of this chapter.

APPLYING THE PRODUCTION FUNCTION: ACHIEVING ECONOMIC GROWTH

The production function allows us to measure how inputs are converted into outputs. The extent to which inputs are converted into outputs is referred to as **productivity.** For example, when worker productivity grows, each worker is producing more output for each hour devoted to production.

Productivity is a key driver of wages and incomes. When workers have access to better tools and equipment or are better educated, productivity increases, resulting in a higher standard of living.

The factors of production discussed in the previous section play an important role in increasing economic growth. As the quantity of each factor rises, output rises according to the production function for each industry. In addition, technology plays an important role in enhancing the productive output of all other resources.

A country's output is measured by the value of the goods and services it produces, which can increase based on their quantity or quality. In other words, highly productive countries are able to produce many goods that are high in value. One reason why Japan remains one of the world's richest countries is that its labor force is highly productive. Using abundant physical capital, human capital, and technology, Japan's labor force produces many high-priced products, such as cars, robots, and advanced electronics.

Let's now look at each factor of production to understand what increases productivity and economic growth.

productivity How effectively inputs are converted into outputs. Labor productivity is the ratio of the output of goods and services to the labor hours devoted to the production of that output. Productivity and living standards are closely related.

Achieving More Land or Natural Resources

Natural resources are the building blocks of production; however, they are not a significant driver of economic growth. Countries that have abundant land and natural resources have an advantage that can translate into economic growth only if such resources are used effectively. Countries that discovered new natural resources have experienced higher rates of growth. For example, new oil deposits have been discovered in Angola and Cameroon over the past decade. These discoveries led to significant investment by oil companies from China, India, and the United States in these countries, which contributed to a higher growth rate.

Growth of the Labor Force

Many countries have experienced significant population growth, leading to an increase in the labor supply. In the United States, population growth has been spurred by a relatively open immigration policy compared to other countries. In addition to population growth, labor force participation increased over the last few decades, as more women entered the workforce and as government policies (such as raising the minimum wage) were implemented to make work more attractive. An increase in the labor force generally leads to greater output but not necessarily more output per person. In order for economic growth to improve the standard of living of its citizens, countries must expand not only the quantity of its labor force but also the quality of labor to ensure that economic growth exceeds population growth.

Increasing the Quality of the Labor Force

investment in human capital Improvements to the labor force from investments in skills, knowledge, and the overall quality of workers and their productivity.

One source of productivity growth comes from improvements to the labor force from **investment in human capital.** Human capital is a term economists use to describe skills, knowledge, and the quality of workers. On-the-job training and general education can improve the quality of labor. In many ways, increasing capital and a highly skilled labor force go together. Well-trained workers are needed to run the highly productive, often highly complex, machines. Unskilled workers are given the least important jobs and earn the lowest wages.

By investing in human capital, nations can ultimately raise their growth rates by improving worker productivity. Government programs that raise the literacy rate, such as universal public education, also raise the rate of economic growth.

Increasing the Capital-to-Labor Ratio

capital-to-labor ratio The capital employed per worker. A higher ratio means higher labor productivity and, as a result, higher wages.

When a farmer in the small Himalayan country of Bhutan plows his field with a crude plow hitched to a couple of yaks, the amount of land he can plant and harvest is minuscule. American farmers, in contrast, use equipment that allows them to plow, plant, fertilize, water, and harvest thousands of acres; they have a high **capital-to-labor ratio.** This raises U.S. farm productivity many orders of magnitude above that of Bhutanese farmers. The ultimate result of this productivity is that American farmers earn a far higher income than their counterparts in the developing world.

Developing countries have large labor forces but little capital. Developed nations like the United States, on the other hand, have limited labor supplies, and each worker works with a large array of capital equipment. As a rule, the more capital employed by workers, the greater their productivity and the higher their earnings.

diminishing returns to capital Each additional unit of capital provides a smaller increase in output than the previous unit of capital.

Although a powerful contributor to productivity, capital is subject to **diminishing returns to capital.** For example, suppose that the farmer in Bhutan buys a tractor to replace his yaks. The increase in productivity would be dramatic. Now suppose that the farmer invests in an irrigation system. Surely, the irrigation system will further increase productivity but likely not as much as the tractor did. In other words, a farmer is likely to purchase the most essential equipment first. Each subsequent piece of equipment will increase production but by a smaller amount than the previous one. For this reason, countries with abundant capital will not gain as much per additional piece of capital than countries with little capital with which to start. This is one reason why developing countries may initially grow faster than developed countries, a phenomenon called the catch-up effect.

catch-up effect Countries with smaller starting levels of capital experience larger benefits from increased capital, allowing these countries to grow faster than countries with abundant capital.

The **catch-up effect** describes the notion that developing countries are able to achieve greater productivity for each unit of capital invested because they have the advantage of using technologies that have already been developed by other countries. This has allowed many developing countries to achieve a higher rate of growth compared to developed countries.

Using expensive tractors and other capital equipment, U.S. farmers are more productive than Bhutanese farmers who rely on wooden plows pulled by yaks.

An example of the catch-up effect is China's remarkable high-speed rail network, the largest in the world. High-speed rail networks were largely invented and perfected by the Japanese, Germans, and French. However, large development costs required substantial government subsidies. China, on the other hand, had the advantage of building its rail network using existing technologies. As a result, China was able to expand its rail network at a lower price per mile, allowing it to catch up and to develop an even more advanced rail network than its predecessors. But because all factors face diminishing returns, the catch-up effect tends to diminish over time unless new technologies are developed to keep the growth rate high.

THOMAS MALTHUS (1766–1834)

Thomas Malthus was raised in Surrey, England, the son of a wealthy eccentric country gentleman. Home-schooled by his father and a tutor, he had learned enough to be accepted to Cambridge University. After attending Cambridge, he spent several years as a clergyman before accepting a teaching post in political economy at the college of the East India Company, making him the first academic economist in history.

In 1793 the pamphleteer William Godwin published *Political Justice,* describing a utopian future with no war, poverty, crime, injustice, or disease. Malthus argued against the book's conclusions during a lengthy discussion with his father, who agreed with the book but nevertheless suggested that Malthus set down his ideas in print.

The result was "An Essay on the Principle of Population, As It Affects the Future Improvement of Society." Malthus argued that the origins of poverty were rooted in an unavoidable contradiction: Population, when allowed to grow without limits, increases geometrically, while the food supply could only increase arithmetically. He argued that English Poor Laws spread pauperism because any improvement in conditions of the poor would simply lead to population increases and to rising food prices and scarcities.

He even went so far as to suggest that "a proclamation should be read out at marriage ceremonies warning couples that they would have to bear the financial burden and consequences of their passion."

His dire predictions about world starvation led Thomas Carlyle a few decades later to describe the economics profession as the "dismal science." Although the predictions of inadequate food supply did not fully materialize due to the invention of agricultural technologies and fertilizer, the "dismal science" remains today as an alternative name for economics.

Information from Paul Strathern, *A Brief History of Economic Genius* (New York: Texere), 2002; Howard Marshall, *The Great Economists: A History of Economic Thought* (New York: Pitman Publishing), 1967; Donald Winch, "Malthus," in *Three Great Economists* (Oxford: Oxford University Press), 1997, pp. 105–218.

Improvements in Technology and Ideas

Technological improvements can come from various sources and play *the* major role in improving productivity, raising the standard of living, and increasing economic growth. These include enterprising individuals who discover innovative products and production methods, from Henry Ford's auto assembly line to Steve Jobs's role in developing the Apple home computer, iPod, iPhone, and iPad that have changed the way we live, work, and socialize. Technology has also improved as a result of advancements in telecommunications, the Internet, and biotechnology.

Technological progress is the primary explanation for the extraordinary economic growth the United States has enjoyed over the last century. In the production function, technology enhances the productive capacity of all other resources.

Technologies that kept our economy expanding have also helped many other countries to grow. In the developing world, growth most often comes from foreign companies building factories that employ locals at low wages. These companies often pay more than workers could have

Did Economic Growth Peak a Century Ago? Prospects for Future Growth

When one thinks of life just 15 years ago, imagine what has changed. GPS technology was very primitive, voice recognition apps were not available, and smartphones and tablets didn't exist, at least in the way we know these products today. Certainly, life has changed from how we lived at the start of the new millennium. But was this a true transformation of our standard of living? According to economist Robert Gordon, the technological advances of the past few decades (including the Internet and social media) do not compare with the effect of inventions over a century ago. In fact, he argues that U.S. economic growth peaked nearly a century ago. Are prospects for future growth in trouble?

In his book *The Rise and Fall of American Growth*, Gordon argues that the true transformation of American standards of living occurred between 1870 and 1940. He points to the five "great inventions," which were (1) electric lights, (2) flush toilets, (3) chemicals and pharmaceuticals, (4) cars, and (5) the telephone. Each of these inventions occurred prior to 1940. Therefore, Gordon argues that life became modernized by the 1940s, and every invention since, while making life more comfortable, has not had the same effect. He makes the point that if a person

Living in the 1940s was "modern" compared to the late 1800s in the sense that people today would find it mostly functional. Have changes in standards of living since the 1940s been as dramatic?

today walked into a 1940s apartment, it would be functional, with indoor plumbing, lights, a refrigerator, and a telephone. But if a person from 1940 walked into an 1870s apartment, the same could not be said.

Is Gordon's pessimistic view on future growth accurate? Only time will tell whether recent and future inventions will measure up to those of a century ago. What would be the contenders of the new "great inventions"? The obvious choices would include personal computers, Internet, social media, biotechnology, and artificial intelligence. But have these inventions so transformed our lives that living without them would be as burdensome as living without lights or the modern toilet? It's a powerful thought to

ponder as one considers the factors that will lead to future growth and the factors that will challenge it.

Prospects for future growth depend largely on the willingness of businesses to innovate and create new products and on the willingness of consumers to demand these new products. Generating another strong and sustained period of growth will not be easy, as many countries face large debts and other problems, making investments in long-term projects more challenging. Yet, just as few predicted the five great inventions of the past century, perhaps a new set of great inventions will occur that might eliminate poverty and diseases and lead to another period of remarkable economic growth.

hoped to earn on their own. These higher earnings become the resources invested to ensure better education and earnings for their children.

Today, new technologies are helping many developing nations accelerate their growth. Wireless service has improved communications, inexpensive vaccinations and health education programs have reduced mortality rates, and the global movement of capital and production facilities has created new job opportunities.

Including Everything Else: Total Factor Productivity

We have shown that productivity can be measured by how well a country uses its resources to produce goods and services. However, a country's productivity is not entirely dependent on the amount of inputs it has. True, a country with more inputs such as physical and human capital will likely produce more output. However, external factors influence the ability of inputs to be used effectively. The measure of output that is not explained by the number of inputs used in production is called **total factor productivity.**

Total factor productivity captures the factors that influence the overall effectiveness of inputs. For example, suppose a major hurricane sweeps through a region, knocking out power and communications for a week. Factories would likely be less productive despite having all of their workers and equipment available. Some equipment might not be able to run without electricity, and the morale of workers after a hurricane might make them less motivated to work. Such effects on output would not be captured by the number of inputs available.

Another factor affecting total factor productivity is the value of new innovations, which increases the efficiency of inputs used in production. For example, social media were originally designed to allow individuals to communicate more easily with one another through sites such as Facebook and Twitter. However, an external effect occurred when firms began to use these sites to market their products, which led to a dramatic change in how people learn about various products and improved the efficiency of production and consumption.

Total factor productivity also is influenced by the institutions in place within a country. For example, a country can have a very educated labor force but policies in place that prevent its human capital from being used efficiently. The country could be engaged in frequent military conflicts, preventing its resources from being used to improve the lives of its citizens. Or a country may have a weak legal system, lack property rights, or lack economic freedom that prevents its markets from producing what people want. These institutional factors are largely influenced by the government. In the next section, we discuss government's role in fostering economic growth.

total factor productivity The portion of output produced that is not explained by the number of inputs used in production.

✅ CHECKPOINT

APPLYING THE PRODUCTION FUNCTION: ACHIEVING ECONOMIC GROWTH

- Productivity is the key driver for economic growth and rises when labor is able to produce greater quantities and higher values of output.

- Increased productivity of labor can come from increases in land and natural resources, the quality of the labor force, the capital-to-labor ratio, and technology.

- Physical capital is subject to diminishing returns, which allows countries with less starting capital to experience a catch-up effect as they acquire more capital.

- Total factor productivity measures the portion of output that is not explained by the amount of inputs placed in use. It captures the external effects that influence the productivity of all inputs.

QUESTION: Several years ago, Warren Buffett, one of the world's richest individuals, pledged that "more than 99% of my wealth will go to philanthropy during my lifetime or at death" and noted that he would give this approximately $30 billion in installments to the Bill & Melinda Gates Foundation. The foundation focuses on grants to developing nations, helping the poorest of the poor. What suggestions would you give the foundation to help these developing nations grow?

Answers to the Checkpoint questions can be found at the end of this chapter.

THE ROLE OF GOVERNMENT IN PROMOTING ECONOMIC GROWTH

Government policies and incentives play an important role in how well a country utilizes its resources, affecting the country's total factor productivity.

Government as a Contributor to Physical Capital, Human Capital, and Technology

The government is the single largest consumer of goods and services in the United States. Each year, the U.S. government spends over $500 billion on purchases including highways, bridges, transportation systems, public education, military equipment, and more. By investing heavily in capital goods, the government promotes a higher level of labor productivity in the country.

Physical Capital: Public Capital and Private Investment One of the reasons why some nations are rich and others are poor lies in the different levels of infrastructure development. The focus on infrastructure means that there is something important that lies behind our aggregate production: We do not just increase capital, increase labor, improve technology, and turn a crank to obtain economic growth.

infrastructure The public capital of a nation, including transportation networks, power-generating plants and transmission facilities, public education institutions, and other intangible resources, such as protection of property rights and a stable monetary environment.

Infrastructure is defined as a country's public capital. It includes: dams, roads, and bridges; transportation networks, such as air and rail lines; power-generating plants and power transmission lines; telecommunications networks; and public education facilities. These items are tangible public goods that can easily be measured, and all are crucial for economic growth.

The government also encourages private investment in physical capital through tax incentives and other subsidies to firms willing to invest in capital projects. Industries that receive the largest tax incentives include aerospace, defense, energy, and telecommunications.

Human Capital: Public Education and Financial Aid The government plays an important role in ensuring that every person has access to a minimum level of education. In the United States, state laws mandate that children stay in school until a minimum age, typically 16. Public schools and universities are highly subsidized by local and state governments to provide affordable access to educational opportunities.

Besides providing funding directly to schools and universities, the government offers various forms of financial assistance directly to students to use toward educational expenses. These include Pell Grants and the G.I. Bill, federal subsidized loans, and various types of tax incentives that allow qualified students (or their parents) to deduct a portion of their tuition and fees from their taxable income, or directly from their taxes. The government also allows teachers to deduct certain expenses from their taxes and provides tax-exempt status for organizations whose mission is to provide scholarships, such as the prestigious National Merit Scholarship Program. These grants, loans, and tax incentives contribute to the government's role in promoting human capital development.

Technology: Government R&D Centers and Federal Grants Some of the largest research centers in the country are funded by the federal government. These include Los Alamos National Laboratory and Sandia National Laboratories (part of the Department of Energy), the National Institutes of Health, the National Aeronautics and Space Administration (NASA), and the National Oceanic and Atmospheric Administration (NOAA), just to name a few. These government research centers employ thousands of scientists, researchers, and doctors for the purpose of advancing knowledge and inventing products that enhance the lives of all citizens and promote economic growth.

Richard Robinson/Los Alamos National Laboratory

The Los Alamos National Laboratory in New Mexico is one of the largest government research centers in the country. During World War II, it was a secret lab that housed the "Manhattan Project," which ultimately produced the world's first atomic bomb.

In addition to running research centers, the federal government provides funds directly to public and private research centers as well as to individual researchers. Among the largest grantors of funds is the National Science Foundation (NSF), founded in 1950. In 2019, the NSF provided nearly $7 billion in grants to approximately 8,000 projects and has maintained its mission of promoting research essential for the nation's economic health and global competitiveness.

Governments that devote substantial resources toward investments in R&D, education, and capital can expect to achieve greater long-run growth. The following Around the World feature focuses on the Central Asian nation of Kazakhstan, whose government has invested heavily in infrastructure and education to promote economic growth.

Government as a Facilitator of Economic Growth

A second major role of government in promoting economic growth is to ensure that an effective legal system is in place to enforce contracts and to protect property rights, and that the financial system is kept stable. These are the less tangible yet equally important components of a country's infrastructure.

Enforcement of Contracts The legal enforcement of contract rights is an important component of infrastructure that promotes economic growth and well-being. Without contract enforcement, people are less likely to be willing to enter into contracts, for example, to produce and deliver goods for payment at some future date. Therefore, contract enforcement promotes economic growth by ensuring that production and purchasing commitments are honored by producers and consumers.

Protection of Property Rights A stable legal system that protects property rights is essential for economic growth. Many developing countries do not systematically record the ownership of real

🌍 AROUND THE WORLD

Kazakhstan: The Next Destination of Growth and Trade

What policies did the government of Kazakhstan implement to promote economic growth over the past decade?

When one thinks of cities experiencing significant economic growth and trade, cities such as Hong Kong, Dubai, and Shanghai often come to mind. But in terms of rapidly growing cities, one city in Central Asia has been overlooked by many: Nur-Sultan, the capital of Kazakhstan.

How did this large country relatively unknown to Americans become a beacon of growth?

Kazakhstan is a melting pot of ethnic cultures, from Russians to Kazakhs who look more like East Asians. Once lampooned by British comedian Sacha Baron Cohen in the

Jose Fuste Raga/Getty Images

movie *Borat* as an impoverished backward nation, Kazakhstan is quite the opposite today. Upon arrival in the capital of Nur-Sultan, one encounters hundreds of construction cranes as new skyscrapers dot the changing city landscape. Kazakhstan is also the launch site of the Russian Federal Space Agency, where Soyuz flights regularly take off and land in the desert steppe at Baikonur Cosmodrome, which today remains the oldest and largest space launch facility in the world.

The emphasis on growth in Kazakhstan can be attributed to several key factors. One surely is abundant natural resources, such as oil. More important are an emphasis on higher education, encouragement of international trade, and significant investment in infrastructure and technology, all backed by government policies. These efforts attracted significant foreign investment from countries around the world, including the United States.

Kazakhstan's strong economic growth, largely due to government efforts, resulted in it achieving the highest average income in Central Asia. A stroll through the modern streets of Nur-Sultan and Almaty (the former capital and home to most historical sites) points to the powerful role that economic growth has on improving the lives of a country's citizens.

📖 GO ONLINE TO PRACTICE THE ECONOMIC CONCEPTS IN THIS STORY

property: land and buildings. Although ownership is often informally recognized, without express legal title, the capital locked up in these informal arrangements cannot be used to secure loans for entrepreneurial purposes. As a result, valuable capital sits idle; it cannot be leveraged for other productive purposes.

In addition, a legal system that recognizes and protects ideas (or intellectual property) is critical to encouraging innovation. Common legal protections for ideas include patents (for inventions), copyrights (for written works, music, and film), and trademarks (for names and symbols). Every country has its innovators; the question is whether these people are offered enough of an incentive to devote their efforts to develop the innovations that drive economic growth. The extent to which countries establish intellectual property rights varies, and even when such protections exist, enforcement of the protections varies.

Stable Financial System Another important component of a nation's infrastructure is a stable and secure financial system. Such a financial system keeps the purchasing power of the currency stable, facilitates transactions, and permits credit institutions to arise. The global economic turmoil that occurred a decade ago was largely caused by financial instability when people lost trust in the institutions that manage our money. More recently, bank runs in Greece and Venezuela highlight the problems of an unstable financial system.

Unanticipated inflations or deflations are both detrimental to economic growth. Consumers and businesses rely on the monetary prices they pay for goods and services for information about the state of the market. If these price signals are constantly being distorted by inflation or deflation, the quality of business and consumer decisions suffers. Unanticipated price changes further lead to a redistribution of income between creditors and debtors. Financial instability is harmful to improving standards of living and generating economic growth.

Government as a Promoter of Free and Competitive Markets

A third role of government in promoting economic growth is maintaining competitive and efficient markets and the freedom for firms and individuals to pursue their interests.

Competitive Markets and Free Trade One challenge facing government is choosing the right mix of policies to keep markets competitive and fair. Regulations are put into place to protect various interests, whether consumer welfare, worker rights and safety, or the environment. But government also must ensure that such regulations do not stand in the way of efficient market operations.

Competitive markets refer to the ability of firms to open and close businesses without unnecessary restrictions or other burdens. Also important is free trade, which refers to the ability to buy and sell products with other countries without significant barriers, such as tariffs or quotas. Allowing the market to function freely within the confines of sensible regulatory laws generally creates more potential for economic growth.

Economic Freedom One of the measures used to gauge the ability of individuals and businesses to make investment and production decisions freely is the Index of Economic Freedom.[1]

Unlike physical infrastructure, such as roads and dams, which are easy to measure, attempting to measure the intangibles of doing business is much harder. The Index of Economic Freedom is a reasonably objective measure that incorporates information about freedoms in twelve categories: property rights, government integrity, judicial effectiveness, taxes, government spending, fiscal health, business, labor, money, trade, investment, and finance.

Clearly, assigning some of these items a numeric value requires a bit of subjective judgment. Even so, this index is one reasonable approach to measuring the overall infrastructure of a country.

Figure 2 portrays the relationship between economic freedom and per capita GDP. Those nations with the most economic freedom have the highest per capita GDP and also the highest growth rates (not shown).

[1] Heritage Foundation, *2019 Index of Economic Freedom* (Washington, D.C.), 2019.

..... Figure 2 • Economic Freedom and per Capita GDP ....

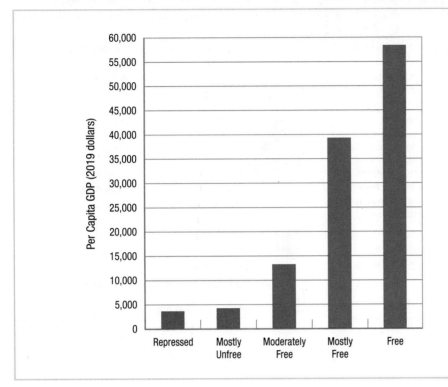

The relationship between economic freedom and per capita GDP in 2019 is shown here. Those nations with the most economic freedom also have the highest per capita GDP.

In this chapter, we have seen that economic growth in the long run comes from improvements in labor productivity, increases in capital, or improvements in technology. Investments in human capital and greater economic freedom also lead to higher growth rates and higher standards of living.

Yet, what are we to do if the economy collapses in the short run? The Great Depression of the 1930s demonstrated that for a reasonably long period (a decade), the economy could be mired in a slowdown with high unemployment rates and negative growth. A deep economy-wide downturn inflicts high costs on both today's citizens and future generations. In the next chapter, we turn to the first of our discussions on managing the economy in the short run.

CHECKPOINT

THE ROLE OF GOVERNMENT IN PROMOTING ECONOMIC GROWTH

- Government has an important role in promoting economic growth by providing physical and human capital, ensuring a stable legal system and financial markets, and promoting free and competitive markets.

- Infrastructure is a country's public capital, including dams, roads, transportation networks, power-generating plants, and public schools.

- Governments provide capital and technology by purchasing public capital and providing incentives for private investment, supporting education through subsidies and financial aid, and supporting research with grants.

- Other less tangible infrastructure elements include protection of property rights, enforcement of contracts, and a stable financial system.

- The Index of Economic Freedom measures the impact of free markets, which supports economic growth.

QUESTION: Imagine a country with a "failed government" that can no longer enforce the law. Contracts are not upheld, and lawlessness is the order of the day. How well could an economy operate and grow in this environment?

Answers to the Checkpoint questions can be found at the end of this chapter.

CHAPTER SUMMARY

SECTION 1 WHY IS ECONOMIC GROWTH IMPORTANT?

7.1 **Economic growth** is the most important factor influencing a country's standard of living. Economic growth is measured by a nation's ability to increase **real GDP** and **real GDP per capita**. Using *real* values instead of *nominal* values allows a country to compare growth from year to year without having to take into account the effects of inflation. Countries with high economic growth have seen rising incomes and better lives for their citizens.

7.2 **The Rule of 70** is a simple tool used to estimate the number of years it takes for a value to double given a constant growth rate.

Number of Years = 70/Growth Rate

Examples: Number of years to double at growth rate of

1%: 70/1 = 70 years
2%: 70/2 = 35 years
5%: 70/5 = 14 years
10%: 70/10 = 7 years
20%: 70/20 = 3.5 years

Small differences in growth rates can result in large differences in value over time due to the power of **compounding.**

7.3 Using the Rule of 70 with 5% and 10% growth rates:

Year	Value at 5%	Year	Value at 10%
2020	$1,000	2020	$1,000
		2027	$2,000
2034	$2,000	2034	$4,000
		2041	$8,000
2048	$4,000	2048	$16,000

In 28 years, the initial $1,000 is worth $16,000 at 10% growth versus $4,000 at 5% growth.

SECTION 2 THINKING ABOUT SHORT-RUN AND LONG-RUN ECONOMIC GROWTH

7.4 **Short-Run Versus Long-Run Growth**

Short-run growth occurs when an economy makes better use of existing or underutilized resources, and is shown as a movement from inside a PPF toward the PPF (such as from point *a* to point *b*).

Long-run growth requires an expansion of production capacity through an increase in resources and/or technology and is shown by an expansion of the PPF (such as from PPF_A to PPF_B).

Short and Long Run

7.5 **Factors of Production**

- **Land (N):** Includes land and natural resources
- **Labor (L):** Within labor is human capital (**H**), labor improved by education or training
- **Capital (K):** Manufactured goods used in the production process
- **Entrepreneurial ability (A):** Includes ideas and the technology that is developed

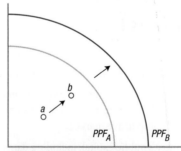

A **production function** is the method by which firms turn factors of production into goods and services.

SECTION 3 APPLYING THE PRODUCTION FUNCTION: ACHIEVING ECONOMIC GROWTH

7.6 **Productivity** is the ability to turn a fixed amount of inputs (factors of production) into more outputs (goods and services).

Ways to Increase Productivity

- Increasing access to natural resources
- Improving quality of labor (human capital)
- Increasing the capital-to-labor ratio
- Promoting innovation and technology

Rising productivity leads to growing incomes and a better standard of living.

7.7 **Total factor productivity** is a measurement of productivity taking into account all other factors beyond the quantity and quality of inputs that could influence production. Examples include natural disasters, climate, or cultural norms that influence the effectiveness of productive inputs.

SECTION 4 THE ROLE OF GOVERNMENT IN PROMOTING ECONOMIC GROWTH

7.8 Government involvement in promoting economic growth occurs by way of investing in physical capital, human capital, and technology.

- **Physical capital:** The building and maintenance of the country's public capital (infrastructure), which includes roads, bridges, airports, power plants, and telecommunications networks
- **Human capital:** Providing subsidized public college education, financial aid grants, and loans
- **Technology:** Funding research via grants and the establishment of major government research labs

West Point, the United States Military Academy, is an example of government promoting physical capital (the campus and buildings), human capital (education), and technology (research by its faculty).

The **Index of Economic Freedom** ranks 186 nations in terms of overall environment for promoting economic growth. In 2019, Hong Kong ranked first, and the United States came in 12th.

7.9 **Government as a Guarantor of Economic Growth**

- **Enforcement of contracts:** A strong legal system
- **Protection of property rights:** Ensuring that monetary rewards are provided to innovators
- **Stable financial system:** A functioning and stable monetary system ensures investment is undertaken when the opportunity arises
- **Promoting free and competitive markets:** International trade allows for specialization and gains from trade, and competitive markets ensure firms do not exploit market power, their ability to set prices for goods and services in a market

Key Concepts

economic growth, p. 166

compounding, p. 166

real GDP, p. 166

real GDP per capita, p. 166

Rule of 70, p. 168

production function, p. 172

productivity, p. 173

investment in human capital, p. 174

capital-to-labor ratio, p. 174

diminishing returns to capital, p. 174

catch-up effect, p. 174

total factor productivity, p. 177

infrastructure, p. 178

Questions and Problems

Check Your Understanding

1. Although having abundant natural resources can be an advantage for a country, are they necessary to ensure economic growth and a prosperous economy?

2. If a country's GDP grows by 10% per year, why isn't the number of years it takes to double the GDP simply 100%/10% = 10 years?

3. What are some ways in which countries can improve labor productivity?

4. In what ways do governments help to build technology and ideas?

5. Why is investment in human capital good for both individuals and fostering economic growth for the economy as a whole?

6. Why is a stable financial system crucial for economic growth?

Apply the Concepts

7. If developing countries such as Vietnam and Ethiopia have growth rates more than double that of the United States or countries in Europe, why do they remain considerably poorer?

8. What role might foreign investment play in helping developing nations improve their growth rates and increase income levels?

9. Higher levels of savings and investment lead to greater rates of economic growth. What can government do to encourage more savings and investment?

10. Per capita income (or output) is the general measure used to compare the standards of living between countries. If a country's population growth is higher than its economic growth, what happens to per capita income? What are some of the limitations to using per capita income as a measure to compare the well-being of different countries?

11. Energy independence has been a goal for many decades. But only in the past decade has the increased focus on renewable energy sources, such as solar, wind, and water, taken on greater significance. How does achieving energy independence contribute to labor productivity and economic growth?

12. When government policymakers debate how to manage a tight budget, they often choose to cut lofty programs such as space exploration, supersonic flights, and reforming the air traffic control system. How might this lead to a tradeoff between short-run and long-run growth?

In the News

13. In 2016, the United Kingdom voted to leave the European Union in a decision referred to as Brexit. By doing so, policies such as the open movement of capital and labor along with free trade may be restricted. Subsequently, the United Kingdom's growth rate slowed. What are some reasons why Brexit may have contributed to the slowing of the United Kingdom's economy?

14. Finland consistently ranks very high in global rankings of educational achievement in science and math. This was a result of a transformation in Finland's public education system to one that focuses on small class sizes and highly trained teachers for primary and secondary education, which is considered a highly prestigious profession. At the college level, many countries fully subsidize college tuition, and in Saudi Arabia, the King Abdullah Scholarship Program offers to send its citizens to study at many of the world's prestigious universities for free. Explain how government investment in education could pay for itself in the long run.

Solving Problems

Work It Out

 interactive activity

15. In 2018, U.S. GDP was approximately $20 trillion, while India's GDP was approximately $2.5 trillion. However, India is growing faster than the United States.

    a. If the U.S. economy grows at 3% per year, in what year will U.S. GDP double to $40 trillion? (*Hint:* Use the Rule of 70 to approximate the number of years needed for GDP to double.)

    b. If India's economy grows at 7% per year, in what year will its GDP double to $5 trillion? In what year would India's economy increase 16-fold to $40 trillion?

    c. If each country's growth rate continues at the same rate, in what year would each country's GDP reach $80 trillion?

16. Suppose a new colony is created on the moon with the following production function: Output $= A \times (L + K + H + N)$. If $L, K, H,$ and N each equal 5 and technology (A) equals 3, how much output would this new colony produce?

 ## Answers to Questions in Checkpoints

Checkpoint: Why Is Economic Growth Important? 169

If incomes in China double every 10 years, Chinese workers would earn $12,000 in 2029, $24,000 in 2039, and $48,000 in 2049, equaling what American workers earned in 2019. If growth continues at the same rate, Chinese workers would earn $96,000 in 2059 and $192,000 in 2069. American workers would earn $96,000 in 2042 and $192,000 in 2065. Therefore, Chinese workers would earn the same as American workers in about 50 years.

Checkpoint: Thinking About Short-Run and Long-Run Economic Growth 173

Every factor of production contributes to economic growth. Although the Ivory Coast has abundant natural resources and labor compared to Iceland, it lacks the human capital, physical capital, and technology that are important components in the production function. In addition, the lack of stability in the country from recent civil and military strife has left many of its resources underutilized for productive purposes, further inhibiting the Ivory Coast from achieving higher long-run growth.

Checkpoint: Applying the Production Function: Achieving Economic Growth 177

An organization such as the Bill & Melinda Gates Foundation can help people improve their health through vaccinations, clean water, and sanitation, thereby enabling them to improve their productivity and earning potential. Then, focus can be put on schools and improving education. All of this focus on human capital can be accomplished with grants to communities or parents (by subsidizing them to send their kids to school) in developing nations.

Checkpoint: The Role of Government in Promoting Economic Growth 181

Not very well. Large-scale businesses that we are accustomed to could not exist. What's left is small individual businesses that serve small local populations. Growth is stymied, and everyone ekes out a small living. Countries such as South Sudan, Somalia, and Yemen are in this no-win situation.

Portland Press Herald/Getty Images

8

Aggregate Expenditures

Understanding the power of spending and how it can multiply income many times over

Madawaska, Maine, near the northern end of U.S. 1 that extends all the way south to Key West, Florida, is like many other idyllic small towns in the United States—picturesque, friendly, and highly dependent on one industry to provide jobs for its residents. For Madawaska, it is the local paper mill, which provides jobs to 620 of its 4,100 residents. The salaries earned by its workers help to keep the rest of the town employed, including workers in restaurants and cafés, pharmacies, banks, and gas stations that serve the paper mill workers and their families.

During the depth of the 2007–2009 recession, when Madawaska's paper mill was on the brink of closure, not only did its workers face potential unemployment, but so did the rest of the community, which depends on people with jobs at the paper mill to support their businesses. Towns such as Madawaska highlight the interdependencies within the economy in that the loss of one job results in a reduction in spending that affects other jobs. In 2010 the workers at the paper mill took the unusual step of accepting an 8.5% wage cut in order to keep the company (and town) from closing down. And the plan worked—the plant survived and was sold to an investment firm in 2013 that promised to keep the paper mill running in Madawaska, where it remains in operation today.

The economic crisis that Madawaska faced during the last recession was one that many cities, big and small, experienced. As unemployment rose across the country, people had less money to spend on clothing, electronics, travel, and cars, which caused a chain reaction downward in consumption, leading to further unemployment and slow or negative economic growth. This chain reaction is what John Maynard Keynes alluded to when he published *The General Theory of Employment, Interest and Money* in 1936, which discussed the importance of aggregate spending and the government's role in stabilizing the macroeconomy. This contrasted with the classical viewpoint prevalent until that time that economic downturns would naturally self-correct if markets were left alone.

In recent years, the U.S. economy has enjoyed a healthy expansion, allowing the chain reaction to work in a positive direction. As economic growth increases incomes, the subsequent increase in spending generates even more economic activity but along with it higher prices or inflation. In this case, the government sometimes needs to intervene to prevent inflation from rising too much, as full employment of resources is achieved.

The key questions facing governments with respect to economic downturns and expansions is *how* it should act and to *what extent* should it act. There is a huge arsenal of tools available to government policymakers: stimulus packages, tax laws, subsidies, financial aid for college students, and much more. These policies are often contentious because they involve the government using tax revenues to achieve its objectives.

Moreover, Keynesian policies have not been without their critics as the size of government grew. Spending by government (federal, state, and local) has increased from 10% of GDP in the 1930s to over 30% today as the size and scope of government programs

BY THE Numbers

The Role of Spending in the Economy

Spending plays a vital role in spurring economic activity and creating growth and jobs. All components of the economy spend: consumers, investors, foreigners, and the government. During economic downturns, the government plays an increasingly important role in spurring economic activity using a variety of policies, including direct purchases of goods and services and indirect purchases through tax cuts and transfer payments. This By the Numbers analyzes the level of government spending in the United States as a percentage of GDP.

DATA:

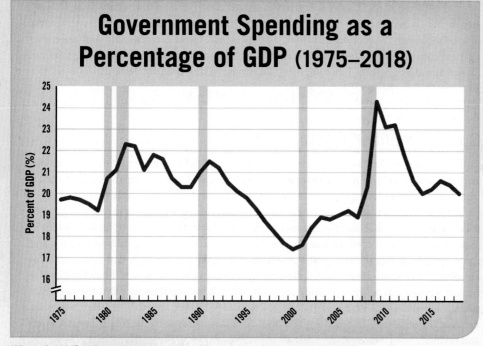

Government Spending as a Percentage of GDP (1975–2018)

y-axis: Percent of GDP (%), values 16 to 25
x-axis: 1975, 1980, 1985, 1990, 1995, 2000, 2005, 2010, 2015

Where Can I Find These Data?

Source: FRED Database, Federal Reserve Bank of St. Louis

Web site: https://fred.stlouisfed.org

Details: Search for "Federal Net Outlays as Percent of Gross Domestic Product"

~ Assessing Your Data Literacy ~

1. In which year did government spending, as a percentage of GDP, reach its highest point? In which year was it at its lowest point?

2. Describe the trend in the chart during times of economic prosperity (such as from 1985 to 1990 and from 1993 to 2000). Describe the trend during economic recessions (indicated by the shaded bars).

3. Explain why the relationship described in question 2 generally exists.

$3,766,276,000,000

Total U.S. private domestic investment spending in 2018

$2,540,600,000,000

Total U.S. spending by foreign consumers (exports) in 2018

WHY ARE THESE DATA IMPORTANT?

When consumers or businesses worry about the health of the economy, they will reduce their spending, which can lead to a significant decrease in output due to the multiplier effect. To offset the reduction in private spending, governments intervene by implementing policies that encourage greater spending, such as tax cuts, subsidies, or direct government spending.

Data *in the News*

"A Big Reason U.S. Economy Is Accelerating: Government Spending" by Kate Davidson; *Wall Street Journal*, October 25, 2018

A stark pickup in government spending, particularly in defense, has helped fuel a broad acceleration in U.S. economic growth.... The U.S. economy has expanded at a 2.9% annual rate since April of 2017, according to the Commerce Department...

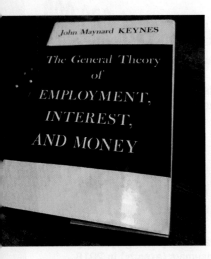

Keynes's famous book published in 1936 led to the development of macroeconomics as a discipline.

expanded. Although many people benefit from these programs, some believe government has overreached, and they would prefer something smaller and simpler.

But this sort of thinking is not new. It is the type of classical viewpoint prevalent among economists over a century ago when government policies were rarely used to intervene in the economy, even during a downturn. The argument that the forces of supply and demand would allow an economy to self-correct is compelling until exceptional circumstances occur.

Keynes challenged the classical framework during the Great Depression by arguing that markets can be sticky (or inflexible, not allowing the economy to adjust quickly), and therefore he focused instead on the economy as a whole and on aggregate spending.

In this chapter, we develop the aggregate expenditures model, which is commonly referred to as the Keynesian model. It can be used to analyze short-run macroeconomic fluctuations and provide policymakers with actions to counteract the effects caused by the business cycle. Keynes focused on aggregate spending, and showed that consumption spending is key to explain how the economy reaches short-term equilibrium employment, output, and income. Using this model, we will see why an economy can get stuck in an undesirable place and why government policies and actions are useful in smoothing out the business cycle.

AGGREGATE EXPENDITURES

Recall that gross domestic product (GDP) can be measured in two ways: total expenditures or total income in the economy. Further, the expenditures were classified into four major categories: consumer spending, business investment spending, government spending, and net foreign spending (exports minus imports). Thus, **aggregate expenditures** (*AE*) are equal to

$$GDP = AE = C + I + G + (X - M)$$

aggregate expenditures
Consist of consumer spending, business investment spending, government spending, and net foreign spending (exports minus imports): $GDP = C + I + G + (X - M)$. *AE* is equal to *GDP* from an expenditures approach.

Some Simplifying Assumptions

In this chapter, we first will focus on a simple model of the private economy that includes only consumers and businesses. Later in the chapter, we will incorporate government spending, taxes, and the foreign sector into our analysis. Second, we will assume that all saving is personal saving as opposed to national saving, which includes business saving and government saving. Third, because Keynes was modeling a depression economy, we follow him in assuming that there is considerable slack in the economy, much like the economy during and in the years following the 2007–2009 recession. Unemployment is high, and other resources are sitting idle, which means that if demand were to rise, businesses could quickly increase output without any upward pressure on costs. We will assume therefore that the aggregate price level (the CPI, PPI, or GDP deflator) is fixed. These simplifying assumptions make the analysis easier but do not affect the key points. Let us begin by looking at consumption and saving.

consumption Spending by individuals and households on durable goods (e.g., autos, appliances, and electronic equipment), nondurable goods (e.g., food, clothing, and entertainment), and services.

saving The difference between income and consumption; the amount of disposable income that is not spent.

Consumption and Saving

Personal consumption expenditures (*C*) represent about 68% of GDP, and for this reason **consumption** is a major component in the aggregate expenditures model. Consumption is closely related to disposable income (Y_d), which is the income households have after subtracting taxes. The portion of disposable income that is not used for consumption is called **saving** (*S*). Therefore, the sum of consumption and saving equals disposable income, or $C + S = Y_d$. From this point on, we will refer to disposable income as income (*Y*).

In the United States over the past century, consumption spending increased nearly every year. A notable exception occurred between 2008 and 2009, when consumption dropped during the depths of the recession. Prior to that, the last time annual consumption spending dropped was in 1933 during the Great Depression.

TABLE 1	HYPOTHETICAL CONSUMPTION AND SAVING, AND PROPENSITIES TO CONSUME AND SAVE					
(1) Income or Output Y (in $)	(2) Consumption C (in $)	(3) Saving S (in $)	(4) APC $C \div Y$	(5) APS $S \div Y$	(6) MPC $\Delta C \div \Delta Y$	(7) MPS $\Delta S \div \Delta Y$
3,000	3,250	−250	1.08	−0.08	0.75	0.25
3,200	3,400	−200	1.06	−0.06	0.75	0.25
3,400	3,550	−150	1.04	−0.04	0.75	0.25
3,600	3,700	−100	1.03	−0.03	0.75	0.25
3,800	3,850	−50	1.01	−0.01	0.75	0.25
4,000	4,000	0	1.00	0.00	0.75	0.25
4,200	4,150	50	0.99	0.01	0.75	0.25
4,400	4,300	100	0.98	0.02	0.75	0.25
4,600	4,450	150	0.97	0.03	0.75	0.25
4,800	4,600	200	0.96	0.04	0.75	0.25
5,000	4,750	250	0.95	0.05	0.75	0.25
5,200	4,900	300	0.94	0.06	0.75	0.25
5,400	5,050	350	0.94	0.06	0.75	0.25
5,600	5,200	400	0.93	0.07	0.75	0.25

Keynes began his theoretical examination of consumption by noting the following:

The fundamental psychological law, upon which we are entitled to depend with great confidence both a priori from our knowledge of human nature and from the detailed facts of experience, is that men are disposed, as a rule and on the average, to increase their consumption as their income increases, but not by as much as the change in their income.[1]

In other words, consumption spending grows as income grows, but not as fast. Therefore, as income grows, saving will grow as a percentage of income. Prior to Keynes's work, classical economists believed that the *interest rate* is the principal determinant of saving, which in turn would drive consumption. Keynes, in contrast, emphasized *income* as the main determinant of consumption and saving.

Table 1 portrays a hypothetical consumption function of the sort Keynes envisioned. As income grows from $4,000 to $4,200, consumption increases by $150 ($4,150−$4,000), and saving grows from $0 to $50. Thus, the *change* in income of $200 is divided between consumption ($150) and saving ($50). Note that at income levels below $4,000, saving is negative; people are spending more than their current income either by using credit or by drawing on existing savings to support consumption.

Average Propensities to Consume and Save The percentage of income that is consumed is known as the **average propensity to consume** (APC); it is listed in column (4) of Table 1. It is calculated by dividing consumption spending by income $(C \div Y)$. For example, when income is $5,000 and consumption is $4,750, APC is 0.95, meaning that 95% of the income is spent.

The **average propensity to save** (APS) is equal to saving divided by income $(S \div Y)$; it is the percentage of income that is saved. Again, if income is $5,000 and saving is $250, APS is 0.05, or 5% is saved. The APS is shown in column (5) of Table 1.

average propensity to consume The percentage of income that is consumed $(C \div Y)$.

average propensity to save The percentage of income that is saved $(S \div Y)$.

[1] John Maynard Keynes, *The General Theory of Employment, Interest and Money* (New York: Harcourt Brace Jovanovich), 1936, p. 96.

Notice that the sum of columns (4) and (5) in Table 1 is always 1. That is because $Y = C + S$; therefore, all income is either spent or saved. Similarly, the two percentages spent and saved must total 100%, or that $APC + APS = 1$.

Marginal Propensities to Consume and Save *Average* propensities to consume and save represent the proportion of income that is consumed or saved. *Marginal* propensities measure what part of *additional* income will be either consumed or saved. This distinction is important because changing policies by government policymakers mean that income changes and consumers' reactions to their *changing* incomes are what drive changes in the economy.

The **marginal propensity to consume** (MPC) is equal to the change in consumption due to a given change in income. Denoting change by the Greek letter delta (Δ), $MPC = \Delta C \div \Delta Y$. For example, when income grows from $5,000 to $5,200 (a $200 change) and consumption rises from $4,750 to $4,900 (a $150 change), MPC is equal to 0.75 ($150 \div $200).

Notice that this result is consistent with Keynes's fundamental psychological law quoted earlier, holding that people "are disposed, as a rule and on the average, to increase their consumption as their income increases, but not by as much as the change in their income." In Table 1, the MPC for all changes in income is 0.75, as shown in column (6).

The **marginal propensity to save** (MPS) is equal to the change in saving associated with a given change in income; $MPS = \Delta S \div \Delta Y$. Therefore, when income grows from $5,000 to $5,200 and saving grows from $250 to $300, MPS is equal to 0.25 ($50 \div $200). Column (7) lists MPS.

Note once again that the sum of the MPC and the MPS will always equal 1 because the only thing that can be done with a change in income is to spend or save it. It is important to note that though $APC + APS = 1$ and $MPC + MPS = 1$, most of the time $APC + MPS \neq 1$ and $APS + MPC \neq 1$. Try adding a few different columns from Table 1, and you will see that this is true.

Figure 1 graphs the consumption and saving schedules from Table 1. The graph in panel A extends the consumption schedule back to zero income, where consumption is equal to $1,000 and saving is equal to –$1,000. (Remember that $Y = C + S$; therefore, if $Y = 0$ and $C = $1,000, then S must equal –$1,000. With no income, people would continue to spend, either borrowing money or drawing down their accumulated savings to survive.) The 45° line in panel A is a reference line where $Y = C + S$. At the point at which the consumption schedule crosses the reference line (point a, $Y = $4,000), saving is zero because consumption and income are equal.

The saving schedule in panel B graphs saving (which is $Y - C$) as a function of income. For example, if income is $4,000, saving is zero (point f in panel B), and when income equals $5,000, saving equals $250 [($b - c$) in panel A, point g in panel B]. Saving is positively sloped, again reflecting Keynes's fundamental law; the more people earn, the greater percentage of income they will save (the average propensity to save rises as income rises). Make a mental note that the saving schedule shows how much people *desire* to save at various income levels.

How much people will *actually* save depends on equilibrium income, or how much income the economy is generating. We are getting a bit ahead of the story here, but planting this seed will help you when we get to the section where we determine equilibrium income in the economy.

Note that the consumption and saving schedules in our example are straight-line functions. This need not be the case, but it simplifies some of the relationships at this point. When the consumption and saving schedules are linear, the MPC is the slope of the consumption function, and the MPS is the slope of the saving function. In this case, $MPC = 0.75$ and $MPS = 0.25$, which tells us that every time income changes by $1,000, consumption will change by $750 and saving will change by $250.

Other Determinants of Consumption and Saving Income is the principal determinant of consumption and saving, but other factors can shift the saving and consumption schedules. These factors include the wealth of a family, their expectations about the future of prices and income, family debt, and taxation.

- *Wealth* An increase in wealth increases consumption at all levels of income, shifting the consumption schedule up. Changes in wealth commonly occur with fluctuations in the stock

marginal propensity to consume The change in consumption associated with a given change in income ($\Delta C \div \Delta Y$).

marginal propensity to save The change in saving associated with a given change in income ($\Delta S \div \Delta Y$).

Kwiatek7/Shutterstock

Suppose you receive some birthday money from your aunt. What portion of this money would you spend, and what portion would you save? These portions are your marginal propensity to consume and marginal propensity to save, respectively.

..... Figure 1 • Consumption and Saving ....

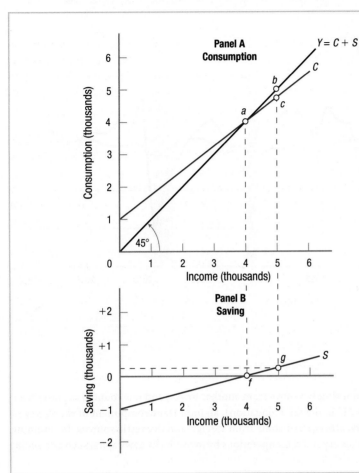

The consumption and saving schedules from Table 1 are graphed here. Panel A graphs the consumption function beginning at $0 income, where consumption is equal to $1,000 and saving is equal to –$1,000. At the point where the consumption function crosses the reference line (point a, Y = $4,000), saving is zero. The saving function in panel B is the difference between the 45° reference line and the consumption function in panel A. Thus, when income = $5,000, saving = $250 [(b − c) in panel A, point g in panel B].

market and the value of housing and other assets. Recessions typically reduce wealth, causing consumption to fall at all levels of income.

- **Expectations** Expectations about future prices and incomes help determine how much a person will spend today. If you anticipate that prices will rise next week, you will be more likely to purchase more products today. Similarly, if you anticipate an increase in income—perhaps you are about to graduate and have already secured a well-paying job—you might want to purchase a new car now, knowing that your income will soon rise.

- **Household Debt** Most households carry some debt, typically in the form of credit card balances, auto loans, student loans, or a home mortgage. The more debt a household has, the less able it is to spend in the current period as it makes payments toward the debt.

- **Taxes** Taxes reduce disposable income, reducing consumption by the reduction in spendable income times the MPC. Saving also falls by the reduction in disposable income times the MPS. Tax reductions have the opposite effect.

Investment

When the town of West Point, Georgia, received the news that South Korean automaker Kia Motors was building a $1 billion car manufacturing facility in its town, its residents couldn't have been happier. Not only was Kia creating thousands of jobs, but the spending by its workers would create even more jobs throughout the region. Kia's manufacturing facility was new to

····· Figure 2 • Changes in Consumption and Gross Private Domestic Investment ·····

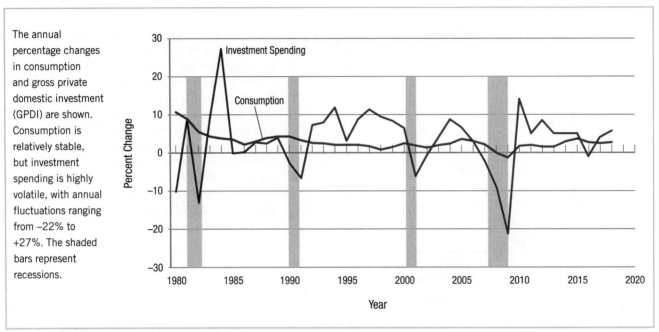

The annual percentage changes in consumption and gross private domestic investment (GPDI) are shown. Consumption is relatively stable, but investment spending is highly volatile, with annual fluctuations ranging from −22% to +27%. The shaded bars represent recessions.

investment Spending by businesses that adds to the productive capacity of the economy. Investment depends on factors such as the rate of return, the level of technology, and business expectations about the economy.

the U.S. economy (and not simply a move from another town), and it is counted as *gross private domestic investment* (the "I" in the GDP equation), an important component of the aggregate expenditures model. **Investment** can come from foreign and domestic sources, for example, when American companies expand their operations by investing in new capital such as building a new factory.

Unlike consumer spending, which at 68% is the largest component of GDP and is relatively stable from year to year, gross private domestic investment is volatile. Large investment deals like Kia's new plant in West Point, Georgia, are a huge boost to the economy, but such investments tend to be sporadic. The annual percentage changes in consumption and investment spending from 1980 to 2018 are shown in Figure 2.

Notice that although consumption rarely changes by more than 5% in any year, investment spending has undergone annual fluctuations ranging from −22% to +27%. Investment constitutes about 17% of GDP; therefore, volatility often drives changes in the business cycle, including recessions and expansions.

The economic expansion of the 1990s was fueled by massive investments in telecommunications and the Internet, but such investments plummeted in 2000 and 2001 when the dot-com bubble burst. Investment then rose again with the housing bubble but collapsed again from 2007 to 2009 as the housing and financial crises took their toll.

Many residents in West Point, Georgia, were excited when South Korean auto manufacturer Kia Motors built a large factory in their town in 2008, saving the town's economy after decades of factory closings and job losses.

Investment Demand Investment levels depend mainly on the rate of return on capital. Investments earning a high rate of return are the investments undertaken first (assuming comparable risk), while those projects offering lower returns find their way into the investment stream later. Interest rate levels also are important in determining how much investment occurs because much of business investment is financed through debt. As interest rates fall, investment rises, and vice versa.

Although the rate of return on investments is the main determinant of investment spending, other factors influence investment demand, including expectations, technological change, capital goods on hand, and operating costs.

- *Expectations* Projecting the rate of return on investment is not an easy task. Returns are forecasted over the life of a new piece of equipment or factory, yet changes in the economy can alter the actual return on these investments. As business expectations improve, investment demand will increase as businesses are willing to invest more at any given interest rate.

- *Technological Change* Technological innovations periodically spur investment. Improvements in communications, digital marketing, and transportation, for example, have spurred investment by companies to ensure that they remain competitive.

Innovations in GPS technology and communications encouraged Amazon to invest heavily in its own delivery services.

- *Operating Costs* When the costs of operating and maintaining machinery and equipment rise, the rate of return on capital equipment declines, and new investment will be postponed.

- *Capital Goods on Hand* The more capital goods a firm has on hand, including inventories of the products it sells, the less the firm will want to make new investments. Until existing capacity can be fully used, investing in more equipment and facilities is less valuable.

Aggregate Investment Schedule To simplify our analysis, we will assume that rates of return and interest rates fully determine investment in the short run. But once that level of investment has been determined, it remains independent of income, or *autonomous,* as economists say. Therefore, unlike consumption, which increases as income rises, we will assume that investment varies not based on income but instead on the rates of return that determine how potentially profitable investment will be. Figure 3 shows the resulting relationship between aggregate investment spending and income.

We have assumed that aggregate investment is I_0 at all income levels, which means the curve is a straight horizontal line. Investment is unaffected by different levels of income. This is a simplifying assumption that we will change later in this chapter.

····· Figure 3 • Investment ······································

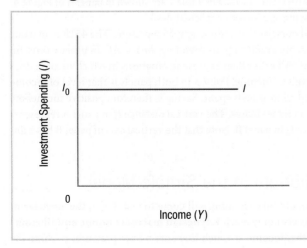

Aggregate investment is shown, relating investment spending to income. The curve is a straight horizontal line because aggregate investment is I_0 at all income levels. This assumption simplifies the aggregate expenditures model.

This section focused on two important components of aggregate spending: consumption and investment. Consumption is relatively stable, but investment is volatile and especially sensitive to expectations about conditions in the economy. We have seen that, on average, some income is spent (APC) and some is saved (APS). But it is that portion of *additional* income that is spent (MPC) and saved (MPS) that is most important for where the economy settles or where it reaches equilibrium, as we will see in the next section.

 CHECKPOINT

AGGREGATE EXPENDITURES

- Aggregate expenditures are equal to $C+I+G+(X-M)$, with consumption being the largest component of aggregate spending.

- Keynes argued that saving and consumption spending are related to income. As income grows, consumption will grow, but not as fast.

- The marginal propensities to consume (MPC) and save (MPS) are equal to $\Delta C \div \Delta Y$ and $\Delta S \div \Delta Y$, respectively. They represent the change in consumption and saving associated with a change in income.

- Other factors affecting consumption and saving include wealth, expectations about future income and prices, the level of household debt, and taxes.

- Investment levels depend primarily on the rate of return on capital.

- Other determinants of investment demand include business expectations, technological change, operating costs, and the amount of capital goods on hand.

- Consumption is relatively stable. In contrast, investment is volatile.

QUESTION: Why is investment spending generally much more volatile than consumption spending?

Answers to the Checkpoint questions can be found at the end of this chapter.

THE SIMPLE AGGREGATE EXPENDITURES MODEL

To this point, we have ignored the government and foreign sectors from our analysis, so aggregate expenditures (AE) consist of the sum of consumer and business investment spending $(AE=C+I)$. Figure 4 shows a simple aggregate expenditures model based on consumption and investment. Aggregate expenditures based on the data in Table 1 are shown in panel A of Figure 4; panel B shows the corresponding saving and investment schedules.

Let us take a moment to remind ourselves what these graphs represent. The 45° line in panel A represents the situation when income exactly equals spending, or $Y = AE$. In other words, no savings occur at any level of income. All other lines represent situations in which income does not exactly equal spending at all levels of income. Point *a* in both panels is that level of income ($4,000) at which saving is zero and all income is spent. Saving is therefore positive for income levels above $4,000 and negative at incomes below. The vertical distance *ef* in panel A represents investment (I_0) of $100; it is equal to I_0 in panel B. Note that the vertical axis of panel B has a different scale from that of panel A.

Keynesian macroeconomic equilibrium The state of an economy at which there are no pressures pushing the economy to a higher or lower level of output.

Macroeconomic Equilibrium in the Simple Model

The important question to ask is where this economy will come to rest. Or, in the language of economists, at what income will this economy reach **Keynesian macroeconomic equilibrium?** By equilibrium, economists mean that income at which there are no net pressures pushing the economy to move to a higher or lower level of output.

····· Figure 4 • Equilibrium in the Aggregate Expenditures Model ················

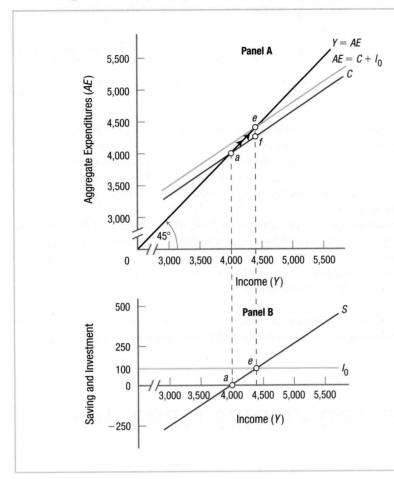

Ignoring government spending and net exports, aggregate expenditures (AE) consist of consumer spending and business investment ($AE = C + I$). Panel A shows AE and its relationship with income (Y); when spending equals income, the economy is on the $Y = AE$ line. Panel B shows the corresponding saving and investment schedules. Point a in both panels shows where income equals consumption and saving is zero. Therefore, saving is positive for income levels above $4,000 and negative at incomes below $4,000. The vertical distance ef in panel A represents investment ($100); it is equal to I_0 in panel B. Equilibrium income and output are $4,400 (point e) because this is the level at which businesses are producing just what other businesses and consumers want to buy.

To find this equilibrium point, let's begin with the economy at an income level of $4,000. Are there pressures driving the economy to grow or decline? Looking at point a in panel A of Figure 4, we see that the economy is producing $4,000 worth of goods and services and has $4,000 in income. At this income level, however, consumers and businesses want to spend $4,100 ($4,000 in consumption and $100 in investment). Because aggregate expenditures (AE) exceed current income and output, there are more goods being demanded ($4,100) than are being supplied at $4,000. As a result, businesses will find it in their best interests to produce more, raising employment and income and moving the economy toward income and output level $4,400 (point e).

Once the economy has moved to $4,400, what consumers and businesses want to buy is exactly equal to the income and output being produced. Businesses are producing $4,400, aggregate expenditures are equal to $4,400, and there are no pressures on the economy to move away from point e. Income of $4,400, or point e, is an equilibrium point for the economy.

Panel B shows this same equilibrium, again as point e. Is it a coincidence that saving and investment are equal at this point where income and output are at equilibrium? The answer is no. In this simple private sector model, saving and investment will always be equal when the economy is in equilibrium.

Remember that aggregate expenditures are equal to consumption plus business investment ($AE = C + I$). Recall also that *at equilibrium,* aggregate expenditures, income, and output are all equal; what is demanded is supplied ($AE = Y$). Finally, keep in mind that income can either be spent or saved ($Y = C + S$). By substitution, we know that, at equilibrium,

$$AE = Y = C + I$$

We also know that

$$Y = C + S$$

Substituting $C + I$ for Y yields

$$C + I = C + S$$

Subtracting the C's from both sides of the equation, we find that, *at equilibrium,*

$$I = S$$

Thus, the location of point e in panel B is not just coincidental; at equilibrium, saving and investment are always equal. Note that at point a, saving is zero, yet investment spending is $100 at I_0. This difference means businesses desire to invest more than people desire to save. With *desired* investment exceeding *desired* saving, businesses want to borrow more funds than are available, and therefore this outcome cannot be an equilibrium. Indeed, income will rise until these two values are equal at point e.

injections Actions that add spending to the economy, including investment, government spending, and exports.

withdrawals Actions that remove spending from the economy, including saving, taxes, and imports.

What is important to take from this discussion? First, when intended (or desired) saving and investment differ, the economy will have to grow or shrink to achieve equilibrium. When desired saving exceeds desired investment—at income levels above $4,400 in panel B—income will decline. When intended saving is below intended investment—at income levels below $4,400—income will rise. Notice that we are using the words "intended" and "desired" interchangeably.

Second, at equilibrium all **injections** of spending (investment in this case) into the economy must equal all **withdrawals** (saving in this simple model). Spending injections increase aggregate

JOHN MAYNARD KEYNES (1883–1946)

In 1935 John Maynard Keynes boasted in a letter to playwright George Bernard Shaw of a book he was writing that would revolutionize "the way the world thinks about economic problems." This was a brash prediction to make, even to a friend, but it was not an idle boast. His *General Theory of Employment, Interest and Money* did change the way the world looked at economics.

Keynes belongs to a small class of economic earth-shakers that includes Karl Marx and Adam Smith. His one-man war on classical theory launched a new field of study known as macroeconomics. His ideas would have a profound influence on theorists and government policies for decades to come.

Keynes was once asked if there was any era comparable to the Great Depression. He replied, "It was called the Dark Ages and it lasted 400 years." His prescription to President Franklin D. Roosevelt was to increase government spending to stimulate the economy. Sudeep Reddy reports that "during a 1934 dinner . . . after one economist carefully removed a towel from a stack to dry his hands, Mr. Keynes swept the whole pile of towels on the floor and crumpled them up, explaining that his way of using towels did more to stimulate employment among restaurant workers" (*Wall Street Journal*, January 8, 2009, p. A10).

During the world economic depression in the early 1930s, Keynes became alarmed when unemployment in England continued to rise after the first few years of the crisis. Keynes argued that *aggregate expenditures,* the sum of consumption, investment, government spending, and net exports, determined the levels of economic output and employment. Because aggregate expenditures were very low during the depression, Keynes argued for policies that directly increase aggregate expenditures which would foster business expansion and higher levels of employment and income growth.

The ideas formulated by Keynes dramatically changed the way government policy is used throughout the world. Many governments have taken a more proactive role in their economies in hopes of avoiding another downturn of the magnitude seen in the 1930s.

····· Figure 5 • Saving and Investment ······································

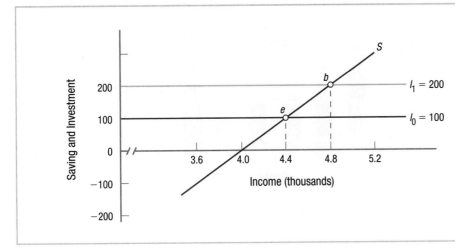

When investment is $100 ($I_0$), equilibrium employment occurs at an output of $4,400 (point e). When investment rises to $200 ($I_1$), equilibrium output climbs to $4,800 (point b). Thus, $100 of added investment spending causes income to grow by $400. This is the multiplier at work.

income, while spending withdrawals reduce it. This fact will become important as we add government and the foreign sector to the model.

Returning to Figure 4, given an initial investment of $100 ($I_0$), equilibrium occurs at the intersection of S and I_0, at an output of $4,400 (point e). Remember that at equilibrium, what people *withdraw* from the economy (saving) is equal to what others are willing to *inject* into the economy (investment). In this case, both values equal $100. Point e is an equilibrium point because there are no pressures in the system to increase or decrease output; the spending desires of consumers and businesses are satisfied.

The Multiplier

Injections and withdrawals in an economy produce an effect that is greater than the initial value of the injection or withdrawal. The following example illustrates why. Assume that *full employment* occurs at output $4,800. How much would investment have to increase to move the economy out to full employment? As Figure 5 shows, investment must rise to $200 ($I_1$), an increase of $100. With this new investment, equilibrium output moves from point e to point b, and income rises from $4,400 to $4,800.

What is remarkable here is that a mere $100 of added spending (investment in this case) caused income to grow by $400. This phenomenon is known as the **multiplier** effect. Recognizing it was one of Keynes's major insights. How does it work?

In this example, we have assumed the marginal propensity to consume is 0.75. Therefore, for each added dollar received by consumers, $0.75 is spent and $0.25 is saved. Thus, when businesses invest an additional $100, the firms providing the machinery will spend $75 of this new income on more raw materials while saving the remaining $25. The firms supplying the new raw materials have $75 of new income. These firms will spend $56.25 of this ($0.75 \times 75.00) while saving $18.75 ($56.25 + $18.75 = 75.00). This effect continues on until the added spending has been exhausted. As a result, income will increase by $100 + $75 + $56.25 \ldots$. In the end, income rises by $400. Figure 6 outlines this multiplier process.

The general formula for the spending multiplier (k) is

$$k = 1/(1 - MPC)$$

Alternatively, because $MPC + MPS = 1$, the $MPS = 1 - MPC$; therefore,

$$k = 1/MPS$$

Thus, in our simple model, the multiplier is

$$1/(1 - 0.75) = 1/0.25 = 4$$

multiplier The factor used to determine the amount by which equilibrium income changes due to a change in spending. The multiplier is calculated as $1/(1 - MPC) = 1/MPS$. The multiplier operates in both directions.

····· Figure 6 • The Multiplier Process ·····

An initial $100 of spending generates more spending because of the multiplier process shown in this figure. With an *MPC* = 0.75 in the second round, $75 is spent and $25 is saved. In the third round, $56.25 of the previous $75 is spent and $18.75 is saved, and so on. Total spending is $400, and total saving is $100 when all rounds are completed.

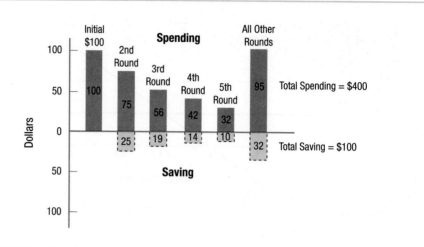

🌍AROUND THE WORLD

Brazil's Beco Do Batman: How Graffiti Revived a Neighborhood

How did the Beco do Batman neighborhood in São Paulo turn graffiti into an economic growth engine?

In cities around the world, graffiti artists exhibit their talents on the sides of buildings, trains, and bridges, turning otherwise pristine areas into unsightly views. Graffiti is also a common tool used by gangs, which increases the perception of neighborhoods with graffiti as unsafe, leading to a reduction in their desirability as a place to live or visit. As a result, neighborhoods and cities have an incentive to clean up graffiti. However, winning the war against graffiti is usually difficult because cleanup costs are expensive and graffiti artists often return.

In one neighborhood in São Paulo, Brazil, instead of pumping more money into a never-ending battle on graffiti, residents decided on a markedly different strategy. What did the residents

of Beco do Batman ("Batman Alley" in Portuguese) choose to do?

Instead of cleaning up the graffiti, residents *encouraged* graffiti artists to come to the area. Since the 1980s, artists from around Brazil and other countries journeyed to Beco do Batman to paint giant murals in its alleyways. The lack of unpainted walls means that new artists must paint over a previous artist's work, thus creating a constantly changing art gallery for visitors to enjoy. How did this strategy of welcoming graffiti affect the neighborhood?

First, overall crime *declined*. Because graffiti in Beco do Batman was no longer a sign of gang power, criminal graffiti artists went elsewhere. This attracted wealthier residents and investors to build homes in the area, raising the property values of all homeowners and businesses.

Second, as Beco do Batman became a unique tourist attraction, money was spent by tourists who visited the shops and restaurants in the area. The economic activity spurred by visitors created jobs and higher wages for its residents, who then had more money to spend. The cycle of increased economic activity generated a multiplier effect that allowed Beco do Batman and its surrounding neighborhoods to thrive, pulling many of its residents out of poverty.

The graffiti art of Beco do Batman is a unique example of how aggregate expenditures and the multiplier effect can lead to higher economic growth.

📉 GO ONLINE TO PRACTICE THE ECONOMIC CONCEPTS IN THIS STORY

As a result of the multiplier effect, new spending will raise equilibrium by 4 times the amount of new spending. Note that any change in spending (consumption, investment—and as we will see in the next section—government spending or changes in net exports) will also have this effect. Spending is spending. The Around the World feature looks at how one community in Brazil uses graffiti art to attract greater spending.

The Multiplier Works in Both Directions

If spending increases raise equilibrium income by the increase times the multiplier, a spending decrease will reduce income in corresponding fashion. In our simple economy, a $100 decline in investment or consumer spending will reduce income by $400.

This is one reason why recession watchers are always concerned about consumer confidence. During a recession, income declines, or at least the rate of income growth falls. If consumers decide to increase their saving to guard against the possibility of job loss, they may inadvertently make the recession worse. As they pull more of their money out of the spending stream, *withdrawals* increase, and income is reduced by a multiplied amount as other agents in the economy feel the effects of this reduced spending. The result can be a more severe or longer-lasting recession.

This was the case when consumer spending peaked in the summer of 2008. After that, auto sales plummeted and housing prices and sales fell. As the recession that started in December 2007 progressed and jobs were lost, consumers reduced their spending. As their confidence in the economy deteriorated, households began to save more, consumer spending declined further, and the economy sank into a deeper recession. Figure 7 shows how consumer spending (downward arrow) fell and saving rose (upward arrow) after September 2008. Leading up to the recession, saving was less than 3% of personal income, but by mid-2009 it had grown to 7%. Before the recession, aggregate household debt had soared, and part of what we are seeing in Figure 7 may reflect households spending less in order to pay down debt and return to more sustainable debt levels.

····· Figure 7 • Consumption and Saving, 2007–2009 ·····························

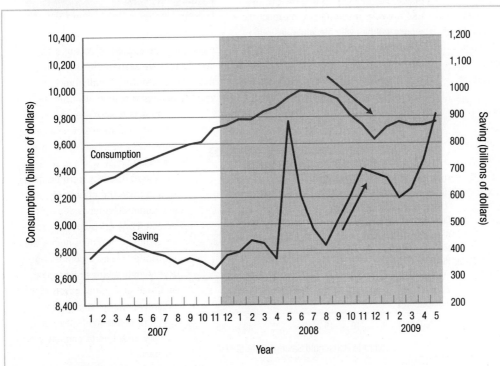

Consumption declined as the recession developed, and consumer worries about job losses and the decline in housing prices resulted in households saving more. The shaded area on the right represents the recession.

paradox of thrift When investment is positively related to income and households *intend* to save more, they reduce consumption. Consequently, income and output decrease, reducing investment such that savings actually end up decreasing.

Paradox of Thrift The implication of Keynesian analysis for actual aggregate household saving and household intentions regarding saving is called the **paradox of thrift.** As we saw in Figure 7, if households *intend* (or desire) to save more, they will reduce consumption, thereby reducing income and output, resulting in job losses and further reductions in income, consumption, business investment, and so on. The end result is an aggregate equilibrium with lower output, income, and investment and, in the final analysis, lower *actual* aggregate saving.

Notice that we have modified our assumption about investment—it now varies with economic conditions and is positively related to income. When the economy improves and income (or output) rises, investment expands as well, and vice versa when the economy sours. This is shown in our simple aggregate expenditures framework in Figure 8.

Initially, the economy is in equilibrium at point *e* with saving equal to S_0. If households *desire* to save more because they feel insecure about their jobs, the savings function will shift leftward

ISSUE

Do High Savings Rates Increase the Risk of a Long Recession?

Everyone has a frugal friend or relative who saves every penny possible or a shopaholic friend who can't seem to save any money at all. These differences in savings rates often are influenced by economic and demographic factors.

People with higher incomes tend to save a larger portion of their incomes than those with lower incomes, and older workers tend to save more than younger workers. Yet, these factors do not fully explain differences in savings rates across countries. In other words, cultural differences play an important role as well.

The following graph shows the average household savings rate in a sample of twelve countries in 2018. China and India rank at the top despite having a lower income per capita than any other country on the list. The United States, which has the highest income per capita among the countries shown, has a relatively low savings rate. And some countries have seen dramatic changes in their savings rate, such as Japan, which had one of the highest savings rates 30 years ago but today

has the lowest savings rate among the countries shown due to its aging population (in which many citizens are using their savings instead of accumulating savings).

The savings rate plays an important role in an economy because it gives a country's banking system a vote of confidence; people trust putting their money into financial institutions and expect the money will be available when desired. Also, savings provide opportunities for others to borrow.

However, a high savings rate can also make a country vulnerable in times of

recession. The adverse effects of a high savings rate are seen in China which has seen its growth rate fall in recent years. The natural reaction by Chinese citizens is to save even more, which may further slow economic growth and eventually lead to a recession.

The ability of governments to minimize the effects of economic downturns depends on the marginal propensity to consume, which determines the multiplier. When a country has a very high savings rate, such as China and India, government incentives to boost consumption and investment may not be very effective to combat a recession.

Average Household Savings Rate (2018)

····· Figure 8 • Paradox of Thrift ································

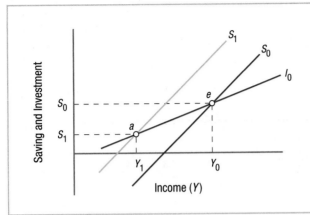

The economy is initially in equilibrium at point *e*. Suppose consumers intend to save more and consume less (the saving function shifts from S_0 to S_1). If investment is a rising function of income, the result is that at equilibrium, households actually end up saving less (point *a*).

to S_1. Now at all levels of income households *intend* to save more. This sets up the chain reaction described previously, leading to a new equilibrium at point *a*, where equilibrium income has fallen to Y_1 and *actual* saving has declined to S_1. The paradox is that if everyone tries to save more (even for good reasons), in the end they may end up saving less.

 CHECKPOINT

THE SIMPLE AGGREGATE EXPENDITURES MODEL

- Ignoring both the government and the foreign sector in a simple aggregate expenditures model, macroeconomic equilibrium occurs when aggregate expenditures are just equal to what is being produced.

- At equilibrium, aggregate saving equals aggregate investment.

- The multiplier process amplifies new spending because some of the new spending is saved and some becomes additional spending. And some of that spending is saved and some is spent, and so on.

- The multiplier is equal to $1/(1 - MPC) = 1/MPS$.

- The multiplier works in both directions. Changes in spending are amplified, changing income by more than the initial change in spending.

- The paradox of thrift results when households *intend* to save more, but at equilibrium they end up saving less.

QUESTION: Business journalists, pundits, economists, and policymakers all pay attention to the results of the Conference Board's monthly survey of 5,000 households, called the Consumer Confidence Index. When the index is rising, this is good news for the economy, and when it is falling, concerns are often heard that it portends a recession. Why is this survey important as a tool in forecasting where the economy is headed in the near future?

Answers to the Checkpoint questions can be found at the end of this chapter.

THE FULL AGGREGATE EXPENDITURES MODEL

With the simple aggregate expenditures model of the domestic private sector (individual consumption and private business investment), we concluded that at equilibrium, saving would equal investment, and that changes in spending lead to a larger change in income. This multiplier effect was an important insight by Keynes. To build the full aggregate expenditures model, we now turn our attention to adding government spending and taxes and the impact of the foreign sector.

····· Figure 9 · Saving, Investment, and Government Spending ················

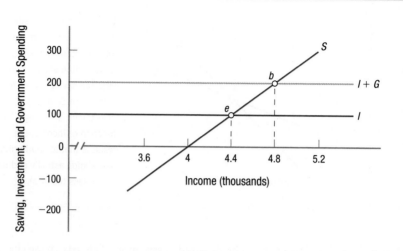

The addition of government spending (G) causes income and output to rise or fall by the spending change times the multiplier.

Adding Government Spending and Taxes

Although government spending and tax policy can get complex, for our purposes it involves simple changes in government spending (G) or taxes (T). As we saw in the previous section, any change in aggregate spending causes income and output to rise or fall by the spending change times the multiplier.

Figure 9 illustrates the addition of government spending. Initially, investment is $100; therefore, equilibrium income is $4,400 (point e), just as in Figure 5 earlier. Rather than investment rising by $100, let's assume that the government decides to add $100 in new spending. As Figure 9 shows, the new equilibrium is $4,800 (point b). This result is similar to the one in Figure 5, confirming that spending is spending; the economy does not care from where it comes.

A quick summary is now in order. Equilibrium income is reached when *injections* (here, $I + G = \$200$) equal *withdrawals* (in this case, $S = \$200$). It did not matter whether these injections came from investment alone or from investment and government spending together. The key is spending.

Changes in spending modify income by an amount equal to the change in spending times the multiplier. How, then, do changes in taxes affect the economy? The answer is not as simple, as we will see.

Tax Changes and Equilibrium When taxes are increased, money is withdrawn from the economy's spending stream. When taxes are reduced, money is injected into the economy's spending stream because consumers and businesses have more to spend. Thus, taxes form a wedge between income and that part of income that can be spent, or disposable income. Disposable income (Y_d) is equal to income minus taxes $(Y_d = Y - T)$. For simplicity, we assume that all taxes are paid in a lump sum, thereby removing a certain fixed sum of money from the economy. This assumption does away with the need to worry now about the incentive effects of higher or lower tax rates.

Returning to the model of the economy we have been developing, consumer spending now relates to disposable income $(Y - T)$, rather than just income. Table 2 reflects this change, using disposable income to determine consumption. With government spending and taxes (fiscal policy) in the model, spending *injections* into the economy include government

TABLE 2	KEYNESIAN EQUILIBRIUM ANALYSIS WITH TAXES					
Income or Output (Y), in $	Taxes (T), in $	Disposable Income (Y_d), in $	Consumption (C)	Saving (S)	Investment (I)	Government Spending (G)
4,000	100	3,900	3,925	−25	100	100
4,100	100	4,000	4,000	0	100	100
4,200	100	4,100	4,075	25	100	100
4,300	100	4,200	4,150	50	100	100
4,400	100	4,300	4,225	75	100	100
4,500	100	4,400	4,300	100	100	100
4,600	100	4,500	4,375	125	100	100
4,700	100	4,600	4,450	150	100	100
4,800	100	4,700	4,525	175	100	100
4,900	100	4,800	4,600	200	100	100
5,000	100	4,900	4,675	225	100	100

spending plus business investment $(G+I)$. *Withdrawals* from the system include saving and taxes $(S+T)$.

Again, equilibrium requires that *injections* equal *withdrawals*, or in this case,

$$G+I=S+T$$

In our example, Table 2 shows that $G+I=S+T$ at income level $4,500 (the shaded row in the table). If no tax had been imposed, equilibrium would have been at the point at which $S=G+I$, and thus at an income of $4,800 (point *b* in Figure 9, not shown in Table 2). Therefore, imposing the $100 tax reduces equilibrium income by $300. Because taxes represent a withdrawal of spending from the economy, we would expect equilibrium income to fall when a tax is imposed. Yet, why does equilibrium income fall by only $300 and not by the tax multiplied by the multiplier, which would be $400?

The answer is that consumers pay for this tax, in part, by *reducing* their saving. Specifically, with the MPC at 0.75, the $100 tax payment is split between consumption, reduced by $75, and saving, reduced by $25. When this $75 decrease in consumption is multiplied by the multiplier, this yields a decline in income of $300 ($75×4). The *reduction* in saving of $25 *dampens* the impact of the tax on equilibrium income because those funds were previously withdrawn from the spending stream. Changing the withdrawal category from saving to taxes does not affect income: Both are withdrawals.

Equilibrium is shown at point *g* in Figure 10. At point *g*, $I+G=S+T$, with equilibrium income equal to $4,500 and taxes and saving equal to $100 each. Note that the value of S in $S+T$ is not equivalent to S by itself. This is because whenever taxes increase, savings decrease to pay for part of the tax.

The result is that a tax increase (or decrease, for that matter) will have less of a direct impact on income, employment, and output than will an equivalent change in government spending. The tax multiplier (calculated as $MPC/(1-MPC)$) is smaller than the spending multiplier $(1/(1-MPC))$ by a value of 1. For example, when the spending multiplier is 4, the tax multiplier would equal 3. Why? The first round of the multiplier effect (see Figure 6) of a tax increase or decrease is eliminated because part of a tax increase is funded by a reduction in savings, while part of a tax decrease is added to savings.

····· Figure 10 • Saving, Investment, Government Spending, and Taxes ···········

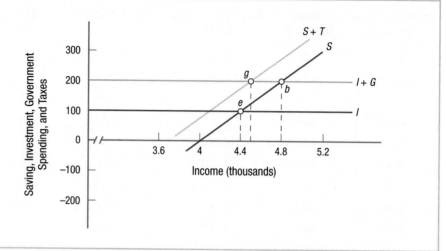

Tax increases or decreases have less of a direct impact on income, employment, and output than an equivalent change in government spending. Some of a tax increase will come from saving and some of a tax decrease will go into saving, thereby reducing the effect of these tax changes.

The Balanced Budget Multiplier By now you have probably noticed something curious. Our original equilibrium income was $4,400, with investment and saving equal at $100. When the government was introduced with a balanced budget ($G = T = \$100$), income rose by $100 to $4,500. The reason for this increase is that part of the $100 increase in taxes ($25 based on the MPS) is paid by a reduction in savings. When this $25 is spent by the government, it becomes $100 in total spending with the multiplier. The remaining $75 in government spending does not affect income because it is transferred from a $75 decrease in consumption. The result is that a $100 increase in government spending that is financed by a $100 increase in taxes results in a $100 increase in income.

This has led to what economists call the **balanced budget multiplier.** Equal changes in government spending and taxation (a balanced budget) lead to an equal change in income. If spending and taxes are increased by the same amount, income grows by this amount, hence a balanced budget multiplier equal to 1. Note that the balanced budget multiplier is 1 regardless of the values of MPC and MPS.

balanced budget multiplier

The balanced budget multiplier is equal to 1. Equal changes in government spending and taxation (a balanced budget) lead to an equal change in income.

Adding Net Exports

Thus far we have essentially assumed a closed economy by avoiding foreign transactions: exports and imports. We now add the foreign sector to complete the aggregate expenditures model.

The impact of the foreign sector in the aggregate expenditures model is through net exports: exports minus imports $(X - M)$. Exports are *injections* of spending into the domestic economy, and imports are *withdrawals*. When Africans purchase grain from American farmers, they are injecting new spending on grain into our economy. Conversely, when we purchase French wine, we are withdrawing spending (as saving does) and injecting these funds into the French economy.

Figure 11 adds net exports to investment and government spending. By adding $100 of net exports to the previous equilibrium at point *b*, equilibrium moves to $5,200 (point *c*). Again, we see the multiplier at work as the $100 in net exports leads to a $400 increase in income.

With the foreign sector included, all injections into the economy must equal all withdrawals; therefore, at equilibrium,

$$I + G + X = S + T + M$$

····· Figure 11 • Saving, Investment, Government Spending, and Net Exports ·····

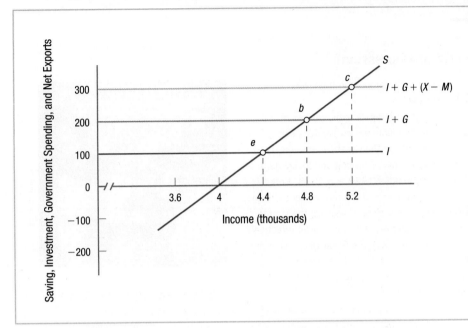

Including investment (I), government spending (G), and net exports ($X - M$) causes income and output to rise or fall by the spending change times the multiplier. In this figure, we add net exports ($X - M$) of $100 to investment and government spending. In sum, an increase of $100 in investment, government spending, or net exports has the same effect on income and output.

Thus, if we import more and all other spending remains the same, equilibrium income will fall. This is one reason why many economists focus on the trade deficit or net exports ($X - M$) figures each month.

The aggregate expenditures model illustrates the importance of spending in an economy. Investment, government spending, and exports all increase income, whereas saving, taxes, and imports reduce it. Further, the fact that consumers spend and save some of the *changes* in income (MPC and MPS) gives rise to a spending multiplier that magnifies the impact of changes in spending on the economy.

GDP Gaps

Keynesian analysis illustrated what was needed to pull the economy out of the Great Depression: an increase in aggregate spending. Without sufficient spending, an economy can be stuck at a point below full employment for an extended period. Therefore, Keynes argued that if consumers, businesses, and foreigners were unwilling to spend, government should. This was also the basic rationale for the extraordinary spending measures implemented during the 2007–2009 recession. But Keynesian analysis is also important when the economy is producing an output that exceeds full employment creating inflationary pressures.

When the macroeconomy is in equilibrium, it is producing the maximum amount of goods and services using its resources efficiently. In other words, it has achieved its potential income. Differences between actual income and potential income (GDP at full employment) are called **GDP gaps**, and can be positive or negative. A positive GDP gap occurs when actual output exceeds the potential output. This might occur when businesses respond to higher-than-normal demand by producing more than what it can do efficiently, such as paying its workers overtime or running its machinery beyond the recommended capacity. A negative GDP gap occurs when actual output falls below the potential output, which means that businesses are not fully utilizing all of their production resources.

GDP gap The difference between actual income and potential income (GDP at full employment).

 ISSUE

Was Keynes Right About the Great Depression?

There is little disagreement that the Great Depression was one of the most important events in the United States in modern history. Good aggregate data were not yet available, but President Roosevelt and congressional leaders knew something was very wrong.

Within a couple of years, 10,000 banks collapsed, farms and businesses were lost, the stock market lost 85% of its value from the beginning of the decade, and soup kitchens fed a growing horde as unemployment soared to nearly 25%, up from 3.2% in 1929. Worse, the Great Depression persisted: It did not look to be temporary; there was no end in sight.

The aggregate expenditures model we have just studied provides some insight into the Great Depression. The figure provides saving and investment functions for 1929 and 1933. Both government and the foreign sector were tiny at this time; therefore, the simple aggregate expenditures model effectively illustrates why the Great Depression did not show signs of much improvement; by 1939 the unemployment rate was still over 17%.

Saving and investment were over $16 billion in 1929, or roughly a healthy 15% of GDP (point a). By 1933 investment collapsed to less than $2 billion (an 87% decline), and the economy was in equilibrium at an income of roughly half of that in 1929 (point b). Government spending remained at roughly the same levels while net exports, a small fraction of aggregate expenditures, fell by more than half of their previous levels.

Keynes had it right: Unless something happened to increase investment or exports (not likely given that the rest of the world was suffering economically as well), the economy would remain mired in the Great Depression. He suggested that government spending was needed. Ten years later (1943), the United States was in the middle of World War II, and aggregate expenditures swelled as government spending rose by a factor of 10. The Great Depression was history.

recessionary gap The increase in spending needed (when expanded by the multiplier) to bring a depressed economy back to full employment.

inflationary gap The decrease in spending needed (when expanded by the multiplier) to bring an overheated economy back to full employment.

GDP gaps are related to but are not the same as a recessionary gap or inflationary gap. A **recessionary gap** is the increase in spending needed (when expanded by the multiplier) to eliminate a negative GDP gap and bring an economy back to equilibrium. An **inflationary gap** is the decrease in spending needed (when expanded by the multiplier) to eliminate a positive GDP gap and bring the economy back to equilibrium. For example, suppose an economy is facing inflationary pressures because its actual GDP is $150 billion and its GDP at full employment is $140 billion. This economy has a positive GDP gap of $10 billion. If the multiplier in this economy is 4 (corresponding to an MPC of 0.75), it would need to reduce spending by $2.5 billion (which is then multiplied by 4) to bring the economy back to equilibrium. Therefore, the inflationary gap is $2.5 billion.

The Keynesian approach to analyzing aggregate spending revolutionized the way economists looked at the economy and led to the development of modern macroeconomics. In the next chapter, we extend our analysis to the aggregate demand and supply model, a modern extension of this aggregate expenditures model that accounts for varying price levels and the supply side of the macroeconomy.

✅ CHECKPOINT

THE FULL AGGREGATE EXPENDITURES MODEL

- Government spending affects the economy in the same way as other spending.

- Tax increases withdraw money from the spending stream but do not affect the economy as much as spending reductions because these tax increases are partly offset by decreases in saving.

- Tax decreases inject money into the economy but do not affect the economy as much as spending increases because tax reductions are partly offset by increases in saving.

- Equal changes in government spending and taxes (a balanced budget) result in an equal change in income (the balanced budget multiplier is 1).

- A recessionary gap is the additional spending required that, when expanded by the multiplier, moves the economy to full employment.

- An inflationary gap is the spending reduction necessary (again when expanded by the multiplier) to bring the economy back to full employment.

QUESTIONS: If the government is considering reducing taxes to stimulate the economy, does it matter if the MPS is 0.25 or 0.33? What if the government reduces government spending by an equal amount to fund the tax cut?

Answers to the Checkpoint questions can be found at the end of this chapter.

CHAPTER SUMMARY

SECTION 1 AGGREGATE EXPENDITURES

8.1 Gross domestic product (GDP) is measured by spending or income. Using the spending approach, GDP is equal to aggregate expenditures (*AE*). Therefore,

$$GDP = AE = C + I + G + (X - M)$$

8.2

45° and Consumption Lines

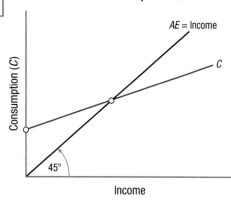

The 45° line shows where total spending (*AE*) equals income. No borrowing or saving exists.

The consumption line (*C*) starts above the origin on the vertical axis (even with no income, one still consumes by borrowing). As income increases, consumption rises, but not as fast as income (the slope of *C* depends on the MPC).

When *C* crosses *AE*, spending equals income (on the 45° line). When *C* is below the *AE* line, saving is positive.

Investment spending fluctuates much more than consumption year to year.

Disposable income, Y_D, is income after all taxes have been paid. Disposable income can either be spent (*C*) or saved (*S*). Thus, $Y_D = C + S$.

The portion that is consumed or saved is an important concept in the aggregate expenditures model:

8.3 **Marginal propensity to consume (*MPC*)** $= \Delta C \div \Delta Y$
Marginal propensity to save (*MPS*) $= \Delta S \div \Delta Y$

$MPC + MPS = 1$ (all money is either spent or saved)

Even with little to no income, college students still consume goods and services, often by borrowing against future income.

8.4 **Determinants of Consumption and Saving**

The aggregate expenditures model states that income is the main determinant of consumption and saving. But other factors also can shift the consumption schedule, such as:

• Wealth
• Expectations
• Household debt
• Taxes

Determinants of Investment Demand

Investment demand is assumed to be independent of income, but certain factors can shift investment demand, such as:

• Expectations
• Technological change
• Operating costs
• Capital goods on hand

SECTION 2 THE SIMPLE AGGREGATE EXPENDITURES MODEL

Ignoring government spending and net exports, aggregate expenditures (AE) are the sum of consumer spending and business investment: $AE = C + I$. Because AE also equals $C + S$ at equilibrium, this means that saving equals investment.

8.5

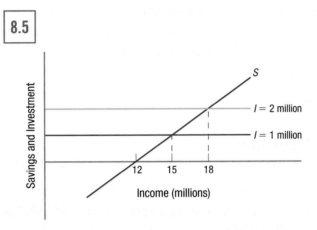

With no investment, Income = $12 million. With $1 million in investment, income rises to $15 million, an increase of $3 million. The multiplier in this example is 3.

8.6 The **multiplier effect** occurs when a dollar of spending generates many more dollars of spending in the economy.

The **multiplier** is equal to $1/(1 - MPC)$ or $1/MPS$.

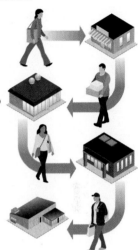

SECTION 3 THE FULL AGGREGATE EXPENDITURES MODEL

8.7 Government spending affects the economy just like any other spending, and so does spending by foreign consumers (exports). In the full aggregate expenditures model, all forms of spending are analyzed, including C, I, G, and $(X - M)$.

If the multiplier for an economy is 5, a $1 million increase in investment increases income by $5 million. The same effect occurs with a $1 million increase in government spending or $1 million increase in net exports. Essentially, spending is spending, no matter from where it comes.

8.8 A general way to analyze policies that increase or decrease aggregate output is to categorize activities as either an **injection** or a **withdrawal:**

- Injections increase spending in an economy and include investment (I), government spending (G), and exports (X).
- Withdrawals decrease spending in an economy and include savings (S), taxes (T), and imports (M).

In equilibrium, all injections must equal all withdrawals:

$$I + G + X = S + T + M$$

8.9 Whenever the economy moves away from its full employment equilibrium, one of two gaps is created:

- **Recessionary gap:** The increase in spending needed (when expanded by the multiplier) to bring a depressed economy back to full employment.
- **Inflationary gap:** The decrease in spending needed (when expanded by the multiplier) to bring an overheated economy back to full employment.

Mark Hryciw/Dreamstime.com

Purchasing an American-made car injects spending into the economy, and the economic benefits are enhanced by the multiplier.

Hupeng/Dreamstime.com

Purchasing a foreign-made car, however, results in a withdrawal because money leaves the country, and this effect is compounded by the multiplier.

Key Concepts

Questions and Problems

Check Your Understanding

1. Describe the important difference between the average propensity to consume (APC) and the marginal propensity to consume (MPC).

2. What are the factors that cause consumption to change at any given level of income?

3. If an economy's spending multiplier is equal to 4, what is its MPC and MPS?

4. What does the paradox of thrift suggest would happen to output, income, and long-run savings if people increased their MPS in preparation for a recession?

5. Explain why a $100 reduction in taxes does not have the same impact on output and employment as a $100 increase in government spending.

6. Explain how injections and withdrawals into an economy affect its income and output.

Apply the Concepts

7. If the economy has an MPC equal to 0.80 and is currently $800 million below its full employment income, will a $150 million increase in investment spending bring the economy to its macroeconomic equilibrium, all else equal?

8. Other than reductions in interest rates that increase the level of investment by businesses, what factors would result in higher investment?

9. The simple aggregate expenditures model argues that one form of spending is just as good as any other; increases in any type of spending lead to equal increases in income. However, is there any reason to suspect that private investment might be better for the economy than government spending?

10. How would a country correct an inflationary gap using changes in government spending? How would it address a recessionary gap?

11. How does the economy today differ from that during the Great Depression, the economy Keynes used as the basis for the macroeconomic model discussed in this chapter?

12. In modern politics, the word "Keynesian" often is synonymous with "big government" spending. Does this characterization accurately reflect the role of government in spurring economic activity? How would a tax cut be characterized today versus in Keynes's time?

In the News

13. The U.S. tax cuts that went into effect in 2018 reduced the corporate tax rate and individual income tax rates. Tax analysts have determined that while most American taxpayers benefit

from the policy, a large portion of the tax cuts is aimed at higher-income households. Explain how the effects of this tax policy might differ, if at all, if more of the tax cuts are aimed at lower-income households based on the multiplier effect.

14. A proposal that has significant support among policymakers regardless of political party is the need to modernize the nation's infrastructure, such as reinforcing thousands of bridges deemed structurally deficient and modernizing airports. Explain why such policies might not be as effective when the economy is experiencing an expansion than when it is in a recession.

Solving Problems

15. Using the following aggregate expenditures table, answer the questions that follow.

Income (Y), in $	Consumption (C), in $	Saving (S), in $
2,200	2,320	−120
2,300	2,380	−80
2,400	2,440	−40
2,500	2,500	0
2,600	2,560	40
2,700	2,620	80
2,800	2,680	120
2,900	2,740	160
3,000	2,800	200

a. Compute the APC when income equals $2,300 and the APS when income equals $2,800.
b. Compute the MPC and MPS.
c. What does the multiplier equal?
d. If investment spending is equal to $120, what will be the level of equilibrium income?
e. On the following grid, graph saving and investment, and determine the equilibrium income.

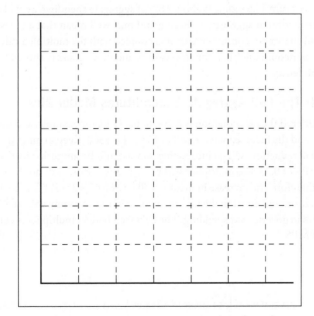

Work It Out

16. Use the figure to answer the following questions.

   a. What are the MPC, the MPS, and the multiplier?

   b. If the economy is currently in equilibrium at point *a* and full employment income is $4,000, how much in *additional* expenditures is needed to move this economy to full employment? What is this level of spending called?

   c. Assume that the economy is currently in equilibrium at point *a* and full employment income is $4,000. How much of a tax decrease would be required to move the economy to full employment?

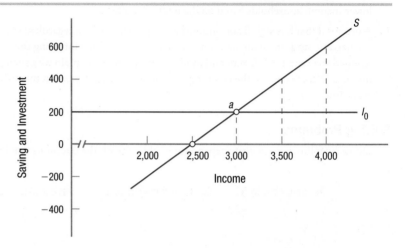

✓ Answers to Questions in Checkpoints

Checkpoint: Aggregate Expenditures 196

Consumer spending, while 5 times larger in absolute size than investment spending, involves many small expenditures by households that do not vary much from month to month, such as rent (or mortgage payment), food, and utilities. Consumers change habits, but slowly. Business investment expenditures are typically on big-ticket items such as new factories and equipment, but such investments occur only when businesses have favorable expectations about the economy. When expectations sour, investment by all firms in an industry typically falls.

Checkpoint: The Simple Aggregate Expenditures Model 203

A decrease in consumer confidence may signal that consumers are going to spend less and save more. Because consumer spending is about 68% of aggregate spending, a small decline represents a significant reduction in aggregate spending and may well mean that a recession is imminent. Relatively small changes in consumer spending coupled with the multiplier can result in relatively large changes in income, and therefore forecasters and policymakers should keep a close eye on consumer confidence.

Checkpoint: The Full Aggregate Expenditures Model 209

Yes, it does matter. If the tax reduction is going to be $100, for example, and the MPS is 0.25, the multiplier is 4, and the income increase will be $75 × 4 = $300. Keep in mind that in this case, one-fourth of the tax reduction will go into saving and will not be amplified by the multiplier. However, with a MPS of 0.33, the multiplier will be 3, and one-third will not be multiplied (will go into saving); therefore, the increase in income will be $66.67 × 3 = $200. If government spending is reduced by an amount equal to the tax cut, income in the economy will fall by exactly the value of the reduction in government spending. The balanced budget multiplier is equal to 1, regardless of the value of MPS.

9

Aggregate Demand and Supply

Understanding how the interaction of total spending and production explains the booms and busts of an economy

Among cities that have changed dramatically over the past two decades is Dubai, a large city in the Middle East that thrived on oil production. But unlike many other oil-rich cities, at the start of the new millennium, Dubai undertook a strategy of transforming its economy to one less dependent on oil, as it foresaw (correctly) a future when oil is no longer an endless source of money. What did Dubai do?

Investors and the government in Dubai invested heavily in infrastructure. They built skyscrapers that became home to multinational corporations, luxury homes and condos (including thousands on artificial islands) to attract wealthy foreigners seeking a vacation home, and lavish shopping malls and attractions to make Dubai a world travel destination.

By diversifying its economy, Dubai ensured that its capacity to produce goods and services that consumers desired extended beyond its oil fields. The takeaway from Dubai's strategy is that the state of an economy cannot be solely based on the performance of a single market, region, or time period. Likewise, government policies are often designed to meet the needs of an entire nation. It would be dangerous to look at just one region or one industry and come to conclusions or make policy recommendations for the nation as a whole.

British economist John Maynard Keynes recognized the need to develop tools to analyze the macroeconomy as a whole. He focused on aggregate expenditures by consumers, businesses, and governments as the key drivers for the economy that determined employment and output. But the model he developed during the Great Depression did not fully consider the effect that changes in the economy would have on prices. Why?

Keynes focused on the problem at hand, when resources were underutilized. For this reason, an expansion of consumption or production did not create much upward pressure on prices. For example, in times of high unemployment, more labor can be hired without raising wages because firms with job openings often are inundated with applicants.

Therefore, the initial Keynesian model was a fixed price model, one that essentially ignored the supply side because increasing production would occur without a rise in prices. The lessons from Keynes, with their focus on spending, formed the foundation of the demand side of the modern macroeconomic model. In this chapter, we add the supply side and move from a fixed price model to a flexible price model, where prices and wages adjust to macroeconomic conditions. We call this model the aggregate demand–aggregate supply (AD/AS) model. This model looks a lot like the supply and demand model for a market, but it has several important differences: It measures real output of the aggregate (overall) economy, it uses the average price level for an economy, and it focuses on short-run fluctuations around a long-run equilibrium output.

Prices and wages do not always change in a consistent manner. As we will see, sometimes prices and wages can be sticky in the short run, a condition that allows an economy to respond positively to economic stimulus policies. But in the long run, prices and wages tend to be very responsive to changing macroeconomic conditions.

This flexible price model expands the analysis that began with Keynes to many more modern problems facing economies. The AD/AS model builds on knowledge you

BY THE Numbers

Contributors to an Economy's Aggregate Demand and Aggregate Supply

Aggregate demand and aggregate supply are made up of many components in the economy. Factors that influence the extent to which consumers (domestic and foreign), businesses, and governments spend make up aggregate demand, while short-run and long-run factors influence producers and aggregate supply. This By the Numbers analyzes homeownership, an important contributor to aggregate demand, and how ownership rates compare across the United States.

DATA:

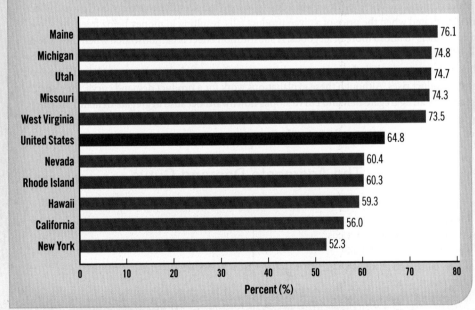

Homeownership Rates (%): The Top Five and Bottom Five States (2018)

State	Rate
Maine	76.1
Michigan	74.8
Utah	74.7
Missouri	74.3
West Virginia	73.5
United States	64.8
Nevada	60.4
Rhode Island	60.3
Hawaii	59.3
California	56.0
New York	52.3

Percent (%)

Where Can I Find These Data?

Source: U.S. Census Bureau, U.S. Department of Commerce

Web site: https://www.census.gov/housing/hvs/data/rates.html

Details: Open the table "Homeownership Rates by State"

~ Assessing Your Data Literacy ~

1. What is the average homeownership rate of the top five states? What is the average homeownership rate of the bottom five states?

2. What is the difference in the homeownership rate between the state with the highest homeownership rate and the state with the lowest homeownership rate?

3. What factors might explain the large difference in homeownership rates between states?

1,184,900

Total number of new homes constructed in the United States in 2018

91.0%

Homeownership rate in Singapore in 2018 (among the highest in the world) fueled by generous government subsidies to encourage its citizens to own homes

WHY ARE THESE DATA IMPORTANT?

Purchasing a home is one of the largest investments people make. When the economy is strong and interest rates and other borrowing conditions are favorable, homeownership will rise. An increase in home construction (which generally rises with homeownership) increases the amount of investment in an economy, leading to an increase in aggregate demand.

Data *in the News*

"Immigrants and Homeownership" by Michael Kolomatsky; *New York Times*, November 15, 2018

A new study examines the share of primary homes owned by the native-born and foreign-born in America's most populated metropolitan areas.... Miami had the highest rate of immigrant homeownership (26 percent).

already have: analyzing changes that affect demand and supply, and determining a new equilibrium. These techniques provide policymakers with a way of looking at the overall economy when many factors and differences in economic performance prevail across regions and industries.

This chapter begins with an analysis of aggregate demand and its determinants. We then turn to aggregate supply, studying the differences between a long-run aggregate supply curve and a short-run aggregate supply curve and the determinants of each. Finally, we put the aggregate demand and aggregate supply curves together to analyze macroeconomic equilibrium. The AD/AS model gives you the tools to analyze tradeoffs between economic output and inflation. It will allow you to understand the causes of recessions and inflation and how government policy is sometimes used to correct these problems.

AGGREGATE DEMAND

aggregate demand The total output of goods and services (real GDP) purchased at different price levels.

The **aggregate demand** (AD) curve (or schedule) shows the total output of goods and services (real GDP) purchased at different price levels. The aggregate demand curve in Figure 1 looks like the product demand curves we studied earlier. They both slope downward, showing how output rises as prices fall, and vice versa. However, it's important to remember that the reasons the product and aggregate demand curves slope downward are different.

Why Is the Aggregate Demand Curve Negatively Sloped?

Product demand curves slope downward due to *income* and *substitution* effects. An income effect is demonstrated when the price of a given product falls, resulting in money being freed up, allowing consumers to afford more of all goods. A substitution effect is demonstrated when the price of a product falls, causing consumers to purchase more of the product because they substitute it for other higher-priced goods. Income and substitution effects work the other way when the price of a given product rises. Although these explanations work for a product demand curve, they do not explain why an aggregate demand curve slopes downward because aggregate demand measures not the demand for just one product but rather the demand for all products. For the latter, we need to look at other factors influencing the aggregate economy.

····· Figure 1 • The Aggregate Demand Curve ··············

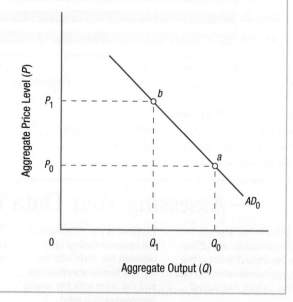

The aggregate demand curve shows the total amount of goods and services (real GDP) that will be purchased at various price levels. As the price level increases from P_0 to P_1, there is a movement along AD_0 from point a to b, corresponding to a change in aggregate output from Q_0 to Q_1.

The Wealth Effect One reason that real output declines when the aggregate price level rises is the **wealth effect.** Households usually hold some of their wealth in financial assets such as savings accounts, bonds, and cash. A rising aggregate price level means that the purchasing power of this monetary wealth decreases. For example, if you have $5,000 in savings and prices rise throughout the economy, that $5,000 will now purchase less than before. This reduction in household purchasing power means that some purchases are put on hold, thereby reducing output demanded. This is represented by a movement from point *a* to point *b* in Figure 1.

Export Price Effect When the U.S. aggregate price level rises, American goods become more expensive in the global marketplace. Higher prices mean that our goods are less competitive with the goods made in other countries. The result is that foreigners purchase fewer American products, and our exports decline. A decrease in exports means that the demand for domestically produced goods and services (the quantity purchased by foreign consumers, a component of real GDP) also declines. However, this effect on real output is mitigated by flexible exchange rates. If the U.S. dollar depreciates in response to inflation, American goods become less expensive in other countries, so U.S. exports will increase.

Interest Rate Effect Interest rates are the prices paid for the use of money. If we assume for a moment that the quantity of money is fixed, then as aggregate prices rise, people will need more money to carry out their economic transactions. As people demand more money, the cost of borrowing money—interest rates—will go up. Rising interest rates mean reduced business investment, which results in a drop in quantity demanded for real GDP, shown in Figure 1 as a movement from point *a* to *b*.

In summary, the aggregate demand curve is negatively sloped because of three factors. When the aggregate price level rises, this lowers household purchasing power because of the wealth effect. A rising aggregate price level also lowers the amount of exports because our goods are now more expensive. Furthermore, a rising aggregate price level increases the demand for money and therefore drives up interest rates. Rising interest rates reduce business investment and reduce the quantity demanded of real GDP. In each case, as aggregate prices rise from P_0 to P_1, quantity demanded of real GDP falls from Q_0 to Q_1.

Determinants of Aggregate Demand

We have seen that the aggregate demand curve is negatively sloped. Everything else held constant, a change in the aggregate price level will change the quantity of real GDP demanded along the aggregate demand curve. The *determinants* of aggregate demand are those factors that shift the *entire* aggregate demand curve when they change. They are the "everything else held constant." These include the components of GDP: consumption, investment, government spending, and net exports.

If one of these components of aggregate spending changes, the aggregate demand curve will shift, as shown in Figure 2. At first, aggregate demand is AD_0; therefore, a shift to AD_1 represents an increase in aggregate demand; more real output is demanded at each price level. If, for example, businesses decide to invest more in new technology, more real output is now demanded at the current price level, P_0, and at all other price levels. For similar reasons, a decrease in aggregate demand from AD_0 to AD_2 means that less real output is being demanded at every price level. If consumers fear the onset of a recession and decide to reduce spending to increase their savings, then less output will be demanded at all price levels.

Let's look at these determinants of aggregate demand more closely. What might cause the various components of aggregate expenditures to change, shifting the AD curve?

Consumer Spending Consumer spending is the largest component of aggregate demand, representing about 68% of total spending in the economy. The level of spending as a percentage of overall output is relatively stable over time. Still, consumer spending is affected by several major factors: wealth, consumer confidence, household debt, interest rates, and taxes. As consumer spending represents such a large part of the economy, even small changes in this factor can have a

wealth effect Households usually hold some of their wealth in financial assets such as savings accounts, bonds, and cash. A rising aggregate price level means that the purchasing power of this monetary wealth declines, reducing output demanded.

····· Figure 2 • Shifts of the Aggregate Demand Curve ·····

The determinants of aggregate demand include the components of GDP and aggregate spending: consumption, investment, government spending, and net exports. A change in one will shift the aggregate demand curve, as shown here. At first, aggregate demand is AD_0; therefore, a shift to AD_1 represents an increase in aggregate demand; more real output is demanded at all price levels. A decline in aggregate demand from AD_0 to AD_2 means that less real output is being demanded at each price level.

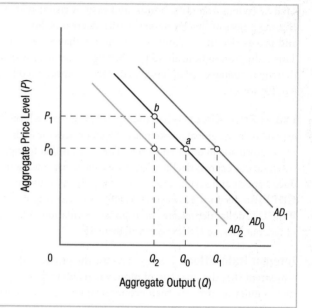

significant impact on the economy. And in times when consumption changes a lot, the effect on the economy can be dramatic.

For example, increases in wealth as a result of rising stock prices or an inheritance may lead to increased consumption *at all price levels*. On the other hand, the financial and housing crisis a decade ago caused a severe decline in wealth as many people saw their home values, investment portfolios, and retirement savings plummet. Note that this effect on wealth is different than the effect described earlier when prices rise. When the price level rises, the purchasing power of a fixed amount of wealth falls. But when some other factor causes wealth to decline, the entire aggregate demand curve shifts from AD_0 to AD_2 in Figure 2.

Consumer expectations and confidence about the economy play a significant role in determining the level of consumer spending. High confidence in the economy eases job security fears and stimulates consumer spending, shifting the aggregate demand curve to the right. High family debt ratios restrict access to future credit, reducing spending on high-ticket items often bought on credit. Higher interest rates increase the cost of borrowing (whether on loans or credit card balances), making purchases more difficult. And finally, higher taxes reduce disposable income, reducing consumer spending and shifting the aggregate demand curve to the left.

Investment Investment (spending, mostly by businesses for structures, equipment, and software) is determined mainly by interest rates and the expected rate of return on capital projects. When interest rates rise, investment will fall and the aggregate demand curve will shift to the left, and vice versa.

When business expectations become more favorable—perhaps some new technology is introduced or excess capacity is reduced—investment will increase, and the aggregate demand curve will increase, or shift to the right. But if businesses see clouds on the horizon, such as new regulations, higher taxes, restrictions on the use of technology, or excess capacity, investment will drop, and the aggregate demand curve will shift to the left.

Investment decisions tend to be larger in magnitude than everyday consumption purchases, which results in investment varying from one year to the next. Therefore, although investment represents a smaller percentage of aggregate demand, its relative instability can result in a significant effect on the aggregate economy.

Government Spending and Net Exports Government spending and net exports have essentially the same effect on the aggregate economy as consumer and investment spending. When government spending or net exports rise, aggregate demand increases, and vice versa.

When the national income of a foreign country rises, some of this money is used to buy more American goods and services. The increase in demand for U.S. goods and services in other countries results in more exports, which increases U.S. aggregate demand.

Foreign exchange rates also affect aggregate demand. An appreciation, or rise, in the value of the euro, for instance, will result in Europeans buying more American goods because a euro will buy more. This change increases U.S. exports and aggregate demand. On the other hand, an appreciation of the U.S. dollar would decrease U.S. exports and aggregate demand.

Another factor that increases net exports in a country is foreign tourism, which is an export of services. The recent increase of American tourists visiting Cuba has boosted aggregate demand in Cuba. The following Around the World feature describes another country, Myanmar, that reopened its border to foreign tourists within the past decade.

A quick summary is now in order. The aggregate demand curve shows the quantities of real GDP demanded at different price levels. (The derivation of the AD curve using the Keynesian fixed price model is shown in the Appendix.) The aggregate demand curve slopes downward because of the wealth effect (the value of monetary assets falls when the price level rises), because exports fall as domestic prices rise, and because rising prices raise interest rates, which reduce investment. On the other hand, changes in one of the determinants of aggregate demand shift the entire aggregate demand curve. Table 1 summarizes the determinants of aggregate demand: consumption, investment, government spending, and net exports. When one of these determinants changes, the entire aggregate demand curve will shift.

A favorable exchange rate for the euro makes shopping trips to New York City for Europeans less expensive, providing a boost to U.S. aggregate demand.

TABLE 1	THE DETERMINANTS OF AGGREGATE DEMAND (THE AGGREGATE DEMAND CURVE SHIFTS WHEN THESE CHANGE)	
Determinant	**AD Increases**	**AD Decreases**
Consumer Spending		
• Wealth	Wealth increases	Wealth decreases
• Consumer expectations	Expectations improve	Expectations worsen
• Household debt	Debt falls	Debt rises
• Interest rates	Lower	Higher
• Taxes	Taxes decrease	Taxes increase
Investment		
• Interest rates	Lower	Higher
• Expected rate of return on investment	Higher	Lower
• Business expectations	More positive	More negative
• Taxes	Taxes decrease	Taxes increase
Government Spending	Increases	Decreases
Net Exports		
• Income in other countries	Rises	Falls
• Foreign exchange rates	U.S. dollar depreciates	U.S. dollar appreciates

AROUND THE WORLD

Myanmar: Opening a Country Causes a Boom in Aggregate Demand

How did Myanmar's transition from an authoritarian regime to a democracy lead to an increase in aggregate demand?

© R.M. Nunes/Alamy Stock Photo

For many nations in Asia and Africa that had been colonized by Europeans in the 19th and 20th centuries, a cultural clash existed between the rich histories of the native inhabitants and the modern influences that were brought by the colonizers. When many of these countries (including major countries such as India and Vietnam) achieved independence in the mid-20th century, the new governments struggled to find a balance between minimizing their colonizer's cultural influences and maintaining the economic developments that were achieved. Often, this led to war and a path toward declining economic growth. For one Southeast Asian nation whose experience under long military rule resulted in one of the most impoverished nations in the world, the

transition to a democratic nation in 2012 was a significant economic event.

What happened in Myanmar since 2012 that caused a significant increase in aggregate demand?

Myanmar (formerly Burma) achieved its independence from the British in 1948, but the transition process was not smooth, as various political organizations (each supported by a segment of the military) competed for power. This culminated in 1962 with a strict authoritarian regime led by a series of political parties that ruled by force. It would take another 50 years before Myanmar held its first democratic elections.

Since 2012 foreign investment has entered the country of 53 million, welcomed by a labor force eager to work, even at low wages, for a chance at a better life. The improved employment picture led to increased consumption and subsequently the opening of new markets and service industries.

Then, a very significant change occurred: the reintroduction of the foreign tourist, largely banned during military rule, who came by the thousands to experience Myanmar's rich 13,000-year history filled with temples and other historical treasures. These tourists brought hard currency (such as dollars, euros, and yen) into a nation seeking to connect with the world that it had long ago abandoned.

Each of these events, which led to an increase in consumption, investment, government spending, and net exports, resulted in a dramatic increase in aggregate demand and subsequently a very high growth rate. Today, Myanmar's future is as bright as its rich historical past centuries ago.

 GO ONLINE TO PRACTICE THE ECONOMIC CONCEPTS IN THIS STORY

Policies are often enacted to change one of the determinants of aggregate demand. For example, a tax reduction is expected to stimulate consumer spending and investment, which then increase aggregate demand and output. But as important as aggregate demand is in determining an economy's output, our analysis would be incomplete without including aggregate supply, which describes the impetus for businesses to produce goods and services.

✓ CHECKPOINT

AGGREGATE DEMAND

- The aggregate demand curve shows the relationship between real GDP and the price level.

- The aggregate demand curve has a negative slope because of the impact of the price level on financial wealth, exports, and interest rates.

- The determinants of aggregate demand are consumer spending, investment spending, government expenditures, and net exports. Changes in any of these determinants will shift the entire aggregate demand curve.

QUESTION: Housing and stock market prices have risen substantially in recent years. Explain how this affects aggregate demand in an economy.

Answers to the Checkpoint questions can be found at the end of this chapter.

AGGREGATE SUPPLY

The **aggregate supply** curve shows the real GDP that firms will produce at varying price levels. Although the definition seems similar to that for aggregate demand, note that we have now moved from the spending side of the economy to the production side. We will consider two different possibilities for aggregate supply: the short run and the long run. In the short run, aggregate supply increases as the price level rises (and vice versa) and is represented by an upward-sloping curve. In contrast, long-run aggregate supply measures the economy at its potential output with full employment and is represented by a vertical curve. Growth occurs in the economy by shifting this vertical aggregate supply curve to the right. Let's begin by looking at the economy from the long-run perspective.

aggregate supply The real GDP that firms will produce at various price levels. The aggregate supply curve is positively sloped in the short run but vertical in the long run.

Long Run

The *vertical* **long-run aggregate supply (LRAS) curve** incorporates the assumptions of classical (pre-1930s) economic analysis. Classical analysis assumes that all variables are adjustable in the long run, where product prices, wages, and interest rates are flexible. As a result, the economy will gravitate to the position of full employment shown as Q_0 in Figure 3.

Full employment is often referred to as the *natural rate of output* or *the natural rate of unemployment* by economists. This long-run output is an equilibrium level at which inflationary pressures are minimal. Once the economy has reached this level, further increases in output are extremely difficult to achieve; there is no one else to operate more machines and no more machines to operate. As we will see later, attempts to expand beyond this output level only lead to higher prices and rising inflation.

In general terms, the vertical LRAS curve represents the full employment capacity of the economy and depends on the amount of resources available for production and the available technology. An economy's productive capacity is determined by the capital available, the size and quality of the labor force, and the technology employed. These are also the big three factors driving economic growth (shifting the $LRAS_0$ curve to the right to $LRAS_1$) once a suitable infrastructure has been put in place.

long-run aggregate supply (LRAS) curve The long-run aggregate supply curve is vertical at full employment because the economy has reached its productive capacity.

Determinants of Long-Run Aggregate Supply

Attempts to improve technology such as automation and digitalization are clear examples of an increase in productive capacity. But so is the enhancement of labor quality. As a greater percentage of people pursue college and postgraduate degrees, productivity increases and leads to economic

····· Figure 3 • Long-Run Aggregate Supply ···············

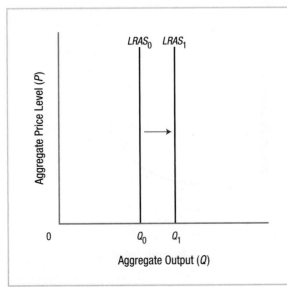

The long-run aggregate supply (LRAS) curve is vertical, reflecting the assumptions of classical economic analysis. In the long run, all variables in the economy can adjust, and the economy will settle at full employment at output Q_0. Changes in the amount of resources available, the quality of the labor force, or technology can shift the LRAS curve to the right to $LRAS_1$, at the new full employment output level Q_1.

growth. Finally, increased trade and globalization have allowed resources to flow more freely, permitting the United States to gain access to better or cheaper inputs and more specialized labor.

Each of the shifts in the LRAS curve takes time. It's not easy to improve the human capital of an entire nation or to develop new production technologies. Therefore, although the LRAS is of concern to the long-term welfare of the country, policymakers are often more concerned about short-run outcomes.

Short Run

short-run aggregate supply (SRAS) curve The short-run aggregate supply curve is positively sloped because many input costs are slow to change (*sticky*) in the short run.

Figure 4 shows a **short-run aggregate supply (SRAS) curve,** which is upward sloping to indicate a positive relationship between the aggregate price level and aggregate output. One of the characteristics of the SRAS curve is that its slope is relatively flat at lower levels of aggregate output and relatively steep at higher levels of aggregate output.

When an economy is experiencing a downturn resulting in lower levels of aggregate output, factors of production are not being fully utilized. This is the type of depressed economy that John Maynard Keynes focused on when he wrote his *General Theory* book. When an economy is producing below its potential output, firms are able to increase production without incurring an immediate increase in input prices, such as wages, rents, or raw materials. In other words, input prices are *sticky*, or slow to change. Sometimes wages and other inputs are sticky as a result of contracts that lock in prices over a period, but they can also be sticky when resources are underutilized. For example, when shopping centers have vacancies, firms can negotiate a better price for rent than when every space is occupied. Sticky prices are reflected in a flatter SRAS curve where increases in aggregate output can be achieved without a large increase in the price level.

Once an economy recovers toward full employment, the prices of inputs will rise as output increases. Therefore, the slope of the SRAS curve increases as the economy approaches full employment and input prices become less sticky. For example, firms will need to pay workers higher wages if unemployment is low and workers have better job opportunities.

And once the economy reaches full employment, any attempt at producing output beyond this level will lead to a sharp increase in the price level. In other words, it is possible to temporarily produce beyond the full employment level of output, but it is not efficient. Businesses may need to pay overtime wages and/or run machinery beyond its recommended capacity and incur costly wear and tear. When an economy produces beyond its potential output, prices rise quickly and act according to the classical theory, which assumes that prices and wages are flexible and quick to react to changes in the economy.

••••• Figure 4 • Short-Run Aggregate Supply ••••••••••••

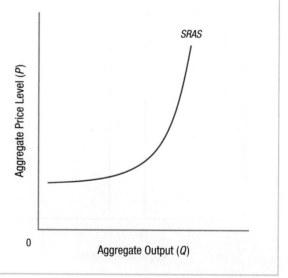

The short-run aggregate supply (SRAS) curve is positively sloped because many input prices are slow to change in the short run (they are *sticky*). The curve is flatter at lower levels of output and steeper at higher levels of output to reflect the reduced stickiness of input prices as aggregate output increases.

A SRAS curve shows the relationship between aggregate output and the price level at different stages in the business cycle. The Keynesian analysis of sticky prices is most evident at lower levels of output, while the classical analysis of flexible prices is most evident at higher levels of output. We now turn our attention to the factors that cause SRAS to change.

Determinants of Short-Run Aggregate Supply

We have seen that, because the aggregate supply curve is positively sloped in the short run, a change in aggregate output, other things held constant, will result in a change in the aggregate price level. The determinants of short-run aggregate supply—those other things held constant—include input prices, productivity, taxes, regulation, the market power of firms, and business and inflationary expectations. When any of these determinants changes, the entire SRAS curve shifts, as Figure 5 illustrates.

The price of copper increased over 300% over the past two decades. This has increased the cost of producing copper products and contributed to a decrease in aggregate supply.

Input Prices Changes in the cost of land, labor, or capital will affect the output that firms are willing to provide to the market. When world crude oil prices rise, it is never long before prices rise at the gasoline pump. Rising input prices are quickly passed along to consumers, and the opposite is true as well. New discoveries of raw materials result in falling input prices, causing the prices for products incorporating these inputs to drop. This means that more of these products can be produced at a price of P_0 in Figure 5 as short-run aggregate supply shifts to $SRAS_1$ (point a), or now output Q_0 can be produced at a lower price on $SRAS_1$ (point b).

Productivity Changes in productivity are another major determinant of short-run aggregate supply. Rising productivity will shift the short-run aggregate supply curve to the right—from $SRAS_0$ to $SRAS_1$ in Figure 5—and vice versa. This is why changes in technology that increase productivity are so important to the economy. Moreover, technological advances often lead to new products that expand short-run aggregate supply. The willingness of firms to invest in new capital

····· Figure 5 • Shifts in Short-Run Aggregate Supply ·····

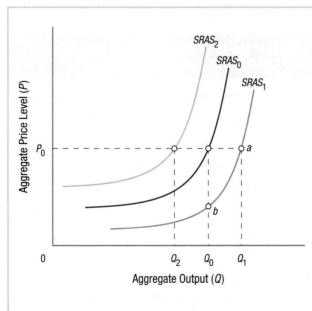

The determinants of short-run aggregate supply include changes in input prices, productivity, taxes, regulation, the market power of firms, and inflationary expectations. If one of these determinants changes, the entire short-run aggregate supply curve shifts. Increasing productivity, for instance, will shift the short-run aggregate supply curve to the right, from $SRAS_0$ to $SRAS_1$. Conversely, raising taxes or adding inefficient regulations can shift the short-run aggregate supply curve to the left, from $SRAS_0$ to $SRAS_2$.

equipment (aided by an improved business outlook) will enhance the productive capacity of an economy, which can also increase long-run aggregate supply.

An example of a technological advancement is the improvement in traffic-enhanced GPS navigational devices, which allows one to select the quickest route to a destination taking into account traffic and roadblocks (such as those caused by construction projects and car crashes) in real time. Such technological enhancements let commercial vehicles reduce their time on the road, reducing transportation costs to the company. These cost reductions lead to an increase in short-run aggregate supply. If these technologies expand the overall productive capacity of the economy, they can also increase long-run aggregate supply.

Taxes and Regulation Rising taxes or increased regulation can shift the short-run aggregate supply curve to the left, from $SRAS_0$ to $SRAS_2$ in Figure 5. Excessively burdensome regulation, though it may provide some benefits, raises costs so much that the new costs exceed the benefits. This results in a decrease in short-run aggregate supply. Often, no one knows how much regulation has increased costs until some sort of deregulation is instituted.

Alternatively, tax reductions, such as investment tax credits, reduce the costs of production, resulting in an increase in short-run aggregate supply. Similarly, improving the process of satisfying regulations, such as reducing required paperwork, also can increase short-run aggregate supply even when the regulations themselves do not change.

Market Power of Firms Monopoly firms charge more than competitive firms. Therefore, a change in the market power of firms can increase prices for specific products, thereby reducing short-run aggregate supply. When the Organization of the Petroleum Exporting Countries (OPEC) proclaimed an oil embargo and reduced the global supply of oil in 1973, oil prices increased by almost 300% in less than a year. Because at that time there were very few substitutes for oil, higher oil prices shifted the SRAS curve to the left.

Today, with many non-OPEC nations (such as Canada, China, Norway, Russia, and the United States) producing large quantities of oil, OPEC's power to raise prices has fallen.

Inflationary Expectations A change in inflationary expectations by businesses or workers can shift the short-run aggregate supply curve. If, for example, workers believe that inflation will increase, they will bargain for higher wages to offset the expected losses to real wages. The intensified bargaining and resulting higher wages will reduce aggregate supply.

To summarize, the short-run aggregate supply curve slopes upward because many input costs are slow to change (i.e., are *sticky*) in the short run. This SRAS curve can shift because of changes in input prices, productivity, taxes, regulation, the market power of firms, or inflationary expectations. Table 2 summarizes the determinants of short-run aggregate supply.

TABLE 2	DETERMINANTS OF SHORT-RUN AGGREGATE SUPPLY (THE SHORT-RUN AGGREGATE SUPPLY CURVE SHIFTS WHEN THESE CHANGE)	
Determinant	**SRAS Increases**	**SRAS Decreases**
Changes in Input Prices	Prices decline	Prices rise
Changes in Productivity		
• Technology	Improvements	Reductions
• Changes in human capital	Improvements	Reductions
Changes in Taxes and Regulations		
• Tax rates	Lower	Higher
• Subsidies	Higher	Lower
• Change in burdensome regulations	Reductions	Additions
Change in Market Power	Decreases	Increases
Changes in Inflationary Expectations	Lower	Higher

✅ CHECKPOINT

AGGREGATE SUPPLY

- The aggregate supply curve shows the real GDP that firms will produce at various price levels.

- The vertical long-run aggregate supply (LRAS) curve represents the full-employment productive capacity of the economy.

- Increasing resources or improving technology shift the LRAS curve, which represents economic growth.

- The short-run aggregate supply (SRAS) curve is upward-sloping, reflecting rigidities in the economy because input and output prices are slow to change (sticky).

- The determinants of short-run aggregate supply include input prices, productivity, taxes, regulations, the market power of firms, and inflationary expectations.

QUESTION: While interest rates had been kept extremely low for almost a decade, many investors worried that access to cheap loans would drive prices higher as more people borrow money for purchases. How might this change in inflationary expectations affect the SRAS curve?

Answers to the Checkpoint questions can be found at the end of this chapter.

MACROECONOMIC EQUILIBRIUM

Let us now put together the aggregate demand and aggregate supply model. A *short-run* **macroeconomic equilibrium** occurs at the intersection of the short-run aggregate supply and aggregate demand curves; see point *e* in Figure 6. In this case, point *e* also represents *long-run macroeconomic equilibrium* because the economy is operating at full employment, producing output Q_f.

Output level Q_f represents full employment. The SRAS curve assumes price level expectations equal to P_e, and thus Q_f is the natural rate of unemployment or output. Remember that the natural rate of unemployment is that unemployment level at which inflation is low and consistent with inflationary expectations in the economy.

macroeconomic equilibrium
The intersection of the short-run aggregate supply and aggregate demand curves. At the corresponding output level, there are no net pressures for the economy to expand or contract.

····· Figure 6 • Macroeconomic Equilibrium ···············

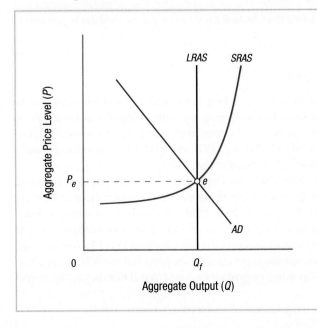

Point *e* represents a short-run macroeconomic equilibrium, the point at which the short-run aggregate supply curve and aggregate demand curve intersect. In this case, point *e* also represents a long-run macroeconomic equilibrium because the economy is operating at full employment, producing output Q_f.

The Spending Multiplier

multiplier Spending changes alter equilibrium income by the initial spending change times the multiplier. One person's spending becomes another's income, and that second person spends some, which becomes income for another person, and so on, until income has changed by $1/(1-MPC)=1/MPS$. The multiplier operates in both directions.

The spending **multiplier** is an important concept introduced into macroeconomics by John Maynard Keynes in 1936. The central idea is that new spending creates more spending, income, and output than just an amount equal to the new spending itself.

For example, let's assume that consumers tend to spend three-quarters and save one-quarter of any new income they receive. Now, assume that good weather encourages a family to spend the day at the annual county fair, spending $100 on food and rides. In other words, $100 of new spending is introduced into the economy. That $100 spent on food and rides adds $100 in income to the operator of the fair because all spending equals income to someone else (whether that be the owner or the workers she hires). Of this additional income, suppose that $25 is saved and $75 is spent by the fair operator to fix a plumbing leak in her home. That $75 in spending becomes $75 in income to the plumber. Now that the plumber has $75 more income, suppose he saves $18.75 (25% of $75) and uses the rest ($56.25) to change the oil in his car, generating $56.25 in income to the mechanic, and so on, round-by-round.

Adding up all of the new spending (equal to the sum of $100 + $75 + $56.25 + . . .) from the initial $100 results in total spending increasing by $400. This represents an increase in output or GDP of $400. Adding up total new saving ($25 + 18.75 + . . .) equals $100, which means that the initial $100 in new spending has increased savings by the same amount through the multiplier process.

marginal propensity to consume The change in consumption associated with a given change in income.

marginal propensity to save The change in saving associated with a given change in income.

The proportion of *additional* income that consumers spend and save is known as the **marginal propensity to consume** and the **marginal propensity to save** (MPC and MPS), respectively. In our example, $MPC = 0.75$ and $MPS = 0.25$. The multiplier is equal to 4, given that $400 of new income was created with the introduction of $100 of new spending. The formula for the spending multiplier is equal to $1/(1-MPC)=1/MPS$ and in this case is $1/(1-0.75)=1/0.25=4$.

The multiplier works as long as the aggregate price level is stable, which is assumed in a Keynesian model with many unemployed resources and excess capacity. This occurs on the flat portion of the SRAS curve. However, once the slope of the SRAS curve increases, the actual multiplier will be smaller because price increases limit the increase in spending that occurs in each round. As a result, the increase in aggregate output rises by less than the multiplier as the price level rises. Once the economy reaches full employment, any further increases in aggregate demand will have little to no effect on output because real output does not change in the long run.

Let's summarize the aggregate demand and supply model before using it to explain important macroeconomic events. Short-run macroeconomic equilibrium occurs at the intersection of AD and SRAS. This output can also represent long-run equilibrium but not necessarily. Short-run equilibrium can occur at less than (or greater than) full employment, as the Great Depression and the 2007–2009 recession has shown. Increases in spending are enhanced by the multiplier, allowing the GDP gap (the difference between current GDP and full-employment GDP) to be closed with a smaller change in spending. The aggregate demand and supply model allows us to examine the effects of policies that can be used during periods of recession and inflation.

Personal consumption is an important part of the multiplier process as money spent in one store generates income that is used to pay its workers and suppliers, who then use this money to make other purchases, and so on. Higher levels of consumer confidence will boost the multiplier in an economy.

The Great Depression

Figure 6 conveniently showed the economy in long-run equilibrium and short-run equilibrium at the same point. However, the Great Depression in the 1930s demonstrated that an economy can reach short-run equilibrium at output levels substantially below full employment. Real GDP dropped by nearly 40% between 1929 and 1933. Unemployment peaked at 25% in 1933 and never fell below 15% throughout the 1930s.

Figure 7 shows actual data for the Great Depression with superimposed aggregate demand and SRAS curves for 1929 and 1933. Investment is the most volatile of the GDP components, and it fell nearly 80% from 1929 to 1933. This drop in investment reduced spending and therefore income and consumption, resulting in a deep depression. The increase in aggregate demand necessary to restore the economy back to 1929 levels was huge, and it was no wonder that a 6% increase in government spending had virtually no impact on the Depression. It wasn't until spending ramped up for World War II that the country moved beyond the Depression.

Figure 7 • Aggregate Demand, Short-Run Aggregate Supply, and the Decline in Investment During the Depression

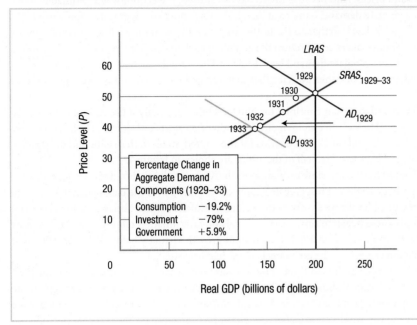

Aggregate demand and short-run aggregate supply are superimposed on the real GDP and price level data for the Great Depression. Investment dropped nearly 80% and consumption declined nearly 20%. Together, these reductions in spending created a depression that was so deep that it took the massive spending for World War II to bring the economy back to full employment.

Percentage Change in Aggregate Demand Components (1929–33)

Consumption	−19.2%
Investment	−79%
Government	+5.9%

Demand-Pull Inflation

Demand-pull inflation occurs when aggregate demand expands so much that equilibrium output exceeds full employment output. Turning to Figure 8, assume that the economy is initially in long-run equilibrium at point *e*. If businesses become overly exuberant and expand investments in some area (such as telecommunications in the late 1990s), this expansion will push aggregate demand out to AD_1. The economy moves to a short-run equilibrium beyond full employment (point *a*), and the price level rises to P_1.

demand-pull inflation

Inflation that occurs when aggregate demand expands so much that equilibrium output exceeds full employment output and the price level rises.

Figure 8 • Demand-Pull Inflation

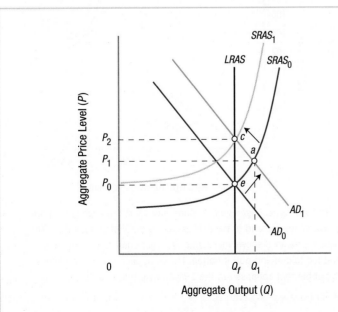

Demand-pull inflation occurs when aggregate demand expands and equilibrium output (Q_1 at point *a*) exceeds full employment output (Q_f). The LRAS curve has not shifted since the capacity has not changed. Thus, the economy will move to a new long-run equilibrium at point *c*. With the new aggregate demand at AD_1, prices have unexpectedly risen. Therefore, short-run aggregate supply shifts to $SRAS_1$ as workers, for example, adjust their wage demands upward, raising the price level further to P_2.

On a temporary basis, the economy can expand beyond full employment as workers work overtime, temporary workers are added, and more shifts are employed. Yet, these activities increase costs and prices. And because LRAS has not shifted, the economy will ultimately move to point c (if aggregate demand remains at AD_1), shifting short-run aggregate supply to $SRAS_1$ and raising the price level further to P_2. In the long run, the economy will gravitate to points such as e and c. Policymakers could return the economy back to the original point e by instituting policies that reduce aggregate demand back to AD_0. These might include reduced government spending, higher taxes, or other policies that discourage investment, consumer spending, or exports.

Demand-pull inflation can continue for quite a while, especially if the economy begins on the SRAS curve well below full employment. Inflation often starts out slow and builds up steam. Decade-long demand-pull inflation scenarios for the United States in the 1960s and for Japan in the last half of the 1980s and first half of the 1990s are shown in Figure 9.

For the United States, the slow escalation of the Vietnam conflict fueled a rising economy along the hypothetical short-run aggregate supply curve placed over the data in panel A. Early in the decade, the price level rose slowly as the economy expanded. But notice how the short-run aggregate supply curve began to turn nearly vertical and how inflation rates rose as the economy approached full employment in 1969. Real output growth virtually halted between 1969 and 1970, but inflation was 5.3%. The economy had reached its potential.

A different example of demand-pull inflation was seen in the Japanese economy from 1987 to 1994. Panel B of Figure 9 shows a steadily growing economy with rising prices throughout the 1980s and early 1990s. Japan ran huge trade surpluses, and the yen appreciated (becoming more valuable). A rising yen would eventually reduce exports (Japanese products would become too expensive). To keep this from happening, the Japanese government kept interest rates artificially low, reducing the pressure on the yen and encouraging investment. But these policies fueled a

Figure 9 • Demand-Pull Inflation, United States (1960s) and Japan (1987–1994)

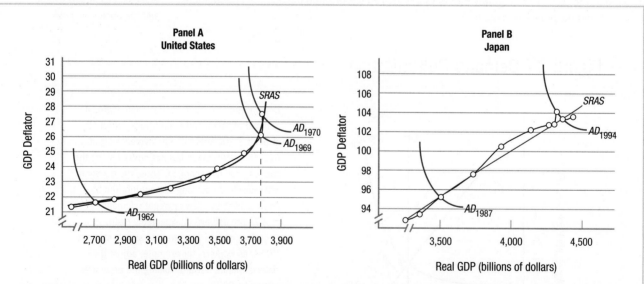

This figure shows two examples of demand-pull inflation, both with hypothetical aggregate demand and short-run aggregate supply curves superimposed over actual data. Panel A shows increasing aggregate demand in the 1960s due to the Vietnam conflict. This resulted in rising inflation in the United States over the entire decade. Panel B shows increasing aggregate demand in Japan as it enjoyed a huge trade surplus, which expanded the economy and led to demand-pull inflation. However, Japanese policymakers kept interest rates artificially low, fueling a real estate and stock bubble that collapsed in the 1990s, resulting in a decade-long recession.

huge real estate and stock bubble that began collapsing in the beginning of the 1990s and led to a decade-long recession that has been called the "lost decade."

Demand-pull inflation can often take a while to become a problem, or to be recognized as a problem. After all, some inflation is good as people like to see increases in their paychecks. But once the inflation spiral gains momentum, it can pose a serious problem for policymakers.

Cost-Push Inflation

Cost-push inflation occurs when a supply shock hits the economy, shifting the short-run aggregate supply curve leftward, from $SRAS_0$ to $SRAS_1$ in Figure 10. The 1973 oil shock is a classic example. Because oil is a basic input in so many goods and services we purchase, skyrocketing oil prices affected all parts of the economy. After a bout of cost-push inflation, rising resource costs push the economy from point e to point b in Figure 10. Note that at point b, real output has fallen (the economy is in a recession) and the price level has risen. Policymakers can increase demand to AD_1 and move the economy back to full employment at point c. For example, they might increase government spending, reduce taxes, or introduce policies that encourage consumption, investment, or net exports. But notice that this means an even higher price level. Alternatively, policymakers could reduce inflationary pressures by reducing aggregate demand, but this leads to an even deeper recession as output and employment fall further.

Figure 11 shows the striking leftward shift in equilibrium points for 1973–1975. Output stood still, while prices rose as the economy adjusted to the new energy prices. Superimposed over the annual data are two hypothetical short-run aggregate supply curves. Notice that it took the economy roughly three years to absorb the oil shock. Only after the economy had adjusted to the new prices did it continue on a path roughly equivalent to the pre-1973 $SRAS_0$ curve.

Before the Great Depression, economic analysis focused on the behavior of individuals, households, and businesses. Little attention was paid to the macroeconomic stabilization potential of government policies. The federal government had its responsibilities under the Constitution in many areas—such as national defense, the enforcement of contracts, and tax collection—but managing the economy was not among them.

The Great Depression of the 1930s and John Maynard Keynes's *The General Theory* drastically changed how economists viewed the role of the federal government. During the Depression, when unemployment reached 25% and bank failures wiped out personal savings, federal

cost-push inflation Inflation that occurs when a supply shock hits the economy, reducing short-run aggregate supply and thus reducing output and increasing the price level.

······ Figure 10 • Cost-Push Inflation ·······················

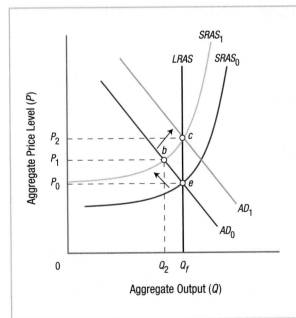

Cost-push inflation is represented by an initial decline in short-run aggregate supply from $SRAS_0$ to $SRAS_1$. Rising resource costs or inflationary expectations will reduce short-run aggregate supply, resulting in a short-run movement from point e to point b. If policymakers wish to return the economy to full employment, they can increase aggregate demand to AD_1 but must accept higher prices as the economy moves to point c. Alternatively, they could reduce aggregate demand, but that would lead to lower output and higher unemployment.

●ISSUE

Why Didn't Stimulus Measures Over the Past Decade Lead to Inflation?

The 2007–2009 recession and the high unemployment that persisted for years after led policymakers to implement many policies to jump-start the economy. These included government spending (stimulus) programs, tax cuts, loan modification programs, and more. Each of these policies was designed to encourage spending by consumers and thereby increase aggregate demand. By doing so, the AD/AS model presented in this chapter predicts that rightward shifts of the AD curve would lead to a higher aggregate price level, or inflation. Yet, inflation rates in the United States remained low. How is that possible?

First, the AD curve might not have moved at all. Much of the government spending to increase aggregate demand was offsetting corresponding decreases in aggregate demand due to high unemployment, low consumer and business confidence, and low foreign demand for American goods. Thus, the role of such

policies may have prevented a worsening of the economy by keeping aggregate demand in the same place as before. Using this explanation, the price level would not be affected at all.

Second, the recession created a large amount of underutilized resources. Keynes argued that during times of poor economic performance, many resources (such as labor and capital) remain underutilized. In such cases, an increase in aggregate demand, which subsequently increases demand for labor and capital, would merely be using resources that had been sitting idle. There would be little pressure on wages and prices to rise.

These reasons help to explain why the government was able to engage in various policies to increase the speed of economic recovery without the immediate threat of inflation. But as the economy recovers and idle

resources become fully employed, further government spending is likely to increase inflation, creating a different set of policy challenges.

····· Figure 11 • Cost-Push Inflation in the 1970s ········

The rise in equilibrium prices following the 1973 oil shocks was striking. From 1973 to 1975, prices rose, yet output did not change as the economy adjusted to the new energy prices. Superimposed over the actual annual data are two hypothetical short-run aggregate supply curves. Notice that it took the economy roughly three years to absorb the oil shock.

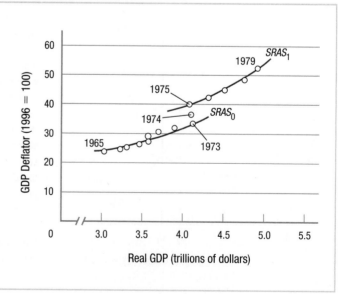

intervention in the economy became imperative. After the 1930s, the federal government's role grew to encompass (1) expanded spending and taxation and the resulting exercise of fiscal policy, (2) extensive new regulation of business, and (3) expanded regulation of the banking sector, along with greater exercise of monetary policy.

The next chapter focuses on how government spending and taxation combine to expand or contract the macroeconomy. When the economy enters a recession, fiscal policy can be used to moderate the impact and prevent another depression. Later chapters will explore the monetary system and the use of monetary policy to stabilize the economy and the price level. The AD/AS model will serve as a tool to analyze both fiscal and monetary policies. As you read these chapters, keep in mind that the long-run goals of fiscal and monetary policy are economic growth, low unemployment, and modest inflationary pressures.

 CHECKPOINT

MACROECONOMIC EQUILIBRIUM

- Macroeconomic equilibrium occurs where short-run aggregate supply and aggregate demand cross.

- The spending multiplier exists because new spending generates new round-by-round spending (based on the marginal propensities to consume and save) that creates additional income.

- The formula for the spending multiplier is $1/(1 - MPC) = 1/MPS$.

- The effect of the multiplier on aggregate output is larger when the economy is in a deep recession or a depression.

- Policymakers can increase output by enacting policies that expand government spending, consumption, investment, or net exports, or by reducing taxes.

- Demand-pull inflation occurs when aggregate demand expands beyond that necessary for full employment.

- Cost-push inflation occurs when a supply shock causes short-run aggregate supply to decrease, causing the price level to rise along with rising unemployment.

QUESTIONS: In recent years, the price of agricultural goods, such as vegetables, fruit, and milk, rose significantly due to severe droughts in several farming regions in the United States. Describe the impact of this price increase on short-run aggregate supply. How might it affect employment, unemployment, and the price level? Would the impact depend on whether consumers and businesses thought the price increase was permanent? Explain.

Answers to the Checkpoint questions can be found at the end of this chapter.

CHAPTER SUMMARY

SECTION 1 AGGREGATE DEMAND

9.1 The **aggregate demand** curve shows the quantity of goods and services (real GDP) demanded at different price levels.

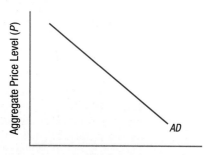

9.2 The aggregate demand curve is downward-sloping for three main reasons:

- **Wealth effect:** When price levels rise, the purchasing power of money saved falls.
- **Export price effect:** Rising price levels cause domestic goods to be more expensive in the global marketplace, resulting in fewer purchases by foreign consumers.
- **Interest rate effect:** When price levels rise, people need more money to carry out transactions. The added demand for money drives up interest rates, causing investment spending to fall.

9.3 The determinants of aggregate demand include the components of aggregate spending:

1. Consumption spending
2. Investment spending
3. Government spending
4. Net exports

Changing any one of these aggregates will shift the aggregate demand curve.

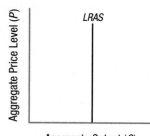

An increase in home construction fueled by rising housing demand results in a boost to aggregate demand.

SECTION 2 AGGREGATE SUPPLY

9.4 The **aggregate supply** curve shows the real GDP firms will produce at varying price levels.

The short-run aggregate supply (SRAS) curve is upward-sloping. Prices and wages are sticky (think of menu prices staying the same for a period of time). Therefore, firms respond by increasing output when prices rise.

The long-run aggregate supply (LRAS) curve is vertical. Prices and wages fully adjust; therefore, output is not affected by the price level.

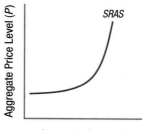

9.5 **Factors that shift the SRAS curve:**
- Input prices
- Productivity
- Taxes and regulation
- Market power of firms
- Inflationary expectations

Factors that shift the LRAS curve:
- Increase in technology
- Greater human capital
- Trade
- Innovation and R&D

Electronic toll collection booths save time and reduce transportation costs to firms, leading to an increase in short-run aggregate supply and potentially long-run aggregate supply.

SECTION 3 MACROECONOMIC EQUILIBRIUM

9.6 A **long-run macroeconomic equilibrium** occurs at the intersection of the LRAS and AD curves, at full employment. A **short-run macroeconomic equilibrium** occurs at the intersection of the SRAS and AD curves. Short-run equilibrium can occur below full employment (recession) or above full employment (inflationary pressure).

Long-Run Macro Equilibrium

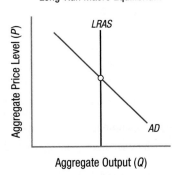

Short-Run Equilibrium (recession)

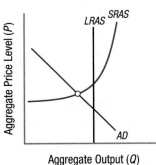

Short-Run Equilibrium (inflation)

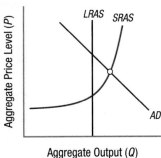

9.7 The spending **multiplier** exists because new spending generates income that results in more spending and income, based on the marginal propensities to consume and save.

Multiplier Example: $MPC = 0.80$ and $MPS = 0.20$

Round 1: $100 in new spending = $100 in new income.

Round 2: $80 is spent and $20 is saved ($80 in new income).

Round 3: $64 is spent and $16 is saved.

Round 4: $51.20 is spent and $12.80 is saved.

Round 5: $40.96 is spent and $10.24 is saved.

Round 6: $32.76 is spent and $8.20 is saved.

$\vdots$

Round n: $0.01 is spent and $0.00 is saved.

Total Effect of $100 in Spending = $500 in Spending and $100 in Savings

Multiplier $= 1/(1 - MPC) = 1/(1 - 0.80) = 5$

9.8 **Demand-pull inflation** occurs when aggregate demand expands so much that equilibrium output exceeds full employment output. Temporarily, the economy can expand beyond full employment as workers work overtime and more workers are added. But as wages rise, the economy will move to a new long-run equilibrium, at a higher price level.

Cost-push inflation occurs when a supply shock hits the economy, shifting the SRAS curve to the left, causing aggregate output to decrease and the price level to increase. Cost-push inflation makes using policies to expand aggregate demand to restore full employment difficult because of the additional inflationary pressures added to the economy.

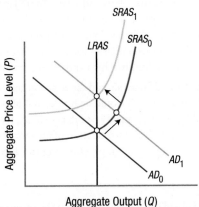

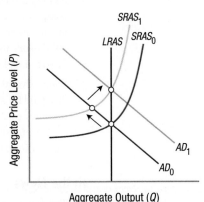

Key Concepts

aggregate demand, p. 218

wealth effect, p. 219

aggregate supply, p. 223

long-run aggregate supply (LRAS) curve, p. 223

short-run aggregate supply (SRAS) curve, p. 224

macroeconomic equilibrium, p. 227

multiplier, p. 228

marginal propensity to consume, p. 228

marginal propensity to save, p. 228

demand-pull inflation, p. 229

cost-push inflation, p. 231

Questions and Problems

Check Your Understanding

1. Describe the impact of rising interest rates on consumer spending.

2. When the economy is operating at full employment, why is an increase in aggregate demand not helpful to the economy?

3. Why is a supply shock (such as sudden rising prices for energy, food, or raw materials), doubly disruptive and harmful to the economy?

4. Explain why the aggregate supply curve is positively sloped during the short run and vertical in the long run.

5. Explain how imports and exports affect aggregate demand.

6. Provide and explain some factors that will shift the long-run aggregate supply curve.

Apply the Concepts

7. There is little doubt that artificial intelligence and automation have changed the economy. Machines are performing manual tasks at a faster and more consistent pace and are becoming better at replacing humans, even in service-oriented jobs, such as customer support. Show the impact of these innovations in production on the economy using an aggregate demand and supply framework.

8. Unemployment can be caused by a reduction in aggregate demand or short-run aggregate supply. Both changes are represented by a leftward shift of the curves. Does it matter whether the shift occurs in aggregate demand or short-run aggregate supply? Use the aggregate demand/aggregate supply framework to support your answer.

9. Why is cost-push inflation a more difficult problem for policymakers than demand-pull inflation?

10. Why is consumer confidence very important in determining the equilibrium level of output and employment?

11. As the Japanese yen appreciated in value during the 1980s and 1990s, more Japanese auto companies built manufacturing plants in other parts of Asia and in the United States. What impact did this have on net exports for the United States? Why did Japanese automakers build plants in the United States? Were the reasons similar to the reasons that American firms build plants (or establish offshore production) in China and other parts of Asia?

12. Some advocates have suggested that the United States should move to a universal health care plan paid for at the federal level, like Medicare, which would be funded out of general tax revenues. Such a plan, it is argued, would guarantee quality health care to all. Ignoring all the controversy surrounding such a plan, how would the introduction of universal health care paid for from tax revenues impact short-run aggregate supply? On long-run aggregate supply?

In the News

13. The U.S. economy has significantly expanded since recovering from the severe effects of the 2007–2009 recession. In 2019 the unemployment rate was under 4%, below the natural rate

of unemployment. Given that the economy was at or beyond full employment, describe the effects of the multiplier when the federal government continued to increase government spending and reduce taxes to boost aggregate demand.

14. In 2018 the United States and China entered into a trade dispute that led both countries to impose import tariffs on each other's goods. Economists have concluded that the tariffs contributed to slower economic growth for both countries, though the effects were greater in China. Using aggregate demand and supply analysis, explain how a trade dispute can lead to a slowing of aggregate output in both countries.

Solving Problems

15. In the following figure, the economy is initially in equilibrium at full employment at point e. Assume that consumption falls by 100, leading to a shift in aggregate demand from AD_0 to AD_1.

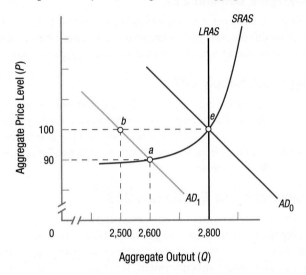

a. What is the new short-run macroeconomic equilibrium price and output?
b. How large is the spending multiplier if there were no changes to the aggregate price level?
c. How large is the spending multiplier if the aggregate price level adjusts to the new equilibrium?

Work It Out

 interactive activity

16. Use the following table and grid to answer the following questions.

Aggregate Price Level	Output (short-run aggregate supply)	Output (aggregate demand)
150	1,000	200
125	800	400
100	600	600
75	400	800
50	200	1,000

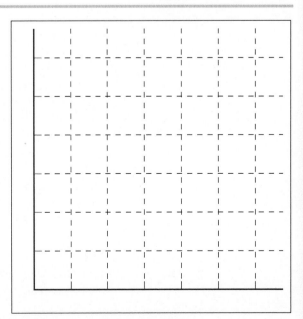

a. On the grid, graph the aggregate demand and short-run aggregate supply curves (label them AD_0 and $SRAS_0$). What are the equilibrium output and the aggregate price level?

b. Assume aggregate demand grows by 200 at each price level. Graph the new aggregate demand curve and label it AD_1. What are the new equilibrium output and the aggregate price level?

c. If full employment output is 600, is the economy experiencing recessionary or inflationary pressures?

d. By how much does the SRAS curve need to shift in order for the economy to return to full employment output at 600? What would be the new equilibrium aggregate price level?

Answers to Questions in Checkpoints

Checkpoint: Aggregate Demand 222

An increase in home prices and stock values would increase the wealth of those who owned these assets. An increase in wealth provides greater financial security, even if income does not change. All else equal, consumption would rise, which would increase aggregate demand.

Checkpoint: Aggregate Supply 227

Low interest rates make it easier for individuals and firms to borrow for consumption and investment, which may lead to higher inflation, especially when the economy fully recovers and production resources are no longer sitting idle. As investors anticipate a rise in inflation, they will adjust production in anticipation of higher input (wages and raw materials) prices, which means that short-run aggregate supply will decrease.

Checkpoint: Macroeconomic Equilibrium 233

Agriculture goods are an important input in our economy. Higher crop prices increase the cost of producing food products as well as operating restaurants and cruise ships, which will reduce short-run aggregate supply. Over time, these cost increases will show up as a higher price level, reduced employment, and higher unemployment. If the economy continues to grow, these impacts will be masked but will still reduce the level of growth. If the change is seen as permanent, consumers and businesses will begin making long-run adjustments to higher prices. For example, consumers might change their diets to include less expensive foods or plant their own crops in gardens, while businesses might consider alternative ingredients when planning menu items. If the price increases are just viewed as temporary, both groups might not adjust much at all.

Appendix

Deriving the Aggregate Demand Curve

The aggregate demand curve shows the quantities of goods and services (real GDP) demanded at different price levels, and can be derived using the aggregate expenditures model. To illustrate, panel A of Figure APX-1 shows aggregate expenditures (AE) curves at two different price levels. Remember that AE curves are drawn assuming fixed prices.

First, consider equilibrium point a on aggregate expenditures curve $AE(P_0)$. This point shows an equilibrium income of Y_0, which is equivalent to a real output of Q_0. Point a in panel B therefore represents a real output of Q_0 and a price level of P_0. However, if the aggregate price level rises to P_1, aggregate expenditures will decline to $AE(P_1)$ because at these higher prices, the same level of expenditures will not buy as much real output as before. The result is a new equilibrium at point b in both panels. Connecting points a and b in panel B, we have constructed aggregate demand curve AD, which represents the relationship between the price level and aggregate output.

••••• Figure APX-1 • Deriving the Aggregate Demand Curve ••••••••••••••••••••••••••

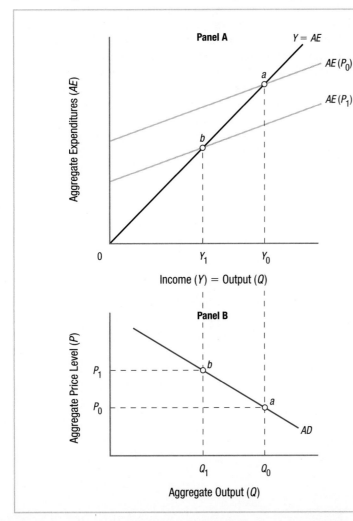

The aggregate demand curve, which shows the quantities of goods and services demanded at different price levels for the entire economy, can be derived using the aggregate expenditures model. Panel A shows aggregate expenditures curves at two different price levels. Point a on aggregate expenditures curve $AE(P_0)$ is associated with real output Q_0 and price level P_0 in panel B. If the aggregate price level rises to P_1, aggregate spending will decline to $AE(P_1)$ in panel A. The result is a new equilibrium at point b in both panels. Connecting points a and b in panel B results in aggregate demand curve AD.

10

Fiscal Policy and Debt

Understanding the role of taxes and spending in addressing fluctuations in the macroeconomy

Learning Objectives

10.1 Describe the tools that governments use to influence aggregate demand.

10.2 Explain how expansionary and contractionary fiscal policy works.

10.3 Determine the influence the multiplier effect has on government spending and aggregate output.

10.4 Describe the fiscal policies that governments use to influence aggregate supply.

10.5 Describe the impact of automatic stabilizers, lag effects, and the propensity toward deficits from fiscal policymaking.

10.6 Identify the different lags that occur when implementing fiscal policy.

10.7 Define deficits and surpluses, and explain the difference between national debt and public debt.

10.8 Describe the potential consequences of maintaining high public debt.

When you apply for a loan to buy a car, you undoubtedly will go through a credit check and receive a credit rating, which is a number that estimates the likelihood that you will pay back the loan. The government is also given a credit rating for the money it borrows. This rating, like yours, estimates the probability of the government paying back its loans.

On August 5, 2011, Standard and Poor's (S&P), a credit rating agency, did something it had never done in its history: lower the debt rating of the U.S. government from a perfect AAA rating to a slightly less than perfect AA+ rating. Although an AA+ rating is still excellent, this change was significant because it suggested for the first time that the U.S. government is not immune from all and any hardships in paying its debts.

Why did the U.S. government lose its perfect debt rating? One reason was its extensive use of fiscal policy in the aftermath of the 2007–2009 recession. Fiscal policy is the use of government revenue collection (mainly taxation) and spending to influence the economy. When the government imposes a tax on something, individuals and businesses have less money to spend. Therefore, taxes put the brakes on various economic activities. However, in terms of spending, think of what it means to local employment if the government decides to improve the roads and bridges in a city. By their very nature, taxation and spending affect the economy.

In extraordinary times, governments use fiscal policy to smooth fluctuations in the business cycle. During the 2007–2009 recession, nearly $800 billion in additional government spending was added in an attempt to pull the economy out of its doldrums. If people would not spend, government would spend in their place. When the economy is overheating, the government uses fiscal policy to decrease spending to reduce inflationary pressures.

When fiscal policy is used to stimulate the economy, deficits will generally occur, adding to the national debt. Most Americans are accustomed to dealing with debt by making periodic payments toward the balance and interest. Governments also deal with debt. The national debt grows when the government spends more than the tax revenues it collects. In 2018, the U.S. government collected $3.33 trillion in taxes but spent $4.11 trillion. The difference of $780 billion represents the federal deficit that was added to the national debt.

Unlike individuals and small companies, a government has a much larger arsenal of tools to prevent it from going bankrupt, including the power to tax and the ever-powerful ability to "print" money. But even those tools can sometimes be rendered useless, causing a government to rack up sizable debt and increase the burden of managing the debt. Further, when a government does default on its debt, havoc in markets throughout the world may result.

In this chapter, we analyze the tools government uses to implement fiscal policy and study their effects on aggregate demand and aggregate supply, which affects income and output. We then analyze whether the amount of the federal debt is a problem and, if so, what the government can do about it. This chapter will give you a good sense of the scope of fiscal policy, and the tradeoffs between relying on public debt and balancing taxes and spending.

BY THE Numbers

Fiscal Policy: The Federal Government and Its Financial Operation

The U.S. government is one of the largest institutions in the world, collecting over $3 trillion each year in revenues. Still, the government (with few exceptions) spends much more, incurring deficits that add to the public debt. The government uses taxes collected primarily from individuals and businesses to fund various government programs in its role as manager of fiscal policy. This By the Numbers analyzes the major sources of government revenue and the major categories of government spending in the United States.

DATA:

U.S. Federal Budget and Expenditures (2018)

Revenues ($3,329 billion)
- Corporate Income Taxes 6%
- Other 8%
- Individual Income Taxes 51%
- Payroll Taxes 35%

Expenditures ($4,108 billion)
- Other 16%
- Social Security 25%
- Income Security Programs 11%
- Net Interest on Debt 8%
- National Defense 15%
- Medicaid 10%
- Medicare 15%

Where Can I Find These Data?

Source: U.S. Congressional Budget Office   **Web site:** https://www.cbo.gov/about/products/budget_economic_data

Details: Look for "Historical Budget Data," which provides an Excel sheet with sources of revenues and categories of expenditures.

~ Assessing Your Data Literacy ~

1. How does the amount of revenue collected from individual income taxes compare to corporate income taxes? Which one produces more government revenue and how much more than the other?

2. Social Security, Medicare, Medicaid, and income security programs are all programs aimed at ensuring senior citizens and low-income households a minimum level of well-being. How much in total was spent on these four categories? How much more is this amount compared to that spent on national defense?

3. In 2018, did the government have a fiscal surplus or a fiscal deficit? What was the magnitude of this surplus or deficit?

WHY ARE THESE DATA IMPORTANT?

Whenever the federal government spends more than it collects in revenues, a fiscal deficit occurs that is added to the national debt. In order to balance the budget over time, the government can raise revenues by increasing taxes and/or rely on a larger tax base (income) when the economy is growing. The government can also reduce spending, but none of these options are popular.

Data *in the News*

"Investors Start to Fret About Ballooning U.S. Public Debt" by Gillian Tett; *Financial Times*, November 8, 2018

U.S. government currently pays $1.43bn each day (yes, day) to service its public debt—10 times more than any other G7 country…. But what is doubly thought-provoking is that this $1bn bill has materialized when interest rates are still fairly low by historical standards.

FISCAL POLICY AND AGGREGATE DEMAND

When an economy faces underutilization of resources because it is stuck in equilibrium well below full employment, we saw that increases in aggregate demand can move the economy toward full employment without generating excessive inflation pressures. However, in normal times, increasing aggregate demand to increase output results in a tradeoff of a higher price level.

In contrast, consider decreasing aggregate demand. When the economy is in an inflationary equilibrium *above full employment*, contracting aggregate demand dampens inflation but leads to another tradeoff: unemployment. Before we examine the theory behind how government actually goes about influencing aggregate demand by using fiscal policy, let's take a brief look at what categories of spending fiscal policy typically alters.

Discretionary and Mandatory Spending

discretionary spending The part of the budget that works its way through the appropriations process of Congress each year and includes spending on national defense, transportation, science, environment, education, and some income security programs.

The federal budget is split into two distinct types of spending: discretionary and mandatory. **Discretionary spending** is the part of the budget that works its way through the appropriations process of Congress each year. Discretionary spending occurs in programs as national defense (primarily the military), transportation, science, environment, income security (some welfare programs and a large portion of Medicaid), education, and veterans benefits and services. As Figure 1 shows, discretionary spending has steadily declined as a percent of the budget since the 1960s, when it was over 60% of the budget, to about 30% of the budget today. Still, this is about $1.3 trillion in spending, and the capacity to alter this spending is a powerful tool for policymakers.

····· Figure 1 • Discretionary and Mandatory Federal Spending ···················

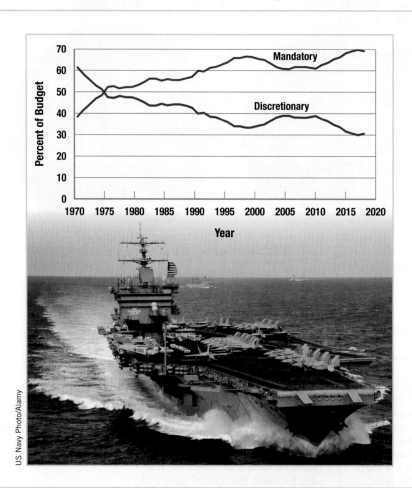

Mandatory spending includes entitlements authorized by law, such as Social Security, Medicare, and the Supplemental Nutrition Assistance Program, along with interest on the national debt. Mandatory spending does not go through the normal congressional appropriations process and have been growing in percentage of the budget. Discretionary spending is authorized each year by the appropriations process of Congress and include national defense, transportation, environment, and education. Discretionary spending has been steadily declining as a percent of the budget.

US Navy Photo/Alamy

Mandatory spending is authorized by permanent laws and does not go through the same appropriations process as discretionary spending. To change one of the entitlements of mandatory spending, Congress must change the law. Mandatory spending includes spending on Social Security, Medicare, part of Medicaid, interest on the national debt, and some means-tested income-security programs, including SNAP (Supplemental Nutrition Assistance Program, formerly known as the Food Stamp Program) and TANF (Temporary Assistance to Needy Families). As Figure 1 illustrates, this part of the budget has been growing, and now accounts for almost 70% of the budget.

Discretionary Fiscal Policy

Discretionary fiscal policy is used to influence aggregate demand. It involves adjusting government spending and/or tax policies to move the economy toward full employment by stimulating economic output or mitigating inflation.

An example of discretionary fiscal policy includes tax cuts implemented to encourage people to spend their tax savings and businesses to invest. This in turn would increase aggregate demand. Tax increases also have occurred, though not as frequently as tax cuts, to address rising deficits and inflationary pressures. But the more common form of discretionary fiscal policy involves changes in government spending.

Government Spending The federal budget authorized by Congress each year comprises spending on thousands of programs and agencies. As we studied previously, changes in government spending or other components of GDP will cause income and output to rise or fall by the spending change *times* the multiplier.

This is illustrated in Figure 2 with the economy initially in a recession at point *e,* with real output at Q_0. If government spending increases, shifting aggregate demand from AD_0 to AD_1, aggregate output will increase from Q_0 to Q_f. Because the short-run aggregate supply curve is upward-sloping, some of the increase in output is absorbed by rising prices, reducing the effect of the spending multiplier.

Once the economy reaches full employment (point *a*), further spending has little to no impact on aggregate output as prices rise quickly as inflationary expectations adjust. Finally, keep in mind that the multiplier works in both directions.

mandatory spending
Spending authorized by permanent laws that does not go through the same appropriations process as discretionary spending. Mandatory spending includes spending on Social Security, Medicare, and interest on the national debt.

discretionary fiscal policy
Policies that involve adjusting government spending and/or tax policies to push the economy toward full employment by stimulating economic output or mitigating inflation.

..... Figure 2 • Fiscal Policy When Output Is Below .... Full Employment

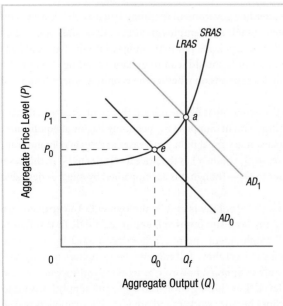

The economy is initially in recession at point *e* (with output Q_0). As new government spending works its way through the economy round-by-round, both income and output are multiplied, but price increases absorb some of the increase in *AD*. Fiscal policy can be used to bring an economy back to full employment at point *a* (with output Q_f). Once the economy reaches full employment, further increases in spending are absorbed by price increases.

Taxes Changes in government spending modify income by an amount equal to the change in spending *times* the multiplier. How, then, do changes in taxes affect the economy? The answer is not quite as simple. Let's begin with a reminder of what constitutes spending equilibrium.

Recall the definition of GDP:

$$GDP = C + I + G + (X - M)$$

When the economy is at equilibrium, all spending *injections* into the economy equal all *withdrawals* of spending. To review, injections are activities that increase spending in an economy, such as investment (I), government spending (G), and exports (X). Withdrawals, on the other hand, are activities that remove spending from the economy, such as saving (S), taxes (T), and imports (M). Therefore, in equilibrium,

$$I + G + X = S + T + M$$

With this equation in hand, let's focus on taxes. When taxes are increased, money is withdrawn from the economy's spending stream. When taxes are reduced, consumers and businesses have more to spend. Disposable income is equal to income minus taxes ($Y - T$).

Because taxes represent a withdrawal of spending from the economy, we would expect equilibrium income to fall when a tax is imposed. Consumers pay a tax increase, in part, by *reducing* their saving. The *reduction* in saving dampens the effect of the tax on equilibrium income because those funds were previously withdrawn from the spending stream. Changing the withdrawal category from saving to taxes does not affect income. A tax decrease has a similar but opposite impact because only the MPC part is spent and multiplied, and the rest is saved and thus withdrawn from the spending stream.

The result is that a tax increase (or decrease, for that matter) has less of a direct impact on income, employment, and output than an equivalent change in government spending. Another way of saying this is that the government tax multiplier is *less* than the government spending multiplier. Therefore, added government spending leads to a larger increase in GDP when compared to the same reduction in taxes.

Transfers Transfer payments are paid directly to individuals, and include, for example, Social Security, unemployment compensation, and welfare. These programs represent part of the country's social safety net. Although these programs are very important in stabilizing the economy, much of this spending is paid as a matter of law, which means they do not play a major role in discretionary fiscal policy.

Expansionary and Contractionary Fiscal Policy

expansionary fiscal policy
Policies that increase aggregate demand to expand output in an economy. These include increasing government spending, increasing transfer payments, and/or decreasing taxes.

Expansionary fiscal policy involves increasing government spending (such as on highways and education), increasing transfer payments (such as unemployment benefits), and/or decreasing taxes to increase aggregate demand. These policies put more money into the hands of consumers and businesses. These additional funds should lead to greater spending, though the precise effect of expansionary fiscal policies depends on whether the economy is at or below full employment.

Referring again to Figure 2, when the economy is below full employment, an expansionary policy will move the economy to full employment. Suppose the economy begins at equilibrium at point e, below full employment. Expansionary fiscal policy increases aggregate demand from AD_0 to AD_1, and equilibrium output rises to Q_f (point a) as the price level rises to P_1. In this case, one good outcome results—output rises to Q_f—though it is accompanied by one less desirable result, the price level rising to P_1.

Figure 3 shows what happens when the economy is at full employment. An expansionary policy raises prices without producing any long-run improvement in real GDP. In this figure, the initial equilibrium is already at full employment (point e); therefore, increasing aggregate demand moves the economy to a new output level above full employment (point a), thereby raising prices to P_1. This higher output is only temporary, however, as workers and suppliers adjust their expectations to the higher price level, thus shifting short-run aggregate supply leftward to $SRAS_1$. Short-run aggregate supply declines because workers and other resource suppliers realize

..... Figure 3 • Expansionary Fiscal Policy ....
at Full Employment

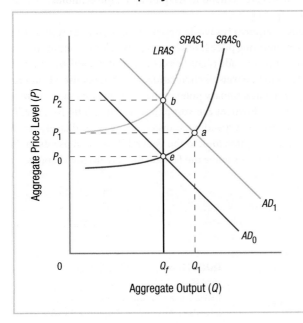

When an economy is already at full employment, expansionary policies lead to higher prices, with no long-run improvement in real GDP. Beginning at full employment (point e), increasing aggregate demand moves the economy to output level Q_1 (point a) above full employment Q_f. However, this higher output is only temporary, however, as workers and suppliers adjust their inflationary expectations. As a result, $SRAS_0$ shifts left to $SRAS_1$, and the economy returns to its long-run equilibrium output level Q_f, and a higher price level P_2 (point b).

that the prices they are paying for products have risen; hence, they demand higher wages or prices for their services. Prices are then pushed up until workers adjust their inflationary expectations and the economy settles into equilibrium at point b. The economy returns to full employment output but at a higher price level of P_2.

Instead of allowing the SRAS curve to shift when the economy is above its full employment output, the government can reduce inflationary pressures by using **contractionary fiscal policy.** These policies include reducing government spending, reducing transfer payments, and/or

contractionary fiscal policy
Policies that decrease aggregate demand to contract output in an economy. These include reducing government spending, reducing transfer payments, and/or raising taxes.

Figure 4 • Contractionary Fiscal Policy ....
to Reduce Inflation

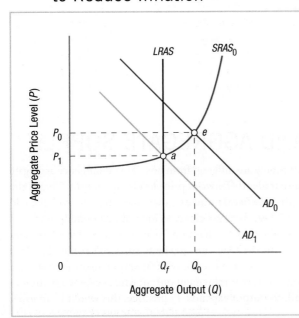

In this figure, the economy is overheating at point e, with output above full employment. Contractionary fiscal policy reduces aggregate demand to AD_1, bringing the economy back to full employment at price level P_1. These policies prevent an inflationary spiral, but result in a decrease in aggregate output.

raising taxes (increasing withdrawals from the economy). Figure 4 shows the result of contractionary policy. The economy is initially overheating at point e, with output above full employment. Contractionary policy reduces aggregate demand to AD_1, bringing the economy back to full employment at price level P_1 and output Q_f.

Implementing demand-side policy requires tradeoffs between increasing output at the expense of raising the price levels, or else lowering price levels by accepting a lower output. When a recession occurs, the public is often happy to trade higher prices for greater employment and output. One would think the opposite would be true when inflationary pressures rise. However, politicians are often reluctant to support contractionary policies that control inflation by reducing aggregate demand because higher unemployment can cost politicians their jobs. As a result, the demand-side fiscal policy tools—government spending, transfer payments, and taxes—may remain unused. In these instances, politicians often look to the Federal Reserve to use its tools and influence to keep inflation in check. We will examine the Federal Reserve in later chapters.

 CHECKPOINT

FISCAL POLICY AND AGGREGATE DEMAND

- Demand-side fiscal policy involves using government spending, transfer payments, and taxes to influence aggregate demand and equilibrium income, output, and the price level in the economy.

- In the short run, government spending raises income and output by the amount of spending times the multiplier. Tax reductions have a smaller impact on the economy than government spending because some of the reduction in taxes is added to saving and is therefore withdrawn from the economy.

- Expansionary fiscal policy involves increasing government spending, increasing transfer payments, and/or decreasing taxes.

- Contractionary fiscal policy involves decreasing government spending, decreasing transfer payments, and/or increasing taxes.

- When an economy is at full employment, expansionary fiscal policy may lead to greater output in the short term but will ultimately just lead to higher prices in the longer term.

- Politicians tend to favor expansionary fiscal policy because it can bring increases in employment even at the cost of higher inflation. Politicians tend to steer away from contractionary fiscal policy because it results in unemployment.

QUESTION: During the 2007–2009 recession, the U.S. government passed a $787 billion stimulus package, which was roughly $2,500 in government spending for every person. The time required for the government to spend that sum on infrastructure projects (funding approvals, environmental clearances, and so on) meant that the spending stretched over several years. Why didn't Congress just send a $2,500 check to every person to speed up the impact on the economy?

Answers to the Checkpoint questions can be found at the end of this chapter.

FISCAL POLICY AND AGGREGATE SUPPLY

supply-side fiscal policies
Policies that focus on shifting the long-run aggregate supply curve to the right, expanding the economy without increasing inflationary pressures. Unlike policies to increase aggregate demand, supply-side policies take longer to impact the economy.

Fiscal policies that influence aggregate supply are different from policies that influence aggregate demand, as they do not always require tradeoffs between price levels and output. That is the good news. The bad news is that **supply-side fiscal policies** require more time to work than do demand-side fiscal policies. The focus of these fiscal policies is on long-run economic growth.

Figure 5 shows the impact that fiscal policy can have on the economy over the long run. The goal of these fiscal policies is to shift the long-run aggregate supply curve to the right, here from $LRAS_0$ to $LRAS_1$. This shift moves the economy's full employment equilibrium from point a to point b, thereby expanding full-employment output while keeping inflation in check. In Figure 5, the price level falls as output expands. In practice, this would be unusual

····· Figure 5 • Fiscal Policy and Aggregate Supply ·······

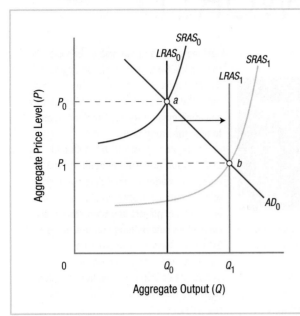

The ultimate goal of fiscal policy directed at aggregate supply is to shift the long-run aggregate supply curve from $LRAS_0$ to $LRAS_1$. This moves the economy's full employment equilibrium from point a to point b, expanding output from Q_0 to Q_1 while reducing the aggregate price level to P_1.

because when the economy grows, aggregate demand typically expands and keeps prices from falling.

Figure 5 may well reflect what happens in general as the world economy embraces trade and globalization. Improvements in technology and communications increase productivity to the point that global long-run aggregate supply shifts outward. These changes, along with freer trade, help increase economic growth and keep inflation low.

Fiscal policies aimed at increasing aggregate supply include increased spending on infrastructure, capital (physical and human), and research and development along with a reduction in tax rates and regulations. These policies aim to expand the supply curves of all businesses and industries.

Investment in Infrastructure, Capital, and Research and Development

Investing in a country's infrastructure, including roads, bridges, and communications networks, can lead to more efficient production and distribution of products. Moreover, higher levels of human capital (from education and training) and improved technology transfer lead to greater productivity. Therefore, long-run economic growth is enhanced through investment in higher education, research and development, and capital goods. Such investments can be encouraged using tax credits, grants, and other monetary incentives.

For example, the U.S. National Institutes of Health invests over $35 billion in health care research each year, mostly in grants to medical schools, universities, and research institutions. These investments have led to new medicines being developed much more quickly, which benefits the entire economy. Improving health care reduces workers' absences and increases productivity in all industries.

Many countries, including China, Kazakhstan, and the United Arab Emirates, have invested huge sums of money to building physical infrastructure, turning its major cities into modern, technologically-advanced cities that attract companies to invest and create jobs. The following Around the World feature focuses on the tiny country of Qatar, which used its oil wealth to build world-class infrastructure, which allowed it to win the right to host the 2022 FIFA World Cup.

AROUND THE WORLD

Qatar: A Nation Built for the Future

How did Qatar, a tiny nation in the Middle East that has never participated in a World Cup soccer match, win its bid to host the biggest sporting event in the world?

Gavin Hellier/Getty Images

In November 2022, soccer fans around the world will focus on the world's most popular sports tournament, the FIFA World Cup. That year's tournament will be held in Qatar, one of the smallest countries in the world in size and population. How did Qatar, whose national soccer team has never qualified for the World Cup in its history, become the host of the 2022 World Cup?

Qatar is located on a peninsula off of the Persian Gulf in the Middle East, with an area smaller than the size of Connecticut and fewer than 2 million residents.

But what it lacks in size and population is offset by its abundance of resources, particularly oil and natural gas. Qatar has a higher GDP per capita than the United States. Its government is flush with cash from its resource exports, which has allowed it to use expansionary fiscal policy with ease.

Over the past two decades, Qatar's government invested heavily to build infrastructure, increase human capital, and attract foreign investment. These policies not only increased Qatar's

aggregate demand but also its capacity to produce through its long-run aggregate supply. While many countries struggle with debt, Qatar's commitment to infrastructure spending made it an excellent candidate to host the World Cup.

In its bid to host the World Cup in 2022, Qatar promised to build at least eight new stadiums, including five high-tech climate-controlled stadiums that are able to keep players and spectators cool even when outside temperatures exceed 100°F. In addition, the government-owned airline, Qatar Airways, will expand its operations to include nonstop flights to nearly all major cities around the world.

Qatar's use of expansionary fiscal policy helped diversify its economy. This strategy is especially important given the volatility of oil prices, which will encourage oil-rich countries such as Qatar to depend on other factors, such as capital and innovation to maintain economic growth.

GO ONLINE TO PRACTICE THE ECONOMIC CONCEPTS IN THIS STORY

Besides government spending, increasing aggregate supply can also be achieved through the reduction of tax rates and regulations.

Reducing Tax Rates and Regulations

Reducing tax rates has an impact on both aggregate demand and aggregate supply. Lower individual tax rates increase aggregate demand because households keep more of what they earn. This in turn allows for more consumption spending and encourages many people to work more. Lower business taxes encourage entrepreneurs to take risks and to invest in businesses.

The highest marginal federal income tax rate for individuals has fallen over the past 60 years from a high of 91% to the current highest rate of 37%. In 1986, President Reagan reduced the top marginal rate to 28%, though later presidents changed the top tax rate to where it is today. Why was President Reagan so aggressive in reducing tax rates? He believed that reducing tax rates would lead to significant growth in incomes that would offset the lower tax collected on each dollar earned. This is the essence of supply-side policies, though it is not without controversy, as lower tax rates resulted in a sharp rise in the national debt beginning in the 1980s. But Reagan's policies were driven in part by a simple tax revenue curve developed by economist Arthur Laffer showing how reducing tax *rates* could increase tax *revenues*.

····· Figure 6 · The Laffer Curve ·······················

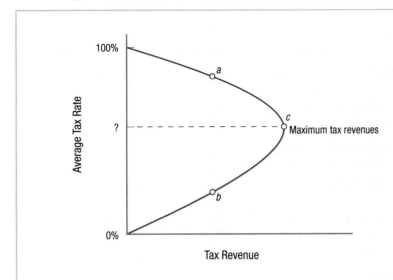

The Laffer curve shows the relationship between average tax rates and total tax revenues. As the tax rate rises from 0%, tax revenues increase. At point *c*, tax revenues are maximized. If tax rates continue to rise, tax revenues will decrease because higher tax rates discourage people from working and firms from producing. A government collects the same tax revenues at points *a* or *b*. The tax rates that correspond to points *b* and *c* are often debated by economists.

The **Laffer curve** in Figure 6 shows that if the tax rate is 0%, tax revenue will be zero because no taxes are collected. If the tax rate is 100%, tax revenue will also be zero because there would be no incentive to earn income. Laffer argued that high rates (such as the rate corresponding to point *a*) create disincentives to work and invest and that a lower tax rate (such as the rate corresponding to point *b*) would generate the same amount of tax revenue. Critics of the Laffer curve argue that individuals who earn high incomes are driven to work hard regardless of the tax rate and therefore the tax rate threshold that causes tax revenues to begin falling (point *c*) is higher than what Laffer and Reagan estimated. Moreover, most economists would argue that the goal of government should not be to maximize tax revenues.

Laffer curve A curve that shows a hypothetical relationship between income tax rates and tax revenues. As tax rates rise from zero, revenues rise, reach a maximum, then decline until revenues reach zero again at a 100% tax rate.

Aside from reducing taxes, supply-side economists also support policies that repeal regulations that hamper business activity. Examples include the trucking and airline industries, both of which were heavily regulated several decades ago but today are mostly deregulated and very competitive. However, the extensive deregulation that occurred in the banking industry contributed to the financial crisis and recession in 2007. Therefore, some regulation is certainly needed, but the amount is still subject to rigorous debate.

For example, the pharmaceutical industry remains one of the most regulated industries. The U.S. Federal Drug Administration's drug approval process is so extensive that bringing a new drug to market can take years and cost over $1 billion. Still, many people argue that these regulations are necessary because people's lives are at stake.

A combination of fiscal policies affecting aggregate demand and/or aggregate supply is used to manage fluctuations in the economy and to encourage long-run economic growth. But the implementation of such policies takes time, as we will see next.

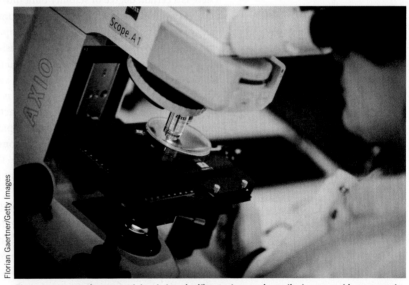

Florian Gaertner/Getty Images

Chromosome genetics research has led to significant advances in medical cures and is an example of how fiscal policy can expand aggregate supply.

✓ CHECKPOINT

FISCAL POLICY AND AGGREGATE SUPPLY

- The goal of fiscal policies that influence aggregate supply is to shift the long-run aggregate supply curve to the right.

- Expanding long-run aggregate supply can occur through higher investments in infrastructure, research and development, and human capital.

- Other fiscal policies to increase long-run aggregate supply include providing tax incentives for business investment and reducing burdensome regulations.

- The Laffer curve suggests that reducing tax rates could lead to *higher* revenues if tax rates are high enough.

- The major limitation of fiscal policies to influence long-run aggregate supply is that they take a longer time to have an impact compared to polices aimed at influencing aggregate demand.

QUESTION: Some economists have suggested that an improved tax structure would entail a reduction in income taxes for individuals, corporations (corporate income tax), and investors (capital gains taxes), which is offset by an increase in consumption taxes (such as sales and excise taxes). Which part(s) of this type of proposal would be consistent with supply-side economics? Explain.

Answers to the Checkpoint questions can be found at the end of this chapter.

IMPLEMENTING FISCAL POLICY

Implementing fiscal policy is often easier said than done. It is frequently a complex and time-consuming process. Three disparate entities—the Senate, House, and the president—must collectively agree on specific spending and tax policies. Ideally, these decisions are made in the open with the public fully informed. The complexities of the budgeting process and its openness (not a bad thing in itself) give rise to several inherent difficulties. We will briefly consider some problems having to do with the timing of fiscal decisions and the political pressures inherent in the process after first looking at the automatic stabilization mechanisms contained in the federal budgeting process.

Automatic Stabilizers

automatic stabilizers Tax revenues and transfer payments automatically expand or contract in ways that reduce the intensity of business fluctuations without any overt action by Congress or other policymakers.

There is a certain degree of stability built into the U.S. macroeconomic system. Tax revenues and transfer payments are the two principal **automatic stabilizers;** without any overt action by Congress or other policymakers, these two components of the federal budget expand or contract in ways that help counter movements of the business cycle.

When the economy is growing at a solid rate, tax receipts rise because individuals and firms are increasing their taxable incomes. At the same time, transfer payments decline because fewer people require welfare or unemployment assistance. Rising tax revenues and declining transfer payments have contractionary effects and act as a brake to slow the growth of GDP, helping to keep the economy from overheating or keeping it from generating inflationary pressures. When the economic expansion ends and the economy goes into a downturn, the opposite happens: Tax revenues decline, and transfer payments rise. These added funds being pumped into the economy help cushion the impact of the downturn, not just for the recipients of transfer payments but also for the economy as a whole.

The income tax is also a powerful stabilizer because of its progressivity. When incomes fall, tax revenues fall faster because people do not just pay taxes on smaller incomes, but they pay taxes at lower rates as their incomes fall. In other words, disposable income falls more slowly than aggregate income. But when the economy is booming, tax revenues rise faster than income, thereby withdrawing spending from the economy. This helps to slow the growth in income, thus reducing the threat of an inflationary spiral.

The key point to remember here is that automatic stabilizers reduce the intensity of business fluctuations. Automatic stabilizers do not eliminate fluctuations in the business cycle, but they render business cycles smoother and less intense. Automatic stabilizers act on their own, whereas discretionary fiscal policy requires overt action by policymakers.

Fiscal Policy Timing Lags

Using discretionary fiscal policy to smooth the short-term business cycle is a challenge because of several lags associated with its implementation. First, most of the macroeconomic data that policymakers need to enact the proper fiscal policies are not available until at least one quarter (three months) after the fact. Even then, key figures are often revised for the next quarter or two. The **information lag** therefore creates a one- to six-month period before informed policymaking can even begin.

Even if the most recent data suggest that the economy is trending into a recession, it may take several quarters to confirm this fact. Short-term (month-to-month or quarter-to-quarter) variations in key indicators are common and sometimes represent nothing more than randomness in the data. This **recognition lag** is one reason why recessions and recoveries are often well under way before policymakers fully acknowledge a need for action.

Third, once policymakers recognize that the economy has trended in a certain direction, fiscal policy requires a long and often contentious legislative process, referred to as a **decision lag.** Not all legislators have the same goals for the economy; therefore, any new government spending must first survive an arduous legislative process. Once some new policy has become law, it often requires months of planning, budgeting, and implementation to develop and start a new program. This process, the **implementation lag,** rarely consumes *less* than 18 to 24 months.

The problem these lags pose is clear: By the time the fiscal stimulus meant to jump-start a sputtering economy kicks in, the economy may already be on the mend. And if so, the exercise of fiscal policy can compound the effects of the business cycle by overstimulating a patient that is already recovering.

Some of these lags can be reduced by expediting spending already approved for existing programs rather than implementing new programs. For example, projects that are "shovel-ready" have already been planned and approved and therefore can have a more immediate impact on the economy. Also, the lags associated with tax changes tend to be shorter because the new rates can go into withholding tables within weeks of enactment, allowing taxpayers to revise their spending sooner.

information lag The time policymakers must wait for economic data to be collected, processed, and reported. Most macroeconomic data are not available until at least one quarter (three months) after the fact.

recognition lag The time it takes for policymakers to confirm that the economy is in a recession or a recovery. Short-term variations in key economic indicators are typical and sometimes represent nothing more than randomness in the data.

decision lag The time it takes Congress and the administration to decide on a policy once a problem is recognized.

implementation lag The time required to turn fiscal policy into law and eventually have an impact on the economy.

The Government's Bias Toward Borrowing and Away From Taxation

Due to the uncertainties surrounding the economy, politicians often take their own interests into account when considering fiscal policy, if not for economic reasons, then very likely for political ones. In times of recessions or slow economic recovery, those on the left tend to favor more government spending and transfer payments, while those on the right tend to favor reductions in taxes. Both policies are expansionary and lead to greater deficits, especially as tax receipts fall due to lower incomes and fewer jobs.

But in order to balance the budget over the long run, such policies generally need to be reversed in good times so that government spending is reduced and taxes raised, along with the generation of more tax receipts from higher incomes and more jobs. But politicians often are reluctant to do so. Even in good economic times, tax hikes are politically dangerous, and so are major cuts to government spending programs and transfer programs. The result is that fiscal policy is financed by deficits. Deficits persist in our system of government.

Public choice theory involves the economic analysis of public and political decision-making, including voting behavior, election incentives on politicians, and the influence of special interest

public choice theory The economic analysis of public and political decision making, looking at issues such as voting, election incentives on politicians, and the influence of special interest groups.

groups. James Buchanan, considered the father of public choice theory, essentially fused the disciplines of economics and political science. Buchanan contrasted Adam Smith's description of social benefits that arise from private individuals acting in their own self-interest with the harm that frequently results from politicians doing the same thing. Competition among individuals and firms for jobs, customers, and profits creates wealth, and thus it benefits the entire society. Self-interested politicians, however, often instigate government interventions that are harmful to the larger economy.

Public choice economists such as Buchanan argue that deficit spending reduces the perceived cost of current government operations. The result is that taxpayers permit some programs to exist that they would oppose if required to pay the full cost today. Public choice economists argue that this situation simply amounts to shifting the cost of government to the next generation. This has resulted in the steady expansion of the federal government.

Public choice analysis helps us to understand why deficits seem inevitable. Simply, we do not pay the full costs of today's programs. In the past 50 years, the federal government has run a deficit in 45 of these years, despite significant growth of the economy over this time. The next section focuses on the role of deficits and public debt on the economy.

 CHECKPOINT

IMPLEMENTING FISCAL POLICY

- Automatic stabilizers reduce the intensity of business fluctuations. When the economy is booming, tax revenues automatically rise and unemployment compensation and welfare payments fall, dampening the expansion. When the economy enters a recession, tax revenues automatically fall and transfer payments rise, cushioning the decline.

- Fiscal policymakers face information lags (the time it takes to collect, process, and provide data on the economy), recognition lags (the time required to recognize trends in the data), decision lags (the time it takes for Congress and the president to decide on a policy), and implementation lags (the time required by Congress to pass a law and see it put in place).

- These lags can often result in government policy being mistimed. For example, expansionary policy taking effect when the economy is well into a recovery or failing to take effect when a recession is under way can make stabilization worse.

- Public choice economists argue that deficit spending reduces the perceived cost of current government operations, and therefore politicians are generally more willing to enact expansionary policies that lead to deficits and a higher public debt.

QUESTION: Suppose that the president wishes to enact fiscal policies that would generate the most immediate effect on the economy, and thus improve his or her chances of reelection. What type of policies would he or she tend to favor and why?

Answers to the Checkpoint questions can be found at the end of this chapter.

FINANCING THE FEDERAL GOVERNMENT

In the late 1990s, an economic expansion fueled by the expansion of the Internet and "dot-com" industries resulted in tremendous economic growth and low unemployment. In 1998 an increase in tax revenues collected as a result of higher incomes and on profits earned from a rising stock market led to tax revenues exceeding government spending for the first time in nearly 30 years. This trend lasted four years until 2002, when the government again spent more than it collected in taxes and has since never reversed course. This section begins by defining deficits and surpluses, national debt, and public debt before studying their impact on the economy.

Defining Deficits and the National Debt

A **deficit** is the amount by which annual government expenditures exceed tax revenues. A **surplus** is the amount by which annual tax revenues exceed government expenditures. In 2000 the budget surplus was $236.2 billion. By 2002, tax cuts, a recession, and new commitments for national defense and homeland security led to a deficit of $157.8 billion. The effects of the deep recession in 2007–2009 and the extent of fiscal policies used changed the magnitude of the deficit picture again. Government intervention and support for the financial and automobile industries and a nearly $800 billion stimulus package to soften the recession, resulted in a 2009 deficit of over $1.4 trillion. And despite a strong economic recovery over the decade since then, large tax cuts and continued increases in spending generated a deficit of $780 billion in 2018.

The gross federal debt, or more commonly known as the **national debt,** is the total accumulation of past deficits less surpluses. The national debt is measured as the total amount of debt issued by the U.S. Treasury. The national debt in 2019 was over $22 trillion. However, a portion of this debt is held by other agencies of government, such as the Social Security Administration, the Treasury Department, and the Federal Reserve, in what is referred to as an intergovernmental transfer. What exactly does this mean?

Suppose you have a savings account with funds to be used to pay your college tuition, but due to an unexpected $2,000 car repair, you temporarily borrowed from your college savings account by withdrawing $800 and borrowed the remaining $1,200 using a credit card. Although you fully intend to pay back the full $2,000 in debt (including your college savings), only $1,200 is owed to someone other than yourself. Similarly, part of the total debt that the government has incurred is owed to itself, and the rest is owed to the public.

The **public debt,** also known as the net debt or federal debt held by the public, is the portion of the national debt that is held by individuals, companies, and pension funds, along with foreign entities and foreign governments. The public debt also represents a real claim on government assets and is the statistic that is often scrutinized when analyzing the health of the macroeconomy.

In sum, the national debt and public debt are distinct measures of the extent to which government spending has exceeded tax revenues over the course of time. Figure 7 shows the public debt as a percentage of gross domestic product (GDP) since 1940. During World War II, public debt exceeded GDP. It then trended downward until the early 1980s, when public debt began to climb again. Public debt as a percentage of GDP fell from the mid-1990s until 2000, first because of growing budget surpluses in the late 1990s, then because of falling interest rates (what the government has to pay on the debt), but it has risen since then. Public debt today exceeds 75% of GDP.

Public debt is held as U.S. Treasury securities, including Treasury bills, notes, bonds, and U.S. Savings Bonds. Treasury bills, or T-bills, as they are known, are short-term instruments with a maturity period of a year or less that pay a specific sum at maturity. T-bills do not pay interest. Rather, they are initially sold at a discount, and their yields are then determined by the time to maturity and the discount. T-bills are the most actively traded securities in the U.S. economy, and they are highly liquid, providing the closest thing there is to risk-free returns.

Treasury notes are financial instruments issued for periods ranging from 1 to 10 years, whereas Treasury bonds have maturity periods exceeding 10 years. Both of these instruments have stated interest rates and are traded sometimes at discounts and sometimes at premiums.

Today, interest rates on the public debt are between 1% and 4%. This relatively low rate has not always been the case. In the early 1980s, interest rates varied from 11% to nearly 15%. Inflation was high and investors required high interest rates as compensation. When rates are high, government interest costs on the debt soar.

deficit The amount by which annual government expenditures exceed tax revenues.

surplus The amount by which annual tax revenues exceed government expenditures.

national debt The total debt issued by the U.S. Treasury, which represents the total accumulation of past deficits less surpluses. A portion of this debt is held by other government agencies, and the rest is held by the public. It is also referred to as the gross federal debt.

public debt The portion of the national debt that is held by the public, including individuals, companies, and pension funds, along with foreign entities and foreign governments. This debt is also referred to as net debt or federal debt held by the public.

Figure 7 • Public Debt as a Percent of GDP

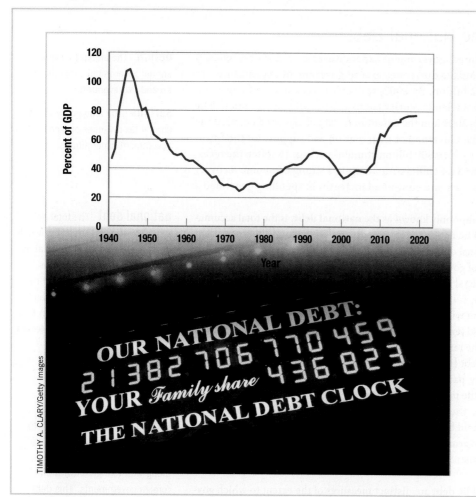

The public debt as a percentage of GDP has varied considerably since 1940. During World War II, public debt exceeded GDP. It then trended downward until the early 1980s, when public debt began to climb again. In 2019 public debt held by the public (as opposed to government institutions) exceeded 75% of GDP.

TIMOTHY A. CLARY/Getty Images

Balanced Budget Amendments

Although federal budget deficits have been the norm for the past 50 years, the 2007–2009 recession led to record deficits, leading many politicians to propose federal balanced budget amendments requiring the federal government to balance its budget every year. Balanced budget amendments are not new. They exist, with varying exceptions, for most state governments. At the federal level, however, such rules have not existed since the 1930s.

annually balanced budget

Expenditures and tax revenues would have to be equal each year.

Most balanced budget amendments require an **annually balanced budget,** which means government would have to equate its revenues and expenditures every year. Most economists, however, believe such rules are counterproductive. For example, during times of recession, tax revenues tend to fall due to lower incomes and higher unemployment. To offset these lost revenues, an annually balanced budget would require deep spending cuts or tax hikes (in other words, contractionary fiscal policy) during a time when expansionary fiscal policies are needed. Many economists believe that balanced budget rules of the early 1930s turned what probably would have been a modest recession into the Great Depression.

cyclically balanced budget

Balancing the budget over the course of the business cycle by restricting spending or raising taxes when the economy is booming and using these surpluses to offset the deficits that occur during recessions.

An alternative to balancing the budget annually would be to require a **cyclically balanced budget,** in which the budget is balanced over the course of the business cycle. The basic idea is to restrict spending or raise taxes when the economy is booming, allowing for a budget surplus. These surpluses would then be used to offset deficits accrued during recessions, when increased

ISSUE

How Big Is the Economic Burden of Interest Rates on the National Debt?

The federal government paid $324 billion in interest payments on the national debt in 2018. This is money that could have been used for other public programs. In fact, interest payments on the debt were greater than the amount the government paid for education, transportation infrastructure, low-income housing, and Homeland Security combined.

Although interest payments on the debt are large, they represent a small portion of the federal budget and an even smaller portion of GDP. Interest on the debt as a percentage of GDP, as shown in the figure, was steady from 1950 to 1980, hovering around 1.5%. This percentage more than doubled during the 1980s because of high inflation and interest rates and rising deficits. In the 1990s, interest rates dropped and deficits fell, allowing interest payments as a percentage of GDP to fall toward the level it was in the 1950s. The rising debt

associated with the 2007–2009 recession increased the percentage again but not by much due to record low interest rates. Today, interest rates remain low, allowing interest payments to remain a small percentage of GDP.

The fact that rising debt has not led to dramatic borrowing costs highlights the important role that interest rates have on the economy. Many individuals, firms, and foreign governments hold long-term (up to 30-year) Treasury bonds. During the economic crisis in the early 1980s, interest rates on 30-year Treasury bonds reached 15%, guaranteeing a bondholder a 15% annual return for 30 years.

Today, those 15% bonds from the 1980s have matured, and new 30-year bonds are paying less than 4%, resulting in tremendous savings to the government in financing the national debt. For example, an average interest rate of 2%

saves the U.S. federal government $500 billion per year compared to a 5% interest rate and saves over $1 trillion per year compared to an 8% interest rate.

Interest rates on the national debt have remained low, as Treasury bonds remain a popular safe asset to hold in retirement and other investment accounts. Foreign governments also continue to buy U.S. Treasury bonds to build up their national reserves.

But despite current favorable borrowing conditions facing the U.S. government, there are headwinds on the horizon. First, interest rates have risen in recent years, increasing the interest payments on the national debt to nearly 2% of GDP. Also, deficits have continued to increase due to tax cuts and increased government spending, adding to the debt. As the national debt and the interest rate to finance that debt continue to rise, the economic burden of the debt will become a greater concern.

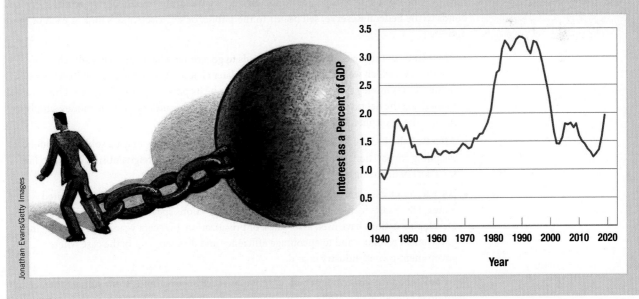

spending or lower taxes are appropriate. To some extent, balancing the budget over the business cycle happens automatically as long as fiscal policy is held constant due to the automatic stabilizers discussed earlier. However, the business cycle takes time to define (due to lags), making it difficult to enforce such a rule in practice.

Finally, some economists believe that balancing the budget should not be the primary concern of policymakers; instead, they view the government's primary macroeconomic responsibility to

functional finance An approach that focuses on promoting economic growth and stable prices while keeping the economy as close as possible to full employment.

promote economic growth and stable prices while keeping the economy as close as possible to full employment. This is the **functional finance** approach to the budget, where governments provide public goods and services that citizens desire (such as national defense and education) and focus on policies that keep the economy growing because rapidly growing economies do not have significant public debt or deficit issues.

In sum, balancing the budget annually or over the business cycle may be either counterproductive or difficult to do. It is not a solution to the previously discussed public choice problem of politicians' incentives to spend and not raise taxes. Consequently, budget deficits begin to look like a normal occurrence in our political system.

Financing Debt and Deficits

Given that deficits are likely to persist, how does the government deal with its debt, and what does this imply for the economy? Government deals with debt in two ways. It can either borrow or sell assets.

Given its power to print money and collect taxes, the federal government cannot go bankrupt per se. But it does face what economists call a **government budget constraint:**

government budget constraint The government budget is limited by the fact that $G - T = \Delta M + \Delta B + \Delta A$.

$$G - T = \Delta M + \Delta B + \Delta A$$

where

G = government spending
T = tax revenues; thus, $(G - T)$ is the federal budget deficit
ΔM = the change in the money supply (selling bonds to the Federal Reserve)
ΔB = the change in bonds held by public entities, domestic and foreign
ΔA = the sales of government assets

The left side of the equation, $G - T$, represents government spending minus tax revenues. A positive $(G - T)$ value is a budget deficit, and a negative $(G - T)$ value represents a budget surplus. The right side of the equation shows how government finances its deficit. It can sell bonds to the Federal Reserve, sell bonds to the public, or sell assets. Let's look at each of these options.

- $\Delta M > 0$: First, the government can sell bonds to government agencies, especially the Federal Reserve, which we will study in depth in a later chapter. When the Federal Reserve buys bonds, it uses money that is created out of thin air by its power to "print" money. This is called monetizing the debt: when the Federal Reserve pumps new money into the money supply to finance the government debt.

- $\Delta B > 0$: If the Federal Reserve does not purchase the bonds, they may be sold to the public, including corporations, banks, mutual funds, individuals, and foreign entities. This also has the effect of financing the government's deficit.

- $\Delta A > 0$: Asset sales represent only a small fraction of government finance in the United States. These sales include auctions of telecommunications spectra and offshore oil leases. Developing nations have used asset sales, or privatization, in recent years to bolster sagging government revenues and to encourage efficiency and development in the case where a government-owned industry is sold.

Thus, when the government runs a deficit, it must borrow funds from somewhere, assuming it does not sell assets. If the government borrows from the public, the quantity of publicly held bonds will rise; if it borrows from the Federal Reserve, the quantity of money in circulation will rise.

The main idea from this section is that deficits must be financed in some form, whether by the government borrowing or selling assets. As we'll see in the next section, rising levels of deficits and the corresponding interest rates raise some important issues about the ability of a country to manage its debt burden.

CHECKPOINT

FINANCING THE FEDERAL GOVERNMENT

- A deficit is the amount that government spending exceeds tax revenue in a particular year.

- The public (national) debt is the total accumulation of past deficits less surpluses.

- Approaches to financing the federal government include annually balancing the budget, balancing the budget over the business cycle, and ignoring the budget deficit and focusing on promoting full employment and stable prices.

- The federal government's debt must be financed by selling bonds to the Federal Reserve ("printing money" or "monetizing the debt"), by selling bonds to the public, or by selling government assets. This is known as the government budget constraint.

QUESTION: State governments have been more willing to pass balanced budget amendments because they do not face large mandatory spending like the federal government. What are some expenses of the federal government that are less predictable or harder to cut that make balanced budget amendments more difficult to pursue?

Answers to the Checkpoint questions can be found at the end of this chapter.

WHY IS THE PUBLIC DEBT SO IMPORTANT?

We have seen that politicians have a bias toward using expansionary fiscal policy and not contractionary fiscal policy and also have a bias toward using debt rather than taxes to finance the ensuing deficits. This explains the persistence of federal debt. We have seen that balancing the federal budget by passing an amendment is not an ideal solution. This leads to the following questions: How big a problem is persistent deficits? Should we be worrying about this now?

Figure 8 shows the debt of mostly developed nations in 2018. Japan, Greece, and Italy had a large debt relative to their GDP, but Greece and Italy have reduced their deficits in recent years, allowing the increase in debt to slow. India has a relatively low debt ratio but has seen higher deficits recently. China, Russia, and Chile have very low debt ratios, but deficits in all three countries have risen in recent years as economic growth slowed. When an economy moves toward the upper right portion of the figure, problems begin to rise. In Japan, an aging population (fact: Japan has more people over the age of 100 than any other country in the world) along with a shrinking working-age population has severely strained government budgets.

Politicians frequently warn that the federal government is going bankrupt or that we are burdening future generations with our own enormous public debt. After all, U.S. public debt of over $16 trillion means that every baby born in the United States begins life saddled with over $50,000 in public debt. Before you start panicking, let's examine the burden of the public debt.

Is the Size of the Public Debt a Problem?

Public debt in the United States represents a little over 75% of GDP. Is this amount of debt a cause for immediate concern? It really depends on the costs of financing the debt. What is the burden of the interest rate payments on the debt?

Think about it another way. Suppose that you earn $60,000 a year and have $45,000 in student loan debt, equal to 75% of your annual income. Is this a problem? It would be if the interest rate on the student loans were 20% a year because interest payments of $9,000 per year would take up a significant portion (15%) of your salary. But if the interest rate were 3%, the

····· Figure 8 • Public Debt and Deficits as a Percent of GDP (2018) ·············

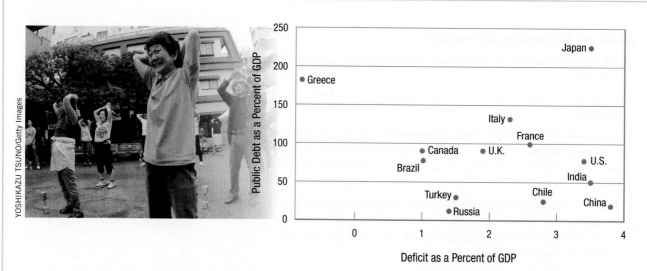

This figure shows the relationship between public debt and deficits for several nations. Japan and Greece have very high debt-to-GDP ratios but differ in their deficit-to-GDP ratios. Greece was forced by the European Union to balance its budget; in Japan, an aging population continues to produce high deficits. However, the willingness of Japan's private sector to hold government bonds allows Japan's government to finance its debt at low interest rates. Still, deficit and debt remain a major problem, so much so that Japan's government has stopped its tradition of bestowing a commemorative silver sake dish when a citizen celebrates his or her 100th birthday.

interest payment of $1,350 per year would not be as substantial, representing a little over 2% of your salary.

For the U.S. national debt, interest payments on the debt were $324 billion in 2018, or about 8% of the federal budget. Although this is a major expense, relatively low interest rates have allowed the government to manage the debt without too much trouble, at least in the near term.

Wouldn't it be wise to pay the debt down or pay it off? Not necessarily. Many people today "own" some small part of the public debt in their pension plans, but many others do not. If taxes were raised across the board to pay down the debt, those who did not own any public debt would be in a worse position than those who did.

Servicing the debt requires taxing the general public to pay interest to bondholders. Most people who own part of the national debt (or who indirectly own parts of entities that hold the debt) tend to be richer than those who do not. This means that money is taken from those across the income or wealth distribution and given to those near the top. Still, the fact that taxes are mildly progressive mitigates some, perhaps even all, of this reverse redistribution problem.

Thus, the public debt is not out of control, at least based on the economy's ability to pay the interest costs. However, rising interest rates will raise the burden of this debt. Even so, at its current size, the public debt is manageable as long as it does not experience another spike in the near term.

Another consideration is whether the debt is mostly held externally (i.e., financed by foreign governments, banks, and investors), as is the case of many developing countries. These countries have discovered that relying on foreign sources of financing has its limits.

Does It Matter if Foreigners Hold a Significant Portion of the Public Debt?

The great advantage of citizens being creditors as well as debtors with relation to the public debt is obvious. Men readily perceive that they can not be much oppressed by a debt which they owe to themselves.

—ABRAHAM LINCOLN (1864)

TABLE 1	DISTRIBUTION OF U.S. NATIONAL DEBT, AS OF JUNE 2019 (TRILLIONS)	
	Amount	Percent
Held by the Federal Reserve and government agencies	$5.865	26.5%
Held by the public	16.251	73.5
Held by foreigners	6.628	30.0
Held domestically	9.623	43.5
Total national debt	22.116	100.00

Data from the U.S. Department of the Treasury.

Consider first, as Abraham Lincoln noted in 1864, that much of the national debt held by the public is owned by American banks, corporations, mutual funds, pension plans, and individuals. As a people, we essentially own this debt—this is **internally held debt.** Hence, the taxes collected from a wide swath of the American public to pay the interest on the debt are paid back out to yet another group of Americans. As Table 1 shows, however, foreigners own a sizable portion of the public debt. This is **externally held debt.**

Of the $22.1 trillion national debt, 26.5% is owed to federal agencies (the Social Security Administration, the Federal Reserve, and other federal agencies), 43.5% is owed to the American private sector, and 30% is owed to foreigners.

The interest paid on externally held debt represents a real claim on our goods and services and thus can be a real burden on our economy. Debt held by the public has grown, and the portion of the debt held by foreigners has expanded. Until the mid-1990s, foreigners held roughly 20% of publicly held debt; this has since doubled.

Traditionally much of the U.S. debt is held internally, but this is changing. In 2019, foreign holdings represent about 40% (30.0/73.5) of the debt held by the public, and about 35% of this is held by China and Japan. Why such a rapid expansion of foreign holdings since the 1990s? One reason is that these countries are buying our debt to keep their currencies from rising relative to the dollar. When their currencies rise, their exports to America are more costly; as a result, sales fall, hurting their economies. It is better to accumulate U.S. debt than to see their export sectors suffer.

However, the increased reliance on external financing of our debt raises some concerns. For example, the significant amount of our debt held by China makes our economy more vulnerable to policy changes by the Chinese government and/or businesses that hold our debt. On the positive side, creditors such as China are likely to maintain strong economic and political ties with the United States; besides, China eventually will want its money back.

Does Government Debt Crowd Out Consumption and Investment?

As we saw in the budget constraint section earlier, when the government runs a deficit, it must sell bonds to either the public or the Federal Reserve. If it sells bonds to the Federal Reserve (prints money) when the economy is near full employment, the money supply will grow and inflation will result.

Alternatively, when the federal government spends more than tax revenues permit, it can sell bonds to the public. But doing so drives up interest rates as the demand for loanable funds (this time by the government rather than the public sector) increases. As interest rates rise, consumer spending on durable goods such as cars and appliances, often bought on credit, falls. It also reduces private business investment. This is the **crowding-out effect** of deficit spending; simply, government borrowing crowds out private borrowing. Therefore, while deficit spending is usually expansionary, the consequence is that future generations will be bequeathed a smaller and potentially less productive economy, resulting in a lower standard of living. However, in a severe

internally held debt Public debt owned by domestic banks, corporations, mutual funds, pension plans, and individuals.

externally held debt Public debt held by foreigners, including foreign industries, banks, and governments.

crowding-out effect When deficit spending requires the government to borrow, interest rates are driven up, reducing consumer spending and business investment.

recession when consumers and businesses are not eager to buy or invest, the crowding-out effect is less pronounced, making fiscal policy more powerful.

The crowding-out effect can also be mitigated if the funds from deficit spending are used for public investment. For example, improvements in the nation's transportation infrastructure, education establishment, and research facilities are aimed at improving the economy's future productive capacity. If the investments expand the nation's productive capacity enough, growth will be such that the debt-to-GDP ratio may fall. But if all or most of the deficit is spent on non-public investment items, growth in GDP may be weak, and the debt-to-GDP ratio will most likely rise.

How Will the National Debt Affect Our Future?

fiscal sustainability A measure of the present value of all projected future revenues compared to the present value of projected future spending.

If the federal debt is not an enormous burden now, what about in the future? Here there is a large cause for concern. Economists have argued that economic growth depends on the **fiscal sustainability** of the federal budget. For a fiscal policy to be fiscally sustainable, the present value (current dollar value) of all projected future revenues must be equal to the present value of projected future spending. If the budget is not fiscally sustainable, an intergenerational tax burden will be created, with future generations paying for the spending of the current generation.

Clearly, some tax burden shifting is sensible. When current fiscal policy truly invests in the economy, future generations benefit, and therefore some of the present costs may justifiably be shifted to them. Investments in infrastructure, education, research, national defense, and homeland security are good examples.

However, the federal government has immense obligations that extend over long periods that are unrelated to economic investment. Its two largest programs, Social Security and Medicare, account for about 40% of all federal spending. People who are just beginning to enter retirement can expect to live for two or three more decades. Add to this the fact that medical costs are growing at rates significantly higher than economic growth as new and more sophisticated treatments are developed and demanded.

The intergenerational impact results from the fact that Social Security and Medicare are pay-as-you-go programs. The current working generation, in other words, funds the older generation's benefits; there are no pooled funds waiting to be tapped as needed. Thus, these two programs represent huge unfunded liabilities to younger (and yet to be born) generations.

With the current national debt held by the public at over $16 trillion and total future liabilities (the money that has been promised, such as for Social Security and Medicare, but has not been paid) estimated to be several times the current public debt, the implications for future budgeting are significant. In other words, without some significant change in economic or demographic growth, taxes will have to be increased dramatically at some point, or else the benefits for Social Security and Medicare will have to be drastically cut.

If these estimates of fiscal imbalance are on track, fiscal policy is headed for a train wreck as the baby boomers keep retiring. The public choice analysis discussed earlier suggests that politicians will try to keep this issue off the agenda for as long as possible, one side fighting tax increases while the other resists benefit reductions. Clearly, given the magnitudes discussed here, this problem will be difficult to solve.

We started this chapter by talking about the government's ability to address fluctuations in the business cycle by using fiscal policy to affect aggregate demand and aggregate supply. But given the government's penchant for expansionary policy, persistent budget deficits tend to result. Unlike for individuals, the federal government has the ability to incur debt for some time because of its ability to print money and borrow from the public. And while the federal government is currently able to safely manage its debt, this picture may change down the road as Social Security and Medicare liabilities continue to grow. The implication is that we are better off dealing with this future problem now rather than later.

CHECKPOINT

WHY IS THE PUBLIC DEBT SO IMPORTANT?

- Interest payments on the debt account for 8% of the federal budget. These funds could have been spent on other programs.

- About 60% of the public debt held by the public is held by domestic individuals and institutions, and 40% is held by foreigners. The domestic portion is internally held and represents transfers among individuals, but that part held by foreigners is a real claim on our resources.

- When the government pays for the deficit by selling bonds, interest rates rise, crowding out some consumption and private investment and reducing economic growth. To the extent that these funds are used for public investment, this effect is mitigated.

- The rising costs of Social Security and Medicare represent the biggest threat to the long-run federal budget. Either the costs of such programs eventually need to be reduced or additional taxes will be required to cover these rising expenses.

QUESTIONS: Suppose China and Japan, the two largest external creditors of U.S. public debt, choose to diversify their asset holdings by selling some of their U.S. Treasury bonds. How will this affect the U.S. government's ability to finance its debt? What might happen to consumption and investment in the United States?

Answers to the Checkpoint questions can be found at the end of this chapter.

CHAPTER SUMMARY

SECTION 1 FISCAL POLICY AND AGGREGATE DEMAND

10.1 **Fiscal policy** describes the use of government taxation and spending to influence the economy. Specifically, it involves three main tools: taxation, government spending on goods and services, and transfer payments.

10.2 **Contractionary fiscal policy** includes reducing government spending, reducing transfer payments, or raising taxes. The effect is a shift of the AD curve to the left, decreasing prices and aggregate output.

Expansionary fiscal policy includes increasing government spending, increasing transfer payments, or reducing taxes. The effect is a shift of the AD curve to the right, increasing prices and aggregate output.

10.3 The **multiplier effect** allows each dollar of government spending to expand aggregate output by a multiple of the amount spent. Changes in government spending have a larger multiplier than changes in taxes.

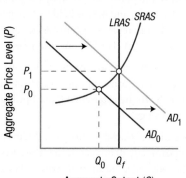

Using expansionary fiscal policy to shift AD during a recession can reduce the time required to achieve full employment. The tradeoff of such policies is potential inflation, although the effect is small when used in a deep recession.

SECTION 2 FISCAL POLICY AND AGGREGATE SUPPLY

The goal of **supply-side fiscal policy** is to shift the LRAS curve to the right. Such policies do not require a tradeoff between output and prices; however, these policies require more time to work.

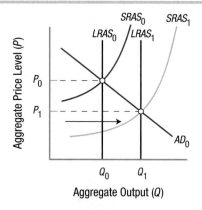

Maintaining highways such as the treacherous Trans-Alaskan Highway can increase aggregate supply if better roads increase productivity.

10.4 **Common Supply-Side Policies**

- **Increase Infrastructure Spending:** Promotes productivity by improving roads and communications networks, stabilizing legal and financial systems, and improving human capital and technologies (R&D).
- **Decrease Tax Rates:** Increases aggregate supply by providing firms incentives to expand or for individuals to work more.
- **Eliminate Burdensome Regulations:** Leads to greater efficiency if the costs of regulation outweigh the benefits.

SECTION 3 IMPLEMENTING FISCAL POLICY

10.5 The economy contains **automatic stabilizers:**

When the economy is strong:

Tax receipts rise   **Transfer payments fall**
(both have contractionary effects to fight inflation)

When the economy is weak:

Tax receipts fall   **Transfer payments rise**
(both have expansionary effects to offset the recession)

10.6 Using fiscal policy involves **timing lags:**

• **Information lag:** Time required to acquire macroeconomic data
• **Recognition lag:** Time required to recognize trends in the data
• **Decision lag:** Legislative process to enact policies
• **Implementation lag:** Time required after laws are passed to develop and start programs

Passing new fiscal policy can take a lot of time, especially in a divided Congress.

SECTION 4 FINANCING THE FEDERAL GOVERNMENT

10.7 The **federal deficit** is the annual amount by which government spending exceeds tax revenues.

A **surplus** occurs when tax revenues exceed government spending. The **national debt** is the accumulation of all past deficits less surpluses. The **public debt** is the portion of the national debt that is held by the public.

How Does the Government Finance Its Deficit ($G - T$)?

• The Federal Reserve prints money to buy bonds: ΔM
• Treasury bonds sold to domestic and foreign entities: ΔB
• Sales of government assets: ΔA

U.S. Savings Bonds are one form of financing government debt.

SECTION 5 WHY IS THE PUBLIC DEBT SO IMPORTANT?

10.8 In 2018 the U.S. government paid $324 billion in interest payments on the public debt. Although this is a manageable expense, higher interest rates and rising future liabilities can make the debt a more significant problem in the future.

Social Security and Medicare liabilities rise each year as Americans live longer and health care costs rise. These two components pose a big concern for future debt.

About 40% of U.S. public debt is held externally, by foreign governments and investors. Of this amount, about 35% ($2.2 billion) is held by China and Japan.

Borrowing money to finance the debt raises interest rates, making it more expensive for individuals and businesses to borrow money. This is the **crowding-out effect.**

Key Concepts

Questions and Problems

Check Your Understanding

1. What is the main difference between discretionary spending and mandatory spending?

2. Explain why increasing government purchases of goods and services is expansionary fiscal policy. Would increasing taxes or reducing transfer payments be contractionary or expansionary? Why?

3. Explain why changes in tax rates affect both aggregate demand and aggregate supply.

4. What is one benefit to businesses when the government budget is in surplus?

5. How might interest paid on the national debt lead to greater income inequality?

6. What factors determine whether the national debt is a cause for immediate concern?

Apply the Concepts

7. One argument against using fiscal policies to smooth fluctuations in the business cycle is that their long lags may end up causing more harm than good. Provide an example that would support this argument and one that would not.

8. What are some major reasons why mandatory spending in the United States is increasing as a share of the federal budget?

9. Our current personal income tax system is progressive: Income tax rates rise with rising incomes and are lower for low-income individuals. Some policymakers favor a "flat tax" as a replacement for our modestly progressive income tax system. Most exemptions and deductions would be eliminated, and a single low tax rate would be applied to personal income. How would such a change in the tax laws alter the automatic stabilization characteristics of the personal income tax?

10. In a speech before the Economic Club of New York in 1962, President Kennedy argued that "it is a paradoxical truth that taxes are too high today and tax revenues are too low—and the soundest way to raise revenues in the long run is to cut rates now." Is President Kennedy's argument consistent with supply-side economics? Why or why not?

11. A balanced budget amendment to the Constitution requiring Congress to balance the budget every year is introduced in Congress every so often. What sort of problems would the

passage of such an amendment introduce for policymakers and the economy? What would be the benefit of the passage of such an amendment?

12. Suppose the economy (gross domestic product) is growing faster than the growth of the national debt held by the public (both domestic and foreign). How does this affect the ability of the government to manage the national debt? What arguments can you make to rebut the common assertion that the national debt is bankrupting the country?

In the News

13. From 2016 to 2019, interest rates on 30-year Treasury bonds rose from around 2.1% to 3.4%. What are the long-term implications of this change in financing the national debt and in managing the annual federal budget?

14. Several years ago, Italy and Spain began to include the estimated output of informal activities (such as the drug trade, prostitution, and other illicit activities) as part of its GDP without actually legalizing these activities. If these activities remain illegal and the government does not collect tax revenues, why would it matter if these activities are counted in official GDP measures?

Solving Problems

15. Suppose a small economy has two income tax rates: 15% for all income up to $50,000 and 30% for any income earned above $50,000. Suppose that prior to the recession, the economy had five workers earning the following salaries:

Amy	$20,000
Betty	$40,000
Charlie	$60,000
Dimitry	$80,000
Evelyn	$100,000

   a. Calculate the total amount of taxes paid by the five workers. What percent of total income does this represent?

   b. Now assume that a recession causes each of the five salaries to fall by 25%. Given the lower salaries, what would be the total amount of taxes paid by the five workers? What percent of total income does this represent?

   c. Explain how this progressive tax structure acts as an automatic stabilizer.

Work It Out

 interactive activity

16. Suppose an economy has a GDP of $40 billion and a national debt of $20 billion, and the average interest rate on this debt is currently 3%.

   a. Calculate the annual interest payments on the debt. What percentage of this economy's GDP is spent on interest payments on its debt?

   b. Suppose that next year one of two events occurs: (1) GDP and interest rates stay the same, but the economy adds $4 billion to its national debt, or (2) GDP and the national debt stay the same, but the average interest rate on the debt increases to 4%. Which of the two events would result in a larger portion of the economy's GDP going toward interest payments on the national debt?

Answers to Questions in Checkpoints

Checkpoint: Fiscal Policy and Aggregate Demand 248

Although the money would have hit the economy sooner, a significant portion of the proceeds would have been saved or used to pay existing bills, potentially limiting the stimulative impact of *added* spending. The other benefit of the infrastructure package is that by being spread out over several years, it won't just be a big jolt to the economy that ends as fast as it began. Thus, the impact on employment and business planning was smoother.

Checkpoint: Fiscal Policy and Aggregate Supply 252

Supply-side economics focuses on providing incentives for individuals to work and for businesses to invest, and therefore advocates lower tax rates. The reduction in the individual, corporate, and capital gains taxes would each be consistent with supply-side economics. However, if a portion of these tax savings is offset through higher consumption taxes, this would not be consistent with supply-side economics because such a tax would discourage consumption and negatively affect business and investment outlook.

Checkpoint: Implementing Fiscal Policy 254

The president would favor policies that could be implemented quickly, such as "shovel ready" infrastructure projects that have already been approved, the expansion of unemployment benefits that can take effect immediately, or tax cuts that can be applied in the current tax year. The president would not favor policies that require a new law to be passed, as such policies may take years before being implemented.

Checkpoint: Financing the Federal Government 259

The federal government must satisfy its mandatory spending requirements, including Social Security, unless it passes a law to reform such spending. Also, the federal government must pay for national defense, including wars, which are unpredictable. Also unpredictable are expenses related to natural disasters, which require action by various federal agencies. Due to the combination of various mandatory spending programs and unpredictable discretionary spending requirements, the federal government would find it difficult in practice to enforce a balanced budget amendment.

Checkpoint: Why Is the Public Debt So Important? 263

If China and Japan reduce their holdings of U.S. debt, interest rates would need to rise in order to attract other investors to purchase these bonds. Rising interest rates would adversely affect consumption and investment in the United States, potentially slowing economic growth.

John Lund/Getty Images

11

Saving, Investment, and the Financial System

Understanding the importance of financial institutions and their role in connecting savers with borrowers

On August 13, 2004, the city of Athens, Greece, celebrated as the Summer Olympic Games returned to its historic homeland, the place where Olympic athletes nearly 3,000 years ago competed on the same land as athletes in the current games were about to compete.

Indeed, it was a proud moment for Greeks and for their government, which had borrowed billions of dollars to build new stadiums, a modern transportation network, a new airport, and to give the city a significant facelift to showcase its growing economic prosperity to a worldwide audience. Where did the government get this money? It borrowed money from banks and from the public by issuing bonds, and there was plenty of money to be borrowed. The Olympics were the ultimate showpiece of a nation on the rise.

No one could have predicted on that proud day that in less than a decade, that same city would be engulfed in financial turmoil, with large government debt, protests and riots, and a country in complete despair. What happened in Greece that led to such a dramatic reversal in fortune?

In short, it was a breakdown of financial institutions caused by a global recession, along with uncontrolled government debt that caused long-term interest rates to skyrocket from 4% in 2009 to 27% in 2012. With interest rates so high, the ability to borrow, whether by the government, by businesses, or by consumers, became prohibitive, leading to a drastic decline in consumption and investment, and subsequently a rise in unemployment. Clearly, Greece headed into a vicious cycle that threatened not only the country but also the stability of the euro, the currency it shares with much of Europe.

Although Greece was not the only country to have undergone a financial crisis, it was one of the most difficult cases because of the challenges that affected the banks, bond market, and stock market—which form what we refer to as a country's financial system. The financial system plays an important role in the health of the macroeconomy, and when the system breaks down, as it did in Greece, the economy often goes down with it.

Up to now, we have studied how the federal government tries to manage the macroeconomy through fiscal policy by using government taxation and spending. We now want to look at the government's other policy approach—monetary policy. To analyze how government uses monetary policy to influence the macroeconomy, we must first

Tim de Waele/Getty Images

Anadolu Agency/Getty Images

BY THE Numbers

The Financial System and Its Sheer Size and Scope

The U.S. financial system consists of commercial banks, money markets, and government institutions that manage money and serve as a bridge between savers and borrowers. It is connected with the global financial system, consisting of banks and financial institutions around the world that influence one another. Many of the world's largest banks are foreign banks. This By the Numbers compares the total assets of the ten largest banks in the world.

$1.7 trillion

Total U.S. currency in circulation in 2019, consisting of Federal Reserve notes (bills) and coins

$6.63 trillion

Total U.S. currency reserves (mostly in electronic form) held around the world, nearly half in China

DATA:

The Ten Largest Banks in the World (2017)

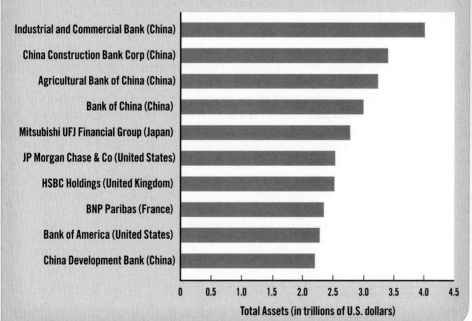

Bar chart showing Total Assets (in trillions of U.S. dollars):
- Industrial and Commercial Bank (China): ~4.0
- China Construction Bank Corp (China): ~3.4
- Agricultural Bank of China (China): ~3.2
- Bank of China (China): ~3.0
- Mitsubishi UFJ Financial Group (Japan): ~2.8
- JP Morgan Chase & Co (United States): ~2.5
- HSBC Holdings (United Kingdom): ~2.5
- BNP Paribas (France): ~2.35
- Bank of America (United States): ~2.25
- China Development Bank (China): ~2.2

X-axis: Total Assets (in trillions of U.S. dollars), 0 to 4.5

Where Can I Find These Data?
Source: Banks Around the World
Web site: https://www.relbanks.com
Details: Select "World's Top Banks" and then select the most recent year for the "Top Banks by Assets."

WHY ARE THESE DATA IMPORTANT?

Banks serve a critical role in the health of an economy by allowing savers to deposit money that is then lent to borrowers to finance investments and other purchases. Twenty-five years ago, Japanese and American banks dominated the largest banks in the world. Today, the world's largest banks are in China. The growth of the Chinese economy and its high savings rate have led to a booming banking industry.

Data *in the News*

"Who's Winning the War for China's Banking Sector?" by Peter Pham; *Forbes*, March 13, 2018

China is home to the world's biggest banking sector. Still, the sector is underdeveloped and not keen to open up, which makes investing in this sector all the more challenging. Even more so if you're not Chinese.

~ Assessing Your Data Literacy ~

1. How many of the ten largest banks in the world are based in China, and what are the combined value of assets of these banks? How many are based in the United States, and what are the combined value of assets?

2. What factors might explain why China's banks are so much larger than U.S. banks?

3. Return to the Web site and select an earlier year (such as 2010). Were Chinese banks dominant back then? Which countries' banks appeared in the top 10?

lay the foundation by examining the financial system and the role of money, which is the subject of this chapter. Building on this foundation, in the following chapters we will see how financial institutions create money and how the government enacts policies that encourage the financial system to do things that mitigate fluctuations in the macroeconomy.

We begin by looking at money: what it is and what it does. Then we examine why people save and why firms borrow. We next show how the market for loanable funds brings together these two groups and how the financial system makes this process easier and better for all. The chapter concludes with an overview of financial tools that illustrates the importance of financial literacy in our everyday lives.

WHAT IS MONEY?

Anything can serve as money, from the cowrie shells of the Maldives to the huge stone discs used on the Pacific islands of Yap. And now, it seems, in this electronic age nothing can serve as money too.
NIALL FERGUSON, *THE ASCENT OF MONEY*

money Anything that is accepted in exchange for goods and services or for the payment of debt.

Money is anything that is accepted in exchange for goods and services or for the payment of debt. For example, we are familiar with currency and coins. Over the ages, however, a wide variety of commodities have served as money—giant circular stones on the island of Yap, wampum (trinkets) among early Native Americans, and cigarettes in prisoner-of-war camps during World War II.

Commodity money consists of objects and materials (such as gold, silver, and trinkets) that have value in and of itself. However, commodities must meet certain criteria to be effectively used as money. First, its value must be easy to determine. Therefore, it must be easily standardized. Second, it must be divisible so that people can make change. Third, money must be durable and portable. It must be easy to carry (so much for the giant circular stones, which today are used only for ceremonial purposes in Yap). Fourth, a commodity must be accepted by many people as money if it is to act as money. As Niall Ferguson makes clear in the quote above, today we have "virtual" money in the sense that digital money is moved from our employer to the bank and then to the retailer for our goods and services in nothing but a series of electronic transactions. This is really the ultimate in **fiat money:** money without any intrinsic value but accepted as money because the government has made it legal tender.

fiat money Money without intrinsic value but nonetheless accepted as money because the government has decreed it to be money.

Money is so important that nearly every society has invented some form of money for its use. We begin our examination of money by looking at its functions.

The Functions of Money

Money has three primary functions in our economic system: medium of exchange, measure of value (unit of account), and store of value. These uses make money unique among commodities.

Medium of Exchange Let us start with a primitive economy. There is no money. To survive, you have to produce everything yourself: food, clothing, housing. It is a fact that few of us can do all of these tasks equally well. Each one of us is better off specializing, providing those goods and services we are more efficient at supplying. Suppose that I specialize in producing dairy products and you specialize in blacksmithing. We can engage in **barter,** which is the direct exchange of goods and services. I can give you gallons of milk if you make me a pot for cooking. A *double coincidence of wants* occurs if, in a barter economy, I find someone who not only has something I want but also wants something I have. What happens if you, the blacksmith, are willing to make the cooking pot for me but want clothing in return? Then I have to search out someone who is willing to give me clothing in exchange for milk; I will then give you the clothing in exchange for the cooking pot. You can see that this system quickly becomes complicated. This is why barter is used primarily in primitive economies.

barter The direct exchange of goods and services for other goods and services.

Consider what happens when money is introduced. Everyone can spend their time producing goods and services rather than running around trying to match up exchanges. Everyone can sell their products for money and then use it to buy cooking pots, clothing, or whatever else they want. Thus, money's first and most important function is a **medium of exchange.** Without money, economies remain primitive.

Unit of Account Imagine the difficulties consumers would have in a barter economy in which every item is valued in terms of the other products offered—12 eggs are worth 1 shirt, 1 shirt equals 3 gallons of gas, and so forth. A 10-product economy of this sort, assigning every product a value for every other product, would require 45 different prices. A 100-good economy would require 4,950 prices.[1] This is another reason why only the most primitive economies use barter.

Once again, money is able to solve a problem inherent to the barter economy. It reduces the number of prices consumers need to know to the number of products on the market; a 100-good economy will have 100 prices. Thus, money is a **unit of account,** or a measure of value. Dollar prices give us a yardstick for measuring and comparing the values of a wide variety of goods and services.

Store of Value Using cherry tomatoes as a medium of exchange and unit of account might be handy, except that they have the bad habit of rotting. Therefore, in order to allow individuals to save money they earn today and use it to buy goods and services in the future, money must serve as a **store of value.** To satisfy this condition, physical money must be durable, while electronic money must be able to be safely deposited in a bank.

Coins are much more durable than banknotes, which can become very worn and dirty as they are circulated. To maintain their function, the Federal Reserve (the central bank of the United States) replaces old banknotes with new ones when they wear out. In order to minimize the cost of replacing banknotes, some countries have replaced banknotes with coins or use polymers (plastic) to make banknotes last longer. The following Around the World feature discusses the history and benefits of polymer banknotes.

Besides money (physical currency or funds stored electronically in banks), other commodities can serve as a store of value. For example, stocks, bonds, real estate, art, and jewelry can be used to store wealth for future use. In fact, many of these assets may rise in value and therefore be preferred to money as a store of value. Why, then, use money as a store of wealth at all?

The answer is that every other type of asset must be converted into money if it is to be spent or used to pay debts. Converting other assets into cash involves transaction costs, and for some assets, these costs are significant. An asset's **liquidity** is determined by how fast, easily, and reliably it can be converted into cash.

Money is the most liquid asset because, as the medium of exchange, it requires no conversion. Stocks and bonds are also liquid, but they do require some time and often a commission fee to convert into cash. Prices in stock and bond markets fluctuate, causing the real value of these assets to be uncertain. Real estate requires considerable time to liquidate, with transaction costs that often approach 10% of a property's value.

Money differs from many other commodities in that its value does not deteriorate in the absence of inflation. However, when price levels do rise, the value of money falls: If prices double, the value of money is cut in half. In times of inflation, most people are unwilling to hold much of their wealth in money. If hyperinflation hits, money will quickly become worthless as the economy reverts to barter.

Money, then, is crucial for a well-functioning modern economy. All of its three primary functions are important: medium of exchange, unit of account, and store of value.

Defining the Money Supply

How much money is in the U.S. economy? One of the tasks assigned to the Federal Reserve System (the Fed), the central bank of the United States, is that of measuring our money supply. The Fed has developed several different measures of monetary aggregates, which it continually

medium of exchange A function of money in which goods and services are sold for money, facilitating exchange and minimizing transaction costs.

unit of account Money provides a yardstick for measuring and comparing the values of a wide variety of goods and services. It eliminates the problem of double coincidence of wants associated with barter.

store of value The function that enables people to save the money they earn today and use it to buy the goods and services they want tomorrow.

liquidity How quickly, easily, and reliably an asset can be converted into cash.

The United States has introduced $1 coins many times throughout its history and in recent decades has included the Susan B. Anthony dollar, the Sacagawea dollar, and the presidential dollar. Yet, the use of dollar coins as a medium of exchange never caught on, with the majority of dollar coins ending up in coin collections rather than in cash registers.

---

[1] The formula for determining the number of prices needed when N goods are in an economy is $[N(N-1)]/2$. Thus, for 10 goods, the result is $[10(10-1)]/2 = 90/2 = 45$.

AROUND THE WORLD

Using Plastic Money (Literally) in Australia

How did a commemorative 1988 Australian $10 banknote made of plastic turn into a trend adopted by over 40 countries?

Take out a few U.S. banknotes of different denominations and notice their characteristics—they are all the same size and are made from the same cotton-and-linen-material used for over a century. Compared to banknotes in many other countries, old U.S. banknotes appear bland and worn out and are sometimes counterfeited using advanced scanners to make realistic copies.

To minimize counterfeiting, new U.S. banknotes contain more security features, such as a watermark and color-shifting ink. And since 2008, new banknotes (other than the $1 bill) contain colors different from the old green and black.

Other countries have transformed their banknotes in more dramatic ways. One such transformation was introduced

in Australia in 1988—money made literally of plastic. How did the introduction of plastic (polymer) banknotes transform the way many countries produce their banknotes?

In 1988 when Australia celebrated the 200th anniversary of the first arrival of Europeans, the Australian Treasury introduced a commemorative $10 banknote made of plastic. The plastic banknote was colorful, was difficult to rip or tear, stayed crisp even after many uses, and, most importantly, was nearly impossible to counterfeit. Due to the popularity of the new design and the subsequent reduction in counterfeiting, Australia

changed all of its banknote denominations to polymer-based materials, becoming the first country to do so but certainly not the last.

Today, over 40 countries (including Mexico and Canada) use polymer banknotes for some or all banknote denominations. Although polymer banknotes cost about twice as much to make as cotton-paper banknotes, they last over twice as long and dramatically reduce counterfeiting. Moreover, the rising cost of cotton in recent years has reduced the difference in cost of producing polymer banknotes.

Are Americans too wed to the paper greenback to accept polymer banknotes? Americans have mostly rejected other ideas, including attempts to eliminate the penny and to replace the $1 bill with a $1 coin. Such aversion to currency changes is ironic, considering that fewer than 25% of U.S. consumer transactions are conducted in cash and over half of Americans do not regularly carry cash at all. In fact, cash may disappear altogether in the future, which might ultimately make this debate obsolete.

 GO ONLINE TO PRACTICE THE ECONOMIC CONCEPTS IN THIS STORY

M1 The narrowest definition of money that measures highly liquid instruments including currency in circulation (banknotes and coins) and checkable deposits.

updates to reflect the innovative new financial instruments our financial system is constantly developing. The monetary aggregates the Fed uses most frequently are M1, the narrowest measure of money, and M2, a broader measure.

More specifically, the Fed defines M1 and M2 as follows:

M1 equals:[2]
- Currency in circulation (banknotes and coins)
+ Checkable deposits

M2 equals:
- M1
+ Savings deposits
+ Money market deposit accounts
+ Small-denomination (less than $100,000) time deposits
+ Shares in retail money market mutual funds

M2 A broader definition of money that includes M1 along with "near monies" that are not as liquid as cash, including deposits in savings accounts, money market accounts, and money market mutual fund accounts.

[2] Traveler's checks are also officially counted as part of M1. However, the improved efficiency of international debit card and credit card transactions has made traveler's checks mostly obsolete. In 2019 traveler's checks represented less than one-tenth of 1% of M1.

Narrowly Defined Money: M1 Because money is used mainly as a medium of exchange, when defined most narrowly, it includes currency in circulation (banknotes and coins) and checkable deposits (including checking accounts and other accounts that have check-writing capabilities). Currency represents slightly less than half of M1, with banknotes constituting more than 90% of currency; coins form only a small part of M1. Checkable deposits (also referred to as demand deposits) represent the other half of the money supply. In 2019, M1 was about $3.7 trillion. It is the most liquid part of the money supply.

Checking accounts can be opened at commercial banks and at a variety of other financial institutions, including credit unions, mutual savings banks, and savings and loan associations. Also, many stock brokerage firms offer checking services on brokerage accounts.

A Broader Definition: M2 A broader definition of money, M2, includes "near monies": money that may not be able to be withdrawn instantaneously but that is nonetheless accessible. This includes deposits in savings accounts, money market deposit accounts, and money market mutual fund accounts. Many of these accounts have check-writing features similar to demand deposits.

Certificates of deposit (CDs) and other small-denomination time deposits can usually be cashed in at any time, although they often carry penalties for early liquidation. Thus, M2 includes the highly liquid assets in M1 and a variety of accounts that are less liquid but still easy and inexpensive to access. In 2019, M2 was about $14.5 trillion.

When economists speak of "the money supply," they are usually referring to M1, the narrowest definition. Economists sometimes disagree on whether M1 or M2 is the better measure of the money supply. Although they tend to have similar trends, they have deviated significantly in certain periods. For the remainder of this book, the money supply will be considered to be M1 unless otherwise specified.

The monetary components that make up the money supply serve many purposes. One of the most important functions of the financial system is to channel funds from savers to borrowers, something barter societies are unable to do. In the next section, we look at a simple model of loanable funds to show how savers and borrowers come together to make moneylending possible and contribute to economic growth.

Cryptocurrency

In recent years, significant attention has been placed on cryptocurrency, also known as virtual currency or Bitcoin (the name of the most familiar cryptocurrency). Unlike traditional money, which is stored in commercial banks and other financial institutions, cryptocurrency is stored in digital *wallets* specific to each cryptocurrency where only the holder has access to it (essentially becoming its own bank). The most secure wallets are stored offline on hardware to prevent hacking.

An important characteristic of cryptocurrency is that it is not managed by any government authority in any country. In terms of its function as money, cryptocurrencies serve the three major functions with varying effectiveness. Although it is designed to be a medium of exchange, cryptocurrency is not widely accepted, and therefore its use in everyday transactions is limited. It serves the unit of account function well. But its function as a store of value is questionable. Because cryptocurrency is stored electronically and under no government authority, money is unrecoverable if stolen by hackers or lost if one forgets the password (there is no password recovery service) or damages the hardware on which the cryptocurrency is stored.

Today, cryptocurrencies are used primarily for speculative purposes, as investors predict whether cryptocurrencies will be legitimized by governments and whether their use as a medium of exchange expands. One factor that has promoted their use is that consumers today are more comfortable paying for purchases with virtual wallets stored on their phones and sending money to others with a few taps on the phone. In order for cryptocurrency to achieve the same level of use, it needs to satisfy the functions of money in an efficient manner.

✅ CHECKPOINT

WHAT IS MONEY?

- Money is anything accepted in exchange for goods and services and for the payment of debts.

- The functions of money include: a medium of exchange, a unit of account, and a store of value.

- Liquidity refers to how fast, easily, and reliably an asset can be converted into cash.

- M1 is currency plus checkable deposits.

- M2 is equal to M1 plus savings deposits plus other savings-like deposits.

QUESTION: The U.S. penny, with Abraham Lincoln's image on the front, has been in circulation since 1909. Back then, pennies were inexpensive to produce and could be used to purchase real items. Today, a U.S. penny actually costs the government more than 1 cent to produce, and it is virtually unusable in any coin-operated machine and impractical to use in stores. How has the role of the penny changed over the past century in terms of its monetary functions (medium of exchange, unit of account, and store of value)?

Answers to the Checkpoint questions can be found at the end of this chapter.

THE MARKET FOR LOANABLE FUNDS

The market for loanable funds is used to analyze the financial market for saving and investment. Initially, we will simplify our analysis by assuming that savers deal directly with investors. We then will bring in financial intermediaries (banks, mutual funds, and other financial institutions) to describe the benefits of a well-functioning financial system.

Supply and Demand for Loanable Funds

Why do people save? Why do they borrow? The first thought might be that people save because they *can* save. Unlike barter economies, money makes saving possible.

People supply funds to the loanable funds market because they do not spend all of their income; they save. There are many reasons why individuals save. People save "for a rainy day": They put away some of their income when times are good to take care of them when times turn bad. Saving behavior is also a cultural phenomenon: Many countries, such as China, India, and France, have savings rates far higher than those in the United States.

The reward for not spending today is the *interest* received on savings, enabling people to spend more in the future. Therefore, in the market for loanable funds shown in Figure 1, the quantity of loanable funds is measured on the horizontal axis, and the price of the funds (interest rate) is measured on the vertical axis. In this market, the supply curve represents savers, while the demand curve represents borrowers.

The supply of funds to the loanable funds market, shown as S_0, is positively related to the interest rate. Because interest rates are the price (reward) that savers receive, higher interest rates result in more saving (funds) supplied to the market. This results in an upward-sloping supply curve much like other supply curves we studied earlier, and is just another example of people reacting to incentives.

The demand for loanable funds is determined by people who want to purchase goods and services, such as taking out a loan to go to college or to buy a car, or who, as entrepreneurs, want to start or expand a business. Firms are borrowers, too. Firms may want to invest in new plants, additional equipment, or expanded warehouse facilities or engage in additional research and development on new products. The specific investment depends on the industry. For firms in the oil industry, it might be for an offshore oil platform or refinery. For a start-up network firm that has a growing number of subscribers but limited financial capital, the loanable funds might be used for another server farm.

····· Figure 1 • The Market for Loanable Funds ···········

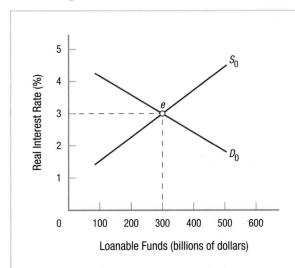

This market represents supply and demand for loanable funds. Savers spend less than they earn and supply the excess funds to the market. Borrowers (primarily businesses) have potential profit-making investment opportunities, and this leads to their demand for funds. The equilibrium is at point *e* at an interest rate of 3% and $300 billion in loanable funds.

The demand for loanable funds, shown as D_0 in Figure 1, slopes downward because when the interest rate is high, fewer projects will have a rate of return high enough to justify the investment. A project will be undertaken only if its expected return (its benefit) is higher than the cost of funding the project. When oil prices fall, for example, an oil platform will not generate enough revenues to justify paying a high interest rate. As interest rates fall, more projects become profitable and the amount of funds demanded rises.

Keep in mind that when we refer to interest rates, we are referring to *real* interest rates (adjusted for inflation) that reflect the real cost of borrowing and the real return to savers.

The loanable funds market reaches equilibrium in Figure 1 at a 3% real interest rate and $300 billion in funds traded in the market. If for some reason the real interest rate *exceeded* 3%, savers would provide more funds to the market than investors want, and interest rates would fall until the market reached point *e*. In a similar way, if the interest rate was *below* 3%, investors would want more funds than savers would be willing to provide. In this case, the market would push up the interest rate to 3% at point *e*.

Building a new server farm requires a substantial amount of cash, often obtained by borrowing in the loanable funds market.

Not surprisingly, the market for loanable funds is similar to a competitive market for goods and services. In the latter, the price changes to achieve equilibrium. In the market for loanable funds, the interest rate changes to achieve equilibrium. In fact, compared to most markets, financial markets are typically more competitive and reach equilibrium more quickly when something changes in the market.

Similar to product markets, the market for loanable funds is subject to factors that shift the supply or demand for loanable funds. When this occurs, interest rates and the level of saving and investment also change.

Shifts in the Supply of Loanable Funds

A shift in the supply curve of loanable funds occurs when a factor increases or decreases the country's willingness to save (either by private individuals or by the public government) at each interest rate. Changes in economic outlook, incentives to save, income or asset prices, and government deficits can influence savings patterns.

Figure 2 • Changes in Supply, Demand, and Interest Rates

Suppose the market for loanable funds is in equilibrium at point *e*. If savers decide to save more, the supply of funds will grow from S_0 to S_1. At the new equilibrium, point *a*, the interest rate falls from 3% to 2.5%, and the amount of loanable funds rises from $300 billion to $400 billion. If instead there were an increase in the rate of return on investment (due to investment tax credits or increased demand for the firm's product), demand for funds will increase from D_0 to D_1. At the new equilibrium, point *b*, the interest rate and loanable funds rise. The interest rate keeps the market in equilibrium between savers and borrowers.

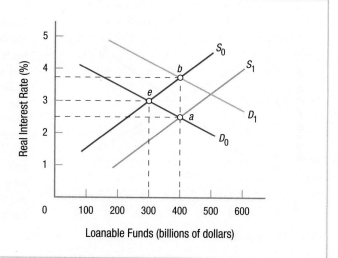

Economic Outlook

Suppose households decide to save a larger proportion of their income because they fear job loss in a recession. If households decide to save more, the amount of funds provided to the market at all interest rates will increase, shifting the supply of loanable funds from S_0 to S_1 in Figure 2. Equilibrium will move from point *e* to point *a*, the real interest rate will fall from 3% to 2.5%, and both saving and investment will rise from $300 billion to $400 billion. On the other hand, if a recession ends and people go on a buying spree, savings will fall. In Figure 2, this would be a shift in the supply curve from S_1 to S_0.

Incentives to Save

Governments and companies offer various incentives to individuals to encourage saving, such as retirement contribution plans and other tax incentives. Adjusting such incentives will change the level of savings accordingly.

Income or Asset Prices

As incomes rise, people generally save a larger proportion of their income, all else equal. Asset prices, however, tend to work the other way. As home prices and stock values increase, people *feel* wealthier (without necessarily having more income) and will spend more and save less. The opposite effects occur when incomes fall or asset prices fall.

Government Deficits

The supply of loanable funds includes both private and public saving. When a government runs a budget surplus, additional loanable funds are provided to the market, increasing the supply of loanable funds. However, governments often incur budget deficits, which means the government becomes a borrower instead of a saver. Governments borrow money by issuing bonds, which are then purchased by individuals and investors using their savings. Therefore, when governments borrow, they do so by reducing the amount that the private sector saves, which decreases the supply of loanable funds. Subsequently, interest rates rise, which crowds out consumption and private investment, an effect discussed in the previous chapter.

Shifts in the Demand for Loanable Funds

We have seen how changes in savings can shift the supply of loanable funds. Now let's turn our attention to the demand side. Anything that changes the rate of return on potential investment will cause the demand for loanable funds to change. Assume saving does not change, and is represented by the initial supply curve, S_0, in Figure 2.

Investment Tax Incentives Investment tax credits effectively reduce tax payments for firms building new factories or buying new equipment. These laws give firms incentives to invest by increasing their *after-tax* rate of return and often are created in bad economic times with the expectation of a quick jolt to investment demand.

An increase in investment demand would shift the demand for loanable funds from D_0 to D_1 in Figure 2 and results in both a higher real interest rate (3.75%) and higher investment ($400 billion). An increase in business taxes would have the opposite effect on demand.

Technological Advances New technologies that increase productivity or create new products give businesses an incentive to increase production, which often results in plant expansion or the need to build an additional facility, increasing the demand for loanable funds.

Regulations Government regulations tend to influence the level of business investment. When regulations reduce corruption and instill confidence in firms and entrepreneurs, demand for investment will rise. But when regulations impose higher costs or make plant expansion difficult, the demand for investment will fall because the return on investment is reduced.

Product Demand When demand for a firm's product or service increases, the return on investment rises. This increases the demand for loanable funds. The opposite is true when product demand falls.

Business Expectations When business sentiment about the economy rises, firms will tend to increase their investment demand, which increases the demand for loanable funds. When business sentiment falls, investment demand decreases, and so does demand for loanable funds.

In summary, the market for loanable funds works just like any other market where one can use the familiar tools of supply and demand analysis. In this market, the price is represented by the real interest rate on loanable funds.

We have seen that when households decide to increase saving, real interest rates fall and investment rises. When the demand by firms for investment funds rises, real interest rates rise along with expanded investment. Together, saving and investment move toward equilibrium in the market for loanable funds.

 **CHECKPOINT**

THE MARKET FOR LOANABLE FUNDS

- Households supply loanable funds to the market when they spend less than their income, and are rewarded with interest for saving.

- Firms demand funds to invest in profitable opportunities.

- The supply curve of funds is positively sloped; higher real interest rates bring more funds into the market. The demand for loanable funds is negatively sloped, reflecting the fact that at higher real interest rates, fewer investment projects are profitable.

- Any policy that provides additional incentives for households to save will increase the supply of loanable funds, resulting in lower interest rates and greater investment.

- Anything that increases the potential profitability (rate of return) of business investments will increase the demand for loanable funds, resulting in higher interest rates and investment.

QUESTIONS: A major downturn in an economy can bring about many consequences, including a reduction in business confidence when firms become reluctant to invest, and an increased fear of job loss among workers. How do these two events affect the supply of savings and the demand for borrowing? What happens to the supply and demand curves in the market for loanable funds? Once the economy recovers, what is likely to happen to these curves?

Answers to the Checkpoint questions can be found at the end of this chapter.

THE FINANCIAL SYSTEM

The previous section discussed how savers and borrowers interact in a market such that those who demand money for various reasons are able to turn to those who have extra money to save. The interest rate is what keeps this market in equilibrium between savers and borrowers. But how does one actually go about saving or borrowing money?

Suppose you have an extra $1,000 that you want to save for the future, and a buddy from your old high school asks you to invest in a new skateboard shop he plans to open on campus. Do you lend your money to him?

Should you invest your money here?

That would depend on a number of factors. First, will your friend be paying you interest or a share of his profits? Second, how risky would such an investment be? Is your friend borrowing from you because he can't qualify for a small business loan elsewhere? Third, when will you expect to get your money back? Next year, or just whenever the business makes enough profit to pay you back? Or perhaps never if the shop goes bust.

These are important questions to evaluate before making financial decisions about your money. Often, the time it takes to evaluate proposals such as lending money to your buddy, and to everyone else you know looking to borrow money, can be significant and costly. For this reason, many individuals instead choose to save by putting money into banks, bonds, and stocks, which together represent the financial system.

The Bridge Between Savers and Borrowers

financial system A complex set of institutions, including banks, bond markets, and stock markets, that allocate scarce resources (financial capital) from savers to borrowers.

The **financial system** is a complex set of institutions that, in the broadest sense, allocates scarce resources (financial capital) from savers, those who are spending less than they earn, to borrowers, those who want to use these resources to invest in potentially profitable projects. Both savers and borrowers can include households, firms, and governments, but our focus is on households as savers and firms as borrowers. As we have seen, savers expect to earn interest on their savings, and borrowers expect to pay interest on what they borrow. Households may save for a down payment on a house or a new car, and firms borrow to invest in new plants, equipment, or research and development.

financial intermediaries Financial firms (banks, mutual funds, insurance companies, etc.) that acquire funds from savers and then lend these funds to borrowers (consumers, firms, and governments).

Financial institutions or **financial intermediaries** are the bridge between savers and borrowers. They include, among others, commercial banks, savings and loan associations, credit unions, insurance companies, securities firms (brokerages), and pension funds. The complexity of a country's financial institutions often is a sign of economic efficiency and growth.

The Roles of Financial Institutions

Financial institutions fulfill three important roles that facilitate the flow of funds to the economy. They (1) reduce information costs, (2) reduce transaction costs, and (3) spread risk by diversifying assets.

Reducing Information Costs Information costs are the expenses associated with gathering information on individual borrowers and evaluating their creditworthiness. Savers (in this case, lenders) would have a difficult time without financial institutions. For example, when deciding whether to lend your buddy money to open his skateboard shop, you might know plenty about your friend's personality and habits but have few ways to determine if his shop is a safe investment or is unsound, or even just a fraud. Financial institutions reduce information costs by screening, evaluating, and monitoring firms to see that they are creditworthy, and that the borrowed funds are used in a prudent manner.

Reducing Transaction Costs Transaction costs are those associated with finding, selecting, and negotiating contracts between individual savers and borrowers. Suppose your buddy needs much more than $1,000 and asks all of his friends to lend him money. Trying to set up contracts individually between many lenders and a borrower can be time-consuming and costly, especially if every lender wants to make sure the business is a sound investment. Financial institutions reduce transaction costs by providing standardized financial products, including savings accounts, stocks, bonds, annuities, mortgages, futures, and options. In your case, you and your friends might put your money into a savings account, while your buddy applies for a loan at that bank.

Diversifying Assets to Reduce Risk Firms need funds for long-term investments, but savers want access to their money at a moment's notice and would want their funds invested in a number of diversified projects to reduce risk. In other words, you might not want to put your entire savings into one risky loan. Financial institutions accept funds from savers and pool this money into a portfolio of diversified financial instruments (stocks, bonds, etc.), reducing overall risk and at the same time permitting savers access to their funds when needed. In addition, they can also offer securities with different risk profiles to savers, from relatively safe CDs and savings accounts to more risky domestic and foreign stocks. In so doing, these institutions allow a greater flow of funds between savers and borrowers, greatly increasing the efficiency of investment in the economy.

The role of financial institutions in channeling funds from savers to investors is essential because the people who save are often not the same people with profitable investment opportunities. Without financial institutions, investment would be more difficult to achieve and the economy significantly smaller.

Types of Financial Assets

Savers have many options when it comes to where to put their money. The primary difference among the many types of financial assets available is the **return on investment (ROI)** one can achieve. A return on investment can be determined by the interest rate earned on savings accounts or CDs, or the capital gains, dividends, and other interest earned from investing in stocks or bonds. The ROI of an asset largely depends on the risk of the asset, with lower-risk assets generally earning a lower ROI and higher-risk assets earning a higher ROI.

The simplest way to save is to deposit money into a checking or savings account at your local bank. This is also the lowest-risk approach to saving because all savings up to $250,000 are insured by the Federal Deposit Insurance Corporation (FDIC) as long as the bank is a member. In its 87-year history, no saver's deposit insured with the FDIC has ever been lost, even when a bank has gone bankrupt.

The advantages of placing savings in banks are clear—savers have easy access to their money (high liquidity) in addition to virtually no risk. The disadvantage is that savings and checking accounts pay very low interest and in some cases no interest at all.

Thus, in order to increase earnings on savings, savers must either (1) choose financial assets with lower liquidity or (2) choose assets that carry a higher level of risk. One way to achieve this is to invest in bonds and stocks, to which we now turn our attention.

Savers can invest their funds *directly* in businesses by purchasing a bond or shares of stock from a firm using one of many brokerage firms easily accessible by ordinary individuals. Savers can also invest *indirectly* by providing funds to a financial institution (such as a bank or mutual fund) that channels those funds to borrowers. A share of stock represents partial ownership of a corporation, and its value is determined by the earning capacity of the firm. A bond, on the other hand, represents debt of the corporation. Bonds are typically sold in $1,000 denominations and pay a fixed amount of interest. If you own a bond, you are a creditor of the firm.

return on investment The earnings, such as interest or capital gains, that a saver receives for making funds available to others. It is calculated as earnings divided by the amount invested.

Bond Prices and Interest Rates

We examined real interest rates when we described the loanable funds market, and we described several direct and indirect financial instruments such as stocks, savings accounts, and bonds. But most of the loanable funds are in the form of corporate or government *bonds*. In 2019, the total value of loans made by U.S. commercial banks was over $13 trillion, the total value of the U.S. bond market was about $41 trillion, and the total value of stocks traded in U.S. stock exchanges was about $34 trillion.

Due to the sheer size of the U.S. bond market, economists frequently look at financial markets from the viewpoint of the supply and demand for bonds. They often consider policy implications by their impact on the price of bonds and the quantity traded. It can be a little confusing because bond prices and interest rates are inversely related—when interest rates go up, bond prices go down, and vice versa. Let's take a quick look at the characteristics of bonds to help you see why interest rates and bond prices move in opposite directions. Understanding this will give you a better understanding of how monetary policy actually works.

To see why bond prices and interest rates are inversely related, we need to analyze bond contracts more closely. A bond is a contract between a seller (the company or government issuing the bond) and a buyer that determines the following:

- Coupon rate of the bond
- Maturity date of the bond
- Face value of the bond

The coupon rate is a fixed rate of interest paid to the holder of a corporate or government bond. The coupon rate is paid on the face value of the bond (usually $1,000 for a corporate bond but often much larger values for government bonds) until a future fixed date (the maturity date of the bond). For example, if XYZ Company issues a bond with a face value of $1,000 at a coupon rate of 5%, it agrees to pay the bondholder $50 per year until the maturity date of the bond. Note that this $50 payment per year is *fixed* for the life of the bond.

Once a bond is issued, it is subject to the forces of the marketplace. As economic circumstances change, people may be willing to pay more or less for a bond that originally sold for $1,000. The *yield* on a bond is the percentage return earned over the life of the bond. Yields change when bond prices change.

Assume, for instance, that when a $1,000 bond is issued, general interest rates are 5% so that the bond yields an annual interest payment of $50. For simplicity, let's assume that the bond is a perpetuity bond—that is, the bond has no maturity date. The issuer of the bond has agreed to pay $50 a year *forever* for the use of this money.

Assume that market interest rates rise to 8%. Just how much would the typical investor now be willing to pay for this bond that returns $50 a year? We can approach this intuitively. If we can buy a $1,000 bond now that pays $80 per year, why would we pay $1,000 for a similar bond that pays only $50? Would we pay more or less for the bond that pays $50? If we can get a bond that pays $80 for $1,000, we would pay *less* for a bond paying $50.

There is a simple formula we can use for perpetuity bonds:

$$\text{Yield} = \frac{\text{Annual Interest Payment}}{\text{Price of Bond}}$$

Or rearranging terms:

$$\text{Price of Bond} = \frac{\text{Interest Payment}}{\text{Yield}}$$

The new price of the bond will be $625 ($50 ÷ 0.08 = $625). Clearly, as market interest rates went up, the price of this bond fell. Conversely, if market interest rates were to fall, say, from 5% to 3%, the price of the bond would rise to $1,666.67 ($50 ÷ 0.03 = $1,666.67).

Keep this relationship between interest rates and bond prices in mind when we focus on the tools of monetary policy in the next couple of chapters, for this approach to bond pricing is important to understanding how the government manages the money supply through the purchase and sale of bonds.

Stocks and Investment Returns

An alternative to placing savings into banks or bonds is to purchase shares of stock (also known as equity) in a company. When one buys a share of stock, this share represents one fraction (of the total shares issued) of ownership in the company and subsequently one vote at shareholder meetings and one share of any dividends (periodic payments to shareholders).

The buying and selling of stock shares occur in stock exchanges (such as the New York Stock Exchange or NASDAQ). The price of a share of stock is determined by supply and demand just as in any other market, and for every buyer of a share of stock there must be a seller.

Compared to bonds, stocks tend to be riskier investments because shares, representing partial ownership as opposed to a creditor of a company, become worthless when a company goes bankrupt. Bonds are generally considered safer investments because bondholders are the first to be repaid when businesses face financial trouble. However, stockholders get to share in the company's profits through dividend payments and the increase in share values, which can be substantial when a company succeeds. Both bonds and stocks are less liquid than savings and checking accounts, as both require the asset to be sold and a small commission paid in order to convert the asset into cash.

Which pays more over the long run, bonds or stocks? Given their higher risk, stocks tend to reward investors with a higher average return on investment over the long run, which follows the general rule of the **tradeoff between lower risk and higher returns.** Riskier assets typically offer a greater return; otherwise, investors would not choose to take such risks. For example, investing in lower-risk assets such as Treasury bonds and CDs means giving up a higher average return on investment. On the other hand, stock market values generally trend upward, allowing investors to earn a higher average return on investment. However, achieving higher average returns means accepting greater risk. Some companies may go bankrupt, or the entire stock market may crash.

The complexity of the financial system offers savers and borrowers many opportunities to conduct economic transactions quickly and efficiently. But because the financial system also can be subject to corruption, financial institutions are heavily regulated to ensure the soundness and safety of the financial system and to increase the transparency and information to investors. The agencies regulating financial markets include the Securities and Exchange Commission (SEC), the Federal Reserve System, the FDIC, and another half dozen or so federal agencies, along with all the state agencies regulating firms in this market.

Although heavily regulated, financial markets are complex environments that occasionally experience crises that can lead the economy into a recession and result in huge losses for the affected firms. When meltdowns occur, the bridge that financial intermediaries bring between savers and lenders can collapse.

tradeoff between lower risk and higher returns When choosing to invest in lower-risk assets, one must give up higher average returns on investment, and vice versa.

✓ CHECKPOINT

THE FINANCIAL SYSTEM

- Financial institutions are financial intermediaries that build a bridge between savers and borrowers.

- Financial institutions reduce information costs, transaction costs, and risk, making financial markets more efficient.

- Efficient financial markets foster growth because they maximize the amount of funds channeled from savers to borrowers.

- Financial assets include savings and checking accounts, certificates of deposit (CDs), bonds, stocks, and mutual funds.

- Bond prices and interest rates are inversely related.

QUESTION: In 2016 Governor Cuomo of New York presented plans to completely renovate LaGuardia airport in New York City at a cost of over $8 billion. A portion of the cost is being financed by investment banks, another portion by Delta Airlines (which operates the most flights out of the airport), and the remainder by state and local governments. Explain how financial intermediation is necessary in order to make this project a reality. Why couldn't the state government just pay for it using tax revenues it collects this year?

Answers to the Checkpoint questions can be found at the end of this chapter.

FINANCIAL TOOLS FOR A BETTER FUTURE

Now that we have discussed the role of money, the market for loanable funds, and financial intermediaries, we should step back and ask ourselves how we can apply what we have learned to our everyday finances and our future. As a caveat, it is always best to seek financial advice from a trusted professional who has your best interests in mind. This section is meant to introduce you to the basic financial concepts encountered when borrowing and saving money.

Short-Term Borrowing

teaser rates Promotional low interest rates offered by lenders for a short period of time to attract new customers and to encourage spending.

As a college student, your income is low to nonexistent as you invest (very wisely) in human capital by pursuing a college degree that will increase your earning potential during your working years. That means that in the near term, you will likely accumulate debt in the form of student loans, credit card balances, and car loans. Eventually, a home mortgage might also necessitate more borrowing.

Interest rates on personal debt vary considerably, with small differences leading to substantial payments over the long run, as we will see shortly. Student loans funded by the government typically offer low interest rates in addition to allowing you to defer payments until after you graduate. These loans often provide the lowest cost of borrowing to get you through until your income rises.

The most common short-term loan, however, comes in the form of credit card debt. Credit card companies typically charge a higher interest rate, although on occasion may provide **teaser rates**—offers of low or even zero interest for a limited time on purchases and/or balance transfers. They are called *teasers* because credit card companies hope that you actually *don't* pay off your balance at the end of the offer period. Interest rates after the offer period increase considerably and often are higher than other borrowing rates. In addition, many credit cards charge balance transfer fees of 3% to 5% of the transferred amount, which means the 0% offer that you enjoy for a limited time is not truly 0%.

Due to the high costs of holding credit card debt, it is generally advisable to:

Plastic surgery for your debt.

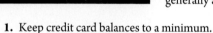

1. Keep credit card balances to a minimum.

2. Find lower cost borrowing opportunities (such as student loans or bank loans) to keep higher interest credit card balances lower.

3. Avoid applying for too many credit cards because fees can rack up and credit scores can be negatively affected by excessive credit applications.

4. Never miss a minimum payment, for *any amount*, even for a month. Every missed payment remains on credit reports for years, potentially raising costs for future car loans and home mortgages and even making insurance and certain jobs harder to find.

The Power (or Danger) of Compounding Interest

compounding effect The effect of interest added to existing debt (or savings) leading to substantial growth in debt (or savings) over the long run.

Interest rates are an important factor in deciding how to go about borrowing or saving money. For the most part, we see interest rates as being quite low, typically less than 10%. The exceptions typically are for credit card debt or high-risk lending when the borrower has a greater likelihood of defaulting on the loan.

But even for low interest rates, the effect on long-run payments can be substantial due to the **compounding effect.** Compounding occurs when interest is calculated and added on a

TABLE 1	COMPOUNDING INTEREST AND DEBT		
Year	Starting Value	10% Interest	Ending Value
1	$1,000.00	$100.00	$1,100.00
2	1,100.00	110.00	1,210.00
3	1,210.00	121.00	1,331.00
4	1,331.00	133.10	1,464.10
5	1,464.10	146.41	1,610.51
...	...	...	...
28	13,109.99	1,311.00	14,420.99
29	14,420.99	1,442.10	15,863.09
30	15,863.09	1,586.31	17,449.40

periodic (often daily) basis to money borrowed or saved, in addition to the interest already charged or earned. Let's use annual terms for simplicity. Suppose you borrow $1,000 at a 10% interest rate. Table 1 shows how compounding interest can add up quickly. After a year, you incur $10\% \times \$1,000 = \$100$ in interest charges. Suppose you do not make any payments on the debt. The next year, you incur $10\% \times \$1,100$ (the original debt + interest already charged) = $110 in interest.

This may not seem like much. But suppose you do not make any payments on the debt for 30 years. Your original $1,000 debt will become $17,449! In fact, in year 30 alone, nearly $1,600 in interest would be added to the debt, more than the original borrowed amount. That is the danger of compounding interest on borrowed debt and an important reason to seek low interest rates and make adequate payments. The good news, however, is that while compounding works against those with debt, it helps those who save, leading to higher future wealth.

Risk Assessment and Asset Allocation

As you work and accumulate savings, an important question is how to go about putting unspent money into assets that will grow over the years until you eventually need it.

The simplest and most liquid means of saving might be to keep money in cash stashed in a safe place or just letting money sit in a checking or savings account at your local bank. Although these methods give you the quickest access to your money, they are unlikely to provide much gain in value. Most checking accounts and even savings accounts pay no interest (and if they do, nowadays it's often less than 1%). With inflation, when you eventually want to use the money, the purchasing power of that money has decreased. How does one go about choosing an asset that pays higher returns?

An important consideration when choosing the type of investment is your tolerance for risk. Would you be frantic if you see your savings fluctuate up and down each day? Would you instead prefer to see steady growth of your savings? Or would you be willing to accept some volatility, the fact that some investments may fall in value, in exchange for a chance of higher growth over the long term?

Risk tolerance should reflect the type of investment instruments purchased. A less risky portfolio would contain a large portion of savings in assets such as CDs and high-rated bonds and "blue chip" stocks. A more risky portfolio would contain a greater portion of savings in growth stocks and high-return bonds.

As described in the previous section, riskier assets typically offer a greater average return. This choice between lower risk and higher returns not only affects one's personal investments but also affects how one goes about saving for the future and for retirement, which we discuss next.

Saving for the Future: Employer-Based Programs

Upon graduating from college, among the exciting challenges facing the new graduate is seeking a good job and earning a salary that allows for a more comfortable life. But besides earning more money, decisions must be made about how to *save* for the future.

Suppose you find your dream job and begin work. Besides the Social Security (FICA) tax that is taken out of each paycheck to fund retirement benefits, you are asked whether you want to contribute to your employer's retirement program. Do you contribute, and if so, how much? 3%? 6%? More? And once you contribute to an account, in what type of assets do you invest that money? Safe or risky assets, or some combination? Tolerance of risk becomes a very important factor in these decisions.

Let's begin by looking at employer-based savings programs, the most common being the 401(k) (offered by most privately held and publicly traded companies), though similar programs exist for government employees and tax-exempt organizations [such as 403(b)].

To Contribute or Not to Contribute? Most retirement savings programs allow (or in some cases require) employees to contribute a certain percentage of their wage earnings into a retirement account. Many companies will then offer a full or partial match of the contribution (often 3% or 4% of one's salary).

vesting period The minimum number of years a worker must be employed before the company's contribution to a retirement account becomes permanent.

If your employer offers to match savings contributions, this is essentially "free money" that is added to your savings, dramatically increasing your return as long as you satisfy the **vesting period,** the minimum years of employment required for the employer-paid portion to become permanent in the account, even if you leave the company.

Suppose you contribute $1,000 into the savings program, and your employer matches it with another $1,000. You will have instantly earned a 100% return on your investment as long as the vesting period has been satisfied. Try finding another financial asset that offers this high a return!

Another benefit of 401(k) (or similar) programs is that contributions are tax-deferred, meaning that an employee does not pay income tax on the contributed amount until the money is eventually withdrawn. Why does this matter?

Suppose you earn $75,000 in taxable income. This means you are in the 22% tax bracket for most income earned. Suppose you increase your 401(k) contribution by $1,000. How much does your take-home pay fall? As you normally would pay 22% in income tax on the $1,000, your take-home pay would fall by only $1,000(1−0.22) = $780. Essentially, you give up $780 now to add an additional $1,000 into your retirement account. That is $220 (or 28% of $780) in extra savings right from the start, on top of the investment earnings on that additional amount compounded over your life until the money is eventually withdrawn.

A downside of most retirement plans is the restriction on when you can use the savings. The minimum age for withdrawing money from most 401(k) accounts is 59.5 years. Withdrawing money before this age incurs (with few exceptions) a 10% early withdrawal penalty.

In What Assets Should One Invest? Suppose you have decided to contribute to your employer's retirement plan and to take advantage of the employer match and tax benefits. Now you are given online access to your account, where you see many options on where to invest your money.

As with all investments, risk assessment is an important consideration when it comes to managing retirement accounts. Most accounts allow you to choose a portfolio of investments ranging from safe assets (such as Treasury bills) to risky assets (such as high-growth stocks). Many financial advisors suggest that you choose a higher risk portfolio in your younger years, then gradually reduce your risk as you approach retirement. Why? Let's use the 2007–2009 stock market crash as an example.

Between October 2007 and March 2009, major stock market indexes fell by nearly 50%. Retirement accounts that were invested fully in stocks fell drastically in value. This had devastating effects on older workers who had not transitioned to safer assets as they approached retirement. However, for younger workers, stock market drops tend to have minimal effects in the long run. In fact, temporary dips in the stock market can even *improve* outcomes over time, as the Issue in this section describes.

Other Retirement Savings Tools: Social Security, Pensions, and IRAs

In addition to employer-sponsored retirement contribution funds, other programs exist that allow individuals to save for their future. These include Social Security, employer-based pension programs, and individual retirement arrangement (IRA, also known as individual retirement account) programs.

Social Security Social Security is another form of retirement savings that nearly every American participates in from the time they start working as a teenager. The payroll tax (FICA) is 12.4% (of which 6.2% is paid by employees and 6.2% is paid by employers) of wage earnings up to $132,900 in 2019. Unlike 401(k) contributions, the money you contribute to FICA is not yours but rather is used to pay the benefits of those currently collecting Social Security benefits. Benefits are determined by a formula based on one's lifetime contributions.

The minimum age to begin collecting Social Security is 62, though if you wait until age 67, monthly benefits will be greater and potentially will pay more overall if you live longer. Of course, if you have a family history of shorter lifespans, it might be a good idea to start collecting sooner.

Some have argued that Social Security is unfair to the poor, who generally have lower life expectancies than the rich. If the minimum age for collecting Social Security rises due to a shortfall of funds, those with lower life expectancies might not collect anything (except for a portion that can be bequeathed to a spouse or heir).

Pension Plans **Pensions** are an alternative to 401(k)-type accounts. Pensions are monthly payments made by your employer from the day you retire until you die, based on the number of years you worked at the company and the salary that you earned. For example, a person who worked at a company 30 years might receive a pension of $3,000 per month upon retirement for the rest of his or her life, while someone who worked only 10 years might receive $1,000 per month.

pensions A retirement plan in which an employer pays a monthly amount to retired employees until they die.

Employers are increasingly switching from pension plans to defined-contribution plans such as a 401(k) to better predict expenses. But a few notable jobs retain comfortable pensions: The president of the United States receives a pension of over $200,000 every year after leaving office.

Finally, in addition to personal savings, investments, 401(k), and pensions plans, many individuals choose to save using individual retirement arrangements (IRAs).

Individual Retirement Arrangements (IRAs) Similar to 401(k) programs, traditional IRA programs allow one to save pretax (tax-deferred) dollars up to a certain limit, which, as discussed earlier, gives an immediate boost to savings compared to posttax dollars. Traditional IRA accounts allow one to invest in a broad range of stocks, bonds, and other assets. The minimum age to withdraw funds without penalty is 59.5 years, and taxes are paid on money withdrawn. (Note that most retirees are in a lower tax bracket compared to their tax bracket during their working years.)

An alternative to a traditional IRA is a Roth IRA, which allows posttax dollars to be contributed up to a certain limit each year. Why would one contribute posttax dollars as opposed to pretax dollars? First, with a Roth IRA, money that you contribute (but not the earnings

ISSUE

Can a Stock Market Crash Increase Long-Term Savings?

From October 2007 to March 2009, major U.S. stock market indices (Dow, NASDAQ, and S&P 500) fell by more than 50% from their peaks. Investment accounts that took decades to accumulate saw their values drop in half in less than 17 months. The same was true for many retirement accounts, such as 401(k) and IRA accounts, which often are heavily invested in stocks. Indeed, this was a bleak period to follow one's retirement savings, not to mention the equally devastating loss in housing values during this period. Would the drop in stock values create long-term consequences for retirement? The answer may be surprising.

Although money invested up to October 2007 suffered a severe decline in value, most workers who continued to contribute to their retirement plans (and with matching employer additions to the new funds) saw their retirement portfolio values bounce back within a few years. How did this happen?

As new money entered retirement plans during the stock market decline, these funds were invested in assets at their new *lower* prices. When stock values recovered, old funds regained their values, while new funds saw healthy gains in value. The following example illustrates two scenarios using hypothetical numbers.

This hypothetical scenario shows that a drop in the stock market may not cause a major problem for retirement savings

over the long run *as long as* one continues to work and contribute toward retirement. Younger workers will feel less of an impact from a stock market correction because they haven't yet accumulated a large amount of investments. Meanwhile, new funds invested at lower prices can earn substantial gains over several decades. Unfortunately, some people sold their stocks after the crash and became hesitant to invest, thereby missing out on the quick recovery that occurred in subsequent years. The moral of the story: Don't panic. Slow and steady wins the race.

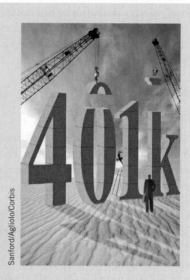

Sanford/Agliolo/Corbis

Scenario 1: Stocks fall 50% over the next year, then fully recover three years later.
Scenario 2: Stock market stays at the same exact level for the entire four-year period.

Description	Scenario 1	Scenario 2
Initial Account Balance:	$100,000	$100,000
Change in Value After Event:	–$50,000	–$0
Scenario 1: 50% fall in stock prices		
Scenario 2: No change in stock prices		
Account Balance After Event:	$50,000	$100,000
New Contributions Over Four Years:	+$30,000	+$30,000
Earnings on New Contributions:	+$20,000	+$0
Scenario 1: Purchased at an average of 40% below peak prices, resulting in a 67% gain		
Scenario 2: Purchased at original stock prices, with no increase in value		
Change in Value of Original Contributions:	+$50,000	+$0
Scenario 1: Full recovery in stock prices		
Scenario 2: No change in stock prices		
Total Value of Account	**$150,000**	**$130,000**

on contributions except in certain circumstances) can be withdrawn anytime without penalty. Second, Roth IRAs do not incur any taxes upon withdrawal after age 59.5, including the interest and capital gains the account accumulates over its life. Thus, while one pays taxes upfront on initial contributions, no taxes are paid on earnings, which can be very substantial with compounding.

Saving for the future is an important financial decision. Fortunately, many programs, such as 401(k), Social Security, and IRAs, make the process easier.

✓ CHECKPOINT

FINANCIAL TOOLS FOR A BETTER FUTURE

- Credit cards typically are an expensive way to finance borrowing, even with teaser rates.

- Debt and savings rise rapidly over the long run due to the compounding effect.

- Riskier assets generally offer a higher average return on investment, whereas safer assets offer a lower average return on investment.

- Company-sponsored retirement accounts, such as a 401(k), allow employees to contribute pretax dollars and receive matching company contributions.

- Social Security is a program into which current contributors (workers) pay for benefits of the recipients (retirees) by way of a payroll tax.

- Individual retirement arrangements (IRAs) are similar to 401(k) programs in that pretax dollars are saved for retirement, lowering one's taxable income. However, IRAs provide greater investment choices.

QUESTIONS: Suppose Nicole is very risk averse with her money, while José likes to invest in riskier assets in hopes of a higher return. What type of assets would be best suited for each person? Assuming that the relationship between risk and return is maintained over the next 30 years, how would Nicole's savings compare to José's given the compounding effect (assuming each saves the same amount)?

Answers to the Checkpoint questions can be found at the end of this chapter.

CHAPTER SUMMARY

SECTION 1 WHAT IS MONEY?

Money is anything that is accepted in exchange for goods and services, or for the payments of debts.

11.1 **Three Primary Functions of Money**

1. **Medium of exchange:** Eliminates the double coincidence of wants common to barter.
2. **Unit of account:** Reduces the number of prices needed to just one per good.
3. **Store of value:** Allows people to save now and spend later.

11.2 **Two Primary Money Supply Measures**

M1 = currency in circulation (banknotes and coins) and checkable deposits.

M2 = M1 + "near monies" (savings accounts, money market deposit accounts, small-denomination time deposits, and money market mutual fund accounts).

An asset's **liquidity** is determined by how fast, easily, and reliably it can be converted into cash.

Most Liquid

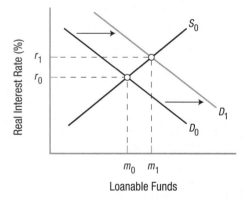

Tom Grill/Corbis · Jeffrey Coolidge/The Image Bank/Getty Images · Cole Perkins

Least Liquid

SECTION 2 THE MARKET FOR LOANABLE FUNDS

11.3 The **market for loanable funds** describes the financial market for saving and investment.

Savers provide more funds to the loanable funds market as interest rates increase. Therefore, S_0 slopes upward.

Firms demand more funds for investment opportunities as interest rates fall. Therefore, D_0 slopes downward.

11.4 Factors affecting the willingness to save or borrow lead to a change in the market for loanable funds. For example, growing business confidence increases firms' willingness to invest, thus shifting the demand curve for loanable funds to the right, causing interest rates to rise and the amount of loanable funds to increase.

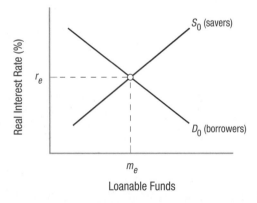

SECTION 3 THE FINANCIAL SYSTEM

James Leynse/Getty Images

Banks, savings and loans associations, credit unions, insurance companies, securities firms (brokerages), and pension funds are all types of financial intermediaries that take savings from savers and loan the funds to borrowers.

11.5 **Financial intermediaries** accept funds from savers and efficiently channel them to borrowers, reducing transaction and information costs, as well as lowering risk.

A bond is a contract between a seller (government or company) and a buyer. As a general rule, as market interest rates rise, the value of bonds (paying a fixed dollar amount of interest) fall, and vice versa.

11.6 **How to Calculate the Price of a Perpetuity Bond**

Price of Bond = Annual Interest Payment ÷ Yield (%)

Example: If a bond pays $100 per year and the yield is 6%, the price of the bond is $100 ÷ 0.06 = $1,667.

SECTION 4 FINANCIAL TOOLS FOR A BETTER FUTURE

11.7 The **compounding effect** is powerful because it causes debt (if no payments are made) and savings to increase dramatically over time.

$10,000 in savings today invested at:
5%: equals $43,219 in 30 years
10%: equals $174,495 in 30 years

$10,000/year saved ($300,000 total over 30 years) invested at:
5%: equals $707,608 in 30 years
10%: equals $1,819,435 in 30 years

11.8 **Tradeoff Between Lower Risk and Higher Returns:** Investing in lower-risk assets means giving up a higher average return on investment. Investing in assets with higher potential returns means accepting greater levels of risk.

U.S. Savings Bonds and Treasury securities are among the safest assets in the world. Due to their low risk, the interest rates paid are very low.

11.9 **Programs for Retirement Savings**

Employer-sponsored programs:

- Defined-contribution plans, such as 401(k) and 403(b), allow workers to contribute pretax dollars and employers to partially match contributions.
- **Pensions** are monthly payments made by employers to their retired employees based on length of employment with the company and salary earned.

Government-sponsored programs:

- Social Security: Current workers pay benefits of retirees through the payroll tax on wages.

Other retirement programs:

- Traditional IRAs use pretax dollars to fund investments; taxes are paid upon withdrawal after age 59.5.
- Roth IRAs use after-tax dollars to fund investments. Contributed funds (but not earnings on those contributions) can be withdrawn anytime without penalty, and no taxes are paid on withdrawals (including earnings on investments) after one reaches the age of 59.5.

Key Concepts

money, p. 272

fiat money, p. 272

barter, p. 272

medium of exchange, p. 273

unit of account, p. 273

store of value, p. 273

liquidity, p. 273

M1, p. 274

M2, p. 274

financial system, p. 280

financial intermediaries, p. 280

return on investment, p. 281

tradeoff between lower risk and higher returns, p. 283

teaser rates, p. 284

compounding effect, p. 284

vesting period, p. 286

pensions, p. 287

Questions and Problems

Check Your Understanding

1. Describe the three functions of money.

2. What is a barter economy? Explain why such an approach is difficult for a modern economy.

3. What is the difference between a pension plan and a defined-contribution plan, such as a 401(k) account?

4. What gives money value if there is no gold or silver backing the currency?

5. What happens to savings if the real interest rate goes up? What happens to the demand for borrowing?

6. What are some similarities and differences between cryptocurrency and U.S. dollars that are stored on a popular phone app?

Apply the Concepts

7. List the following assets from most liquid to least liquid: a house (real estate); cash; a one-carat diamond; savings account deposits; 100 shares of Google stock; a Harley-Davidson motorcycle; a checking account; your old leather jacket.

8. At many game centers (such as Dave & Buster's), it is common for kids to play carnival-type games to win prize tickets, which are then redeemed for a variety of prizes based on the number of tickets earned. In what ways do these prize tickets illustrate the three functions of money?

9. During an economic expansion when businesses are increasing their investment spending and individuals are more willing to increase their consumption, what happens to the demand and supply of loanable funds? What is the effect on real interest rates?

10. Most individuals with average wealth choose to save their money using a financial intermediary such as a bank or a mutual fund. However, individuals with greater wealth are more likely to invest in individual stocks or directly in new or existing businesses. Explain why persons of different wealth are likely to show differences in how they save and how financial intermediaries play a role.

11. Why would it be better to put $1,000 each year into a retirement account than to wait ten years and put in $10,000 all at once? Would it make much of a difference in the long run?

12. If the stock market and bond market are substitutes for one another, what is expected to happen to bond prices if the stock market increases sharply and investors move more money from bonds into stocks? If this occurs, what will happen to interest rates on bonds?

In the News

13. One of the proposals put forth by economists to address the future expected shortfall in Social Security funding is to raise the minimum age when one can begin collecting benefits from 62 to 65. The rationale is that as people live longer, the benefits being collected exceed the amounts contributed during one's working years, which is unsustainable. If such a proposal becomes law, how would this affect the incentives to work and save? How would this impact the market for loanable funds?

14. In late 2018, SpaceX CEO Gwynne Shotwell announced the company's goal of sending people to the Moon by 2023 and to Mars within a decade. This announcement was tied to another round of investment funding from which the company hoped to raise $500 million from investors and to borrow $250 million from banks. How does investing in SpaceX compare to other investments (such as buying stocks or bonds in well-known companies) in terms of risk? What would be the expected return on investment?

Solving Problems

15. Suppose a small country has the following monies in circulation:

> Cash/currency: $5 million
> Checkable deposits: $14 million
> Small-denomination time deposits: $15 million
> Savings deposits: $20 million
> Money market deposit accounts: $25 million

Calculate the value of M1 and M2 for this country.

Work It Out

 interactive activity

16. The yield for a perpetuity bond is determined by the simple formula

$$\text{Yield} = \frac{\text{Annual Interest Payment}}{\text{Price of Bond}}$$

a. Calculate the yield on a $1,000 perpetuity bond that pays $40 a year forever to the bondholder.

b. Suppose that actions taken by the Fed cause interest rates in the economy to fall by 2%. How will this affect the price of the bond that still pays $40 a year in interest?

c. Now suppose that one purchases a new $1,000 perpetuity bond at the lower interest rate. What will the annual interest payment be equal to?

d. If interest rates were to rise back to the original level determined in part (a), how will that affect the price of the new bond purchased in part (c)?

✓ Answers to Questions in Checkpoints

Checkpoint: What Is Money? 276

Because the purchasing power of the penny has fallen significantly since its first introduction, its monetary role also has diminished. The penny still serves as a medium of exchange, though the ease of its use has become so difficult that pennies often are left in coin jars, tip jars, and charity bins, as opposed to being kept for everyday use. Its function as a unit of account remains since most prices are still quoted to the nearest penny. And its function as a store of value remains, though a substantial jar of pennies would be needed before taking the time to bring it to a coin exchange machine or the bank.

Checkpoint: The Market for Loanable Funds 279

A fall in business confidence would reduce the demand for loanable funds, shifting the demand curve to the left in Figure 2. Meanwhile, increased insecurity about jobs will encourage people to save more, shifting the supply of savings to the right. These shifts create a huge surplus of funds at the original interest rate, and therefore interest rates would fall until a new equilibrium is reached. As the economy recovers, businesses resume their investments and consumers begin spending again, and the demand curve will shift back to the right and the supply curve would shift to the left. Interest rates would then trend upward.

Checkpoint: The Financial System 283

The renovation of LaGuardia airport is a costly multiyear project that is too large to be paid for using taxes from any one year. Even if the state government pays for it using taxes over many years, it still must borrow the money first. Therefore, financial intermediation by banks and other financial institutions is required. But financing the airport renovation requires more than just financial institutions. It also relies on the bond market, where investors lend money and expect to be paid back with interest. It also relies on the equity market by selling partial ownership of the airport to investors in exchange for a share of earnings from airport operations. Finally, a substantial amount of money was provided by Delta Airlines, which will benefit from more efficient operations as well as improved customer satisfaction.

Checkpoint: Financial Tools for a Better Future 289

Because Nicole is more risk averse with her money, she would choose a low-risk portfolio containing safer bonds and stocks, while José, being more risk preferring, would invest in growth stocks and high-yield bonds. If the tradeoff between lower risk and higher returns holds, José's savings would grow at a higher average annual rate than Nicole's. With compounding, José's savings over the long run will likely be substantially larger than Nicole's. One exception might be if a stock market crash occurs at the end, in which José's savings would fall if he didn't reduce the riskiness of his portfolio in the later years. Even so, with the power of compounding, José's portfolio would likely be much higher than Nicole's even if a stock market crash did occur.

12

Money Creation and the Federal Reserve

Understanding how banks play a powerful role in the economy by accepting deposits and lending money

Learning Objectives

12.1 Explain how banks create money by accepting deposits and making loans.

12.2 Define fractional reserve banking and explain why banks can lend much more than they keep in reserves.

12.3 Explain how the money multiplier works and how it makes monetary policy decisions very powerful.

12.4 Define a money leakage and explain how it reduces the effect of the money multiplier.

12.5 Describe the history and structure of the Federal Reserve System.

12.6 List the important banking functions conducted by the Federal Reserve regional banks and their branches.

12.7 Describe the Federal Reserve's principal monetary tools.

12.8 Analyze the federal funds rate and how it affects all other interest rates.

12.9 Explain why the Federal Reserve's policies take time to affect the economy.

I n small towns and villages throughout Central and South Asia, Africa, and Latin America, entrepreneurship is flourishing. These are not your typical high-tech start-ups or research and development centers but rather primitive small shops selling basic goods and services. Many got their start using a microloan—a small loan (as little as $50) offered by organizations aiming to promote business enterprise among individuals who would not qualify for traditional bank loans.

These small loans and the new businesses they help create (largely by women in the poorest parts of the world) have been credited with bringing more people out of poverty in recent years than direct foreign aid has. How can a tiny loan of $50 have such a positive effect on the economy?

Quite easily, in fact. In Bangladesh, Fatima takes her $50 loan and buys cotton to make a dozen sharis. She sells the sharis at the local outdoor market for a total of $120, of which she uses $50 to pay back her microloan and $70 to buy more cotton to make even more sharis. Only this time, she is debt-free, allowing her to use all her proceeds to expand her business and provide income for her family. Meanwhile, the $50 she paid back will be loaned to another entrepreneur, allowing another small business to get its start.

When a small loan is used to create a new business, jobs are created, which allows people to spend money at other businesses (also likely started from a microloan). The collective power of new businesses, jobs, and increased spending leads to healthy economic growth in the village, and it all started from a single microloan. Now, multiply this one case by the thousands of microloans being made available throughout the developing world, and the effect on reducing poverty is staggering. This example represents a microcosm of the global economy and the money creation process in which financial intermediaries play an important role.

This chapter will explain how banks and financial institutions create money through the process of accepting deposits and making loans. This is an important part of maintaining a healthy economy and promoting economic growth. However, in times of economic

A microloan bank in Burkina Faso.

Afghan women attend a village meeting to make payments on their microloans.

BY THE Numbers

$3,346,896,000,000

Size of the U.S. monetary base in January 2019

The Federal Reserve: *Its Role in Managing the Money Supply and Interest Rates*

Banks create money by accepting deposits and making loans. This process is aided by the Federal Reserve (Fed), which influences interest rates and sets reserve requirements for member banks. The Fed serves as the bank for all commercial banks as well as the lender of last resort for financial institutions facing insolvency. The Fed's role increased significantly during and after the 2007–2009 recession and financial crisis. Its actions dramatically affected the monetary base, which consists of all currency in circulation and reserves held by banks. This By the Numbers analyzes the U.S. monetary base over the last 30 years.

85

Total number of months (from December 2008 to January 2016) that the federal funds rate was targeted at 0% to 0.25%, the lowest rate in over 50 years

DATA:

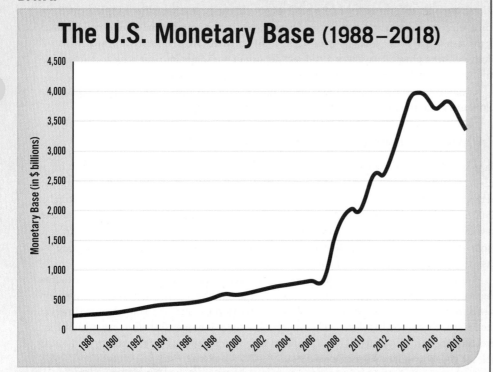

The U.S. Monetary Base (1988–2018)

Where Can I Find These Data?

Source: FRED Database; Federal Reserve Bank of St. Louis
Web site: https://fred.stlouisfed.org
Details: Search for "Monetary Base" and select "Monetary Base; Total"

WHY ARE THESE DATA IMPORTANT?

The Federal Reserve plays an important role in stabilizing the economy through its role as the lender of last resort. When banks were struggling to remain solvent during the 2007–2009 recession and financial crisis, the Fed purchased many high-risk assets (such as mortgage-backed securities) from banks using reserves that it created electronically. The increase in reserves led to the increase in the monetary base.

Data *in the News*

"Fed's Brainard Says Balance-Sheet Runoff Should Probably End This Year" by Nick Timiraos; *Wall Street Journal*, February 14, 2019

The process of passively shrinking the Fed's $4 trillion holdings of bonds and other assets "has really done the work that it was supposed to do."

~ Assessing Your Data Literacy ~

1. By approximately how much (in dollars and in percentage) did the U.S. monetary base increase from 2007 to 2014?

2. By approximately how much (in dollars and in percentage) did the U.S. monetary base decrease from 2014 to 2018?

3. Why did the U.S. monetary base continue to increase even after the recession ended in 2009?

downturn or a slow recovery, banks and other financial institutions are less willing to lend money because of the greater likelihood of loans not being repaid. In response, the government will often take action.

The Federal Reserve (or Fed), the central bank of the United States, has extensive power in controlling the supply of money and interest rates, key elements in its arsenal of tools to jump-start the economy when markets fail to do so on their own. After the 2007–2009 recession, the Fed took dramatic steps to make borrowing less expensive for consumers and homeowners and to provide banks with more capital and the confidence to lend to qualified borrowers.

The latter half of this chapter studies the history and structure of the Fed along with its role as the guarantor of our money and our financial system. We analyze the policies and tools the Fed can use to influence the money supply and interest rates.

HOW BANKS CREATE MONEY

When most people think of money being created, one typically imagines large machines at government institutions printing sheets of crisp new banknotes or a large mint hammering out shiny new coins. Although this is indeed money creation in the literal sense, in reality currency represents less than half of the money supply, as we saw in the previous chapter.

Most money that we use every day involves not cash and coins but rather a sophisticated system of electronic debits and credits to our bank accounts. For example, unless one works primarily for cash tips or runs a small business where most purchases are paid for in cash, most of us will receive either a physical paycheck or a direct deposit of our wages into our bank accounts. Similarly, when we make purchases, most of us might use a debit or a credit card.

Given that most transactions today do not involve cash, the idea of *creating money* takes on an additional meaning, a process in which banks play a very important role.

Creating Money as if Out of Thin Air

Suppose that you run a small tutoring service helping students at your school succeed in (or at least pass) their economics courses. Some of your clients pay you with a personal check at the end of their session, while others give you cash. Let's assume that this month, you received a total of $500 in checks, which you deposit into your checking account, and $500 in cash, which you keep in your safe at home. Your goal is to save as much of your tutoring earnings as possible in order to buy a new car. Aside from the potential forgone interest earnings and the temptation to spend the cash, does it really matter whether you put the cash in the bank or not?

To you, it doesn't. If you need the money, you could just as easily go to an ATM to withdraw the cash as you could take the cash out of your safe. But for the economy, there is in fact an important difference. The $500 you hold in cash is available to you—and only you—to use. However, the $500 in checks you had deposited in your bank account is money that *others* can use until you eventually need it. How is it that other people can use your money and yet this money is still available for you to withdraw when you need it?

Banks hold deposits from many customers at any moment in time. On any given day, only a small portion is withdrawn; the banks service this need for cash by using the reserves they keep on hand (also called vault cash). The rest is loaned out to borrowers who pay interest to the bank, part of which is then used to pay interest on the deposits the bank holds. The deposits and lending that occur in a bank start the money creation process.

To illustrate the power of the money creation process, suppose you decide to take your $500 in cash and deposit it into your checking account. Let's analyze how the bank uses this money using a simplified balance sheet comparing a bank's assets (money the bank claims) and liabilities (money the bank owes) called a T-account. Liabilities are shown on the right side of the T-account. When you deposit money into the bank, it becomes a liability for the bank—the bank owes you this money. However, to balance out this liability, the bank now has an asset consisting of the cash from your deposit. Assets are shown on the left side of the T-account.

The following T-account shows an increase in the bank's assets by $500, the cash that you deposit that the bank now holds. On the right side, the bank's liabilities increase by $500 because it must give back the $500 when you ask for it.

T-Account After Initial Cash Deposit	
Assets	**Liabilities**
Cash +$500	Increase in your checking account balance +$500

It is important to note that based on this initial transaction, no new money has been created in the economy. Why? Cash and demand deposits (checking accounts) are both components of the money supply measured as M1. By taking cash and converting it into a checkable deposit, there is now $500 less cash in circulation but $500 more in checkable deposits, resulting in no change in M1.

But the process is just beginning. Now that the bank has additional reserves, it can lend some of this money to someone else. Suppose another customer at the same bank, Jenna, is running low on cash and needs to take out a small loan of $300 to cover bills that are coming up at the end of the month. How would the bank handle this?

The bank would create a $300 loan for Jenna (which becomes an asset to the bank) and add $300 to Jenna's checking account for her to use when needed. The following shows the updated T-account for the bank.

T-Account After Loan to Jenna	
Assets	**Liabilities**
Cash +$500	Increase in your checking account +$500
Loan to Jenna +$300	Increase in Jenna's checking account +$300

After the loan to Jenna is made, the total amount of checkable deposits has now increased by $800 based on the initial $500 cash deposit. In other words, the bank has *created* $300 in money, as if out of thin air, simply by making a loan to Jenna. And the process doesn't stop there. When Jenna writes a check to the veterinarian for her cat's annual checkup, her veterinarian deposits the check into her bank, which allows that bank to start another round of lending and money creation.

One might now wonder why banks could not just continue making an infinite amount of loans. The reason is that the bank needs to have enough funds in place should you, Jenna, or the veterinarian decide to make a withdrawal to pay bills or make purchases. Thus, a bank's ability to make loans is limited to a certain percentage of its total customer deposits. In other words, a bank must keep some reserves (such as cash) on hand to cover day-to-day withdrawals. The level of reserves a bank holds as a percentage of total deposits is called its **reserve ratio.** Further, the government requires that banks maintain a minimum level of reserves called the **reserve requirement.**

In our example, the reserve ratio is calculated by dividing total reserves by total deposits. In this case, the reserve ratio is $\$500/(\$500 + \$300) = 62.5\%$. Because most reserve requirements are much lower than this percentage, this bank is considered highly liquid. Therefore, the bank may continue to make more loans using your initial cash deposit until the reserve ratio decreases to the reserve requirement.

Until now, we have assumed that all loans and deposits occurred at the same bank, but this need not be true. In fact, most money transactions in our economy take place between banks. But the way in which we analyze loans and deposits and how that leads to money being created does not change. The example above describes the process of a fractional reserve banking system.

reserve ratio The percentage of a bank's total deposits that are held in reserves.

reserve requirement The required ratio of funds that commercial banks and other depository institutions must hold in reserves against deposits.

Fractional Reserve Banking System

Banks loan money for consumer purchases and business investments. Assume that you deposit $1,000 into your checking account and the bank then loans this $1,000 to a local business to purchase some machinery. If you were to go to the bank the next day and ask to withdraw your funds, how would the bank pay you? The bank could not pay you if you were its only depositor. Banks, however, have many depositors, and the chance that everyone would want to withdraw their money on the same day is very small.

Such "runs on the bank" are rare, normally occurring only when banks or a country's currency are in trouble. In the United States, the Federal Deposit Insurance Corporation (FDIC) protects bank deposits (up to $250,000) from bank failure. When a bank gets into financial trouble, the FDIC typically arranges for another (healthy) bank to take over the failing bank, resulting in virtually no interruption of services to the bank's customers. The bank takeover usually occurs late on a Friday, and the bank reopens on Monday morning under a new name. Because most accounts are insured, it is business as usual on Monday.

It was the possibility of bank runs that led to the **fractional reserve banking system.** When someone deposits money into a bank account, the bank is required to hold part of this deposit in its vault as cash, or on deposit with the regional Federal Reserve Bank. We will learn more about the Federal Reserve System later in this chapter, but for the moment, let us continue to concentrate on how fractional reserve banking permits banks to create money.

The Money Creation Process Banks create money by lending some or all of their **excess reserves,** the reserves above the reserve requirement. When a bank makes a loan, the money eventually is deposited back into the original bank or some other bank. The bank will again hold some of these new deposits as reserves, loaning out the rest. This process continues until the entire initial deposit is held as reserves somewhere in the banking system.

Assume that the Federal Reserve sets the reserve requirement at 20%. This means that banks must hold 20% of each deposit in reserve, whether in their vault or in accounts with the regional Federal Reserve Bank. Now assume that you take $1,000 out of your personal safe at home and take it to Bank A. Bank A puts 20% of your $1,000 into its vault as reserves and loans out the rest. Its T-account balance sheet now reads:

Bank A			
Assets		**Liabilities**	
Reserves	+$200	Deposits	+$1,000
Loans	+$800		

As the balance sheet indicates, your $1,000 deposit is now a liability for Bank A. But the bank also has new assets, split between reserves and loans. In each of the transactions that follow, we assume banks become fully *loaned-up*, loaning out all they can and keeping in reserve only the amount required by law.

Assume that Bank A loans out the $800 it has in excess funds to a local gas station, and assume that this money is deposited into Bank B. Bank B's balance sheet now reads:

Bank B			
Assets		**Liabilities**	
Reserves	+$160	Deposits	+$800
Loans	+$640		

Individual bank accounts are protected against bank failure by the FDIC. No FDIC insured deposit has ever been lost in its history.

fractional reserve banking system Describes a banking system in which a portion of bank deposits are held as vault cash or on deposit with the regional Federal Reserve Bank, while the rest of the deposits are loaned out to generate the money creation process.

excess reserves Reserves held by banks above the legally required amount.

Bank B, in other words, has new deposits totaling $800. Of this, the bank must put $160 into reserves; the remaining $640 is loaned out, say to a local winery. The winery deposits these funds into its bank, Bank C, whose balance sheet now shows:

Bank C			
Assets		**Liabilities**	
Reserves	+$128	Deposits	+$640
Loans	+$512		

Summing up the balance sheets of the three banks shows that total reserves have grown to $488 ($200+$160+$128), loans have reached $1,952 ($800+$640+$512), and total deposits are $2,440 ($1,000+$800+$640). Your original $1,000 cash deposit has caused the money supply to grow.

Banks A, B, C			
Assets		**Liabilities**	
Reserves	+$488	Deposits	+$2,440
Loans	+$1,952		

This process continues until the entire $1,000 of the original deposit has been placed in reserves, thus raising total reserves by $1,000. By this point, all the banks together will have loaned out a total of $4,000. A summary balance sheet for all banks reads:

All Banks			
Assets		**Liabilities**	
Reserves	+$1,000	Deposits	+$5,000
Loans	+$4,000		

Notice what has happened. Keeping in mind that demand deposits form part of the money supply, your original deposit of $1,000—cash that was injected into the banking system—has turned into $5,000 in deposits, a $4,000 increase in the money supply. Bank reserves have increased by your initial deposit, but beyond this, an added $4,000 has been created. This was made possible because banks were allowed to loan part of your deposit to consumers and businesses.

The ability of banks to take an initial deposit of cash and turn it into loans and deposits many times over (5 times the initial deposit in our example) demonstrates the power of the banking system to create money. Moreover, the initial deposit of cash need not come from an individual; in fact, much of the money creation that occurs in the economy begins with deposits made by the government, as we will see later in this chapter.

✅ CHECKPOINT

HOW BANKS CREATE MONEY

- Money is created when banks make loans to customers which are eventually deposited into other banks as checkable deposits.

- The fractional reserve system permits banks to create money by accepting deposits and loaning out their excess reserves.

- The reserve ratio is the fraction of total customer deposits held in reserves.

- The reserve requirement is the minimum reserve ratio banks must follow.

- A T-account is a simplified balance sheet showing assets (money banks lay claim to) and liabilities (money banks owe).

QUESTIONS: Suppose that you go to your bank and withdraw $1,000 from your checking account to spend on your spring break vacation to the Caribbean. If the bank has plenty of cash to pay you without falling below its reserve requirement or changing the amount of loans it has, would the money supply M1 change? Would the money supply change if the bank had planned to loan out its excess reserves?

Answers to the Checkpoint questions can be found at the end of this chapter.

THE MONEY MULTIPLIER AND ITS LEAKAGES

We have just seen how banks create money when they make loans using the deposits of their customers. As money is deposited and loaned out over and over, an initial amount of money can generate new deposits and loans many times over. Just how much money can an initial deposit actually create? We use the money multiplier to find the answer.

Bank Reserves and the Money Multiplier

In theory, money creation can be infinite if banks loaned out 100% of all money deposited and all loaned money found its way back into another bank following their business transactions. But this is highly unlikely due to several factors, the most important being reserves held by the bank.

All banks are required to hold a certain percentage of their deposits as reserves in their vault or at their regional Fed bank. This limits the maximum amount of money that can be created.

Given a bank's reserve requirement, the *potential* or *maximum* amount the money supply can increase (or decrease) when a dollar of new deposits enters (or exits) the system is called the **money multiplier.** The money multiplier is calculated as:

money multiplier The *potential* or *maximum* amount the money supply can increase (or decrease) when a dollar of new deposits enters (or exits) the system and is calculated as 1 divided by the reserve requirement.

$$\text{Money Multiplier} = \frac{1}{\text{Reserve Requirement}}$$

Thus, if the reserve requirement is 20%, as in our example in the previous section, the money multiplier is $1/0.20 = 5$. Therefore, an initial deposit of $1,000 will create an additional $4,000 in money for a total of $5,000, a 5-fold increase.

The money multiplier is important to economic policy because money can be initially deposited into the banking system in two ways. The first approach, described earlier, is a cash deposit made by a bank customer. The second approach occurs when the government injects new money into the banking system through the power it has to print money.

When the government "prints money," it does not mean it is printing banknotes and spending it at the mall. Instead, the government typically adds reserves electronically to banks in exchange for bonds and other assets. This money did not exist before the Fed created it by just a stroke of a computer key. When these funds are added to bank reserves, that in itself increases the money supply (unlike a customer's cash that is already counted in the money supply). Further, the effect is compounded by the money multiplier. The government therefore possesses tremendous power in influencing the money supply through its ability to print money, which is then enhanced by the money multiplier.

But the ability of the government to expand the money supply is affected by various factors preventing the full money multiplier from taking place. In other words, the money multiplier formula gives us the *potential* money multiplier. The actual money multiplier will be smaller because of leakages from the banking system. How much smaller?

Money Leakages

The potential money multiplier and the actual money multiplier are rarely the same because of money **leakages.** A leakage is money that leaves the money creation process of deposits and loans due to an action taken by a bank, an individual, a business, or a foreign entity.

leakages A reduction in the amount of money that is used for lending that reduces the effect of the money multiplier. It is caused by banks choosing to hold excess reserves and from individuals, businesses, and foreigners choosing to hold cash.

Bank Leakages Banks are in the business of making loans. If they don't, they likely will not stay in business for long, especially if all they do is accept deposits and pay interest on those deposits. For any bank, profits come from the interest charged on loans made to borrowers. For this reason, it is generally presumed that banks will be loaned-up, or maximize the amount of loans they can make given the reserve requirement.

However, many banks choose not to be loaned-up. Instead, banks hold excess reserves, or reserves above the legally required amount. Why would a bank choose not to loan out the maximum amount of money allowed?

The lessons from the last financial crisis point to the answer. The recession caused many loan defaults and foreclosures as workers were laid off or faced wage cuts. Whenever a borrower defaults on a loan, the amount of that loan is removed (written off) from the bank's assets; however, the bank still owes the people whose deposits made those funds available. Banks absorb these losses through the profits they earn from charging interest to those who pay back their loans. If a large number of borrowers default on their loans, the bank risks becoming **insolvent,** when its liabilities exceed its assets. This means that the bank owes more than what is owed to it, increasing the likelihood of bankruptcy.

insolvent A situation when a bank's liabilities exceed its assets.

Returning to our earlier example, suppose that Jenna used her $300 loan to pay off her bills (transferring money from her account to her creditor's account) but then defaults on her loan. The bank's balance sheet would now read:

Assets		Liabilities	
Cash	+$500	Increase in your checking account	+$500
Loan to Jenna	+$300	Increase in Jenna's creditor's account	+$300
Jenna's default	–$300	*Bank equity*	*–$300*

The difference between assets and liabilities is a bank's equity, or value that is shared by the bank's shareholders. A healthy bank has a positive amount of bank equity as it earns profit from its business. Although equity is not a liability, it appears in the liabilities column because ultimately any gains are distributed to shareholders like a liability. When liabilities exceed assets, as in the case above, the bank has negative equity (shown as –$300 on the right-hand side of the T-account). When this occurs, the bank is insolvent; in other words, it's broke.

To reduce the risk of becoming insolvent, banks often hold excess reserves during tough economic times to ensure that they have the ability to absorb a higher rate of default. Each time a borrower defaults on a loan, a bank's assets fall by the amount of the loss, which reduces the bank's equity. By being more cautious about to whom a bank lends money (which often means not being fully loaned-up), it can reduce the number of defaults to avoid losing its entire equity and becoming insolvent.

When banks choose not to loan all of their excess reserves, the actual money multiplier is reduced because the reduction in loans recirculates less money back through the banking system.

As we saw in the chapter opener, the willingness of banks to lend generates a powerful effect on the economy. We now know that this is due to the money multiplier. However, the lack of lending creates the opposite effect, which makes bank leakages an extremely important obstacle to economic growth.

Got jars of coins? Coins represent a cash leakage. Businesses such as Coinstar convert coins into banknotes or gift cards that are more likely to be spent, helping to bring money back into the banking system.

Leakages by Individuals and Businesses Earlier in the chapter, we saw how holding cash reduces the ability of banks to create money. Why would people choose to hold more cash?

One factor might be the interest rate the bank pays on deposits. If interest rates paid on savings and checking accounts at the bank are near 0, as they has been for much of the past decade, one might choose to hold more savings in cash out of convenience or make fewer trips to the bank by making larger withdrawals from an ATM. Another factor might be a general rise in fear about the financial system. Despite the existence of the FDIC, when banks are in trouble, people begin to believe that their money is less safe in banks and start to hold more cash.

When individuals choose to keep money in cash rather than deposit it in a bank, a leakage in the money supply occurs because that money is not available to be loaned to someone else. The cycle of lending and saving that would be generated from that money comes to a halt, and the actual money multiplier is reduced.

Individuals are not the only ones to hold cash. Most businesses conduct a portion of their transactions using cash. Therefore, at any one time, a business will be holding a certain fraction of its money in cash rather than in a bank. The percentage of cash holdings varies by business but regardless represents a leakage in the money supply. As businesses hold more cash, as do individuals, this diminishes their deposits, thus reducing the effect of the money multiplier and therefore the money creation process.

The Effect of Foreign Currency Holdings Most Americans are accustomed to using debit and credit cards for daily transactions, reducing the need to hold cash. Yet, surprisingly, the U.S. government continues to print billions of new U.S. dollars each year. If Americans generally are holding smaller amounts of cash, who then is holding all of these dollars?

The answer is foreign consumers, businesses, and governments. Due to the relative stability of the U.S. dollar, many countries hold U.S. dollars in reserves in order to provide support to their own currencies. Some countries, such as El Salvador and Ecuador, have abandoned their own currency altogether, choosing to use the U.S. dollar as their only legal form of currency. The prominent role that the U.S. dollar plays as the world's most popular reserve currency causes the majority of U.S. dollars (about two-thirds, in fact) to be held outside of the United States.

The following Around the World feature discusses the role that Swiss banks play in holding cash from individuals and companies seeking a safe place to store their money.

The sheer volume of U.S. currency being held as cash throughout the world has reduced the actual money multiplier relative to its potential. But keep in mind that this is not necessarily a bad thing. A popular currency allows the U.S. government to print more without worrying about a significant decrease in its value relative to other currencies.

What Is the Actual Money Multiplier in the Economy?

Given the leakages described earlier, economists have studied and estimated the actual value of the money multiplier that ultimately influences economic growth. What they have found is that leakages in the U.S. economy tend to be large due to significant cash holdings by foreigners and banks' unwillingness to lend when the perceived risks of default are high.

To study the effect of leakages on the money multiplier, it is useful to modify our original money multiplier formula (1/Reserve Requirement). We incorporate bank and cash leakages to create a leakage-adjusted money multiplier [1/(Reserve Requirement + Excess Reserves + Cash Holdings)], where each component in the denominator is expressed as a percentage.

A leakage-adjusted money multiplier takes into account the required reserve requirement along with excess reserves held by banks and cash held by individuals, businesses, and foreigners. Higher values of these components translate to greater leakages and therefore a lower actual money multiplier.

For example, suppose that the reserve requirement is 20%, but the existence of leakages doubles the percentage held in reserves and cash to 40%. These money leakages cause the money multiplier to drop from 5 (1/0.20) to 2.5 (1/0.40), a significant reduction in money creation in the economy.

Empirical data have shown that money leakages tend to increase during economic recessions, when banks are more reluctant to lend and people are more likely to hold cash. We will see in the next chapter that the resulting decrease in the money multiplier adds to the challenges of using monetary policy to pull the economy out of a recession.

During the 2007–2009 recession, the actual money multiplier fell precipitously from 1.7 to less than 1, which means that fewer loans were being made than the new money introduced into the economy. This is very important because actions by the government to increase the money supply are less effective when the money multiplier is smaller. Such an effect renders monetary policy much more challenging.

The fact that banks can create money by making loans represents a great deal of power. This power is mitigated by leakages and their effect on the money multiplier. Governments can encourage this money creation process by injecting banks with new money. But how do governments go about doing this? Once we understand how the government, meaning the Fed, creates money, we can then go on in the next chapter to discuss the short- and long-run results of this monetary policy.

The institution charged with overseeing the money supply and creating money out of thin air is the Federal Reserve System. The next section describes the Federal Reserve System: how it is organized, what purposes it serves, and what functions it has. The next chapter takes a closer look at the Fed in action.

AROUND THE WORLD

The Rise and Fall of the Famous (and Infamous) Swiss Bank Account

How did Switzerland become the preferred destination of the world's offshore funds, and how is that changing today?

For centuries, people around the world, including the rich and famous as well as the powerful and infamous, looked to Switzerland to deposit their wealth. Swiss banks today remain the world's largest holder of offshore funds (holding about one-third of the world's total), which are deposits of money by people outside of their country of citizenship. But times are changing, as banks in other countries, especially in Hong Kong and Singapore, experience vastly higher growth rates in offshore deposits.

What made Swiss banks so popular with foreigners, and how is that changing today?

The popularity of Swiss banking derives largely from its secrecy laws, which date back several centuries. The ability of people to store money (regardless of where that money came from) without scrutiny or risk of disclosure made Swiss banks a magnet for the world's wealthy. These secrecy laws were further cemented with the 1934 Federal Act on Banks and Savings Banks, which made it a criminal offense for banks to disclose names of account holders. It also led to the development of *numbered bank accounts* in which people accessed their accounts using code words instead of their names. Moreover, Switzerland is a centrally located, neutral nation that hasn't been invaded in centuries, adding confidence to those seeking a safe place to store money.

But times have changed. Worldwide efforts to crack down on tax evaders using Swiss bank accounts to hide profits and criminal organizations hiding stolen money led to changes in how Swiss banks do business. Although Swiss banks still have strict secrecy laws, most no longer accept hidden profits or ill-gotten gains on behalf of individuals or corporations. Moreover, Swiss banks with branches in other countries are subjected to those countries' banking laws. This has made life more difficult for the world's criminals and tax evaders.

Today, banks remain a prominent fixture in Swiss cities such as Geneva and Zurich and an important source of economic activity for the country as a whole. But how Swiss banks operate today resembles how most banks in the world operate: by accepting deposits and making loans, creating money in the process.

GO ONLINE TO PRACTICE THE ECONOMIC CONCEPTS IN THIS STORY

✅ CHECKPOINT

THE MONEY MULTIPLIER AND ITS LEAKAGES

- The money multiplier is equal to 1 divided by the reserve requirement. This is the maximum value for the multiplier.

- Money leakages are caused by banks choosing to hold excess reserves and by individuals, businesses, and foreigners holding a portion of their funds in cash rather than depositing it in a bank. Leakages reduce the effect of the money multiplier.

- The leakage-adjusted money multiplier takes leakages into account and provides a more realistic estimate of the money multiplier in the economy.

QUESTIONS: In the following table, calculate the potential money multiplier for each of the following reserve requirements if banks fully loan out all of their excess reserves. If banks were not required to hold any reserves, how big could the money multiplier potentially be? Is this a realistic money multiplier? Why or why not?

Reserve Requirement	Potential Money Multiplier
50%	
33.3%	
25%	
20%	
10%	

Answers to the Checkpoint questions can be found at the end of this chapter.

THE FEDERAL RESERVE SYSTEM

Federal Reserve System

The central bank of the United States.

The **Federal Reserve System** is the central bank of the United States. It controls an immense power to create money in the economy.

Early in U.S. history, banks were private and chartered by the states. In the 1800s and early 1900s, bank panics were common. After an unusually severe banking crisis in 1907, Congress established the National Monetary Commission. This commission proposed one central bank with sweeping powers. But a powerful national bank became a political issue in the elections of 1912, and the commission's proposals gave way to today's Federal Reserve System.

The Federal Reserve Act of 1913 was a compromise between competing proposals for one large central bank and for no central bank at all. The act declared that the Fed is "to provide for the establishment of Federal Reserve Banks, to furnish an elastic currency, to afford means of rediscounting commercial paper, to establish a more effective supervision of banking in the United States, and for other purposes."

Since 1913, other acts have further clarified and supplemented the original act, expanding the Fed's mission. These acts include the Employment Act of 1946, the International Banking Act of 1978, the Full Employment and Balanced Growth Act of 1978, the Depository Institutions Deregulation and Monetary Control Act of 1980, and the Federal Deposit Insurance Corporation Improvement Act of 1991.

The original Federal Reserve Act, the Employment Act of 1946, and the Full Employment and Balanced Growth Act of 1978 all mandate national economic objectives. These acts require the Fed to promote economic growth accompanied by full employment, stable prices, and moderate long-term interest rates. As we will see in the next chapter, meeting all of these objectives at once has often proved difficult.

The Federal Reserve is considered to be an independent central bank in that its actions are not subject to executive branch control. However, the entire Federal Reserve System is subject to oversight from Congress. The Constitution gives Congress the power to coin money and set its value, and the Federal Reserve Act delegated this power to the Fed, subject to congressional oversight. Though several presidents have disagreed with Fed policy over the years, the Fed has managed to maintain its independence from the executive branch.

Experience in this country and abroad suggests that independent central banks are better at fighting inflation than are politically-controlled banks. The main reason is that an independent central bank is less likely to be influenced by short-term political pressures to engage in excessive expansionary monetary policy to hasten a recovery.

The Structure of the Federal Reserve

The Federal Reserve Act of 1913 passed by Congress led to the establishment of *regional* banks governed by a central authority. The intent was to provide the Fed with a broad perspective on the economy. Regional Federal Reserve Banks contribute economic analysis from all parts of the country while a central authority carries out a national monetary policy.

The Fed is composed of a central governing agency, the Board of Governors, located in Washington, D.C., and twelve regional Federal Reserve Banks in major cities around the nation. Figure 1 shows the twelve Fed districts and their bank locations.

The Board of Governors The Fed's Board of Governors consists of seven members who are appointed by the president and confirmed by the Senate. Board members serve one 14-year term, after which they cannot be reappointed. Appointments to the Board are staggered such that one term expires on January 31 of every even-numbered year. Vacancies can arise when members choose to leave before their term ends. In these cases, a new member can be appointed to serve the remainder of the term plus one full 14-year term.

Members of the Board of Governors have historically been academic economists (university professors) who take a long leave of absence from their universities to serve in this prestigious role. However, recent confirmations, such as Jerome Powell, Randal Quarles, and Michelle Bowman, who are lawyers by profession, have deviated from this tradition.

The chair and the vice chair of the Board must already be members. They are appointed to their leadership positions by the president, subject to Senate confirmation, for a four-year term but can be reappointed for as long as they remain members of the Board. The Board of Governors' staff of nearly 2,000 helps the Fed carry out its responsibilities for monetary policy and banking and consumer credit regulation.

Federal Reserve Banks Twelve Federal Reserve Banks and their branches perform a variety of functions, including providing a nationwide payments system, distributing coins and currency, regulating and supervising member banks, and serving as the banker for the U.S. Treasury. Table 1 lists all regional banks and their main locations. Each regional bank has a number and letter

····· Figure 1 • Regional Federal Reserve Districts ····························

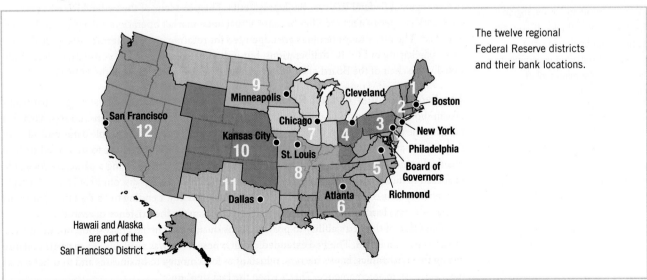

The twelve regional Federal Reserve districts and their bank locations.

TABLE 1	FEDERAL RESERVE REGIONAL BANKS	
Number	**Bank**	**Letter**
1	Boston	A
2	New York	B
3	Philadelphia	C
4	Cleveland	D
5	Richmond	E
6	Atlanta	F
7	Chicago	G
8	St. Louis	H
9	Minneapolis	I
10	Kansas City	J
11	Dallas	K
12	San Francisco	L

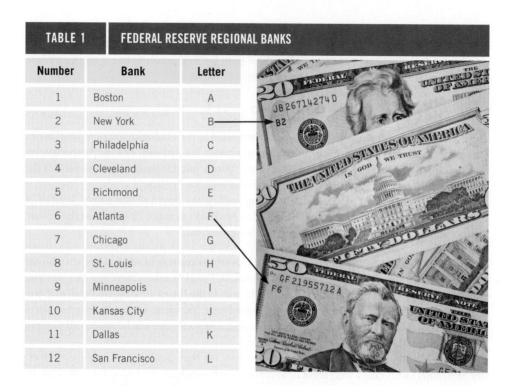

associated with it. If you look at your money, you will see that all U.S. currency bears the designation of the regional bank where it was first issued, as shown in Table 1.

Each regional bank also provides the Federal Reserve System and the Board of Governors with information on economic conditions in its home region. Eight times a year this information is compiled into a report—called the Beige Book—that details the economic conditions around the country. These reports are provided to the Board of Governors first and later released to the public. The Board and the Federal Open Market Committee use information from the Beige Book to determine the course of the nation's monetary policy.

Federal Open Market Committee The **Federal Open Market Committee (FOMC)** oversees open market operations, the main tool of monetary policy. Open market operations involve the buying and selling of government securities. How these open market operations influence reserves available to banks and other thrift institutions will become clear shortly.

The FOMC is composed of the seven members of the Board of Governors and five of the twelve regional Federal Reserve Bank presidents. The president of the Federal Reserve Bank of New York is a permanent member because actual open market operations take place at the New York Fed. The other four members are appointed for rotating one-year terms. All regional presidents participate in FOMC deliberations, but only those serving on the committee vote. Traditionally, the chair of the Board of Governors has also served as the chair of the FOMC.

The Fed as Lender of Last Resort As we have seen, the essence of banking is that banks take in short-term deposits (liabilities) and make long-term, often illiquid, loans (assets). This puts banks in the unique position of facing extraordinary withdrawals when people panic and all want their money at the same time. Banks typically do not have sufficient reserves to stem a full-fledged financial panic. They cannot turn these long-term loans into cash. During a panic, banks would be forced to dump the securities or loans onto the market at a deep discount (or "take a haircut" in financial parlance), potentially forcing them into insolvency. Lending to banks during financial panics—being a lender of last resort—is a principal reason for the existence of central banks.

The value of the Fed's ability to provide loans during a financial crisis stood out during the financial panic in 2008. The Fed extended credit where none was available. As markets collapse during financial panics, banks become reluctant to lend money to businesses and to other banks that need cash in an emergency. This is when the Fed steps in.

Federal Open Market Committee (FOMC) A twelve-member committee that is composed of members of the Board of Governors of the Fed and selected presidents of the regional Federal Reserve Banks. It oversees open market operations (the buying and selling of government securities), the main tool of monetary policy.

In just a few months, the Fed extended more than $2 trillion in loans to banks and other financial institutions and by doing so changed the allocation of assets in its balance sheet in ways not seen since it was created in 1913. Specifically, instead of holding primarily government Treasury securities, the Fed began buying up large sums of risky mortgage-backed securities from banks struggling to sell them as investor confidence fell. By the end of 2008, the Fed held more bank assets than Treasury securities.

Had the Fed and its lender of last resort capability not been available, the 2007–2009 recession would have been much deeper and could possibly have resulted in another depression. The ability of the Fed to make loans and inject the banking system with new money allows the fractional banking process to work and prevents the economy from facing a much worse financial crisis.

 **CHECKPOINT**

THE FEDERAL RESERVE SYSTEM

- The Federal Reserve System is the central bank of the United States.

- The Federal Reserve is structured around twelve regional banks and a central governing agency, the Board of Governors.

- The Federal Open Market Committee (FOMC) oversees open market operations (the buying and selling of government securities) for the Federal Reserve.

- The Federal Reserve serves as the lender of last resort, stepping in to loan money to banks that are facing emergency cash shortages or other financial difficulties.

QUESTION: If a large portion of a bank's customers want their money back at the same time and other banks won't lend to it, what can the Federal Reserve do to prevent a run on the bank?

Answers to the Checkpoint questions can be found at the end of this chapter.

THE FEDERAL RESERVE AT WORK: TOOLS, TARGETS, AND POLICY LAGS

With an ability to alter the money supply, both directly and indirectly through the money multiplier, the Federal Reserve has remarkable powers to conduct monetary policy, its primary role. And because it acts independently of political parties, the Fed is able to set monetary policy with remarkable efficiency, especially compared to fiscal policy, which involves the ever common wrangling between political parties in Congress and the president. For this reason, monetary policy is often looked at as a way to provide quicker remedies to economic conditions facing the country.

But how is monetary policy actually carried out? Quite remarkably, the Federal Reserve uses just three primary tools for conducting monetary policy:

- **Reserve requirements**—The required ratio of funds that commercial banks and other depository institutions must hold in reserve against deposits.

- **The discount rate**—The interest rate the Federal Reserve charges commercial banks and other depository institutions to borrow reserves from a regional Federal Reserve Bank.

- **Open market operations**—The buying and selling on the open market of U.S. government securities, such as Treasury bills and bonds, to adjust reserves in the banking system.

Reserve Requirements

The Federal Reserve Act specifies that the Fed must establish reserve requirements for all banks and other depository institutions. As we have seen, this law gives rise to a fractional reserve system that enables banks to create new money, expanding demand deposits through loans. The potential expansion depends on the money multiplier, which in turn depends on the reserve requirement. By altering the reserve requirement, the Fed changes reserves in the system, which affects the supply of money in the economy.

Banks hold two types of reserves: required reserves and excess reserves (above what is required). Roughly 13,000 depository institutions, ranging from banks to thrift institutions, are bound by the Fed's reserve requirements. Reserves are kept as vault cash or in accounts with the regional Federal Reserve Bank. These accounts not only help satisfy reserve requirements but are also used to clear many financial transactions.

Banks are assessed a penalty if their accounts with the Fed are overdrawn at the end of the day. Given the unpredictability of the volume of transactions that may clear a bank's account on a given day, most banks choose to maintain excess reserves.

federal funds rate The interest rate financial institutions charge each other for overnight loans used as reserves.

At the end of the day, banks and other depository institutions can loan one another reserves or trade reserves in the federal funds market. One bank's surplus of reserves can become loans to another institution, earning interest (the **federal funds rate**). A change in the federal funds rate reflects changes in the market demand and supply of excess reserves.

In 2008 the Fed changed its long-standing law of not paying interest on reserves. The new law allowed banks to earn interest on the reserves it deposits at the Fed. This law changed the incentives faced by banks by reducing the opportunity cost of choosing not to lend. In other words, in tough economic times, banks may choose to forgo making loans (especially risky ones) in favor of earning interest on their excess reserves deposited at the Fed. As we saw in the previous section, when banks hold more excess reserves, the money multiplier falls.

By raising or lowering the reserve requirement, the Fed can add reserves to the system or squeeze reserves from it, thereby altering the supply of money. Yet, changing the reserve requirement is almost like doing surgery with a bread knife; the impact is so massive and imprecise that the Fed rarely uses this tool.

Discount Rate

discount rate The interest rate the Federal Reserve charges commercial banks and other depository institutions to borrow reserves from a regional Federal Reserve Bank.

The **discount rate** is the rate regional Federal Reserve Banks charge depository institutions for short-term loans to ensure the reserve requirement is met. The discount window also serves as a backup source of liquidity for individual depository institutions.

The Fed extends discount rate credit to banks and other depository institutions typically for overnight balancing of reserves. The rate charged is roughly 0.5 percentage point higher than the FOMC's target federal funds rate. However, most banks avoid using the discount window out of fear that it might arouse suspicion by both their customers and the Fed that they are facing financial trouble. Still, the Fed prefers that banks use the discount window when needed as opposed to making imprudent decisions that could increase the risk of bankruptcy.

Although setting the discount rate and reserve requirement are both important tools used by the Fed, neither gives the Fed as much power to implement monetary policy as open market operations. Open market operations allow the Fed to alter the supply of money and system reserves by buying and selling government securities.

Open Market Operations

open market operations The buying and selling of U.S. government securities, such as Treasury bills and bonds, to adjust reserves in the banking system.

When one private financial institution buys a government security from another, funds are redistributed in the economy; the transaction does not change the amount of reserves in the economy. However, when the Fed buys a government security, it pays some private financial institution for this bond. Therefore, it adds to aggregate reserves by putting new money into the financial system.

Open market operations are powerful because of the dollar-for-dollar change in reserves that comes from buying or selling government securities. When the FOMC buys a $100,000 bond, $100,000 of new reserves is instantly put into the banking system. These new reserves have the potential to expand the money supply as banks make loans.

Open market operations are the most important of the Fed's tools. When the Fed decides on a policy objective, the volume of bonds being traded in open market operations to achieve that objective can be staggering. With the bond market valued in the trillions, it requires billions of dollars in bond transactions in order for the FOMC to push the federal funds rate toward its target.

The Federal Funds Target The target federal funds rate is the Fed's primary approach to monetary policy. As we will see in the next chapter, targeting the federal funds rate through open market operations gives the Fed an ability to influence the price level and output in the economy, a very powerful tool. The FOMC meetings result in a decision on the target federal funds rate, which is announced at the end of the meeting. Keep in mind that the federal funds rate is not something that the Fed directly controls. Banks lend overnight reserves to each other in this market, and the forces of supply and demand set the interest rate.

The Fed uses open market operations to adjust reserves and thus affect nominal interest rates with the goal of nudging the federal funds rate toward the Fed's target. When the Fed buys bonds, its demand raises the price of bonds, lowering nominal interest rates in the market. The opposite occurs when the Fed sells bonds and adds to the market supply of bonds for sale, lowering prices and raising the nominal interest rate. The Fed has been very precise at keeping the federal funds rate near the target, as Figure 2 illustrates.

In summary, the Fed sets a target for the federal funds rate and then uses open market operations to manipulate reserves to alter the money supply. Changing the money supply alters market interest rates to bring the federal funds rate in line with the Fed's target. Open market purchases increase reserves, reducing the need for banks to borrow, lowering the federal funds rate, and vice versa for open market sales. The key point to note here is that the Fed does not directly control the money supply. It proceeds indirectly, though it has been very successful in meeting its goals.

Monetary Policy Lags

Although the Fed has a remarkable ability to use tools that have important impacts on interest rates, bank reserves, and the money supply, they can still take time to have an effect on the economy. Like fiscal policy, monetary policy is subject to four major lags: information, recognition, decision, and implementation. The combination of these lags can make monetary policy difficult for the Fed. Not only does the Fed face a moving bull's-eye in terms of its economic targets, but often it can be difficult for the Fed to know when its own policies will take effect and what their effect will be.

····· Figure 2 • The Federal Funds Rate and Target Federal Funds Rate ···········

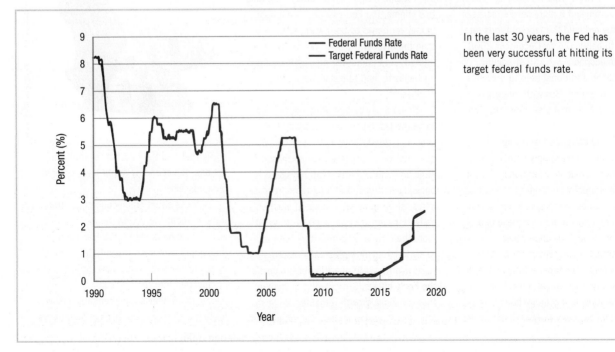

In the last 30 years, the Fed has been very successful at hitting its target federal funds rate.

Information Lags We discussed information lags when we discussed fiscal policy lags. Economic data are available only after a lag of one to three months. Therefore, when an economic event takes place, changes may ripple throughout the economy for up to three months before monetary authorities begin to see changes in their data. Moreover, many economic measures published by the government are subject to future revision. It is not uncommon for these revisions to be so significant as to render the original number meaningless. Thus, it might take the Fed several quarters to identify clearly a changing trend in prices or output.

Recognition Lags Simply seeing a decline in a variable in one month or quarter does not necessarily mean that a change in policy is warranted. Data revisions upward and downward are common. In the normal course of events, unemployment rates can fluctuate by small amounts, as can GDP. A quarter-percent decline in the rate of growth of GDP does not necessarily signal the beginning of a recession, although it could. Nor does a quarter-percent increase in GDP mean that the economy has reached the bottom of a recession; double-dip recessions are always a possibility. Due to this recognition lag, policymakers are often unable to recognize problems when they first develop.

Decision Lags The Federal Reserve Board meets regularly to determine broad economic policy. Therefore, once a problem is recognized, decisions are made to steer the economy towards full employment with stable prices. Decision lags for monetary policy are shorter than for fiscal policy. Once the Fed makes a decision to, say, avert a recession, the FOMC can begin to implement that decision almost immediately. As Figure 2 illustrates, once the Fed decides on a federal funds target, nominal interest rates track that target in a hurry. In contrast, fiscal policy decisions typically require administrative proposals and then congressional action, which can take a long time.

ISSUE

What Can the Fed Do When Interest Rates Reach 0%?

At the height of the 2007–2009 recession, the Federal Reserve took aggressive action to prevent a more severe recession. It rapidly reduced the federal funds rate target to nearly 0% by December 2008. Yet, the economy was still struggling and needed additional help to prevent a deeper recession. But with interest rates already at 0%, what else could the Fed do?

The Fed developed new ways to expand the money supply without using its regular open market operations. First, it purchased poorly performing assets from banks, such as mortgage-backed securities, in an effort to remove these bad assets from bank balance sheets.

Second, the Fed reduced the difference between the federal funds target rate and the discount rate and used *term auction facilities* to encourage borrowing by banks that typically would not borrow from

the Fed out of fear it would signal that the bank was in trouble. In an effort to reduce this stigma, the Fed essentially auctioned money for banks to borrow at rates lower than the discount rate. In doing so, bank liquidity was improved, making it easier for banks to lend to individuals and businesses.

Then came the tool often considered to be the last resort to stimulating the economy, *quantitative easing*, or QE. With quantitative easing, the Fed purchased large amounts of bank debt, mortgage-backed securities, and long-term Treasury notes, all with money it created electronically. Between 2008 and 2014, the Fed more than tripled the monetary base (currency in circulation plus bank reserves).

It is difficult to quantify the success of the Fed's efforts. Critics point to the fact that economic growth remained sluggish after the recession ended. But supporters

argue that had the Fed not taken these actions, the economy might have entered a depression.

In these situations, economists often wonder about the *counterfactual*, or what would have happened if the Fed hadn't intervened with such magnitude. The reality is that we will never know. Still, there is no question that the Fed's power in influencing the money supply remains a powerful tool that affects our lives in many ways.

Implementation Lags Once the FOMC decides on a policy, there is another lag associated with the reaction of banks and financial markets. Monetary policy affects bank reserves, interest rates, and decisions by businesses and households. As interest rates change, investment and buying decisions are altered, but often not with any great haste. Investment decisions hinge on more than just interest rate levels. Rules, regulations, permits, tax incentives, and future expectations (what Keynes called "animal spirits") all enter the decision-making process.

Economists estimate that the average lag for monetary policy is between a year and 18 months, with a range varying from a little over one quarter to slightly over two years. Using monetary policy to fine-tune the economy requires more than skill—some luck helps.

This chapter began with a discussion of how banks create money by lending excess reserves from their customer deposits. The power of the fractional banking system to generate money many times over allows the Fed to wield this power in several ways, mainly by targeting the federal funds rate using open market operations. The next chapter looks more deeply into how the Fed uses its monetary tools to balance its goals of keeping income growing and prices stable.

 CHECKPOINT

THE FEDERAL RESERVE AT WORK: TOOLS, TARGETS, AND POLICY LAGS

- The Fed's tools include altering reserve requirements, changing the discount rate, and open market operations (the buying and selling of government securities).

- The Fed uses open market operations to keep the federal funds rate at target levels.

- The Fed's policies, as with fiscal policy, are subject to information, recognition, decision, and implementation lags. Unlike fiscal policy, the Fed's decision lags tend to be shorter because Fed policies do not involve lengthy legislative processes.

QUESTIONS: Of the three tools used by the Fed, open market operations are the most common. Why is the Fed more hesitant about adjusting the reserve requirement and the discount rate? What can go wrong?

Answers to the Checkpoint questions can be found at the end of this chapter.

CHAPTER SUMMARY

SECTION 1 HOW BANKS CREATE MONEY

12.1 Money is created when banks make loans that eventually are deposited back into the system, generating checkable deposits. Part of these deposits are held as new reserves while the rest is again loaned out, creating even more money as these loans are spent and funds are deposited back into the system.

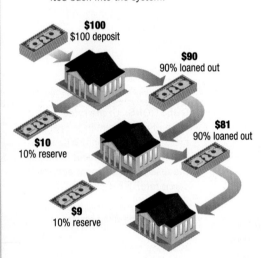

$100
$100 deposit

$90
90% loaned out

$10
10% reserve

$81
90% loaned out

$9
10% reserve

12.2 In a **fractional reserve banking system,** banks accept deposits and hold only a certain portion in reserves, loaning out the rest.

T-Accounts and Reserve Ratios

A T-account is a simple balance sheet showing a bank's assets (money the bank claims) on the left side and liabilities (money the bank owes) on the right side.

Assets	Liabilities
Cash reserves	Deposits by customers
Loans made	

A bank can continue to make loans as long as its **reserve ratio,** calculated as its reserves as a percentage of its total customer deposits, is greater than the **reserve requirement.**

$$\text{Reserve Ratio} = \frac{\text{Reserves}}{\text{Customer Deposits}}$$

SECTION 2 THE MONEY MULTIPLIER AND ITS LEAKAGES

12.3 The **money multiplier** is used to determine the maximum amount the money supply can increase (or decrease) when a dollar of new deposits enters (or exits) the system.

$$\text{Money Multiplier} = \frac{1}{\text{Reserve Requirement}}$$

Examples:

If the reserve requirement is 25%, the money multiplier = 1/0.25 = 4.

If the reserve requirement is 15%, the money multiplier = 1/0.15 = 6.67.

A **leakage-adjusted money multiplier** takes into account the excess reserves and cash holdings that reduce the loans made and therefore reduces the effect of the money multiplier.

12.4 The actual money multiplier found in the economy is often lower than the potential money multiplier due to **leakages** caused by:

1. Banks choosing to hold excess reserves by not lending out the maximum amount allowed.
2. Individuals and businesses holding money in cash rather than in a bank.
3. Foreign consumers, businesses, and governments holding cash in reserves or as a medium of exchange.

Stashing cash under the mattress creates a leakage in the money supply because this money cannot be loaned out to another borrower.

SECTION 3 THE FEDERAL RESERVE SYSTEM

12.6 The Fed is composed of a seven-member Board of Governors and twelve regional Federal Reserve Banks. The regional banks and their branches conduct the following services:

1. Provide a nationwide payments system.
2. Distribute coins and currency.
3. Regulate and supervise member banks.
4. Serve as the banker for the U.S. Treasury.

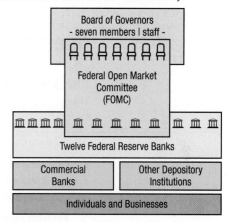

12.5 The **Federal Reserve System** is the central bank of the United States. It was established by the Federal Reserve Act of 1913 and is required by law to promote economic growth accompanied by full employment, stable prices, and moderate long-term interest rates.

The Federal Reserve Is the Guarantor of the Financial System

Its actions are not subject to executive branch oversight, although the entire Federal Reserve System is subject to oversight by Congress.

SECTION 4 THE FEDERAL RESERVE AT WORK: TOOLS, TARGETS, AND POLICY LAGS

12.7 The Fed uses three major tools to conduct monetary policy:

1. **Reserve requirements:** Establishing the minimum level of reserves banks must hold.
2. **Discount rate:** Setting the interest rate at which banks can borrow from the Fed.
3. **Open market operations:** Buying and selling government securities to target the federal funds rate.

12.8 The Fed targets the **federal funds rate,** an interest rate that influences nearly all other interest rates. The federal funds rate was near 0% from 2008 to 2015.

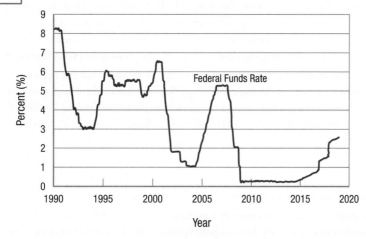

12.9 Monetary policy is subject to lags:

- **Information lag:** The time it takes for economic data to become available.
- **Recognition lag:** The time before a trend in the data is certain enough to warrant a change in policy.
- **Decision lag:** The time it takes for the Federal Reserve Board to meet and make policy decisions.
- **Implementation lag:** The time it takes for banks and financial markets to react to the policy change.

Compared to fiscal policy lags, monetary policy lags, especially decision lags, are often shorter because decisions do not require the cooperation of Congress and the president.

Key Concepts

reserve ratio, p. 299

reserve requirement, p. 299

fractional reserve banking system, p. 300

excess reserves, p. 300

money multiplier, p. 302

leakages, p. 303

insolvent, p. 303

Federal Reserve System, p. 306

Federal Open Market Committee (FOMC), p. 308

federal funds rate, p. 310

discount rate, p. 310

open market operations, p. 310

Questions and Problems

Check Your Understanding

1. Describe the role required reserves play in determining how much money the banking system creates.

2. Why are checking account deposits considered a liability to the bank?

3. How do leakages reduce the money multiplier from its potential?

4. What is the most common tool used by the Federal Reserve to conduct monetary policy, and how does it affect interest rates?

5. For what type of borrowing do the federal funds rate and the discount rate apply? Which rate is used in more transactions in the United States?

6. Why are monetary policy lags generally shorter than fiscal policy lags?

Apply the Concepts

7. The U.S. government produces billions of dollars in banknotes and coins for use in everyday transactions. Explain why issuing currency alone does not represent money creation.

8. During an economic expansion, banks tend to increase their willingness to lend. How does this trend influence the actual money multiplier?

9. The Federal Deposit Insurance Corporation (FDIC) insures individual bank accounts up to $250,000. Does the existence of this insurance eliminate the need for reserve requirements? Does it essentially prevent "runs" on banks?

10. If the Fed announces that it has no plans to raise the federal funds rate in the following year, how might this announcement affect the actions of individuals and businesses, and what impact might this have on the economy?

11. Alan Greenspan, a former Fed Chair, noted that "the Federal Reserve has to be independent in its actions and as an institution, because if Federal Reserve independence is in any way compromised, it undercuts our capability of protecting the value of the currency in society." What is so important about protecting the value of the currency? How does Fed independence help?

12. The reserve requirement sets the required percentage of deposits that must be held by the bank in cash or on deposit at the regional Federal Reserve Bank. Many banks have widespread branches and ATMs. How would the existence of branches and ATMs affect the level of excess reserves (above those required) that banks hold, and how would it affect the actual money multiplier?

In the News

13. Eric Keetch offered an interesting anecdote in the *Financial Times*:

    In a sleepy European holiday resort town in a depressed economy and therefore no visitors, there is great excitement when a wealthy Russian guest appears in the local hotel reception, announces that he intends to stay for an extended period and places a €100 note on the counter as surety while he demands to be shown the available rooms.

While he is being shown the room, the hotelier takes the €100 note round to his butcher, who is pressing for payment.

The butcher in turn pays his wholesaler who, in turn, pays his farmer supplier.

The farmer takes the note round to his favorite "good time girl" to whom he owes €100 for services rendered. She, in turn, rushes round to the hotel to settle her bill for rooms provided on credit.

In the meantime, the Russian returns to the lobby, announces that no rooms are satisfactory, takes back his €100 note and leaves, never to be seen again.

No new money has been introduced into the local economy, but everyone's debts have been settled.

What's going on here? In the end, no new money was introduced into the town, but all debts were paid. How do you explain what has happened? Did local GDP increase as a result of all debts being paid? Is the money multiplier infinite?

14. Increased skepticism about the role of the Federal Reserve as well as the spread of misinformation (e.g., that increasing the money supply devalues the dollar and amounts to counterfeiting) have led some politicians to propose that the Federal Reserve be abolished. If this happens, monetary policy would essentially cease to exist, as the money supply would no longer be flexible. This was the case about 50 years ago when the money supply was still tied to the amount of gold in reserves. Given your knowledge of the role of the Fed, what are some risks to the economy if the Fed is abolished?

Solving Problems

Work It Out

 interactive activity

15. Assume that First Purity Bank begins with the balance sheet below and is fully loaned-up. Answer the questions that follow.

First Purity Bank			
Assets		**Liabilities**	
Reserves	+$700,000	Deposits	+$2,000,000
Loans	+$1,300,000		

a. What is the reserve requirement?

b. If the bank receives a new deposit of $1 million and the bank wants to remain fully loaned-up, how much of this new deposit will the bank loan out?

c. What is the money multiplier in this case?

d. When the new deposit to First Purity Bank works itself through the entire banking system (assume all banks remain fully loaned-up), by how much will total deposits, total loans, and total reserves increase?

16. Suppose that the leakage-adjusted money multiplier can be calculated using a modification of the money multiplier formula:

$$\frac{1}{(\text{Reserve Requirement} + \text{Excess Reserves} + \text{Cash Holdings})}$$

where each component in the denominator is expressed as a percentage.

Suppose that the reserve requirement is 25%, but banks, on average, hold an additional 10% of their deposits as excess reserves. Further, assume that individuals and businesses choose to hold 15% of their borrowed funds in cash. Compare the money multiplier with the leakage-adjusted money multiplier. Does the existence of leakages make a significant impact on the ability to conduct monetary policy? Explain why or why not.

✅ Answers to Questions in Checkpoints

Checkpoint: How Banks Create Money 302

The basic transaction reduces your checking account by $1,000 and adds $1,000 in cash for your trip. Therefore, M1 would stay the same because cash and checkable deposits are both part of M1. However, by withdrawing $1,000 from the bank, this is $1,000 that could be loaned out by the bank and lead to money creation. Therefore, by making the withdrawal, the money supply would drop if the bank had planned to loan out its excess reserves.

Checkpoint: The Money Multiplier and Its Leakages 306

The potential money multipliers are 2, 3, 4, 5, and 10, respectively. If banks were not required to hold any reserves, the money multiplier could theoretically be infinite if every bank loans out 100% of its deposits. However, this is not likely due to the many leakages that occur in the banking system. Banks would still hold some reserves, just as banks currently hold excess reserves over the required limit. No bank would want to be at the mercy of a small bank run that would lead to its ruin. Therefore, it would keep some currency reserves on hand. Also, individuals, businesses, and foreign entities may choose to hold a portion of their assets in cash, preventing this money from working its way through the money creation process.

Checkpoint: The Federal Reserve System 309

The Federal Reserve has the power to loan the struggling bank the money to satisfy the withdrawals. However, such withdrawals are often a sign of deeper underlying troubles at the bank. The question then becomes whether to let the bank fail and be taken over by a solvent bank or to help it survive by purchasing bad debts and recapitalizing the bank.

Checkpoint: The Federal Reserve at Work: Tools, Targets, and Policy Lags 313

Open market operations are very effective because they influence virtually all interest rates. Reducing the reserve requirement can certainly boost lending; however, reducing it too much can put banks at risk should defaults rise. Adjusting the discount rate is generally less effective because bank customers and investors often view borrowing from the discount window as a warning sign of the bank's deteriorating financial health. As a result, the Fed typically keeps the discount rate at a fixed level slightly above the federal funds rate.

Monetary Policy

*Understanding how central banks alter the money supply to
minimize fluctuations in the macroeconomy*

Learning Objectives

13.1 Explain the importance of interest rates on the economy and how they affect our daily lives.

13.2 Explain the goals of monetary policy and how the Fed uses policies to expand or contract the economy.

13.3 Contrast classical monetary theory with Keynesian and monetarist theories.

13.4 Describe the equation of exchange and its implications for monetary policy in the long run.

13.5 Determine the effectiveness of monetary policy when demand or supply shocks occur.

13.6 Describe the debate on whether the Fed should have discretion or be governed by simple monetary rules.

13.7 Describe the federal funds target, the Taylor rule, and how they are used in modern monetary policymaking.

13.8 Explain why extraordinary powers were used in response to the financial crisis of 2008.

13.9 Discuss the monetary policy challenges faced by the European Central Bank following the financial crises affecting individual Eurozone members.

Information received since the Federal Open Market Committee met in December indicates that the labor market has continued to strengthen and that economic activity has been rising at a solid rate. Job gains have been strong . . . and the unemployment rate has remained low . . . and overall inflation remains near 2 percent. . . . The Committee decided to maintain the target range for the federal funds rate at 2-1/4 to 2-1/2 percent. . . . In light of global economic and financial developments and muted inflation pressures, the Committee will be patient as it determines what future adjustments to the target range for the federal funds rate may be appropriate.

—Excerpt from the FOMC Statement of January 30, 2019

At 2:00 P.M. EST on an ordinary weekday afternoon, the Federal Reserve (Fed) concludes its meeting of the Federal Open Market Committee, and just 15 minutes later, at 2:15 P.M., a meeting statement is released. To the twelve voting members of this committee, which meets about every six weeks, it's just another day on the job. But this is not your ordinary everyday job.

On Wall Street, millions of investors, physically present at a stock exchange or virtually present via their online brokerage accounts, anxiously await this Fed statement. Corporate executives, just coming back from lunch, immediately search their news app for the latest statement release.

Government policymakers in Ecuador, El Salvador, Panama, and Timor-Leste tune in to the news to hear the Fed statement because it affects their countries' interest rates and their currency, which in fact is *the U.S. dollar*. And markets in the rest of the world await the Fed statement to determine how their own economies will be affected.

Indeed, in a matter of minutes after the release of the Fed statement, the twelve members of the Federal Open Market Committee will have affected the lives of hundreds of millions of people. How do such ordinary people carry such tremendous power?

The Federal Open Market Committee is the body within the Federal Reserve that controls U.S. monetary policy. Their economic policy decisions affect not only the U.S. economy but also the entire world economy.

Although not every Fed meeting statement produces a dramatic flurry of reactions, the ability of the Fed to exert powerful policy action in times of economic fluctuation makes its meeting statement the most dissected piece of economic news in the world. Even the most slightly nuanced wording of the statement can generate mass market activity as people attempt to predict how the Fed will act not only today but also in the months and years ahead.

Mario Tama/Getty Images

An investor awaiting the Fed statement.

BY THE Numbers

Monetary Policy in Action

Among the tools used by the Federal Reserve to conduct monetary policy are setting the discount rate and conducting open market operations targeting the federal funds rate. The interest rates targeted by the Fed have a profound impact on the entire economy. The federal funds rate affects the prime rate, which is the interest rate charged by banks to their best customers, and also serves as a benchmark for determining home equity lines of credit and other lending rates. It also influences mortgage rates used to finance homeownership. This By the Numbers compares four key interest rates over the last 15 years.

$15,419,529,000,000

Total amount of mortgage debt outstanding in the United States in 2019

$1,058,200,000,000

Total amount of outstanding credit card balances in the United States in 2019

DATA:

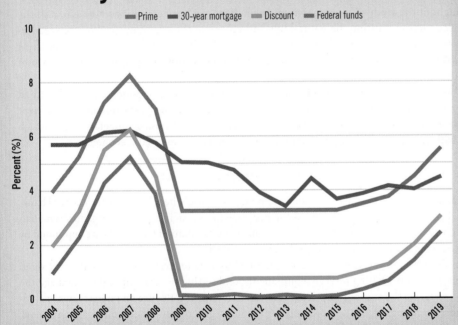

Four Key U.S. Interest Rates (2004–2019)

— Prime — 30-year mortgage — Discount — Federal funds

Where Can I Find These Data?

Source: FRED Database; Federal Reserve Bank of St. Louis

Web site: https://fred.stlouisfed.org

Details: Search for "prime rate," "30 year fixed mortgage rate," "discount rate," and "federal funds rate"

WHY ARE THESE DATA IMPORTANT?

The Federal Reserve plays an important role in stabilizing the economy by targeting interest rates to promote economic growth and minimize inflation. Moreover, nearly everybody borrows in order to purchase a home or car, to pay for college tuition and expenses, or to spread out payments on one's credit card balances over time. Interest rates affect the cost of borrowing and therefore influence our ability to make purchases.

Data *in the News*

"Seeking Middle Ground, Fed Raises Rates, Will Be Careful with Increases Next Year" by Larry Edelman; *Boston Globe*, December 20, 2018

Walking a fine line between being overly optimistic and too pessimistic, the Federal Reserve bumped up its benchmark interest rate . . . and said the U.S. economy remained strong, but it warned of possible headwinds next year.

~ Assessing Your Data Literacy ~

1. Which interest rate tends to change most in tandem with changes in the federal funds rate? Which one is least in tandem with the federal funds rate?

2. Describe the trend in interest rates as the economy went into the 2007–2009 recession and the trend in interest rates as the economy expanded from 2015 to 2019.

3. Explain why interest rates would follow the trends described in question 2.

In the previous chapter, we saw how the Federal Reserve System is organized, and we described the three monetary policy tools the Fed uses, which are setting reserve requirement, setting the discount rate, and conducting open market operations. This chapter studies the remarkable influence the Fed has to alter the macroeconomy using these tools. The Federal Reserve Act mandates that the Fed implement monetary policies that will promote economic growth accompanied by high employment, stable prices, and moderate long-term interest rates. We look at what monetary policy aims to achieve and how the Fed undertakes monetary policy to deal with economic fluctuations.

The first part of this chapter describes how monetary policy is used during economic downturns and during economic expansions. We then consider the question: How do changes in the money supply affect the economy? We will see that money has no effect on the economy's real growth in the long run but can have sizable effects in the short run. We then examine the impact of monetary policy on controlling demand and supply shocks and how the Fed actually tries to manage the economy, a process that is considered both art and science. The chapter concludes by looking at monetary policy challenges faced by the Fed and the European Central Bank.

WHAT IS MONETARY POLICY?

Throughout the study of macroeconomic principles, we have emphasized the effect of the business cycle in creating the natural ups and downs in the economy, which often lead to inflation or unemployment. The rest of our study has dealt largely with ways to manage these fluctuations and to limit the harm from deviating too far from the long-run growth path of the economy.

One way of managing economic fluctuations is the use of fiscal policy, which we studied earlier. Fiscal policy uses the tools of taxation, government transfer payments, and government spending. The other way of managing economic fluctuations is the use of monetary policy, which deals with how the money supply is controlled to target interest rates in an economy.

The Twin Goals of Monetary Policy

The authority to control a nation's monetary policy is typically held by a country's central bank. In the United States, the central bank is the Federal Reserve, an independent organization unaffiliated with any political party. The seven members of its Board of Governors are appointed by the president for a 14-year term, rather than being elected.

As discussed in the previous chapter, the Fed uses its primary tools of conducting open market operations, setting reserve requirements, and setting the discount rate to manage the money supply in the economy. By doing so, it has tremendous influence on interest rates, including those on savings accounts, money market accounts, government bonds, mortgage payments, student loans, car loans, and credit card balances.

The Fed uses these tools to promote its twin goals of economic growth with low unemployment and stable prices with moderate long-term interest rates. When the economy enters an expansion or a recession that threatens the stability of these factors, the Fed can step in to enact an appropriate policy to counteract the effect.

Examples of Monetary Policy in Action

The business cycle of the economy produces frequent ups and downs, and the Fed is kept busy anticipating and reacting to prevent major economic crises from occurring. The following summarizes the Fed's major actions over the past two decades.

1998–1999: The peak of the Internet growth, when new "dot-com" companies sprouted up daily, led to tremendous economic growth. But along with growth came inflationary pressures, and the Fed responded by raising interest rates.

2001–2003: With the dramatic collapse in the price of technology stocks along with the short recession in 2001, the Fed lowered interest rates to stimulate employment.

2004–2006: The housing bubble led to strong growth throughout the economy and inflationary pressures crept up (especially in industries related to housing), leading the Fed to raise interest rates again.

2007–2009: When the housing bubble collapsed, unemployment rose significantly, and the Fed dramatically reduced interest rates to record lows.

2010–2015: A slow economic recovery with lackluster employment growth encouraged the Fed to hold interest rates at record lows until late 2015.

2016–2019: An economic expansion leads to concerns about rising inflation. The Fed raises interest rates.

Why Is the Interest Rate So Important to the Economy?

Examine the economic decisions you make every day, and you might discover how interest rates play a powerful role. Interest rates affect the manner in which we borrow and consume, and the way in which we save and invest.

Suppose you are looking to buy a new car and have budgeted $2,000 for a down payment and $400 a month toward the monthly payment on a five-year loan. How much of a car can you afford with this budget?

It depends a great deal on the interest rate. Suppose the current interest rate on a car loan is 8.99%. Using the money you have, you would be able to afford a car costing up to $21,275. But now suppose that the interest rate on a car loan is 2.99%. At the lower interest rate, you would be able to afford a car costing up to $24,265, or almost $3,000 in extra spending without changing your monthly payment.

This extra $3,000 in potential spending resulting from the lower interest rate adds to the amount of consumption in the economy. Recall that aggregate demand is the sum of consumption, investment, government spending, and net exports. Just as lower interest rates make cars more affordable, they also make homes more affordable, along with equipment purchases by businesses. Therefore, a reduction in interest rates promotes greater consumption and investment, which leads to an increase in aggregate demand, shifting the aggregate demand curve to the right.

When Is It Optimal to Loosen or Tighten Monetary Policy?

By influencing interest rates, the Fed influences aggregate demand. Specifically, the Fed loosens monetary policy in times of recessionary concerns and tightens monetary policy in times of inflationary concerns.

- **Loosening monetary policy:** Reducing interest rates → increases consumption and investment → increases aggregate demand.
- **Tightening monetary policy:** Raising interest rates → decreases consumption and investment → decreases aggregate demand.

Let's explore "loosening" and "tightening" a bit more.

Expansionary Monetary Policy During times of economic downturn, the Fed will engage in **expansionary monetary policy** by conducting open market operations. By buying government bonds from banks using money it creates, the Fed puts more money into the economy, thus expanding the money supply and reducing interest rates. Lower interest rates tend to reduce the proportion of income people save and increase the amount they consume or invest, all else equal. The increase in consumption and/or investment results in an increase in aggregate demand (AD).

As interest rates are lowered, consumers and businesses find the cost of borrowing decreasing as well. For a business, this reduces the financing cost for an expansion of a factory or the building of a new restaurant or store. To a consumer, a lower interest rate on a home or car purchase can

A lower interest rate allows one to afford a better car (or at least fancier rims) with the same monthly payment.

expansionary monetary policy Fed actions designed to increase the money supply and lower interest rates to stimulate the economy (expand income and employment).

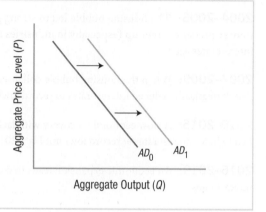

Figure 1 • Expansionary Monetary Policy

Expansionary monetary policies reduce interest rates, which lead to greater aggregate demand, shifting the aggregate demand curve to the right.

significantly reduce monthly payments, freeing up some money for other purchases. As borrowing increases to finance consumption or investment, AD again increases.

Further, a reduction in interest rates, in particular on Treasury securities, means that the government is spending less on financing the national debt. By spending less on financing the debt, the government is then able to spend more on other purchases, which contributes to an increase in AD.

Finally, as the interest rate falls, American bonds become less attractive to foreign investors, and this often leads to a decline in the value of the U.S. dollar in foreign exchange markets. A falling dollar makes American products cheaper relative to foreign products, which stimulates exports and reduces imports, increasing AD.

In sum, expansionary monetary policy is used when the economy faces a recessionary gap, in which output is below the level needed to reach full employment. By engaging in expansionary policy, the aggregate demand curve shifts to the right as shown in Figure 1, expanding output at every price level.

Contractionary Monetary Policy The opposite of expansionary monetary policy is **contractionary monetary policy,** which occurs when the Fed sells bonds, taking money out of the economy to reduce the money supply and raise interest rates. The Fed uses contractionary monetary policy when inflationary pressures build up. When do inflationary periods typically occur?

Inflationary pressures usually follow a period of strong economic growth. For example, the recent economic expansion has resulted in higher growth and lower unemployment. As consumers and businesses become more confident about the economy, demand for goods and services increases, pushing the overall price level higher. If prices rise too much, this would have consequences on the economy as the purchasing power of savings erodes.

To stem the growth of inflation, the Fed would reduce the money supply, thereby increasing the interest rate to slow the growth of demand. In this case, rising interest rates would lead to a fall in consumption and investment. The government would spend more financing the national debt, reducing what it can spend on other goods and services. Moreover, a rise in the value of the dollar from increased demand for higher interest bonds makes American goods more expensive, reducing net exports. Each of these effects causes the aggregate demand curve to shift to the left as shown in Figure 2, reducing output at every price level and putting downward pressure on prices.

Up until now, we have assumed that monetary policy affects the interest rate, which subsequently influences aggregate demand. But how does a simple change in the money supply influence the amount of goods and services in the real economy? The next section explores this question by analyzing how prices and output change in the short run and long run.

contractionary monetary policy Fed actions designed to decrease the money supply and raise interest rates to shrink income and employment, usually to fight inflation.

····· Figure 2 · Contractionary Monetary Policy ············

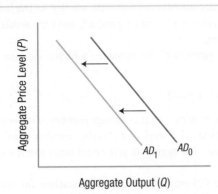

Contractionary monetary policies raise interest rates, which lead to lower aggregate demand, shifting the aggregate demand curve to the left.

✅ CHECKPOINT

WHAT IS MONETARY POLICY?

- Monetary policy involves controlling the money supply by targeting interest rates in order to stabilize fluctuations in the business cycle.

- The Federal Reserve implements monetary policy. Its goals are to promote economic growth by maintaining full employment, stable prices, and moderate long-term interest rates.

- Interest rates are crucial because they directly influence the components of aggregate demand, including consumption and investment.

- Expansionary monetary policy is used during times of recession and involves expanding the money supply to reduce interest rates.

- Contractionary monetary policy is used during times of rising inflation and involves reducing the money supply to raise interest rates.

QUESTION: Suppose the government passes legislation limiting the maximum interest rate that can be charged on student loans, reducing the monthly payment on your loans. How is this legislation similar to an expansionary monetary policy?

Answers to the Checkpoint questions can be found at the end of this chapter.

MONETARY THEORIES

In discussing the theories that justify the use of monetary policy, it is best to differentiate the long run from the short run. We will see that money has no effect on the real economy (such as employment and output) in the long run but can have an effect in the short run.

The Short Run Versus the Long Run

One of the important concepts covered in a previous chapter is the comparison between the short-run aggregate supply curve (SRAS) and the vertical long-run aggregate supply curve (LRAS). Recall that the LRAS curve is vertical because economic output is always fixed in the long run at the full employment output when wages and prices are flexible. Only factors that increase the productivity of inputs can shift the LRAS curve. The SRAS curve, however, is upward-sloping because higher prices can cause temporary increases in output. This is due to sticky wages and prices.

We now build on the AD/AS model by explaining how changes in the money supply, which directly affect the aggregate demand curve, might change prices and output in the economy. Let's begin by looking at the long run, which is the analysis most commonly associated with the classical theory.

The Long Run: The Classical Theory

Classical economists focused on long-run adjustments in economic activity. In the long run, wages, prices, and interest rates are flexible, allowing the labor, product, and capital markets to adjust to keep the economy at full employment.

A product of the classical theory is the *quantity theory of money*, which is defined by the **equation of exchange:**

$$M \times V = P \times Q$$

equation of exchange The heart of classical monetary theory uses the equation $M \times V = P \times Q$, where M is the supply of money, V is the velocity of money (the average number of times per year a dollar is spent on goods and services), P is the price level, and Q is the economy's real output level.

where M is the supply of money, V is the velocity of money (the average number of times per year a dollar is spent on goods and services), P is the price level, and Q is the economy's real output level. Note that the right side of the equation—the aggregate price level times the level of real output—is equal to nominal GDP.

In the long run, when the economy is at full employment, the implications for monetary policy are straightforward. Because velocity (V) is assumed to be fixed by existing monetary institutions (e.g., the amount of cash you use on a monthly basis is generally consistent) and real aggregate output (Q) is assumed to be fixed at full employment, any change in the money supply (M) will translate directly to a change in prices (P), or, in other words, inflation.

Suppose you sell your grandma's old LP records on eBay. Last month you listed five records for sale and sold them at an average winning bid of $20 each. Now suppose that this month a 10% increase in the money supply causes more people to want to buy records. If you again list only five records for sale, what will likely happen? There is more money to spend on the same amount of goods. Buyers might bid up the price to, say, $22. In the end, prices rise in the exact proportion to the rise in the money supply. This is the essence of the classical theory—that increases in the money supply translate into an immediate and proportional rise in the aggregate price level with no change in real output (Q). As a result, monetary policy is ineffective.

IRVING FISHER (1867–1947)

Irving Fisher was one of the ablest mathematical economists of the early 20th century. He was a staunch advocate of monetary reform, and his theories influenced economists as different as John Maynard Keynes and Milton Friedman.

Born in upstate New York in 1867, Fisher studied mathematics, science, and philosophy at Yale University. In 1905 Fisher was in a phone booth in Grand Central Terminal in New York City when someone stole his briefcase, which contained his manuscript of *The Nature of Capital and Income*, one of the first economics books about the stock market. He rewrote the book over the next year, making copies of each chapter as it was finished and always closing the doors to phone booths after that.

Monetarists owe a great debt to Fisher's next great book, *The Purchasing Power of Money,* in which he offered an "equation of exchange": $MV = PT$ (where T is the total goods and services transacted, or output). Classical economists have used variations of the formula to suggest that inflation is caused by increases in the money supply.

Fisher was prim and straight-laced and disciplined and did not drink alcohol or coffee or tea, smoke, eat chocolate, or use pepper. His lack of humor and sometimes controversial economic beliefs (such as 100% bank reserves) led some to regard him as quite odd.

But among his many skills and interests, Fisher was a successful inventor and businessman. In 1925 he patented the "visible card index" system that allowed users to organize addresses, from which he earned a fortune. Unfortunately, within a few years he would lose everything in the stock market crash of 1929, an event that he famously failed to predict. His insistence of an imminent recovery during the early Depression years caused irreparable damage to a well-earned reputation as one of America's greatest economists.

Information from Robert Allen, *Irving Fisher: A Biography* (Cambridge, MA: Blackwell), 1993.

Figure 3 • The Impact of a Change in the Money Supply in the Long Run: Theory and Evidence

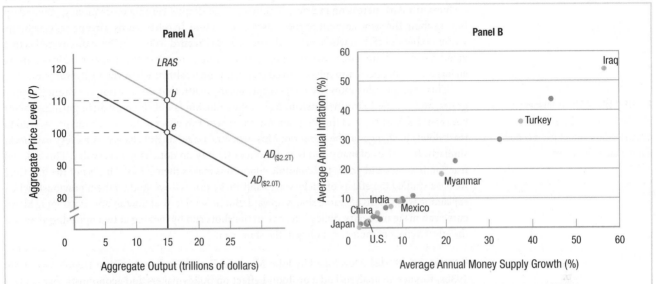

The quantity theory of money is shown using aggregate demand and aggregate supply. The economy is initially in equilibrium at point *e*. The long-run aggregate supply curve is vertical at the full employment output of $15 trillion, while the aggregate demand curve reflects a money supply of $2.0 trillion. Increasing the money supply to $2.2 trillion (a 10% increase) shifts aggregate demand upward to $AD_{(\$2.2T)}$, resulting in a new equilibrium at point *b*, where the aggregate price level rises by 10%, yet real output remains constant. The price level rise is equal to the percentage increase in the money supply. Money supply growth and inflation for thirty countries from 1992 to 2017 support this theory.

Panel A of Figure 3 illustrates how the quantity theory works within an aggregate demand and aggregate supply model. The economy is initially in long-run equilibrium at point *e* with full employment output of $15 trillion and an initial money supply of $2.0 trillion. Increasing the money supply to $2.2 trillion (a 10% increase) shifts aggregate demand upward to $AD_{(\$2.2T)}$, resulting in a new equilibrium at point *b*, where the aggregate price level increases to 110 (a 10% increase), yet real output remains constant at $15 trillion. This positive relationship between changes in the supply of money and inflation is evident in the scatter diagram shown in panel B, which shows the strong correlation between average growth in the money supply and inflation for 30 countries from 1992 to 2017. This suggests that any central bank that wants to avoid high inflation must avoid rapid growth of its money supply.

The quantity theory of money provides a good explanation of the long-run impact of monetary growth in the larger economy. But do people really catch on so quickly to money growth? Typically not. The realization that wages and prices can be "sticky" led economists to develop theories of how prices and output can change in the short run, leading to a SRAS curve that differs from a LRAS curve. The most notable theories include the Keynesian and monetarist models.

Short-Run Effects of Monetary Policy

If the short-run effects of money supply were the same as in the long run, that would be the end of the story. In contrast to the long run, changes in the money supply can have an effect on the real economy in the short run, not just on the price level. To explain this, let's start by returning to our earlier example to show how money supply growth can affect economic output.

Money Illusion and Sticky Wages and Prices Suppose you continue to sell your grandma's records on eBay, listing five for sale each month. And every month, you notice that the average winning bids keep rising, first to $22, then to $25, then to $30, or even higher. This increase in the sales price makes you happy because you feel richer each month compared to the previous month. You think you are benefiting from the growing popularity of your grandma's good taste in music.

How would you use your additional income? Most people would spend it by going out to eat more or buying more clothes. This extra spending (by you and everyone who *feels* richer) results in a temporary increase in economic output. But then you notice that the items you typically buy each month start increasing in price, so much so that despite earning more money, you end up buying about the same amount of goods as you did before. In other words, after prices caught up, you're no better off than when you made only $20 per record. What you have discovered is that grandma's records are not growing in popularity. Rather, growth in the money supply is causing an increase in all prices. You misperceived that you were wealthier when you really were not.

money illusion A misperception of wealth caused by a focus on increases in nominal income but not increases in prices.

This example illustrates the misperceptions in wealth that occur when the money supply grows, and is called **money illusion.** But money illusion is not the only distinguishing factor between the short run and the long run. Another short-run effect is that wages and prices tend to react slowly to changes in the economy. Most workers' wages do not change with every paycheck; similarly, the prices of many goods and services we buy do not change every day. This delayed reaction in wages and prices to economic conditions makes them *sticky*. This is not the first time we have studied the effects of sticky wages and sticky prices—we studied them previously when explaining why the SRAS curve slopes upward. But now we look at how an upward-sloping SRAS curve can make monetary policy effective in the short run by looking at two opposing views on the effectiveness of monetary policy in the short run.

Keynesian Model Developed by John Maynard Keynes during the Great Depression of the 1930s, Keynesian analysis had a profound effect on policymakers and economists that continues today. According to Keynesian theory, an increase in the money supply leads more people to buy interest-earning assets (bonds), causing the price of bonds to rise and the interest rate to fall. Lower interest rates should normally lead to an increase in investment that increases aggregate demand, which increases income, output, and employment.

However, Keynesians believed this outcome occurs only when the economy is healthy. During times of recession, people become fearful and don't buy as much, leading to massive excess capacity for businesses. Reducing interest rates might not lead to greater investment because firms are

NOBEL PRIZE
MILTON FRIEDMAN (1912–2006)

Milton Friedman may be the best-known economist of the latter half of the 20th century. During the 1980s, his advocacy of free market economics and "monetarist" theories had a dramatic impact on policymakers, notably President Ronald Reagan and British Prime Minister Margaret Thatcher. His book *A Monetary History of the United States, 1867–1960*, coauthored with Anna Schwartz, is considered a modern classic of economics.

Born in 1912 in Brooklyn, New York, to poor immigrant parents, Friedman was awarded a scholarship to Rutgers University but paid for his additional expenses by waiting on tables and clerking in a store. He eventually went on to graduate school at the University of Chicago to study economics and then to Columbia University.

In 1946 he accepted a professorship at the University of Chicago, where he delved into the role of money in business cycles. In 1950 Friedman worked in Paris for the Marshall Plan, studying a precursor to the Common Market. He came to believe in the importance of flexible exchange rates between members of the European community.

Friedman's views were explicitly counter to the Keynesian belief in a range of activist government policies to stabilize the economy. He emphasized the importance of monetary policy in determining the level of economic activity and advocated a consistent policy of steady growth in the money supply to encourage stability and economic growth.

Friedman was awarded the Nobel Prize in Economics in 1976 for his work on monetary theories and also for his concept of "permanent income," the idea that people based their savings habits on the typical amount they earn instead of on increases or decreases they may view as temporary.

unable to sell what they were currently producing. With a decline in business expectations, firms would be reluctant to invest more.

Further, when interest rates fall to very low levels, Keynes argued that people simply hoard money because it's not worth holding bonds that pay so little interest. Keynes referred to this phenomenon as the **liquidity trap.** In a liquidity trap, an increase in the money supply does not result in a decrease in interest rates; there is no change in investment and consequently no change in income or output. Monetary policy is totally ineffective. This was one reason Keynes argued that fiscal policy, especially government spending, was needed to get the economy out of the Depression.

liquidity trap When interest rates are very low, people hold money rather than invest in bonds due to their expectations of a declining economy or an unforeseen event such as war.

Monetarist Model Milton Friedman challenged the Keynesian view by arguing that government spending inherent to fiscal policy must be financed by either increased taxation and/or increased borrowing. His monetarist theory states that higher taxation means consumers and firms have less money to consume and invest, while increased borrowing leads to higher interest rates, which also reduces consumption and investment. Thus, monetarists believe that the crowding-out effect makes fiscal policy ineffective.

Friedman pioneered the notion that consumption is based not only on income but also on wealth, an idea he referred to as the *permanent income hypothesis*.

With Friedman's approach, when the money supply increases, interest rates fall, and individuals rebalance their asset portfolios by exchanging money for other assets, including real estate and consumer durables, such as cars and recreational equipment. Therefore, falling interest rates will lead to higher investment and/or consumption. This leads to an increase in aggregate demand and ultimately an increase in income, output, and/or the price level.

Therefore, monetarists believe that monetary policy can be effective in the short run. But, like classical economists, monetarists believe that an increase in the money supply will ultimately increase prices in the long run. As Milton Friedman famously remarked: "Inflation is always and everywhere a monetary phenomenon."

Figure 4 illustrates the monetarist approach that a change in output will occur only in the short run. The economy is initially in long-run equilibrium at point e, with output at \$15 trillion and a price level of 100. A 10% increase in the money supply from \$2.0 trillion to \$2.2 trillion shifts the aggregate demand curve from AD_0 to AD_1, initially raising output to \$16 trillion and the aggregate price level to 105 (point b). Over time, as prices adjust, the SRAS curve will shift left to $SRAS_1$ and the economy will move back to its full employment output (\$15 trillion), raising prices in the long run by 10% to 110 (point c).

•••••• Figure 4 • Monetarist Theory on Money Supply •••••••••••••••••••••••••••

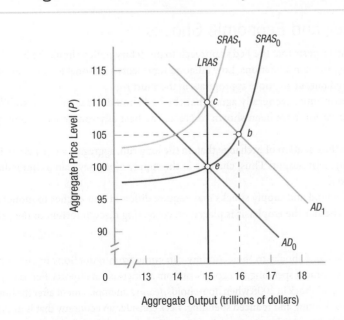

Monetarists argue that a change in output will last only in the short run; in the long run, the economy will move back to full employment. The economy begins in equilibrium at point e. An increase in the money supply of 10% shifts the aggregate demand curve from AD_0 to AD_1, resulting in higher short-run output, \$16 trillion, and a higher price level at point b. Over time, the economy will move back to full employment output (\$15 trillion), increasing the price level in the long run to 110 (a 10% increase) at point c. The long-run aggregate supply curve is vertical at the full employment output of \$15 trillion.

Summary of the Effectiveness of Monetary Policy

Let's summarize the theories of the effectiveness of monetary policy.

Long Run: Changes in the money supply show up directly as increases in the price level because both velocity and output are considered fixed in the equation of exchange $(M \times V = P \times Q)$. Classical economists saw no use for monetary policy because in the long run, the economy would self-correct to equilibrium.

Short Run: Keynes believed that when the economy is well below full employment, monetary policy is ineffective because investment is more influenced by business expectations about the economy than interest rates. Further, Keynes suggested that once interest rates become very low, monetary policy might confront a "liquidity trap," where money is just hoarded. Thus, Keynesian economists favor fiscal policy to move the economy toward full employment.

Monetarists, on the other hand, do see a role for monetary policy. In the short run, changes in the money supply reduce interest rates, which in turn stimulate both investment and consumption. Consumer spending is related to wealth (not just income), and changes in interest rates lead to changes in consumer spending for durable goods.

A summary of the three theories is provided in Table 1.

TABLE 1	SUMMARY OF MONETARY THEORIES	
	Short Run	**Long Run**
Classical Theory	Monetary policy is ineffective. The economy always self-adjusts.	The economy self-adjusts due to flexible prices. Changes in the money supply lead only to price changes.
Keynesian Theory	Fiscal policy is effective, while monetary policy is ineffective in times of deep recession.	The economy adjusts to long-run equilibrium; increased money supply leads to higher prices.
Monetarist Theory	Fiscal policy is ineffective because government spending crowds out consumption and investment, while monetary policy is effective.	The economy adjusts to long-run equilibrium; increased money supply leads to higher prices.

Monetary Policy and Economic Shocks

Our discussion thus far suggests that the Fed's approach to monetary policy should be based on both short-run and long-run considerations. Low inflation represents a reasonable long-run goal, while greater income and output are more appropriate in the short run.

In the long run, economists generally agree that the Fed should focus on price stability because low rates of inflation have been shown to create the best environment for long-run economic growth.

We have seen from the equation of exchange that, in the long run, aggregate supply is vertical and fixed at full employment output. Thus, changes in the supply of money lead to immediate changes in the price level.

In the short run, demand and supply shocks may require different approaches to monetary policy, depending on whether the emphasis is placed on correcting disequilibrium in the price level, output, or both.

Demand Shocks Demand shocks to the economy can come from reductions in consumer demand, investment, government spending, or exports, or from an increase in imports. For example, the economy faced a demand shock in 2008 when households, fearing unemployment after the housing bubble burst, increased saving and reduced spending. Let's consider an economy that is initially in full employment equilibrium at point *e* in panel A of Figure 5. A *demand shock* then reduces aggregate demand to AD_1. At the new equilibrium (point *a*), the price level and output both fall.

····· Figure 5 • Demand Shocks, Supply Shocks, and Monetary Policy ············

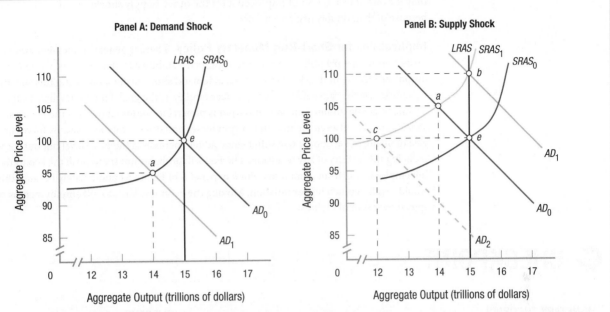

Monetary policy can be effective in counteracting a demand shock. In panel A, the economy begins in full employment equilibrium at point e, and then a demand shock reduces aggregate demand to AD_1, resulting in a new equilibrium (point a). Expansionary monetary policy will shift aggregate demand back to AD_0, restoring full employment output ($15 trillion) and prices (100). Monetary policy is less effective in counteracting a supply shock. In panel B, a negative supply shock shifts $SRAS_0$ to $SRAS_1$. The new equilibrium (point a) is at a *higher* price level, 105, and *lower* output, $14 trillion, a doubly negative result. The Fed could use expansionary monetary policy to shift AD_0 to AD_1 to restore full employment output (point b), but at an even higher price level (110). Alternatively, the Fed could focus on price level stability, using contractionary monetary policy to shift aggregate demand to AD_2, but this would further deepen the recession as output falls to $12 trillion (point c).

An expansionary monetary policy will increase the money supply, lower interest rates, and thereby shift aggregate demand back to AD_0, restoring employment and output to full employment levels. In this case, targeting either a stable price level (100) or the original income and output level ($15 trillion) will bring the economy back to the same point of equilibrium, point e, where *both* targets are reached.

A positive demand shock produces a corresponding, though opposite, result. The positive demand shock will jolt output and the price level upward. Contractionary monetary policy will reduce both of them, restoring the economy to its original equilibrium.

Therefore, demand shocks create no conflict between the twin goals of monetary policy. Not only is the objective of full employment compatible with the objective of stable prices, but by the Fed targeting either one of these objectives, the other objective also will be achieved.

Supply Shocks Supply shocks can arise due to many reasons, including changes in resource costs such as a drought causing a rise in food prices, changes in inflationary expectations, or changes in technology. Looking at panel B of Figure 5, let us again consider an economy initially in full employment equilibrium at point e. Assume that a negative shock to the economy, say, a spike in crop prices, shifts short-run aggregate supply from $SRAS_0$ to $SRAS_1$. The new equilibrium (point a) occurs at a *higher* price level (105) and a *lower* output of $14 trillion.

This doubly negative result means that a supply shock is very difficult to counter. The Fed could use expansionary monetary policy to shift aggregate demand from AD_0 to AD_1; this would restore the economy to full employment output of $15 trillion (point b), but at an even higher price level (110). Alternatively, the Fed could focus on price level stability, using contractionary monetary policy to shift aggregate demand to AD_2, but this would further deepen the recession by pushing output down to $12 trillion (point c).

For a negative supply shock, not only has price level stability worsened, but so have output and income. Contrast this with the situation earlier, when a demand shock worsened the economy for one of its targets but improved it for the other. Supply shocks are difficult to counteract because of their doubly negative results.

Implications for Short-Run Monetary Policy There is general agreement among economists that monetary policy should focus on price stability in the long run while focusing on output or income in the short run. When a demand shock occurs, following this short-run policy course has the same effect as using price stability as the goal. However, when a supply shock occurs, targeting nominal income or output is preferable because it permits the Fed to spread the shock's impact between income and output losses and price level increases. By increasing aggregate demand, the economy will suffer some added increase in the price level but output will rise, reducing the severity of any recession. The Fed will probably not try to push the economy back to full employment (from point *a* to point *b* in panel B of Figure 5) immediately because this action would result in much higher inflation. Moving the economy back to full employment is typically spread over several periods.

CHECKPOINT

MONETARY THEORIES

- The classical equation of exchange is $M \times V = P \times Q$. In the long run, velocity (V) and output (Q) are assumed to be fixed. Therefore, changes in the money supply translate directly into changes in the price level: $\Delta M = \Delta P$.

- In the short run, Keynesian monetary analysis suggests that changes in the money supply change interest rates, leading to changes in investment and aggregate demand when the economy is healthy. However, in a deep recession, changes in the money supply have no effect, and therefore fiscal policy is preferred to monetary policy.

- Monetarists suggest that in the long run, the economy functions in the way that classical economists described, but they see monetary policy affecting interest rates in the short run, which in turn affects investment and/or consumption.

- In the long run, the Fed targets price stability. Low rates of inflation are most conducive to long-run economic health.

- Monetary policy can offset demand shocks because the objective of full employment is compatible with the objective of stable prices.

- Supply shocks present a more challenging problem for monetary policy. A negative supply shock reduces output but increases the price level. Expansionary monetary policy to increase output further increases the price level, and contractionary policy to reduce the price level worsens the recession.

QUESTION: A common debate on dealing with rising national debt involves those who prefer a smaller government (reduced taxation with a dramatic reduction in government spending) versus those who prefer increased government spending funded by higher taxes. Which general theories described in this section best resemble the two sides of the debate?

Answers to the Checkpoint questions can be found at the end of this chapter.

easy money, quantitative easing, or accommodative monetary policy Fed actions designed to increase the money supply to stimulate the economy (increase income and employment). *See also* expansionary monetary policy.

MODERN MONETARY POLICY

When the Fed engages in expansionary monetary policy, it is buying bonds from banks using money that it creates out of thin air. By adding this money to the bank's existing reserves, banks have more money to lend. Other terms used to describe this process include **easy money, quantitative easing,** and **accommodative monetary policy.** These actions increase the money supply and reduce interest rates in order to stimulate the economy and expand income and employment. The opposite of an expansionary policy is contractionary monetary policy, also referred to as **tight money** or **restrictive monetary policy.** Tight money policies are designed to shrink income and employment, usually in the interest of fighting inflation. The Fed brings about tight monetary policy by selling bonds, thereby reducing reserves from the financial system.

The Federal Reserve Act gives the Board of Governors significant discretion over conducting monetary policy. It sets goals but leaves it up to the discretion of the Board of Governors how best to reach these objectives. As we have seen, the Fed attempts to frame monetary policy to keep inflation low over the long run but also to maintain enough flexibility to respond in the short run to demand and supply shocks.

tight money or restrictive monetary policy Fed actions designed to decrease the money supply to shrink income and employment, usually to fight inflation. *See also* contractionary monetary policy.

Rules Versus Discretion

The complexities of monetary policy, especially in dealing with a supply shock, have led some economists to call for a **monetary rule** to guide policymakers. Other economists argue that modern economies are too complex to be managed by a few simple rules. Constantly changing institutions, economic behaviors, and technologies means that some discretion, and perhaps even complete discretion, is essential for policymakers. Also, if policymakers could use a simple and efficient rule on which to base successful monetary policy, they would have enough incentive to adopt it voluntarily because it would guarantee success and their job would be much easier.

Milton Friedman argued that variations in monetary growth were a major source of instability in the economy. To counter this problem, which is compounded by the long and variable lags in discretionary monetary policy, Friedman advocated the adoption of monetary growth rules. Specifically, he proposed increasing the money supply by a set percentage every year, at a level consistent with long-term price stability and economic growth.

Friedman and other monetarists, like the classical economists before them, believed the economy to be inherently stable. If a demand shock is small or temporary, a monetary growth rule will probably function well enough. But if the shock is large or persistent, as was the case during the 2007–2009 recession, a discretionary monetary policy aimed at bringing the economy back to full employment more quickly would probably be preferred.

In some cases, a monetary rule keeps policymakers from making things worse by preventing them from taking imprudent actions. Yet, the monetary rule also prevents policymakers from aiding the economy when a policy change is needed, as was the case during the oil crisis in the 1970s when the Fed's practice of setting a fixed rate for money supply growth wasn't considered successful.

The alternative to setting money growth rules that modern monetary authorities around the world have tried is the simple rule of **inflation targeting,** which sets targets on the inflation rate, usually around 2% per year. If inflation (or the forecasted rate of inflation) exceeds the target, contractionary policy is employed; if inflation falls below the target, expansionary policy is used. Inflation targeting has the virtue of explicitly iterating that the long-run goal of monetary policy is price stability.

But while inflation targeting may work well to combat negative demand shocks, the same is not true when a negative supply shock occurs. Inflation targeting means that contractionary monetary policy should be used to reduce the inflation spiral. But contractionary policy would deepen the recession, and, in reality, few monetary authorities would stick to an inflation-targeting approach in this situation. They would be more likely to stimulate the economy slightly, hoping to move it back to full employment with only a small increase in inflation. The result is that inflation targeting would be less effective in dealing with a negative supply shock.

monetary rule Keeps the growth of money stocks such as M1 on a steady path, following the equation of exchange to set a long-run path for the economy that keeps inflation in check.

inflation targeting The central bank sets a target inflation rate (usually around 2% per year) and adjusts monetary policy to keep inflation near that target.

The Federal Funds Target and the Taylor Rule

If not a monetary rule or inflation targeting, what other rule can the Fed use? We know that the Fed alters the federal funds rate as its primary monetary policy instrument. Under what circumstances will the Fed change its federal funds target? The Fed is concerned with two major factors: preventing inflation and preventing and moderating recessions. Professor John Taylor of Stanford University studied the Fed and how it makes decisions, and he empirically found that the Fed tended to follow a general rule that has become known as the **Taylor rule** for federal funds targeting:

Taylor rule A rule for setting the federal funds target equal to the target inflation rate + current inflation rate + ½(inflation gap) + ½(output gap).

$$\text{Federal Funds Target Rate} = \text{Target Inflation Rate} + \text{Current Inflation Rate}$$
$$+ \tfrac{1}{2}(\text{Inflation Gap}) + \tfrac{1}{2}(\text{Output Gap})$$

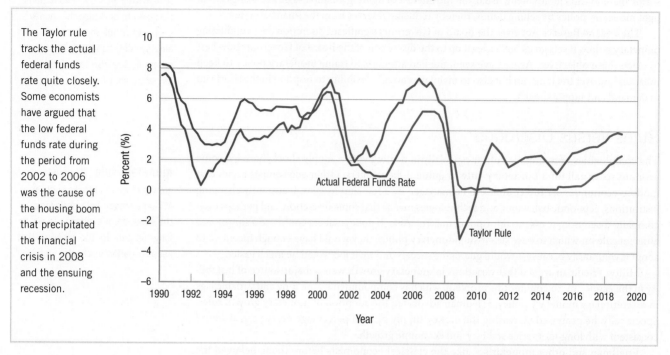

····· Figure 6 • Actual Federal Funds Rate and the Taylor Rule ·················

The Taylor rule tracks the actual federal funds rate quite closely. Some economists have argued that the low federal funds rate during the period from 2002 to 2006 was the cause of the housing boom that precipitated the financial crisis in 2008 and the ensuing recession.

The Fed's inflation target is typically 2%, the inflation gap is the current inflation rate minus the Fed's inflation target, and the output gap is current GDP minus potential GDP[1]. If the Fed tries to target inflation around 2%, the current inflation rate is 4%, and output is 3% below potential GDP, then the target federal funds rate according to the Taylor rule is

$$FF_{Target} = 2+4+\frac{1}{2}(4-2)+\frac{1}{2}(-3)$$
$$= 2+4+\frac{1}{2}(2)+\frac{1}{2}(-3)$$
$$= 2+4+1-1.5$$
$$= 5.5\%$$

Notice that the high rate of inflation (4%) drives the federal funds target rate upward, while the fact that the economy is below its potential reduces the rate. If the economy were operating at its potential, the federal funds target would be 7% because the Fed would not be worried about a recession and would be focused on controlling inflation.

Figure 6 shows how closely the Taylor rule tracks the actual federal funds rate. Some economists have blamed the large spread between the two rates during the period between 2002 and 2006 for the housing boom that precipitated the financial crisis in 2008. They argue that the extremely low interest rates fueled the housing boom.

More important, what the Taylor rule tells us is that when the Fed meets to change the federal funds target rate, the two most important factors are whether inflation is different from the Fed's target (typically 2%) and whether output varies from potential GDP. If output is below its potential, a recession threatens, and the Fed will lower its target. Conversely, when output exceeds its potential, inflation threatens, and the Fed will raise its target.

A Recap of the Fed's Policy Tools

Now is a good time to summarize the monetary policy actions that the Fed can take to achieve its twin goals of price stability and full employment.

---

[1] The original Taylor rule used logarithms to measure the output gap. For simplicity, we use the percentage difference between current and potential GDP.

When output exceeds potential output, firms are operating above their capacities and costs will rise, adding an inflationary threat that the Fed wants to avoid. Therefore, the Fed would increase the real interest rate to cool the economy. When output is below potential, the Fed's goal is to drive the economy back to its potential to avoid a recession along with the losses associated with an economy below full employment. The Fed does this by lowering the real interest rate. This reflects the Fed's desire to fight recession when output is below full employment and to fight inflation when output exceeds its potential.

Today, monetary authorities set a target interest rate and then use open market operations to adjust reserves and keep the federal funds rate near this level. The Fed's interest target is the level that will keep the economy near potential GDP and/or keep inflationary pressures in check. When GDP is below its potential and a recession threatens the economy, the Fed uses expansionary policy to lower interest rates, expanding investment, consumption, and exports. When output is above potential GDP and inflation threatens, the Fed uses a higher interest rate target to slow the economy and reduce inflationary pressure.

Raising interest rates is never a politically popular act, but the Fed will be forced to balance future economic growth against rising inflationary expectations. As former Fed Chair William McChesney Martin said, "The job of a good central banker is to take away the punchbowl just as the party gets going."

When faced with the challenge of targeting economic growth and controlling inflation, two general strategies arise. Those who advocate for policies that prevent inflation from rising as their top priority

ISSUE

The Record of the Fed's Performance

Measuring the impact of Federal Reserve policy on our large, complex economy is not easy. The figure shows how three variables—unemployment, inflation, and interest rates (effective federal funds rate)—have fared during the tenure of the six* Fed chairs over the last four decades.

Before 1980, when Arthur Burns headed the Fed, inflation was rising. Oil supply shocks in the 1970s along with expansionary monetary policy caused inflation to increase sharply, peaking at over 14% in 1980. Paul Volcker, the head of the Fed at that time, tightened monetary policy to induce a recession (1981–1982)

to reduce inflation. By the end of his term, inflation had been reduced to little more than 4%, a remarkable feat.

During the 1990s, the Alan Greenspan Fed alternated between encouraging output growth (mid-1990s) and fighting inflation (early and late 1990s). Interest rates trended down, and inflation was moderate during the 1990s and early 2000s. But a housing bubble, partly the result of the extremely low interest rates from 2002 to 2005, followed by its collapse in 2007, brought on a financial panic and a deep recession.

The problems stemming from the housing collapse and financial crisis became a challenge for Fed Chair Ben Bernanke. In 2008 the Fed lowered the Fed funds rate to almost 0% and continued to expand the monetary base by purchasing long-term assets from banks.

As unemployment trended down following the recession, Bernanke and Janet Yellen continued to keep interest rates low until the end of 2015. By that time, the economy had recovered and began to expand. In response, Yellen and Jerome Powell raised interest rates to keep inflation from rising.

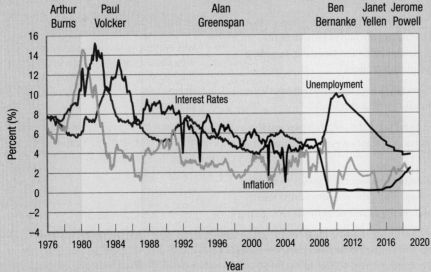

*Technically, there were seven Fed chairs over this period. However, G. William Miller's tenure lasted just over a year from 1978 to 1979 and therefore is not included in this graph.

monetary hawk A policymaker who advocates for monetary policies that emphasize keeping inflation low as its top priority.

monetary dove A policymaker who advocates for monetary policies that emphasize low unemployment and high growth as its top priorities.

are referred to as **monetary hawks.** Those who advocate for policies that emphasize low unemployment and higher growth as their top priorities are referred to as **monetary doves.** In the aftermath of the last recession, the Fed was seen as mostly dovish by keeping interest rates at record lows for many years. But the Fed has been more hawkish in recent years as inflation became more of a concern.

Transparency and the Federal Reserve

How does the Fed convey information about its actions, and why is this important? For many years, decisions were made in secrecy, and often they were executed in secrecy. The public did not know that monetary policy was being changed. As monetary policy affects the economy, the Fed's secrecy stimulated much speculation in financial markets about current and future Fed actions. Uncertainty often led to various counterproductive actions by people guessing incorrectly. These activities were highly inefficient.

When Alan Greenspan became head of the Fed in 1987, this policy of secrecy started to change. By 1994 the Fed released a policy statement each time it changed interest rates, and by 1998 it included a "tilt" statement forecasting what would probably happen in the next month or two. By 2000 the FOMC released a statement after each of its eight meetings per year even if policy remained the same. As the chapter opener describes, the FOMC statement is now one of the most anticipated pieces of economic news.

This new openness has come about because the Fed recognized that monetary policy is less effective when financial actors take counterproductive actions when they are uncertain about what the Fed will do. In the words of William Poole, former president of the Federal Reserve Bank of St. Louis,

> *Explaining a policy action—elucidating the considerations that led the FOMC to decide to adjust the intended funds rate, or to leave it unchanged—is worthwhile. Over time, the accumulation of such explanations helps the market, and perhaps the FOMC itself, to understand what the policy regularities are. It is also important to understand that many—perhaps most—policy actions have precedent value.... One of the advantages of public disclosure of the reasons for policy actions is that the required explanation forces the FOMC to think through what it is doing and why.*[2]

Fed transparency helps the public understand why it is taking certain actions. This helps the market understand what the Fed does in certain circumstances and what the Fed is likely to do in similar situations in the future. The Fed's "tilt" comment after each meeting provides a summary of the Fed's outlook on the economy and information on the target federal funds rate. Transparency helps the Fed implement its monetary policy.

 **CHECKPOINT**

MODERN MONETARY POLICY

- In the past, monetary rules were used to control the rate of growth of the money supply. Later, an alternative approach of inflation targeting, targeting the inflation rate to around 2%, became more prevalent.

- The Fed sets a target federal funds rate and then uses open market operations to adjust reserves to keep the federal funds rate near this level.

- The Taylor rule ties the federal funds rate target to the inflation gap and the output gap for the economy, and has done a good job in estimating the actual federal funds rate target set by the Fed.

- When inflation rises, the Fed uses contractionary monetary policy to increase the federal funds rate to slow the economy. When the economy drifts into a recession, the Fed does the opposite and reduces the federal funds rate, giving the economy a boost.

- Fed transparency helps us to understand why the Fed makes particular decisions and also what the Fed will probably do in similar circumstances in the future.

QUESTION: After years of quantitative easing, many worry that inflation will eventually become a problem. Why should bond investors sell when the Fed or other central bankers decide that inflation is a growing problem?

Answers to the Checkpoint questions can be found at the end of this chapter.

[2] William Poole, "Fed Transparency: How, Not Whether," The Federal Reserve Bank of St. Louis, *Review*, November/December 2003, p. 5.

MONETARY POLICY CHALLENGES

For much of the past century since the Federal Reserve Act created the Federal Reserve and with it monetary policy, policies were quite predictable. The Fed was seen as an important but not overreaching government body. A similar sentiment was felt toward the European Central Bank (ECB), which was established on June 1, 1998 by 11 countries using the euro as their common currency. As of 2019, 19 countries are members.

These perceptions changed when the financial crisis affected the economies of the United States and Europe beginning in 2007. In the years that followed, the Fed and the ECB took extraordinary actions to prevent their economies from collapsing. This section briefly summarizes the challenges faced by the Fed and the ECB during the financial crisis and its recovery and concludes by describing the new challenges faced as economic expansion generates worries of inflationary pressures and a growing skepticism of the role of central banks.

The Fed's Role in Dealing With the Financial Crisis

The financial meltdown that plagued the global economy beginning in 2007 was caused by a perfect storm of conditions. Low interest rates from 2002 to 2005 encouraged home buying. Financial risk was not properly managed, as consumers were eager to buy homes (sometimes more than one) and banks were eager to lend even to those who had poor credit or insufficient incomes as long as housing values kept increasing. Moreover, investors and financial institutions bought trillions of assets tied to the value of homes, assets that were given excellent ratings (despite their risk) by bond rating agencies. When borrowers began to default on their loans due to rising interest rates and lending contracts that increased monthly payments over time, the resulting foreclosures caused housing values to plummet along with the mortgage-backed securities tied to them. As a result, homeowners, investors, and financial institutions found themselves in trouble, leading to the worst recession since the Great Depression.

In response to the financial crisis, the Fed used its normal monetary policy tools by lowering the federal funds target to 0% in December 2008. But that wasn't enough to stop the economy from faltering. The Fed then took extraordinary measures by buying large amounts of risky assets from banks (in a series of purchases called *quantitative easing*) to prevent banks from becoming insolvent. From 2008 to 2012, the Fed's balance sheet ballooned from less than $1 trillion to over $3 trillion, and its allocation changed from one that consisted about 90% of safe Treasury securities to one comprising nearly half in risky mortgage-backed securities.

Although many people credit the Fed for preventing the economy from further collapse, its aggressive actions in raising the monetary base led to criticism by some who believe the Fed overstepped its authority and risked higher inflation in the future. But as former Fed Chair Ben Bernanke said, if your neighbor's house is on fire because he was smoking in bed, you deal with the fire first because if you don't, your own house can burn down. You deal with your neighbor's smoking problem later. The Fed was not alone in taking drastic action during the financial crisis. The ECB took extraordinary action as well.

The Eurozone Crisis and the Role of the European Central Bank

The Eurozone was created during a 1992 meeting in the Netherlands by twelve European countries that envisioned a single currency that would reduce transaction costs and facilitate and expand trade. The meeting resulted in the signing of the Maastricht Treaty, which set the monetary criteria that each country had to satisfy before joining the Eurozone. These criteria included, among others, the following:

1. Maintaining an inflation rate no higher than 1.5% above the average of the three member countries with the lowest inflation rates

2. Maintaining long-term interest rates (on 10-year bonds) no higher than 2% above the average of the three member countries with the lowest interest rates

Figure 7 • A Timeline of Eurozone Countries Facing a Financial Crisis From 2008 to 2013

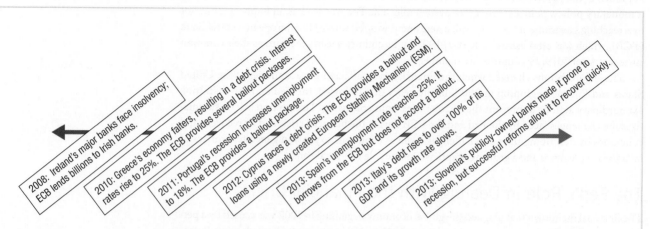

2008: Ireland's major banks face insolvency; ECB lends billions to Irish banks.

2010: Greece's economy falters, resulting in a debt crisis. Interest rates rise to 25%. The ECB provides several bailout packages.

2011: Portugal's recession increases unemployment to 18%. The ECB provides a bailout package.

2012: Cyprus faces a debt crisis. The ECB provides a bailout and loans using a newly created European Stability Mechanism (ESM).

2013: Spain's unemployment rate reaches 25%. It borrows from the ECB but does not accept a bailout.

2013: Italy's debt rises to over 100% of its GDP and its growth rate slows.

2013: Slovenia's publicly-owned banks made it prone to recession, but successful reforms allow it to recover quickly.

This timeline shows the sequence of major events that occurred within the Eurozone from 2008 to 2013 that led to the European Central Bank taking extraordinary actions to prevent a financial collapse.

3. Maintaining annual deficits of less than 3% of GDP
4. Maintaining total debt of less than 60% of GDP
5. Having no major currency devaluation in the preceding two years

When the euro was adopted on January 1, 1999 eleven of the twelve treaty members met the monetary criteria. Greece took two extra years to satisfy the criteria and joined the Eurozone on January 1, 2001.

Why were such stringent criteria needed? When a common currency is adopted, monetary policy becomes shared by all members. Therefore, a monetary crisis in one country can quickly spread to all countries. Germany, the largest member of the Eurozone, traditionally had maintained low inflation and a stable economy. Although Germany had much to gain from the Eurozone, it also faced risks by integrating its monetary policy with countries whose economies were less stable.

For much of the first decade, the euro was a success, with member nations keeping their debt under control while the ECB implemented monetary policy for the entire Eurozone. Moreover, the euro established itself as a major reserve currency, giving it significant clout among world financial institutions.

However, conditions began changing in 2007 when several member countries experienced rising debt as the global financial crisis began to spread. From 2008 to 2013, nearly half of the Eurozone members faced a financial crisis, requiring the ECB to use its normal monetary policy tools in addition to extraordinary measures to prevent countries from defaulting on their debt. Figure 7 presents a timeline showing the countries that faced a crisis and some of the actions used by the ECB in response.

The ECB took extraordinary actions to prevent financial crises in individual countries from causing the collapse of the Eurozone. The ECB provided loans to banks, bought government debt, and created the European Stability Mechanism (ESM) in 2012 to facilitate the funds being disbursed. The ECB also negotiated with private banks and investors to write off portions of debt and to restructure existing loans to governments. It also demanded that governments enact structural reforms and be subjected to greater scrutiny. Like the Fed, the ECB's balance sheet ballooned from about 1 trillion euros in 2007 to over 3 trillion euros in 2012.

In addition to dealing with crises in individual countries, the ECB had another worry: that countries might

bildbroker.de/Alamy

Ireland went from being the second wealthiest member of the Eurozone (after Luxembourg) to one facing the biggest financial crisis in 2008.

decide to withdraw from the Eurozone and cause a global loss of confidence in the euro. Investors would be less willing to invest in euro-denominated bonds and assets if the long-term viability of the euro came into question. Imagine what would happen if a U.S. state became so much in debt that it chose to give up the U.S. dollar and create its own, much devalued state currency. The impact would be significant. Fortunately, this will never happen given the long history of the U.S. dollar and laws preventing such action. But in Europe, countries might be more willing to give up on the euro and return to their previous currencies along with independent monetary policy. Greece is a recent example of a country that nearly decided to leave the Eurozone.

Joining Versus Leaving a Common Currency

The challenges facing a central bank in managing a currency is already difficult when a recession affects many countries (in the Eurozone) or many states (in the United States). But even more challenging is when one country or state experiences a recession while another experiences an economic expansion. In this situation, a shared monetary policy becomes difficult because using expansionary monetary policy to mitigate the effects of a recession in one area may exacerbate inflationary pressures in another area that is expanding. The following Issue discusses the challenges facing a central bank when there are regional differences in economic performance.

The Challenges of Monetary Policy With Regional Differences in Economic Performance

The Eurozone crisis of 2008–2013 led many to point to Europe as an experiment with monetary policy integration gone wrong. Members of the Eurozone were too different, not only culturally but also economically. Prior to its formation in 1999, the richest member of the Eurozone, Luxembourg, had a GDP per capita that was more than twice the level of that of Portugal, which at the time was the poorest member of the original eleven countries, until Greece joined in 2001. In 2007 countries in Eastern Europe began joining, further spreading the difference between the richest and poorest members, which would all share the same currency and monetary policy determined by the European Central Bank (ECB).

Although each member nation would have representation in the ECB based on population, Germany and France, the two largest members, dominate decisions. The challenge faced by the ECB is formulating a common monetary policy that best fits the economic conditions faced by its members. This is not easy.

Choosing a common monetary policy involves placing the priority of one country's economic concerns over another's. For example, if one part of the Eurozone is booming while another part is struggling with debt, the appropriate policy for one country might be in direct conflict with that for the other.

But is the situation in Europe the only one in which a common monetary policy needs to address wide variations in economic performance? The answer is no, and the best example of another monetary zone facing similar problems may surprise you: the United States.

The United States shares many similarities with the Eurozone when it comes to monetary policy. Although the United States is one country, wide variations in economic performance still exist. In 2018, Connecticut's per capita income of about $72,000 was twice that of Mississippi's $36,000.

Further, U.S. monetary policy also must take into account territories that use the U.S. dollar, such as Puerto Rico, as well as countries, such as Ecuador, El Salvador, Panama, and Timor-Leste, all of which have a per capita income even lower

European Central Bank in Frankfurt, Germany.

than Mississippi's. The Fed's decisions have a direct impact on all economies that use the U.S. dollar.

In sum, large monetary unions such as the Eurozone and the United States must weigh the priorities of one region against another when considering the policies they implement. Such a task makes the statement that *monetary policy is as much art as science* a realistic description facing central banks today.

When regional differences occur, there is increased desire by countries to pursue their own monetary policy, as was the case in Greece in 2017. Greece had experienced rampant debt and was forced to drastically cut wages and other government benefits in exchange for bailouts from the ECB. But such reforms were highly unpopular among Greeks who felt they were being punished. Many Greeks wanted to leave the Eurozone in a process coined "Grexit" and reintroduce the drachma, the currency used prior to the euro. But austerity measures did ultimately reduce Greece's debt, as the government managed to generate a fiscal surplus. And the overall improved economy helped mitigate concerns of Greece leaving the Eurozone.

Retaining independent monetary policy is one reason why several members of the European Union, including the United Kingdom, Sweden, and Denmark, chose not to adopt the euro. In 2016, voters in Britain elected to leave the European Union altogether (coined "Brexit"), which has caused much uncertainty in financial markets as policymakers in Britain and the rest of the Europe grapple with how to manage their separation.

Another situation that may occur when a country (often developing) faces an economic crisis or uncontrollable inflation is giving up its monetary policy altogether. The following Around the World feature describes why some countries decided to adopt another country's currency (such

AROUND THE WORLD

Why Would a Country Give Up Its Monetary Policy?

What factors led Ecuador, El Salvador, and Panama to give up their ability to use monetary policy in favor of adopting the U.S. dollar?

Traveling to Ecuador? No need to exchange money. The official currency is the U.S. dollar.

One of the first tasks when traveling abroad is to exchange currency. In most countries, this is an easy task: Just visit a foreign exchange booth or withdraw money from a local ATM. Some countries that depend on tourism, such as Jamaica and Costa Rica, readily accept U.S. dollars despite having their own national currency. But for American tourists visiting Ecuador, El Salvador, Panama, or Timor-Leste, exchanging money isn't even an option because the official currency in these countries *is* the U.S. dollar.

Why would a country adopt the U.S. dollar as its official currency, and what effect does it have on its monetary policy?

The decision for a country to use a foreign currency (in this case, the U.S. dollar) as its own official currency,

called dollarization, is not in any way influenced or dictated by the United States. Ecuador, El Salvador, and Panama willingly gave up their own currency to adopt the U.S. dollar. And by doing so, these countries relinquished their ability to set monetary policy because the supply of dollars and the interest rate are managed by the U.S. Federal Reserve. Why would a country give up control of its monetary policy?

Panama adopted the U.S. dollar over a century ago to facilitate trade, given its strategic geographic location that

attracts cargo ships from around the world crossing the Panama Canal. In the case of Ecuador and El Salvador, which adopted the U.S. dollar in 2000 and 2001, respectively, their situations were different than Panama's. Prior to adopting the U.S. dollar, both countries had rampant inflation, caused by the inability of their central banks to keep money growth under control. High inflation decreases investor confidence because profits quickly lose their value. By adopting the U.S. dollar (and thereby preventing the government from adjusting the money supply), Ecuador and El Salvador sent a signal that they were serious about maintaining low inflation, which subsequently led to greater foreign direct investment.

Still, problems persist in countries that dollarize, and the lack of an independent monetary policy makes it difficult to address fluctuations in the economy, especially when they differ from those of the United States. But for these countries and others that have dollarized their economies, the potential benefits outweigh the costs.

Johner Images/Alamy

GO ONLINE TO PRACTICE THE ECONOMIC CONCEPTS IN THIS STORY

as the U.S. dollar) as their official medium of exchange. When a country chooses to adopt the U.S. dollar, it is adopting U.S. monetary policy as well. But the benefit of doing so is a commitment to investors that money earned in the country will retain its value (as long as the U.S. dollar remains a dominant reserve currency).

The Politicization of Monetary Policy

This section has shown that a strong central bank can implement monetary policy to mitigate even the worst financial crises. By doing so, its influence in the macroeconomy is enhanced, which has led to some criticism that the central bank holds too much power. In fact, some policymakers have recently questioned the need for central banks and instead yearned for a return to a fixed monetary base, such as the gold standard.

Part of the criticism stems from the fact that central banks such as the Fed are independent bodies tasked with smoothing the business cycle. This means using expansionary monetary policy during times of recession and contractionary monetary policy during times of economic expansion. Yet, much like no politician wants to implement contractionary fiscal policy because it can slow economic growth, some politicians have criticized contractionary monetary policy being used to reduce inflationary pressures.

An important reason for the criticism is that contractionary monetary policy raises interest rates, which slows economic growth. This consequence is experienced in the short run (when politicians are trying to be reelected), but the benefits of lower inflation are enjoyed mostly over the long run. Therefore, even when a strong economy calls for contractionary monetary policy, as has been the case in the United States in recent years, some politicians would rather keep using expansionary monetary policy because of the short-run economic and political benefits. But just as using expansionary fiscal policy when the economy is already at full employment can lead to an overheated economy, using expansionary monetary policy when unnecessary can lead to long-term inflation, which reduces the standard of living. For that reason, maintaining the Fed's independence is seen as vital to maintaining a healthy economy.

 **CHECKPOINT**

MONETARY POLICY CHALLENGES

- To control the financial panic of 2008, the Fed used its normal monetary policy tools and some that it hadn't used in many decades.

- The European Central Bank is the Fed's counterpart in Europe, setting the monetary policy for the nineteen-member Eurozone.

- A long and severe debt crisis occurred when several European nations neared default on their loans, requiring extraordinary actions, including bailout loans, by the ECB to keep the effects of the crisis from spreading to the entire Eurozone.

- The Fed's and the ECB's aggressive actions have led to some criticism of the powerful role of monetary policy.

QUESTION: As the economies of the United States and Europe expand, what are some of the challenges facing the Fed and the ECB in implementing monetary policy to prevent inflation from rising?

Answers to the Checkpoint questions can be found at the end of this chapter.

CHAPTER SUMMARY

SECTION 1 WHAT IS MONETARY POLICY?

 13.1 **Monetary policy** is the process by which a country's money supply is controlled to target interest rates that subsequently influences economic output and prices.

Importance of Interest Rates on the Economy

Higher interest rates affect aggregate demand by:

1. Making borrowing more expensive, forcing consumers and firms to cut spending and investing
2. Giving people more incentive to save than spend
3. Forcing the government to spend more on financing the national debt
4. Increasing the value of the U.S. dollar, making U.S. exports more expensive

Lower interest rates affect aggregate demand in the opposite way.

13.2 **Twin Goals of Monetary Policy**

1. Economic growth and full employment
2. Stable prices and moderate long-term interest rates

Bills, bills, bills. Higher interest rates cause debt payments to take a bigger portion of each paycheck, leaving less to spend on other goods.

Cultura Creative (RF)/Alamy

Expansionary Monetary Policy: More money → lower interest rates → higher C, I, G, and $(X - M)$ = increase in aggregate demand and output

Contractionary Monetary Policy: Less money → higher interest rates → lower C, I, G, and $(X - M)$ = decrease in aggregate demand and output

SECTION 2 MONETARY THEORIES

13.3 The **quantity theory of money** is a product of the classical school of thought, which concludes that the economy will automatically tend toward equilibrium at full employment in the long run.

Classical theorists do not believe that monetary policies are effective at all.

Keynesians and monetarists believe that monetary policy can be effective in the short run, but not in the long run.

13.4 **Equation of Exchange (Classical Theory)**

$$M \times V = P \times Q$$

$$\uparrow \qquad \uparrow$$
$$\text{Fixed} \qquad \text{Fixed}$$

$$\Delta M = \Delta P$$

Velocity (V) and output (Q) are believed to be fixed in the long run, so any change in the money supply (M) directly affects the price level (P).

Keynesian Money Theory

Increasing the money supply leads to greater investment when the economy is healthy. In times of severe recession, however, monetary policy is ineffective.

Fiscal policy is the preferred approach to restore full employment output.

Tim Gidal/Getty Images

John Maynard Keynes

Monetarist Theory

Increasing the money supply reduces interest rates, which leads to greater consumption and investment. Monetary policy is therefore effective in the short run.

Fiscal policy is ineffective as it crowds out consumption and investment.

Bettmann/Getty Images

Milton Friedman

13.5 **Demand Shocks Versus Supply Shocks**

Demand shocks affect the AD curve.

- Caused by factors such as consumer confidence, business sentiment, or export demand.
- Monetary policy is more effective because targeting one goal automatically targets the other.

Supply shocks affect the SRAS curve.

- Caused by factors such as changing input prices or technological innovation.
- Monetary policy is less effective because targeting one goal makes the other target worse.

Rising food prices cause a negative supply shock that is difficult to counteract with monetary policy.

SECTION 3 MODERN MONETARY POLICY

13.6 **Rules:** Money grows by a fixed amount each year, preventing monetary policy from causing too drastic an effect because the economy is inherently stable in the long run.

versus

Discretion: A flexible money approach based on current economic conditions. It is useful in severe recessions when constant money growth might not be enough.

An alternative to money targeting is **inflation targeting:** implementing policy to keep inflation at about 2% to facilitate long-term economic growth.

Magictorch/Getty Images

13.7 **Taylor rule:** Used to approximate the Fed's actions on interest rates based on economic conditions:

Fed Funds Target Rate = Target Inflation Rate + Current Inflation Rate
$+ \frac{1}{2}$(Inflation Gap) $+ \frac{1}{2}$(Output Gap)

SECTION 4 MONETARY POLICY CHALLENGES

13.8 The U.S. financial crisis that began in 2007 created a major challenge for the Fed, which had lowered the federal funds rate to near 0% but still faced an economy in deep recession.

To continue expansionary monetary policy with interest rates at 0%, the Fed engaged in various **quantitative easing** strategies, including purchasing long-term assets from banks to expand the monetary base.

13.9 The nineteen member nations that form the Eurozone share a monetary policy set by the European Central Bank (ECB). In recent years, the ECB has used aggressive monetary policy actions to prevent the effects of financial crises in individual nations from engulfing the entire region.

Andy Rain/Epa/Shutterstock

Protests on quantitative easing arose because people feared high potential inflation, which would reduce the value of money and savings. The aggressive actions taken by the Fed and the ECB led to growing criticism of the powerful role of monetary policy.

Key Concepts

expansionary monetary policy, p. 323

contractionary monetary policy, p. 324

equation of exchange, p. 326

money illusion, p. 328

liquidity trap, p. 329

easy money, quantitative easing, or
    accommodative monetary policy, p. 332

tight money or restrictive monetary policy, p. 333

monetary rule, p. 333

inflation targeting, p. 333

Taylor rule, p. 333

monetary hawk, p. 336

monetary dove, p. 336

Questions and Problems

Check Your Understanding

1. Why is it important for the Federal Reserve Board to be independent of the executive branch of the federal government?

2. When the interest rate falls, why do people desire higher money balances?

3. Describe how open market operations alter the supply of money.

4. What does the equation of exchange, $M \times V = P \times Q$, help to explain?

5. How is the impact of expansionary monetary policy different when the economy is considerably below full employment compared to when it is at full employment?

6. How do sticky wages and prices make monetary policy effective in the short run?

Apply the Concepts

7. Suppose a rise in consumer confidence causes aggregate demand to increase, resulting in a short-run equilibrium that is above full employment output. What type of monetary policy might the Fed use to reduce inflationary pressures and to bring the economy back to full employment?

8. It seems that each time the Fed raises interest rates, the stock market has an awful few days. Why do higher interest rates have such an impact on the stock market?

9. If the Fed persistently uses expansionary monetary policy to keep interest rates very low, what are some of the risks that may occur?

10. When NASA scientists were operating the Mars rovers to make them drive across the Martian landscape and collect and analyze rocks and crevices, the scientists complained that the 20-minute delay between when they issued a command and when the rovers responded made their job more challenging. Isn't this somewhat similar to what monetary policymakers face? How is it different?

11. Suppose another spike in energy prices causes a negative supply shock. What type of monetary policy should the Fed use if the goal is to maintain price stability in the economy? What are the consequences of doing so?

12. Explain how the housing bubble at the beginning of the 21st century led to the Taylor rule target exceeding the actual federal funds rate. How might the severity of the Great Recession been reduced had the federal funds rate been adjusted?

In the News

13. In 2019 President Trump nominated individuals to fill vacancies in the Federal Reserve's Board of Governors who have been critical of the Fed in the past, even questioning its existence during the height of the quantitative easing years. How might bringing in

nominees with strong political views about the Fed play a role in the type of monetary policy decisions that result?

14. When Greece faced a debt crisis in 2017, it was forced to adopt austerity measures that reduced wages of government workers as well as benefits enjoyed by much of the population. By cutting government spending, particularly investments in public projects, Greece managed to achieve a budget surplus in 2017 and 2018 as well as maintain positive economic growth. However, some worried that such austerity measures would push Greece back into a recession in the near future. Explain how this might occur.

Solving Problems

15. Suppose a major earthquake disrupts production in many industries, causing $SRAS_0$ to shift to $SRAS_1$ in the following figure. What happens to the aggregate price level and aggregate output in this economy? If the government's objective is to return aggregate output back to full employment as quickly as possible using monetary policy, what policy would it use? Show the effect of the government's action in the figure. How does it affect the aggregate price level?

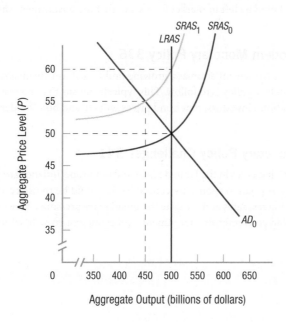

Work It Out

 interactive activity

16. In 2016 U.S. inflation was 1.2%, and output was 0.6% below its long-run potential. In 2019, an expanding U.S. economy caused inflation to increase to 1.6%, and output was 0.4% above its long-run potential.

    a. If the inflation target is 2%, what was the federal funds target in 2016 using the Taylor rule?

    b. If the actual federal funds rate was 0.75% in 2016, did the Taylor rule estimate the target accurately?

    c. Again assuming an inflation target of 2%, what was the federal funds target in 2019 using the Taylor rule?

    d. If the actual federal funds rate was 2.5% in 2019, did the Taylor rule do a better job predicting interest rates compared to 2016? Explain your answer.

Answers to Questions in Checkpoints

Checkpoint: What Is Monetary Policy? 325

Expansionary monetary policy reduces interest rates in order to spur consumption and investment, leading to an increase in aggregate demand. A reduction in interest rates placed on student loans by the government, although technically not monetary policy, produces a similar effect. When your monthly payments are reduced due to the interest rate reduction, you now have extra money to spend on other items. This extra consumption contributes to an increase in aggregate demand, much like an expansionary monetary policy.

Checkpoint: Monetary Theories 332

Those who prefer a large government role in the economy would best resemble Keynesians who believe in fiscal policy to increase aggregate demand. Keynesians would support raising tax revenues to reduce the debt. Those who advocate for a smaller government might be considered monetarists, who believe that fiscal policy tends to crowd out consumption and investment. Monetarists would support a reduction in spending to reduce the debt. Those who do not believe in either fiscal or monetary policy interventions might resemble classical theorists who believe that the economy should be left to market forces and that the government should be as small as possible.

Checkpoint: Modern Monetary Policy 336

When the Fed begins to view inflation as a growing problem, it usually means that some form of contractionary monetary policy is to follow. This typically means that interest rates will rise and, most important for bond investors, that bond prices will *fall* and bondholders will incur capital losses.

Checkpoint: Monetary Policy Challenges 341

As economic growth increases in the United States and in Europe, inflationary pressures are likely to increase. The appropriate response by central banks would be to use contractionary monetary policy to raise interest rates and mitigate the inflationary pressures. However, raising interest rates leads to reduced consumption, investment, and economic growth, which is not politically popular.

ZRS Management

Macroeconomic Policy: Challenges in a Global Economy

Understanding the obstacles facing our economy and the policy tools that are available to overcome them

Learning Objectives

Since the start of the new millennium, the U.S. economy has experienced periods of rapid economic growth along with a severe recession caused by a major financial crisis. Although such ups and downs are a normal part of the business cycle for a healthy economy, the severity of the fluctuations over the past two decades has made macroeconomic policy more relevant in our public discourse. The effects of the business cycle were not limited to the United States. Countries around the world experienced similar fluctuations as an increasingly globalized economy makes no country completely immune from the prosperity or troubles of others.

One of the unique aspects of the last financial crisis and recession was that it was caused largely by aggressive actions related to the housing market that led to a bubble. Once that bubble burst in 2007, the consequences spread to all sectors of the economy, especially the financial sector, which led to the most severe recession in over a generation.

What does macroeconomics have to say about the effects of a deep economic recession and a slow economic recovery? Quite a bit, actually. We have seen in previous chapters how the Fed and the federal government intervene in markets to promote long-term economic growth and stability in employment and prices. But this is much harder than it might appear to be: There is no magic formula easily discernible to all that will correct each problem.

Before the 1930s, common wisdom was that the economy was best left alone. The Great Depression changed that, and ever since then the government's role in economic stabilization—smoothing the business cycle—expanded substantially.

This chapter studies the economic policies that address the macroeconomic issues facing the world today: rising debt, long-run inflation, and structural unemployment resulting from technological change. One challenge is the existence of a potential tradeoff between inflation and unemployment. Another is the potential tradeoff between debt reduction and economic growth. These potential tradeoffs influence the macroeconomic policies chosen to guide the economy.

The chapter begins with a broad overview of the factors leading to the 2007–2009 Great Recession (as it is now known) and the slow recovery. The chapter then studies several theories regarding the effectiveness of macroeconomic policy, including the Phillips curve on the potential tradeoff between unemployment and inflation, the rational expectations argument about the ultimate ineffectiveness of policy, and the new Keynesian response.

Finally, we discuss the economic issues that influence the future of our economy. We focus on the effects of rising debt, globalization, and automation. We use the macroeconomic tools discussed throughout this book to analyze how economic policies affect our economy and our standard of living.

BY THE Numbers

7,163,000

Total jobs lost during the Great Recession (December 2007–June 2009)

17,981,000

Total jobs created over nine years of economic recovery and expansion (July 2009–July 2018)

Macroeconomic Challenges:
Managing an Expanding Economy

After the Great Recession of 2007–2009 led to the near collapse of the housing and financial markets, consumer sentiment and business expectations were deflated. It took many years for the economy to recover. Once it did, the economy continued to expand as consumer and business confidence increased and led to a record-setting 10-year period of growth that reduced the unemployment to levels not seen in over 50 years. This By the Numbers analyzes the University of Michigan's Index of Consumer Sentiment, an important gauge for measuring the health of the economy.

WHY ARE THESE DATA IMPORTANT?

Consumption represents about 68% of total U.S. gross domestic product. Although consumption does not vary significantly from year to year compared to investment spending, even small changes in consumer confidence can result in substantial changes in the growth rate for the economy. When combined with more volatile investment spending, recessions can result when consumers become more pessimistic about the economy.

DATA:

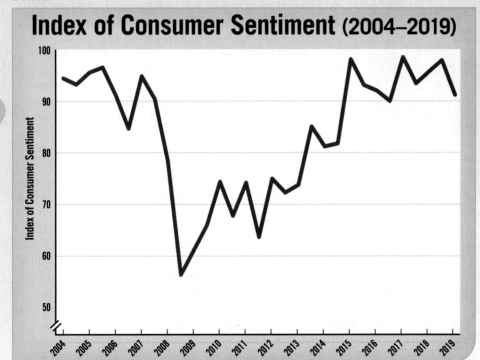

Index of Consumer Sentiment (2004–2019)

Where Can I Find These Data?

Source: FRED Database; Federal Reserve Bank of St. Louis

Web site: https://fred.stlouisfed.org/

Details: Search for "Consumer Sentiment" and select "University of Michigan: Consumer Sentiment"

Data *in the News*

~ Assessing Your Data Literacy ~

1. What was the lowest level of the Index of Consumer Sentiment during the depth of the 2007–2009 recession? In which year did that occur?

2. In which year did the Index of Consumer Sentiment reach its peak prior to the 2007–2009 recession? Has consumer confidence returned to that level since the 2007–2009 recession?

3. How closely does the Index of Consumer Sentiment follow the trend of other measures of the macroeconomy (such as real GDP) over the business cycle?

FROM RECESSION TO RECOVERY: GOVERNMENT IN ACTION

The 18-month recession that lasted from December 2007 to June 2009 was dubbed the Great Recession not because of its length but rather for its severity and impact on individuals, businesses, and countries. Further, it took many years for major economic indicators to return to their pre-recession levels. This section presents an overview of the Great Recession and the macroeconomic policies that were used to mitigate its effects.

From the Housing Bubble to the Financial Crisis

During the first few years of the 21st century, two key factors contributed to low interest rates: a glut of worldwide savings and the Fed's aggressive expansionary monetary policies, set in response to the 2001 recession. Demand for homes subsequently increased, causing home prices to rise and enticing more people to become speculators—purchasing homes with the intention of selling them quickly for a profit.

Meanwhile, banks became eager to cash in on the lucrative housing market and loosened their lending standards, allowing people with poor credit and/or lower incomes to qualify for loans. Instead of the traditional 30-year mortgage with a fixed interest rate, banks offered a variety of attractive adjustable-rate mortgages (ARMs) to encourage home buying. These mortgages offered a below-market interest rate for a short period (usually three to five years) and then would adjust to a much higher rate.

The housing boom of 2003 to 2007 saw even more innovations in the mortgage market as banks felt competitive pressure from mortgage brokers and investors. For example, banks dramatically increased the use of **subprime mortgages**, loans made to borrowers with poor credit. These loans carried high interest rates and were profitable for banks as long as borrowers made payments on time. Moreover, banks minimized their risk by selling many of these high-risk loans to investors in the form of **collateralized debt obligations** (CDOs), also known as mortgage-backed securities (the most common asset in CDOs during that time).

First homes, bigger homes, and second homes were the goals of many Americans during the housing bubble of the early 21st century.

subprime mortgage Mortgages that are given to borrowers who are a poor credit risk. These higher-risk loans charge a higher interest rate, which can be profitable to lenders if borrowers make their payments on time.

collateralized debt obligation A collection of assets, primarily mortgages with varying risk, sold as a security to investors.

CDOs are essentially bonds backed by a collection of mortgages: prime, subprime, home equity, and other ARMs. Banks could reduce risk by selling loans to consolidators who put together large packages of CDOs with the mortgaged homes serving as the collateral. Wall Street then sold slices of these mortgage pools to investors interested in the steady income from mortgage payments. Because high-risk subprime mortgages were combined with solid mortgages, risk was somewhat mitigated, much like diluting poison into a large lake to dissipate its effects.

The consequence of CDOs was that banks were now evaluating mortgage clients for loans that they did not intend to keep. They could make the loan, collect the fees, and then sell the loans to investors. Banks could advertise and sell loans quickly and then transfer the risk elsewhere.

Trouble started in 2007 when some people with subprime mortgages started to default. Many subprime borrowers did not fully understand the conditions of their loans, which often involved ARMS that reset after a few years, causing monthly payments to double or triple. Moreover, the rise in foreclosures caused the value of houses to fall and started the collapse of the housing market. Borrowers wishing to refinance their homes (to make mortgage payments affordable again) were often turned away because the amount they were seeking to borrow exceeded the value of their now lower-value home. This led to even more defaults.

Another problem was that bond rating agencies misled investors by inflating the ratings of risky CDOs, manipulating the standards to provide the highest possible AAA rating. Why would they do this? One key reason was that ratings firms were paid up to six times their normal fee to give the AAA rating to mortgage packages. Investors wanted bonds with the security of a AAA rating, which gave the appearance of high-yield, low-risk investments. As a result, the risk was highly underestimated.

TABLE 1	THE MAGNIFIED RISK OF LEVERAGED INVESTMENTS
Nonleveraged Investment	**Leveraged Investment**
Initial account value: $10,000	Initial account value: $10,000
Leverage ratio: 1:1	Leverage ratio: 10:1
Value of invested assets: $10,000 ($10,000 × 1)	Value of invested assets: $100,000 ($10,000 × 10)
Event: 10% drop in invested assets	Event: 10% drop in invested assets
Drop in value of investment: $1,000 ($10,000 × 10%)	Drop in value of investment: $10,000 ($100,000 × 10%)
New account value: $9,000	New account value: $0

Two more problems added to the growing house of cards. Many investors **leveraged** their money to earn greater returns because CDOs were viewed as a low-risk investment. This means that a small amount of money is used to support a larger amount of investment by borrowing. But leveraging adds risk: A small drop in prices can cause severe losses. Table 1 shows how a leveraged investment magnifies the risk of losing money. In this case, a 10% decrease in the price of the security wipes out the leveraged account, while the value of the nonleveraged account falls by just 10%. A leveraged account magnifies both gains and losses.

To protect against this risk, investors purchased **credit default swaps**, an instrument developed by the financial industry to act as an insurance policy against defaults. The biggest issuer of credit default swaps, the American International Group (AIG), sold several *trillion* dollars of these swaps with only a few *billion* dollars in capital to back them up. Again, risk was underestimated and therefore mispriced.

In 2007, the house of cards finally fell, leading to the financial crisis. Around $25 *trillion* in American CDOs were held worldwide. As subprime mortgage defaults skyrocketed, investors panicked and sold CDOs, causing prices to plummet. AIG could not cover the losses it had insured and went bankrupt. Banks that held CDOs became insolvent. Credit lines dried up, and the money supply decreased, contracting the economy and leading to the worst recession in over a generation.

leverage Occurs when a small amount of capital is used to support a larger amount of investment by borrowing. The risk of highly leveraged investments is that a small decrease in price can wipe out one's account.

credit default swap A financial instrument that insures against the potential default on an asset. Due to the extent of defaults in the last financial crisis, issuers of credit default swaps could not repay all of the claims, bankrupting these financial institutions.

The Government's Policy Response

The financial crisis that began in 2007 was among the worst in U.S. history. For the Fed, it was crucial to maintain public confidence in order to prevent the widespread bank failures that plagued the economy during the Great Depression and during the savings and loan crisis in the 1980s. To keep the recession from worsening, the Fed stepped far outside of its normal role of managing the money supply and took extraordinary measures to prevent a financial sector meltdown.

In July 2007, investment bank Bear Sterns liquidated two hedge funds that invested in mortgage-backed securities as they started to collapse. By March 2008, a near bankrupt Bear Sterns was bailed out by the Fed, which arranged its takeover by Chase Bank. A few months later, Lehman Brothers, the fourth largest commercial bank, went bankrupt. Stung by criticism of its Bear Sterns bailout, the Fed let Lehman Brothers fail on September 15, 2008. This inaction sent financial markets into turmoil as banks lost faith in other banks and insolvencies rose. Adding fuel to the fire, the following day AIG announced it was bankrupt, turning AAA-rated CDO bonds into highly discounted junk bonds. To stem the panic, the Fed loaned AIG over $100 billion.

In addition to these bailouts, the government used unprecedented fiscal policies to save the economy. In October 2008, Congress passed the $700 billion

The collapse of the housing market forced many homeowners out of their homes and contributed to the severity of the 2007–2009 recession.

Troubled Asset Relief Program (TARP), authorizing the U.S. Treasury to purchase CDOs from banks to increase the banks' capital. To reduce the risk of bank runs, the Federal Deposit Insurance Corporation (FDIC) increased its guarantee on deposits from $100,000 to $250,000 in 2008. In 2009, the $787 billion American Recovery and Reinvestment Act was passed, a fiscal stimulus package aimed at boosting aggregate demand. Finally, the government responded to support industries that suffered from depressed consumer demand during the crisis. For example, in 2009 the government loaned money to General Motors, Chrysler, and Ford and bought stock in General Motors and Chrysler to save the U.S. automobile industry. The auto industry eventually recovered and became highly profitable, allowing the government to earn a profit on its investment.

Finally, because the recovery from the recession was very slow and weak, the Fed continued to buy risky mortgage-backed securities from banks using money it created in a sequence of what were referred to as quantitative easing (QE) programs. When QE ended in 2014, the Fed had accumulated over $1.7 trillion in mortgage-backed securities.

The U.S. Economy: A Decade Later

The magnitude of the fiscal and monetary policies used during and after the financial crisis changed the way many people view the role of government. Many people (including economists) lauded the government's efforts as necessary to avert a larger financial crisis and recession. But critics of the government's actions argue that such extreme actions will lead to rising debt and inflation, among other effects, that will hamper future economic growth.

In recent years, the economy has fully recovered from the last recession and experienced significant economic growth. But that doesn't mean the economy is free from problems. The national debt continues to rise both in nominal terms as well as a percentage of GDP. Recent tax reforms and increased mandatory government spending have increased the debt, posing greater concern. Also, rising inflationary pressure as the economy expands has led the Fed to raise interest rates more aggressively.

The tools we learned in previous chapters help us understand how and when the government acts to smooth fluctuations in the business cycle. The next section takes a further look at the effectiveness of macroeconomic policy by considering the Phillips curve and the rational expectations model.

 CHECKPOINT

FROM RECESSION TO RECOVERY: GOVERNMENT IN ACTION

- A world savings glut and low interest rates in the early 21st century led to a housing price bubble. Consumers were eager to buy homes, developers were eager to build them, banks were eager to lend money to purchasers, and investors were eager to invest in CDOs.

- Financial risk was not properly considered in the period leading up to the financial crisis, and ratings agencies gave too many CDOs a AAA rating that wasn't deserved.

- When the housing bubble collapsed, foreclosures on subprime mortgages sent the economy into a recession.

- To control the panic, the Fed used its normal monetary policy tools and some that it hadn't used in a long time in its role as lender of last resort.

- Congress used fiscal policy to mitigate the drop in aggregate demand caused by the financial crisis.

QUESTION: The U.S. housing bubble in the early 21st century was caused by a number of factors that provided incentives to individuals to buy houses, to businesses to build and sell houses, and to financial institutions to loan money. In hindsight, what are some policies that the government could have implemented to mitigate this housing bubble?

Answers to the Checkpoint questions can be found at the end of this chapter.

PHILLIPS CURVES AND RATIONAL EXPECTATIONS

The severe recession of 2007–2009 and its slow recovery had economists debating the right policy to use. Fiscal policy was implemented to boost market activity, at the cost of rising debt. In addition, significant monetary policy actions were taken to inject the economy with more money, at the cost of potential inflation. Questions that arise from these policies include whether the effort to reduce unemployment could result in higher inflation or whether macroeconomic policy has any short-term effects at all. We address these issues in this section by studying two theories developed in the 1950s and 1960s: the Phillips curve and rational expectations.

With Phillips curve analysis, it first seemed that fiscal policy was easy: Pick an unemployment rate from column A and obtain a corresponding inflation rate from column B. Unfortunately, reality turned out to be much more complex. With rational expectations, the question was whether policy could ever be effective at all.

Unemployment and Inflation: Phillips Curves

Does a relationship exist between unemployment and inflation? In his early work, A. W. Phillips compared the rate of change in money wages to unemployment rates in Britain over the years from 1861 to 1957. The negatively sloped curve shown in Figure 1 reflects his estimate of how these variables were related and has been called a **Phillips curve** in his honor. As you can see, when unemployment rises, wages are negatively affected.

What explains this negative relationship between changes in wage rates and unemployment? Labor costs or wages are typically a firm's largest cost component. When labor demand rises as recently seen in the health care and Internet security industries, labor markets will tighten, and firms will offer higher wages to attract workers. On the other hand, when labor demand falls, unemployment rises and wages decline.

The market relationship between wages and unemployment will clearly affect prices. But worker productivity also plays an important role in determining prices.

Productivity, Prices, and Wages We might think that whenever wages rise, prices must also rise. Higher wages mean higher labor costs for employers—costs that businesses then pass along in the form of higher prices. But this is not always the case. If worker productivity increases

Phillips curve The original curve posited a negative relationship between wages and unemployment, but later versions related unemployment to inflation rates.

····· Figure 1 • The Original Phillips Curve for Britain (1861–1957) ·············

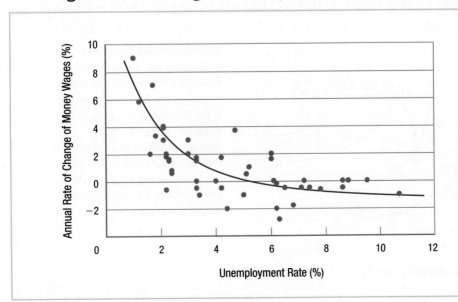

A. W. Phillips compared the rate of change in money wages to unemployment rates in Britain from 1861 to 1957. The resulting nonlinear, negatively sloped curve is the first example of a Phillips curve. When unemployment rises, changes in wage rates fall, and vice versa. Note that some dots represent multiple years.

····· Figure 2 • The Phillips Curve ···

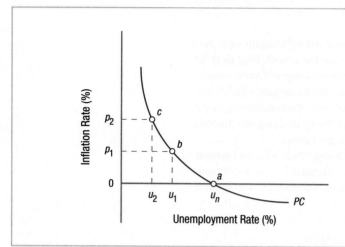

A rise in wages may cause a rise in prices, but if worker productivity increases sufficiently to offset the wage increase, product prices can remain stable. When the rates of change in productivity and wages are equal, inflation is zero (point *a*). This is the natural rate of unemployment. If policymakers want to use expansionary policy to reduce unemployment from u_n to u_1, they must be willing to accept inflation of p_1. Reducing unemployment further to u_2 would raise inflation to p_2 as labor markets tighten and wages rise more rapidly than productivity.

enough to offset the wage increase, then product prices can remain stable. The basic relationship among wages, prices, and productivity is:

$$\text{Inflation} = \text{Increase in Nominal Wages} - \text{Rate of Increase in Labor Productivity}$$

For example, when wages increase by 5% and productivity increases by 3%, inflation is 2%. Given this relationship, the Phillips curve can be adapted to relate productivity to inflation and unemployment, as shown in Figure 2.

When the rates of change in productivity and wages are equal, inflation is zero (point *a*). This occurs at the natural rate of unemployment, the unemployment rate when inflationary pressures are nonexistent. Therefore, higher rates of productivity growth mean that for a given level of unemployment, inflation will be less (the Phillips curve would shift in toward the origin).

If policymakers want to use expansionary policy to reduce unemployment from u_n to u_1, then according to the curve shown in Figure 2, they must be willing to accept inflation of p_1. To reduce unemployment further to u_2 would raise inflation to p_2 as labor markets tighten and wages rise more rapidly.

Figure 3 shows the Phillips curve for the United States from 1961 to 1981. During the 1960s, a smooth negative relationship existed between inflation and unemployment, much like that in

····· Figure 3 • The Phillips Curve from 1961–1981 ·················

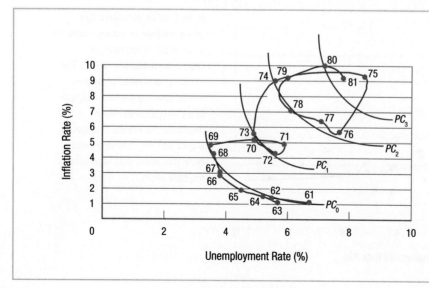

Data from the 1960s presented policymakers with a clear inverse relationship between inflation and unemployment. But this changed in the 1970s when oil supply shocks and rising inflationary expectations shifted the Phillips curve outward, causing both inflation and unemployment to rise. By 1980, annual inflation was over 10% and unemployment over 7%.

Figures 1 and 2. As unemployment fell, inflation rose. This empirical relationship led policymakers to believe that the economy presents them with a menu of choices. By accepting a minor rise in inflation, they could keep unemployment low. Alternatively, by accepting a rise in unemployment, they could keep inflation near zero.

But just as policymakers were getting used to the ease of making policy by accepting moderate inflation in exchange for lower unemployment rates, the economy played a big trick on them. The entire Phillips curve began shifting outward during the early 1970s.

What looked to be an easy tradeoff between inflation and unemployment turned ugly. Unemployment rates that had been associated with modest inflation of 2% to 3% in the 1960s began requiring twice that rate in the early 1970s. By the late 1970s, these same unemployment rates were generating annual inflation rates approaching double digits. The reason for these shifts turned out to be the oil supply shocks of the mid-1970s and the rising inflationary expectations that followed.

The Importance of Inflationary Expectations

Higher prices reduce real wages, or what nominal wages will buy. Therefore, when workers determine their willingness to work, they take into account their expectations of inflation.

Taking **inflationary expectations** into account, wage increases can be connected to unemployment and expected inflation by adding a variable, p^e, representing inflationary expectations, to the inflation equation introduced earlier:

$$\text{Inflation} = \text{Increase in Nominal Wages} - \text{Rate of Increase in Labor Productivity} + p^e$$

In other words, the same tradeoff between inflation and unemployment in the short-run Phillips curve existed as we saw before, but there is a unique tradeoff for each level of inflationary expectations.

For example, suppose there are no inflationary expectations, and productivity is growing at a 3% rate when the economy's unemployment rate is 4%. In this scenario, if nominal wages increase by 5%, inflation would be $5\% - 3\% + 0\% = 2\%$. However, if inflationary expectations (p^e) grow to, say, 4%, the Phillips curve will shift outward and the inflation rate now associated with 4% unemployment will be $5\% - 3\% + 4\% = 6\%$.

Inflationary Expectations and the Phillips Curve

Panel B of Figure 4 shows a Phillips curve augmented by inflationary expectations. The economy begins in equilibrium at full employment with zero inflation (point a in panel B). Panel A shows the aggregate demand and supply curves for this economy in equilibrium at point a. Note that the economy is producing at full employment output of Q_f, and this translates to the natural rate of unemployment, u_n, in panel B.

The Phillips curve in panel B is initially PC_0 $(p^e = 0\%)$. Thus, inflation is equal to zero and so are inflationary expectations (p^e). Now assume that policymakers want to reduce unemployment below u_n. Using expansionary policies, they shift aggregate demand in panel A from AD_0 to AD_1. This moves the economy to point b; real output and the price level rise, to Q_1 and P_1.

In panel B, the unemployment rate has declined to u_1 (point b) but inflation has risen to 5%. Workers had anticipated zero inflation; this *unanticipated inflation* means that real wages have fallen. Therefore, workers will begin asking for raises, and employers wanting to keep turnover at a minimum may well offer higher wages.

The Long-Run Phillips Curve

The long-run Phillips curve (LRPC), shown in panel B of Figure 4 as the vertical line at full employment (unemployment = u_n), shows the long-term relationship between inflation and unemployment when the inflation rate and the expected inflation rate are equal. The LRPC is the Phillips curve counterpart to the vertical long-run aggregate supply curve (LRAS) in panel A.

Accelerating Inflation

As nominal wages rise over time as shown in panel A, the short-run aggregate supply curve shifts leftward to $SRAS_1$, moving the economy back to full employment at price level P_2 (point c). In panel B, with inflation now at 5%, the Phillips curve shifts outward to PC_1 $(p^e = 5\%)$. Unemployment moves back to the natural rate as inflationary expectations rise to 5%.

inflationary expectations
The rate of inflation expected by workers for any given period. When inflationary expectations rise, workers will demand higher nominal wages.

Figure 4 • Aggregate Demand, Aggregate Supply, and the Expectations-Augmented Phillips Curve

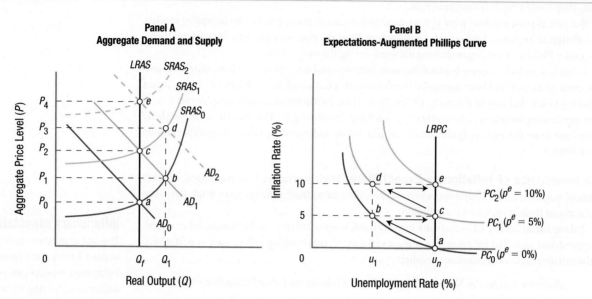

Panel A
Aggregate Demand and Supply

Panel B
Expectations-Augmented Phillips Curve

Panel A shows the economy's aggregate demand and aggregate supply curves, and panel B shows the economy's Phillips curve, augmented by inflationary expectations. Using expansionary policies to reduce unemployment below u_n in panel B, policymakers shift aggregate demand in panel A from AD_0 to AD_1. This moves the economy to point b in panel A, with real output and the price level rising to Q_1 and P_1, respectively. Unemployment declines to u_1 (point b in panel B), but inflation rises to 5%. If policymakers attempt to hold unemployment below the natural rate, the economy will endure accelerating inflation. The long-run Phillips curve (LRPC) in panel B shows the relationship between inflation and unemployment when the inflation rate is just equal to inflationary expectations.

At this point, if policymakers move the economy back to u_1 (or Q_1) again, they must repeat the process of expanding aggregate demand, only this time, the economy is starting from a higher Phillips curve because inflationary expectations are already elevated.

The implications of this analysis for fiscal and monetary policymakers who want to keep unemployment below the natural rate are not pleasant. To do so, they must continually increase aggregate demand so that inflation will always exceed what is expected. Thus, policymakers must be willing to incur a permanently *accelerating* rate of inflation—hardly a popular idea.

In the late 1970s and early 1980s, oil price shocks and rising inflationary expectations caused both inflation and unemployment to rise, creating what economists call **stagflation**. While the original Phillips curve concluded that rising unemployment would correspond with *falling* inflation, the 1970s witnessed rising unemployment and *rising* inflation as the Phillips curve shifted outward. By 1980 inflation was over 10% and unemployment was over 7%.

stagflation Simultaneous occurrence of rising inflation and rising unemployment.

An oil crisis in the 1970s caused inflation to spike and unemployment to rise, creating what economists call stagflation.

Bill Pierce/Getty Images

Returning Inflation to Normal Levels To eliminate inflationary pressures when they arise, policymakers must be willing to curtail growth in aggregate demand and accept higher unemployment in the short run. As aggregate demand falls, wage and price pressures will soften, reducing inflationary expectations. The Phillips curve shifts inward back to a position with lower inflation at the natural rate of unemployment. The time it takes for this process to occur depends on how rapidly the economy adjusts its inflationary expectations. Policymakers can speed this process along by ensuring their policies are credible by issuing public announcements that are consistent with contractionary policy.

The stagflation of the early 1980s required almost a decade to be resolved. Former Fed Chair Paul Volcker, who insisted on keeping interest rates high in the face of fierce public opposition, deserves much of the credit for this triumph over inflation. The next Fed chair, Alan Greenspan, maintained a tight watch on inflation, which fell from around 4% to near 1% in the 1990s.

Today, policymakers are generally willing to use expansionary policy to promote economic growth and reduce unemployment as long as the threat of inflation remains low. This was seen in the aftermath of the 2007–2009 recession when aggressive fiscal and monetary policies were used. These policies assume that inflationary expectations adjust with a lag, allowing some tradeoff between inflation and unemployment. However, some economists argue that consumers and businesses adapt their expectations so rapidly that policies become ineffective.

Rational Expectations and Policy Formation The use of expectations in economic analysis is nothing new. Keynes believed that expectations are driven by emotions. He suggested that investors in the stock market will follow trends without attempting to understand the underlying market dynamics. Milton Friedman developed his model of expectations using what are known as **adaptive expectations**, whereby people use past events to predict the future. Adaptive expectations are represented by a *backward-looking* model of expectations, which contrasts with the rational expectations model.

In the **rational expectations** model developed by Robert Lucas, individuals are assumed to make the best possible use of all publicly available information about what the future holds before making decisions. This does not mean that every individual's predictions about the future will be correct. Those errors that do occur will be randomly distributed such that the expectations of large numbers of people will average out to be correct.

Assume that the economy has been in equilibrium for several years with low inflation (2%) and unemployment (6%). In this situation, the average person would expect the inflation rate to be stable. But now assume that the Fed announces it is going to increase the rate of growth of the money supply significantly, which will eventually lead to higher inflation. Knowing this, households and businesses will immediately revise their inflationary expectations upward.

adaptive expectations
Inflationary expectations are formed from a simple extrapolation from past events.

rational expectations
Individuals are assumed to make the best possible use of all publicly available information, then make informed, rational judgments on what the future holds. Any errors in their forecasts will be randomly distributed.

NOBEL PRIZE
ROBERT LUCAS JR.

In the 1970s, a series of articles by Robert Lucas Jr. changed the course of contemporary macroeconomic theory and profoundly influenced the economic policies of governments throughout the world. His development of the rational expectations theory challenged decades of assumptions about how individuals respond to changes in fiscal and monetary policies.

Lucas was born in 1937 in Yakima, Washington. At age 17, he was awarded a scholarship to the University of Chicago, where he studied history. He then went on to the University of California, Berkeley, to pursue a Ph.D. in history, but while there he developed a keen interest in economics. Without funding from Berkeley's Economics Department, he returned to the University of Chicago, where he earned his Ph.D. in 1964. One of his professors was Milton Friedman, whose skepticism about interventionist government policies influenced a generation of economists. Lucas began his teaching career at Carnegie-Mellon University and later became a professor at the University of Chicago.

Before Lucas, economists accepted the Keynesian idea that expansionary policies could lower the unemployment rate. However, Lucas argued that the rational expectations of individual workers and employers would adjust to the changing inflationary conditions, and unemployment rates would rise again. Lucas developed mathematical models to show that temporarily cutting taxes to increase spending was not a sound policy because individuals would base their decisions on expectations about the future, and these temporary tax cuts would find their way into savings and not added spending. In other words, individuals were rational, forward-thinking, and perfectly able to adapt to changing economic information.

When the Royal Swedish Academy of Sciences awarded Lucas the Nobel Prize in 1995, it credited Lucas with "the greatest influence on macroeconomic research since 1970."

····· Figure 5 • Rational Expectations: The Policy Ineffectiveness Hypothesis ·····

Rational expectations theory suggests that macroeconomic policy will be ineffective, even in the short run. Assume that the economy is operating at full employment (point *a*) and short-run aggregate supply curve $SRAS_0$ ($P = 100$). Suppose that the Fed announces that it intends to increase the money supply. Expanding the money supply will shift aggregate demand from AD_0 to AD_1, raising nominal wages and prices (point *b*). Yet, as soon as the Fed announces the increase in the money supply, individuals will use this information to raise their inflationary expectations, shifting $SRAS_0$ to $SRAS_1$. Thus, output will remain unchanged, though the price level rises immediately to 110 (point *c*).

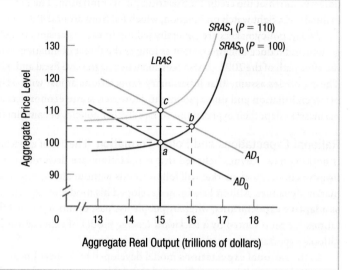

In this model, people do not rely only on past experiences to formulate their expectations of the future but instead use all information available to them. If adaptive expectations are *backward-looking*, rational expectations are *forward-looking*.

Policy Implications of Rational Expectations Do individuals and firms really form their future expectations as the rational expectations hypothesis suggests? If so, it would imply that macroeconomic policy is ineffective.

To illustrate, assume that the economy depicted in Figure 5 is operating at full employment at point *a*. Short-run aggregate supply curve $SRAS_0$ ($P = 100$) reflects current inflationary expectations. Suppose the Fed announces that it intends to increase the money supply, which shifts aggregate demand from AD_0 to AD_1. This will raise nominal wages and prices. But what happens next?

Natural rate theorists, using adaptive expectations, would argue that workers will be fooled into thinking that the increase in money wages represents a real raise, thus driving output and employment up to $16 trillion (point *b*). However, workers will eventually realize that real wages have not risen because prices have risen by at least as much as wages. Aggregate supply will then fall to $SRAS_1$ ($P = 110$) as price expectations climb and the economy gradually moves back to full employment at a higher price level (point *c*). In this scenario, the Fed's policy succeeds in raising output and employment in the short term, but at the expense of a long-term rise in the cost of living.

Contrast this with the rational expectations model. When the Fed announces that it is going to increase the money supply, perfectly rational individuals and firms will immediately raise their inflationary expectations. In Figure 5, output will remain unchanged because the price level will rise immediately to 110. No one is fooled into temporarily increasing output, even though the increase in the money supply still drives up prices. Therefore, any macroeconomic policy announcement will result in an immediate move to a new long-run equilibrium, leaving the short-term aspects of the policy change ineffective.

This suggests that if the Fed wants to use an increase in the money supply to raise output and employment in the short run, the only way it can do so is by *not* announcing its plans; it must essentially force individuals and firms to make decisions with incomplete information.

Assessing the Rational Expectations Model Empirical assessments of the ineffectiveness of macroeconomic policy based on rational expectations have yielded mixed results. Most studies do not find monetary policy to be ineffective. In other words, macroeconomic policies do have a real impact on the economy, and monetary policies are credited with keeping inflation low.

New Keynesian economists have taken a different approach to critiquing rational expectations theory. Both the adaptive and the rational expectations models assume that labor and product markets are highly competitive, with wages and prices adjusting quickly to expansionary or contractionary policies. However, new Keynesians point out that labor markets often have imperfect information and that efficiency wages lead to short-run wage stickiness.

Imperfect information occurs when firms and workers do not have full information on economic fluctuations due to timing lags, causing wages and prices to not react quickly. **Efficiency wage theory** disputes the notion that labor markets are like competitive commodity markets with equal prices. In other words, all labor is not equal. People need incentives to work hard, and paying workers an efficiency wage, or a wage above the market-clearing level, is one form of motivation to improve morale and productivity.

Imperfect information and efficiency wages suggest that wages and prices may be sticky because workers and firms are either unable or unwilling to make adjustments quickly to changes in monetary or fiscal policy. And this would give such policies a chance of a short-run impact.

Still, rational expectations as a concept has profoundly affected how economists approach macroeconomic problems. Nearly all economists agree that policy changes affect expectations and that this affects the behavior of individuals and firms. As a result, the effectiveness of monetary and fiscal policy is potentially reduced.

efficiency wage theory
Employers often pay their workers wages above the market-clearing level to improve morale and productivity, reduce turnover, and create a disincentive for employees to shirk their duties.

CHECKPOINT

PHILLIPS CURVES AND RATIONAL EXPECTATIONS

- The Phillips curve represents the inverse relationship between the unemployment rate and the inflation rate. When the unemployment rate goes up, inflation goes down, and vice versa.

- Rising inflationary expectations by the public shifts the Phillips curve to the right, worsening the tradeoff between inflation and unemployment.

- If policymakers use monetary and fiscal policy to push unemployment below the natural rate, they will face accelerating inflation. Reducing inflation requires that policymakers curtail aggregate demand and temporarily accept higher rates of unemployment.

- Adaptive expectations assume that individuals and firms extrapolate from past events; it is a *backward-looking* model. Rational expectations assume that individuals and firms make the best possible use of all publicly available information; it is a *forward-looking* model of expectations.

- Rational expectations analysis leads to the conclusion that policy changes will be ineffective; however, market imperfections and information problems are two reasons why rational expectations analysis has met with mixed results empirically.

QUESTIONS: If an economy has high unemployment but low inflation, what would the Phillips curve suggest to be an appropriate macroeconomic policy? Would your answer change if inflationary expectations rise? If we assume that all individuals and firms have excellent foreknowledge as described by the rational expectations model, would that change your answer?

Answers to the Checkpoint questions can be found at the end of this chapter.

MACROECONOMIC ISSUES THAT CONFRONT OUR FUTURE

Macroeconomic theory developed largely during the 85 years after Keynes wrote his famous book detailing the role of government in smoothing fluctuations in the economy. But as the previous two sections have shown, choosing the right macroeconomic policy to use in a given situation is neither easy nor one that generates a consensus among policymakers and the general public. However, it is clear that monetary policy has taken an increasingly important role in keeping the economy on a steady low-inflation growth path. Meanwhile, fiscal policy continues to be debated as issues of efficiency versus equity arise when the government uses taxpayer money to finance programs it deems essential for society. If you take one idea away from this course, it should be that there is not one economic model or one economic policy that fits all situations. Different circumstances call for different approaches.

In this section, we describe the key aspects surrounding three important issues facing our economy today and likely in the future: (1) growing debt and the threat of long-run inflation, (2) the importance of achieving economic growth in a globalized economy, and (3) the role of automation in changing the type of jobs that are available today and in the future.

Will Rising Debt and Future Debt Obligations Lead to Inflation?

Much of the debate among policymakers in recent years has centered on rising deficits and national debt. Indeed, fiscal deficits and national debt (at least in nominal terms) have risen to levels not seen in our history. The concern over debt has changed the politics in Washington, as a bitter debate ensued regarding the use of expansionary policies (such as corporate tax cuts and quantitative easing) to promote economic growth versus austerity measures (cost cutting) to reduce the deficit and the burden of the debt on future generations.

Rising Future Debt Obligations: Health Care and Social Security Even if the current deficits are brought under control using a combination of government spending cuts and tax increases, the long-term debt obligations relating to Social Security payments and rising health care costs pose a bigger question about the ability to keep deficits and debt under control over the long term.

As greater numbers of baby boomers (those born in the years following the end of World War II) retire, more will begin receiving Social Security and Medicare benefits. In addition to greater numbers of beneficiaries, the cost of the benefits also rises. Social Security benefits increase based on the rate of inflation, while Medicare payments rise as the cost of health care increases.

Recent legislation has slowed the rise in health care costs, but the overall cost remains difficult to sustain in the long term. In addition, the long-term debt obligations stemming from health care and Social Security do not fully appear in current deficit statistics because these expenses are budgeted and paid out during the year in which the costs are incurred. Therefore, if costs rise faster than revenues, deficits will persist, adding to the national debt.

The Cost of Financing Debt The cost of financing debt depends on the interest rate. Fortunately, the United States has enjoyed very low interest rates for much of the past decade. This not only helps individuals and firms looking to borrow but also the government in financing its debt. A new 30-year Treasury bond issued in 2019 paid about 3% per year. In 1989 a new 30-year Treasury bond paid about 8% per year. A difference of 5% in the interest rate represents a tremendous savings to the government.

Another factor in the cost of financing debt is the willingness of countries to hold U.S. debt. Part of this depends on the demand for the U.S. dollar. The U.S. dollar remains the most widely held currency in the world. When U.S. dollars are held by foreigners, this amounts to an interest-free loan to the U.S. government (also referred to as *seigniorage*) because no interest is paid on currency. The willingness of people around the world to use and hold dollars allows the government to print these dollars without the immediate worry of inflation.

The Effects of Debt on Inflation Addressing debt can be undertaken with fiscal policy as well as monetary policy. Fiscal policy to curb debt includes raising taxes or reducing government spending. However, neither of these policies is popular, especially the reduction of Social Security or health care benefits that account for over half of government spending. Further, contractionary fiscal policy can curtail economic growth, which is especially dangerous when recovering from a severe recession. For this reason, policymakers have turned to monetary policy.

One of the dangers of using monetary policy to help address deficit and debt issues occurs with **monetized debt**, which is debt that is paid for by an increase in the money supply. In other

monetized debt Occurs when debt is reduced by increasing the money supply, thereby making each dollar less valuable through inflation.

words, debt is reduced by way of a lower real value of the dollar. Because U.S. Treasury securities have long been desired as a safe investment by individuals, firms, as well as governments around the world, the U.S. government has not had to worry about the inflationary effects of its monetary policy in recent years.

However, should world demand for U.S. Treasury securities fall as countries diversify their holdings to other assets (such as euro-denominated assets or gold-backed assets), the value of the U.S. dollar may fall. A weaker dollar would increase the price Americans pay for foreign goods, and lead to inflation. Although a weaker dollar and inflation both reduce the burden on the existing debt, a higher rate of inflation reduces the purchasing power of one's income and savings, thereby reducing the standard of living.

In order to stem the effects of higher inflation, contractionary monetary policy is needed once the economy has recovered enough to withstand an increase in interest rates. However, such policies are not popular. But in order to keep rising inflation from causing more severe problems for the economy, the Fed has raised interest rates in recent years.

American Mint, LLC

One wild idea floated a number of years ago to reduce the national debt was to mint a *trillion-dollar coin* that would be used to pay off the government's annual deficit. But doing so would cause significant inflation as more money chases a relatively fixed output. Holders of dollar-denominated assets, such as bonds and savings and retirement accounts, would lose.

Will Globalization Lead to Increased Obstacles to Economic Growth?

Economic growth has been the driving force in improving our standard of living. However, the world is changing, and emerging countries such as China and India have experienced higher growth rates than the United States, Japan, and countries in Europe over the past two decades. Further, smaller developing countries, such as Cambodia, Ethiopia, and Vietnam, have seen stellar growth rates that have pulled millions out of poverty.

Why has economic growth spread throughout the world in this way, and what does this entail for developed nations such as the United States?

One of the most important changes to the world economy over the past generation has been the dramatic increase in international trade, international factor movements (foreign investment and immigration), offshoring (the movement of factories overseas), and international banking. The integration of the world's economies through mutual cooperation and free trade agreements has allowed more countries to specialize and reap the gains from trade that result.

For developed countries such as the United States, Japan, and countries in Europe, increased globalization means increased competition for resources, especially talented labor, which now has many more opportunities than it did in the past. Therefore, pressures to innovate and to increase productivity have increased with globalization.

What does this mean for macroeconomic policy? Not only does fiscal and monetary policy need to be tailored to fit the problems inherent in our own country, but how these policies affect other countries becomes important as well. The following Around the World feature describes how Germany managed its economy following its reunification in 1990 and in its role as a leader in the European Union.

Fiscal policies such as implementing trade restrictions or providing support for domestic industries tend to help one country at the expense of its trading partners. Taking these policies too far may encourage other countries to take similar actions, which would lead to fewer exports and a reduction in trade and economic growth.

Monetary policies also affect other nations through trade and the exchange rate. Expansionary monetary policy, such as reducing the interest rate, has the effect of lowering the value of one currency against others. When this occurs, the price of imports rises and the price of exports falls, helping to improve the trade balance as consumers react by purchasing more domestically-produced goods than foreign-made goods. But again, such policies can lead to retaliatory actions if taken too far.

The next two chapters on international trade and open economy macroeconomics deal with how countries interact with other countries, either through the trade of goods and services or through the exchange of currencies. Both have important implications for the ability of countries to grow and to improve their standards of living.

imageBROKER/Alamy

Ethiopia, which experienced one of the worst famines in world history in 1985, today has an emerging economy with a high growth rate as it focuses on infrastructure, manufacturing, and trade.

🌍 AROUND THE WORLD

Life on the Autobahn: Germany's Role in European Growth and Stability

How did Germany maintain a strong economy after its reunification in 1990 and then in a Eurozone that faced many financial crises?

The autobahn has long been a symbol of Germany's quest for economic strength and prosperity. Led by its successful auto industry, Germany achieved much economic growth over the last 50 years, and its corporate brands are among the most recognizable and respected in the world. Even more remarkable is how Germany withstood many challenges over the last 30 years that tested its ability to maintain its economic strength.

What are some major events that shaped Germany's economy over the last 30 years?

One major test of Germany's resilience came with the fall of the Berlin Wall in 1989 and the reunification of West Germany with East Germany in 1990. At the time of reunification, West Germany's

The autobahn has no speed limit in most areas, symbolizing Germany's strength in the face of many economic challenges.

GDP per capita was more than twice that of East Germany. Despite vast economic differences, the reunified Germany invested heavily in capital improvements in the East, where marginal returns to capital were strong, increasing labor productivity that led to rising incomes.

Another major test was the formation of the European Union, which allowed workers and capital to move between member countries, along with the

introduction of the euro, which merged the monetary policies of countries with different economic conditions. When nearly half of the Eurozone members faced financial crises between 2008 and 2013, Germany led the European Central Bank's efforts to increase lending while mandating reforms to put countries back on a path to growth.

Finally, Germany played a vital role in the resettlement of refugees and migrants that began flooding into Europe in 2015 to escape war and/or poverty. In the following year Germany accepted more than 1 million asylum seekers. Germany demonstrated its ability to show compassion to the plight of others while continuing to maintain economic growth and low inflation.

Today, Germany remains a strong economic power that embraces diversity and has become a land of opportunity for many in a time when other countries are shutting their doors. It is a symbol of globalization that has given millions a new chance at life.

© Val Thoermer/Alamy Stock Photo

🖿 GO ONLINE TO PRACTICE THE ECONOMIC CONCEPTS IN THIS STORY

---

automation The use of capital, such as a robot, to perform a task that a human worker previously performed.

Automation and Its Effect on the Macroeconomy

In 2017 the company CafeX made headlines for opening an automated coffee shop in San Francisco that uses robots to make coffee much faster and, according to some of its loyal customers, better tasting than a human barista. This prompted Starbucks, which operates more than 24,000 stores and employs more than 250,000 people, to issue an announcement that it has no plans to replace its human baristas with robots. However, the announcement did not say whether it would *ever* consider such an action. Still, rising concerns about **automation** replacing human workers prompted the company to ease worries among its workers and customers who prefer a human to prepare their favorite coffee drink.

Competitive pressures in the market along with improved capital innovations have allowed automation to take a larger role in manufacturing and service industries. Although replacing a human with a robot requires a substantial fixed cost, the savings in wages generally far exceed the maintenance and depreciation costs of the robot. Moreover, for many mundane tasks, robots are often faster and more accurate, can work longer hours, and will never call in sick (though they *can* break down). However, there are still many industries in which humans are preferred to robots, such as in service industries noted in the story above. Customers often prefer to speak to a human customer service representative to solve a problem than to enter a seemingly endless series of automated prompts. In the coffee industry, most coffee is still picked by hand due to the delicate nature of

Justin Sullivan/Getty Images

Automated coffee shops in San Francisco have generated fans who value their efficiency and consistency, and critics who dislike the lack of human interaction that is part of the coffee culture.

the plant and the need to distinguish between ripe and unripe coffee cherries that are processed into coffee beans.

The impact of automation on the macroeconomy is very significant. One of the main effects of automation is the structural unemployment that it causes. Recall from an earlier chapter that structural unemployment occurs when workers are no longer needed due to a technological change in an industry or when a good or service becomes obsolete. For example, structural unemployment has occurred in the toll collecting industry, as most tolls collected on highways and at entrances to bridges are now automated using toll responders and license plate readers. Structural unemployment requires workers to seek new jobs that use similar skills or requires workers to be retrained to pursue a different career. For toll collectors, the skill set is transferrable to many other service jobs. But for certain manufacturing jobs, such as automobile mechanics, the transition is more dramatic. Many vocational schools and colleges aim to help workers transition to new careers, while other organizations help specific people, such as veterans, transition into a changing workforce.

The VOW to Hire Heroes Act is an example of fiscal policy used to encourage employers to hire veterans returning from active duty.

Another consequence of automation is that it has contributed to a phenomenon called a **jobless recovery** after the last three U.S. recessions. A jobless recovery occurs after a recession when output begins to rise but employment growth does not. An explanation for this effect is that many companies are hesitant to lay off a worker for the direct purpose of replacing him or her with automation. However, when a recession occurs, many workers lose their jobs due to weakness in demand. When the recession ends, companies then find it easier to invest in automation instead of rehiring the workers they laid off.

jobless recovery A phenomenon that takes place after a recession, when output begins to rise, but employment growth does not.

The promising news for human workers is that automation has generated a large demand for high-skilled workers that can build and/or maintain the equipment being used. Moreover, software engineers are needed to program robots, and Internet security experts are needed to ensure that malware and other risks do not harm the company's operations.

Automation will become even more prevalent as new technologies, such as artificial intelligence, improve. For example, self-driving cars will potentially replace millions of drivers of ride-sharing services, trucking, and delivery services. As more consumers become comfortable communicating with their voice assistants, such as Amazon Echo or Google Assistant, they may be more open to communicating with virtual assistants for customer service transactions. Regardless of how automation affects our daily lives, the effects on the economy are significant and will need to be considered when choosing macroeconomic policies.

✓ CHECKPOINT

MACROECONOMIC ISSUES THAT CONFRONT OUR FUTURE

- No single macroeconomic model can solve all economic problems.

- Jobless recoveries are spurred by increases in labor productivity, changes in employment patterns, and increased use of offshoring. Fiscal and monetary policies provide incentives to consume and invest, leading to job growth.

- Rising deficits were caused by expansionary fiscal policies used to stem the effects of the financial crisis. Future concerns of deficits and debt center on the rising costs of Social Security and Medicare, making the use of fiscal policy to mitigate rising debt difficult.

- Rising interest rates in the future will increase borrowing costs, making it more difficult to finance debt. Increased use of expansionary monetary policy can lead to long-run inflation, reducing the debt burden but also reducing the purchasing power of savings.

- Globalization has led to economic growth throughout the world, especially in developing countries. However, increased competition from abroad has made it more challenging for developed nations to maintain high growth rates over time.

QUESTIONS: In 2009 inflation was negative (also known as deflation); average prices *fell* mostly due to a sharp decline in consumer spending and business investments from the recession. In early 2015, deflation occurred again, but this time it was caused by a sharp drop in energy prices. How does deflation affect the ability of households and businesses to manage debt? Does the cause of the deflation matter? Explain.

Answers to the Checkpoint questions can be found at the end of this chapter.

CHAPTER SUMMARY

SECTION 1 FROM RECESSION TO RECOVERY: GOVERNMENT IN ACTION

14.1 **Events Leading to the Great Recession**

- A glut in worldwide savings in the early years of the 21st century reduced interest rates.

- Low interest rates and easy bank loans fueled a housing bubble.

- Risky subprime mortgages were packaged into securities that were inadequately investigated and given perfect AAA ratings.

- Loan defaults led to a reduction in home prices and the collapse of mortgage-backed securities.

- Banks lost money from poor investments, insurance companies could not cover losses, and the downward spiral spread to other industries and eventually to the entire economy.

philip gangler/Shutterstock

14.2 **The Government's Policy Response**

- Passed the $700 billion Troubled Asset Relief Program (TARP) to bail out banks nearing bankruptcy.

- Loaned over $100 billion to AIG to prevent its insolvency in insuring risky assets by financial institutions.

- Passed the $787 billion American Recovery and Reinvestment Act (stimulus package).

- Bailed out the U.S. automobile industry.

- Reduced the federal funds target rate to 0% and began a series of quantitative easing (QE) programs to purchase risky assets from banks.

SECTION 2 PHILLIPS CURVES AND RATIONAL EXPECTATIONS

14.3 The **Phillips curve** shows an inverse relationship between unemployment rates and inflation. As unemployment falls, firms bid up the price of labor. Greater employment increases aggregate demand, pushing prices higher.

The Phillips curve presented policymakers with a menu of choices. By accepting modest inflation, they could keep unemployment low.

14.4 Phillips curves are affected by **inflationary expectations.** Rising inflationary expectations by the public would be reflected in a shift in the Phillips curve to the right, worsening the tradeoff between inflation and unemployment.

If policymakers use monetary and fiscal policy to attempt to keep unemployment continually below the natural rate, they will face accelerating inflation.

Once inflation reaches a high level, the risk of **stagflation** occurs, in which high inflation is coupled with high unemployment. Reducing stagflation requires tough contractionary monetary policies to bring down inflation.

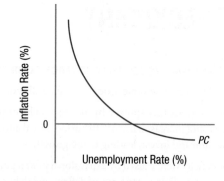

14.5 **The adaptive expectations model** assumes that people form their future expectations based on their past experiences. Therefore, it is a backward-looking model of expectations.

The rational expectations model suggests that policymakers cannot stimulate output in the short run by raising inflation unless they keep their actions secret.

Market imperfections and information problems are two reasons why the policy ineffectiveness conclusions of rational expectations analysis have met with mixed results empirically.

The rational expectations model assumes that individuals use all publicly available information in forming their expectations and is a forward-looking model of expectations.

Efficiency wages are paid in many professions as a way to keep employees from shirking their duties or leaving the company. The existence of efficiency wages brings about wage stickiness, which makes rational expectations less likely.

SECTION 3 MACROECONOMIC ISSUES THAT CONFRONT OUR FUTURE

14.6 The use of fiscal policy or monetary policy, or both, depends on the type of issues confronting our economy. Important issues facing our country today and in the future include:

- Rising deficits and debt
- Higher long-term inflation
- Globalization and its effect on economic growth
- The effect of automation on structural unemployment

Technological improvements in self-driving vehicles will lead to greater automation, potentially causing structural unemployment as human drivers are replaced with machines.

14.7 Globalization affects what we buy and what we produce, as goods and inputs move across borders.

Disney's Epcot World Showcase gives tourists a brief tour of the world. Although Epcot is located entirely in the United States, evidence of globalization abounds. Disney hires thousands of foreign workers, exports services to foreign tourists, imports millions of dollars worth of foreign-made merchandise, and invests in theme parks and companies overseas.

14.8 **Automation** is the use of capital to complete tasks that previously were completed by human workers. The structural unemployment that results requires workers to find new work using similar skills or be retrained.

Jobless recoveries have resulted after the last three recessions as companies invest in automation instead of rehiring its previous workers. However, new jobs have been created in building and maintaining capital equipment along with software programming and Internet security.

Key Concepts

subprime mortgage, p. 350

collateralized debt obligation, p. 350

leverage, p. 351

credit default swap, p. 351

Phillips curve, p. 353

inflationary expectations, p. 355

stagflation, p. 356

adaptive expectations, p. 357

rational expectations, p. 357

efficiency wage theory, p. 359

monetized debt, p. 360

automation, p. 362

jobless recovery, p. 363

Questions and Problems

Check Your Understanding

1. Why does the Phillips curve become very steep when unemployment is low and rather flat when unemployment is high?

2. Explain why the long-run Phillips curve makes it difficult (if not impossible) for policymakers to increase output and employment beyond full employment in the long run.

3. Explain why inflation accelerates if policymakers use monetary and fiscal policy to keep unemployment below the natural rate.

4. Explain why rational expectations does not mean that all individuals act rationally and are always correct.

5. Would policymakers prefer a Phillips curve with a steep or a flat slope? Why?

6. How does a negative supply shock (a huge natural disaster or significant energy price spike) affect the short-run Phillips curve? How does it affect the long-run Phillips curve?

Apply the Concepts

7. Why would policymakers want to drive unemployment below the natural rate, given that inflation would result?

8. Why are inflationary expectations so important for policymakers to keep under control? When a supply shock such as an oil price spike occurs, does it matter how fast policymakers attempt to bring the economy back to full employment? Explain.

9. Describe a few government policies that could have prevented the financial crisis in 2007.

10. Explain how the credibility of policymakers' (Congress and the Fed) commitment to keeping inflation low affects inflationary expectations when the economy is beset by a supply shock.

11. Explain why those who favor the rational expectations approach to modeling the economy do not favor discretionary policymaking.

12. Explain how the rise of automation in many industries can lead to both job gains and job losses in the overall economy.

In the News

13. Over the last 25 years, the Fed has increased its transparency by providing more detailed policy announcements after its meetings. In response, investors have reacted more quickly in response to the announcements. Does greater transparency provide more or less support to the conclusions of the rational expectations model? Explain how greater transparency might cause monetary policy to become less effective.

14. Almost every year, Congress is tasked with increasing the debt ceiling that allows the government to continue borrowing. In past decades, such legislation would pass easily because it was authorizing the payment of expenses already incurred. However, in recent years, some congressional leaders took the drastic approach of opposing to raise the debt ceiling as a way to reign in government spending. What are some benefits and costs of preventing the debt ceiling from being raised?

Solving Problems

15. The Phillips curve of the 1960s showed an inverse relationship between the inflation rate and unemployment. Use the following data on inflation and unemployment to plot a Phillips curve from 2014 to 2018. Does the same relationship between inflation and unemployment hold in 2014 to 2018 as it did in the 1960s?

Year	Inflation Rate	Unemployment Rate
2014	1.6	6.2
2015	0.1	5.3
2016	1.3	4.9
2017	2.1	4.4
2018	2.4	3.9

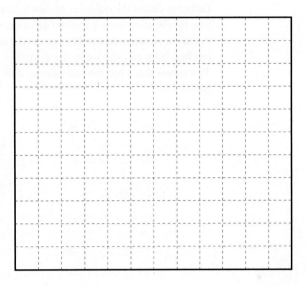

Work It Out

 interactive activity

16. During the recession from December 2007 to June 2009, the U.S. economy lost a total of 7,163,000 jobs. How many jobs were lost per month, on average? Suppose that a healthy economy generates an average of 200,000 jobs per month. At this rate, how long would it take the economy to gain back the number of jobs it had lost? According to data from the Bureau of Labor Statistics, the U.S. economy gained 5,485,000 jobs from June 2009 to June 2013. What was the average number of jobs per month created during the first four years of recovery? Given your answers to the previous two questions, what does this suggest about the pace of economic recovery after the 2007–2009 recession?

Answers to Questions in Checkpoints

Checkpoint: From Recession to Recovery: Government in Action 352

Had it been known that the collapse of the housing market bubble would have caused a severe financial crisis, the government could have implemented macroeconomic policies to slow the rise in housing prices. For example, the government could: (1) use contractionary monetary policy to push interest rates higher, making it more expensive to borrow money; (2) pass regulations on financial institutions requiring greater scrutiny of potential borrowers; (3) limit the types of risky loans that could be created; and (4) eliminate tax incentives on housing market profits to limit the buying and selling of homes for profit.

Checkpoint: Phillips Curves and Rational Expectations 359

The Phillips curve would suggest that unemployment can be reduced by accepting a higher rate of inflation. As long as inflation is very low, a small rise in inflation would be a small cost to pay for pushing the unemployment rate down. However, if inflationary expectations rise, it would require a greater inflation rate to achieve a lower unemployment rate. Here, policymakers must be careful not to let inflation exceed a level that might cause larger problems for the economy. Finally, if individuals and firms acted according to the rational expectations model, any increase in inflation would never lead to a reduction in unemployment. In this case, macroeconomic policy is ineffective in the short run, and the best prescription would be to leave the market alone to correct itself over time.

Checkpoint: Macroeconomic Issues That Confront Our Future 363

Deflation causes the real value of debt to rise, making it more difficult to repay. Yes, it does matter how the deflation occurs. In 2009 deflation resulted from a decrease in aggregate demand (from a decline in consumption and investment), causing both prices and output to fall. In 2015 deflation resulted from an increase in the short-run aggregate supply curve (from falling input prices). This means that while the real value of debt rises, rising output and income make it easier to pay back debt.

15

International Trade

*Understanding why trade with other countries
is beneficial for consumers and producers*

Every day at the Port of Los Angeles, up to ten mega container ships arrive, each containing 10,000 to over 20,000 TEU (*20-foot equivalent units*, or 20 feet × 8 feet × 8.5 feet standard containers) of goods from around the world. A standard tractor trailer can transport two TEUs, which means that up to 100,000 tractor trailers full of goods are brought into the United States each day, *at just one port.*

These cargo ships and trucks transport the goods we enjoy that are made in China, France, Brazil, Kenya, Australia, and the 180 other countries with which the United States has trading relations.

Take a quick look in your closet and count how many countries contributed to your wardrobe—shirts tailored in Hong Kong, shoes made in Italy, sweaters made in Norway, jackets made in China, and so on. On occasion, you might come across something made in the United States, although it is a rarity in the apparel industry. Most Americans wear foreign-made clothing, over half drive foreign cars, and even American cars contain many foreign components. Australian wines, Swiss watches, Chilean sea bass, and Brazilian coffee have become common in the United States. We also buy services from other countries, for example, when we travel to Europe and stay in hotels and use its high-speed trains. The opportunity to buy goods and services from other countries gives consumers more variety to choose from and also provides an opportunity to buy products at lower prices.

Although the United States buys many goods from other countries, it also sells many goods to other countries—just not clothing. The "Made in USA" label is highly respected throughout the world, and the United States sells commercial airplanes, cars and trucks, tractors, high-tech machinery, and pharmaceuticals to individual consumers and businesses in other countries. It also sells agricultural goods and raw materials, such as soybeans, copper, and wood pulp. And it sells services, too, such as medical care, tourist services when foreigners visit the United States, higher education when foreign students study at American schools, and entertainment, including movies, software, and music.

Trade is now part of the global landscape. Worldwide foreign trade has quadrupled over the past 25 years. In the United States today, the combined value of exports and imports exceeds $5 trillion a year. Twenty-five years ago, trade represented about 20% of gross domestic product (GDP); today, it accounts for nearly 30% of GDP. Nearly a tenth of American workers owe their jobs to foreign consumers. Figure 1 shows the current composition of U.S. exports and imports. Note that the United States imports and exports a lot of capital goods—that is, the equipment and machinery used to produce other goods. Also, we export about 50% more services than we import, services such as education and health care. Moreover, exports of petroleum products are roughly equal to imports as the United States relies less on imports of oil as domestic oil production increases.

Improved communication and transportation technologies have worked together to promote global economic integration. In addition, most governments around the world have reduced their trade barriers in recent years.

BY THE Numbers | 20

Number of countries in which the United States has a free trade agreement with as of 2018

International Trade Balances:
A Focus on the U.S. Trade Deficit

The United States exports and imports a tremendous amount of goods and services each year. Total trade represents nearly one-quarter of the entire economy's annual output. But for most of the past half-century, the United States has imported more than it has exported, resulting in a trade deficit. Reasons for the trade deficit include demand for products unavailable domestically, lower input costs overseas that incentivize offshore production, a strong demand for foreign brands, and differences in trade protection policies. Despite the trade deficit, U.S. exports have grown significantly, especially in services in which the United States has a trade surplus. Millions of American jobs depend on exports of goods and services. Moreover, American consumers benefit from lower prices of imported goods. This By the Numbers looks more closely at the trade deficit and its effect on the economy.

$269,214,000,000

U.S. trade surplus in services in 2018, including tourism, education, financial services, defense contracts, and royalties

WHY ARE THESE DATA IMPORTANT?

According to the discussion of trade in the text, a trade deficit means that more money is flowing out of the country in order to pay for the greater value of imports relative to the value of exports. Although this is generally good for consumers who benefit from lower prices of imported goods, a large trade deficit may not be ideal for domestic businesses that compete against imports.

DATA:

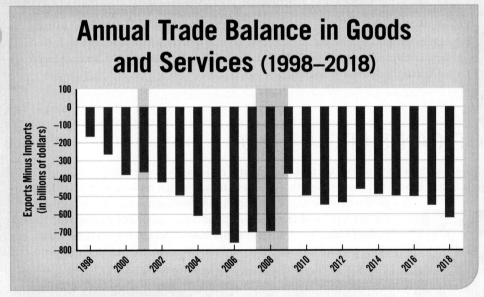

Annual Trade Balance in Goods and Services (1998–2018)

y-axis: Exports Minus Imports (in billions of dollars)

Where Can I Find These Data?

Source: U.S. Census Bureau (U.S. Department of Commerce)

Web site: https://www.census.gov/foreign-trade/data/index.html

Details: Select "Historical Series," then "U.S. International Trade in Goods and Services," and finally "Annual" data.

Data *in the News*

"US Trade Deficit Drops to $43.1 Billion in May, but Deficit With China Jumps" by Martin Crutsinger; *USA Today*, July 6, 2018

The U.S. trade deficit dropped in May to the lowest level in 19 months as U.S. exports rose to a record level. But the trade gap between the United States and China increased sharply, underscoring the economic tensions between the world's two biggest economies.

~ Assessing Your Data Literacy ~

1. In what year (from 1998 to 2018) was the U.S. trade deficit the smallest? Largest?

2. In terms of dollars, between which two years did the trade balance improve the most? Between which two years did the trade balance worsen the most?

3. The last two recessions occurred in 2001 and 2007–2009 (shaded vertical bars). What was the general trend in the trade balance during these recessions? Why do you think this trend occurs?

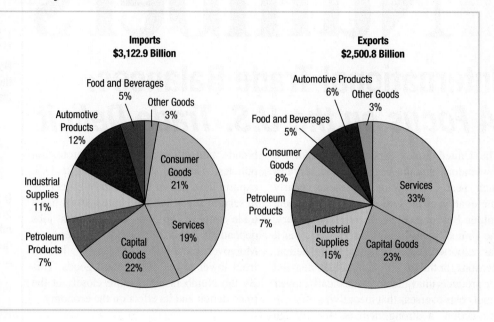

····· Figure 1 • U.S. Trade by Sector (2018) ·····················

This figure shows trade by sector. The United States imports and exports large amounts of capital goods, the equipment and machinery used to produce other goods. Also, one-third of U.S. exports are services such as education and health care.

Source: U.S. Census Bureau; U.S. Department of Commerce

Imports
$3,122.9 Billion

Food and Beverages 5%
Other Goods 3%
Automotive Products 12%
Consumer Goods 21%
Industrial Supplies 11%
Petroleum Products 7%
Services 19%
Capital Goods 22%

Exports
$2,500.8 Billion

Automotive Products 6%
Other Goods 3%
Food and Beverages 5%
Consumer Goods 8%
Petroleum Products 7%
Services 33%
Industrial Supplies 15%
Capital Goods 23%

autarky A country that does not engage in international trade, also known as a closed economy.

imports Goods and services that are purchased from abroad.

exports Goods and services that are sold abroad.

Trade must yield significant benefits, or it would not exist. After all, there are no laws requiring countries to trade, just agreements permitting trade and reducing impediments to it. This chapter begins with a discussion of why trade is beneficial. We look at the terms of trade between countries. Then we look at tariffs and quotas, which are used to restrict trade, and add these costs into the analysis. Finally, we consider some arguments critics have advanced against increased trade and globalization.

THE GAINS FROM TRADE

Economics studies voluntary exchange. People and nations do business with one another because they expect to gain through these transactions. Foreign trade is nearly as old as civilization. Centuries ago, European merchants were already sailing to the Far East to obtain spices, silk, and porcelain. Today, people in the United States buy cars from South Korea and electronics from China, along with millions of other products from countries around the world.

Virtually all countries today engage in some form of international trade. Those that trade the least are considered *closed economies.* A country that does not trade at all is called an **autarky.** Most countries, however, are *open economies* that willingly and actively engage in trade with other countries. Trade consists of **imports,** goods and services purchased from other countries, and **exports,** goods and services sold abroad.

Many people assume that trade between nations is a zero-sum game: a game in which, for one party to gain, the other party must lose. Poker games fit this description; one person's winnings must come from another player's losses. This is not true of voluntary trade. Voluntary exchange and trade is a positive-sum game, meaning that both parties to a transaction can gain.

To understand how this works and thus why nations trade, we need to consider the concepts of absolute and comparative advantage. Note that

International trade allows consumers to buy goods (such as televisions) produced in other countries. Competition from trade allows for greater variety and lower prices.

Yuri Arcurs/age fotostock

nations per se do not trade; individuals in specific countries do. We will refer to trade between nations but recognize that individuals, not nations, actually engage in trade.

Absolute and Comparative Advantage

Table 1 presents a hypothetical production rate for South Korea and Thailand, two countries with similar populations that can produce cars and ultra-HD televisions. As shown in the table, South Korea is able to produce either 30,000 cars or 120,000 televisions using its resources over a fixed time period, while Thailand is able to produce either 15,000 cars or 90,000 televisions over the same time period. Based on this comparison, South Korea has an **absolute advantage** over Thailand in producing both products. An absolute advantage exists when one country can produce more of a good than another country using the same amount of resources.

At first glance, one might wonder why South Korea would trade with Thailand if it's able to produce more of both goods. Wouldn't South Korea just produce all of its own cars and televisions? The answer lies in comparative advantage. One country has a **comparative advantage** in producing a good if its opportunity cost is lower than another country's opportunity cost for that good.

In Table 1, the opportunity cost to produce each good is calculated for each country. The opportunity cost of producing one car in South Korea is 4 televisions (because it can produce either 30,000 cars or 120,000 televisions, it gives up 4 televisions for each car produced). In Thailand the opportunity cost of one car is 6 televisions. Because South Korea's opportunity cost of producing a car is lower than Thailand's opportunity cost, South Korea has the comparative advantage in car production.

Conversely, the opportunity cost of producing 1 television is 0.25 car in South Korea and 0.17 car in Thailand (Table 1 shows the calculations). Thailand has a lower opportunity cost to produce each television and therefore has the comparative advantage in television production.

In any example with two countries, each country will have a comparative advantage in producing one good even if one country has an absolute advantage in producing both goods. The rare exception is if the opportunity costs in the two countries are identical. As long as opportunity costs differ between trading partners, there will always be an opportunity to gain from trade if each country specializes in producing the good in which it has a comparative advantage.

absolute advantage A country can produce more of a good than another country using the same amount of resources.

comparative advantage A country has a lower opportunity cost of producing a good than another country.

TABLE 1	COMPARING PRODUCTION AND OPPORTUNITY COSTS FOR CARS AND TELEVISIONS (IN THOUSANDS)			
	Absolute Advantage		Comparative Advantage	
	Cars	Televisions	Opportunity Cost of 1 Car	Opportunity Cost of 1 Television
South Korea	30	120	120 ÷ 30 = 4 televisions	30 ÷ 120 = 0.25 cars
Thailand	15	90	90 ÷ 15 = 6 televisions	15 ÷ 90 = 0.17 cars
Advantage	South Korea	South Korea	South Korea	Thailand

A country has an absolute advantage if it can produce more of a good than another country using the same amount of resources. South Korea has the absolute advantage in producing both cars and televisions. Even so, Thailand has the comparative advantage over South Korea in producing televisions because its opportunity cost of producing 1 television is 0.17 car, which is lower than the opportunity cost of 0.25 car for South Korea. However, South Korea has a lower opportunity cost to produce 1 car (4 vs. 6 for Thailand), thus giving South Korea the comparative advantage in car production.

····· Figure 2 • Production Possibilities and Trade for South Korea and Thailand ·····

South Korea and Thailand initially produce and consume at point *a* (in autarky) on their respective PPFs. When each country specializes according to their comparative advantage, each country moves to point *b* on their PPF. Finally, by trading with each other, each country ends up at point *c*, which is beyond their original PPFs. Specialization and trade based on comparative advantage leads to gains for both countries.

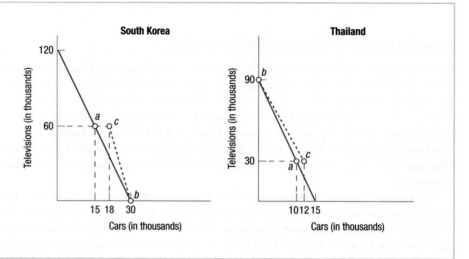

Gains From Trade

To see how specialization and trade can benefit both countries even when one has an absolute advantage in producing both goods, we draw a production possibilities frontier (PPF) for each country in Figure 2 using the production rates shown in Table 1. We assume that the amount of resources and time used in Table 1 is the same in Figure 2, which means the intercepts represent the maximum amount of output that each country can produce if all resources are devoted to producing that one product. For example, South Korea can produce 30,000 cars *or* 120,000 televisions or any combination along its PPF. Similarly, Thailand can produce 15,000 cars *or* 90,000 televisions or any combination along its PPF. The slopes of the PPFs for each country correspond to the opportunity cost, which we assume is constant. This means that the PPFs will be straight lines.

Assume that South Korea and Thailand are at point *a* in Figure 2. This is the autarky situation in which both countries produce and consume their own cars and televisions. South Korea will produce and consume 15,000 cars and 60,000 televisions, while Thailand will produce and consume 10,000 cars and 30,000 televisions. The left column of Table 2 summarizes these conditions before specialization and trade.

Now assume both countries specialize and produce only the good in which it has the comparative advantage. South Korea will produce 30,000 cars while Thailand will produce 90,000 televisions. These amounts are shown in the middle columns of Table 2 and points labeled *b* in Figure 2. Although the combined production of televisions did not increase, the total production of cars increased by 5,000.

TABLE 2	PRODUCTION AND CONSUMPTION BEFORE AND AFTER TRADE (IN THOUSANDS)					
	Before Specialization and Trade		After Specialization		After Trade	
	Cars	Televisions	Cars	Televisions	Cars	Televisions
South Korea	15	60	30	0	18	60
Thailand	10	30	0	90	12	30
Total Production	25	90	30	90	30	90

Now suppose that the two countries agree to trade according to the following terms: South Korea will trade 12,000 cars in exchange for 60,000 televisions. The resulting mix of products consumed in each country is shown in the right columns of Table 2 and points labeled *c* in Figure 2. Compared to the autarky situation, both countries are now better off, having engaged in specialized production and trade. In fact, both countries are now consuming at points beyond their PPFs, which means trade allows countries to achieve an outcome that could not be achieved on their own given the amount of resources they have. The important point to remember here is that even when one country has an absolute advantage over another, both countries can still benefit from trading with one another.

The Terms of Trade

How much can a country charge when it sells its goods to another country? How much must it pay for imported goods? As we saw in the previous example, South Korea exported 12,000 cars to Thailand in exchange for 60,000 televisions. This means that the price of each car was 5 times greater than the price of each television. This 5 to 1 price ratio represents the **terms of trade** between South Korea and Thailand. The terms of trade is the ratio of the price of exported goods to the price of imported goods (P_x/P_m). Because the price of South Korea's export was 5 times larger than the price of its import, the terms of trade would equal 5. For Thailand, its terms of trade would be 1/5, or 0.2, because the price of its export, televisions, is one-fifth the price of its import, cars.

terms of trade The ratio of the price of exported goods to the price of imported goods (P_x/P_m).

 ISSUE

The Challenge of Measuring Imports and Exports in a Global Economy

Before the growth of globalization of manufacturing, the brand names of products would indicate their origin. For example, Sony televisions were made in Japan, Nokia telephones were made in Finland, and a Ford car would be made in the United States using American steel, engines, cloth, and, of course, American labor.

Today, a product's brand name does not tell the entire story. Production has become very complex, with parts sourced from around the world. With such complexities in trade, how then are imports and exports measured?

Do sales of Levi's jeans count as U.S. exports? Although Levi's are an American brand that has for much of its history been produced in the United States, today nearly all Levi's jeans are made in Asia. Therefore, the American-brand jeans we buy count as an *import*. On the other hand, we also consume many products

that may seem foreign but are made in the United States. The majority of Toyota and Honda cars, for example, are assembled in American factories using American steel, glass, and other materials. The same is true to a lesser extent for luxury brands such as BMW, which produces many cars in South Carolina. For all but a few parts (such as the engine and transmission) that are made in Japan or Germany, these cars are as American as apple pie and are not counted as imports.

In order to measure imports and exports accurately, the U.S. Bureau of Economic Analysis tabulates data from documents collected by U.S. Customs and Border Protection, which details the appraised value (price paid) for all shipments of goods into and out of the ports of entry (whether by land, air, or sea). The value of imported and exported services is more difficult to measure and is based on a survey of monthly government and

A domestic content label of an "imported" Toyota truck.

industry reports to determine the value of all services bought from and sold to foreigners.

The globalized economy has been spurred in large part by falling transportation and communication costs in the past few decades. Companies face ever greater competition, applying more pressure to reduce production costs. The expansion of the production process to a worldwide factory is just one way our economy has changed, and this trend is likely to continue into the future.

When countries trade many commodities, the terms of trade are defined as an index of export prices over an index of import prices. This can get a bit complicated given that the price of each import and export is quoted in its own national currency, while the exchange rate between the two currencies may be constantly changing. We will ignore these complications by translating currencies into dollars, focusing our attention on how the terms of trade are determined and the impact of trade on consumers and producers.

✅ CHECKPOINT

THE GAINS FROM TRADE

- An absolute advantage exists when a country can produce more of some good than another country using the same amount of resources.

- A comparative advantage exists when one country can produce a good at a lower opportunity cost than another country.

- Both countries gain from trade when each specializes in producing goods in which they have a comparative advantage.

- The terms of trade are determined by the ratio of the price of exported goods to the price of imported goods.

QUESTIONS: When two individuals voluntarily engage in trade, they both benefit, or the trade wouldn't occur—one party wouldn't choose to be worse off after the trade. Is the same true for nations? Is everyone in both nations better off?

Answers to the Checkpoint questions can be found at the end of this chapter.

THE IMPACT OF TRADE ON CONSUMERS AND PRODUCERS

Our analysis of comparative advantage has highlighted the overall benefits of trade. But that doesn't mean that everybody benefits equally from trade. In fact, some consumers and producers may be worse off with trade, especially when trade policies are determined by governments and trading decisions are determined by businesses that end up impacting many consumers and workers. Moreover, additional factors can limit the benefits of trade, including transportation and communications costs and the effect of diminishing returns to specialization when resource costs rise due to scarcity.

To understand why some people are skeptical of international trade, we need to analyze the impact of trade on different stakeholders. Trade produces both winners and losers within each country. However, there are many more winners than losers; otherwise, countries would not choose to trade. Figure 3 shows four key stakeholders that are affected by trade: consumers of imported goods, consumers of exported goods, producers of exported goods, and producers of import-competing goods.

The first stakeholders are consumers of imported goods. This includes individuals like ourselves who buy clothes, video games, and countless other items that are imported. Some products, like coffee or cocoa used to make chocolate, *must* be imported because of the inability to produce these products efficiently in the United States. Moreover, nearly all manufacturers buy some of their raw materials from other countries. Therefore, even a product that is "Made in USA" still often contains components that are imported. These consumers and producers who buy imported goods and inputs are clearly winners from trade. Not only do many imported goods have lower prices, but there is a greater variety of products from which to choose.

The second stakeholders are consumers of exported goods. For example, Tesla is a popular manufacturer of electric plug-in cars. These cars are popular not only in the United States (where

..... Figure 3 • The Four Major Stakeholders of International Trade ....

Import Consumer

Export Consumer

Import-Competing Producer

Export Producer

Trade affects many consumers and producers. Much of the attention on trade policy has focused on import-competing producers, such as American furniture manufacturers. But consumers of imported goods benefit from lower prices and a greater variety of goods. Trade also affects export producers, such as Boeing which sells large airplanes to airlines in many countries. Lastly, trade affects export consumers when foreigners demand American-made goods and services, increasing their prices.

they are manufactured) but also all around the world. For example, in Amsterdam many taxi companies use large Tesla fleets to promote zero-emissions transportation. But as demand for U.S. goods abroad increases, so do prices. Therefore, products that are exported abroad will generally cost more with trade, making domestic consumers somewhat worse off. This effect applies to services as well. Part of the reason that Disneyland and Universal Studios can charge high admission prices is because many of their visitors come from other countries, increasing the demand and thereby pushing up prices (money spent by foreign tourists counts as a service export). Although there are many other examples of buying products that are exported, generally we buy many more imported products, and therefore trade overall makes consumers better off.

The third stakeholders are producers of exported goods. U.S. soybean farmers benefit tremendously from trade because soybeans represent one of the largest U.S. exports, especially to Asia, where large quantities of soybeans are used to make animal feed and where many people consume soy products, such as tofu and soy sauce. Also, the U.S. aerospace industry sells aircraft to airlines around the world, the U.S. film and music industry licenses its products to moviegoers and music fans around the world, and the U.S. automobile industry now sells more cars to foreign consumers than to American consumers! Indeed, trade is extremely valuable to these exporting industries because they generate substantial income from other countries that support millions of well-paying jobs in high-skilled and technical industries. Many recent trade policies being debated in government involve the desire to open new markets for American products, especially in countries such as China and India, which combined have 2.8 billion potential customers, or over 8 times the population of the United States. Clearly, there are huge opportunities for American companies to benefit from trade.

The final stakeholders are industries that compete against imported goods, such as the steel industry, furniture industry, medical device industry, and others. Because many of these industries manufacture goods that require a significant amount of labor, foreign companies can often produce these products at lower cost than American companies. As a result, industries that compete against imported goods face very tough price competition, making it difficult to stay in business. Many U.S. companies are forced to move their production plants to other countries with lower wages, thereby forcing many U.S. workers to lose their jobs. In other cases, U.S. companies have gone out of business altogether, such as television manufacturing (Zenith and RCA were the last two major American television brands, and both are no longer in existence).

Much like how there are more winners than losers from trade among consumers, there are also more winners than losers among producers. Certainly, millions of workers have been displaced or laid off from manufacturing jobs, but millions of jobs have been created in high-skilled industries producing goods and services that are exported. As someone pursuing a college degree and perhaps an advanced degree later, it's very likely you may end up working for a company that exports goods and therefore will benefit from trade. However, we cannot ignore the concerns of companies and workers that have been hurt from trade. In fact, they are a very vocal group, often hiring lobbyists to encourage politicians to do more to protect their industries from trade. This has resulted in trade restrictions, which we turn to next.

How Trade Is Restricted

Trade restrictions can range from subsidies provided to domestic firms to protect them against lower-priced imports to embargoes by which the government bans any trade with a country. Between these two extremes are more intermediate policies, such as exchange controls that limit the amount of foreign currency available to importers or citizens who travel abroad. Regulation, licensing, and government purchasing policies are all frequently used to promote or ensure the purchase of domestic products. The main reason for these trade restrictions is simple: The industry and its employees actually feel the pain and lobby extensively for protection, while the huge benefits of lower prices are diffused among millions of consumers whose benefits are each so small that fighting against a trade barrier isn't worth their time.

tariff A tax on imported products.

quota A government-set limit on the quantity of imports into a country.

The most common forms of trade restrictions are tariffs and quotas, though tariffs are used more frequently than quotas. A **tariff** is a tax on imported products. A **quota** is a government-set limit on the quantity of imports into a country. Figure 4 shows the average U.S.

····· Figure 4 • Average U.S. Tariff Rates, 1900–2019 ·····························

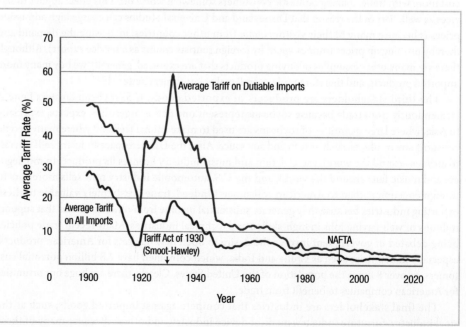

Tariffs and quotas are the most common forms of trade restrictions. Tariff rates in the United States peaked during the Great Depression. Over the last several decades, tariff rates have steadily declined to an average of about 2% today.

tariff rates since 1900. Some economists have suggested that the tariff wars that erupted in the 1920s and culminated in the passage of the Smoot-Hawley Act of 1930 were an important factor underlying the severity of the Great Depression. The high tariffs of the 1930s reduced trade, leading to a reduction in income, output, and employment, and added fuel to the worldwide depression. Since the 1930s, the United States has, with few exceptions, moved toward freer trade with much of the world, decreasing the average tariff rate imposed on imported goods to about 2% today. Tariffs and quotas are still used extensively in the agricultural industry, certain imported luxury goods (such as alcohol and perfume), and against countries due to trade or political disputes. Still, trade today is much more open compared to the past.

Effects of Tariffs and Quotas

What exactly are the effects of tariffs and quotas? **Tariffs** are often *ad valorem taxes*. *Ad valorem* is Latin for "in proportion to the value," and *ad valorem taxes* means that the product is taxed by a certain percentage of its price (value) as it crosses the border. Other tariffs are unit taxes (also known as *specific tariffs*); a fixed tax per unit of the product is assessed at the border. Tariffs are designed to generate revenues and to drive a wedge between the domestic price of a product and its price on the world market. The effects of a tariff are shown in Figure 5.

Domestic supply and demand for the product are shown in Figure 5 as *S* and *D*. Assume that the product's world price of $400 is lower than its domestic price of $600. At $400, domestic quantity demanded (10,000 units) will consequently exceed domestic quantity supplied (6,000 units). Imports to this country will therefore be 4,000 units.

Now assume that the firms and workers in the industry hurt by the lower world price lobby for a tariff and are successful. The country imposes a tariff of $100 per unit on this product. The results are illustrated in Figure 5. The product's price in this country rises to $500, and imports fall to 2,000 units (9,000−7,000). Domestic consumers buy less of the product at the higher price, which causes a reduction in consumer surplus by areas A+B+C+D.

⋯⋯ Figure 5 • Effects of a Tariff ⋯⋯⋯⋯⋯⋯⋯⋯⋯⋯⋯⋯⋯

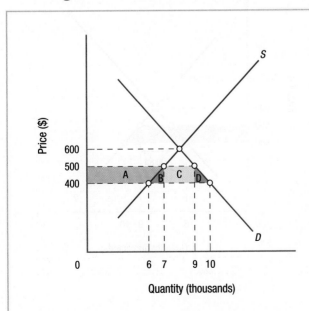

Supply and demand curves *S* and *D* represent domestic supply and demand. Assume the product's world price of $400 is lower than its domestic price of $600. Imports will therefore be 4,000 units. If the country imposes a tariff of $100 on this product, the domestic price of imports rises to $500, and the import quantity falls to 2,000 units. Domestic consumers now buy less (9,000 units) of the product at the higher price ($500), and lose areas A + B + C + D in consumer surplus. Domestic producers gain area A in producer surplus because the price and output have risen. The government collects area C in tariff revenue. Areas B + D represent deadweight loss, the inefficiency from the tariff.

Domestic producers, however, are pleased with the higher price, which allows them to increase production, resulting in an increase in producer surplus by area A. Meanwhile, the government collects revenue equal to $200,000 ($100 tariff × 2,000 imported units), which is area C. These revenues can be significant as evidenced in the 1800s when tariffs were the federal government's dominant form of revenue, but over the past century, the government has relied more on income taxes.

Notice that while consumers lost areas A + B + C + D, only areas A and C are transferred to producers and the government, respectively. Areas B and D represent the inefficiency of the tariff, also referred to as deadweight loss.

Figure 6 shows the effects of a **quota.** They are similar to what we saw in Figure 5, except that the government restricts the quantity of imports into the country to 2,000 units. Imports fall to the quota level, and consumers again lose areas A + B + C + D in terms of reduced consumer surplus because they must pay higher prices for less output. Producers gain area A in greater producer surplus as prices and employment in the domestic industry rise. For a quota, however, the government does not collect revenue. Then who gets this revenue? The foreign exporting company receives it in the form of higher prices for its products. Therefore, the importing country has deadweight loss of B + C + D. This explains why government prefer tariffs over quotas.

The United States imposed quotas on Japanese automobiles in the 1980s. The primary effect of these quotas was initially to raise dramatically both the minimum standard equipment and price for some Japanese cars. Ultimately, the number of Japanese cars made in American factories increased. If a firm is limited in the number of vehicles it can sell, why not sell higher-priced ones whose profit margins are higher? The Toyota Land Cruiser, for instance, was originally a bare-bones SUV selling for under $15,000. With quotas, this vehicle was transformed into a luxury behemoth that sells for over $80,000 today, with all the bells and whistles standard. Although quotas on Japanese automobiles have long expired, Japanese automakers continue to produce a wide array of luxury automobiles.

Figure 6 • Effects of a Quota

The effects of a quota are similar to a tariff except that the government restricts the quantity of imports into the country to 2,000 units. Imports fall to the quota level, and again consumers lose areas A + B + C + D in consumer surplus, as they must pay higher prices for less output. Producers gain area A in producer surplus as prices and employment in the domestic industry rise. With a quota, however, the government does not collect revenues, and therefore areas B + C + D represent a deadweight loss.

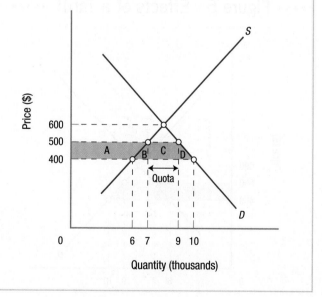

One problem with tariffs and quotas is that when they are imposed, large numbers of consumers pay just a small amount more for the targeted products. Few consumers are willing to spend time and effort lobbying Congress to end or forestall these trade barriers from being introduced. Producers, however, are often few in number, and they stand to gain tremendously from such trade barriers. It is no wonder that such firms have large lobbying budgets and provide campaign contributions to political candidates.

ISSUE

Do Foreign Trade Zones Help or Hurt American Consumers and Workers?

Driving through the gates of the Cartago *Zona Franca* in Costa Rica, one encounters a remarkable sight in a historic Central American town: large factories adorned with the names of large American companies in industries including pharmaceuticals, semiconductors, medical supplies, and household products. What are these companies doing in Costa Rica, and why did they choose to locate within this small gated compound?

In Cartago, as well as in other cities throughout the world, clusters of multinational companies engage in manufacturing activities. These companies are taking advantage of the benefits offered by foreign trade zones, also commonly known as free trade zones or export processing zones.

A foreign trade zone is a designated area in a country where foreign companies can import inputs, without tariffs, to be used for product assembly by local workers who are often paid a fraction of what equivalent workers would be paid in the company's home country. By operating in a foreign trade zone, all inputs coming into a country are exempted from tariffs as long as the finished products (with some exceptions) are then exported from the country. Further, companies are often exempted from other taxes levied by the government.

Countries such as China, the Philippines, and Costa Rica establish foreign trade zones to attract foreign investment, which creates well-paying jobs relative to wages paid by domestic companies. Countries with high literacy rates, like Costa Rica, are especially attractive because their workers can perform semi-skilled tasks such as assembling electronic and computer products or handling customer service calls. Foreign trade zones also are prevalent along border towns, such as those in Mexico, where easy transportation to and from the United States allows inputs and products to flow rapidly.

Although companies operating in foreign trade zones benefit from lower production costs and the host country benefits from jobs created, not everyone is in favor of foreign trade zones. Various unions in the United States view foreign trade zones as facilitating the offshoring of American jobs. Offshoring occurs when part of the production process (typically, the labor-intensive portions) is sent to countries with lower input costs.

What may be surprising, however, is that foreign trade zones and offshoring are not one-way streets. The United States has many foreign trade zones established for the same purpose: to attract foreign

The entrance to the free trade zone in Cartago, Costa Rica.

companies to invest in manufacturing plants. By moving production to the United States, European and Japanese companies produce goods such as cars while enjoying the same tax benefits as American companies operating abroad. Today almost as many jobs are created by foreign companies in the United States as jobs lost from American companies moving production overseas.

There are both winners and losers in trade. But when all impacts are considered, including savings to consumers from lower product costs, imports of U.S. goods by foreigners, profits to U.S. affiliates, and the value of labor reemployed, the benefits tend to outweigh the costs. Clearly, those who lose their jobs suffer. But with a policy to provide training to displaced workers, the savings from offshoring can lead to greater investment and growth in the long run.

✅ CHECKPOINT

THE IMPACT OF TRADE ON CONSUMERS AND PRODUCERS

- Trade leads to winners and losers in each country and in each market.

- Trade restrictions vary from subsidies to domestic firms to government bans on the import of foreign products.

- Tariffs are taxes on imports that protect domestic producers and generate revenue for the government.

- Quotas represent restrictions on the volume of particular imports that can come into a country. Quotas do not generate revenue for governments and are infrequently used.

QUESTION: When the government imposes a quota on foreign trucks, who benefits and who loses?

Answers to the Checkpoint questions can be found at the end of this chapter.

ARGUMENTS AGAINST FREE TRADE AND REBUTTALS BASED ON EVIDENCE

We have seen the benefits of trade and have looked at how trade undoubtedly benefits some and harms others. Those who are harmed by trade often seek to restrict trade, primarily in the form of tariffs and quotas. Because trade leads to some loss, those who are harmed by trade have made arguments against free trade.

The arguments against free trade fall into two camps. Traditional economic arguments include protection for infant industries, protection against dumping, low foreign wages, and support for industries judged vital for national defense. More recent arguments focus on globalization (social and economic) concerns that embody political-economy characteristics. These include domestic employment concerns, environmental concerns, and the impact of globalization on working conditions in developing nations. In what follows, we take a critical look at each of these arguments, showing that most of these arguments do not have a solid empirical basis.

Traditional Economic Arguments

Arguments against trade are not new. Despite the huge gains from trade, distortions (subsidies and trade barriers) continue because changing current policies will hurt those dependent on subsidies and trade restrictions, and these firms and workers will show their displeasure in the voting booth. All of these traditional economic arguments against free trade seem reasonable on their face, but on closer examination, they look less attractive.

infant industry An industry so underdeveloped that protection is needed for it to become competitive on the world stage or to ensure its survival.

Infant Industry Argument An **infant industry,** it is argued, is one that is too underdeveloped to achieve comparative advantage or perhaps even to survive in the global market. Such an industry may be too small or undercapitalized, or its management and workers may be too inexperienced, to compete. Unless the industry's government provides it with some protection through tariffs, quotas, or subsidies, it might not survive in the face of foreign competition.

In theory, once the infant industry has been given this protection, it should be able to grow, acquiring the necessary capital and expertise needed to compete internationally. Germany and the United States used high tariffs to protect their infant manufacturing sectors in the 1800s, and Japan continued to maintain import restrictions up until the 1970s.

Although the infant industry argument sounds reasonable, it has several limitations. First, protecting an industry must be done in a way that makes the industry internationally competitive. Many countries coddle their firms, and these producers never seem to develop into "mature," internationally viable firms. Once protection is provided (typically, a protective tariff), it is difficult to remove after an industry has matured. The industry and its workers continue to convince policymakers of the need for continued protection.

Second, infant industry protection often tends to focus on capital manufacturing. Countries with huge labor supplies would do better to develop their labor-intensive industries first, letting more capital-intensive industries develop over time. Every country, after all, should seek to exploit its comparative advantages, but it is difficult to determine which industries have a chance of developing a comparative advantage in the future and should be temporarily protected.

Third, many industries seem to be able to develop without protections; therefore, countries may be wasting their resources and reducing their incomes by imposing protection measures.

Clearly, the infant industry argument is not a compelling one for advanced economies such as those of the United States, much of Europe, and Japan. The evidence for developing nations shows some benefits but is mixed for the reasons noted above.

Antidumping Argument **Dumping** means that goods are sold at lower prices (often *below cost*) abroad than in their home market. This is typically a result of government subsidies.

In the same way that price discrimination improves profits, firms can price discriminate between their home markets and foreign markets. Let's assume that costs of production are $100 per unit for all firms (domestic and foreign). A subsidy of $30 a unit, for example, reduces domestic costs to $70 per unit and permits the firm to sell its product in world markets at these lower prices. These subsidies give these firms a cost advantage in foreign markets.

Firms can use dumping as a form of predatory pricing, using higher prices in their domestic markets to support unrealistically low prices in foreign markets. The goal of predatory pricing is to drive foreign competitors out of business. When this occurs, the firm doing the dumping then comes back and imposes higher prices. In the long run, these higher prices thereby offset the company's short-term losses.

Dumping violates U.S. trade laws. If the federal government determines that a foreign firm is dumping products in the United States, it can impose antidumping tariffs on the offending products. However, the government must distinguish among dumping, legitimate price discrimination, and legitimate instances of lower-cost production arising from comparative advantage.

Low Foreign Wages Some advocates of trade barriers maintain that domestic firms and their workers need to be protected from displacement by cheap foreign labor. They argue that without this protection, foreign manufacturers that pay their workers very low wages will flood the market with low-cost products. As we already saw has happened in the American textile industry, workers in advanced economies can be displaced by low-wage foreign workers.

Once a handful of American clothing manufacturers began moving their production facilities overseas, thereby undercutting domestic producers, other manufacturers were forced to follow. American consumers have benefited from lower clothing prices, but many displaced textile workers are still trying to obtain training and adapt to work in other industries. More recently, many manufacturing jobs have drifted overseas, and high-technology firms today are shifting some help desk facilities and computer programming to foreign shores.

However, the benefits of lower-priced goods considerably exceed the costs of lost employment. The federal government has resisted imposing protection measures for the sake of protecting jobs, instead funding programs that help displaced workers transition to new lines of work.

National Defense Argument In times of national crisis or war, the United States must be able to rely on key domestic industries, such as oil, steel, and defense. Some have argued that these industries may require some protection even during peacetime to ensure that they are already well established when a crisis strikes and importing key products may be impossible. Within limits, this argument is sound. However, the United States has the capacity to produce such a wide variety of products that protections for specific industries are usually unnecessary. In 2018, the United States raised the tariff on steel imports from Canada, calling the imports a national security threat, a position that seemed preposterous given the close ties between the United States and Canada. Still, the argument of national defense continues to be used as a way to justify the use of tariffs in certain industries.

dumping Selling goods abroad at lower prices than in home markets and often below cost.

The steel industry is one of several that are considered key domestic industries vital in times of national crisis. Therefore, industry executives frequently argue for protection against foreign competition.

So what are we to make of these traditional arguments? Although they all seem reasonable, they all have deficiencies. Infant industries may be helped in the short run, but protections are often extended well beyond what is necessary, resulting in inefficient firms that are vulnerable on world markets. Dumping is clearly a potential problem, but distinguishing real cases of dumping from comparative advantage has often proven difficult in practice. Low foreign wages are often the only comparative advantage a developing nation has to offer the world economy, and typically, the benefits to consumers vastly outweigh the loss to a particular industry. Maintaining (protecting) industries for national defense has merit and may be appropriate for some countries, but for a country as large and diversified as the United States, it is probably unnecessary.

Recent Globalization Concerns

Expanded trade and globalization have provided the world's producers and consumers with many benefits. Some observers, however, have voiced concerns about globalization and its effects on domestic employment, the global environment, and working conditions in developing nations. Let's look at each one of these globalization concerns.

Trade and Loss of Domestic Employment Some critics argue that increased trade and globalization spell job losses for domestic workers. We have seen that this can be true. Some firms, unable to compete against cheaper imports, will be forced to lay off workers or even close their doors. Even so, increased trade usually allows firms that are exporters to expand their operations and hire new workers. These will be firms in industries with comparative advantages. For the United States, these industries tend to be those that require a highly skilled workforce, resulting in higher wages for American workers.

Clearly, the industries that are adding workers are not the industries that are losing jobs. For workers who lose their jobs, switching industries can be difficult and time consuming, and often it requires new investment in human capital. U.S. trade policy recognizes this problem, and the Trade Adjustment Assistance (TAA) program provides workers with job search assistance, job training, and some relocation allowances. In some industries sensitive to trade liberalization, including textiles and agriculture, trade policies are designed to proceed gradually, thus giving these industries and their workers some extra time to adjust.

Possible employment losses in some noncompetitive industries do not seem to provide enough justification for restricting trade. By imposing trade restrictions such as tariffs or quotas in one industry, employment opportunities in many other industries may be reduced. Open, competitive trade encourages producers to focus their production on those areas in which the country has a comparative advantage. Free trade puts competitive pressure on domestic firms, forcing them to be more productive and competitive, boosting the flow of information and technology across borders, and widening the availability of inputs for producers. At the end of the day, consumers benefit from these efficiencies, having more goods to choose from and enjoying a higher standard of living.

Trade and Harm to the Environment Concerns about globalization, trade, and the environment usually take one of two forms. Some people are concerned that expanded trade and globalization will lead to increased environmental degradation as companies take advantage of lax environmental laws abroad, particularly in the developing world. Others worry that attempts by the government to strengthen environmental laws will be challenged by trading partners as disguised protectionism.

Domestic environmental regulations usually target a product or process that creates pollution or other environmental problems. One concern in establishing environmental regulations, however, is that they not unfairly discriminate against the products of another country. This is usually not a serious problem. Nearly all trade agreements, including the World Trade Organization agreements and USMCA, have provisions permitting countries to enforce measures "necessary to protect human, animal or plant life or health" or to conserve exhaustible natural resources. Nothing in our trade agreements prevents the United States from implementing environmental regulations as long as they do not unreasonably discriminate against our trading partners.

Will free trade come at the expense of the environment? Every action involves a tradeoff. Clearly, there can be cases in which the benefits of trade accruing to large numbers of people result in harm to a more concentrated group. However, trade policies can also be complementary to good environmental policies. For example, increased free trade in agriculture encourages countries with fertile lands to specialize in growing crops while discouraging countries from farming marginal lands that require the use of environmentally damaging pesticides and chemicals.

We have seen that trade raises incomes in developed and developing countries. How rising incomes affect environmental protections depends on the state of a country's development. In poor, developing countries, environmental protection will not at first be a priority. Critics of globalization argue that rich nations will exploit weaker environmental regulations with trade and foreign direct investment. Yet many studies have found that not to be the case. In fact, as countries develop and incomes rise, the demand for environmental protection rises as the issue takes on added importance even in poorer nations. The result is what economists refer to as an environmental Kuznets curve, in which economic development initially harms the environment but then improves as incomes rise. An increased emphasis on environmental issues can be seen in countries such as Costa Rica, Brazil, and even India and China, as people in these countries demand a cleaner environment as incomes rise.

Trade and Its Effect on Working Conditions in Developing Nations Some antiglobalization activists argue that trade between the United States and developing countries, where wages are low and working conditions may be deplorable, exploits workers in these developing countries. Clearly, such trade does hurt American workers in low-wage, low-skilled occupations who cannot compete with the workers paid an even lower wage overseas. But it is not clear that workers in developing countries would be helped if the United States were to cut off its trade with those countries that refuse to improve wages or working conditions. For these workers, producing goods for export may be the only job opportunity they have.

Restricting trade with countries that do not raise wages to levels we think acceptable or bring working conditions up to our standards would probably do more harm than good. Low wages reflect, among other factors, small investments in human capital, low productivity, and meager living standards characteristic of developing nations. Blocking trade with these nations may deprive them of their opportunity to grow and to improve in those areas in which we would like to see change.

Liberalized trade policies, economic freedom, and a legal system that respects property rights and foreign capital investment probably provide the best recipe for rapid development, economic growth, environmental protection, and improved wages and working conditions.

In summary, trade does result in job losses in some industries, but the gain for consumers and the competitive pressures that trade puts on domestic companies are beneficial to the economy as a whole. Trade raises incomes in developing nations, resulting in a growing demand for more environmentally-friendly production processes. Trade brings about higher levels of income and better working conditions. For example, decades of strong economic growth in China has resulted in higher wages and a vibrant middle class that enjoys luxuries such as cars and vacations. The following Around the World describes an interesting phenomenon when residents of the world's most populous country take a few weeks of vacation all at the same time.

🌍AROUND THE WORLD

Can One Country's Festival Disrupt World Trade?

How is China's export sector so important that it can disrupt global trade during its annual Spring Festival?

Between late-January and mid-February of each year (depending on the lunar calendar), one of the largest mass migrations of people begins in China—hundreds of millions of people pack onto crowded trains, airline seats sell out, and highways are jammed with cars in the world's largest auto market. Although this might sound typical of a Memorial Day or Thanksgiving weekend in the United States, the sheer scale of the Spring Festival in China (its largest holiday) makes most other holidays around the world appear minuscule.

Just how big of an impact on the world does this Chinese festival have?

The 15-day Spring Festival, which coincides with the Lunar New Year and culminates with the Lantern Festival, is so large that it actually disrupts

Calvin Chan/Alamy

global trade each year. Because China is the world's largest exporter of goods, consumers and producers around the world depend on Chinese exports to stock their shelves and to provide parts for manufacturing. Moreover, many companies depend on custom orders, such as custom tote bags for a large conference or custom racing medals to be handed out to runners after a marathon. Often these orders are made months in advance to allow time for production as well as shipping, usually by cargo ship.

Because nearly everyone celebrates the Spring Festival in China, most workers take long vacations during this period. Factories that employ migrants from the countryside become empty as workers leave to visit their families and friends. As a result, many factory orders are delayed or placed on hold during the festival, which can affect markets around the world as stores and customers wait for their orders to arrive.

The sheer size and influence of China's export sector can disrupt global trade when there is a halt in production. As a result, distributors anticipate delays by placing orders extra early whenever possible around that time of year. One might wonder why factory managers do not provide incentives for workers to forgo the festival in order to fill customer orders. Most likely it's because the managers themselves are leaving to see their families! The Spring Festival is a 4,000-year-old tradition and one not to be missed, even at the cost of disrupting world trade.

📖 GO ONLINE TO PRACTICE THE ECONOMIC CONCEPTS IN THIS STORY

 **CHECKPOINT**

ARGUMENTS AGAINST FREE TRADE AND REBUTTALS BASED ON EVIDENCE

- The infant industry argument claims that some industries are so underdeveloped that they need protection to survive in a global competitive environment.

- Dumping involves selling products at different prices in domestic and foreign markets (even below cost), often with the help of subsidies from the government. This is a form of predatory pricing to gain market share in the foreign market.

- Some suggest that domestic workers need to be protected from the low wages in foreign countries. This puts the smaller aggregate loss to small groups ahead of the greater general gains from trade. Also, for many countries, a low wage is their primary comparative advantage.

- Some argue that select industries need protection to ensure that they will exist for national defense reasons.

- Globalization displaces some workers due to foreign competition, and some advocates suggest restricting trade on these grounds alone. However, trade has led to higher overall employment as exports expand and the economy grows.

- Concern about the environment is often a factor in trade negotiations. But as trade increases incomes in developing countries, environmental awareness rises.

- Some believe that trade exploits workers in developing countries. However, trade has typically resulted in higher wages for these workers.

QUESTION: Trade between the United States and China increased significantly over the last two decades. China is now the United States' largest trading partner. Expanding trade has led to significant reductions in the price of many goods, including technology goods such as computers and tablets. However, some people have been vocal against policies that promote freer trade with China. What are some reasons why people would be against greater trade with China?

Answers to the Checkpoint questions can be found at the end of this chapter.

CHAPTER SUMMARY

SECTION 1 THE GAINS FROM TRADE

15.1 **Absolute advantage:** Occurs when one country can produce more of a good than another country using the same amount of resources.

Comparative advantage: Occurs when a country can produce a good at a lower opportunity cost than another country.

Fotokostic/Shutterstock

The United States has a comparative advantage in both soybean production (due to an abundance of fertile land and farming technology) and commercial aircraft production (due to an abundance of technology and human capital).

15.2 Trade is a **positive-sum game**, which means that both countries in a trading relationship can benefit, compared to not trading.

SECTION 2 THE IMPACT OF TRADE ON CONSUMERS AND PRODUCERS

15.3 The **terms of trade** describe the relative prices of imports and exports. When countries trade many commodities, the terms of trade are defined as an index of export prices over an index of import prices.

15.4 **The Effect of Trade on Prices**

Before trade, the prices charged for one good may be different in the two countries. The country with the lower price is likely to export the good; greater demand for that country's good pushes prices higher. The country with the higher price is likely to import the good; lesser demand for that country's good pushes prices lower. Market forces therefore push prices toward an equilibrium under free trade.

Price in Country A

Imports Push Prices Down

Equilibrium Price With Trade

Exports Push Prices Up

Price in Country B

15.5 **Tariffs** are a tax on imports. They raise the domestic price of the good to the *world price + tariff*.

Winners: Domestic producers gain area A. Government gains area C in tariff revenues.

Losers: Domestic consumers lose areas A + B + C + D due to a higher price and lower quantity.

Net Loss: Areas B + D (deadweight loss from the tariff)

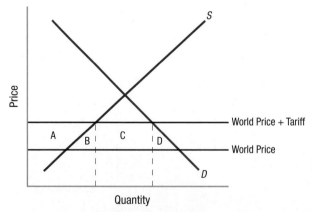

Quotas are an alternative to tariffs that limit imports directly. They have a similar effect on price and quantity as tariffs, but the government does not receive any revenue. Area C goes to foreign producers.

Historically, trade barriers have been high. The Smoot-Hawley Act of 1930 placed an average tax of 60% on most imported goods, arguably prolonging the Great Depression. Trade barriers have fallen since and in the past three decades have fallen dramatically to nearly free trade with all countries.

SECTION 3 ARGUMENTS AGAINST FREE TRADE AND REBUTTALS BASED ON EVIDENCE

15.6 Many strong arguments against free trade exist. In each case, trade protection in the form of a tariff, quota, or subsidy is sought to protect the domestic industry.

Infant industry argument: States that a new industry requires protection to survive against established foreign competition. The problem is determining when these industries mature.

Antidumping argument: Argues that protection is needed when a foreign firm sells its goods below cost or at a price below what it charges in its domestic market.

National defense argument: States that a country must be able to rely on its domestic industries for critical goods such as food, oil, steel, and defense equipment in times of conflict when trade might not be possible.

15.7 **Environmental degradation argument:** States that countries producing large quantities of goods in factories that pollute allow their environments to deteriorate. However, studies show that as countries develop and incomes grow, demand for environmental protection rises.

In the early 1980s, Harley-Davidson sought infant industry protection against competition from established lower-cost Japanese motorcycles, giving it time to retool its factories to become more competitive.

Protection against cheap labor argument: Argues that domestic workers need to be protected from cheap foreign labor. Most economists estimate that the benefits from lower-priced imports from free trade exceed the costs of lost employment. Further, increased trade generates jobs in export industries.

15.8 **Exploitation of foreign workers argument:** Argues that trading with developing countries where wages are low and working conditions are deplorable exploits workers in these countries. But restricting trade would probably do more harm than good. Producing goods for export provides opportunities for these economies to grow and the workers to improve their standard of living.

South Korea sustained environmental degradation during its economic development in the 1980s and 1990s. Today, South Korea makes large investments in environmental protection, which can be seen in sustainable cities like Songdo, located outside the capital of Seoul.

Although working conditions in factories in developing countries look miserable, they often are better than working conditions before trade. In addition, trade increases demand for workers, which leads to higher wages.

Key Concepts

autarky, p. 372

imports, p. 372

exports, p. 372

absolute advantage, p. 373

comparative advantage, p. 373

terms of trade, p. 375

tariff, p. 378

quota, p. 378

infant industry, p. 382

dumping, p. 383

Questions and Problems

Check Your Understanding

1. What is the difference between absolute and comparative advantage? Why would Stephen Curry, who is better than you at both basketball and mowing grass, still hire you to mow his lawn?

2. If the United States has a comparative advantage in the production of strawberries compared to Iceland, how might trade affect the prices of strawberries in the two countries?

3. Who are the beneficiaries from a large U.S. tariff on French and German wines? Who are the losers?

4. Why does a quota generate a larger loss to the importing country than a tariff that restricts imports to the same quantity?

5. What is the difference between an infant industry and a key industry? Why do producers in both industries desire protection against foreign imports?

6. How could free trade between the United States and China lead to *more* jobs in the United States?

Apply the Concepts

7. Some American politicians claim that China's trade policies are unfair to the United States and that a large tax (tariffs) should be placed on Chinese imports to protect American workers and industries. Why might such a policy sound better than it actually is in practice? What are the dangers of imposing large taxes on Chinese imports?

8. Expanding trade in general benefits all countries, or they would not willingly engage in trade. But we also know that consumers and society often gain while particular industries or workers lose. Because society and consumers gain, how might the government compensate the few losers for their loss?

9. Some activist groups are calling for "fair trade laws" by which other countries would be required to meet or approach our environmental standards and provide wage and working conditions approaching those of developed nations in order to be able to trade with us. Is this just another form of rent seeking by industries and unions for protection from overseas competition?

10. Why is there free trade between states in the United States but not necessarily between countries?

11. Remittances from developed countries amount to over $500 billion each year. Most of these funds are sent by foreign workers and migrants to their home countries. Is this similar to the gains from trade discussed in this chapter, or are these workers just taking jobs that workers in developed countries would be paid more to do in the absence of the migrants?

12. Suppose Brazil developed a secret process that effectively quadrupled its output of coffee from its coffee plantations. This secret process enabled it to significantly undercut the prices of U.S. domestic producers. Would domestic producers receive a sympathetic ear to calls for protection from Brazil's lower-cost coffee? How is this case different from that of protection against cheap foreign labor?

In the News

13. Migrant workers obtain temporary work permits to do jobs that most American workers avoid (such as picking fruit at the minimum wage), allowing U.S. farms to compete against low-cost imports. However, critics claim that if farm wages increase, these jobs can be filled by American workers. Given these viewpoints, is there a connection between restricting migrant workers and restricting international trade? Are the effects similar?

14. Since before the Civil War, Hawaii had been a major producer and exporter of sugarcane. About the time Hawaii became a U.S. state in 1959, the sugar industry had already started its decline, and in 2016, the last sugar plantation in Hawaii closed. Explain how the sugar industry in Hawaii was affected by reductions in tariffs, world competition, and the opportunity costs of production relative to other states. Why does sugar continue to be produced in Florida and Louisiana but not in Hawaii?

Solving Problems

Work It Out

interactive activity

15. The following figure shows the production possibilities frontiers (PPFs) for Italy and India for their domestic production of olives and tea. Without trade, assume that each is consuming olives and tea at point *a*.

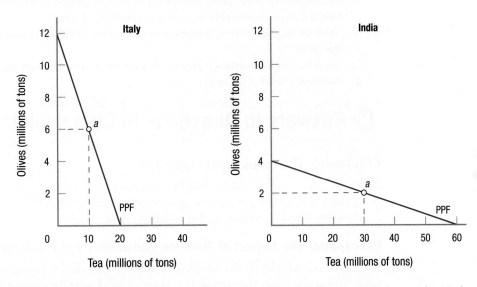

a. If Italy and India were to consider specialization and trade, in what commodity would each specialize? What is India's opportunity cost for tea? For olives? What is Italy's opportunity cost for tea? For olives?

b. Assume that the two countries agree to specialize entirely in one product (the one for which each country has a comparative advantage) and agree to split the total output between them. Complete the following table. Are both countries better off after trade?

Country and Product	Before Specialization	After Specialization	After Trade
Italy			
Olives	6 million tons	_____	_____
Tea	10 million tons	_____	_____
India			
Olives	2 million tons	_____	_____
Tea	30 million tons	_____	_____

16. The following figure shows the annual domestic demand and supply for 64-GB flash drives.

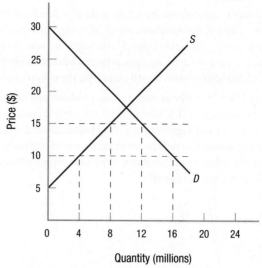

a. Assume that the worldwide price of these 64-GB flash drives is $10. What percent of sales in the United States is imported?
b. Assume the U.S. government puts a $5 tariff per unit on flash drive imports. How many 64-GB flash drives would be imported into the United States?
c. Given the tariff in question b, how much revenue would the government collect from this tariff?
d. Given the tariff in question b, how much more revenue would domestic companies receive as a result of the tariff?

✅ Answers to Questions in Checkpoints

Checkpoint: The Gains From Trade 376

Yes, in general, nations would not trade unless they benefit. However, as we have seen, even though nations as a whole gain, specific groups—industries (and their workers) that do not have a comparative advantage relative to other countries—lose.

Checkpoint: The Impact of Trade on Consumers and Producers 382

When a quota is imposed, the first beneficiary is the domestic industry. Foreign competition is curtailed. If the market is important enough (e.g., automobiles), foreign companies will build new plants in the United States and compete as if they were domestic firms. A second beneficiary is foreign competitors in that they can increase the price or complexity of their products and increase their profit. Losers are consumers and, to some extent, the government because a tariff could have accomplished the same reduction in imports and the government would have collected some revenue.

Checkpoint: Arguments Against Free Trade and Rebuttals Based on Evidence 387

Growth in the volume of trade with China has led to lower prices on many goods Americans enjoy. Although trade with China has led to significant benefits to Americans, the sentiment is not always positive for a number of reasons. First, many believe that China's low prices (through its low wages as well as government efforts to keep the value of the U.S. dollar strong) forced many American factories to close or move overseas, causing job losses. Second, some believe China holds an unfair advantage due to poor working conditions and low environmental standards. Third, some believe that quality standards for Chinese products are low, leading to safety issues. These and other reasons have created a backlash against efforts to further reduce trade barriers between the two nations. However, these concerns have not diminished the benefits of low prices and the many American jobs generated through increased exports of American-made products to a growing consumer market in China.

16

Open Economy Macroeconomics

Understanding how fluctuations in exchange rates affect what we pay for goods and services in a globalized economy

Learning Objectives

16.1 Define the current account and the financial account in the balance of payments between countries.

16.2 Explain the difference between nominal and real exchange rates.

16.3 Describe the effects of currency appreciation or depreciation on imports and exports.

16.4 Describe the effects of changes in inflation rates, disposable income, and interest rates on exchange rates.

16.5 Explain the differences between fixed and flexible exchange rate systems.

16.6 Describe the implications for fiscal and monetary policies when used with fixed and flexible exchange rate systems.

You probably are aware of international finance if you have traveled abroad. To purchase goods and services in another country, you need to have some of that country's currency. True, you can use credit cards for most purchases, but you still need some currency for daily transactions. In Britain, you need to pay in British pounds; in France, you need euros. British and French shopkeepers and public transportation officials will not accept U.S. dollars. This means that at the beginning of your trip, whether at the airport or at a bank, you have to exchange your dollars for the currency of the country you are visiting.

This process of exchanging money applies to international trade as well. You may pay dollars for your Burberry scarf or Louis Vuitton handbag in a store in the United States, but eventually your dollars have to be converted to pounds or euros when your payments make their way back to Britain or France, respectively. Similarly, if U.S. companies export goods abroad, they will want to bring dollars back to the United States, whether the goods are originally purchased with dollars or not.

Furthermore, in today's open economies, individuals can hold domestic and foreign financial assets. Financial portfolios might include foreign stocks, bonds, and currency, as well as domestic stocks and bonds. Buying and selling foreign securities and goods involves the buying and selling of foreign currency, also known as foreign exchange.

We can see that foreign exchange transactions for tourism, trade, and investment would seem to be large in number and amount. In fact, foreign exchange transactions dwarf the

BY THE Numbers

Foreign Exchange: *The Role of Currency Trading in the International Economy*

The foreign exchange market is the world's largest trade exchange, far surpassing the total value of all bond and stock transactions throughout the world. Currencies are traded 24 hours a day from Sunday 5:00 P.M. EST to Friday 5:00 P.M. EST in major foreign exchanges in Sydney, Tokyo, London, and New York. The U.S. dollar fluctuates in value against many currencies, and the overall trend is measured by the U.S. Dollar Index. This By the Numbers analyzes the U.S. Dollar Index over the 24-year period from 1995 to 2019.

$5.1 trillion

Total value of currency traded *each day* **in foreign exchange markets**

88%

The percentage of all foreign exchange transactions that include the U.S. dollar as one of the two currencies being traded

---

DATA:

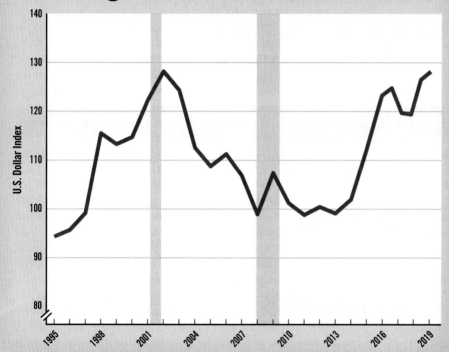

Trade-Weighted U.S. Dollar Index (1995–2019)

(Y-axis: U.S. Dollar Index, 80 to 140; X-axis: 1995, 1998, 2001, 2004, 2007, 2010, 2013, 2016, 2019)

Where Can I Find These Data?

Source: FRED Database; Federal Reserve Bank of St. Louis

Web site: https://fred.stlouisfed.org

Details: Search for "Trade Weighted U.S. Dollar Index" and use the "Broad, Goods" measure

---

WHY ARE THESE DATA IMPORTANT?

The value of the U.S. dollar affects how much American consumers pay for imported goods and foreign travel, as well as how much American businesses receive when exporting goods to other countries. A strong dollar makes imports and international travel less expensive. But it also makes American goods and services relatively more expensive to foreign consumers, which may depress sales.

Data *in the News*

"Stronger Dollar Poses Challenge for Wall Street Blue Chips" by Nicole Bullock and Chloe Cornish; *Financial Times*, May 30, 2018

Currency strength seen hurting foreign revenues for multinational companies. . . . Many of the leading lights in the S&P 500 rely on foreign-based revenues and thus face an unfavorable conversion when the dollar strengthens.

~ Assessing Your Data Literacy ~

1. Name two periods over which the U.S. dollar appreciated in value. By approximately what percentage did the U.S. Dollar Index increase in each period?

2. By approximately what percentage did the U.S. Dollar Index decrease from its peak in 2002 to its low point in 2008?

3. How does economic growth explain why the U.S. dollar appreciated from 2014 to 2019?

volume of exports and imports, often by as much as 30 to 40 times, in the same way that the annual value of all stock transactions far surpasses the market value of all companies on the New York Stock Exchange. Most foreign exchange transactions are conducted not for trade but for financial or speculative purposes. The social benefit to emerge from this speculation is a highly liquid foreign exchange market that ensures the possibility of trade. The large volume of speculative trade in currencies means that there will always be a market for international trade.

In this chapter, we will look at foreign exchange markets to obtain a sense of how policymaking in the United States is affected by an open worldwide economy. We start with the balance of payments accounts, which are to open economy macroeconomics what national income accounts are to an individual country's macroeconomic accounts. This accounting structure is the basis for open economy analysis. We then examine the foreign exchange market in detail, looking at both the trade and financial aspects of currency appreciation and depreciation. Finally, we put this all together when we view fixed and flexible exchange rate systems and discuss how an open economy affects monetary and fiscal policymaking.

THE BALANCE OF PAYMENTS

All open economies have balance of payments accounts. Open financial markets permit economies to run trade surpluses and deficits.

A simplified version of the U.S. balance of payments accounts for 2018 is shown in Table 1. These accounts were compiled by the Bureau of Economic Analysis of the U.S. Department of Commerce. The balance of payments represents all payments received from foreign countries

TABLE 1	THE BALANCE OF PAYMENTS 2018 (BILLIONS OF U.S. DOLLARS)	
Current Account		
Exports	2,500.8	
Imports	3,122.9	
Balance of trade (exports − imports)		−622.1
Income received (inflow)	1,060.4	
Income payments (outflow)	816.1	
Balance on income (inflow − outflow)		244.3
Net transfers		−110.7
Current account balance		−488.5
Financial Account		
Change in foreign-owned assets in the United States	800.9	
Change in U.S.-owned assets abroad	301.6	
Net increase in foreign-owned holdings		499.3
Statistical discrepancy		−10.8
Financial account balance		488.5

Data from Bureau of Economic Analysis.

and all payments made to them. Notice that the accounts are split into two broad divisions: the current account and the financial account.

The Current Account

The **current account** includes payments for imports and exports of goods and services, incomes flowing into and out of the country, and net transfers of money.

Imports and Exports In 2018, U.S. exports of goods and services totaled $2,500.8 billion, with imports totaling $3,122.9 billion. This exchange produced a trade deficit of $622.1 billion because we imported more than we exported. Some balance of payments accounts break exports and imports into separate categories of goods and services; here, they are combined. This component of the current account is known as the balance of trade.

Income Another source of foreign payments to the United States comprises income flows, which include wages, rents, interest, and profit that Americans earn abroad ($1,060.4 billion in 2018) minus the corresponding income foreigners earn in the United States ($816.1 billion). On balance, foreigners earned $244.3 billion less in the United States than U.S. citizens and corporations earned abroad in 2018.

Transfers Direct transfers of money also take place between the United States and other countries. These transfers include foreign aid, funds sent to such international organizations as the United Nations, and stipends paid directly to foreign students studying in the United States or U.S. students studying abroad. These transfers also include remittances, money that people working in the United States send back to their families in foreign countries. Net transfers of money for 2018 from all sources totaled –$110.7 billion.

Adding all current account categories for 2018 yields a current account deficit of $488.5 billion. This means that in 2018, the United States paid out $488.5 billion more than it received. Therefore, the United States had to borrow $488.5 billion from the rest of the world, or the net holdings of U.S. assets by foreigners must have increased by that same amount, or some combination of the two.

The Financial Account

The **financial account** summarizes the flow of money into and out of domestic and foreign assets. This account includes investments by foreign companies in domestic plants or subsidiaries—a Toyota truck plant in Tennessee, for example. Note that the profit from such investments flow abroad, and thus they are in the income payments (outflow) category of the current account. Other foreign holdings of U.S. assets include portfolio investments such as mutual funds, stocks, bonds, and deposits in U.S. banks. American investors hold foreign financial assets in their portfolios, including foreign stocks and bonds. And American companies own plants and other assets in foreign countries.

The United States ran a current account deficit in 2018, which means it must run a financial account surplus. Net financial inflows into the United States must equal $488.5 billion to offset the current account deficit. Indeed, foreign-owned assets in the United States increased by $800.9 billion, while U.S. ownership of foreign assets increased by $301.6 billion, resulting in a net increase in foreign-owned asset holdings of $499.3 billion. Many accounts are prone to estimation errors, which necessitates a statistical discrepancy value of –$10.8 billion added to bring the financial account surplus to $488.5 billion.

To clarify, the balance of payments actually includes three components: the current account, the financial account, and the capital account. The capital account is a relatively tiny value that includes financial transactions that have no effect on income, such as debt forgiveness. For simplicity, we focus only on the financial account to offset the current account. The key point to remember in balance of payments accounts is that a deficit in the current account must be offset by a corresponding surplus in the financial account, and vice versa.

current account Includes payments for imports and exports of goods and services, incomes flowing into and out of the country, and net transfers of money.

The iconic Plaza Hotel in New York City, which has appeared in several dozen movies, was sold to a Qatari company in 2018. The inflow of funds to the United States used to purchase the hotel appeared in the U.S. financial account that year.

financial account Summarizes the flow of money into and out of domestic and foreign assets, including investments by foreign companies in domestic plants or subsidiaries, and other foreign holdings of U.S. assets, including mutual funds, stocks, bonds, and deposits in U.S. banks. Also included are U.S. investors' holdings of foreign financial assets, production facilities, and other assets in foreign countries.

✅ CHECKPOINT

EXCHANGE RATES

As we saw in the chapter opening, if you wish to go abroad or to buy a product directly from a foreign firm, you need to exchange dollars for foreign currency. Today, credit cards automatically convert currencies for you, making the transaction more convenient. However, this conversion does not alter the transaction's underlying structure.

When you decide to travel abroad, the value of the dollar compared to the currency where you are going determines how expensive your trip will be. The value of the dollar fluctuates continuously against most foreign currencies that are traded in the foreign exchange market. This section looks at the issues of exchange rates and their determination.

Defining Exchange Rates

exchange rate The rate at which one currency can be exchanged for another.

The **exchange rate** is defined as the rate at which one currency, such as U.S. dollars, can be exchanged for another, such as British pounds. The exchange rate is nothing more than the price of one currency for another. Table 2 shows exchange rates for selected countries for a specific date (April 18, 2019), as found on the Web site xe.com. Exchange rates can be quoted in one of two ways: (1) the price (in domestic currency) of 1 unit of foreign currency, or (2) the number of units of a foreign currency required to purchase 1 unit of domestic currency. As Table 2 illustrates, exchange rates are often listed from both perspectives.

Nominal Exchange Rates According to Table 2, 1 British pound will buy 1.30 dollars. Equivalently, 1 dollar will purchase 0.77 pound. These numbers are reciprocal measures of each other ($1 \div 1.30 = 0.77$). A **nominal exchange rate** is the price of one country's currency in terms of another country's currency. It is the most common way of stating exchange rates. However, nominal exchange rates do not take into account changes in prices between countries. Therefore, economists often use an alternative measure of exchange rates, called the real exchange rate, when analyzing their effects on the economy.

nominal exchange rate The price of one country's currency in terms of another country's currency.

real exchange rate A measure of a currency's value relative to another, taking into account the price levels of both countries. It is equal to the nominal exchange rate multiplied by the ratio of the price levels of the two countries.

Real Exchange Rates The **real exchange rate** takes the price levels of both countries into account. Real exchange rates become important when inflation is an issue in one country. The real exchange rate between two countries is defined as

$$e_r = e_n \times (P_d/P_f),$$

where e_r is the real exchange rate, e_n is the nominal exchange rate, P_d is the domestic price level, and P_f is the foreign price level.

TABLE 2	EXCHANGE RATES (APRIL 18, 2019)	
	U.S. Dollars	Currency per U.S. Dollar
Australia (dollar)	0.718	1.393
Brazil (real)	0.254	3.939
Britain (pound)	1.304	0.767
Canada (dollar)	0.749	1.335
China (yuan)	0.149	6.695
France (euro)	1.129	0.885
India (rupee)	0.014	69.520
Japan (yen)	0.009	111.898
Mexico (peso)	0.053	18.846
Russia (ruble)	0.016	63.891
Switzerland (franc)	0.990	1.010

Data from xe.com.

The nominal value of a currency does not mean much until exchange rates and prices are considered. For example, $1 U.S. can be exchanged for about 1,100 South Korean won but only 0.30 Kuwaiti dinar. But this doesn't mean that the U.S. dollar can buy more in Seoul than in Kuwait City.

The real exchange rate is the nominal exchange rate multiplied by the ratio of the price levels of the two countries. In other words, the real exchange rate tells us how many units of the foreign good can be obtained for the price of 1 unit of that good domestically. The higher this number, the cheaper the good abroad becomes. If the real exchange rate is greater than 1, prices abroad are lower than at home. In a broad sense, the real exchange rate may be viewed as a measure of the price competitiveness between the two countries. When prices rise in one country, its products are not as competitive in world markets.

Let us take British and American cars as an example. Assume that Britain suffers significant inflation, which pushes the price of Land Rovers up by 15% in Britain. Meanwhile, the United States experiences no such inflation of its price level. If the dollar-to-pound exchange rate remains constant for the moment, the price of Land Rovers in the U.S. market will climb, while domestic auto prices remain constant.

Land Rovers become less competitive due to the higher prices, resulting in fewer sales. Note that the resulting reduction in U.S. purchases of British cars and other items will reduce the demand for British pounds. This puts downward pressure on the pound, reducing its exchange value and restoring some competitiveness. Markets do adjust! We will look at this issue in more detail later in the chapter.

Purchasing Power Parity **Purchasing power parity** (PPP) is the rate of exchange that allows a specific amount of currency in one country to purchase the same quantity of goods in another country. Absolute PPP would mean that nominal exchange rates equaled the same purchasing power in each country. As a result, the real exchange rate would be equal to 1. For example, PPP would exist if $4 bought a meal in the United States and the same $4 converted to British pounds (about £3.1) bought the same meal in London.

If you have traveled abroad, you know that PPP is not absolute. Some countries, such as India and Thailand, have a relatively low average cost of living while in other countries, such as Norway and Switzerland, many goods and services are more expensive. *The Economist* provides an online interactive tool called the "Big Mac Index," a lighthearted attempt to capture the notion of PPP.

Table 3 presents some recent estimates of PPP and the Big Mac Index. It also shows the PPP implied by the relative cost of Big Macs, along with the actual exchange rate. When comparing these two, we obtain an approximate over- or understating of the exchange rate. Keep in

purchasing power parity The rate of exchange that allows a specific amount of currency in one country to purchase the same quantity of goods in another country.

Prices of fast food in different nations often do not result in purchasing power parity.

TABLE 3	MEASURES OF PURCHASING POWER PARITY: BIG MAC INDEX				
	In Local Currency	In Dollars	Implied PPP of the Dollar	Actual Dollar Exchange Rate (January 2019)	Under (−)/Over (+) Against the Dollar (%)
United States	US$ 5.58	5.58	1.00	—	—
Australia	AUD$ 6.10	4.36	1.09	1.40	−22
Britain	Pound 3.19	4.09	0.57	0.78	−27
Canada	CAD$ 6.77	5.09	1.21	1.33	−9
China	Yuan 20.9	3.05	3.75	6.85	−45
India	Rupee 178	2.55	31.90	69.69	−54
Japan	Yen 390	3.60	69.89	108.44	−36
Mexico	Peso 49	2.54	8.78	19.31	−55
Norway	Krone 50	5.86	8.96	8.53	+5
Switzerland	CHF 6.5	6.63	1.16	0.98	+19
Taiwan	NT$ 69	2.24	12.37	30.80	−60
Thailand	Bhat 119	3.72	21.33	32.01	−33
United Arab Emirates	Dirham 14	3.81	2.51	3.67	−32

Data from the Big Mac Index interactive tool: economist.com/content/big-mac-index.

mind that the cost of a McDonald's Big Mac may be influenced by many unique local factors (trade barriers on beef, customs duties, taxes, competition), and therefore it may not reflect real PPP. Also, in some countries where beef is not consumed, chicken, fish, or vegetable patties are substituted.

According to the Big Mac Index, in 2019 most currencies were undervalued to the U.S. dollar, with the exception of the Norwegian krone and Swiss franc. Although not perfect, changes in the Big Mac Index often are reflective of movements in true PPP. Changes in various factors that distort the index often reflect real changes in the economy.

An hour-long massage in Bangkok, Thailand, can cost as little as $10, while a quick 10-minute cab ride in Geneva, Switzerland, can run $30. Exchange rates often do not result in purchasing power parity between nations.

Exchange Rate Determination

We have seen that people and institutions have two primary reasons for wanting foreign currency. The first is to purchase goods and services and conduct other transactions under the current account. The second is to purchase foreign investments under the financial account. These transactions create a demand for foreign currency and give rise to a supply of domestic currency available for foreign exchange.

A Market for Foreign Exchange Figure 1 shows a representative market for foreign exchange. The horizontal axis measures the quantity of dollars available for foreign exchange, and the vertical axis measures the exchange rate in British pounds per U.S. dollar. The demand for dollars as foreign exchange is downward-sloping; as the exchange rate falls, U.S. products become more attractive, and more dollars are desired.

Suppose that the exchange rate at first is $1 = £1 and that the U.S. game company Electronic Arts manufactures and sells its games at home and in Britain for $50 (£50). Then suppose that the dollar *depreciates* by 50% such that $1.00 = £0.50. If the dollar price of a game remains at $50 in the United States, the pound price of games in Britain will fall to £25 because of the reduction in the exchange rate. This reduction will increase the sales of games in Britain and increase the quantity of dollars British consumers need for foreign exchange.

The supply of dollars available for foreign exchange reflects the demand for pounds because to purchase pounds, U.S. firms or individuals must supply dollars. Not surprisingly, the supply curve for dollars is positively sloped. If the dollar were to *appreciate*, say, moving to $1 = £2, British goods bought in the United States would look attractive because their dollar price would be cut in half. As Americans purchase more British goods, the demand for pounds would grow, and the quantity of dollars supplied to the foreign exchange market would increase.

Flexible Exchange Rates Assume that exchange rates are fully flexible such that the market determines the prevailing exchange rate and that the exchange rate in Figure 1 is initially e_1. At this exchange rate, the quantity of dollars demanded (Q_2) exceeds the quantity supplied (Q_1). As a result, the dollar will **appreciate**, or rise in value relative to other currencies, and the exchange rate will move in the direction of e_0 (more pounds are required to purchase a dollar). As the dollar appreciates, it becomes more expensive for British consumers, thus reducing the demand for U.S. exports. Due to the appreciating dollar, British imports are more attractive for

appreciation (currency)
When the value of a currency rises relative to other currencies.

····· Figure 1 • The Foreign Exchange Market for Dollars ·························

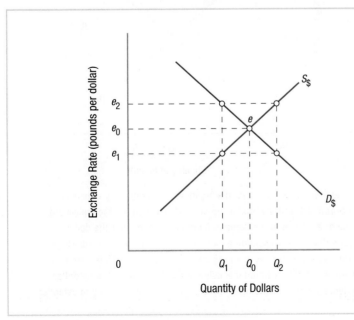

A market for foreign exchange is shown here. The horizontal axis measures the quantity of dollars available for foreign exchange, and the vertical axis measures the exchange rate in pounds per dollar. If exchange rates are fully flexible and the exchange rate is initially e_1, the quantity of dollars demanded (Q_2) exceeds the quantity supplied (Q_1). As a result, the dollar will appreciate, and the exchange rate will move to e_0. Alternatively, if the exchange rate is initially e_2, the quantity of dollars supplied (Q_2) exceeds the quantity demanded (Q_1). In this case, the dollar will depreciate. Eventually, the market will settle at the equilibrium exchange rate of e_0, where precisely the quantity of dollars supplied is the quantity demanded.

depreciation (currency)
When the value of a currency falls relative to other currencies.

U.S. consumers, increasing U.S. imports. These forces work to move the exchange rate to e_0, closing the gap between Q_2 and Q_1.

Alternatively, if the exchange rate begins at e_2, the quantity of dollars supplied (Q_2) exceeds the quantity demanded (Q_1). The value of dollars relative to British pounds will decline, or **depreciate**, because more dollars are being offered than demanded. American goods become less expensive in Britain, increasing American exports and the quantity of dollars demanded, while British goods become more expensive for American consumers. Eventually, the market will settle at the exchange rate of e_0, where the quantity of dollars supplied is equal to the quantity demanded.

Currency Appreciation and Depreciation A currency appreciates when its value rises relative to other currencies and depreciates when its value falls. This concept is clear enough in theory, but it can become confusing when we start looking at charts or tables that show exchange rates. The key is to be certain of which currency is being used to measure the value of other currencies. Does the table you are looking at show the pound price of the dollar or the dollar price of the pound?

Figure 2 shows the exchange markets for dollars and pounds. Panel A shows the market for dollars, where the price of dollars is denominated in pounds (£/$), just as in Figure 1. This market is in equilibrium at £0.56 per dollar (point e). Panel B shows the equivalent market for pounds; it is in equilibrium at $1.78 per pound (again at point e). Note that $1 \div 0.56 = 1.78$; therefore, panels A and B represent the same information, just from different viewpoints.

Assume that foreign exchange traders exchange pounds for dollars. In panel A, rising demand for dollars leads to its appreciation from £0.56 to £0.75 per dollar (point a). In panel B, the corresponding increase in the supply of pounds (from S_0 to S_1) leads to a depreciation of the pound and a fall in the exchange rate from $1.78 to $1.33 per pound (point b). Notice that the pound's depreciation in panel B produces a decline in the exchange rate, but this decline simultaneously results in appreciation of the dollar. An appreciation of one currency is the same as a depreciation

Figure 2 • The Foreign Exchange Market

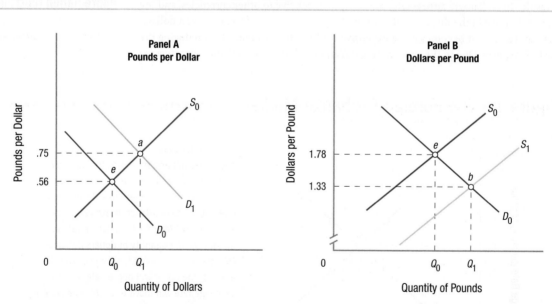

Data for dollars and pounds are graphically represented here. Panel A shows a market for dollars in which the price of dollars is denominated in pounds (£/$). In panel A, the market is in equilibrium at £0.56 per dollar (point e). Panel B shows the equivalent market for pounds in equilibrium at $1.78 per pound (again at point e). A rise in the demand for dollars means that the dollar appreciates to £0.75 per dollar (point a in panel A). Panel B shows that the corresponding increase in the supply of pounds (from S_0 to S_1) leads to a depreciation of the pound as the exchange rate falls from $1.78 to $1.33 per pound (point b). Note that a depreciating pound in panel B indicates a decline in the exchange rate, but this simultaneously represents an appreciating dollar. Thus, graphs can be viewed as reflecting either appreciation or depreciation, depending on which currency is being used to establish the point of view.

of the other. These graphs could be viewed as showing either an appreciation or a depreciation, depending on which currency represents your point of view.

For our purposes, we will try to use figures that show the exchange rate rising when the focus currency appreciates. Still, you need to be aware that exchange rates can be represented in two different ways. Exchange rate graphs are difficult and sometimes confusing; therefore, you will need to think through each graph you encounter.

Determinants of Exchange Rates What sort of conditions will cause currencies to appreciate or depreciate? First, a change in our tastes and preferences as consumers for foreign goods will result in currency appreciation or depreciation. For example, if we desire to purchase more foreign goods, this will lead to an increase in the demand for foreign currency and result in the depreciation of the dollar.

Second, if our income growth exceeds that of other countries, our demand for imports will grow faster relative to the growth of other nations. This will lead again to an increase in demand for foreign currency, resulting in the depreciation of the dollar.

Third, rising inflation in the United States relative to foreign nations makes our goods and services relatively more expensive overseas and foreign goods more attractive here at home. This results in growing imports and reduced exports and again leads to a depreciation of the dollar.

Fourth, falling interest rates in the United States relative to foreign countries make financial investment in the United States less attractive. This reduces the demand for dollars, leading once again to a depreciation of the dollar.

Note that if we reverse these stories in each case, the dollar will appreciate.

Exchange Rates and the Current Account

As we have already seen, the current account includes payments for imports and exports. Also included are changes in income flowing into and out of the country. In this section, we focus on the effect that changes in real exchange rates have on both of these components of the current account. We will assume that import and export demands are highly elastic as prices change due to fluctuations in the exchange rate.

Changes in Inflation Rates Let's assume that inflation increases in Britain such that the British price level rises relative to U.S. prices. Production costs rise in Britain; therefore, British goods are more expensive. American goods become relatively less expensive for British customers, which leads to an increase in U.S. exports, improving the U.S. current account. American consumers purchase more domestic goods and fewer British imports because of rising British prices, further improving the American current account. The opposite is true for Britain: British imports rise and exports fall, hurting the British current account.

These results are dependent on our assumption that import and export demands are highly elastic with real exchange rates. Thus, when exchange rates change, exports and imports will change proportionally more than the change in exchange rates.

Changes in Domestic Disposable Income If domestic disposable income rises, U.S. consumers will have more money to spend, and given existing exchange rates, imports will rise because some of this increased consumption will go to foreign products. As a result, the current account will worsen as imports rise. The opposite occurs when domestic income falls.

Exchange Rates and the Financial Account

The financial account summarizes flows of money or capital into and out of U.S. assets. Each day, foreign individuals, companies, and governments put billions of dollars into Treasury bonds, U.S. stocks, companies, and real estate. Today, foreign and domestic assets are available to investors. Foreign investment possibilities include direct investment in projects undertaken by multinational firms, the sale and purchase of foreign stocks and bonds, and the short-term movement of assets in foreign bank accounts.

Investors must balance their risks and returns because these transactions all involve capital. Two factors essentially incorporate both risk and return for international assets: interest rates and expected changes in exchange rates.

Interest Rate Changes If the exchange rate is assumed to be constant and the assets of two countries are *perfectly substitutable*, then an interest rate rise in one country will cause capital to flow into it from the other country. For example, a rise in interest rates in the United States will cause capital to flow from Britain, where interest rates have not changed, into the United States, where investors can earn a higher rate of return on their investments. Because the assets of both countries are assumed to be perfectly substitutable, this flow will continue until the interest rates (r) in Britain and the United States are equal, or

$$r_{US} = r_{UK}$$

Everything else being equal, we can expect capital to flow in the direction of the country that offers the highest interest rate, and therefore the highest return on capital. But "everything else" is rarely equal.

Expected Exchange Rate Changes Suppose that the exchange rate for U.S. currency is *expected to appreciate* ($\Delta\varepsilon > 0$). The relationship between the interest rates in the United States and Britain becomes

$$r_{US} = r_{UK} - \Delta\varepsilon$$

Investors demand a higher return in Britain to offset the expected depreciation of the British pound relative to the U.S. dollar. Unless interest rates rise in Britain, capital will flow out of Britain and into the United States until U.S. interest rates fall enough to offset the expected appreciation of the dollar.

If capital is not perfectly mobile and substitutable between two countries, a *risk premium* can be added to the relationship just described; thus,

$$r_{US} = r_{UK} - \Delta\varepsilon + x$$

where x is the risk premium. In this case, a higher x implies greater risk for holding the U.S. dollar. Therefore, a higher interest rate, r_{US}, is required. Expected exchange rate changes and risk premium changes can produce enduring interest rate differentials between two countries.

If the dollar falls relative to the yen, the euro, and the British pound, this is a sign that foreign investors were not as enthusiastic about U.S. investments. Low interest rates and high deficits may have convinced foreign investors that it was not a good time to invest in the United States.

The United States is more dependent on foreign capital than ever before. Today, about 40% of U.S. Treasury debt held by the public is held by foreigners. Changes in inflation, interest rates, and expectations about exchange rates are important.

Exchange Rates and Aggregate Supply and Demand

How do changes in nominal exchange rates affect aggregate demand and aggregate supply? A change in nominal exchange rates will affect imports and exports. Consider what happens when the value of the dollar depreciates. The dollar is weaker, and thus the pound (or any other currency) will buy more dollars. American products become more attractive in foreign markets; therefore, American exports increase and aggregate demand expands. Yet, because some inputs into the production process may be imported (raw materials, computer programming services, or call center services), input costs will rise, causing aggregate supply to contract.

Let us take a more detailed look at this process by considering Figure 3. Assume that the economy begins in equilibrium at point e, with full employment output Q_f and the price level at P_e. A depreciating dollar will spur an increase in exports, thus shifting aggregate demand from AD_0 to AD_1 and raising prices to P_1 in the short run. Initially, output climbs to Q_1, but because some of the economy's inputs are imported, short-run aggregate supply will decline, mitigating this rise in output (not shown in the figure). In the short run, the economy will expand beyond Q_f, and prices will rise.

In the longer term, as domestic prices rise, workers will realize that their real wages do not purchase as much as they did before because import prices are higher. As a result, workers will start demanding higher wages just to bring them back to where they were originally. This shifts short-run aggregate supply from $SRAS_0$ to $SRAS_1$, thereby moving the economy from point a

Figure 3 • Exchange Rates and Aggregate Demand and Supply

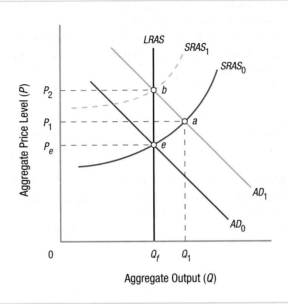

Assume that the economy initially begins in equilibrium at point e, with full employment output Q_f and the price level at P_e. Assume that the dollar then depreciates. This will increase exports, shifting aggregate demand from AD_0 to AD_1 and raising prices to P_1 and output to Q_1 in the short run. In the long run, short-run aggregate supply will shift from $SRAS_0$ to $SRAS_1$ as workers readjust their wage demands, thus moving the economy to point b. As the economy adjusts to a higher price level, the benefits from currency depreciation are greatly reduced.

●ISSUE

Would a Stronger Chinese Yuan Be Good for Americans?

Much discussion in recent years has focused on the accusation that the Chinese government intentionally undervalues its currency, the yuan.

When Americans purchase goods from China (and we purchase a tremendous amount), normally dollars must be exchanged for yuan to pay for these goods. Factories in China need to pay their workers in yuan so that their workers can pay their rent and buy groceries. When dollars are exchanged for yuan, demand for yuan increases, which raises its value. Therefore, the yuan should appreciate against the dollar.

When the yuan appreciates, it takes more dollars to obtain the same amount of yuan as before. Therefore, goods made in China, from toys you buy for your nephews and nieces to shoes, clothes, and electronics you buy for yourself, become more expensive.

To prevent the prices of China's exports from rising too much in the United States, the Chinese government bought up many of these dollars flowing into China, preventing them from being sold on the foreign exchange market. By holding U.S. dollars, the dollar value is kept from falling. In 2019, China held about 2 trillion in U.S. dollars.

Who benefited from this policy and who lost out? The actions by the Chinese government to prevent the yuan from appreciating keeps prices of Chinese-made goods low for ordinary American consumers, especially benefiting those with limited budgets. China's efforts make many U.S. consumers better off.

Who lost out? China's policy made it harder for American (and other non-Chinese) companies to compete against Chinese imports.

If the winners from this policy are American consumers and the losers are American businesses and their workers, policymakers are faced with a dilemma. Pressuring the Chinese to let its currency appreciate might be good for American

Are you ready to pay more for everyday purchases? When the Chinese yuan appreciates, you will.

companies, though it will lead to higher prices for many goods that we buy. Are we ready to see the cost of this policy come out of our pockets? Many Americans would be reluctant to support such an outcome because it would have a similar effect as an increase in taxes or inflation. Both reduce the purchasing power of our income and savings.

Indeed, you can see that the debate about currency manipulation goes beyond whether one side is playing by the rules. Sometimes, fairness can be a costly proposition.

in the short run to point *b* in the long run. As the economy adjusts to a higher price level, the original benefits accruing from currency depreciation will be greatly reduced.

Currency depreciation works because imports become more expensive and exports less so. When this happens, consumer income no longer goes as far because the price of domestic goods does not change but the cost of imports rises. In countries where imports form a substantial part of household spending, major depreciations in the national currency can produce significant declines in standards of living. Such depreciations (or devaluations) have occasioned strikes and, in some cases, even street riots; examples in recent decades include such actions in Argentina, Brazil, Mexico, and Indonesia.

What are the implications of all this for policymakers? First, a currency depreciation or devaluation can, after a period, lead to inflation. However, in most cases the causation probably goes the other way: Macroeconomic policies or economic events force currency depreciations.

Trade balances usually improve with an exchange rate depreciation. Policymakers can improve current account balances without inflation by pursuing devaluation first, then pursuing fiscal contraction (reducing government spending or increasing taxes), and finally moving the economy back to point *e* in Figure 3. But again, the real long-run benefit is more stable monetary and fiscal policies.

CHECKPOINT

EXCHANGE RATES

- Nominal exchange rates define the rate at which one currency can be exchanged for another.

- Real exchange rates are the nominal exchange rates multiplied by the ratio of the price levels of the two countries.

- Purchasing power parity (PPP) is a rate of exchange that permits a given level of currency to purchase the same amount of goods and services in another country.

- A currency appreciates when its value rises relative to other currencies. Currency depreciation causes a currency to lose value relative to others.

- Inflation causes depreciation of a country's currency, worsening its current account. Rising domestic income typically results in rising imports and a deteriorating current account.

- Rising interest rates cause capital to flow into the country with the higher interest rate, and expectations about a future currency appreciation or depreciation affect the financial account.

- Currency appreciation and depreciation can affect aggregate supply and demand. For example, currency depreciation expands aggregate demand as exports increase, but some (now higher-priced) imported inputs increase the cost of domestic production, reducing aggregate supply.

QUESTION: Cities along the U.S.– Canadian border, such as Vancouver, Niagara Falls, Detroit, and Buffalo, receive a substantial number of day visitors. For example, Americans might cross the border into Niagara Falls for a day of sightseeing, while Canadians might cross the border into Detroit to shop. Suppose that the value of the Canadian dollar appreciates against the U.S. dollar. How does this change affect tourism, businesses that depend on day-trippers, and the current account of the United States and Canada?

Answers to the Checkpoint questions can be found at the end of this chapter.

MONETARY AND FISCAL POLICY IN AN OPEN ECONOMY

How monetary and fiscal policy is affected by international trade and finance depends on the type of exchange rate system in existence. There are several ways that exchange rate systems can be organized. We will discuss the two major categories: fixed and flexible rates.

Fixed and Flexible Exchange Rate Systems

A **fixed exchange rate** system is one in which governments determine their exchange rates, then adjust macroeconomic policies to maintain these rates. In contrast, a **flexible** or **floating exchange rate** system relies on currency markets to determine the exchange rates consistent with macroeconomic conditions.

Before the Great Depression, most of the world economies were on the gold standard. According to Peter Temin, the gold standard was characterized by "(1) the free flow of gold between individuals and countries, (2) the maintenance of fixed values of national currencies in terms of gold and therefore each other, and (3) the absence of an international coordinating organization."[1]

Under the gold standard, each country had to maintain enough gold stocks to keep the value of its currency fixed to that of others. If a country's imports exceeded its exports, this balance of payments deficit had to come from its gold stocks. Due to gold backing the national currency, the country would have to reduce the amount of money circulating in its economy, thereby reducing expenditures, output, and income. This reduction would lead to a decline in prices and wages, a rise in exports (which were getting cheaper), and a corresponding drop in imports (which were becoming more expensive). This process would continue until imports and exports were again equalized and the flow of gold ended.

In the early 1930s, the U.S. Federal Reserve pursued a contractionary monetary policy intended to cool off the overheated economy of the 1920s. This policy reduced imports and increased the flow of gold into the United States. With France pursuing a similar deflationary policy, by 1932 these two countries held more than 70% of the world's monetary gold. Other countries attempted to conserve their gold stocks by selling off assets, thereby spurring a worldwide monetary contraction. As other monetary authorities attempted to conserve their gold reserves, bank failures were inadvertently created as bank liquidity fell. As a result, the Depression in the United States spread worldwide.

As World War II came to an end, the Allies met in Bretton Woods, New Hampshire, to design a new and less troublesome international monetary system. Exchange rates were set, and each country agreed to use its monetary authorities to buy and sell its own currency to maintain its exchange rate at fixed levels.

The Bretton Woods agreements created the International Monetary Fund to aid countries having trouble maintaining their exchange rates. In addition, the World Bank was established to loan money to countries for economic development. In the end, most countries were unwilling to make the tough adjustments required by a fixed rate system, and it collapsed in the early 1970s. Today, we operate on a flexible exchange rate system in which each currency floats in the market.

Pegging Exchange Rates Under a Flexible Exchange Rate System

Although most currencies fluctuate in value based on their relative demand and supply on the foreign exchange market, a number of countries use macroeconomic policies to peg the exchange rate of their currency (i.e., maintain a fixed exchange rate) to another currency, most commonly the U.S. dollar or the euro.

A common reason for a country to peg its currency to another is to maintain a close trade relationship because fixed exchange rates prevent fluctuations in prices due to changes in the exchange rate. For example, most OPEC nations peg their currencies to the U.S. dollar as a result of their dependency on oil exports. Many Caribbean nations that depend on tourism and trade with the United States also peg their currencies to the U.S. dollar.

Some countries do not maintain a strict fixed exchange rate with the U.S. dollar but will intervene to control the exchange rate. For example, China has intervened in foreign exchange markets for strategic purposes, propping up the value of the U.S. dollar by holding dollars instead of exchanging them on the foreign exchange market. By keeping the U.S. dollar strong, the price of Chinese

fixed exchange rate Each government determines its exchange rate, then uses macroeconomic policy to maintain the rate.

flexible or floating exchange rate A country's currency exchange rate is determined in international currency exchange markets.

---

[1] Peter Temin, *Lessons from the Great Depression: The Lionel Robbins Lectures for 1989* (Cambridge, MA: MIT Press), 1989, p. 8.

Alvaro Leiva/AGE Fotostock

When traveling to Panama, it is not necessary to exchange money. Panama's official currency is the U.S. dollar.

dollarization Describes the decision of a country to adopt another country's currency (most often the U.S. dollar) as its own official currency.

exports is kept low for American consumers, allowing China to continue expanding its export volume, and therefore its economy.

Another reason for maintaining a fixed exchange rate is to improve monetary stability and to attract foreign investment. For example, several countries in western Africa peg their unified currency, the CFA franc, to the euro. By maintaining a fixed exchange rate, a country is essentially giving up its ability to conduct independent monetary policy. However, some countries, such as Mexico and Argentina, both of which had pegged their currencies to the U.S. dollar in the past, were forced to abandon their efforts due to high inflation, which made their products too expensive in world markets.

Finally, some countries chose to abandon their currency altogether by adopting another country's currency as their own. Panama, Ecuador, El Salvador, Timor-Leste, and others all chose to adopt the U.S. dollar as their official currency, a process known as **dollarization**. Although these countries gave up their ability to use monetary policy, they also eliminated the risk of being unable to maintain fixed exchange rates with their original currencies. The following Around the World feature describes a unique situation in which an American town chooses to conduct transactions using a foreign currency.

There clearly are many approaches to foreign exchange. But how does a fixed versus a flexible exchange rate system affect each country's ability to use fiscal and monetary policy? We answer this question next.

AROUND THE WORLD

Hyder, Alaska: An American Town That Uses the Canadian Dollar

How did an American town end up using Canadian currency, utility services, and schools?

In a number of countries throughout the world, the U.S. dollar is more than just a valuable reserve currency. It's actually used as a medium of exchange. A few countries, including Panama, Ecuador, El Salvador, and Timor-Leste, have adopted the U.S. dollar as their official currency. But in many other countries, including Costa Rica, Bahamas, and Cambodia, the U.S. dollar is accepted as legal tender as easily as their own currencies. In these countries, circumstances such as tourism or political instability encourage businesses to conduct transactions more often in U.S. dollars than in their own currency.

But in one remote American town, the situation is reversed. Circumstances led its residents to conduct transactions in a foreign currency. Where is this place?

The residents of Hyder, Alaska, live more like Canadians than Americans due to the town's isolated location.

Hyder, Alaska, is a town of about 100 residents in the southeastern point of Alaska. There are no airports and very few boats that come in and out of its small harbor. In fact, there is just one road going in and out of Hyder, and that road leads to Canada. Hyder is so economically wed to its larger sister city across the border, Stewart, British Columbia, that it relies on Canadian

police, hospitals, utility services, and telecommunications (it has a Canadian area code). It also celebrates Canadian holidays because Hyder's children attend schools in Canada.

Most interestingly, Hyder adopted the Canadian dollar as its preferred currency. Although the American dollar is still legal tender in Hyder, its few businesses (with the exception of the U.S. Postal Service) conduct transactions in Canadian dollars. Much like why some countries use the U.S. dollar for convenience, businesses in Hyder use the Canadian dollar to reduce transaction costs by not having to exchange currency frequently. Because most of Hyder's product suppliers are located in Canada, conducting transactions in Canadian dollars also means that the effects of exchange rate fluctuations are minimized.

Hyder's economic ties with its Canadian neighbor exemplify the importance of strong global relations and how that can benefit individuals and businesses.

GO ONLINE TO PRACTICE THE ECONOMIC CONCEPTS IN THIS STORY

Figure 4 • Monetary and Fiscal Policy in an Open Economy Under Fixed Exchange Rates

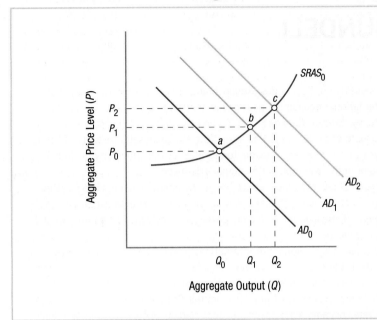

The use of expansionary monetary or fiscal policy increases aggregate demand from AD_0 to AD_1. The resulting higher domestic price level reduces exports while rising incomes increase imports, worsening the current account. An expansionary monetary policy (holding fiscal policy constant) increases the money supply and reduces interest rates. The resulting capital outflow decreases aggregate demand back toward AD_0. An expansionary fiscal policy (holding monetary policy constant) increases interest rates, leading to capital inflow, pushing aggregate demand farther to the right to AD_2.

Policies Under Fixed Exchange Rates

When the government engages in expansionary policy, aggregate demand rises, resulting in output and price increases. Figure 4 shows the result of such a policy as an increase in aggregate demand from AD_0 to AD_1, with the economy moving from equilibrium at point *a* to point *b* in the short run and the price level rising from P_0 to P_1. A rising domestic price level means that U.S. exports will decline as they become more expensive. As incomes rise, imports will rise. Combined, these forces will worsen the current account, moving it into deficit or reducing a surplus, as net exports decline.

An expansionary monetary policy, combined with a fiscal policy that is neither expansionary nor contractionary, will result in a rising money supply and falling interest rates. This causes aggregate demand to rise to AD_1 as shown in Figure 4. Lower interest rates result in capital flowing from the United States to other countries, which reduces aggregate output.

The greater the capital mobility, the more aggregate demand moves back in the direction of AD_0. With perfect capital mobility, monetary policy would be ineffective. The amount of capital leaving the United States would be just equal to the increase in the money supply to begin with, and interest rates would be returned to their original international equilibrium.

Keeping exchange rates fixed and holding the money supply constant, an expansionary fiscal policy will produce an increase in interest rates. As income rises, there will be a greater transactions demand for money, resulting in higher interest rates. Higher interest rates mean that capital will flow into the United States.

As more capital flows into U.S. capital markets, the expansionary impact of the original fiscal policy increases. Expansionary fiscal policy is reinforced by an open economy with fixed exchange rates as aggregate demand increases to AD_2.

Policies Under Flexible Exchange Rates

Expansionary monetary policy under a system of flexible exchange rates, again holding fiscal policy constant, results in a growing money supply and falling interest rates. Lower interest rates lead to a capital outflow and a balance of payments deficit, or a declining surplus. With flexible exchange rates, consumers and investors will want more foreign currency; thus, the domestic currency

NOBEL PRIZE
ROBERT MUNDELL

Awarded the 1999 Nobel Prize in Economics, Robert Mundell is best known for his ground-breaking work in international economics and for his contribution to the development of supply-side economic theory. Born in Canada in 1932, he attended the University of British Columbia as an undergraduate and earned his Ph.D. from the Massachusetts Institute of Technology in 1956. For a year, he served as a postdoctoral fellow at the University of Chicago, where he met the economist Arthur Laffer, his collaborator in the development of supply-side theory.

Supply-side economists advocated reductions in marginal tax rates and stabilization of the international monetary system. This approach was distinct from the two dominant schools of economic thought, Keynesianism and monetarism, although it shared some ideas with both. Mundell's work had a major influence on the economic policies of President Ronald Reagan and Federal Reserve chair Paul Volcker, whose tight money policies helped curb inflation.

Mundell's early research focused on exchange rates and the movement of international capital. In a series of papers in the 1960s that proved to be prophetic, he speculated about the impacts of monetary and fiscal policy if exchange rates were allowed to float, emphasizing the importance of central banks acting independently of governments to promote price stability. At the time, his work may have seemed purely academic. However, within 10 years the Bretton Woods system of fixed exchange rates tied to the dollar broke down, exchange rates became more flexible, capital markets opened up, and Mundell's ideas were borne out.

In another feat of near prophecy, Mundell wrote about the potential benefits and disadvantages of a group of countries adopting a single currency, anticipating the development of the European currency, the euro, by many years. Since 1974, Mundell has taught at Columbia University.

will depreciate. As the dollar depreciates, exports increase; U.S. exports are more attractive to foreigners as their currency buys them more. The net result is that the international market works to reinforce an expansionary policy undertaken at home.

Permitting exchange rates to vary and holding the money supply constant, an expansionary fiscal policy produces a rise in interest rates as rising incomes increase the transactions demand for money. Higher interest rates mean that capital will flow into the United States, generating a balance of payments surplus or a smaller deficit, causing the domestic currency to appreciate as foreigners value dollars more. As the dollar becomes more valuable, exports decline, moving aggregate demand back toward AD_0 in Figure 4. With flexible exchange rates, therefore, an open economy can hamper fiscal policy.

These movements are complex and go through several steps. Table 4 summarizes them for you. The key point to note is that under our current flexible exchange rate system, an open economy reinforces monetary policy and hampers fiscal policy. No wonder the Fed has become more important.

TABLE 4	THE EFFECTS OF AN OPEN ECONOMY ON MONETARY AND FISCAL POLICY IN A FIXED AND FLEXIBLE EXCHANGE RATE SYSTEM	
	Flexible Exchange Rate	**Fixed Exchange Rate**
Monetary policy (fiscal policy constant)	Reinforced	Hampered
Fiscal policy (monetary policy constant)	Hampered	Reinforced

Several decades ago, presidents and Congress could adopt monetary and fiscal policies without much consideration of the rest of the world. Today, economies of the world are vastly more intertwined, and the macroeconomic policies of one country often have serious impacts on others. Today, open economy macroeconomics is more important, and good macroeconomic policy-making must account for changes in exchange rates and capital flows.

During the financial crisis and recession of 2007–2009, the implications of monetary policy on exchange rates became important, as countries throughout the world were eager to use expansionary monetary policy to curtail the severity of the crisis. However, taking such action unilaterally can lead to adverse effects in other countries due to its effect on exchange rates, which affect trade and current accounts.

Therefore, in October 2008, six central banks, including the Fed and the European Central Bank, took a rare action of coordinated monetary policy in which the central banks jointly announced a reduction in their target interest rates. As a result, countries engaging in a similar level of expansionary policy would prevent instability in exchange rates. As former Fed chair Ben Bernanke put it, "The coordinated rate cut was intended to send a strong signal to the public and to markets of our resolve to act together to address global economic challenges."[2] The coordinated efforts of central banks continued over several years, especially when the Eurozone crisis intensified in 2011.

The global economy is connected not only through trade and currency exchanges. Nearly all economic decisions have effects that extend beyond our country's borders, from the types of goods that consumers purchase, to the goods firms produce and where they produce them, to how governments set policies that affect their citizens and those in other countries. As you complete your degree and prepare for your career, keep in mind the statement from Chapter 1 that has been illustrated throughout this book: *Economics is all around us.*

✅ CHECKPOINT

MONETARY AND FISCAL POLICY IN AN OPEN ECONOMY

- A fixed exchange rate is one in which governments determine their exchange rates and then use macroeconomic policy to maintain these rates.

- Flexible exchange rates rely on markets to determine exchange rates consistent with macroeconomic conditions.

- Some countries peg the exchange rate of their currency to another currency to facilitate trade, to promote foreign investment, or to maintain monetary stability.

- Fixed exchange rate systems hinder monetary policy but reinforce fiscal policy.

- Flexible exchange rates hamper fiscal policy but reinforce monetary policy.

QUESTION: The United States seems to rely more on monetary policy to maintain stable prices, low interest rates, low unemployment, and healthy economic growth. Does the fact that the United States has really embraced global trade (imports and exports combined are nearly 30% of GDP) and has a flexible (floating) exchange rate help explain why monetary policy seems more important than fiscal policy?

Answers to the Checkpoint questions can be found at the end of this chapter.

[2] Ben Bernanke, *Policy Coordination Among Central Banks,* Speech at the Fifth European Central Banking Conference, The Euro at Ten: Lessons and Challenges, Frankfurt, Germany, November 14, 2008, http://www.federalreserve.gov/newsevents/speech/bernanke20081214a.htm.

CHAPTER SUMMARY

SECTION 1 THE BALANCE OF PAYMENTS

16.1

The **current account** includes payments for imports and exports of goods and services, incomes flowing into and out of the country, and net transfers of money.

The **financial account** includes flows of money into and out of domestic and foreign assets.

The sum of the current account and financial account balances must equal zero.

Foreign investment in the United States includes foreign ownership of domestic plants or subsidiaries; investments in mutual funds, stocks, and bonds; and deposits in U.S. banks. Similarly, U.S. investors hold foreign financial assets in their portfolios and own interests in foreign facilities and companies.

gingercprice/Getty Images

When foreign tourists visit Miami Beach, the money that is spent adds to the U.S. current account. When a foreign tourist purchases a vacation condo, the purchase of this asset increases the U.S. financial account.

SECTION 2 EXCHANGE RATES

16.2

The **exchange rate** defines the rate at which one currency can be exchanged for another.

A **nominal exchange rate** is the price of one country's currency for another.

The **real exchange rate** takes price levels into account. The real exchange rate (e_r) is the nominal exchange rate (e_n) multiplied by the ratio of the price levels of the two countries:

$$e_r = e_n \times (P_d/P_f)$$

If exchange rates are fully flexible, markets determine the prevailing exchange rate. If the quantity of dollars demanded exceeds the quantity supplied, the dollar will appreciate, or increase in value. If the quantity of dollars supplied exceeds the quantity demanded, the dollar will depreciate, or decrease in value.

Purchasing power parity is the rate of exchange that allows a specific amount of currency in one country to purchase the same quantity of goods in another country.

Many services, such as playing a video game at a gaming center, are not easily traded. Therefore, price differences will exist based on the country's standard of living, and often will not reflect purchasing power parity with other countries.

16.3 It is important to keep in mind which currency is being used to measure the price of others. Graphs can be viewed as showing either an appreciation or a depreciation, depending on which currency is being considered.

In the figure, an increase in demand for U.S. dollars leads to its appreciation from 0.60 pounds per dollar to 0.75 pounds per dollar.

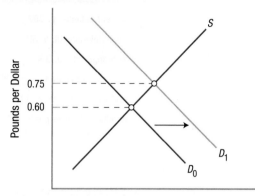

A shopping trip to the United States by British tourists increases demand for the dollar.

Interest rates and exchange rate expectations affect the financial account. An interest rate rise in one country will cause capital to flow into it from another country.

16.4 Real exchange rates affect the payments for imports and exports and also affect the current account. Inflation leads to higher prices for exports, reducing their demand and worsening the current account. Also, greater domestic disposable income worsens the current account as consumers increase spending on imports.

Interest rates can differ between countries due to expected exchange rate changes ($\Delta\varepsilon$) and a risk premium (x) when capital is not perfectly substitutable between countries.

$$r_{US} = r_{UK} - \Delta\varepsilon + x$$

SECTION 3 MONETARY AND FISCAL POLICY IN AN OPEN ECONOMY

16.5 A **fixed exchange rate system** is one in which governments determine their exchange rates, then use macroeconomic adjustments to maintain these rates.

A **flexible** or **floating exchange rate system** relies on currency markets to determine the exchange rates, given macroeconomic conditions.

Some countries choose to peg the exchange rate of their currency to another currency in order to facilitate trade, attract foreign investment, or promote monetary stability.

Ecuador took an extreme form of fixed exchange rate by adopting the U.S. dollar as its official currency (a process known as dollarization).

16.6 The ability of a country to use fiscal policy and monetary policy is affected by the type of foreign exchange system in place.

- A fixed exchange rate system hinders expansionary monetary policy because lower interest rates lead to capital outflows, which slow the economy.

- A fixed exchange rate system reinforces expansionary fiscal policy because higher interest rates lead to capital inflows, which expand the economy.

- Flexible exchange rates hamper expansionary fiscal policy because higher interest rates lead to currency appreciation, which reduces net exports.

- Flexible exchange rates reinforce expansionary monetary policy because lower interest rates lead to currency depreciation, which increases net exports.

Key Concepts

current account, p. 397

financial account, p. 397

exchange rate, p. 398

nominal exchange rate, p. 398

real exchange rate, p. 398

purchasing power parity, p. 399

appreciation (currency), p. 401

depreciation (currency), p. 402

fixed exchange rate, p. 407

flexible or floating exchange rate, p. 407

dollarization, p. 408

Questions and Problems

Check Your Understanding

1. Explain what the balance of trade is, and how it is calculated. What factors contribute to our trade deficit?

2. If the price of one euro changes from $1.10 to $1.20, does the value of the euro appreciate or depreciate against the dollar? Does the value of the U.S. dollar appreciate or depreciate against the euro?

3. What is the important difference between the current account and the financial account, given that the sum of the two values must equal 0?

4. If the euro appreciates by 30%, what will happen to exports of Mercedes-Benz automobiles (manufactured in Germany) to the United States?

5. Describe the difference between fixed and flexible exchange rates.

6. Describe the difference between the nominal and real exchange rates. What does rising inflation do to a country's real exchange rate?

Apply the Concepts

7. Assume that global warming and especially high temperatures in Northern California have rendered it impossible for wine grapes in the Napa Valley (and all over California) to grow properly. Unable to get California wines, demand jumps dramatically for Australian wines. How would this affect the Australian dollar? Is this good for other Australian exports?

8. If European economies have a serious bout of stagflation—high rates of both unemployment and inflation—will this affect the value of the dollar? Explain.

9. If a country prefers to use fiscal policy to smooth fluctuations in its business cycle, would a fixed or flexible exchange rate system be more conducive to this objective? Explain.

10. Mexican migrant workers in the United States often send money (known as remittances) to Mexico to support their families. In 2018, these remittances surpassed $30 billion. How are these transfers recorded in the balance of payments accounts?

11. If it costs 300 U.S. dollars to purchase an iPad in the United States and 400 Australian dollars to purchase one in Sydney, then according to purchasing power parity, the exchange rate between the Australian dollar and the U.S. dollar should be 4:3. Why might purchasing power parity be different from the exchange rate?

12. When the dollar becomes stronger against major foreign currencies, does the price of French wine rise or fall in the United States? Would this be a good time to travel to Australia? What happens to U.S. exports?

In the News

13. From 2014 to 2018, the annual number of tourists visiting Iceland more than doubled, attracted by its natural beauty, which includes hot springs, volcanoes, waterfalls, glaciers, and a chance of spotting the aurora borealis. How does this tourism boom affect the foreign exchange market for Icelandic krona, all else equal? How does it affect Iceland's current account?

14. The loosening of travel restrictions by the U.S. government for travel to Cuba has led to a large increase in American tourists. However, when tourists exchange U.S. dollars for Cuban pesos, the Cuban government charges a 10% tax. This tax is not levied on any other foreign currency being exchanged for Cuban pesos. What could American tourists do to avoid the 10% tax on foreign exchange transactions (keeping in mind that U.S.-issued credit and debit cards are difficult to use in Cuba)? What are the costs of trying to avoid this tax?

Solving Problems

15. Assume that the following exchange rates prevail:

	Value of U.S. Dollar
Brazil (real)	0.2545
Canada (dollar)	0.7492
Mexico (peso)	0.0531
New Zealand (dollar)	0.6697

How many Mexican pesos does it take to buy 1 New Zealand dollar? If you had 20 U.S. dollars, could you take a ferry ride in Canada if it costs 25 Canadian dollars? If someone gave you a 100 Brazilian real note to settle a 500 Mexican peso bet, would it be enough?

Work It Out

 interactive activity

16. Suppose that you are given an opportunity to work in Tokyo over the summer as an English tutor, and you are provided with all living expenses and a 500,000-yen cash stipend that you plan to save and bring home. If the exchange rate is 120 yen per U.S. dollar, how much would your stipend be worth in dollars if you exchanged your money right away? Suppose you predict that the exchange rate will change in the next few months to 110 yen per U.S. dollar. Would you receive more dollars if you exchanged the yen now or later? Show your calculations.

 # Answers to Questions in Checkpoints

Checkpoint: The Balance of Payments 398

When a country has a high savings rate (relative to domestic investment), its exports will probably exceed imports, resulting in a trade surplus. Both China and Russia are net exporters, which shows up as a current account surplus in their balance of payments accounts.

Checkpoint: Exchange Rates 406

When the Canadian dollar appreciates against the U.S. dollar, Canadian tourists visiting the United States receive more U.S. dollars for each Canadian dollar. Therefore, purchases by Canadian tourists in the United States become cheaper. As a result, demand rises, helping American businesses that depend on Canadian tourists. Also, the increased flow of money into the United States helps improve the U.S. current account. Meanwhile, the opposite occurs for American tourists to Canada, who find it more expensive to visit Canada. The higher cost of travel will discourage some Americans from visiting Canada, and Canadian businesses, such as those in Niagara Falls, Ontario, will suffer. Also, the reduction in money being spent by Americans in Canada will hurt Canada's current account.

Checkpoint: Monetary and Fiscal Policy in an Open Economy 411

As noted in this section, monetary policy is reinforced when exchange rates are flexible, while fiscal policy is hindered. This is probably only a partial explanation because fiscal policy today seems driven more by "events" and other priorities and less by stabilization issues.

The Great Recession from 2007 to 2009 required heavy doses of both monetary and fiscal policy to keep the economy from a devastating downturn. Additional government spending, while significant, did not impact the economy as strongly as many had anticipated. Maybe flexible exchange rates kept it from being as effective as anticipated.

absolute advantage A country can produce more of a good than another country using the same amount of resources.

adaptive expectations Inflationary expectations are formed from a simple extrapolation from past events.

aggregate demand The output of goods and services (real GDP) demanded at different price levels.

aggregate expenditures Consist of consumer spending, business investment spending, government spending, and net foreign spending (exports minus imports): $GDP = C + I + G + (X - M)$.

aggregate supply The real GDP that firms will produce at varying price levels. The aggregate supply curve is positively sloped in the short run but vertical in the long run.

allocative efficiency The mix of goods and services produced is just what society desires.

annually balanced budget Expenditures and tax revenues would have to be equal each year.

appreciation (currency) When the value of a currency rises relative to other currencies.

asymmetric information Occurs when one party to a transaction has significantly better information than another party.

autarky A country that does not engage in international trade, also known as a closed economy.

automatic stabilizers Tax revenues and transfer payments automatically expand or contract in ways that reduce the intensity of business fluctuations without any overt action by Congress or other policymakers.

automation The use of capital, such as a robot, to perform a task that a human worker previously performed.

average propensity to consume The percentage of income that is consumed $(C \div Y)$.

average propensity to save The percentage of income that is saved $(S \div Y)$.

balanced budget multiplier Equal changes in government spending and taxation (a balanced budget) lead to an equal change in income (the balanced budget multiplier is equal to 1).

barter The direct exchange of goods and services for other goods and services.

business cycles Alternating increases and decreases in economic activity that are typically punctuated by periods of recession and recovery.

capital Includes manufactured products such as tractors, welding equipment, and computers that are used to produce other goods and services. The payment to owners of capital is interest.

capital-to-labor ratio The capital employed per worker. A higher ratio means higher labor productivity and, as a result, higher wages.

catch-up effect Countries with smaller starting levels of capital experience larger benefits from increased capital, allowing these countries to grow faster than countries with abundant capital.

change in demand Occurs when one or more of the determinants of demand changes, shown as a shift of the entire demand curve.

change in quantity demanded Occurs when the price of the product changes, shown as a movement along an existing demand curve.

change in quantity supplied Occurs when the price of the product changes, shown as a movement along an existing supply curve.

change in supply Occurs when one or more of the determinants of supply change, shown as a shift in the entire supply curve.

circular flow diagram Illustrates how households and firms interact through product and resource markets and shows that economic aggregates can be determined by examining either spending flows or income flows to households.

collateralized debt obligation A collection of assets, primarily mortgages with varying risk, sold as a security to investors.

comparative advantage A country has a lower opportunity cost of producing a good than another country.

complementary goods Goods that are typically consumed together. When the *price* of a complementary good rises, the *demand* for the other good declines, and vice versa.

compounding The ability of growth to build on previous growth. It allows variables such as income and GDP (as well as debt) to increase significantly over time.

compounding effect The effect of interest added to existing debt or savings leading to substantial growth in debt or savings over the long run.

consumer price index (CPI) An index of the average prices paid by urban consumers for a typical market basket of consumer goods and services.

consumer surplus The difference between what consumers (as individuals or collectively as the market) would be willing to pay and the market price. It is equal to the area above market price and below the demand curve.

consumption Spending by individuals and households on both durable goods (e.g., autos, appliances, and electronic equipment) and nondurable goods (e.g., food, clothing, and entertainment).

contractionary fiscal policy Policies that decrease aggregate demand to contract output in an economy. These include reducing government spending, reducing transfer payments, and/or raising taxes.

contractionary monetary policy Fed actions designed to decrease the money supply and raise interest rates to shrink income and employment, usually to fight inflation.

cost-push inflation Results when a supply shock hits the economy, reducing short-run aggregate supply and thus reducing output and increasing the price level.

credit default swap A financial instrument that insures against the potential default on an asset. Because of the extent of defaults in the last financial crisis, issuers of credit default swaps could not repay all of the claims, bankrupting these financial institutions.

crowding-out effect When deficit spending requires the government to borrow, interest rates are driven up, reducing consumer spending and business investment.

current account Includes payments for imports and exports of goods and services, incomes flowing into and out of the country, and net transfers of money.

cyclical unemployment Unemployment that results from changes in the business cycle and where public policymakers can have their greatest impact by keeping the economy on a steady, low-inflationary, solid growth path.

cyclically balanced budget Balancing the budget over the course of the business cycle by restricting spending or raising taxes when the economy is booming and using these surpluses to offset the deficits that occur during recessions.

deadweight loss The reduction in total surplus that results from the inefficiency of a market not in equilibrium.

decision lag The time it takes Congress and the administration to decide on a policy once a problem is recognized.

deficit The amount by which annual government expenditures exceed tax revenues.

deflation A decline in overall prices throughout the economy. This is the opposite of inflation.

demand The maximum amount of a product that buyers are willing and able to purchase over some time period at various prices, holding all other relevant factors constant (the *ceteris paribus* condition).

demand curve A graphical illustration of the law of demand, which shows the relationship between the price of a good and the quantity demanded.

demand-pull inflation Results when aggregate demand expands so much that equilibrium output exceeds full employment output and the price level rises.

demand schedule A table that shows the quantity of a good a consumer purchases at each price.

depreciation (currency) When the value of a currency falls relative to other currencies.

determinants of demand Nonprice factors that affect demand, including tastes and preferences, income, prices of related goods, number of buyers, and expectations.

determinants of supply Nonprice factors that affect supply, including production technology, costs of resources, prices of related commodities, expectations, number of sellers, and taxes and subsidies.

diminishing returns to capital Each additional unit of capital provides a smaller increase in output than the previous unit of capital.

discount rate The interest rate the Federal Reserve charges commercial banks and other depository institutions to borrow reserves from a regional Federal Reserve Bank.

discouraged workers Discouraged workers are the portion of marginally attached workers who have given up actively looking for work and, as a result, are not counted as unemployed.

discretionary fiscal policy Policies that involve adjusting government spending and tax policies to push the economy toward full employment by stimulating economic output or mitigating inflation.

discretionary spending The part of the budget that works its way through the appropriations process of Congress each year and includes national defense, transportation, science, environment, education, and some income security programs.

disinflation A reduction in the rate of inflation. An economy experiencing disinflation still faces inflation, but at a declining rate.

dollarization Describes the decision of a country to adopt another country's currency (most often the U.S. dollar) as its own official currency.

double-dip recession A recession that begins after only a short period of economic recovery from the previous recession.

dumping Selling goods abroad at lower prices than in home markets and often below cost.

easy money, quantitative easing, or accommodative monetary policy Fed actions designed to increase excess reserves and the money supply to stimulate the economy (increase income and employment). *See also* expansionary monetary policy.

economic growth A change in a country's output or income that leads to an improvement in the standard of living.

economics The study of how individuals, firms, and society make decisions to allocate limited resources to many competing wants.

efficiency How well resources are used and allocated. Do people obtain the goods and services they want at the lowest possible resource cost? This is the chief focus of efficiency.

efficiency wage theory Employers often pay their workers wages above the market-clearing level to improve morale and productivity, reduce turnover, and create a disincentive for employees to shirk their duties.

entrepreneurs Entrepreneurs combine land, labor, and capital to produce goods and services. They absorb the risk of being in business, including the risk of bankruptcy and other liabilities associated with doing business. Entrepreneurs earn profit for their effort.

equation of exchange The heart of classical monetary theory uses the equation $M \times V = P \times Q$, where M is the supply of money, V is the velocity of money (the average number of times per year a dollar is spent on goods and services, or the number of times it turns over in a year), P is the price level, and Q is the economy's real output level.

equilibrium Market forces are in balance when the quantities demanded by consumers just equal the quantities supplied by producers.

equilibrium price The price at which the quantity demanded is just equal to the quantity supplied.

equilibrium quantity The output that results when the quantity demanded is just equal to the quantity supplied.

equity The fairness of various issues and policies.

excess reserves Reserves held by banks above the legally required amount.

exchange rate The rate at which one currency can be exchanged for another.

expansionary fiscal policy Policies that increase aggregate demand to expand output in an economy. These include increasing government spending, increasing transfer payments, and/or decreasing taxes.

expansionary monetary policy Fed actions designed to increase the money supply and lower interest rates to stimulate the economy (expand income and employment).

exports Goods and services that are sold abroad.

externally held debt Public debt held by foreigners, including foreign industries, banks, and governments.

federal funds rate The interest rate financial institutions charge each other for overnight loans used as reserves.

Federal Open Market Committee (FOMC) A twelve-member committee that is composed of members of the Board of Governors of the Fed and selected presidents of the regional Federal Reserve Banks. It oversees open market operations (the buying and selling of government securities), the main tool of monetary policy.

Federal Reserve System The central bank of the United States.

fiat money Money without intrinsic value but nonetheless accepted as money because the government has decreed it to be money.

financial account Summarizes the flow of money into and out of domestic and foreign assets, including investments by foreign companies in domestic plants or subsidiaries, and other foreign holdings of U.S. assets, including mutual funds, stocks, bonds, and deposits in U.S. banks. Also included are U.S. investors' holdings of foreign financial assets, production facilities, and other assets in foreign countries.

financial intermediaries Financial firms (banks, mutual funds, insurance companies, etc.) that acquire funds from savers and then lend these funds to borrowers (consumers, firms, and governments).

financial system A complex set of institutions, including banks, bond markets, and stock markets, that allocate scarce resources (financial capital) from savers to borrowers.

fiscal sustainability A measure of the present value of all projected future revenues compared to the present value of projected future spending.

fixed exchange rate Each government determines its exchange rate, then uses macroeconomic policy to maintain the rate.

flexible or **floating exchange rate** A country's currency exchange rate is determined in international currency exchange markets.

fractional reserve banking system Describes a banking system in which a portion of bank deposits are held as vault cash or in an account with the regional Federal Reserve Bank, while the rest of the deposits are loaned out to generate the money creation process.

frictional unemployment Unemployment resulting from workers who voluntarily quit their jobs to search for better positions or are moving to new jobs but may still take several days or weeks before they can report to their new employers.

functional finance An approach that focuses on fostering economic growth and stable prices while keeping the economy as close as possible to full employment.

GDP deflator An index of the average prices for all goods and services in the economy, including consumer goods, investment goods, government goods and services, and exports. It is the broadest measure of inflation in the national income and product accounts (NIPA).

GDP gap The difference between actual income and potential income (GDP at full employment).

GDP per capita A country's GDP divided by its population. GDP per capita provides a useful measure of a country's relative standard of living.

government budget constraint The government budget is limited by the fact that $G - T = \Delta M + \Delta B + \Delta A$.

government spending Includes the wages and salaries of government employees (federal, state, and local), the purchase of products and services from private businesses and the rest of the world, and government purchases of new structures and equipment.

gross domestic product (GDP) A measure of the economy's total output; it is the most widely reported value in the national income and product accounts (NIPA) and is equal to the total market value of all final goods and services produced by resources in a given year.

gross private domestic investment (GPDI) Investments in such things as structures (residential and nonresidential), equipment, and software and changes in private inventories.

horizontal summation The process of adding the number of units of the product purchased or supplied at each price to determine market demand or supply.

hyperinflation An extremely high rate of inflation; above 100% per year.

implementation lag The time required to turn fiscal policy into law and eventually have an impact on the economy.

imports Goods and services that are purchased from abroad.

incentives The factors that motivate individuals and firms to make decisions in their best interest.

infant industry An industry so underdeveloped that protection is needed for it to become competitive on the world stage or to ensure its survival.

inferior goods Goods that have income elasticities that are negative. When consumer income increases, demand for inferior goods falls, and vice versa.

inflation A general rise in prices throughout the economy. It is a measure of changes in the cost of living.

inflation targeting The central bank sets a target on the inflation rate (usually around 2% per year) and adjusts monetary policy to keep inflation near that target.

inflationary expectations The rate of inflation expected by workers for any given period. When inflationary expectations rise, workers will demand higher nominal wages.

inflationary gap The spending reduction necessary (when expanded by the multiplier) to bring an overheated economy back to full employment.

informal economy Includes all transactions that are conducted but are not licensed and/or generate income that is not reported to the government (for tax collection).

information lag The time policymakers must wait for economic data to be collected, processed, and reported. Most macroeconomic data are not available until at least one quarter (three months) after the fact.

infrastructure The public capital of a nation, including transportation networks, power-generating plants and transmission facilities, public education institutions, and other intangible resources, such as protection of property rights and a stable monetary environment.

injections Increments of spending, including investment, government spending, and exports.

insolvent A situation when a bank's liabilities exceed its assets.

internally held debt Public debt owned by domestic banks, corporations, mutual funds, pension plans, and individuals.

investment Spending by businesses that adds to the productive capacity of the economy. Investment depends on factors such as its rate of return, the level of technology, and business expectations about the economy.

investment in human capital Investments such as education and on-the-job training that improve the productivity of labor.

jobless recovery A phenomenon that takes place after a recession, when output begins to rise, but employment growth does not.

Keynesian macroeconomic equilibrium The state of an economy at which all injections equal all withdrawals. There are no pressures pushing the economy to a higher or lower level of output.

labor Includes the mental and physical talents of individuals who produce products and services. The payment to labor is wages.

labor force The total number of those employed and unemployed. The unemployment rate is the number of unemployed divided by the labor force, expressed as a percent.

labor force participation rate The percentage of the adult non-institutionalized population that is in the labor force.

Laffer curve A curve that shows a hypothetical relationship between income tax rates and tax revenues. As tax rates rise from zero, revenues rise, reach a maximum, then decline until revenues reach zero again at a 100% tax rate.

laissez-faire A market that is allowed to function without any government intervention.

land Includes natural resources such as mineral deposits, oil, natural gas, water, and land in the usual sense of the word. The payment for use of land as a resource is rent.

law of demand Holding all other relevant factors constant, as price increases, quantity demanded falls, and as price decreases, quantity demanded rises.

law of supply Holding all other relevant factors constant, as price increases, quantity supplied rises, and as price declines, quantity supplied falls.

leakages A reduction in the amount of money that is used for lending that reduces the money multiplier. It is caused by banks choosing to hold excess reserves and from individuals, businesses, and foreigners choosing to hold cash.

leverage Occurs when a small amount of capital is used to support a larger amount of investment by borrowing. The risk of highly leveraged investments is that a small decrease in price can wipe out one's account.

liquidity How quickly, easily, and reliably an asset can be converted into cash.

liquidity trap When interest rates are very low, people hold on to money rather than invest in bonds due to their expectations of a declining economy or an unforeseen event such as war.

long-run aggregate supply (LRAS) curve The long-run aggregate supply curve is vertical at full employment because the economy has reached its capacity to produce.

M1 The narrowest definition of money that measures highly liquid instruments including currency (banknotes and coins), demand deposits (checks), and other accounts that have check-writing or debit capabilities.

M2 A broader definition of money that includes "near monies" that are not as liquid as cash, including deposits in savings accounts, money market accounts, and money market mutual fund accounts.

macroeconomic equilibrium Occurs at the intersection of the short-run aggregate supply and aggregate demand curves. At this output level, there are no net pressures for the economy to expand or contract.

macroeconomics The study of the broader issues in the economy such as inflation, unemployment, and national output of goods and services.

mandatory spending Spending authorized by permanent laws that does not go through the same appropriations process as discretionary spending. Mandatory spending includes Social Security, Medicare, and interest on the national debt.

marginal propensity to consume The change in consumption associated with a given change in income $(\Delta C \div \Delta Y)$.

marginal propensity to save The change in saving associated with a given change in income $(\Delta S \div \Delta Y)$.

marginally attached workers Workers who were available for work and actively looked for it during the last 12 months but not in the last four weeks.

market failure Occurs when a free market does not lead to a socially desirable level of output.

markets Institutions that bring buyers and sellers together so that they can interact and transact with each other.

medium of exchange A function of money in which goods and services are sold for money, then the money is used to purchase other goods and services.

microeconomics The study of the decision-making by individuals, businesses, and industries.

misallocation of resources Occurs when a good or service is not consumed by the person who values it the most and typically results when a price ceiling creates an artificial shortage in the market.

monetary dove A policymaker who advocates for monetary policies that emphasize low unemployment and high growth as its top priorities.

monetary hawk A policymaker who advocates for monetary policies that emphasize keeping inflation low as its top priority.

monetary rule Keeps the growth of money stocks such as M1 on a steady path, following the equation of exchange (or quantity theory) to set a long-run path for the economy that keeps inflation in check.

monetized debt Occurs when debt is reduced by increasing the money supply, thereby making each dollar less valuable through inflation.

money Anything that is accepted in exchange for goods and services or for the payment of debt.

money illusion A misperception of wealth caused by a focus on increases in nominal income but not increases in prices.

money multiplier A formula that measures the *potential* or *maximum* amount the money supply can increase (or decrease) when

a dollar of new deposits enters or exits the system and is defined as 1 divided by the reserve requirement.

multiplier Spending changes alter equilibrium income by the spending change times the multiplier. One person's spending becomes another's income, and that second person spends some (the MPC), which becomes income for another person, and so on, until income has changed by $1/(1-MPC)=1/MPS$. The multiplier operates in both directions.

national debt The total debt issued by the U.S. Treasury, which represents the total accumulation of past deficits less surpluses. A portion of this debt is held by other government agencies, and the rest is held by the public. It is also referred to as the gross federal debt.

national income All income, including compensation of employees, profits (from sole proprietorships, partnerships, and corporations), rental income, net interest, and taxes on production and imports collected by the government.

natural rate of unemployment The level of unemployment at which price and wage decisions are consistent; a level at which the actual inflation rate is equal to people's inflationary expectations and where cyclical unemployment is zero.

net exports Exports minus imports for the current period. Exports include all goods and services we sell abroad, while imports include all goods and services we buy from other countries.

nominal exchange rate The price of one country's currency in terms of another country's currency.

normal goods Goods that have positive income elasticities less than 1. When consumer income increases, demand for normal goods rises, but less than the rise in income.

normative question A question whose answer is based on societal beliefs on what should or should not take place.

open market operations The buying and selling of U.S. government securities, such as Treasury bills and bonds, to adjust reserves in the banking system.

opportunity cost The value of the next best alternative; what you give up to do something or purchase something.

paradox of thrift When investment is positively related to income and households *intend* to save more, they reduce consumption. Consequently, income and output decrease, reducing investment such that savings actually end up decreasing.

pensions A retirement program into which an employer pays a monthly amount to retired employees until they die.

personal consumption expenditures Goods and services purchased by residents of the United States, whether individuals or businesses; they include durable goods, nondurable goods, and services.

Phillips curve The original curve posited a negative relationship between wages and unemployment, but later versions related unemployment to inflation rates.

positive question A question that can be answered using available information or facts.

price ceiling A maximum price established by government for a product or service. When the price ceiling is set below equilibrium, a shortage results.

price floor A minimum price established by government for a product or service. When the price floor is set above equilibrium, a surplus results.

price level The absolute level of a price index, whether the consumer price index (CPI; retail prices), the producer price index (PPI; wholesale prices), or the GDP deflator (average price of all items in GDP).

price system A name given to the market economy because prices provide considerable information to both buyers and sellers.

producer price index (PPI) An index of the average prices received by domestic producers for their output.

producer surplus The difference between the market price and the price at which firms are willing to supply the product. It is equal to the area below market price and above the supply curve.

production The process of converting resources (factors of production)—land, labor, capital, and entrepreneurial ability—into goods and services.

production efficiency Goods and services are produced at their lowest resource (opportunity) cost.

production function Measures the output that is produced using various combinations of inputs and a fixed level of technology.

production possibilities frontier (PPF) Shows the combinations of two goods that are possible for a society to produce at full employment. Points on or inside the PPF are attainable, and those outside of the frontier are unattainable.

productivity How effectively inputs are converted into outputs. Labor productivity is the ratio of the output of goods and services to the labor hours devoted to the production of that output. Productivity and living standards are closely related.

public choice theory The economic analysis of public and political decision making, looking at issues such as voting, election incentives on politicians, and the influence of special interest groups.

public debt The portion of the national debt that is held by the public, including individuals, companies, and pension funds, along with foreign entities and foreign governments. This debt is also referred to as net debt or federal debt held by the public.

purchasing power parity The rate of exchange that allows a specific amount of currency in one country to purchase the same quantity of goods in another country.

quota A government-set limit on the quantity of imports into a country.

rational expectations Individuals are assumed to make the best possible use of all publicly available information, then make informed, rational judgments on what the future holds. Any errors in their forecasts will be randomly distributed.

real exchange rate A measure of a currency's value relative to another, taking into account the price levels of both countries. It is equal to the nominal exchange rate multiplied by the ratio of the price levels of the two countries.

real GDP The total value of final goods and services produced in a country in a year measured using prices in a base year.

real GDP per capita Real GDP divided by population. Provides a rough estimate of a country's standard of living.

recessionary gap The increase in aggregate spending needed (when expanded by the multiplier) to bring a depressed economy back to full employment.

recognition lag The time it takes for policymakers to confirm that the economy is in a recession or a recovery. Short-term variations in key economic indicators are typical and sometimes represent nothing more than randomness in the data.

reserve ratio The percentage of a bank's total deposits that are held in reserves.

reserve requirement The required ratio of funds that commercial banks and other depository institutions must hold in reserve against deposits.

resources Productive resources include land (land and natural resources), labor (mental and physical talents of people), capital (manufactured products used to produce other products), and entrepreneurial ability (the combining of the other factors to produce products and assume the risk of the business).

return on investment (ROI) The earnings, such as interest or capital gains, that a saver receives for making funds available to others. It is calculated as earnings divided by the amount invested.

Rule of 70 Provides an estimate of the number of years for a value to double and is calculated as 70 divided by the annual growth rate.

saving The difference between income and consumption; the amount of disposable income not spent.

scarcity Our unlimited wants clash with limited resources, leading to scarcity. Everyone (rich or poor) faces scarcity because, at a minimum, our time on earth is limited. Economics focuses on the allocation of scarce resources to satisfy unlimited wants as fully as possible.

shortage Occurs when the price is below market equilibrium and quantity demanded exceeds quantity supplied.

short-run aggregate supply (SRAS) curve The short-run aggregate supply curve is positively sloped because many input costs are slow to change (*sticky*) in the short run.

short-run supply curve The marginal cost curve above the minimum point of the average variable cost curve.

stagflation Simultaneous occurrence of rising inflation and rising unemployment.

store of value The function that enables people to save the money they earn today and use it to buy the goods and services they want tomorrow.

structural unemployment Unemployment caused by changes in the structure of consumer demands or technology. It means that demand for some products declines and the skills of this industry's workers often become obsolete as well. This results in an extended bout of unemployment while new skills are developed.

subprime mortgage Mortgages that are given to borrowers who are a poor credit risk. These higher-risk loans charge a higher interest rate, which can be profitable to lenders if borrowers make their payments on time.

substitute goods Goods consumers will substitute for one another. When the *price* of one good rises, the *demand* for the other good increases, and vice versa.

supply The maximum amount of a product that sellers are willing and able to provide for sale over some time period at various prices, holding all other relevant factors constant (the *ceteris paribus* condition).

supply-side fiscal policies Policies that focus on shifting the long-run aggregate supply curve to the right, expanding the economy without increasing inflationary pressures. Unlike policies to increase aggregate demand, supply-side policies take longer to impact the economy.

surplus Occurs when the price is above market equilibrium and quantity supplied exceeds quantity demanded.

tariff A tax on imported products.

Taylor rule A rule for the federal funds target that suggests the target is equal to Target Inflation Rate + Current Inflation Rate + $1/2$(Inflation Gap)$+1/2$(Output Gap).

teaser rates Promotional low interest rates offered by lenders for a short period of time to attract new customers and to encourage spending.

terms of trade The ratio of the price of exported goods to the price of imported goods (P_x / P_m).

tight money or **restrictive monetary policy** Fed actions designed to decrease excess reserves and the money supply to shrink income and employment, usually to fight inflation. *See also* contractionary monetary policy.

total factor productivity The portion of output produced that is not explained by the number of inputs used in production.

total surplus The sum of consumer surplus and producer surplus; it is a measure of the overall net benefit gained from a market transaction.

tradeoff between lower risk and higher returns When choosing to invest in lower-risk assets, one must give up higher average returns on investment, and vice versa.

underemployed workers Workers who are forced to take jobs that do not fully utilize their education, background, or skills. Underemployed workers often hold part-time jobs.

unit of account Money provides a yardstick for measuring and comparing the values of a wide variety of goods and services. It eliminates the problem of double coincidence of wants associated with barter.

vesting period The minimum number of years a worker must be employed before the company's contribution to a retirement account becomes permanent.

wealth effect Households usually hold some of their wealth in financial assets such as savings accounts, bonds, and cash, and a rising aggregate price level means that the purchasing power of this monetary wealth declines, reducing output demanded.

willingness-to-pay An individual's valuation of a good or service, equal to the most an individual is willing and able to pay.

withdrawals Activities that remove spending from the economy, including saving, taxes, and imports.

yield curve Shows the relationship between the interest rate earned on a bond (measured on the vertical axis) and the length of time until the bond's maturity date (shown on the horizontal axis).

Index

Note: Page numbers followed by f indicate figures; those followed by n indicate footnotes; those followed by t indicate tables.

A

AARP, 143
Absolute advantage, 43–44, 43t, 373, 373t
Accommodative monetary policy, 332
Account, money as unit of, 273
AD. *See* Aggregate demand (AD) curve
AD/AS model. *See* Aggregate demand-aggregate supply (AD/AS) model
Adjustable-rate mortgages (ARMs), housing bubble and, 350
Ad valorem taxes, 379
Aerospace industry, 377
Africa. *See also specific countries*
   economic growth of, 169
Aggregate demand (AD) curve, 218–222, 218f
   determinants of, 219–222, 220f, 221t
   exchange rates and, 404, 405f, 406
   negative slope of, 218–219
   shifts of, 219, 220f
Aggregate demand-aggregate supply (AD/AS) model
   aggregate demand and, 218–222, 218f
   aggregate supply and, 223–227
Aggregate expenditures, 123, 187–212
   consumption and saving and, 190–193, 191t
   investment and, 193–196, 194f
   models of. *See* Full aggregate expenditures model; Simple aggregate expenditures model
   simplifying assumptions and, 190
Aggregate investment schedule, 195, 195f
Aggregate supply, 223–227
   determinants of, 225–226, 226t
   exchange rates and, 404, 405f, 406
   fiscal policy and, 248–252, 249f
   in long run, 223–224, 223f
   in short run, 224–225, 224f
Agricultural price supports, 96–97
AIG. *See* American International Group (AIG)
Allen, Robert, 326n
Allocative efficiency, 6, 35
Amazon, 56
American International Group (AIG), 351
American Recovery and Reinvestment Act of 2009, 352. *See also* Stimulus package, following recession of 2007–2009
Annually balanced budget, 256
Antidumping argument against free trade, 383
APC. *See* Average propensity to consume (APC)
Appreciation, of currencies, 401–403, 402f
APS. *See* Average propensity to save (APS)
ARMs. *See* Adjustable-rate mortgages (ARMs), housing bubble and
Assets
   allocation of, risk assessment and, 285–286
   choosing for investment, 286–287
   diversification of, by financial institutions, 281
   financial, types of, 281
   prices of, supply of loanable funds and, 278
Asymmetric information, market failure and, 98
Athens, Greece, Olympic Games at, 270
Australia, plastic money of, 274
Autarky, 45, 372
Auto industry, 46, 377, 380
Automatic stabilizers, 252–253
Automation, 362–363

Average propensity to consume (APC), 191–192
Average propensity to save (APS), 191–192

B

Bahamas, acceptance of U.S. dollar in, 408
Balanced budget amendments, 256–258
Balanced budget multiplier, 206
Balance of payments, 396–397, 396t
Bangladesh, GDP per capita in, 127
Bank(s)
   central. *See* European Central Bank (ECB); Federal Reserve System
   leakages from, 303
   loaned-up, 300
   money creation by, 298–302
   reserves and. *See* Reserve(s)
   Swiss, 305
Banking system, fractional reserve, 300–301
Bar charts, 22–23, 22f
Barter, 272
Basic economic questions, 32–33
BEA. *See* Bureau of Economic Analysis (BEA)
Bear Stearns, 351
Beige Book, 308
Benefits, 2
Bernanke, Ben, 337
Big Max Index, 399–400, 400t
Bitcoin, 56, 275
"Black Friday," 59
Black market, 128
BLS. *See* Bureau of Labor Statistics (BLS)
BMW, 375
Board of Governors of Federal Reserve System, 307
Bonds, 273
   prices of, interest rates and, 282
Borrowing. *See also* Loan(s); Mortgage(s), subprime
   Fed as lender of last resort and, 308–309
   financial system as bridge between savers and borrowers and, 280
   government bias toward, 253–254
   microloans and, 296
   short-term, 284
   subprime mortgages and, 350
Bottled water industry, 54
Branson, Richard, 11
Brazil, economic growth of, 164
Bretton Woods agreements, 407
BRIC countries. *See* Brazil, economic growth of; China; India; Russia
Bronco Wine Company, 74
Budget(s)
   annually balanced, 256
   cyclically balanced, 256–257
Budget deficits
   financing, 258
   supply of loanable funds and, 278
Bureau of Economic Analysis (BEA), 116, 166–167, 397
Bureau of Labor Statistics (BLS)
   consumer spending and inflation measurement by, 139, 140
   employment data collected by, 146–147, 149
Business(es). *See* Corporations, profits of, in GDP; Firms

Business cycles, 112–117. *See also* Great Depression; Great Recession; Recession(s)
   alternative measures of, 114–116
   dating, 114
   definition of, 112–114, 113f, 114t
Business expectations, demand for loanable funds and, 279
Busts. *See* Business cycles
Buyers, number of, demand and, 61–62

C

CafeX, 362
Cambodia, acceptance of U.S. dollar in, 408
Canada
   international trade of, 384
   tradeoffs in Nunavut and, 10
   USMCA agreement with, 46, 385
Canterbery, E. Ray, 43n, 71n
Capital
   accumulation of, economic growth and, 40, 40f
   diminishing returns to, 174
   human. *See* Human capital
   physical. *See* Physical capital, government as contributor to
Capital account, exchange rates and, 403–404
Capital goods, on hand, investment and, 195
Capital investment, fiscal policy and, 249
Capitalist economies, 32, 33
Capital-to-labor ratio, economic growth and, 174–175
Catch-up effect, 174–175
Causation, correlation vs., 28
CDOs. *See* Collateralized debt obligations (CDOs)
Census Bureau, employment surveys of, 146, 149
Central banks. *See* European Central Bank (ECB); Federal Reserve System
CES. *See* Current employment Statistics (CES) Survey
Ceteris paribus assumption, 6, 26–27
Chad, GDP per capita in, 127
Change in demand
   change in quantity demanded vs., 62, 63f
   equilibrium and, 73, 73f, 74f, 75, 75t
Change in quantity demanded, changes in demand vs., 62, 63f
Change in quantity supplied, change in supply vs., 67–68, 67f, 68f
Change in supply
   changes in quantity supplied vs., 67–68, 67f, 68f
   equilibrium and, 71, 72f, 73, 74f, 75, 75t
Charles Shaw wines, 74
Chase Bank, 351
Cheap foreign labor argument against free trade, 384
Chicago Fed National Activity Index, 115
Chile, public debt of, 259
China
   American car consumption in, 46
   comparative advantage in, 47
   currency of, 405
   economic growth of, 164, 166, 169, 175
   economy of, 32–33
   international trade of, 381, 386
   public debt of, 259
   savings rate in, 202
   U.S. trade with, 377